Law of Tort

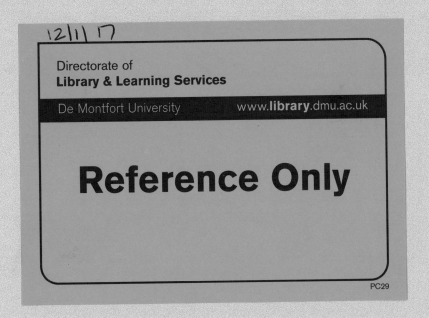

foundations series

Written with learning in mind, these texts allow students to gain a solid understanding of the law. Each book presents the subject clearly and accessibly for effective and satisfying study.

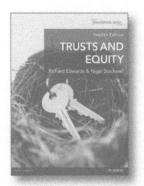

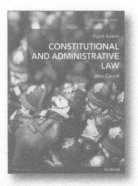

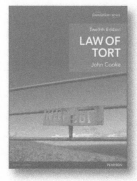

All our texts within the Foundations Series can be supported by MyLawChamber which provides online study support through the interactive Pearson eText, Case Navigator, Virtual Lawyer, practice questions, online glossary and legal updates, all located at **www.mylawchamber.co.uk.**

Available from all good
bookshops or order online at:
www.pearsoned.co.uk/law

MyLawChamber

Twelfth Edition

Law of Tort

JOHN COOKE
Emeritus Professor of Common Law
Liverpool John Moores University

PEARSON

Harlow, England • London • New York • Boston • San Francisco • Toronto • Sydney • Auckland • Singapore • Hong Kong
Tokyo • Seoul • Taipei • New Delhi • Cape Town • São Paulo • Mexico City • Madrid • Amsterdam • Munich • Paris • Milan

PEARSON EDUCATION LIMITED
Edinburgh Gate
Harlow CM20 2JE
United Kingdom
Tel: +44 (0)1279 623623
Web: www.pearson.com/uk

First published 1992 (print)
Second edition published 1995 (print)
Third edition published 1997 (print)
Fourth edition published 1999 (print)
Fifth edition published 2001 (print)
Sixth edition published 2003 (print)
Seventh edition published 2005 (print)
Eighth edition published 2007 (print)
Ninth edition published 2009 (print)
Tenth edition published 2011 (print)
Eleventh edition published 2013 (print and electronic)
Twelfth edition published 2015 (print and electronic)

© Pearson Professional Limited 1992, 1997 (print)
© Pearson Education Limited 1999, 2011 (print)
© Pearson Education Limited 2013, 2015 (print and electronic)

ISBN: 978-1-292-06282-2 (print)
     978-1-292-06287-7 (PDF)
     978-1-292-06283-9 (eText)

British Library Cataloguing-in-Publication Data
A catalogue record for the print edition is available from the British Library

Library of Congress Cataloging-in-Publication Data
A catalog record for the print edition is available from the Library of Congress

ARP Impression 98

Cover: © Fuse / Getty Images

Print edition typeset in 9/12pt Stone Serif ITC Std by 35
Printed by Ashford Colour Press Ltd

NOTE THAT ANY PAGE CROSS-REFERENCES REFER TO THE PRINT EDITION

Brief contents

Contents

Part 5 Miscellaneous torts

Preface

The major area of change since the last edition has been defamation. The Defamation Act 2013 is now in force. Whether it will make a substantial difference to litigation in defamation is still a matter of controversy. Perhaps the major legal innovations have yet to come in the area of new technology. What was noticeable in the Leveson Report was that it shone a spotlight on what is a fading and obsolete method of reporting, newspapers. The more complex area of new technology must wait for another day.

Nuisance has also had a relatively lively period with decisions in *Lawrence* v *Fen Tigers* and *Barr* v *Biffa*.

The structural change to the book is the addition of an extra chapter on Liability of public authorities (Chapter 7). This topic was previously dealt with in the old Chapter 6. The much litigated area of liability of the police in negligence has moved from Chapter 3 to the new Chapter 7.

Thanks go to the editorial and sales staff at Pearson for their great assistance.

My thanks go to my wife Joan for her support and to my former colleagues and students at Liverpool John Moores University for everything they have taught me.

I have attempted to state the law as it was at 20 July 2014.

John Cooke
22 July 2014

Table of cases

Table of statutes and other statutory material

Acknowledgements

We are grateful to the following for permission to reproduce copyright material:

Text

The Incorporated Council of Law Reporting for England and Wales (ICLR) for extracts from law reports published by the ICLR; Contains Parliamentary information licensed under the Open Parliament Licence v3.0; Contains public sector information licensed under the Open Government Licence v3.0.

In some instances we have been unable to trace the owners of copyright material, and we would appreciate any information that would enable us to do so.

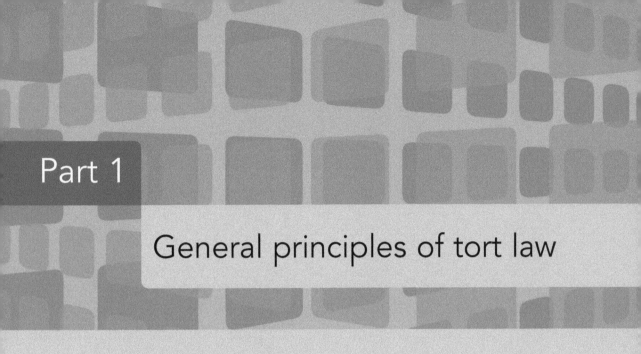

Part 1

General principles of tort law

1

General principles

Objectives

After reading this chapter you will:

1. Understand the elements of a tort.
2. Have a knowledge of the interests protected by tort law.
3. Understand the distinctions between fault and strict liability.
4. Have a knowledge of the objectives of tort law.
5. Have a critical knowledge of alternative systems of compensation.
6. Have a critical knowledge of whether England and Wales have a compensation culture.
7. Have a critical understanding of the boundaries of tort law and its links with contract.
8. Understand the relationship between tort and human rights legislation.

Introduction

This chapter will attempt to explain some of the basic principles which underlie the law of tort. Introductory chapters in textbooks are notoriously difficult for students to understand as they are written by people with a detailed knowledge of the subject for people who are new to it. The author will inevitably assume knowledge which the reader will probably not have. Readers are therefore asked to read the chapter and pick up what they can but not to agonise at this stage over material which appears impenetrable. As you progress through the book you will be able usefully to refer back to the introductory chapter.

What is a tort?

Objective 1

A tort is a civil wrong in the sense that it is committed against an individual (which includes legal entities such as companies) rather than the state. The gist of tort law is that a person has certain interests which are protected by law. These interests can be protected by a court awarding a sum of money, known as damages, for infringement of a protected

3

See 'The boundaries of tort' in this chapter for the relationship between tort law and other branches of law.

interest. Alternatively, by the issuing of an injunction, which is a court order, to the defendant to refrain from doing something. There are increasingly limited circumstances where the victim of a tort may avail himself of self-help.

Other branches of law also defend protected interests and the relationship between these and tort law will be discussed later.

Elements of a tort

Tort is a remarkably wide-ranging subject and probably the most difficult of all legal areas to lay down all-embracing principles for.

The approach that will be taken at this stage is to lay down a general pattern and then to show some of the main deviations from this pattern.

The basic pattern

The paradigm tort consists of an *act* or *omission* by the defendant which *causes damage* to the claimant. The damage must be caused by the fault of the defendant and must be a *kind of harm* recognised as attracting legal liability.

This model can be represented:

act (or omission) + causation + fault + protected interest + damage = liability.

An illustration of this model can be provided by the occurrence most frequently leading to liability in tort, a motor accident.

Example

A drives his car carelessly with the result that it mounts the pavement and hits *B*, a pedestrian, causing *B* personal injuries. The act is *A* driving the vehicle. This act has caused damage to *B*. The damage was as a result of *A*'s carelessness, i.e. his fault. The injury suffered by *B*, personal injury, is recognised by law as attracting liability. *A* will be liable to *B* in the tort of negligence and *B* will be able to recover damages.

Variations

We will be looking at these elements of a tort in more detail shortly. Now we will look at some of the common variations on the basic model. The elements of act (or omission) and causation are common to all torts. There are certain torts which do not require fault. These are known as torts of strict liability.

Example

For breach of statutory duty see Chapter 13.

An Act of Parliament makes it compulsory for employers to ensure that their employees wear safety helmets. The employer may be liable in a tort called breach of statutory duty if the employee does not wear a helmet and is injured as a result. This is the case even if the employer has done all they could to ensure the helmet was worn. (See also 'The mental element in tort'.)

In some cases the act or omission of the defendant may have caused damage to the claimant but the claimant may have no action as the interest affected may not be one protected by law. Lawyers refer to this as *damnum sine injuria* or harm without legal wrong.

> ### Example
>
> *A* opens a fish and chip shop in the same street as *B*'s fish and chip shop. *A* reduces his prices with the intention of putting *B* out of business. *A* has committed no tort as losses caused by lawful business competition are not actionable in tort.

Just in case you thought this was straightforward, there are also cases where conduct is actionable even though no damage has been caused. This is known as *injuria sine damno* and where a tort is actionable without proof of damage it is said to be actionable *per se*.

> ### Example
>
> If *A* walks across *B*'s land without *B*'s permission then *A* will commit the tort of trespass to land, even though he causes no damage to the land.

For trespass to land see Chapter 16.

The interests protected

Personal security

Objective 2

People have an interest in their personal security. This is protected in a number of ways. If one person puts another in fear of being hit, then there may be an action in the tort of assault. If the blow is struck, then the person hit may have an action in the tort of battery. A person whose freedom of movement is restricted unlawfully may be able to sue for false imprisonment. If personal injury is caused negligently, then the claimant may have an action in the tort of negligence.

The scope given to the personal security interest expands as society becomes more advanced. Until the last century little attention was paid to the psychiatric damage that can be caused to a person. Someone who witnesses a traumatic event can incur serious mental suffering. The advance of psychiatric medicine and changing views on what is tolerable have led the courts to protect certain aspects of mental suffering, such as psychiatric damage caused by witnessing a negligently caused accident. This is an area of law which is still being worked out by the courts in the context of disasters, such as the Hillsborough football stadium disaster.

In the area of medical treatment, patients have become less willing to accept the word of doctors without question. Litigation in this area has led to the courts having to examine difficult issues such as consent to treatment and the right to life. Here law and morality are inextricably mixed. What, for example, is the legal position if a doctor needs to give a blood transfusion to a patient who will die if they do not receive it, but the patient refuses to have the blood transfusion because of his religious beliefs?

Interest in property

For trespass to land see Chapter 16; nuisance see Chapter 17; *Rylands v Fletcher* see Chapter 18 and negligence Chapters 2–10.

Property in the broad sense of the word is protected by tort law. A person has an interest in their land which is protected by a number of torts such as nuisance, *Rylands* v *Fletcher* and *trespass to land*. Interests in personal property are protected by torts such as *trespass to goods* and *conversion*. Where clothing or a car is damaged in a negligently caused accident, then a person may have an action for damages in *negligence*.

Economic interests

Tort law will give limited protection to economic interests where the defendant has acted unlawfully and has caused economic loss to the claimant. These are known as the economic torts. Such protection is limited because the common law has been cautious in drawing the line between lawful and unlawful business practice. This is a line which is largely left to statute to draw. (See *OBG Ltd* v *Allan* [2007] 2 WLR 920.)

See 'The boundaries of tort' later in this chapter for the relationship between contract and tort.

A controversial area, and one which will be dealt with in the chapter on negligence, is the extent of liability for *negligently* caused economic loss. This is an area where tort and contract intersect.

A distinction is drawn between economic loss which is consequential on physical damage (to the person or to property) and 'pure' economic loss.

> ### Example
>
> *A* is driving an excavator and negligently severs an electricity cable which leads to a factory. The factory is forced to close down for a day and production is lost as a result. Any production which had been started at the time of the interruption of the supply and is damaged will be classed as damage to property and can be claimed in a negligence action. Any production which has not been started but cannot be carried out and results in loss of profit will be classed as economic loss and will be irrecoverable. Do you think that this distinction makes sense?

Reputation and privacy

See Chapter 21 for defamation and Chapter 22 for privacy.

Increasingly important are a person's interests in their reputation and privacy. Where a person's reputation is damaged by untrue speech or writing, then they may have an action in the tort of *defamation*. There is no specific tort in English law to defend privacy but there have been some interesting developments in this area which are dealt with in the chapter on privacy.

The role of policy

Lawyers are used to dealing in concepts such as duty of care, remoteness of damage and fault, etc. When cases are analysed in these terms and there is held to be no liability as there was no duty or the damage was too remote, or the defendant was not at fault, this is referred to as formal conceptualism or black letter law. What is frequently concealed in this terminology is the policy reason behind the decision. Although the lawyer must know the relevant rules of law, and these will be the main area of study in this book, a clear picture will not emerge unless the student is aware of the policy issues which have shaped the decision.

Take another look at the example given in the previous section. The court has the choice of allowing the loss to lie on the factory owner by saying that *A* is not liable, or of shifting the loss to *A* by holding him liable. The court's decision will be explained by saying, for example, that *A* owes no duty to the factory owner in terms of certain kinds of loss or that certain kinds of loss are too remote. But the decision can also be explained in terms of two policy factors. The courts are concerned with opening the floodgates of litigation: for example, if the electricity cable was connected to 50 factories. Closely connected to this is the role of insurance. Most damages in tort are in practice paid by insurance companies. The court's decision will act as a signal to firms as to who will have to insure against this risk. The decision may also be based on who they think is the best insurer.

Traditionally, English judges did not refer to policy when giving decisions but they are now increasingly prepared to state these reasons. The floodgates argument has been prevalent in the development of the law on both **nervous shock** and the recovery of economic loss in negligence. When you study these sections, bear in mind that one of the factors governing the legal rules imposed is the fear of the courts being swamped by a large number of actions and too heavy a burden being placed on the defendant or their insurers.

The role of insurance

Without insurance the tort system would simply cease to operate. Where a claimant is successful in an action, the damages will normally be paid by an insurance company.

In cases of property damage, insurance may take the form of 'loss', or first-party insurance, which covers loss or damage to the property insured from the risks described in the policy, whether or not the loss occurs through the fault of another party. There is also 'liability', or third-party insurance. This is a matter of contract between the insurer and the insured whereby the insurer promises to indemnify the insured against all sums the insured becomes liable to pay as damages to third parties. The third party must establish the insured's liability to them.

Both first- and third-party insurance are also relevant in cases of personal injuries or death. Three types of first-party insurance are relevant. These are life assurance, personal accident insurance and permanent health insurance. An accident victim who recovers tort damages in respect of the accident will not normally have any first-party insurance money received deducted from the damages. Third-party insurance operates in a similar way to cases of property damage.

The operation of the insurance system can be seen in relation to motor accidents.

Example

A has taken out first- and third-party (comprehensive) insurance on his car with *B* insurance company. *C* has taken out similar insurance on his vehicle with *D* insurance company. Due to *C*'s negligent driving, *A*'s car is damaged and *A* suffers serious personal injuries. If *A* successfully sues *C* for negligence, then under the third-party insurance of *C*, *D* will become liable to pay *A*'s damages. If *C*'s car was damaged in the accident, then *D* may be liable to reimburse *C* for this damage under *C*'s first-party insurance.

If *A*'s negligence action was unsuccessful, then he could claim for the damage to his car from *B* under his first-party insurance, but unless he carried personal accident insurance (which is relatively rare) he would go uncompensated for the personal injuries.

In practice, most cases do not go to court but are settled by the parties. The largest element in *A*'s claim in the above example is likely to be for his personal injuries. If his lawyers have assessed his claim as £500,000, any action may well be settled if fault is not at issue.

The fact that a party is insured is, strictly speaking, disregarded by the court when liability and quantum of damages are assessed. However, it is suspected that the tort system would be unable to operate without the underpinning of insurance and that the presence of insurance may have shaped some liability rules. Not many people would be able to meet a damages award of £500,000 and, without insurance, it would be likely that many claimants would go uncompensated or receive only partial compensation. The fact that the defendant is insured in certain types of cases means that the court can set the standard of care at a higher level so as to compensate more people. This is particularly the case where insurance is compulsory, such as in motor accident cases. A driver must carry third-party insurance by law. Similarly, an employer must be insured against any damages an employee may recover against him in respect of injury at work.

This advantage has a price in the control which insurance has over the conduct of litigation. The insurer's right of subrogation combined with the terms of insurance policies will give the insurer complete control over the litigation process, although the case will be brought in the insured's name.

Example

A runs into the back of *B*'s car while *B* is stationary at traffic lights. This causes £1,000 worth of damage to *B*'s car. *B* is comprehensively insured and the insurer pays for the repairs to the car. Normally, *A* would allow his insurers to deal with the claim and, assuming liability is admitted, either a 'knock for knock' agreement between the insurance companies would operate, or *A*'s insurers would reimburse *B*'s insurers. If *A* decides not to use his insurance company as he thinks it would badly affect his no-claims discount, then *A* can be sued for the £1,000 by *B*'s insurers exercising their right of subrogation. The action would be brought in *B*'s name.

The insurance principle can also be seen at work in professional indemnity policies. A solicitor or accountant will carry indemnity insurance in case they are sued for professional negligence. The damages in such actions can be very high and insurance is essential to the operation of the system.

Insurers pay out 94 per cent of tort compensation and in some areas of tort law have a considerable influence on the tort system. This may happen in one of two ways. The first is the impact on legislation and judicial decisions. If legislative change is being contemplated, the impact on insurance will be taken into account by Parliament. Impact on judicial decisions is harder to assess, as few judges acknowledge the effect of insurance on their

See Chapter 9 for *Barker* v *Corus UK Ltd*.

decisions. (But see ***Barker* v *Corus UK Ltd*** [2006] 3 All ER 785.) The second is in the actual operation of the tort system. As the insurance companies are effectively the paymasters, they have a large say in its operation. Insurers determine which cases go to court. Only 1 per cent of all claims made go to court and far fewer go on appeal and appear in the law reports. Which cases are appealed may be determined by the insurer and one factor in their decision not to appeal may be that they want a point of law to remain uncertain. Other cases are settled by the insurers. For reasons of cost an insurer may wish to settle a case where in strict legal terms the claim might not succeed in court. Conversely, a party might be coerced by the insurer into accepting less on a settlement than they would have received if they had gone to court.

The rules of law as stated in this book may bear little resemblance to the practice of tort law, particularly in the area of personal injuries.

Fault and strict liability

Objective
3

As we saw previously, it may not be sufficient for claimants to prove that the defendant's act or omission caused them damage in order to succeed in an action. It may also be necessary for the claimant to show that the defendant was at fault. Fault in tort means malice, intention or negligence. Where fault does not have to be proved it is said to be a strict liability tort.

The history of fault in tort law is connected to policy and stems from the nineteenth century. At this time the availability of insurance was extremely limited and damages would usually be paid personally by the defendant. In order to protect developing industries, the courts evolved a system of tort that usually required proof of fault in order for an action to succeed. The economic argument in favour of fault was supported by the moral and social arguments that fault-based liability would deter people from anti-social conduct and it was right that bad people should pay. One consequence of this development was that workers in industry who suffered industrial accidents were largely deprived of compensation.

English law has never succeeded in ridding itself of this nineteenth-century legacy and fault remains as the basis of most tort actions. Understanding of the principle is made more difficult as the spread of insurance has meant that the courts have been able to increase the standard of conduct required in certain situations, while retaining the language of moral wrongdoing. It has been shown that many errors by car drivers which are classed as being negligence (fault) are statistically unavoidable. Where this is the case, the moral and deterrent arguments for fault are certainly reduced if not extinguished. Further problems are caused by the fact that a tort judgment is rarely paid by the defendant themselves but by their insurer. What has happened is that fault has often moved away from being a state of mind to being a judicially set standard of conduct which is objectively set for policy reasons.

Example

A was operated on by surgeon *B*. Something went wrong during the operation and *A* is now incapable of looking after himself. *A* sues *B* for negligence. If the action is successful, then *A* will be awarded £500,000 damages. The question in the case will be whether *B* was negligent (at fault). At what level should the court set the standard? In order to compensate as many victims of medical accidents as possible, the standard should obviously be set very high. But if this is done, the damages which are paid out by the health authority will remove money which could otherwise be used for patient treatment. The standard will therefore be set at a level which is dictated by policy.

There are three states of mind which a student needs to be aware of in tort law. These are *malice, intention* and *negligence*. Where a tort does not require any of these it is said to be a tort of strict liability.

Malice

Malice in tort has two meanings. It may be: (a) the intentional doing of some wrongful act without proper excuse; (b) to act with some collateral or improper motive. It is (b) which is usually referred to.

In the sense of (b) above there is a basic principle that malice is irrelevant in tort law. If a person has a right to do something then their motive in doing it is irrelevant.

Bradford Corporation v *Pickles* [1895] AC 587

The defendant extracted percolating water in undefined channels with the result that the water supply to the claimant's reservoir was reduced. The defendant's motive in doing this was to force the claimant to buy his land at his price. The action failed, as the defendant had a right to extract the water. As he had such a right, his motive, even if malicious, was irrelevant.

In some countries, such as the USA and Germany, a bad motive is a ground for liability but, as can be seen in the above case, this is not the rule in English law.

> Some writers regret the failure of English law to accept bad motive as a ground for liability, as it is in the United States and Germany: see for example Heydon, *Economic Torts*, 2nd ed (1978), p. 28. But I agree with Tony Weir's opinion, forcibly expressed in his Clarendon Law Lectures on *Economic Torts* (1997) that we are better off without it. It seems to have created a good deal of uncertainty in the countries which have adopted such a principle. Furthermore, the rarity of actions for conspiracy (in which a bad motive can, exceptionally, found liability) suggests that it would not have made much practical difference. (***OBG Ltd*** v ***Allan*** [2007] 2 WLR 920 at 927, per Lord Hoffmann.)

There are two groups of exceptions to the basic principle that malice is irrelevant:

1 Where malice is an essential ingredient of the tort, for example, in *malicious prosecution*, the claimant must prove not only that the defendant had no grounds for believing that the claimant was probably guilty, but also that the defendant was activated by malice. The reason for this requirement is that policy in this area favours law enforcement over individual rights. The result of the requirement is that there are few successful cases of malicious prosecution.

2 There are also torts where malice may be relevant to liability. For example, in *nuisance* malice may convert what would have been a reasonable act into an unreasonable one.

Christie v *Davey* [1893] 1 Ch 316

See also Chapter 16.

Claimant and defendant lived in adjoining houses. The claimant gave music lessons and this annoyed the defendant. In retaliation the defendant banged on the wall and shouted while the lessons were in progress. The claimant was held to be entitled to an injunction because of the defendant's malicious behaviour.

See Chapter 17 for nuisance.

The distinction between this case and ***Bradford Corporation*** v ***Pickles*** is difficult. ***Pickles*** was thought to have established a principle that a lawful act does not become unlawful when done with malice. However, this case was concerned with water rights to which special rules apply and was concerned with a prospective, rather than existing, amenity. This is not to suggest that malicious interference with an existing amenity is always actionable.

Also, in defamation cases, malice may destroy a defence of honest opinion or qualified privilege and may affect the defence of justification where spent convictions are in issue.

See Chapter 21 for defamation.

Intention

The meaning of intention varies according to the context in which it is used.

> I do not resile from the proposition that the policy considerations which limit the heads of recoverable damage in negligence do not apply equally to torts of intention. If someone actually intends to cause harm by a wrongful act and does so, there is ordinarily no reason why he should not have to pay compensation. But I think that if you adopt such a principle, you have to be very careful about what you mean by intend. (Lord Hoffmann in *Wainwright v Home Office* [2003] 4 All ER 969.)

Intention is relevant in three groups of torts:

For trespass to the person, see Chapter 20.

1 Torts derived from the writ of trespass. Here intention means where a person desires to produce a result forbidden by law and where they foresee it and carry on regardless of the consequences. The defendant must intend to do the act, but need not intend harm: for example, if a person has a fit and strikes another person this would not amount to trespass to the person. But the test will catch the practical joker who intends to frighten a person but ends up causing them severe psychiatric damage.

See Chapter 23 for deceit and malicious falsehood.

2 In cases of fraud and injurious falsehood. In these torts the defendant must make a statement which they know is untrue.

3 In cases of conspiracy. If *X* and *Y* combine together and act to cause injury to *Z*, then *Z* will have an action provided that they can prove that their primary motive was to cause them damage. If the primary motive of *X* and *Y* was to further their own interests, then even if they realised that their act would inevitably damage *Z*, they will not be liable in conspiracy.

Crofter Hand Woven Harris Tweed Co Ltd v *Veitch* [1942] AC 435

Yarn for making Harris Tweed was spun by mills on Harris. Crofters who made Harris Tweed began importing cheaper yarn from the mainland. The millworkers' union ordered its members at the docks to refuse to handle the imported yarn after the millworkers' employers had refused a pay rise because of competition from the crofters. The crofters' action for conspiracy failed as the union's predominant motive was to advance the interests of its members and not to damage the crofters.

Negligence

For the tort of negligence, see Chapters 2–10.

Negligence in tort has several meanings. It may refer to the *tort of negligence* or it may refer to *careless behaviour*. It is in the latter sense that the word is used here. In this sense it does not refer to a state of mind. When a court finds that a person has been negligent it is making an *ex post* assessment of their *conduct*. A person who totally disregards the safety of others but does not injure them is not guilty of negligence, although they may be morally reprehensible. On the other hand, the person who tries their best, but falls below the standard set by the court and causes damage, will be liable.

For standard of care in negligence, see Chapter 8.

The standard set is an objective one. The court will apply the test of what a 'reasonable man' would have done in the defendant's position. One effect of this test is that no account is taken of individual disabilities.

Nettleship v *Weston* [1971] 2 QB 691

The defendant was a learner driver who was given lessons by the claimant. The claimant was injured as a result of the defendant's negligent driving. The court held that all drivers, including learner drivers, would be judged by the standards of the average competent driver.

The setting of the standard depends on what the objective of the negligence formula is. If the objective is to compensate the claimant for their loss, then it is clearly in the claimant's interests to set the standard as high as possible. But if the objective is to deter the defendant, then it is counter-productive to set a standard which is too high to be attainable. Research has shown that the standard set for drivers is unattainable, even by safe drivers, with the result that the defendant may have been unable to avoid the accident but is still classed as having been negligent.

Strict liability

Whereas fault is a positive idea, strict liability is a negative one. It means liability without fault. In the last century the emphasis was placed by the courts on fault-based liability, and strict liability was generally frowned on. Some areas of strict liability have survived and Parliament has created others.

See Chapter 19 for liability for animals.

See Chapter 18 for *Rylands v Fletcher*.

No coherent theme links these areas. There are historical relics such as strict liability for trespassing livestock, which harks back to a predominantly agricultural society. The rule in *Rylands* v *Fletcher* represents a largely failed attempt by the judiciary to deal with the problems created by the Industrial Revolution. The rule that an employer is vicariously liable for the negligence of their employee in the course of their employment, in the absence of any fault on the part of the employer, is a pragmatic response to a particular problem.

See Chapter 24 for vicarious liability.

In the area of industrial safety, Parliament has passed legislation which imposes strict as opposed to fault-based liability on an employer.

See Chapters 13 and 14 for breach of statutory duty and employer's liability.

The standard of liability imposed, even within the context of strict liability, varies from tort to tort. There is one example of absolute liability, where no defence is available. This is the Nuclear Installations Act 1965. Most actions, however, permit some defences or exemptions from liability.

See the Consumer Protection Act 1987, Chapter 12.

What is common to all tort actions is the idea of causation. The claimant must always prove that the defendant caused their injury. There are frequently calls for drug manufacturers to be made strictly liable for injury caused by their products. If this were to occur then the claimant would no longer have to prove negligence but would still be faced with the difficult task of proving that it was that drug which caused their injury.

Objectives of tort

Objective 4

Tort law has two main objectives: compensation and deterrence. It is generally thought that tort law normally has no punitive function and that this job is performed by the criminal law. There are very limited circumstances, though, where exemplary damages may be awarded in tort and these do have a punitive function. The fact that the judiciary has kept the award of this type of damages within such narrow parameters means that they are wary of tort law performing this function.

See Chapter 28 for exemplary damages.

Deterrence

Individual deterrence

The theory behind individual deterrence is that the possibility of a civil sanction, such as damages, will cause the defendant to alter their behaviour and avoid inflicting damage.

This theory depends on two factors. First, will the sanction actually affect the defendant? We have seen that most awards of damages are paid out by insurance companies. The only financial effect of an award of damages on an insured defendant may be to increase the premium which they have to pay for their insurance. But reputation is also important to some people. A finding of negligence against a doctor or lawyer may adversely affect their career. The second factor is whether the defendant could have avoided the accident. We have seen that it is impossible for a car driver to avoid committing driving errors which the law will label as negligence. If a person cannot avoid an error then they cannot be said to be deterred by a liability rule.

It is now generally accepted that individual deterrence has little part to play in many tort actions. The legal reason that most people drive as safely as they can is the fear of criminal, not civil, sanctions. Individual deterrence does have a role where a person's professional reputation is at stake, and the reason why most newspapers try to avoid libelling people is the fear of an action for defamation.

General or market deterrence

Academic work on the economic effects of tort liability rules has renewed interest in the role of deterrence in tort law. This form of deterrence is not individual deterrence but what is known as market deterrence. The idea behind this is that tort law should aim to reduce the costs of accidents. This is achieved by imposing the costs of accidents on those who participate in accident-causing activities.

Example

If a car manufacturer were to be charged the accident costs of cars in which seat belts were not installed, then the price of cars without seat belts would reflect the accident costs. Rather than impose a law which states that cars must be fitted with seat belts, the market, through the cost of cars without seat belts, would enable people to make a choice between the cheaper cars with seat belts or the more expensive ones without.

Compensation

One of the major aims of tort law is to compensate those who have suffered personal injury. The present system shifts losses from the claimant to the defendant when the defendant has been shown to have been at fault. In recent years this system has come under increasing criticism as being an inefficient method of compensating accident victims.

There are three systems which provide for accident victims. These are tort law, public insurance (social security) and private insurance. The largest part in compensation is now played by public insurance. A person who is injured in an accident may become entitled to payments by the state, such as sickness benefit.

Tort damages are distinguished from payments by the state in that the former are payable only on proof that a person caused an injury and was at fault in doing so. The latter are payable on the occurrence of an event and according to need.

The third system is private insurance. This plays a small but growing part in accident compensation. Personal accident insurance or permanent health insurance may be taken out against the possibility of indisposition. This is still relatively expensive in the United Kingdom but is being taken up by employers for their key personnel.

A number of criticisms are levelled at the tort system. It is very expensive to administer in comparison with social security. It has been calculated that the cost of operating the tort system accounts for 85 per cent of the sums which are paid to accident victims. For claimants the system is unpredictable, as they do not know whether they will receive any compensation or not. This results in pressure on claimants to settle actions for less than they would receive if they went to trial. The system is also slow and a claimant may have to wait years before receiving compensation. The more serious the accident then generally the longer the claimant has to wait. Finally, damages have historically been paid in a lump sum. This created difficulties as inflation may erode the value of the award and no account can be taken of improvement or deterioration in the claimant's medical condition. The

See Chapter 28. situation is now changing, however.

The civil justice system was subjected to a radical overhaul as a result of the Woolf Report on *Access to Justice* (1996). The reforms were introduced in 1999 with a view to saving costs and speeding up litigation. Judges are given greater powers in case management in order to attempt to bring down costs and speed up cases.

Alternative systems of compensation

Objective 5

We have already seen that tort damages are only part of the overall picture of compensation for accidents and are a junior partner to state benefits. The position in England and Wales is complex, with a number of possible avenues of compensation open to an injured person. They may be able to obtain tort damages, be covered by private insurance and be entitled to state benefits. Because of the haphazard and uncoordinated way in which the system has evolved, the victim may end up being over-compensated. On the other hand, a victim may have no insurance cover, not be able to prove fault against a person and may not have a sufficient contribution record to claim contributory state benefits. This victim will only have the safety net of income support benefit at subsistence level to support them.

One other source of compensation which should be mentioned at this point is the Criminal Injuries Compensation Scheme. Payments may be made for injuries directly attributable to crimes of violence. If the victim goes on to obtain tort damages, then any award made under the scheme must be repaid.

In some countries the role of compensating for accidents has been removed from the tort system. In New Zealand, a comprehensive no-fault accident compensation scheme was set up in 1974 to replace tort damages in personal accident cases. Where a person suffers injury through accident they make a claim through the Accident Compensation Commission. The victim may claim up to 80 per cent of earnings before the accident. Payments are made on a weekly basis and can be adjusted to reflect inflation and the victim's medical condition. The victim does not have to prove fault and a wider range of accidents are therefore covered by the scheme than by tort law. The system of periodical payments avoids problems which are caused by lump sum awards of damages in tort cases. In tort cases it is not generally possible for the court to take into account future inflation or to allow for changes in the victim's medical condition. Under the scheme, a victim may also claim for non-pecuniary loss in the form of an independence allowance for persons who have a permanent disability above 10 per cent. Such awards are low compared with those which would be received under a tort system. The advantage of the scheme is that all accident victims receive some compensation and are not put to the trauma, cost and delay of having to sue someone. The drawbacks which have been discovered from experience of running the scheme are the cost, which is clearer and therefore more political than the tort system, and the possibilities of fraud. A further problem, which is common to most legal compensation systems, is that a distinction is drawn between the covered area of personal injury by accident (including occupational disease) and the uncovered areas of disease and ageing. A number of writers have pointed out that in a no-fault compensation scheme the concentration should not be on the cause of the accident but on the disability itself.

The New Zealand experience has been that a no-fault system that tries to replace tort damages across the board is extremely expensive and the government was forced to reduce the level of benefits available.

In England, the thalidomide tragedy in the 1960s and 1970s aroused interest in the question of compensation. The Pearson Commission (Royal Commission on Civil Liability and Compensation for Personal Injury, Cmnd 7054 (1978)) was established and the report proposed a no-fault scheme limited to accidents caused by motor vehicles. Some 188 other proposals were made but it is doubtful whether any reform can be traced directly to these. Despite the political neglect of this report it remains the most far-reaching piece of research on the tort system carried out.

A no-fault scheme does involve spending money and the implementation of such a scheme depends on the political will to do so. Opponents of such schemes argue that the removal of tort actions will remove an important deterrent to careless conduct.

The question of taking medical 'accidents' out of the legal system has been discussed for a number of years. The option of a comprehensive no-fault scheme was dismissed in 2003 when the cost was estimated at £4 billion per annum.

<table>
<tr><td>See Chapter 15 for more on NHS Redress Act 2006.</td><td>The Department of Health has now come up with an alternative to tort law in the form of the NHS Redress Act 2006. The Act established an NHS redress scheme which enables the settlement of certain low value claims arising after adverse incidents without the need for court proceedings. It came into effect in 2008. The scheme applies only to claims under £20,000 and will apply where the claim is by the estate or **dependants** of a deceased patient. The objectives are to take the 'heat' out of disputes and remove any financial disadvantage from the patient. This is not a 'no-fault scheme', as it applies only to claims in tort, but it is anticipated that it will remove the need for patients to go to court in low-cost claims.</td></tr>
</table>

On similar lines a 'quick and simple compensation scheme for road traffic accidents' for claims valued at between £1000 and £10,000 came into effect for personal injury claims from April 2010.

One influential writer in England favours the abolition of the action for personal injuries and its replacement by private insurance. Professor Atiyah, who was once a strong supporter of state-funded no-fault schemes, has declared his lack of faith in such schemes and his faith in the market (*The Damages Lottery* (1997)). This view is open to the criticism that the poor would be excluded from a market-based system.

A compensation culture?

<table>
<tr><td>Objective 6</td><td>There is renewed interest in the personal injury litigation system, partly as a result of claims that England and Wales now have a 'compensation culture' similar to that in the United States. A compensation culture can be loosely defined as a propensity to respond to injury by legal redress. Such claims have been partly driven by changes in the way in which the legal system operates in this area.</td></tr>
</table>

Lawyers have become increasingly adept at identifying and developing claims for personal injuries. Increasing specialisation and the foundation of the Association of Personal Injury Lawyers in 1990 has enabled lawyers to coordinate claims and share expertise.

Social awareness of the right to claim has been raised, partially as a result of the ability of lawyers to advertise and the advent of claims management companies that act as intermediaries between the client and lawyers and aggressively advertise the availability of claims.

The availability of conditional fee arrangements (CFAs) allowed lawyers to work for clients on a 'no-win no-fee' basis and may also have been a factor. CFAs meant that if a claim fails the client does not have to pay his own lawyer's costs. An insurance policy could be taken out to cover the costs of the other side. If the claim is successful, the claimant lawyer's own costs and a 'success fee' can be recovered from the defendant. The financial risks of litigation were therefore considerably reduced. CFAs became widely available after the implementation in 2000 of the Access to Justice Act 1999. However, such figures as are available for the period 2000–13 do not suggest that claims in accident cases have risen appreciably since then. CFAs have now been replaced by after the event insurance. (See 'Access to justice' below.)

One problem with assessing the current position is that there has been no comprehensive empirical study of the system since the Pearson Commission in 1978 and the Oxford Study in 1984. (D. Harris *et al.*, *Compensation and Support for Illness and Injury* (1984).) Recent research on the available data suggests that although there has been a threefold rise in claims since 1978, this is not a recent phenomenon and claims for accidents (as opposed to disease) have not risen in the last decade. The total number of claims has rose by 3 per cent between 2001–06. However, there was a 5 per cent fall in the number of accident claims in the same period. Motor claims remained stable, whereas clinical negligence claims fell by 34 per cent and employer's liability claims by 21 per cent. Motor accident claims accounted for 70 per cent of the total. What has increased is the total cost of claims, probably as a result of changes to the way damages are calculated and legal costs. (R. Lewis, A. Morris and K. Oliphant, 'Tort Personal Injury Claims Statistics: Is There a Compensation Culture in the United Kingdom?' (2006) 2 JPIL 87–103.)

The view of the UK government, following the conclusions of its Better Regulation Task Force in *Better Routes to Redress* (Cabinet Office Publications, 2004) is that the compensation culture is a myth but that the public's erroneous belief that it exists results in real and costly burdens. This underlies the rather strange provision of s 1 of the Compensation Act 2006 which, according to the government, simply reiterates the current test for breach of duty in negligence and then establishes a framework for the regulation of claims management companies.

Section 1 of the Act is intended to deal with the effect of negligence on social activities where people might be inhibited from involving themselves or allowing their land to be used:

> A court considering a claim in negligence or breach of statutory duty may, in determining whether the defendant should have taken particular steps to meet a standard of care (whether by taking precautions against a risk or otherwise), have regard to whether a requirement to take those steps might:
>
> (a) prevent a desirable activity from being undertaken at all, to a particular extent or in a particular way, or
>
> (b) discourage persons from undertaking functions in connection with a desirable activity.

See Chapter 8 for more on *Tomlinson* v *Congleton Borough Council*.

It is difficult to see what this will achieve, as there is stated to be no change to the common law test for breach of duty and the courts are already alert to this problem as is shown in cases such as ***Tomlinson* v *Congleton Borough Council*** [2003] 3 All ER 1122.

The boundaries of tort

The boundary between tort and contract is an area which has caused the courts considerable problems in recent years.

A number of distinctions between contract and tort can be offered, but it remains the case that there are still substantial areas of overlap between these two strands of common law liability. At best, it can be said that there are differences between contractual and tortious obligations, but that the two interact and complement each other and in many instances they overlap.

Legally imposed and voluntarily assumed obligations

One of the most commonly offered distinctions is that tortious duties are fixed by law, whereas the contractual obligations of the parties are fixed by the parties themselves. However, like most generalisations, this is apt to mislead. For example, many contractual obligations are legally imposed, not the least of which is the duty not to break a promise which forms the basis for a remedy for breach of contract. In addition, there are a number of contractual duties which can only be described as arising by operation of law. For example, in the field of product liability, terms are implied in contracts for the supply of goods which owe little to voluntary choice. Sellers have terms of fitness for the purpose and satisfactory quality included in the contract by virtue of the Sale of Goods Act 1979 (as amended by the Sale and Supply of Goods Act 1994).

Likewise, the courts are able to imply terms into contracts so as to make sense of the arrangement. Ostensibly the purpose of such implication is to give effect to the presumed intent of the parties, but one might be forgiven for taking the view that the court is actually legislating by imposing duties upon the parties to the contract. Sometimes, a court may 'create' a contract for the parties. In such cases, the court would appear to have imposed an obligation upon the 'promisor'. Frequently, it will be found that the collateral contract device is used to fill a gap which has appeared in the law. For example, it was used to create liability in damages for negligent misrepresentations before the Misrepresentation Act 1967 was passed. It was also used to render liable the supplier of goods under a hire purchase contract for statements made by him during the course of negotiations. An explanation of these cases is that the court used the collateral contract as a means of disapproving of the defendant's conduct by ordering him to compensate the claimant for the loss he had suffered. In this way, the court effectively imposed an obligation upon the defendant.

Just as it is misleading to say that contractual obligations are voluntarily assumed, it is also a mistake to ignore the relevance of voluntary choice when considering the issue of tortious liability. Some tortious duties arise out of a relationship which has been voluntarily entered into. For example, the duties owed by an employer to his employees and that owed by an occupier of premises is partly dependent on the relationship between the parties. Moreover, liability for economic loss caused by negligently prepared advice will involve a consideration of the relationship between the adviser, the advisee and any relevant third party and it will be necessary to take account of any contractual undertaking which might have been given. In contract the statement is made voluntarily and must be supported by consideration from the recipient. In tort the maker of the statement must voluntarily assume responsibility for it. The only distinction is that no consideration is required in tort.

While tortious duties are imposed by law, it does not always follow that they are immovable, since it is possible for such duties to be modified by an agreement between the parties.

Consent

Does the distinction between contract and tort make sense if one approaches this question from the point of view of consent (i.e. that a contractual duty can only be imposed where a party consents, but a tortious duty may be imposed in the absence of consent)? Whether a contractual duty exists or not is determined on the basis of objective criteria, not on the subjective intention of the parties. This means that although consent plays a part in contract, it is not all-important. Conversely, in tort consent may play a role. Where a person is injured during a sporting contest, such as football, there may be no action in tort, as the injured person may have consented to the risk of injury by taking part in the contest. Tort law also imposes duties on an occupier of land to a visitor to the land. Whether a person is a visitor or not, and therefore whether such a duty may be imposed, depends on the consent of the occupier to the presence of that person.

Strict and fault-based liability

A further generalisation is that contractual liability is strict, whereas tortious liability is fault-based. Although it is true that many contractual duties are strict, there are many that require the defendant to exercise reasonable care and are therefore fault-based. Many tortious duties are said to be fault-based, but the problem is to decide what is meant by fault. It is clear that the word fault has different meanings. For example, very rigorous standards are imposed in areas where liability insurance is compulsory. Furthermore, there are a number of strict liability torts in which it is not necessary to show that the tortfeasor is blameworthy in causing harm to the claimant.

The interest protected when granting a remedy

The common law recognises a number of interests which it regards as deserving of protection. Traditionally, the fulfilment of expectations is perceived to be the function of the law of contract with the result that an award of contract damages is supposed to put the claimant in the position he would have occupied had the defendant's undertaking been fulfilled. The claimant's expectations may be protected in other ways, for example where a defaulting buyer is ordered to pay for goods he has agreed to purchase, or if the court grants a decree of specific performance. Compensating a claimant for wrongfully inflicted harm is seen to be the role of the law of tort and requires the claimant to be returned to the position they were in before the defendant's wrong was done. Accordingly, in general terms, tort damages are not supposed to take account of what would have happened to the claimant. Instead, damages are assessed on the 'out of pocket' principle.

> ### Example
>
> If *A* sold *B* a motor car for £5,000 which was worth £4,000 but *A* said it was worth £6,000, *B*'s contract damages would in theory be the difference between what the car was worth and what he had been led to believe it was worth, i.e. £2,000. But *B*'s damages in tort would be the amount required to put him in the position he was in before the tort was committed, i.e. £1,000.

But these distinctions are apt to mislead and it is important not to say that only the law of contract is concerned with expectations, and that only the law of tort is concerned with compensating wrongful harm. In some instances the so-called 'contract measure' is relevant in a tort action, for example where the claimant in a personal injuries case is awarded damages for loss of future earnings or where a solicitor has negligently drafted a will depriving the beneficiaries of their bequest.

The traditional role of tort law has been to protect people against damage to their person and property. This is done by making an award of damages for any loss incurred by the victim. The problem comes, as in the above example, where tort is used to protect *economic* interests. Some people believe that this should be the role of contract and that tort should have no role to play. Contract law aims to make things better and tort to avoid making things worse. But consider the following case.

See Chapter 5 for economic loss and more on *Ross* v *Caunters*.

Ross v *Caunters* [1979] 3 All ER 580

The defendant solicitor acted negligently in the execution of a will, with the result that the claimant was unable to take a bequest under the will. The testator (person making the will) had a contract with the solicitor but the claimant did not, because of the contractual doctrines of consideration and privity. The court decided that the defendant was liable in the tort of negligence and the claimant was able to recover the value of his lost bequest from the solicitor. But was this a case of the solicitor making the claimant worse off or failing to make him better off? Would it not be easier in these circumstances to alter the law of contract so that there is a contract in favour of a third party (in this case the beneficiary)?

Some writers have pointed out that the extent to which contract protects the expectation interest is in practice limited by the rules which restrict the amount of damages which may be claimed. The two most important are the rules that a claimant may not recover items of loss which are too remote and the claimant must take reasonable steps to mitigate their loss. The effect of these rules is that in many cases a claimant will only be able to recover their reliance or status quo loss.

Concurrent liability

See Chapter 2 for concurrent liability.

There are situations where a claimant may have a choice between contract and tort. If a person receives private medical treatment and is negligently injured, they may sue the doctor in negligence or for breach of contract. The substance of the action will not differ, as in negligence the doctor must take reasonable care and in contract there is an implied term that the doctor will take reasonable care. It is unlikely that the doctor will have guaranteed a cure, so there is no advantage to the claimant in suing in contract to protect their expectation interest. The damages in either case will be the same.

See Chapter 26 for limitation of actions.

There are a number of technical distinctions between contract and tort. The limitation period (the time in which the claimant has to start proceedings) is different and there are different rules on when writs may be served outside the jurisdiction.

Change

The dividing line between the two areas is never static and a student can observe the changes from a historical perspective. The rigidity of contract law through the doctrines of consideration and privity may give rise to an expansion in tort law. This can be clearly observed in the law relating to defective buildings. As a purchaser of a defective building may not have a contract with the builder or a sub-contractor if there is no privity of contract, there may be no breach of contract action against the builder. To compensate for

See Chapter 11 for defective buildings.

this perceived injustice, tort law developed an action in the tort of negligence against the builder. However, the senior judiciary turned against this action and it was rejected. This has now led to developments in contract law to create a contract action in the case of sub-contractors.

Tort and crime

One of the main functions of the criminal law is to identify and provide punitive sanctions for behaviour that is categorised as criminal because it is damaging to the good order of society. It is fundamental to criminal law and procedure that everyone charged with criminal behaviour should be presumed innocent until proven guilty and that, as a general rule, no one should be punished for a crime that he or she did not intend to commit or be punished for the consequences of an honest mistake. There are, of course, exceptions (strict liability crimes, for example).

The same conduct can amount to both a crime and a tort. An example would be driving a car recklessly and hitting another vehicle. The driver could be prosecuted for a motoring criminal offence and sued for negligence in tort.

Ashley v Chief Constable of Sussex Police [2008] UKHL 25

In cases of assault and battery it is possible for criminal and civil proceedings to be brought but it is important to remember that the rules are different. This is illustrated by a case where a police officer shot and killed a man. A civil action was brought by the family and the police officer pleaded self-defence. The House of Lords held that the ends to be served by the two systems were very different. One of the main functions of the criminal law was to identify and provide sanctions for behaviour that was categorised as criminal because it was damaging to the good order of society. It was fundamental to criminal law and procedure that everyone charged with criminal behaviour should be presumed innocent until proven guilty and that as a general rule no one should be punished for a crime that he or she did not intend to commit or be punished for the consequences of an honest mistake. This explained why a person who honestly believed that he was in danger of an imminent deadly attack and responded violently in order to protect himself from that attack should be able to plead self-defence as an answer to a criminal charge, whether or not he had been mistaken in his belief and whether or not his mistake had been, objectively speaking, a reasonable one for him to have made. The greater the unreasonableness of the belief, however, the more unlikely it might be that the belief was honestly held. The function of the civil law of tort was different. Its main function was to identify and protect the rights that every person was entitled to assert against, and require to be respected by, others. It was one thing to say that if a person's mistaken belief was honestly held he should not be punished by the criminal law. It would be quite another to say that his unreasonably held mistaken belief would be sufficient to justify the law in setting aside the victim's right not to be subjected to physical violence by that person.

For assault and battery, see Chapter 20.

The position of minors

As a general principle, anyone may sue in tort. A minor may bring an action through a next friend.

The position of minors as defendants has not been considered very much, probably because they would not normally be able to satisfy a judgment. In principle, there is no reason why a person of any age cannot be sued. In practice, it may be that the courts set the standard of care according to the age of the child (see Chapter 8), although in theory the standard of care in negligence is an objective one.

Damage caused before birth has always posed a problem in tort law. It was one of the principal hurdles that the parents of the thalidomide children had to face in their litigation. Legislation has since improved the position.

The Congenital Disabilities (Civil Liability) Act 1976 gives a child a cause of action where it was born disabled as the result of an occurrence which: affected the ability of either parent to have a normal healthy child; or affected the mother during the pregnancy; or affected the child in the course of its birth; or there was negligence in the selection or handling of an embryo or gametes for the purpose of assisted conception during treatment for infertility. In any of these cases the child must be born with disabilities which it would otherwise not have had.

The child's action is unusual as it is derived from a tortious duty to the parents. The defendant will be liable to the child if he would have been liable to the parent but for the fact there was no actionable injury to the parent.

The child's mother is not liable under the Act unless the injury can be attributed to her negligent driving of a motor vehicle.

Example

Christine became pregnant and suffered badly from nausea. She consulted her doctor, who prescribed a drug to relieve the nausea. Christine gave birth to a daughter who suffered from physical and mental disabilities. Both the doctor and the manufacturer of the drug owed a duty of care to Christine. If the doctor was negligent in prescribing the drug or the drug company in making or marketing it, then all the elements of a negligence action by Christine are present except damage. It is the baby who has suffered the damage and has the action under the Act. The stumbling-block will be causation. It will be necessary to prove that the drug was the cause of the child's disabilities.

Where the disability is a result of a pre-conception event which affected the ability of the parents to have a normal healthy child, the defendant is not responsible if either or both of the parents knew of the risk. If the child's father is the defendant and he knew of the risk but the mother did not, then the father will be answerable to the child.

The Human Rights Act 1998

Objective
8

A further layer of complexity has been introduced to tort law by the passing of the Human Rights Act 1998, which came into force in October 2000.

The United Kingdom was an original signatory to the European Convention on Human Rights, but until the Act the rights contained in the Convention did not form a part of national law. A person who alleged that their rights under the Convention had been infringed by the United Kingdom had to take a case to the Commission and then to the European Court of Human Rights in Strasbourg. If the decision of the Strasbourg court was against the United Kingdom, then national law would be changed to accommodate the judgment.

Under the 1998 Act the Convention applies either directly or indirectly. Most of the rights in the Convention are now directly enforceable against public bodies in English law.

A new remedy is created against public authorities which act in a way which is incompatible with the Convention. A public authority is defined by s 6(3) as a court or tribunal or any person certain of whose functions are of a public nature. If proceedings are against a private person or body then the Act may have an indirect effect. A court is in itself a public authority and must therefore ensure compatibility with Convention rights by an appropriate interpretation of the law. As far as legislation is concerned, a court or tribunal must interpret legislation in accordance with the Convention (s 3). A court which is considering any question which has arisen in connection with a Convention right must take account of decisions of the European Commission and the European Court of Human Rights (s 2). It is important to note that a court may find that there has been a breach of a Convention right by a public authority and award compensation. This breach may or may not also amount to a tort. If it does amount to a tort then the claimant cannot be doubly compensated for the same injury.

Example

See Chapter 17 for nuisance.

A landowner suffers a reduction in the value of his property and interference with his peaceful enjoyment of it as a result of low flying aircraft from the Royal Air Force. This may amount to the tort of nuisance and it may also be a breach of Article 8. If the claimant has been compensated for loss of peaceful enjoyment (loss of amenity) in nuisance then he will not be compensated for breach of Article 8 for the same loss.

How this will affect the different parts of tort law is difficult to predict, but in some areas such as defamation and negligence the courts had been working towards compatibility with the Convention in their decisions before the Act came into effect.

Example

See Chapter 7 for liability of local authorities.

Mark is a 10-year-old boy who has been taken into care following allegations that he has been sexually abused by his stepfather. Two years later it is discovered that social workers on Mark's case had been negligent and Mark should not have been taken into care. As the social workers are employed by the local authority, which is a public authority under the Act, Mark will have a direct action under the Human Rights Act against the local authority for possible breaches of the Convention. He may also have an action in the law of tort for negligence and the court must take into account the jurisprudence of the Convention when determining the action.

Example

See Chapter 22 for privacy.

A celebrity is photographed leaving a drugs clinic and the photograph is published in a newspaper. The celebrity cannot bring a direct action against the newspaper for breach of a Convention right, as the newspaper is not a public authority. However, in any other action the court must take account of relevant articles of the Convention and any relevant jurisprudence of the European Court of Human Rights.

More detailed treatment of the relevant parts of the Convention will be given in the appropriate chapters. At this stage of the book an indication will be given of the articles likely to affect tort law and where their impact will be felt.

Convention jurisprudence is different from English law but normally works on the basis of a right being given by an article (such as freedom of speech) and then the state being permitted to make derogations from that right for particular purposes (such as the protection of reputation). In making these derogations the state is allowed a 'margin of appreciation', in the sense that not all national laws need be identical. However, any derogations may be subjected to a test of whether the derogation was 'necessary' for the protection of one of the stated aims. This involves the court performing a balancing act between the harm done by a breach of the right and the harm which will be caused by upholding it. One of the difficulties posed for English law by the new law is that tort law is generally based on the commission of a *wrong* whereas Strasbourg jurisprudence is based on *rights*. The tension between these concepts creates problems for courts.

Example

A newspaper wishes to publish a political corruption story about X. They are not able to prove that all their allegations are true. The relevant right is freedom of speech. The newspaper should be free to expose political wrongdoing. However, one of the permitted derogations is the protection of reputation. The question for English law will be whether the existing law of defamation draws the correct balance in the sense that any restriction on the newspaper's freedom to publish is necessary in a democratic society to protect X's reputation.

See Chapter 21 for defamation.

Article 6

This gives the right to a fair trial. The most serious effect of Article 6 will be in negligence, where the granting of immunity from negligence actions to certain groups of public or quasi-public bodies such as the police and advocates had already come under scrutiny. The previous system of the defendant having the action 'struck out' at an early stage because the defendant had immunity came under attack from the Strasbourg court. (***Osman* v *UK** [1999] FLR 193.) This was on the basis of a lack of proportionality, as on a striking out application there was no opportunity of balancing the claimant's interests against the defendant's immunity claim. This decision caused difficulties to the English courts (see ***Barrett* v *Enfield London Borough Council** [1999] 3 All ER 193), which had difficulties in determining how an article which appears to be concerned with procedural rights could affect a substantive right as to whether a claimant was entitled to bring a claim in negligence on these facts at all. The Strasbourg court then acknowledged in a later case (***Z* v *UK** [2001] 2 FLR 612) that their decision in ***Osman*** had been based on a misunderstanding of the English rules of negligence and the working of the striking out procedure.

See Chapter 7 for liability of public authorities.

Matthews v *Ministry of Defence* [2003] 1 All ER 689

The claimant brought proceedings for negligence after serving in the Royal Navy and alleging that he had suffered personal injury as a result of exposure to asbestos fibres. At the time of his service the Crown Proceedings Act 1947 s 10(1) precluded certain claims for personal injury against the Crown. The claimant contended that s 10(1) was incompatible with Article 6 of the Convention, which gives the right to a fair trial. The House of Lords ruled that it was compatible as it was a substantive limitation on claims against the Crown, not a procedural bar.

See Chapter 7 for liability of public authorities.

The collision between two different legal systems, the pragmatic English common law and rights-based Strasbourg law will cause tensions and problems for many years. Subtly and gradually it appears likely that some areas of English tort law where there was no duty owed may be affected by the Convention. The courts, for example, now appear more prepared to weigh the various interests in cases involving public authorities and children more carefully.

Article 2

See Chapter 15 for medical law.

See Chapter 7 for Van Colle v Chief Constable of the Hertfordshire Police.

See Chapter 7 for liability of the police.

See Chapter 7 for liability of public authorities.

Article 2 provides a right to life. This is most pertinent to medical law and to date English law has been found to comply with the right. The major right to life decision is that food and water may lawfully be withdrawn from a patient in a permanent vegetative state. (*Airedale NHS Trust v Bland* [1993] 1 All ER 821.) This decision has been held to be compatible with the Convention. (*NHS Trust A v M; NHS Trust B v H* [2001] 2 WLR 942.)

The most interesting area under Article 2 may be where an individual is unable to obtain treatment. Would the courts be prepared to sanction a right to treatment?

One way in which the right to life can be invoked and the principles to be applied by a court is illustrated by *Van Colle v Chief Constable of the Hertfordshire Police* [2008] UKHL 50. A prosecution witness in a criminal case was murdered by the person charged with the offence. An action under the Human Rights Act by his estate and dependants failed on the facts against the police for neglect of duty leading to loss of life contrary to Article 2. It is important to note that this was not a tort case but a direct action under the human rights legislation. (See also *Mitchell v Glasgow City Council* [2009] UKHL 11 for an action against a local authority.)

Article 3

See Chapter 7 for liability of public authorities.

This is the right not to be subjected to degrading treatment. There are instances where a claimant can be prevented from claiming a remedy in tort law for policy reasons. Such a prohibition applied to actions against social workers for negligence in relation to care decisions on children. Even if no tort action exists, it may be possible to claim damages for a breach of Article 3.

Article 5

See Chapter 20 for trespass to the person.

Article 5 provides a right to liberty and security. This right is likely to operate in actions for trespass to the person and whether English law provides satisfactory remedies.

Article 10

See Chapters 21 and 22.

Article 10 provides a right to freedom of speech. This will be particularly relevant to actions in defamation and privacy.

Article 8

Article 8 provides a right to a family life and privacy. There was previously no direct right to privacy in English law but the courts have had to confront this gap and balance the right to privacy against the right to freedom of speech.

The right to privacy also applies to cases of medical treatment and to nuisance actions.

Human rights and tort law

Conflicts inevitably arise between the rights-based human rights regime and the wrongs-based English tort law. These problems will continue to arise for a considerable period of time. One example of the stresses raised was considered by the House of Lords in the following case:

Watkins v *Secretary of State for the Home Department* [2006] 2 All ER 353

The claimant was a prisoner serving a sentence of life imprisonment. The confidentiality of his legal correspondence was protected by the Prison Rules. The claimant complained that prison staff had breached those rules by opening and reading mail when they were not entitled to do so. He brought an action against the Secretary of State and certain prison officers for damages for misfeasance in public office. The judge found that three of the officers had acted in bad faith but he dismissed the claims against those officers on the ground that misfeasance in public office was not a tort actionable *per se*, and that the claimant had failed to prove actual loss. The Court of Appeal allowed the claimant's appeal, holding that if there was a right which could be identified as a constitutional right, then there could be a cause of action in misfeasance in public office for infringement of that right without proof of damage. They held that the prison officers had infringed the claimant's constitutional right of unimpeded access to the courts and to legal advice. A nominal award of general damages was made.

The House of Lords held that the tort of misfeasance in public office was never actionable without proof of material damage, which included financial loss, or physical or mental injury and psychiatric illness but not distress, injured feelings, indignation or annoyance. The importance of the claimant's right to enjoyment of his right to confidential legal correspondence did not require or justify the modification of the rule that material damage had to be proved to establish the cause of action. Modification would open the door to argument as to whether other rights less obviously fundamental, basic or constitutional were sufficiently close or analogous to be treated, for damage purposes, in the same way and in the absence of a codified constitution the outcome of such argument in other than clear cases would necessarily be uncertain. The lack of a remedy in tort for someone in the position of the claimant, who had suffered a legal wrong but no material damage, did not leave him without a legal remedy. It could reasonably be inferred that Parliament had intended that infringements of the core human and constitutional rights protected by the Human Rights Act 1998 should be remedied under it and not by development of parallel remedies.

The Court of Appeal had made a bold attempt to create something akin to 'constitutional torts' which would have their own rules but the House of Lords were not convinced that the structure of English tort law could be changed in this manner and numerous problems would arise particularly with determining what a constitutional tort was.

Access to justice

The cost of litigation is high and one of the problems with justice is who pays? A litigant may have the money to pay and we have already seen that a high proportion of cases are funded by insurance companies.

An alternative is state funded litigation in the form of legal aid. At one time this was seen as the way forward but as pressure has come on government budgets so legal aid has been drastically cut.

A third way of funding litigation is through 'no win no fee' arrangements backed up by insurance (CFAs). An extensive review of fees and access (*Review of Civil Litigation Costs* TSO, 2010 (The Jackson Report)) recommended the abolition of CFAs and after the event insurance (ATE) and allowed the use of damages based arrangements (DBAs). The review also proposed a 10 per cent increase in general non-pecuniary damages to assist in paying the success fee. A number of proposals in the review were brought into force by the Legal Aid, Sentencing and Punishment of Offenders Act 2012. The effect appears to be that fewer claims are being made and the cost of actions has been reduced.

Summary

This chapter deals with the general principles of the law of tort:

What is a tort?

- A civil wrong committed against an individual.
- Interests which are protected by law.
- Protected by an award of damages or an injunction.

Elements of a tort

- The basic pattern is an act (or omission) by the defendant which causes damage to the claimant.
- The damage must be caused by the fault of the defendant and must be a recognised form of harm.
- Some torts do not require fault and are known as torts of strict liability.
- Some interests are not protected by tort law – *damnum sine injuria*.
- Some torts do not require damage – *injuria sine damno* – these are known as torts actionable *per se*.

Interests protected

- Personal security by assault, battery, false imprisonment and negligence.
- Interests in property by nuisance, ***Rylands* v *Fletcher***, trespass to land and negligence.
- Economic interests by the economic torts and negligence.
- Reputation and privacy by defamation and breach of confidence.

Role of policy

- Factors which influence a decision such as insurance.
- Role of insurance.
- Damages usually paid by an insurance company.
- May be first-party or third-party insurance.
- Most cases are settled.
- Tort system unable to operate without insurance.
- Insurers have considerable control over the conduct of litigation.

Fault and strict liability

- Moral and social arguments in favour of fault – 'bad people pay'.
- Fault has now moved to being a judicially set standard of conduct.

Malice

- Basic principle is that it is irrelevant – ***Bradford Corporation v Pickles***.
- Exceptions where malice is an essential ingredient of the tort.
- Exceptions where malice may be relevant to liability – nuisance (***Christie v Davey***) and defamation in the defences of fair comment and qualified privilege.

Intention

- Trespass – where a person desires a result and foresees it – the person must intend to do the act but need not intend to do harm.
- Fraud and injurious falsehood.
- Conspiracy.

Negligence

- Careless behaviour.
- An objective standard – reasonable person – ***Nettleship v Weston***.
- Objective of the negligence formula – deterrence or compensation.

Strict liability

- Liability without fault.
- No coherent theme.
- Applies in cases of trespassing livestock, vicarious liability, breach of statutory duty and (arguably) ***Rylands v Fletcher***.

Objectives of tort

- Deterrence – may be individual deterrence – but damages paid by insurers – or general (market) deterrence.
- Compensation.
- Three types of compensation – tort law, public and private insurance.
- Tort law compensation in the area of personal injuries criticised as it is slow, expensive and unpredictable.
- Alternatives include no fault schemes such as that in New Zealand.

Compensation culture?

- Specialised lawyers, Conditional Fee Arrangements and claims management companies.
- Appears to be no great increase in claims but there is in the amount of damages.
- Section 1 of the Compensation Act 2006 appears to add little to the common law.

Boundaries of tort

- Contract and tort.
- Tortious duties fixed by law – contract duties voluntarily assumed – not always clear cut – some contractual duties imposed by law and some tortious duties arise from a voluntary relationship.

- Contract protects the expectation interest and tort the status quo interest – but there are examples in case law where this is not so – **Ross v Caunters**.
- Tort law usually protects against damage to person and property.
- Contract law is primarily concerned with economic interests.
- There may be concurrent liability where the claimant has a choice between contract and tort.

Minors

- Anyone may sue in tort.
- Defendant minors pose a problem with the setting of the standard of care.
- A duty is owed to an unborn child.

Human rights

- European Convention on Human Rights applies against public bodies.
- A new remedy is created and compensation may be awarded for breach of a Convention right but no double compensation.
- Human Rights Act 1998.
- Tort law is based on commission of a wrong – Strasbourg (Convention) jurisprudence is based on rights.
- Article 6 gives the right to a fair trial and is relevant in negligence.
- Article 2 gives the right to life and is relevant to medical law.
- Article 3 gives the right not to be subjected to degrading treatment and is relevant to child care cases.
- Article 5 gives a right to liberty and security and is relevant to trespass to the person.
- Article 10 gives a right to freedom of speech and is relevant to defamation.
- Article 8 gives a right to privacy.
- Legislation must be interpreted in accordance with the Convention.

Further reading

Introductory reading

Fleming, J. G. (1985), *An Introduction to the Law of Torts* (2nd edn), Clarendon.

Williams, G. L. and Hepple, B. A. (1985), *Foundations of the Law of Tort* (2nd edn), Butterworths.

Compensation schemes

Atiyah, P. S. (1997), *The Damages Lottery*, Hart Publishing.

Atiyah, P. S. (2006), *Accidents, Compensation and the Law* (6th edn by P. Cane), Weidenfeld & Nicolson.

Conaghan, J. and Mansell, W. (1998), 'From the Permissive to the Dismissive Society' 25 JLS 284.

Genn, H. (1987), *Hard Bargaining*, Clarendon.

Harris, D. (1974), 'Accident Compensation in New Zealand: A Comprehensive Insurance System' 113 LQR 195.

Harris, D. *et al.* (1984), *Compensation and Support for Illness and Injury*, Oxford University Press.

Report of the Royal Commission on Civil Liability and Compensation for Personal Injury (The Pearson Report) Cmnd 7054 (1978) chs 3 and 4.

Civil procedure reforms

Zander, M. (1998), 'The Government's Plan on Civil Justice' 61 MLR 382.

Compensation culture

Better Regulation Task Force (2004), *Better Routes to Redress*, Cabinet Office Publications.

Hand, J. (2010) 'Compensation Culture: Fact or Fantasy?' 37(4) JLS 569.

Lewis, R., Morris, A. and Oliphant, K. (2006), 'Tort Personal Injury Claims Statistics: Is There a Compensation Culture in the United Kingdom?' 2 JPIL 87.

Morris, A, (2007) 'Spiralling or Stabilising? The Compensation Culture and our Propensity to Claim Damages in Personal Injury' 70(3) MLR 349.

The Human Rights Act 1998

Buxton, R. (2000), 'The Human Rights Act and Private Law' 116 LQR 48.

Damages under the Human Rights Act 1998, Law Commission Report No 266 (2000).

Gearty, C. (2002), 'Osman Unravels' 65 MLR 87.

Wade, W. (2000), 'Horizons of Horizontality' 116 LQR 217.

Insurance

Stapleton, J. (1995), 'Tort, Insurance and Ideology' 58 MLR 520.

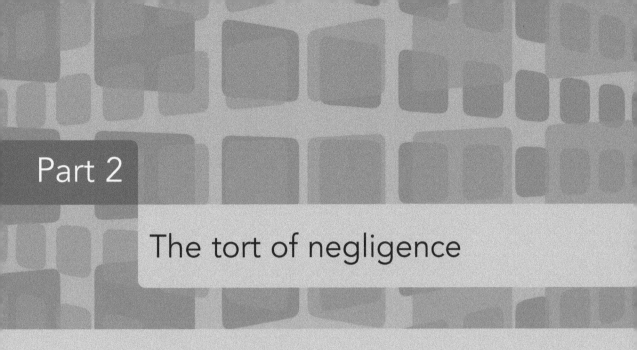

Part 2

The tort of negligence

General principles of negligence

Objectives

After reading this chapter you will:

1. Have a knowledge of the elements of the tort of negligence.

2. Understand the interests protected by the tort of negligence.

3. Appreciate the problem areas that the tort of negligence has to deal with.

4. Have a critical knowledge of the problems created by concurrent liability in contract and tort.

Elements of the tort

Objective 1

See Chapter 3 for duty of care.

See Chapter 8 for breach of duty.

See Chapter 9 for causation and remoteness.

See Chapter 10 for defences to negligence.

Negligence is the most important of the modern torts. This chapter will attempt to explain the structure of the tort, the problem areas and the issues of concurrent liability with contract law.

To succeed in a negligence action the claimant must prove three things:

1 That the defendant owed him a duty of care.

2 That the defendant was in breach of that duty; and

3 That the claimant suffered damage caused by the breach of duty, which was not too remote.

The defendant may raise certain defences to the action. The most important defences are that the claimant consented to run the risk of the injury (*volenti*) or that the defendant was contributorily negligent.

Example

A drove his car over the speed limit and failed to keep a proper lookout, as he was talking to the passenger next to him. *A*'s car struck *B*, a pedestrian, causing personal injuries to *B*. Analysing this event in terms of the legal categories, *A* owed a duty of care to *B* as one road user to another. *A* was in breach of the duty in speeding and failing to keep a proper lookout (i.e. *A* was 'negligent'). *B* has suffered damage as a result of *A*'s negligence.

If *B* had failed to look before stepping into the road, it would be open to a court to find that *B* had been contributorily negligent and reduce his damages by the proportion in which he was held to be responsible for the accident.

History of negligence

The nineteenth century saw the beginnings of the modern tort of negligence. Two concepts had to be fused in order to produce this. These were liability for positive acts causing damage, known as misfeasance, and liability for neglect of a duty to act, known as nonfeasance. In the eighteenth century, these were actionable as case for misfeasance and case for negligence respectively. The action for nonfeasance covered the neglect to perform various duties which were imposed by law, and included duties imposed by undertakings, and customs of the realm, local custom and those arising out of an office. The development of the action for misfeasance outside of pre-existing relationships was limited and was largely confined to road accidents, which were classified as actions on the case (negligence) because of the assumption of risk theory.

Development in negligence liability was stifled by the new law of contract being fashioned by the judges in the early years of the nineteenth century and by the doctrine of *laissez-faire*. The abolition of the writ system saw a clear distinction emerge between three branches of the common law of obligations, with contract emerging as the strongest partner because of the prevailing economic and philosophical influences. This dominance of contract restricted and closely defined the emergence of tort and restitution. The Industrial Revolution increased the likelihood of accidents arising out of industrial construction and the operation of the railways.

Nineteenth-century values had encouraged the view that obligations could only be voluntarily assumed through the free choice of individuals. There was little room for legally imposed obligations, such as the modern tort of negligence. For example, nineteenth century employment relationships were largely governed by the contract between the parties, but given the employee's weak bargaining position he would be unlikely to have secured the employer's agreement to bear responsibility for an accident at work. Initially the courts were reluctant to impose tortious duties on the employer to protect the employee's safety because this would be inconsistent with the contract which did not allocate responsibility. Devices used to secure this end included the doctrines of common employment and *volenti non fit injuria*. So intractable was the common law on this issue that legislative intervention was necessary to provide an insurance scheme for injured workmen.

Although the judges rapidly developed a unified theory of contract, there was nothing to unite the various negligence actions until an authoritative statement in 1932 by Lord Atkin in **Donoghue v Stevenson** [1932] AC 562. This was the famous 'neighbour test', which required a man to take 'reasonable care to avoid acts or omissions which he can reasonably foresee would be likely to injure his neighbour'. In answer to the question, 'Who is a neighbour?' Lord Atkin's answer was, 'persons who are so closely and directly affected by my act that I ought reasonably to have them in contemplation as being so affected when I am directing my mind to the acts or omissions which are called into question'. This test was not the first attempt to articulate a general theory of duty in negligence, but it was the first one to gain general acceptance.

In the nineteenth century, a right to due care was seen as something which a person had to pay for. Where there was a pre-existing relationship between the parties, the action was seen to have a contractual flavour. The tendency had been to restrict liability within the newly-defined contractual parameters. The judiciary may have been reluctant to stifle the development of nascent industries by imposing on employers and manufacturers liability to compensate an injured claimant. At that time, there was no strong insurance market, accordingly liability was generally only imposed where there was a pre-existing relationship of some kind between the claimant and the defendant.

The 'neighbour test' did not explain why certain duties were recognised but not others. At this time, there was no liability for pure nonfeasance in the absence of a pre-existing relationship between the parties. Certain positive acts which caused damage to others were not actionable in negligence. If a person ruined another financially by legitimate trade competition, then there was no liability. The duty only extended to physical damage to the person or property, and not to 'pure' economic harm which might be caused.

The values of the twentieth century differed. There was the emergence of the welfare state and a consumer-orientated society. The assumption of equality of bargaining power made in the nineteenth century was not always possible. Twentieth-century values placed more emphasis upon egalitarianism. The shift is also illustrated in the emergence of the modern law of negligence and the greater willingness of the courts to order that benefits received should be paid for. These changes can be put down to an alteration in the values which govern modern social relations. Individualism and the preservation of personal freedoms coupled with minimal market regulation were the order of the day in the nineteenth century. But we can now say that the values of the twentieth century were those of paternalism, fairness and cooperation.

While there is a difference between the values of the nineteenth and twentieth centuries, there has been a resurgence of political belief in the workings of the free market. This has led, in particular, to the emergence of a powerful body of academic opinion which argues for greater individual choice.

In tort, the major development has been in the tort of negligence. Beginning in 1932, and against a background of widely available indemnity insurance, the judiciary fashioned a remedy for physical harm caused by fault. The catalyst for this development was the neighbour test established by Lord Atkin in **Donoghue v Stevenson**. Although slow to be adopted by the judiciary, this test for whether one person owed another a duty to take reasonable care has had a remarkable history. In terms of consumer protection it provided a remedy for those persons who had no contractual protection, such as donees. In doing this it was filling a gap left by the rigidity of the contractual doctrines of consideration and privity. However successful negligence was in dealing with compensation for physical harm, it has great difficulties in providing a remedy for economic loss. The courts have regarded economic loss caused by negligent acts as the proper province of contract law and with rare exceptions have refused a remedy in negligence. This process is illustrated in the defective buildings cases (see, for example, **Murphy v Brentwood District Council** [1990] 2 All ER 908) where no remedy lies in tort against careless builders and building supervisors whose negligence has resulted in structural defects in property owned by the consumer. The loss to the building owner has been regarded by the courts as pure economic loss which is actionable only where there is a contract between the parties.

Whatever the doctrinal problems of negligence, it has created severe difficulties for consumers seeking a remedy. The expense and time of litigating and the difficulties of proving negligence are sufficient to deter all but the most determined claimant. The common law's partial success in this area has been to provide a legal framework against which producers and providers of services can work out self-regulatory codes of practice and complaints procedures. A good example is the Association of British Travel Agents code, under which, initially, a dissatisfied customer does not have to take legal proceedings but can go through a relatively swift and inexpensive complaints procedure.

However, whatever the defects of negligence it became the governing principle in tort law and replaced strict liability with a fault-based principle.

Why did negligence and the fault principle succeed as the core principle in tort law? The reasons for this are not particularly clear. One reason was the prevailing intellectual ideas in the nineteenth century when the writ system broke down and the judges forged the laws of contract and tort. At this time the emphasis was on individual responsibility and generally against state interference. The former was reflected in the principle that you should only be responsible for those losses which were caused by your *fault*.

A number of commentators have emphasised the effect of the Industrial Revolution and the great increase in the number of accidents at work as a result of industrial processes. However, there is a conflict of opinion. One viewpoint is that the development of negligence was a positive response by the law by shifting the loss. The contrary view is that the courts were concerned to protect infant industries by moving away from strict liability which might have crippled the developing industries.

The history and arguments on this subject are fascinating and complex. Although the mainstream philosophy was individualistic, there was a considerable amount of state intervention in areas such as safety at work and in transport. (For a full history see Atiyah, P., *The Rise and Fall of Freedom of Contract* (Clarendon Press 1979).)

The interests protected

Objective 2

See Chapter 17 for nuisance.

See Chapter 21 for defamation.

Negligence is the most important modern tort. Other torts are normally identified by the particular interest of the claimant which is protected: for example, defamation protects interests in reputation, and nuisance protects a person's use and enjoyment of land. Negligence, on the other hand, protects a number of interests and the only unifying factor is the defendant's conduct, which must be labelled as negligent if liability is to arise.

Three interests can be identified as being protected by the tort of negligence. These are: protection against personal injury, damage to property and economic interests. Economic losses consequential on damage to the person and damage to property may also be recovered.

> ### Example
>
> *A* drives his car negligently and collides with *B*'s car. This causes personal injuries to *B* and damage to his car (property damage). *B* may recover damages from *A* for both these losses. *B* may lose wages as a result of his injuries and may have to hire a car while his own is being repaired. Both these losses are recoverable as consequential economic loss.
>
> *A* asks his solicitor, *B*, to draw up a will leaving *A*'s property to *C*. *B* negligently drafts the will with the result that *C* is unable to take his bequest under the will. *C* may sue *B* in negligence, for the value of his lost bequest. The interest protected here is *C*'s economic interest and *C* is said to recover damages for pure economic loss.

Note the difference between consequential and pure economic loss. In the example of the will, *C* has suffered no personal injuries or property damage and his loss is said to be damage to the pocket or pure economic loss.

Readers are reminded that most defendants in tort actions will be insured and any damages awarded will be paid by an insurance company and not by the defendant themselves. When a judge says that they will not impose liability as it would impose too heavy a burden on the defendant, they usually mean that it would impose too heavy a burden on the defendant's insurers. In the car example above, *B*'s damages would be paid by *A*'s motor insurers, and *C*'s damages would be paid by *B*'s liability insurers. In both cases it is compulsory for the defendant to carry insurance against these risks.

Where a court finds the defendant is liable in negligence this is loss-shifting. However, because of the system of compulsory insurance negligence more often operates as a loss-spreading device. The loss is spread across premium payers with the insurance company.

See Chapter 1 for relevance of insurance.

A defendant cannot be liable in this tort unless the court judges him to have been negligent (i.e. at fault). This means that the defendant's conduct must have dropped below a standard set by law. Where there is liability insurance the court can set the standard at a fairly high level, as the award of damages will not directly penalise the defendant. But as one of the purposes of the negligence formula is said to be deterrence, the presence of insurance distorts the actual deterrence to the defendant.

Problem areas

Objective 3

Negligence expanded so quickly in the twentieth century that, at one time, it appeared possible that it would make other torts redundant. Its popularity was based on a fairly simple formula of fault, backed by insurance. The structure is now creaking due to problems in the insurance market and negligence no longer seems to be the simple panacea for all legal problems that it once did.

Personal injuries

In statistical terms, most negligence actions are brought for personal injuries suffered by the claimant. The majority of personal injury actions are brought in the areas of motor accidents and accidents at work.

See Chapter 1 for the Pearson Commission.

An injured person requires compensation for their injuries and the more serious the injury, the greater the need for compensation. It has already been observed that the insurance factor dilutes the personal deterrence objective of negligence. As the other objective of tort law is compensation for the victim, the negligence system can only be supported if it is an efficient and fair method of delivering compensation to the victims. The Pearson Commission established that this was not the case.

The inefficiency and apparent unfairness of the tort system at delivering compensation has led to calls for it to be replaced in whole or in part by a no-fault scheme of compensation or by private insurance. No such scheme is perfect and the introduction of such a scheme is a question of political will.

Medical negligence

See Chapter 15 for medical negligence.

There have been claims that England is suffering a medical malpractice crisis similar to that in the United States. Doctors claim that the threat of litigation leads to 'defensive medicine': i.e. carrying out procedures in order to avoid being sued, rather than for the benefit of the patient. The rise in the Caesarean section rate is often pointed to as an example of defensive medicine. Research shows that the number of claims for clinical negligence has dropped but the overall cost of claims is rising due to changes in the way in which damages are calculated. The number of claims dropped from 10,980 in 2000–01 to 7,196 in 2004–05. The cost of claims rose from £415 million in 2000–01 to £503 million in 2004–05. (R. Lewis, A. Morris and K. Oliphant, 'Tort Personal Injury Claims Statistics: Is There a Compensation Culture in the United Kingdom?' (2006) 2 JPIL 87–103.) (See **www.nhsla.com** for information on current claims figures.)

Victims of medical accidents are not happy with the negligence system. Numerous problems stand in the way of a person who wishes to sue for medical negligence. The action is expensive and legal aid is not easily available; lawyers with the necessary skills in this specialised area are not always easy to find; the system leads to a closing of ranks on the part of the medical profession, which makes it difficult for the patient to find out what went wrong; even if the victim does obtain compensation, this may be many years after the event.

Disenchantment with the system on the part of both doctors and patients led to calls for medical negligence to be replaced by a no-fault scheme of compensation. This was supported by the medical insurers, doctors, professional bodies and victim support agencies. The Department of Health's proposal for an alternative to tort law, in the form of the NHS Redress Act 2006, is discussed elsewhere.

See Chapters 1 and 15.

 ## Economic loss

See Chapter 5 for details on economic loss.

Complaints about negligence in the area of personal injuries are concentrated on inefficiency and unfairness, but at least the law in that area is relatively clear and mature, except in cases of psychiatric damage. The tort of negligence has only recently ventured into the area of economic loss and the law on this subject is unclear and at an early stage of development.

Historically, contract was the proper action where a person suffered economic loss and if a person had no contract they had no action. The reason that negligence (tort) law moved into this area was the perceived injustice created by the doctrine of *privity* in contract law. This doctrine states that only a party to a contract may sue or be sued on the contract. A party to a contract is a person who provides consideration.

> ### Example
>
> *A* instructs *B*, his solicitor, to draft a will leaving *A*'s property to *C*. When *A* dies, it is discovered that *B* has drafted the will negligently with the result that *C* is unable to take his bequest. *C*'s loss is economic loss and in theory *C* should sue for breach of contract. But *C* has no contract. The contract is between *A* and *B*. The doctrine of privity means that *C* cannot sue *B* in contract, which leaves tort law to decide whether *C* should have a negligence action against *B*.

It is often useful to consider economic loss cases in diagrammatic form:

$$A \;\text{———}\; \text{Contract} \;\text{———}\; B$$
$$\vdots$$
$$C$$

Many of the economic loss cases fall into this triangular pattern. The question for the court is usually whether tort law is prepared to complete the triangle by granting *C* a negligence action against *B*.

Omissions

See Chapter 6 for omissions.

Negligence actions are usually concerned with the situation where *A* commits a negligent act and causes damage to *B*. But could *A* be liable in negligence to *B* where they omit to do something and *B* suffers damage?

NB: In legal terminology, a positive act is known as misfeasance and a failure to act as nonfeasance.

Liability for failing to take positive steps to safeguard another is traditionally the role of contract. If you want a person to assist you then you have to pay them (provide consideration).

If *A* sees *B* drowning then they are under no duty in tort to attempt a rescue. But what if *A* has some relationship with *B*? For example, *A* is *B*'s parent or *B* is a visitor to *A*'s premises. Would *A* then be under a duty to attempt a rescue?

Liability in contract and tort

Objective 4

See also Chapter 1 'The boundaries of tort'.

See Chapter 26 for limitation.

See Chapter 9 for remoteness.

See Chapter 10 for contributory negligence.

See Chapter 5 for details on *Hedley Byrne*.

Where the parties have a contractual relationship, can there also be tortious liability? This is known as *concurrent liability*. The answer to this question has practical importance as, if the answer is yes, the claimant will be able to take advantage of tortious rules which may be more advantageous.

The most important of these will be the rules on limitation. These rules govern the time period within which a claimant must bring an action. In contract, time periods generally run from the time a contract is made and in tort from the time damage is suffered.

Other rules are those on *causation* and *remoteness*. Remoteness principles in tort are generally thought to be more favourable to the claimant than those in contract.

Not all concurrent liability principles will run in the claimant's favour. If the claimant chooses to sue in negligence, then the defendant has the opportunity of raising the defence of contributory negligence by the claimant. If the action is brought in contract, then the opportunity to raise contributory negligence is limited by the current law and is not available where the contractual duty is stricter than negligence.

Two competing principles have been at work in English law since the courts started to grapple with this problem. The first is the solution adopted by French law, that a party to a contract should pursue the remedy in contract alone. This has the advantage of simplicity. The second is the principle followed in German law that concurrent remedies are permissible. At first, English courts refused to allow professional people, such as solicitors and architects, to be sued in tort by their contractual clients. This created a problem as certain professional people, such as doctors, could be sued in contract or tort.

The decision in *Hedley Byrne* v *Heller* [1964] AC 465, changed the basis on which English law operated. It was now possible for a person who did not have a contract to sue in respect of negligent advice leading to economic loss. This raised the question of why a person who had a contractual relationship should not be able to take advantage of tortious principles and might be worse off than a person who had received gratuitous advice.

The case sparked off a series of decisions sympathetic to the existence of concurrent duties. These included: *Esso Petroleum Co Ltd* v *Mardon* [1976] QB 801 (petrol company and tenant); *Batty* v *Metropolitan Realisations Ltd* [1978] QB 554 (property developer and purchaser); *Midland Bank Trust Co Ltd* v *Hett, Stubbs & Kemp* [1979] Ch 384 (solicitor and client).

Doubt was cast on these developments by a statement by Lord Scarman in *Tai Hing Cotton Mill* v *Liu Chong Bank Ltd* [1986] AC 80 at 107:

Their Lordships do not believe that there is anything to the advantage of the law's development in searching for liability in tort where the parties are in a contractual relationship. Though it is possible as a matter of legal semantics to conduct an analysis of the rights and duties inherent in some contractual relationships . . . either as a matter of contract law when the question will be what, if any, terms are to be implied or as a matter of tort law when the task will be to identify a duty arising from the proximity and character of the relationship between the parties, their Lordships believe it to be correct in principle and necessary for the avoidance of confusion in the law to adhere to the contractual analysis: on principle because it is a relationship in which the parties have, subject to a few exceptions, the right to determine their obligations to each other, and for the avoidance of confusion because different consequences do follow according to whether liability arises in contract or tort, e.g. in the limitation of action.

In *Tai Hing*, the claimant was seeking to establish liability in tort which went further than the liability established by the contract between the parties. The court had refused to imply a term into a contract between banker and customer whereby the customer would be obliged to take reasonable care of the bank's interests. They also refused to recognise a similar obligation based in tort. The case does not deal with the position between professional and client and is probably best interpreted as meaning that liability in tort cannot be imposed which contradicts the express terms of the contract. (See *Johnstone* v *Bloomsbury Health Authority*, below.) The case does not prevent a claimant from taking advantage of a tortious duty which is the same as a contractual duty in order to use advantageous rules such as limitation periods.

The case posed difficulty in the area of employer's liability to their employees. This area is a complex mixture of contract and tort. There is a contract of employment between the employer and employee which will contain express terms. There are also implied terms in the contract and the employer owes tortious duties. The next case is concerned with the interaction of the express and implied terms and the tortious duties.

Johnstone v *Bloomsbury Health Authority* [1991] 2 All ER 293

The claimant was employed by the defendant health authority as a junior doctor. The essence of his claim was that, by his contract, he was obliged to work 88 hours per week and that this was in breach of the employer's duty to take reasonable care for his safety and well-being. The Court of Appeal heard cross appeals on the question of striking out the claim.

It was held (Leggatt LJ dissenting) that although the defendants were entitled to require the claimant to work up to 88 hours per week under his contract of employment, they had to exercise that discretion in such a way as not to injure the claimant. The health authority therefore had to exercise its power in such a way as not to injure the claimant's health. The authority could not require the claimant to work so much overtime in a week that his health might reasonably foreseeably be damaged.

Two of the judges also stated that an implied contractual term in a contract of employment, such as the implied duty to take reasonable care for the health of employees, is subject to any express terms in the contract. It was only because the defendants had a discretion to get the claimant to work 88 hours, rather than an absolute obligation, that the Vice-Chancellor was able to consider the interaction of the express and implied terms. Stuart-Smith LJ dissented on this point. To him it was a question of the interaction of the two terms, the express and implied one. The contract gave the authority the power to require the claimant to work up to 88 hours per week, but only if this could be done in such a way as not to breach the implied term of reasonable care for the employee's health.

If the approach of the majority were adopted on the point of express terms overriding implied terms, this would reduce the whole of the law of negligence on employer's liability to a question of contract. It is unlikely that the judiciary would take such an approach. One problem may be that the judges were trying too hard to follow Lord Scarman in *Tai Hing*. However, in that case his Lordship stressed that his quote was particularly apt for commercial relationships where the allocation of commercial risks should not be disturbed by an escape out of contract into tort. What is appropriate for a commercial case may not be so for an employer's liability one.

Where there is no contradiction between the contractual and the tortious duties, it is now clear that concurrent liability does exist and that a claimant can take advantage of favourable tortious rules.

Henderson v Merrett Syndicates Ltd [1994] 3 All ER 506

See also Chapter 5 for *Henderson* v *Merrett*.

Lloyd's names sued their managing agents. Some of the names had a contract with their agents but this was held not to preclude a duty of care in tort.

Lord Goff in a detailed judgment reviewed the authorities and upheld the analysis in favour of concurrent liability.

[L]iability can, and in my opinion should, be founded squarely on the principle established in **Hedley Byrne** itself, from which it follows that an assumption of responsibility coupled with the concomitant reliance may give rise to a tortious duty of care irrespective of whether there is a contractual relationship between the parties, and in consequence, unless his contract precludes him from doing so, the claimant, who has available to him concurrent remedies in contract and tort, may choose that remedy which appears to him the most advantageous.

This case established that concurrent liability in contract and tort is generally available. There will not be concurrent liability in all cases where there is a contract between the parties. The contractual duty must require the exercise of reasonable care and not be a strict liability duty. The tortious duty must be co-extensive with the contractual one and be freestanding in the sense that the claimant cannot build on the contract to establish a duty where no tortious duty is recognised. This would be the case where a person had a contract with a builder and suffered economic loss. There is no duty of care on a builder to avoid economic loss. However, the tortious duty may be more extensive than the contractual one, for example, where a professional gives advice which is outside his retainer. (**Holt v Payne Skillington** [1996] PNLR 179.)

It is possible that this decision may lead to a review of other cases. What is the position now, for instance, of the following case?

Reid v Rush & Tompkins Group plc [1989] 3 All ER 228

The claimant was employed by the defendants and was sent abroad to work. He was injured in a motor accident by a hit-and-run driver. The claimant sued his employers, claiming (among other things) that they were in breach of duty in tort to take all reasonable steps to protect his economic welfare, arising out of personal injury, while he was acting in the course of his employment. The breach of duty was alleged to be in failing to take out appropriate insurance cover for him or advising him to take it out for himself. Relying on Lord Scarman's dicta in *Tai Hing*, the Court of Appeal held that as there was no term in the contract providing for this, the claimant was precluded from suing for economic loss in tort.

This was an attempt by the claimant to expand the employer's duties beyond the express and implied terms of the contract and the existing boundaries of the law of torts. The decision must now be read in the light of **Henderson** and **Spring v Guardian Assurance** [1994] 3 All ER 129 and **Scally v Southern Health and Social Services Board** [1992] 1 AC 294. **Spring** imposes liability for economic loss on an employer for giving a negligent reference and **Scally** imposes liability on an employer through the implied term contractual route for failure to give information regarding valuable pension rights.

Summary

This chapter deals with the general principles of the tort of negligence.

- The claimant must prove duty, breach and damage to establish the tort of negligence.
- The usual defences to a negligence action are *volenti* and contributory negligence.
- Unlike other torts, negligence protects various interests.
- Three interests are protected: personal injuries; property damage; and economic loss.
- Insurance is crucial in underpinning the tort of negligence.
- The presence of insurance may explain the standard of care set by a court.
- The alternative to compensating for personal injuries through the tort system would be a no-fault scheme or private insurance.
- Some areas of negligence pose particular problems. These include medical negligence, liability for economic loss and liability for omissions (nonfeasance).
- It is possible for there to be concurrent liability in contract and tort based on the same facts. (**Henderson v Merrett Syndicates** (1994).)
- In order for there to be concurrent liability, there must be a contractual duty based on reasonable care; the tortious duty must be a freestanding one; and the tortious duty must not have been excluded by the contract.
- The advantages of a tort action for a claimant are principally in the more generous limitation rules and the rules on remoteness of damage.

Further reading

Atiyah, P. (1979), *The Rise and Fall of Freedom of Contract,* Clarendon Press.

Burrows, A. (1995), 'Solving the Problem of Concurrent Liability' Current Legal Problems 103.

Fleming, J. (1984), 'Comparative Law of Torts' 4 OJLS 235.

Lewis, R., Morris, A. and Oliphant, K. (2006), 'Tort Personal Injury Claims Statistics: Is There a Compensation Culture in the United Kingdom?' 2 JPIL 87.

Markesinis, B. S. (1987), 'An Expanding Tort Law – The Price of a Rigid Contract Law' 103 LQR 354.

www.nhsla.com for litigation against the National Health Service.

Stapleton, J. (1985), 'Compensating Victims of Diseases' 5 OJLS 248.

Stapleton, J. (1988), 'The Gist of Negligence' 104 LQR 213.

3

Duty of care

Objectives

After reading this chapter you will:

1. Understand the legal rules governing the imposition of a duty of care and appreciate the significance of insurance in the law of negligence.
2. Have a knowledge of the concepts of proximity and assumption of responsibility.
3. Have a critical knowledge of the policy factors which influence the courts in deciding whether to impose a duty of care.

Introduction

Objective 1

The first element in the claimant's case negligence is whether the defendant owed him a duty to take reasonable care. This chapter will look at the general principles applicable to duty of care. Subsequent chapters will concentrate on particularly difficult areas such as nervous shock and economic loss. The reader who is new to the subject may well find it difficult at first. It is advisable to read this chapter in conjunction with the following three.

It is accepted that negligence does not exist in a vacuum and that there is no all-embracing duty owed to the whole world in all circumstances. If it were otherwise, a person who saw someone walking near the top of a cliff could be liable if they then failed to shout a warning and there was a fall.

Duty of care, therefore, exists as a control device in order to determine who can bring an action for negligence and in what circumstances. Because society changes so rapidly, this area of law will never be static. Changes in technology, business practices and the rapid growth of the service industries, coupled with increasing consumer demands, present problems. Demands for protection against negligent conduct are virtually limitless. When a person suffers loss as a result of negligent conduct, they will want to shift that loss on to the person who caused it through a negligence action. But negligence will only be successful as long as the insurance market is able to cover new forms of liability at premiums which people can afford. The appeal courts, therefore, have to set a limit on the boundaries of when one person will owe another a duty to take reasonable care. It will be seen in this chapter that this boundary has moved backwards and forwards with startling rapidity.

A court may not be explicit about the socio-economic reasons for a change in the law. Conceptual tools such as reasonable **foreseeability**, **proximity**, policy and assumption of responsibility are used by the judges to determine whether a duty of care exists.

When a negligence action is brought to court, the judge will usually be able to rely on a precedent to determine whether a duty exists. But what if there is no precedent? What test should the judge use to determine whether a duty exists in this particular case?

See Chapter 5 for detail on economic loss.

The law in this area has grown to be extremely complex, particularly with regard to economic loss.

Historical development

Negligence liability has existed in one form or another for centuries, but until the nineteenth century there was no concept of duty as we now know it. Liability existed within defined relationships such as doctor–patient, ferryman–passenger, blacksmith–customer. Where a case fell outside a recognised relationship, there was no test for determining whether liability existed or not.

The need for such a test was brought about by the social, industrial and technological changes wrought by the Industrial Revolution. However, the economic and philosophical views which were prevalent during this period meant that the law of contract played the dominant part in the law of obligations. *Laissez-faire* ideology led to the view that an obligation should not be imposed on a person unless they had agreed to it. As tortious obligations were generally thought to be imposed by law, rather than being based on agreement, the law of tort played a minor part at this stage.

Although there were some attempts in the late nineteenth century to develop a general test, there was no accepted test until 1932.

The neighbour test

Donoghue v *Stevenson* [1932] AC 562

A friend of the claimant purchased ginger beer in an opaque bottle. The claimant poured half of the ginger beer into a glass and drank it. She then poured the remainder into the glass and saw the remains of a decomposed snail. She claimed to have suffered illness as a result. She sued the manufacturers of the ginger beer in negligence as she had no contract with either the retailer or the manufacturer. The House of Lords laid down that a duty was owed by the defendant to the claimant.

This is probably the most famous case in legal history. Why?

1 It destroyed the privity fallacy. This idea laid down that where the defendant was liable to one person for breach of contract, they could not be liable to a third party in tort for the same act or omission. On the facts of the case the café proprietor would have been liable to the friend for breach of contract in selling him a defective product, if the friend had suffered damage. By creating a tortious duty to the claimant, the House of Lords began the removal of the privity fallacy from English law.

See Chapter 12 for defective products.

2 A new category of duty was created: that of manufacturers of dangerous products to their ultimate consumers. This is known as the narrow rule and is the *ratio decidendi* of the case.

3   The fame of the case rests on the *obiter dicta* (things said by the way). Lord Atkin stated his famous neighbour test as a general test for determining whether a duty of care existed. This is known as the wide rule:

> You must take reasonable care to avoid acts or omissions which you can reasonably foresee would be likely to injure your neighbour. Who, then, in law is my neighbour? The answer seems to be – persons who are so closely and directly affected by my act that I ought reasonably to have them in contemplation as being so affected when I am directing my mind to the acts or omissions which are called in question.

Lord Macmillan stated:

> In the daily contacts of social and business life human beings are thrown into, or place themselves in, an infinite variety of relations with their fellows; and the law can refer only to the standards of the reasonable man in order to determine whether any particular relation gives rise to a duty to take care as between those who stand in that relation to each other. The grounds of action may be as various and manifold as human errancy; and the conception of legal responsibility may develop in adaptation to altering social conditions and standards. The criterion of judgment must adjust and adapt itself to the changing circumstances of life. The categories of negligence are never closed.

Controversy exists as to how influential the neighbour test has been in the development of duty of care principles. The test has been much cited and gave the law a starting point for the question of whether a duty of care existed, based on reasonable foreseeability of damage to the claimant. What has always been clear is that this test alone was not sufficient to explain cases where the court found that no duty existed. There were numerous cases after *Donoghue* where the damage to the claimant was clearly foreseeable but the courts refused to find a duty. One example was that of the builder who negligently constructed a house. The courts, until the 1970s, refused to find that the builder was liable in negligence to the house owner for the cost of repair. There were also cases of **psychiatric damage** where foreseeable shock did not give rise to a duty. Some other factor was clearly required to explain these cases.

The expansion of negligence liability

See Chapter 5 for *Hedley Byrne* v *Heller*.

The neighbour test was originally confined to cases where physical damage was caused to the claimant by the defendant's negligence. But in *Hedley Byrne & Co Ltd* v *Heller & Partners Ltd* [1964] AC 465 the House of Lords allowed, in principle, a duty of care not to cause economic loss. They rejected the neighbour test as giving rise to potentially too wide a liability and instead stated that there had to be a special relationship between the parties.

A more elaborate test was put forward in *Anns* v *Merton* in an attempt to rationalise developments since *Donoghue* and provide a framework within which judges could develop the law. (*Anns* v *Merton London Borough Council* [1978] AC 728 at 751–2 per Lord Wilberforce.)

A two-stage test was established. The first stage was to establish that the parties satisfied the requirements of the neighbour test. If this was done then a duty would exist unless the court found that policy dictated that there should be no duty.

The two-stage test altered the way in which the neighbour test was used. Previously, the courts had used it to justify new areas of liability if there were policy reasons for doing so. Now, it would apply unless there were policy reasons for excluding it. In other words, policy was now to operate as a long stop.

Lord Wilberforce's dicta were followed by a brief but dramatic expansion in negligence liability as the courts applied the two-stage test. The high-water mark of this expansion was reached in ***Junior Books Ltd* v *Veitchi Co Ltd*** [1983] 1 AC 520, where the House of Lords apparently extended liability for economic loss to encompass traditional contract liability.

See Chapter 5 for *Junior Books* v *Veitchi*.

Retraction of negligence

The expansion of liability which took place in the 1970s and early 1980s caused some alarm to the appellate courts, who set about trying to check it and pull it back. The alarm was set off by a number of factors, including the difficulties in obtaining adequate insurance to cover the new types of liability and the incursion of tort into traditionally contractual areas.

When changes are made to the law by the judiciary, they are usually not explicit about the socio-economic factors which make these changes necessary, but they do need conceptual tools in order to make these changes. Highly influential in judicial reasoning during the period of retraction was a statement by Brennan J in the Australian case of ***Sutherland Shire Council* v *Heyman*** (1985) 60 ALR 1:

> Of course, if foreseeability of injury to another were the exhaustive criterion of a prima facie duty to act to prevent the occurrence of that injury, it would be essential to introduce some kind of restrictive qualification – perhaps a qualification of the kind stated in the second stage of the general proposition in *Anns*. I am unable to accept that approach. It is preferable, in my view, that the law should develop novel categories of negligence incrementally and by analogy with established categories, rather than by a massive extension of a prima facie duty of care restrained only by indefinable 'considerations which ought to negative, or to reduce or limit the scope of the duty or the class of persons to whom it is owed'. The proper role of the 'second stage', . . . embraces no more than those 'further elements' [in addition to the neighbour principle] which are appropriate to the particular category of negligence and which confine the duty of care within narrower limits than those which would be defined by an unqualified application of the neighbour principle.

The approach taken by Brennan J was to reject a broad general principles approach as taken by Lord Wilberforce and instead adopt an incremental approach. This would develop by looking at the particular category that the case fell into and developing specific rules within that category. So a psychiatric damage case, for example, would attract different rules from a straightforward physical damage one, as the former creates different problems and is not susceptible to an approach based on reasonable foreseeability alone.

This approach has been adopted a number of times by the House of Lords and you will find it referred to in the case reports as one of the tests for whether a duty of care exists. For example, Lord Keith in ***Yuen Kun-yeu* v *Attorney-General of Hong Kong*** [1987] 2 All ER 705:

> Their Lordships venture to think that the two-stage test formulated by Lord Wilberforce for determining the existence of a duty of care in negligence has been elevated to a degree of importance greater than it merits, and greater perhaps than its author intended. Further, the expression of the first stage of the test carries with it a risk of misinterpretation . . . there are two possible views of what Lord Wilberforce meant. The first view . . . is that he meant to test the sufficiency of proximity simply by the reasonable contemplation of likely harm. The second view . . . is that Lord Wilberforce meant the expression proximity or neighbourhood to be a composite one, importing the whole concept of necessary relationship between plaintiff and defendant . . . In their Lordships' opinion the second view is the correct one . . . foreseeability does not of itself, and automatically, lead to a duty of care . . . The truth is that the

trilogy of cases referred to by Lord Wilberforce (***Donoghue* v *Stevenson*** (1932); ***Hedley Byrne* v *Heller*** (1963); ***Home Office* v *Dorset Yacht*** (1970)) each demonstrate particular sets of circumstances, differing in character, which were adjudged to have the effect of bringing into being a relationship apt to give rise to a duty of care. Foreseeability of harm is a necessary ingredient of such a relationship, but it is not the only one . . . The speech of Lord Atkin stressed not only the requirement of foreseeability of harm but also that of a close and direct relationship of proximity . . . The second stage of Lord Wilberforce's test is one which will rarely have to be applied. It can arise only in a limited category of cases where, notwithstanding that a case of negligence is made out on the proximity basis, public policy requires that there should be no liability . . . their Lordships consider that for the future it should be recognised that the two-stage test in ***Anns*** is not to be regarded as in all circumstances a suitable guide to the existence of a duty of care.

See also Chapter 5 for *Caparo* v *Dickman*.

Further consideration was given to this question by Lord Bridge in ***Caparo Industries plc* v *Dickman*** [1990] 1 All ER 568 when he reviewed the necessary ingredients of a duty of care:

> What emerges is that, in addition to the foreseeability of damage, necessary ingredients in any situation giving rise to a duty of care are that there should exist between the party owing the duty and the party to whom it is owed a relationship characterised by the law as one of proximity or neighbourhood and that the situation should be one in which the court considers it fair, just and reasonable that the law should impose a duty of a given scope on the one party for the benefit of the other . . . the concepts of proximity and fairness . . . are not susceptible of any such precise definition as would be necessary to give them utility as practical tests, but amount in effect to little more than convenient labels to attach to the features of different specific situations . . . I think the law has now moved in the direction of attaching greater significance to the more traditional categorisation of distinct and recognisable situations as guides to the existence, the scope and the limits of the varied duties of care which the law imposes.

See Chapter 5 for *Murphy* v *Brentwood DC*.

Finally, it should be noted that in ***Murphy* v *Brentwood District Council*** [1990] 2 All ER 908, the House of Lords overruled ***Anns* v *Merton***.

By 1990 the courts had arrived at a position where the standard test for duty of care was a three- or four-stage test:

1 *reasonable foreseeability* of damage to the claimant (the 'neighbour test');

2 *proximity* between the defendant and claimant;

3 was it *fair, just and reasonable* to impose a duty;

4 policy.

The third stage is sometimes taken to include policy considerations and the courts usually consider it as a three-stage test.

Reasonable foreseeability + proximity + fair, just and reasonable = duty of care

Has there been another swing of the pendulum? The statement by Lord Bridge in ***Caparo*** appeared to have taken the law back to a pre-***Donoghue*** position, although ***Donoghue*** itself is probably too well entrenched to be overturned judicially. However, developments since See Chapter 5 for the extended *Hedley Byrne* principle. ***Caparo*** indicate that the period of retraction may well be over and an era of, albeit cautious, expansion begun. This is apparent in House of Lords decisions with regard to: liability for negligent references (***Spring* v *Guardian Assurance plc*** [1994] 3 All ER 129); liability of solicitors to third parties (***White* v *Jones*** [1995] 1 All ER 691); and concurrent liability in contract and tort (***Henderson* v *Merrett Syndicates Ltd*** [1994] 3 All ER 506). In each of these cases the result was in the claimant's favour with regard to the issue of duty of care.

A different conceptual test was used by some judges in these cases. In determining whether a duty of care was owed, the court asked whether the defendant had 'assumed responsibility' to the claimant on the facts of the case. There is now, therefore, a third test used by the courts, usually in cases of pure economic loss, 'assumption of responsibility'.

Set against this trend is the House of Lords decision in *The Nicholas H (Marc Rich & Co v Bishop Rock Marine)* [1995] 3 WLR 227, which is one of the most conservative decisions on duty of care. It was held in this case that the four requirements necessary for a duty of care in economic loss cases were equally applicable to cases of physical damage to property. Any student wishing to see the disarray and disagreement among the senior judiciary on this issue should read the majority judgment of Lord Steyn and compare it with the dissenting judgment of Lord Lloyd.

See Chapter 5 for economic loss.

The present position

It can be seen from the above extracts that there are now four requirements for the existence of a duty of care based on the *Caparo* case. These are: foresight of damage, proximity, policy and whether it is just and reasonable to impose a duty. A court will not necessarily refer to them all in the same case.

In some cases, particularly those involving pure economic loss, the courts will apply a different test, that of assumption of responsibility.

Before looking at these concepts, it is necessary to note the major change that has taken place. Instead of applying the two-stage test to the facts of the case, the court will look at the particular relationship between claimant and defendant in the context of the type of damage caused (i.e. whether it is physical damage or economic loss).

> ### Example
>
> An accountant negligently prepares a firm's accounts. He could of course be liable for breach of contract to the firm but could he be liable to a third party in negligence? On a *Caparo* analysis the court will start by looking at the relationship between the accountant and the third party. Was it reasonably foreseeable that this party would suffer financial loss as a result of the negligently prepared accounts? If it was not foreseeable that the third party would see the accounts (for example, if they were leaked) then no duty is owed. The next stage is to determine whether there is proximity between the parties. Various factors will go towards this element, such as whether it was reasonable of the claimant to rely on the accounts and whether he was entitled to do so in the circumstances in which he received the information. Would it be just and reasonable to impose a duty? The court might take into account any other (for example, statutory) obligation which the defendant might be under. Finally, the court could deny the existence of a duty on policy grounds.
>
> The alternative approach would be for the court to ask whether the accountant had assumed responsibility to the third party for the accuracy of the accounts. This is usually a factual issue and could occur if the accountant has made a statement to the third party in a meeting.

See Chapter 5 for liability of accountants.

It should be noted that the court's concern is with attempts to extend duty areas into new relationships and types of loss, particularly economic loss. Where a duty, such as that between highway users, has been traditionally recognised, this will normally be unaffected but caution should be exercised in cases of damage to property following the decision in *The Nicholas H.*

Proximity and foreseeability

Objective
2

Foreseeability means that the defendant must have foreseen some damage to the claimant at the time of their alleged negligence. The important factor is that the claimant has to establish that the duty was owed to them. They cannot build on a duty owed to another. The damage must also be of a kind which is foreseeable. A defendant may therefore be able to foresee physical injury but not psychiatric damage.

Bourhill v Young [1943] AC 92

The claimant was descending from a tram when she heard a motor accident. She did not see the accident, but later saw blood on the road and suffered nervous shock. It was reasonably foreseeable that some people would suffer damage as a result of the defendant's negligent driving, but the claimant was not foreseeable as she was so far from the accident and was owed no duty of care. The test for foreseeability is an objective one; it is the foresight of the reasonable man that counts, not the foresight of the defendant.

Lord Thankerton:

> Clearly [the duty of the motor-cyclist] is to drive the cycle with such reasonable care as will avoid the risk of injury to such persons as he can reasonably foresee might be injured by failure to exercise such reasonable care. It is now settled that such injury includes injury by shock, although no direct physical impact or lesion occurs. If, then, the test of proximity or remoteness is to be applied, I am of opinion that such a test involves that the injury must be within that which the cyclist ought to have reasonably contemplated as the area of potential danger which would arise as the result of his negligence, and the question in the present case is whether the appellant was within that area.
>
> I am clearly of opinion that she was not . . .

Lord Wright:

> This general concept of reasonable foresight as the criterion of negligence or breach of duty . . . may be criticized as too vague, but negligence is a fluid principle, which has to be applied to the most diverse conditions and problems of human life. It is a concrete, not an abstract idea. It has to be fitted to the facts of the particular case. . . . It is also always relative to the individual affected. This raises a serious additional difficulty in the cases where it has to be determined, not merely whether the act itself is negligent against someone, but whether it is negligent vis-à-vis the plaintiff. This is a crucial point in cases of nervous shock. Thus, in the present case John Young was certainly negligent in an issue between himself and the owner of the car which he ran into, but it is another question whether he was negligent vis-à-vis the appellant.

See Chapter 4 for liability for psychiatric damage.

The damage in this case was psychiatric damage and this kind of damage presents particular difficulties. The case establishes that damage to that claimant of the kind suffered (psychiatric damage here) must have been reasonably foreseeable to the defendant. Where workmen have dug a trench in the pavement then safety measures have to be taken for sighted and blind people as blind people are a foreseeable class of highway users. (**Haley v London Electricity Board** [1965] AC 778.) Also, where a caterer supplied food with eggs in it to a Sikh wedding (Sikhs are not permitted to eat eggs as a result of their religion) and was therefore in breach of his duty of care, he was held liable for the death of a guest at the wedding who had an allergy to eggs. Personal injury as a result of eating eggs was not in itself reasonably foreseeable but the special facts of the case created a duty of care. (**Bhamra v Dubb** [2010] EWCA Civ 13.)

It can be seen from the extracts above that there was for a time some confusion as to whether there was any distinction between foresight and proximity. It can equally be seen that this problem has been resolved. The two are distinct, although foresight of damage is a necessary ingredient of proximity. If a person drives their car carelessly then it is reasonably foreseeable that damage will be caused to other road users. What makes a fellow road user foreseeable is the spatial proximity to the negligent driver.

What will constitute proximity will vary from case to case. Where the case is a road accident and physical damage is caused to the claimant, then mere foreseeability of damage will be sufficient to establish proximity. If the claimant is not struck by the vehicle or placed in danger but suffers nervous shock as a result of witnessing the accident, then factors such as the relationship between the claimant and the person placed in physical danger, and the closeness of the claimant to the scene of the accident, will determine proximity.

Proximity is clearly a complex idea and means different things in different types of case. It may be used in the sense of a prior relationship between the parties and whether that relationship is sufficient to found a legal relationship giving rise to a duty of care. This is the sense in which it is used in some of the economic loss cases where the parties have a relationship close to contract and in the occupier's liability cases. However, in many negligence cases it is simply confusing to discuss liability in terms of relationship. The negligent driver does not have a duty of care imposed because of a prior relationship with a pedestrian. A manufacturer of goods does not have a prior relationship with the ultimate consumer of the goods.

Whether the concept is of any use as a conceptual tool is arguable and some critics have argued that the term is devoid of meaning. In many negligence cases the issue of 'proximity' is really an issue of whether the defendant was the effective or legal cause of the claimant's damage. This can be seen in the defective products cases.

There are cases where proximity is distinctive from the other limbs of the test. These are in cases of omissions and liability arising from failure to control a third party.

See Chapter 12 for defective products.

See Chapter 6 for omissions.

Just and reasonable and policy

Objective 3

The basis of any decision as to duty of care will be policy. It can therefore fairly be asked whether there is any difference between proximity, just and reasonable, and policy. Would a court be prepared to find that there was proximity and then say it was not just and reasonable to impose a duty or vice versa?

No clear answer can be given to this question as yet. But the indication in *Caparo* v *Dickman* was that proximity could be used as a comprehensive term embracing all three.

Lord Oliver:

> [L]imits have been found by the requirement of what has been called the 'relationship of proximity' between the plaintiff and defendant and by the imposition of a further requirement that the attachment of liability for harm which has occurred be 'just and reasonable'. But although the cases in which the courts have imposed or withheld liability are capable of an approximate categorisation, one looks in vain for some common denominator by which the existence of the essential relationship can be tested. Indeed it is difficult to resist a conclusion that what have been treated as three separate requirements are, at least in most cases, in fact merely facets of the same thing, for in some cases the degree of foreseeability is such that it is from that alone that the requisite proximity can be deduced, whilst in others the absence of that essential relationship can most rationally be attributed simply to the court's view that it would not be fair and reasonable to hold the defendant responsible. 'Proximity' is, no doubt, a convenient expression so long as it is realised that it is no more than a label which embraces not a definable concept but merely a description of circumstances from which, pragmatically, the courts conclude that a duty of care exists.

The expression 'policy' appears to have changed in meaning with the recent cases. Under the old *Anns* v *Merton* test, policy had a broad meaning which encompassed proximity, fair and reasonable and public policy in the narrow sense in which it is now used.

This can best be explained through the so-called 'floodgates' problem. This is a difficulty which the courts have grappled with in this area for a long time. The accepted definition of 'floodgates' was given by Cardozo CJ in the US case of *Ultramares Corp* v *Touche* (1931) 174 NE 441 at 444 as the undesirability of exposing defendants to a potential liability 'in an indeterminate amount for an indeterminate time to an indeterminate class'. Take two examples of this problem, one involving physical damage and the other economic loss.

See Chapter 4 for psychiatric injury.

Example A

Arthur drives his car negligently with the result that he crashes into a group of small children waiting to cross the road outside a primary school at 9 a.m. The injuries to the children struck by the car present no difficulties in terms of duty of care. The neighbour test can be applied. The problem will come from persons who suffer psychiatric damage as a result of witnessing the accident. These may include parents, teachers, school crossing patrol and strangers who just happen to be passing. These will make up Cardozo's 'indeterminate class'. The common law needs to draw a line limiting those who can recover. The old law would have asked whether psychiatric damage was reasonably foreseeable to a particular person and then whether there were any 'policy' grounds why that person should not be owed a duty. The 'new' law will ask the four questions. But a duty could be denied on any of these grounds. Assume that it is reasonably foreseeable that anyone would suffer psychiatric damage at the sight of a horrific accident. Does it make any difference whether the court denies a duty on the grounds of lack of proximity between Arthur and the claimant; that it would not be just and reasonable to impose a duty; or that a duty should not be imposed on the grounds of public policy?

Using the term 'policy' in its narrow modern sense, there are no policy grounds for denying liability for nervous shock generally. It may not be just and reasonable to impose a duty because of the burden that would fall on Arthur (or rather his insurers) but the reason that would be given by the court would be that there was no proximity between the claimant and Arthur. It could well be argued here of course that there are no grounds for denying a claim to anyone who suffers identifiable psychiatric damage. Opponents of the floodgates theory argue that it should not be used to deny a claim to a large but foreseeable class of persons in cases of physical damage.

See Chapter 5 for economic loss.

Example B

Arthur fails to have his car serviced and, as a result, it breaks down in the Mersey Tunnel causing an enormous traffic jam. As a result, large numbers of people are late for work and lose wages. Others are on their way to business meetings and lose contracts as a result of being held up. This loss may continue to ripple down a chain. The late employee may cause his firm to lose business, etc. No duty of care is owed by Arthur in respect of these claims for economic loss. The number of claims would be indeterminate as it would depend on what time of day the car broke down. The extent of the claims would also be indeterminate, as it would depend upon who was stuck there. Finally, if a duty was recognised, where would it end? With the people in the tunnel? With the people with whom they had or expected to have contractual relations?

The same question may be asked again. On what grounds should the courts deny a duty of care? If you say that there is no proximity between Arthur and persons suffering economic loss, you can see that this may introduce elements of justness and reasonableness and perhaps public policy.

Hemmens v Wilson Browne [1993] 4 All ER 826

See also Chapter 5.

Defendant solicitors drafted a document at the request of *P*, giving the claimant the right to call on *P* to pay her (the claimant) £110,000 to buy a house. The document did not give the claimant any enforceable rights as it was not a contract (no consideration), did not create a trust (no identifiable fund) and was not a deed (no seal). The claimant asked *P* to carry out the promise and *P* refused.

It was held that a solicitor could owe a duty of care in carrying out an *inter vivos* transaction. There was reasonable foreseeability of damage to the claimant and proximity between the parties. However, it would not be fair, just or reasonable to impose a duty as the claimant was still alive and able to rectify the situation by instructing another solicitor to draft an enforceable document. The claimant could then sue for breach of contract.

The defendant had made it clear that he was acting for *P* and not for the claimant and that the claimant should seek independent legal advice. (Therefore, the assumption of responsibility test could not apply.)

The conclusion to be drawn is that the headings indicated by the appellate courts are not watertight and run into each other. In fact, it could even be said that the courts have replaced the old uncertain terminology with new, equally uncertain terminology.

A series of cases concerning the liability of fire brigades heard together by the Court of Appeal illustrates some of the difficulties.

Capital & Counties plc v Hampshire County Council; John Monroe (Acrylics) Ltd v London Fire and Civil Defence Authority; Church of Jesus Christ of Latter Day Saints (Great Britain) v West Yorkshire Fire and Civil Defence Authority [1997] 2 All ER 865

In the **Hampshire** case the brigade had switched off the sprinkler system in a burning building. If the system had not been turned off, the building would not have been so badly damaged. In the **London** case the brigade left the scene of an explosion without noticing smouldering debris close to inflammable material on the claimant's neighbouring premises. This later turned into a serious fire. In **West Yorkshire** the brigade attended a fire in a room adjoining a chapel. Because of failure to inspect and maintain hydrants, the brigade was unable to obtain sufficient water until it was too late to save either building.

The Court of Appeal said that there were three potential duties on a fire brigade: a duty owed to respond to an emergency call (duty 1); a duty to fight a fire in a reasonable manner once it has responded to a call (duty 2); a duty to take reasonable care not to create any additional danger (duty 3).

Duty 1 – fire brigades are not under a common law duty to answer an emergency call, nor under a duty to take reasonable care to do so. This is because there is insufficient proximity between the emergency services and the maker of a call. (**Alexandrou v Oxford** [1993] 4 All ER 328.) The number of emergency callers who would otherwise be owed duties was persuasive. The concept of general reliance was rejected as a possible way of establishing proximity. The court's view was that there was not a general expectation that fires would necessarily be extinguished by the fire brigade and that people generally relied on insurance for indemnification of loss. (Would this be the case if the action were for personal injury?)

> Duty 2 – a fire brigade did not assume a duty to fight a fire with reasonable skill and care merely by responding to a call out, nor by assuming control of fire-fighting operations. One reason was a lack of proximity and the number of persons who would otherwise be owed a duty. There was no assumption of responsibility by the fire brigade, as apparently they did not undertake to apply a special skill for the benefit of another. An analogy was drawn with the duty owed by a doctor to a patient who attends casualty in a hospital, and the very limited duty owed by an off-duty doctor at the roadside not to make a person's condition worse. (But why should an on-duty fire officer owe the same duty as an off-duty doctor?) Perhaps the only convincing reason given was that fire brigades take control of fires for the benefit of the public generally and not for the benefit of a particular property owner. If a duty was owed to a particular property owner, this could inhibit fire brigades.
>
> Duty 3 – fire brigades do owe a duty to take reasonable care not to make a victim's condition worse. This would cover the creation of a danger additional to the fire and also substantially increasing the risk of harm from the fire (as in the *Hampshire* case).
>
> On the basis of proximity, a duty was held to exist in the *Hampshire* case, but not in the *London* or *West Yorkshire* cases.

The court also considered the issues of public policy and none was found for rejecting a duty. What is noticeable is that the court dismissed two claims for want of proximity for what appear to be policy reasons (floodgates), but because proximity is 'policy-free' was able to give what are somewhat unconvincing formalistic reasons. For example, the court (at 1043–4) dismissed the floodgates argument as unconvincing, but found this a good reason for rejecting proximity.

The case is linked to the rules governing the duty to rescue. Where there is no duty to rescue (as here), the defendant cannot be liable for failing in a rescue attempt. He must have made the defendant's situation worse before liability can be attached.

Public policy

The courts showed willingness to invoke public policy principles of immunity where certain groups of defendants were sued in negligence. In most cases these groups of defendants carried out (or failed to carry out) what might be called 'public service' duties such as the police, fire services and local authority services such as education and social work. The standard argument was that it would be in the public interest for these bodies to go about their business without the threat of litigation that might encourage defensive practices or threaten a precarious financial base. The immunity was justified by the courts on the basis that it would not be fair, just and reasonable to impose a duty on 'policy' grounds. The

See also Chapter 7 for public policy.

overall reason for the immunity was that the harm to the public in general in granting a duty of care would outweigh the loss suffered by the individual claimant.

Human rights and policy

In cases where a policy immunity was thought to apply, the defence would apply at an early stage to have the claimant's case 'struck out' as it disclosed no cause of action. A striking out hearing does not involve a full hearing of the facts and appeal judges (hearing the appeal against the striking out) complained that they were having to make decisions while not in possession of all the facts. (See Lord Browne-Wilkinson in *Barrett* v *Enfield London Borough Council* [1999] 3 All ER 193.)

The enactment of the Human Rights Act 1998 and a judgment from the European Court of Human Rights concentrated judicial minds on the problems created by public policy

See also Chapter 7 for public policy and police liability.

immuity and the practice of striking out in the context of Article 6 of the European Convention (the right to a fair trial).

The immunity given to the police was successfully challenged in the European Court of Human Rights.

Osman v United Kingdom [1999] FLR 193 (ECHR)

Ahmet Osman was a pupil at a London school, where one of the teachers formed a disturbing attachment to him. Eventually Ahmet Osman was shot by the teacher, who was subsequently convicted of two charges of manslaughter and sentenced to be detained in a mental hospital. Civil proceedings for negligence were begun against the police and the case was struck out by the Court of Appeal on the ground that no action lay because of the public policy reason stated in **Hill v Chief Constable of West Yorkshire Police** [1988] 2 All ER 238. An application was made to Strasbourg on the ground that this constituted a breach of Article 6 of the European Convention on Human Rights (the right to a fair trial); specifically, that under Article 6(1) everyone should have the right of access to a court. The complaint was upheld by the European Court of Human Rights as there was never any determination of the claim on its merits. The court found that although the aim of the rule, to protect the effectiveness of the police, was a legitimate one, there had been no balancing of other competing public interests. A litigant was entitled to a full hearing where the facts would be found and the proportionality of the immunity to the claimant's rights weighed in the balance.

The decision in **Osman** caused great difficulties to the English judiciary. (See **Barrett v Enfield London Borough Council** [1999] 3 All ER 193.) In essence, Article 6 was thought to confer procedural rights on a litigant, rather than substantive legal rights, such as whether a cause of action existed. It subsequently transpired that the European Court of Human Rights had misunderstood English tort law in **Osman**. They had failed to accept that a decision on the third limb of the test for duty of care is a part of substantive law. If a court decides that it would not be fair, just and reasonable to impose a duty of care, this is different to having a procedural immunity which bars a litigant's access to the court in breach of Article 6. (**Z v UK** [2001] 2 FLR 612.)

Was this much ado about nothing? For a litigant who is struck out at an early stage of the action, the distinction made in **Z** between substance and procedure might well seem artificial. It may be, however, that the reluctance of the courts to strike out on blanket policy grounds, favourable to the defendant, in the post-**Osman** period, will survive. Claimants faced with a striking out application could advance the policy issue that where there is a wrong there should be a remedy. (See **Hall v Simons** below.) It should also be noted that a case can still be struck out on the grounds that there was no proximity between the parties. (**Palmer v Tees Health Authority** [1999] Lloyd's Rep Med 351.) The argument that proximity is policy neutral is rather suspect. Look at the reasoning used in the fire brigade cases and try to determine whether the real issues were proximity or policy issues.

See also Chapter 7 for public authority liability.

The Human Rights Act 1998 brings a very different perspective to tort law which in time may well reshape its perspectives. In **Z v UK** [2001] 2 FLR 612, the issue was whether a local authority welfare system which broke down, resulting in children suffering neglect and abuse, rendered the local authority liable in negligence. The House of Lords and the European Court of Human Rights held that no duty of care was owed by the local authority in these circumstances but the Strasbourg Court found a breach of Article 3 (prohibiting torture and inhumane or degrading treatment). There was also a breach of Article 13, as at that time there was no appropriate remedy for a breach of Article 3.

See Chapter 6 for details.

One effect of this decision is that English courts have now held that a duty of care is owed to children by child care professionals (although not to the parents) in making decisions regarding taking a child into care and child abuse. (*D* v *East Berkshire Community Health NHS Trust; K and another* v *Dewsbury Healthcare NHS Trust; K and another* v *Oldham NHS Trust* [2003] 4 All ER 796 (CA); [2005] 2 All ER 443 (HL).)

Advocate's immunity

The organisation of the legal profession in England and Wales means that a person requiring legal assistance must normally approach a solicitor. The client will have a contract with the solicitor. If a barrister is needed then they are 'briefed' by the solicitor. This means that the client has no contract with the barrister. Any liability of the barrister to the client must sound in tort.

Rondel v *Worsley* [1969] 1 AC 191

The House of Lords held that a barrister does not owe a duty of care to their client in connection with the conduct of a case in court. The public policy ground for this decision was that a barrister owes a duty to the court which transcends that of their duty to their client. Fear of being sued for negligence by their client might lead them to neglect the duty to the court. Further, if a barrister was successfully sued, this might lead to cases being re-opened.

In practice, the immunity became extremely complex to apply. Increasingly fine distinctions were drawn such as: whether the negligence was 'intimately connected' with the conduct of the case in court; whether a settlement of the case was covered; and whether an advocate's strategy or tactics were covered.

The difficulties created by the extent of the immunity and the amount of litigation that this lack of clarity created led a specially constituted seven-judge House of Lords to sweep away the immunity.

Hall v *Simons* [2000] 3 All ER 673

Clients brought proceedings for negligence in three separate cases against their former solicitors. In each case the solicitors relied on the immunity of advocates and the claims were struck out. The Court of Appeal held that the claims fell outside the scope of the immunity and should not have been struck out.

Held (House of Lords) (7 judges – 3 dissents):

Advocates no longer enjoyed immunity from suit in respect of their conduct of civil proceedings. Such an immunity was no longer needed to deal with collateral attacks as these would normally be struck out as an abuse of process. A collateral attack is where a negligence action is started against a lawyer with the ulterior purpose of having a previous decision of a court overturned. If X is charged and convicted of a criminal offence and then wishes to sue his barrister Y for negligence, this may involve what is in effect a retrial of the original case. (For the law on collateral challenge see *Hunter* v *Chief Constable of West Midlands* [1981] 3 All ER 727.)

The House based its decision on other professions, such as doctors, who owed dual duties and experience in other jurisdictions.

1 A collateral civil challenge to a subsisting criminal conviction would ordinarily be struck out as an abuse of process, but the public policy against such a challenge would no longer bar an action in negligence by a client who had succeeded in having his conviction set aside. (See *Acton* v *Graham Pearce* [1997] 3 All ER 909.)

2 The principles of *res judicata*, issue estoppel and abuse of process should be sufficient to cope with the risk of challenges to civil decisions.

3 The immunity was not needed to ensure that advocates would respect their duty to the court. There were a number of examples of dual duties owed by professionals and the experience in Canada, where there was no advocate immunity, had demonstrated that removal of the immunity would not undermine this aspect of the advocate's duty.

4 It would bring to an end the anomalous exception to the premise that there should be a remedy for a wrong and there was no floodgates risk.

5 Mere performance by an advocate of their duty to the court, to the detriment of their client, could never be called negligent.

6 Courts would take into account the difficult situations faced daily by barristers working in demanding situations to tight timetables. Courts could be trusted to differentiate between errors of judgement and true negligence and a claimant would have to establish a causative link between poor advocacy and outcome.

It is possible to speculate that the removal of the immunity of advocates in this case was as a result of the Human Rights Act, as the immunity might not have survived scrutiny in Strasbourg. Whether this is the case or not, students may wish to consider point 6 in the reasons given by the House of Lords. This has the effect of moving the emphasis in these cases from duty of care to breach of duty and causation.

Police

See also Chapter 7 for police liability.

A second example covers the liability of the police when investigating crime and they fail to apprehend a suspect. What is the position if they are negligent and a member of the public suffers loss as a result?

This area provides an interesting aspect to some of the developments in negligence and the impact of human rights legislation. The issue is whether the police should be exposed to litigation if they are judged to have been negligent in their investigation of a crime and a person has suffered damage as a result. The traditional approach of the English courts has been to refuse an action, either on policy grounds or because there is no proximity between the injured person and the police. The implementation of the Human Rights Act 1998 means that there is now a direct action under the legislation against the police if they are found to be in breach of one of the relevant articles. Such an action might be brought by the estate or dependants of a person who has died as a result of an alleged breach by the police of Article 2 (the right to life).

Other emergency services

See also Chapter 7 for liability of emergency services.

In relation to the other emergency services a very limited duty of care has been imposed on the fire brigade. (See ***Capital & Counties plc v Hampshire County Council*** [1997] 2 All ER 865.) Note that in cases where no duty is imposed on a fire brigade this is on the grounds of proximity and not policy.

The coastguards have immunity on similar lines to the fire brigade without the necessity of resorting to public policy. (***OLL Ltd v Secretary of State for Transport*** [1997] 3 All ER 897.)

The ambulance service does owe a duty of care to respond within a reasonable time once a 999 call has been made. The accepting of the call establishes proximity between the parties. An analogy is drawn with medical services provided by a hospital rather than with the emergency services. (***Kent v Griffiths*** [2000] 2 WLR 1158.)

The incoherence of the present law is illustrated by a road accident attended by the ambulance service and the fire brigade. The duties owed by each to victims of the accident are completely different although both are there for the same reason: saving life.

Local authorities

One of the issues involved in the complex question of whether local authorities and other public authorities can be sued in negligence is the policy issue. However, a number of other issues such as omissions and liability for economic loss are involved and this question will be dealt with elsewhere.

See Chapter 7.

 ## Other policy issues

In a book of this nature it is not possible to discuss all the policy issues which might affect a court in reaching its decision. However, one issue which might sway a court is the fact that liability already exists in another tort which has its own rules on checks and balances which could be disturbed by the interference of the tort of negligence. Consider the following House of Lords decision on whether a person owes a duty of care in giving a reference.

Spring v *Guardian Assurance plc* [1994] 3 All ER 129

See also Chapter 5 for *Spring* v *Guardian Assurance*.

The claimant sued his former employers in negligence for a reference which he claimed had prevented him from obtaining employment. The claim was for economic loss. The question for the House of Lords was whether an employer owed a duty of care in giving a reference on a present or past employee.

The defendants argued public policy as a reason for not finding a duty of care. In the first place that to give a cause of action in negligence would distort and subvert the tort of defamation. If an action is brought in defamation regarding a reference then the referee will normally have a defence of qualified privilege which can only be defeated by malice on the part of the referee. There is no defence of qualified privilege in negligence. The House decided that the two torts were different. Defamation exists in order to protect reputation and proof of actual financial loss is not necessary in a libel action. The claimant's claim in this case was for financial loss. To recognise a duty of care would not be to extend defamation by removing the necessity for malice but would bring a different principle into play. This would operate in a limited number of situations where foreseeability and proximity existed and, of course, negligent conduct would be required. Defamation is in one sense a tort of strict liability as it is the fact of the defamation rather than the state of mind, in the sense of intention or negligence, that renders the defendant liable.

A second argument on public policy was that a person who makes a reference should be free to express their own views, otherwise referees might be inhibited from giving frank references, or indeed any references at all. The House balanced this against the damage caused to the subject of the reference by negligence and came down in favour of a duty of care in certain situations. Lord Keith dissented and specifically raised the question of people working with children and the need for free and frank disclosure in those circumstances:

> In these circumstances it is, I consider, necessary to approach the question as a matter of principle. Since, for the reasons I have given, it is my opinion that in cases such as the present the duty of care arises by reason of an assumption of responsibility by the employer to the employee in respect of the relevant reference, I can see no good reason why the duty to exercise due skill and care which rests upon the employer should be negatived because, if the plaintiff were instead to bring an action for damage to his reputation, he would be met by the defence of qualified privilege which could only be defeated by proof of malice. It is not to be forgotten that the **Hedley Byrne** duty arises where there is a relationship which is, broadly speaking, either contractual or equivalent to contract. In these circumstances, I cannot see that principles of the law of defamation are of any relevance.

It is true that recognition of a duty of care to an employee in cases such as the present, based on the **Hedley Byrne** principle, may have some inhibiting effect on the manner in which references are expressed, in the sense that it may discourage employers from expressing views . . . For my part, however, I suspect that such an inhibition exists in any event. Employers may well, like many people, be unwilling to indulge in unnecessary criticism of their employees . . . In all the circumstances, I do not think that we may fear too many ill effects from the recognition of the duty. The vast majority of employers will continue, as before, to provide careful references. But those who, as in the present case, fail to achieve that standard, will have to compensate their employees or former employees who suffer damage in consequence. Justice, in my opinion, requires that this should be done; and I, for my part, cannot see any reason in policy why that justice should be denied.

For these reasons I would allow the appeal; but I would nevertheless remit the matter to the Court of Appeal to consider the issue of the extent to which the damage suffered by the claimant was caused by the breach of duty of the defendants.

Other tests

The vast sprawl of negligence and the different circumstances in which the courts have to determine duty situations have given rise to a number of tests. There is a considerable difference between road accidents, economic loss cases and whether a public authority owed a duty. It must be remembered that the tests used by the courts are merely tools used to the end of determining the question of whether a duty of care is owed by the defendant. An analogy can be drawn with a mechanic who, faced with a problem, will reach into his toolbox and try a number of tools until he finds the one that works.

Reasonable reliance

The relevance of reliance to duty of care has had a chequered history. Some cases have stated that it is vital while others have denied its relevance.

What is understood by 'reliance' varies. There is detrimental and non-detrimental reliance, although it is difficult to see how non-detrimental reliance could found an action in negligence because of the requirement of damage.

There are also concepts of specific and general reliance. Specific reliance will be present when the parties have communicated with each other, whereas general reliance will arise when the parties are more remote. The classic specific reliance case concerns the giving of advice or information. This version of reliance operates as a check on liability becoming too wide. For example, in the surveyor cases, a surveyor acting for a building society will owe a duty only to the building society and the person who has paid the building society for the valuation. If that person chose to show it to someone else, who relied on it, then no duty would arise. The concept of specific reliance can be seen at work in the emergency services cases as well. Although the police do not generally owe a duty of care to the public in investigating crime, they may have given assurances to a member of the public who has reasonably relied on them. In this area reliance is often coupled with assumption of responsibility.

General reliance operates in the sense that the defendant had some power which could have been exercised carefully in the claimant's favour and the claimant was aware of that fact and relied on the careful exercise of the power. An example of this is in the area of public authorities exercising statutory powers or duties in connection with building

See Chapter 5 for surveyor cases.

See Chapter 11.

regulations. This approach has been rejected in England in this area and in the area of the emergency services. Even if the public generally count on the police to investigate crime and apprehend criminals and the fire brigade to respond to emergency calls, it does not follow that it is reasonable for the public to rely on scarce resources being committed in each case.

Assumption of responsibility

See also Chapter 5 for assumption of responsibility.

The concept of assumption of responsibility has given rise to considerable problems for the judiciary. Lord Reid in *Hedley Byrne* v *Heller & Partners* [1964] AC 465 at 486 explained that a reasonable man who knew he was being trusted to give careful advice had three courses of action open: refuse to answer, answer with a disclaimer or answer without a disclaimer. 'If he chooses the last course he must, I think, be held to have accepted some responsibility for his answer being given carefully, or to have accepted a relationship with the inquirer which requires him to exercise such care as the circumstances require.'

Since then doubt has been expressed as to whether this criterion was necessary or useful (see, for example, *Smith* v *Eric S Bush* [1990] 1 AC 831) but this scepticism was expressed within the context of whether the claimant was within the category of those owed a duty of care. However, in *Henderson* v *Merrett Syndicates Ltd* [1994] 3 All ER 506 at 521, Lord Goff was quite clear that in cases which were concerned with situations equivalent to contract, including negligent provision of a service, once the defendant was found to have assumed responsibility there was no problem with recovery of economic loss. What Lord Goff meant here, however, was a very broad definition of voluntary assumption, to mean voluntary assumption of a *task* not voluntary assumption of the *legal risk*.

In *White* v *Jones* [1995] 1 All ER 691 at 706, Lord Browne-Wilkinson thought that the phrase was concerned with whether some duty of care existed, not with the extent of the duty which could vary with the circumstances. He felt that the concept originated with breach of fiduciary duty, where a duty came into existence not because of any mutual dealing between the parties (the 'equivalent to contract' concept) but because the defendant had assumed a commitment to act in the claimant's affairs. A trustee is under a duty to a beneficiary whether or not he has had any dealings with him. On this basis it is not necessary that there be any reliance on the defendant. The important factor is that the defendant knows that the claimant's economic well-being depends on the careful conduct of his affairs.

Lennon v *Metropolitan Police Commissioner* [2004] 2 All ER 266

The claimant had been a member of the Metropolitan Police Force and wished to transfer to the Royal Ulster Constabulary. The arrangements for the transfer were handled by a personnel officer (*B*) who told the claimant to leave everything to her. In response to a specific enquiry from the claimant, *B* negligently informed him that his service would be continuous, whereas there was in fact a three-week break in service. This caused economic damage to the claimant. The Court of Appeal held that even where the parties were in a relationship of employer and employee (or in a situation akin to employment or equivalent to another kind of contract), there was nothing to prevent the voluntary assumption of responsibility principle applying to an omission to give advice in circumstances where, if not handled carefully, the matter for which the defendant had voluntarily assumed responsibility could result in the claimant suffering economic loss. In this case a duty of care had arisen from the express assumption of responsibility by the defendant, for a particular matter, on which the claimant had relied.

The House of Lords has warned against trying to find any general principle:

> circumstances may differ infinitely and . . . there can be no necessary assumption that those features which have served in one case to create the relationship between the plaintiff and the defendant on which liability depends will necessarily be determinative of liability in another case. (*Caparo Industries plc* v *Dickman* [1990] 1 All ER 568 at 587 per Lord Oliver.)

This still leaves the question as to what is the relationship between the three-stage *Caparo* test and the assumption of responsibility test. This question was addressed by the Court of Appeal in *Merrett* v *Babb* [2001] 3 WLR 1, where it was recognised that the two tests were complementary and should produce the same result.

However, in *Customs and Excise Commissioners* v *Barclays Bank plc* [2006] 4 All ER 256 the House of Lords held that assumption of responsibility was a sufficient but not necessary condition of liability. If the objective test for assumption of responsibility was satisfied, it was not necessary for the court to go any further. If not, then the court had to go on to apply the three-stage test.

Lord Bingham:

> the authorities disclose three tests which have been used in deciding whether a defendant sued as causing pure economic loss to a claimant owed him a duty of care in tort. The first is whether the defendant assumed responsibility for what he said and did vis-à-vis the claimant, or is to be treated by the law as having done so. The second is commonly known as the threefold test: whether loss to the claimant was a reasonably foreseeable consequence of what the defendant did or failed to do; whether the relationship between the parties was one of sufficient proximity; and whether in all the circumstances it is fair, just and reasonable to impose a duty of care on the defendant towards the claimant (what Kirby J in *Perre* v *Apand Pty Ltd* (1999) 198 CLR 180, para 259, succinctly labelled 'policy'). The third is the incremental test, based on the observation of Brennan J in *Sutherland Shire Council* v *Heyman* (1985) 157 CLR 424, 481, approved by Lord Bridge of Harwich in *Caparo Industries plc* v *Dickman* [1990] 2 AC 605, 618, that:
>
> > It is preferable, in my view, that the law should develop novel categories of negligence incrementally and by analogy with established categories, rather than by a massive extension of a prima facie duty of care restrained only by indefinable considerations which ought to be negative, or to reduce or limit the scope of the duty or the class of person to whom it is owed.

He went on to make five general observations:

> First there are cases in which one party can accurately be said to have assumed responsibility for what is said or done to another, the paradigm situation being a relationship having all the indicia of contract save consideration . . . I think it is correct to regard an assumption of responsibility as a sufficient but not a necessary condition of liability, a first test which, if answered positively, may obviate the need for further inquiry. If answered negatively, further consideration is called for.
>
> Secondly, however, it is clear that the assumption of responsibility test is to be applied objectively . . . and is not answered by consideration of what the defendant thought or intended . . .
>
> The problem here is, as I see it, that the further this test is removed from the actions and responsibilities of the actual defendant, and the more notional the assumption of responsibility becomes, the less difference there is between this test and the threefold test.
>
> Thirdly, the threefold test itself provides no straightforward answer to the vexed question of whether or not, in a novel situation, a party owes a duty of care . . .

Fourthly, I incline to agree with the view . . . that the incremental test is of little value as a test in itself, and is only helpful when used in combination with a test or principle which identifies the legally significant features of a situation. The closer the facts of the case in issue to those of a case in which a duty of care has been held to exist, the readier a court will be, on the approach of Brennan J adopted in **Caparo Industries plc**, to find that there has been an assumption of responsibility or that the proximity and policy conditions of the threefold test are satisfied. The converse is also true.

Fifthly, it seems to me that the outcomes (or majority outcomes) of the leading cases cited above are in every or almost every instance sensible and just, irrespective of the test applied to achieve that outcome. This is not to disparage the value of and need for a test of liability in tortious negligence, which any law of tort must propound if not to become a morass of single instances. But it does in my opinion concentrate attention on the detailed circumstance of the particular case and the particular relationship between the parties in the context of their legal and factual situation as a whole.

In practice, therefore, the courts seem to prefer to use voluntary assumption of responsibility in cases involving economic loss, although it remains open to the court to check the result by referring to the three-stage test.

Conclusion

A large amount of House of Lords' time has been spent on the issue of duty of care and it is easy to forget that this is merely a starting point in the negligence equation. Indeed, French law manages to do without an English-style concept of duty and imposes a general principle in favour of liability (Article 1382 of the French Civil Code) without producing greatly differing results. It is important to remember that the 'gist' of negligence is the defendant's conduct (is it negligent?) and the link between that and the claimant's damage (causation and remoteness). What English law has done is to move many of the problems into duty of care where the conceptual tools to answer the questions are apparently not readily available. It may be useful, therefore, to conclude a difficult chapter with some of the major arguments for not imposing a duty.

The claimant's interest is not protected

See Chapter 4 for psychiatric damage.

See Chapter 5 for economic loss.

The argument that the claimant's interest is not protected is deployed on either a full or a partial basis. It can be seen in full operation in psychiatric damage cases where liability for emotional distress falling short of psychiatric injury is denied, and partially in the rules on whether a secondary victim of nervous shock can recover. In actions for 'pure' economic loss, English law started with a denial of such liability in negligence on the basis that the right to protection from such loss has to be bought and must therefore be contractual. There is then a movement into partial denial of such loss and the case law becomes extremely complex.

There are areas where modern English law is reluctant to find any protected interest at all. One of these was privacy.

Kaye v Robertson [1991] FSR 62

The claimant was a well-known TV actor who suffered severe head injuries from being struck by an advertising hoarding during a storm. He was on a life-support machine in hospital and required complete peace and quiet. The defendant newspaper sent a photographer into the intensive care unit and took a flashlight photograph of Mr Kaye. The Court of Appeal held that the torts of battery,

See Chapter 22 for the HRA 1998.

passing off and libel had not been committed but was able to grant a partial injunction against publication on the grounds of malicious falsehood.

No negligence action could be brought against the newspaper on these facts, as there was no actionable damage. The courts have now started to close this lacuna in English law, having been stimulated by the Human Rights Act 1998.

There was not a sufficiently close relationship between the parties

The argument that there was not a sufficiently close relationship between the parties takes a number of forms including the 'unforeseeable claimant' and lack of proximity.

The immediate question begged is whether a prior relationship between the parties should be necessary at all in order to found a negligence action.

In some cases it is clearly not. The commonest form of negligence is the road traffic accident where, excepting cases of psychiatric damage, duty issues rarely play a part and there is clearly no need for a prior relationship.

See also Chapter 4 for *Alcock*.

Where the damage to the claimant is nervous shock other considerations come into play, including the 'floodgates' problem of too many potential claimants. The courts then use restrictive devices such as 'unforeseeable claimant' (see *Bourhill* v *Young*) and lack of proximity (see *Alcock* v *Chief Constable of the South Yorkshire Police*) to restrict the ambit of liability.

The issue frequently arises in cases of 'pure' economic loss and is often resolved by saying there was no 'proximity' between the parties. In this sense it often means that the parties did not have a relationship sufficiently close to contract and suggests that in that context the courts are expanding the boundaries of contract rather than fashioning a free-standing tort-based obligation.

In many cases there may be a question as to who was actually responsible for the damage. This will arise, for example, where the defendant has failed to warn against a risk created by a third party. In these cases it could be argued that the damage was too remote or was not caused by the defendant's negligence. Examples of this arise where a regulatory agency is alleged to have been negligent in failing to warn the claimant. (See *The Nicholas H.*)

See Chapter 5 for assumption of responsibility.

The argument can be extended and used in support of the proposition that there is no liability for pure omissions or nonfeasance. In the absence of a prior relationship between the parties (such as employer–employee) there is in theory no liability for inaction. The difficulties here are distinguishing misfeasance and nonfeasance and when there is a sufficient prior relationship to require action on the part of the defendant. There is a recent movement led by Lord Goff to impose liability where there is an 'assumption of responsibility' by the defendant. This can be used to impose liability for omission to act and may succeed in removing the distinction between omission and commission.

Defendant is immune (policy)

Defendant immunity is rare in England and is largely confined to the administration of justice. Judges, and arbitrators, have varying degrees of immunity from negligence actions.

Such immunity is controversial and it is difficult to see why it should exist in any circumstances if the standard of care is set at the appropriate level.

Negligence would undermine other legal rules

The argument that negligence would undermine other legal rules is an old one and applies in areas such as negligence and contract and negligence and public law.

The negligence undermining contract argument can be seen in the pre-*Donoghue* cases in the sense that if a person had contracted with another then the balance of the risks should not be upset by allowing a third party to bring a non-contractual action. The point is still raised by defendants and was argued in the *White* v *Jones* case on the lines that a beneficiary under a will should not have an action against the solicitor for negligence.

It takes a slightly different form in the concurrent liability cases, but although the courts have now accepted the existence of concurrent liability, it is unlikely that they would allow the terms of the contract, such as an exclusion clause, to be undercut by a duty in negligence.

Public law and negligence raise some difficult problems. The normal remedy for abuse of an administrative process is judicial review. However, there are no damages available following a successful judicial review. These are only available in a private law action. To what extent should a public body be exposed to liability for damages when there may be internal administrative procedures available and their proceedings subject to judicial review?

See Chapter 7 for public authority liability.

The 'purpose' of the advice given

The argument concerning the 'purpose' of the advice given has been deployed in cases of liability for negligent statements causing economic loss. In *South Australia Asset Management Corp* v *York Montague Ltd* [1996] 3 All ER 365 the House of Lords ruled that the court had to look at the purpose of a valuation given by a valuer to a lender and hence what loss the valuer would be liable for if the property was negligently overvalued.

See Chapter 5 for economic loss.

Summary

This chapter deals with the tests used by the courts to determine whether a duty of care exists.

- Duty of care exists as a control device to determine who can bring an action for negligence and in what circumstances.

- No single test for duty of care existed until *Donoghue* v *Stevenson* (1932). The *obiter dicta* in the case were that a person owes a duty of care when they can reasonably foresee damage to their neighbour. This is known as the 'neighbour test'.

- Negligence liability expanded and a two-stage test of reasonable foreseeability of damage with a limiting factor of policy issues was adopted in *Anns* v *Merton*.

- The expansion in negligence caused problems and the courts took steps to rein back the ambit of the tort. Influential in this was the 'incremental test' from the Australian case of *Sutherland Shire Council* v *Heyman*.

- In a series of cases culminating in *Caparo Industries* v *Dickman* the courts laid down a four-part test for duty of care: (i) reasonable foreseeability of damage to the claimant (see *Bourhill* v *Young*); (ii) proximity between the parties (see *Bourhill* v *Young*); (iii) whether it was fair, just and reasonable to impose a duty; (iv) policy. The third and fourth parts of the test are frequently taken together so as to make a three-stage test.

- In cases of pure economic loss, particularly those involving the negligent performance of services, the courts frequently use a test of 'assumption of responsibility'.

- One of the major reasons for denying a duty of care is 'floodgates', where the defendant might be exposed to liability for an indeterminate amount to an indeterminate class. This may be countered by the use of proximity to limit the potential number of claimants. For example, the fire brigade cases: *Capital & Counties plc* v *Hampshire County Council*.

- Alternatively, the problem may be dealt with by denying a duty of care on policy grounds. The use of immunity from negligence actions of particular groups is now in retreat as a result of the influence of Strasbourg judgments such as *Osman* v *UK* and *Z* v *UK*. The immunity of advocates from negligence actions has now been abolished by *Hall* v *Simons*. However, the immunity of the police in the investigation of crime appears to have survived. (*Van Colle/Smith*.)

- The Human Rights Act 1998 has had an effect on this area of law as it concentrates on rights rather than wrongs. Other policy issues include not undermining legal rules in other torts (*Spring* v *Guardian Assurance*) and not undermining contract law.

- Reliance has played a part in duty of care, primarily as specific reliance in the advice cases. General reliance has been rejected in English law.

- The alternative test of assumption of responsibility means assumption of responsibility for a task, not assumption of the legal risk. If an objective test of assumption of responsibility is satisfied it is not necessary for the court to go any further.

- Reasons for denying a duty of care include: the claimant's interest was not protected; there was not a sufficiently close relationship between the parties; the defendant is immune; negligence would undermine other legal rules.

Further reading

Howarth, D. (1991), 'Negligence After *Murphy*: Time To Rethink' CLJ 58.

Markesinis, B. A. (1987), 'An Expanding Tort Law – The Price of a Rigid Contract Law' 103 LQR 354.

Posner, R. A. (1972), 'A Theory of Negligence' 1 JLS 29.

Smith, J. C. and Burns, P. (1983), '*Donoghue* v *Stevenson*: The Not So Golden Anniversary' 46 MLR 147.

Stapleton, J. (1995), 'Duty of Care: Peripheral Parties and Alternative Opportunities for Deterrence' 111 LQR 301.

Witting, C. (2005), 'Duty of Care: An Analytic Approach' 25 OJLS 33.

4

Psychiatric damage

Objectives

After reading this chapter you will:

1. Understand the concept of psychiatric damage.
2. Have a critical knowledge of the medical background to psychiatric damage claims in negligence.
3. Have a critical knowledge of the legal rules and policy factors governing the recovery of damages for psychiatric damage.
4. Understand the distinction between primary and secondary victims.

Introduction

Objective 1

This chapter is concerned with one particular type of damage which arises in some negligence claims. This is where there is damage to the mind rather than to the body. Lawyers have traditionally used the expression nervous shock to describe this condition. However, the Court of Appeal has indicated that the expression psychiatric damage is preferable. (*Attia* v *British Gas plc* [1987] 3 All ER 455 at 462.)

This is a relatively recent development in English law. During the nineteenth century the law of negligence concerned with accidents developed around personal injuries, often in industrial cases. The severity of working conditions and lack of scientific knowledge of the working of the mind meant that little, if any, attention was paid to psychiatric damage. The rise of psychology as a science led to greater concentration by the law on this type of damage.

In these cases the claimant must establish harm over and above ordinary grief and distress. No damages are recoverable for the ordinary grief, sorrow or distress which is suffered as a result of a traumatic event. Before a person can claim, they have to establish, on the basis of medical evidence, that they have suffered a definite and identifiable psychiatric illness.

Originally claims in this area were typically where a person suffers a reaction when they witness an accident in which a loved one is injured.

> **Example**
>
> A mother is walking her five-year-old child to school. She leaves the child with the school crossing lollipop person. A car tries to drive through while the sign to stop is raised, narrowly misses the child and hits the lollipop person. The mother suffers psychiatric damage as a result of fearing for the safety of her child.

The law has developed slowly in this area and now divides claimants into two categories, primary and secondary victims. In the example the child and the lollipop person are primary victims as they are actually in physical danger and the mother is a secondary victim. It is easier for a primary victim to sue for psychiatric damage so claimant lawyers will try to fit their clients into this category. The courts have been very restrictive with secondary victims and introduced control devices to cut down on the number of potential claims.

Problems raised

Psychiatric damage is dealt with separately for a number of reasons. Initially, the courts had difficulty in distinguishing a genuine claim from a fictitious one. Advances in psychiatry mean this is no longer a major problem and it is rarely referred to by the courts.

There is a problem in placing a monetary value on this type of harm. A successful claimant will recover for pecuniary losses, such as loss of earnings, in the normal way. But damages for non-pecuniary loss have to be assessed by the court. However, this is a problem which the courts have to deal with in all personal injuries claims. Is it any more difficult to assess these damages in psychiatric damage cases than in, for example, paralysis cases?

See also Chapter 3 for 'floodgates'. A further difficulty is the 'floodgates' problem. Ordinary physical damage caused by negligent conduct will by its nature be limited to those within the range of impact. Psychiatric damage is not so limited, as persons not within the range of impact may be affected. The courts have been conscious of this problem as they developed the law and have imposed restrictions on those who can recover.

The medical background and public scepticism

Objective 2 The initial problem in psychiatric illness cases is the difficulty in analysing and accepting these illnesses. Traditional physical damage cases involve injuries either visible to the eye or diagnosable with established medical tests such as blood tests or X-rays. The two questions of whether the claimant suffers from a disability sounding in damages and whether this was caused by the defendant's breach of duty can therefore normally be answered in the affirmative. At the easier end of the spectrum, if the claimant had two legs before the accident caused by the defendant's negligent driving and one leg after the accident, it is straightforward to allocate the loss of the leg to the defendant's negligence. If the claimant's claim is for post-traumatic stress disorder (PTSD), this raises the problems of whether there is such a thing, whether the claimant is suffering from it and whether it was caused by the defendant's negligent act. Judicial and public scepticism about the genuineness of psychiatric illnesses and controversy in the medical profession about their diagnosis have held back this area of law and led to it being treated as a separate area with its own rules. The courts are now being faced with similar problems in the area of 'physical' illnesses such as non-symptomatic repetitive strain injury (RSI) and myalgic encephalomyelitis (ME).

English law does not give damages for the shock itself, which is the primary response to a traumatic event. Compensation is awarded for the secondary, more long-lasting effects of trauma. The illness must be shock-induced. Psychiatric illness which is brought about by a cumulative effect on the nervous system, such as watching a relative die slowly after negligent medical treatment, is not generally compensatable. However, where the claimant has suffered a psychiatric illness partly caused by the defendant's negligence in causing the death of his children in a road accident and partly by pathological grief at the deaths, the claimant is entitled to full damages with no discount for the consequences of the grief. (***Vernon*** v ***Bosley (No 1)*** [1997] 1 All ER 577.)

How is psychiatric illness diagnosed? There are two diagnostic systems used by psychiatrists. These are DSM-IV (American Diagnostic and Statistical Manual of Mental Disorders) and ICD-10 (International Classification of Diseases and Related Health Problems). The claimant may claim to be suffering from more than one psychiatric illness following a traumatic event but a significant proportion of claimants now formulate their claims in terms of PTSD. The reasons for this are apparent when one looks at the correlation between PTSD diagnosis and the legal rules governing recovery of damages for psychiatric illness.

The identifying feature of PTSD is that it requires an external event or stressor which triggers characteristic symptoms. The event has to be of a psychologically distressing nature or a situation of an exceptionally threatening or catastrophic nature. Common experiences such as divorce, bereavement and business losses are not acceptable as stressors. The stressor must have been extreme and have had two characteristics. First, the person in question must have experienced, witnessed or been confronted with an event that involved actual or threatened death or serious injury, or a threat to the physical integrity of self or others. Second, their response must have involved intense fear, helplessness or horror. A diagnosis of PTSD may involve internal factors such as the claimant's personality but the key factor is the external stressor. Once this is established, there is an explicit assumption that the cause of the disorder is known. It is therefore unlikely that, once a diagnosis of PTSD has been made, the claimant's case will fail on causation grounds.

Other psychiatric illnesses do not depend on an external trigger, making causation harder to establish, and personality plays an important role. This is likely to bring the claimant into conflict with the 'customary phlegm' principle applied in secondary victim cases, where the claimant is of a sensitive disposition.

A distinction is made in PTSD diagnosis between those events which are directly experienced, those which are witnessed and those which are learnt about. The first category includes natural or man-made disasters, a severe automobile accident and being diagnosed with a life-threatening illness. The second includes seeing someone being seriously injured or killed in an accident or unexpectedly witnessing a dead body. The third category includes learning about a serious accident or injury to a member of one's family. In legal terms, the first category correlates to primary victims; the second to secondary victims, incorporating both geographical proximity and aftermath; and the third to the generally irrecoverable area of learning of the event through third parties.

Historical development

The initial response of the common law to claims for psychiatric damage was to deny liability until the early part of the twentieth century.

Dulieu v *White & Sons* [1901] 2 KB 669

> The claimant, who was pregnant, was working behind the bar of a public house when the defendant's servant negligently drove a horse van into the public house. The claimant suffered shock resulting in the premature birth of her child. The claimant was entitled to recover as the shock was due to fear for her own personal safety. (See also *McFarlane* v *EE Caledonia Ltd* [1994] 1 All ER 1; *Page* v *Smith* [1995] 2 All ER 736.) Shock suffered as a result of fear for the safety of another would not be compensated.
>
> *NB.* In modern terms the claimant in this case would be classified as a primary victim.

Hambrook v *Stokes Bros* [1925] 1 KB 141

> The defendants left a lorry unattended at the top of a hill with the brake off. The lorry ran down the hill and eventually crashed. The claimant's wife had just left her children round a bend in the road. She saw the lorry and feared for the safety of her children. She was told that a girl with glasses had been injured and thinking it was her daughter she suffered nervous shock leading to her death. Damages were awarded, although she was not within the foreseeable area of impact and the shock was suffered as a result of fear for another's safety. A new limitation was imposed, that the shock should occur as a result of what the claimant witnessed as a result of her own unaided senses, rather than as a result of what others later told her.
>
> *NB.* The claimant in this case would now be classified as a secondary victim. This is the first reported case in England where a secondary victim recovered damages.

Following this case two factors became important in determining whether a person owed a duty not to cause psychiatric damage. One was the closeness of the claimant to the accident and whether the defendant was aware of the claimant's presence. The other was the relationship between the person suffering psychiatric damage and the person placed in danger. It became apparent that close family ties, such as parent–child or spouse, would suffice. For some time other relationships appeared to be recognised on various grounds.

1 Fellow employees in danger:
   Where a crane driver witnessed a load dropping into the hold of a ship and feared injury to his workmates, a duty was held to be owed. (*Dooley* v *Cammell Laird & Co Ltd* [1951] 1 Lloyd's Rep 271.)

2 Rescuers:
   The relationship between a rescuer and his victims gave rise to a duty to the rescuer on the grounds that rescue invited danger. (*Chadwick* v *British Railways Board* [1967] 1 WLR 912.)

In the 1980s there appeared to be a relaxing of the requirements for a successful claim following the House of Lords decision in *McLoughlin* v *O'Brian* [1983] AC 410 and the law seemed to be moving in the direction of a test of reasonable foreseeability. What has to be foreseeable in cases involving strangers is assessed *ex post facto* (after the event) on the basis of what a reasonable man would have foreseen. If the parties are in a contractual relationship and the claim arises out of concurrent liability, such as an employer imposing stressful conditions on his workforce, the question is based on those features of the claimant's personal life and disposition of which the defendant was aware. (***McLoughlin v Jones*** [2002] 2 WLR 1279.) This principle will also apply to professional advisers such as solicitors where, for example, a solicitor's negligence results in a person being wrongfully sent to prison. (***McLoughlin v Jones***.)

However, the 1990s saw a tightening of controls on nervous shock and a distinction between **secondary victims** (three-party cases) and **primary victims** (two-party cases). In the former, the House of Lords affirmed control tests of geographical proximity to the accident and closeness of relationship to the primary victim. (***Alcock v Chief Constable of South Yorkshire Police*** [1991] 4 All ER 907.) In the latter, where the person claiming is the person placed in danger, the House of Lords recognised a different test based on foreseeability of physical damage. (***Page v Smith*** [1995] 2 All ER 736.) Finally, a rather exasperated House of Lords gave a narrow ruling in the area and ignored the liberal proposals of the Law Commission. This case involved police officers who had been present at the scene of the Hillsborough football disaster and their claims in the capacity of employees of the defendant and as rescuers failed. (***White and others v Chief Constable of South Yorkshire Police*** [1999] 1 All ER 1.)

Types of claim

Psychiatric damage can arise in a number of ways and the law applied to a case will depend on what category it falls into:

1 A person who suffers physical injury as a result of a negligent act may suffer psychiatric injury as a result (primary victim).

2 The victim of an accident may be badly treated after the accident and develop psychiatric injury (primary victim).

3 A person is involved in an accident where they suffer no physical injury but develop psychiatric injury as a result of their fear (primary victim).

4 A person may witness an accident to others and suffer from psychiatric injury as a result of fear for another's safety (secondary victim).

Primary and secondary victims

Objective
4

The term primary victim was introduced by Lord Oliver in *Alcock v Chief Constable for the South Yorkshire Police* [1991] 4 All ER 907 at 923.

A distinction was made between primary and secondary victims:

> Broadly [the cases] divide into two categories, that is to say, those cases in which the injured plaintiff was involved, either mediately or immediately, as a participant and those in which the plaintiff was no more than a passive and unwilling witness of injury caused to others.

Three examples were given of claimants who would be classified as primary victims: claimants who feared for their own safety; rescuers; and involuntary participants. There are two points worth noting about this classification. First, Lord Oliver appeared to draw the distinction for the purposes of proximity as the primary victim cases illustrate 'a directness of relationship which is almost self-evident from a mere recital of the facts'. Once classified as a secondary victim, it was necessary for the claimant to go on and establish factors such as closeness of relationship and closeness to the accident to establish proximity. Secondly, the definition attempts to define both primary and secondary victims in positive terms. Some definitions have defined primary victims and left secondary victims as a residual category.

The second attempt at definition was by Lord Lloyd in *Page* v *Smith* [1995] 2 All ER 736 at 755:

> In all these cases the plaintiff was the secondary victim of the defendant's negligence. He or she was in the position of a spectator or bystander. In the present case, by contrast, the plaintiff was a participant. He was himself directly involved in the accident, and well within the range of foreseeable physical injury. He was the primary victim.

Lord Lloyd's concept of primary victim would therefore appear to be narrower and to exclude rescuers and involuntary participants unless they came within the range of foreseeable physical injury.

This narrower definition has subsequently been supported by the majority in *White and others* v *Chief Constable of South Yorkshire Police and others* [1999] 1 All ER 1. In the context of that case it was to deny compensation to police officers at the Hillsborough football disaster. The officers failed to qualify as primary victims as they were not within the range of foreseeable physical injury. The fact that they were rescuers and employees of the defendant was not sufficient to lift them into that privileged category of claimants. Having failed this test, they clearly failed the control tests for secondary victims.

The wider definition was used to compensate those who came to the rescue of the injured and those who believed they were the cause of another person's death. (*Hunter* v *British Coal Corp* [1998] 2 All ER 97.) It was also relied on by Lord Goff in his dissenting speech in *White* v *Chief Constable of South Yorkshire Police*. Lord Goff doubted whether Lord Lloyd meant that, to qualify as a primary victim, the claimant had to be within the range of foreseeable physical injury as this meaning would contradict a number of well-known cases and is a sufficient condition of liability for psychiatric injury but not a necessary condition of such liability.

Primary victims

The distinction between primary and secondary victims has been controversial. (See above.) The significance of this distinction became clear with the House of Lords decision in *Page* v *Smith*.

Page v *Smith* [1995] 2 All ER 736

The claimant was driving his car when he was involved in an accident caused by the defendant's negligence. He suffered no physical injury and no compensatable nervous shock. His claim was for the activation of his myalgic encephalomyelitis (ME). He had suffered from ME for a number of years, but at the time of the accident was in remission and claimed that the accident, described as one of modest severity, had reactivated the ME.

The House of Lords held (Lords Keith and Jauncey dissenting) that in primary victim cases the duty of care was established by the reasonable foreseeability of physical damage to the claimant. Nervous shock or psychiatric damage was encompassed within this definition of physical damage and no

> distinction was to be drawn between psychiatric damage and traditional personal injuries. The control factors which were necessary in secondary victim cases were not necessary where the claimant was a primary victim. The claimant's physical proximity to the accident dispenses with the need for rules limiting the ambit of the duty of care. What will be crucial in primary victim cases is not the ability of the event to shock but the reasonable foreseeability of physical injury. The case itself was referred back on causation grounds as the claimant had failed to establish, on the balance of probabilities, that his ME had been reactivated by the accident. (See *Page* v *Smith (No 2)* [1996] 3 All ER 272.)

This case raises almost as many questions as it answers. Great weight is placed on reasonable foreseeability. Lord Lloyd, who gave the leading majority judgment, stated that in primary victim cases hindsight played no part in assessing what was reasonably foreseeable. Hindsight will, however, continue to play a part in what was reasonably foreseeable in secondary victim cases. The only thing that has to be reasonably foreseeable in primary victim cases is physical damage. This means that there is no longer any difference between a case involving a broken leg following a motor accident and one where the primary victim suffers PTSD. Provided some physical damage is foreseeable to the claimant, the full extent of the claimant's damage is recoverable. There may be some cases where the question of whether the claimant was in the area of physical danger will raise questions of fact.

McFarlane v *EE Caledonia Ltd* [1994] 1 All ER 1

> The claimant was employed as a painter on an oil rig in the North Sea owned and operated by the defendants. The claimant was in his bunk on a support vessel 550 metres away, when a series of massive explosions occurred on the oil rig. For an hour and three-quarters the claimant witnessed the explosions and consequent destruction of the rig before he was evacuated by helicopter. The closest the claimant came to the fire, in which 164 men were killed, was 100 metres. This was when the support vessel moved towards the rig in an attempt to fight the fire and render assistance. The claimant claimed damages for psychiatric illness suffered as a result of the events he had witnessed.
>
> The Court of Appeal held that on the facts no duty of care was owed to the claimant in respect of psychiatric illness.
>
> A person who was in the actual area of danger created by the event would have a claim. Such a person would have been on the Piper Alpha rig. The claimant did not come into this category. On the evidence, the support vessel never was in actual danger. No one sustained physical injury and no one except the claimant sustained psychiatric illness. Where the claimant is not actually in danger but because of the sudden and unexpected nature of the event they reasonably (objectively) think that they are, a duty will be owed. An example of this is *Dulieu* v *White*. Again, on the evidence, this was not the case. The claimant could have taken steps to take shelter unless he was rooted to the spot with fear, which he was not. Many of the claimant's professed fears appeared to be based not on what he actually saw and felt but on an *ex post facto* rationalisation.
>
> A claimant cannot be categorised as a primary victim because he feels himself (wrongly) to be responsible for the death of a fellow employee. Where a workman ran to turn off a water hydrant after an explosion and discovered a quarter of an hour later that his workmate had been killed, he was not a primary victim. (*Hunter* v *British Coal Corp* [1998] 2 All ER 97.)

Is this broadening of the foreseeability test to eradicate the physical/psychiatric distinction justifiable? The leading textbook on nervous shock (Mullany and Handford, *Tort Liability for Psychiatric Damage* (1993), p. 323) argues that: 'as a general observation an injured mind is far more difficult to nurse back to health than an injured body and is arguably more debilitating and disruptive of a greater number of aspects of human existence.' If this is accepted, then any distinction between psychiatric illness and physical damage must rest on diagnosis problems and, although the issue is not clear-cut, there is evidence to show that psychiatrists are as consistent in their diagnosis as other physicians. If PTSD is taken in isolation with its emphasis on an external stressor, there would appear to be no diagnostic reasons to distinguish it from physical damage. Beyond PTSD there may be evidential problems and it is perhaps significant that the claimant in *Page* v *Smith* was suffering from a controversial illness.

Was the removal of the control tests in primary victim cases justifiable? The necessary relationship and geographical proximity tests are self-evidently not required, but what of the customary phlegm test? A secondary victim has to overcome a threshold test for psychiatric damage before they can recover. If a normal person would not have suffered shock in these circumstances, then a sensitive claimant can recover nothing. In primary victim cases there would no longer appear to be such a threshold and, so long as some physical damage is foreseeable, the claimant can recover, subject to causation, for the full extent of any psychiatric damage suffered. This allows 'walking time bombs', such as the claimant in *Page*, to recover.

Further problems can be envisaged as secondary victims attempt to reclassify themselves as primary victims in order to benefit from the more advantageous rules and, if Lord Lloyd's approach is adopted, there is apparently nothing to prevent the principles being applied in cases other than motoring accidents. Lord Browne-Wilkinson's view appears more likely to find favour as he restricted his approach to the point that psychiatric illness is foreseeable as a result of a motoring accident.

Rothwell v *Chemical and Insulating Co Ltd* [2007] 4 All ER 1047

See Chapter 28 for *Rothwell* v *Chemical and Insulating Co Ltd.*

The House of Lords was invited to depart from *Page* v *Smith* in a case where the claimant had suffered anxiety at the prospect that he might suffer illness as a result of being negligently exposed to asbestos.

Lord Hoffmann:

> Counsel for the defendants invited the House to depart from the decision in *Page*'s case on the ground that it was wrongly decided. It has certainly had no shortage of critics, chief of whom was Lord Goff of Chieveley in *White* v *Chief Constable of South Yorkshire Police* [1999] 1 All ER 1, supported by a host of academic writers. But I do not think that it would be right to depart from *Page*'s case. It does not appear to have caused any practical difficulties and is not, I think, likely to do so if confined to the kind of situation which the majority in that case had in mind. That was a foreseeable event (a collision) which, viewed in prospect, was such as might cause physical injury or psychiatric injury or both. Where such an event has in fact happened and caused psychiatric injury, the House decided that it is unnecessary to ask whether it was foreseeable that what actually happened would have that consequence. Either form of injury is recoverable.
>
> In the present case, the foreseeable event was that the claimant would contract an asbestos-related disease. If that event occurred, it could no doubt cause psychiatric as well as physical injury. But the event has not occurred. The psychiatric illness has been caused by apprehension that the event may occur. The creation of such a risk is, as I have said, not in itself actionable. I think it would be an unwarranted extension of the principle in *Page*'s case to apply it to psychiatric illness caused by apprehension of the possibility of an unfavourable event which had not actually happened.

In *Yearworth* v *North Bristol NHS Trust* [2009] EWCA Civ 37 it was held that the negligent destruction of semen stored by a hospital did not amount to personal injury and therefore could not give rise to a claim for psychiatric damage. It did, however, give rise to a claim for bailment and damages on a contractual basis.

White and others v Chief Constable of South Yorkshire Police
[1999] 1 All ER 1

This case involved police officers who had been present at the scene of the Hillsborough football disaster and claimed in the capacity of employees of the defendant and as rescuers.

The House of Lords ruled against the police officers.

1 They were held to have no claim as employees as they were not primary victims and had no close relation of love and affection with the victims. The mere fact that the claimants were employees of the defendant did not make them primary victims.

2 They had no claim as rescuers. A rescuer was in no special position regarding psychiatric damage and had to show that they had been objectively exposed to physical danger. (The decision in *Chadwick* would appear to survive on the basis that the claimant was foreseeably exposed to physical danger.)

Lord Hoffmann:

Should then your Lordships take the incremental step of extending liability for psychiatric injury to 'rescuers' (a class which would now require definition) who give assistance at or after some disaster without coming within the range of foreseeable physical injury? It may be said that this would encourage people to offer assistance. The category of secondary victims would be confined to 'spectators and bystanders' who take no part in dealing with the incident or its aftermath. On the authorities, as it seems to me, your Lordships are free to take such a step.

In my opinion there are two reasons why your Lordships should not do so. The less important reason is the definitional problem to which I have alluded. The concept of a rescuer as someone who puts himself in danger of physical injury is easy to understand. But once this notion is extended to include others who give assistance, the line between them and bystanders becomes difficult to draw with any precision. For example, one of the plaintiffs in the *Alcock's* case, a Mr O'Dell, went to look for his nephew. 'He searched among the bodies . . . and assisted those who staggered out from the terraces'. He did not contend that his case was different from those of the other relatives and it was also dismissed. Should he have put himself forward as a rescuer?

But the more important reason for not extending the law is that in my opinion the result would be quite unacceptable. I have used this word on a number of occasions and the time has come to explain what I mean. I do not mean that the burden of claims would be too great for the insurance market or the public funds, the two main sources for the payment of damages in tort. The Law Commission may have had this in mind when they said that removal of all the control mechanisms would lead to an 'unacceptable' increase in claims, since they described it as a 'floodgates' argument. These are questions on which it is difficult to offer any concrete evidence and I am simply not in a position to form a view one way or the other. I am therefore willing to accept that, viewed against the total sums paid as damages for personal injury, the increase resulting from an extension of liability to helpers would be modest. But I think that such an extension would be unacceptable to the ordinary person because (though he might not put it this way) it would offend against his notions of distributive justice. He would think it unfair between one class of claimants and another, at best not treating like cases alike and, at worst, favouring the less deserving against the more deserving. He would think it wrong that policemen, even as part of a general class of persons who rendered assistance, should have the right to compensation for psychiatric injury out of public funds while the bereaved relatives are sent away with nothing.

The plaintiffs say that they were primary victims because they were not 'spectators or bystanders'. The defendants say that the plaintiffs were secondary victims because they were not 'within the range of foreseeable physical injury'. Both arguments have some support from the speeches in *Page v Smith*, which did not have the present question in mind. Essentially, however, as I said at the beginning of this speech, the plaintiffs draw two distinctions between their position and that of spectators or bystanders. The first is that they had a relationship analogous to employment with the chief constable. Although constitutionally a constable holds an office rather than being employed, there is no dispute that his chief constable owes him the same duty of care which he would to an employee. The plaintiffs say that they were therefore owed a special duty which required the chief constable and those for whom he was vicariously liable to take reasonable care not to expose them to unnecessary risk of injury, whether physical or psychiatric. Secondly, the plaintiffs (and in this respect there is no difference between the police and many others in the crowd that day) did more than stand by and look. They actively rendered assistance and should be equated to 'rescuers', who, it was said, always qualify as primary victims.

My Lords, I shall consider first the claim to primary status by virtue of the employment relationship. Mr Hytner QC, for the plaintiffs, said that prima facie an employer's duty required him to take reasonable steps to safeguard his employees from unnecessary risk of harm. The word 'unnecessary' must be stressed because obviously a policeman takes the risk of injury which is an unavoidable part of his duty. But there is no reason why he should be exposed to injuries which reasonable care could prevent. Why, in this context, should psychiatric injury be treated differently from physical injury? He referred to *Walker* v *Northumberland CC* [1995] 1 All ER 737 where an employee recovered damages for a mental breakdown, held to have been foreseeably caused by the stress and pressure of his work as a social services officer. This, he said, showed that no distinction could be made.

I think, my Lords, that this argument really assumes what it needs to prove. The liability of an employer to his employees for negligence, either direct or vicarious, is not a separate tort with its own rules. It is an aspect of the general law of negligence. The relationship of employer and employee establishes the employee as a person to whom the employer owes a duty of care. But this tells one nothing about the circumstances in which he will be liable for a particular type of injury. For this one must look to the general law concerning the type of injury which has been suffered. It would not be suggested that the employment relation-ship entitles the employee to recover damages in tort (I put aside contractual liability, which obviously raises different questions) for economic loss which would not ordinarily be recoverable in negligence. The employer is not, for example, under a duty in tort to take reasonable care not to do something which would cause the employee purely financial loss, e.g. by reducing his opportunities to earn bonuses. The same must surely be true of psychiatric injury. There must be a reason why, if the employee would otherwise have been regarded as a secondary victim, the employment relationship should require him to be treated as a primary one. The employee in *Walker* v *Northumberland CC* was in no sense a secondary victim. His mental breakdown was caused by the strain of doing the work which his employer had required him to do.

Lord Hoffmann concluded that it would not be fair to give police officers the right to a larger claim merely because their injuries were caused by other police officers and rejected the employment relationship as in itself a sufficient basis for liability.

See Chapter 14 for employer's liability for occupational stress.

When set against the employer's liability for occupational stress to employees this looks odd. If an employer has negligently subjected an employee to a work regime which gradually built up to foreseeably cause stress to the employee, then that employee is categorised as a primary victim. (*Hatton* v *Sutherland* [2002] 2 All ER 1.) Why should an employee, such as the police officers at Hillsborough, who suffers a sudden and violent assault on their senses be a secondary victim?

The decision in *Dooley* v *Cammell Laird* would appear to be in doubt although it was not expressly overruled and it is possible that it could be supported on a primary victim basis. (See below.)

The decision preserves the distinction between primary victims and secondary victims. The former are not subject to the control devices and what needs to be foreseeable is physical injury. Foreseeability of shock is not necessary. The intended effect of *White* would appear to be to attempt to prevent creeping expansion of claimants in this category.

The strong policy element which surrounds this area can be seen where, as a result of their own negligence, a primary victim causes psychiatric damage to a third party. If *X* drives his car negligently and causes a traffic accident in which he is injured and *Y* (*X*'s father) attends the scene of the accident as a fireman and suffers psychiatric damage, *X* owes no duty to *Y*. (*Greatorex* v *Greatorex* [2000] 4 All ER 769.) The reasons for this are that to hold otherwise would impose a significant limitation on an individual's freedom of action and would encourage litigation between family members.

Is the category of primary victims closed?

The advantages of a claimant being classified as a primary victim are obvious from the point of view of the likely success of their case. The intention of the majority in the House of Lords in *White* was clearly to keep this as a tightly defined category of those exposed to a risk of physical harm, with a limited number of claimants qualified to occupy this privileged position. How successful have they been?

The question of occupational stress victims has already been mentioned, together with the possible interpretation of *Dooley* v *Cammell Laird*.

Further developments have come in the area of medical negligence. A father who was wrongly told that his baby had died and was given a dead baby to hold was classed as a primary victim (*Farrell* v *Avon Health Authority* [2001] Lloyd's Rep Med 458), as was a mother who gave birth to a disabled child as a result of the defendant's negligence. (*Farrell* v *Merton, Sutton and Wandsworth Health Authority* (2000) 57 BMLR 158.) The mother in this case had herself suffered physical injury.

In cases of local authority negligence, the increasing reluctance of the courts to strike out actions extends to cases where the claim is for psychiatric damage. Where a known sexual abuser was placed with a foster family (without the authority informing them he was an abuser) and abused the foster parents' own children, the striking out of the claimant's case for psychiatric damage by the Court of Appeal was overturned by the House of Lords (*W* v *Essex County Council* [2000] 2 All ER 237), as it was arguable that at trial the parents might be held to be owed a duty of care.

On the same basis that psychiatric damage need not be foreseeable to a primary victim in a road accident case, neither need it be to a person who has been falsely imprisoned as a result of their solicitor's negligence. Such a person is a primary victim. (*McLoughlin* v *Jones* [2002] 2 WLR 1279.)

It is worth noting at this stage that there may be cases where the court feels that a duty of care should be owed but is reluctant to classify the claimant as either a primary or secondary victim. This was the case where a claimant was injected with human growth hormone which carried the risk that the claimant could develop Creutzfeldt-Jakob disease (CJD). It was foreseeable by the defendants that the claimant would develop a psychiatric condition on being informed of the risk of this invariably fatal illness. The judge held that a duty of care did exist but declined to find that the claimant was a primary victim because of the effect that such a ruling would have on other cases. People who had been exposed to radiation or asbestos would then have been able to claim for psychiatric damage. The basis of the duty found was said by the judge to be similar to that between doctor and patient. (*CJD Litigation: Group B Plaintiffs* v *Medical Research Council* [2000] Lloyd's Rep Med 161.)

It is important to remember that these specific rules on psychiatric damage do not exist in a vacuum and that they may be affected by other legal rules on matters such as employer–employee liability.

Secondary victims

The modern law on secondary victims is largely drawn from one case. This was the litigation arising from a disaster at a football match. The case is reported at length because of its importance.

The Hillsborough litigation

Jones v *Wright* [1991] 2 WLR 814 (QBD); [1991] 3 All ER 88 (CA)

On 15 April 1989 the FA Cup semi-final was due to be played between Liverpool and Nottingham Forest at Hillsborough stadium in Sheffield. The match was a sell-out and television cameras were at the ground to record the football for transmission later that evening. The match was halted after six minutes as the weight of numbers of people in the Leppings Lane pens had created such pressure that spectators were being trapped against the wire separating the pens from the pitch. Ninety-five people died as a result of their injuries and another 400 needed hospital treatment. Thousands witnessed the horrific events from other parts of the ground and millions more witnessed what was happening on live television broadcasts or heard the news on radio. Many of those watching or listening had loved ones at the match. Inevitably, a large number of people suffered psychological disorders and some cases within well-accepted categories of psychiatric damage were settled. Sixteen test cases were brought to determine whether the defendant (the Chief Constable of the police force responsible for policing the ground) owed them a duty of care. These cases were representative of 150 similar claims.

Four of the claimants had actually attended the match and witnessed the events and had friends or relatives in the Leppings Lane pens. One claimant was outside the ground and watched the events on television in a coach. He later identified the body of his son-in-law in a mortuary. Nine of the claimants witnessed the disaster on television and had loved ones at the match. One claimant heard the news on the radio and later saw recorded highlights on television. The final claimant heard the news while out shopping, heard the news again on the radio some two hours later and at 10 p.m. saw it on recorded television.

The claimants had all been examined by the same medical expert and the trial judge accepted his evidence that they were all suffering from at least one psychiatric illness.

The issue for the court was therefore whether the defendant owed each claimant a duty of care. Two issues were pertinent as to proximity.

1 First, the necessary degree of relationship between the claimant and the person in danger.
2 Second, the question of geographical proximity to the accident.

The question of simultaneous television transmission arose for decision for the first time.

On necessary relationship, the first instance judge held that parents, spouses and siblings of a victim had a close enough relationship to be foreseeable. The Court of Appeal was split on this point. Stocker and Nolan LJJ were prepared to accept that a person who fell outside the accepted categories of parent–child, spouse or rescuer, could claim, provided they could establish a sufficient degree of relationship and care. Parker LJ agreed that the claim was based on relationship and care. On this basis the accepted categories had a presumptive claim, but the presumption could be rebutted if the necessary degree of care was not present. Thus spouses who were separated and hated each other could have the presumption in their favour defeated. The result in the instant case was that all persons who did not fall within the parent–child or spouse categories had their claims rejected as no evidence had been led to establish the necessary degree of care required. An example of such a relationship would be where a grandparent had brought up a child from being a baby.

On the question of geographical proximity, the trial judge considered that all persons in, or immediately outside, the stadium were sufficiently proximate in terms of time and space. Those persons who witnessed the scenes on television and had the necessary degree of relationship could also claim. Claimants who were told of the disaster or heard it on the radio had no claim. The Court of Appeal, however, took the view that those persons who suffered shock as a result of watching live television had no claim. While it was reasonably foreseeable that television pictures would be broadcast, the intervention of a third party between the accident and the claimant meant that television was not equivalent to sight or sound of the accident.

The Court of Appeal also took a narrow view of the immediate aftermath test. They regarded the events in *McLoughlin* as being equivalent to viewing the accident. Stress was placed on the fact that the family were still in the same state as they had been at the time of the accident. In cases where claimants had viewed the corpse of a loved one some hours after the disaster, this was not regarded as the immediate aftermath.

Alcock v *Chief Constable of the South Yorkshire Police* [1991] 4 All ER 907

Ten of the original claimants appealed to the House of Lords and the House unanimously dismissed their appeals.

Counsel for the claimants based his case on the argument that the sole test for duty in nervous shock cases was whether such illness was reasonably foreseeable. The House rejected this, in line with Lord Wilberforce's point in *McLoughlin* that foreseeability alone did not give rise to a duty.

Lord Keith:

As regards the class of persons to whom a duty may be owed to take reasonable care to avoid inflicting psychiatric illness through nervous shock sustained by reason of physical injury or peril to another, I think it sufficient that reasonable foreseeability should be the guide. I would not seek to limit the class by reference to particular relationships such as husband and wife or parent and child. The kinds of relationship which may involve close ties of love and affection are numerous, and it is the existence of such ties which leads to mental disturbance when the loved one suffers a catastrophe. They may be present in family relationships or those of close friendship, and may be stronger in the case of engaged couples than in that of persons who have been married to each other for many years. It is common knowledge that such ties exist, and reasonably foreseeable that those bound by them may in certain circumstances be at real risk of psychiatric illness if the loved one is injured or put in peril. The closeness of the tie would, however, require to be proved by a plaintiff, though no doubt being capable of being presumed in appropriate cases. The case of a bystander unconnected with the victims of an accident is difficult. Psychiatric injury to him would not ordinarily, in my view, be within the range of reasonable foreseeability but could not perhaps be entirely excluded from it if the circumstances of a catastrophe occurring very close to him were particularly horrific.

In the case of those within the sphere of reasonable foreseeability the proximity factors mentioned by Lord Wilberforce in *McLoughlin* v *O'Brian* must, however, be taken into account in judging whether a duty of care exists. The first of these is proximity of the plaintiff to the accident in time and space. For this purpose the accident is to be taken to include its immediate aftermath, which in *McLoughlin's* case was held to cover the scene at the hospital which was experienced by the plaintiff some two hours after the accident. In *Jaensch* v *Coffey* (1984) 54 ALR 417 the plaintiff saw her injured husband at the hospital to which he had been taken in severe pain before and between his undergoing a series of emergency operations, and the next day stayed with him in the intensive care unit and thought he was going to die. She was held entitled to recover damages for the psychiatric illness she suffered as a result. Deane J said: . . . the aftermath of the accident extended to the hospital to which the injured person was taken and persisted for so long as he remained in the state produced by the accident up to and including immediate post-accident treatment . . . Her psychiatric injuries were the result of the impact upon her of the facts of the accident itself and its aftermath while she was present at the aftermath of the accident at the hospital.

As regards the means by which the shock is suffered, Lord Wilberforce said in *McLoughlin's* case that it must come through sight or hearing of the event or of its immediate aftermath. He also said that it was surely right that the law should not compensate shock brought about by communication by a third party. On that basis it is open to serious doubt whether *Hevican* v *Ruane* [1991] 3 All ER 65 and *Ravenscroft* v *Rederiaktiebolaget Transatlantic* [1991] 3 All ER 73 were correctly decided, since in both of these cases the effective cause of the psychiatric illness would appear to have been the fact of a son's death and the news of it.

The requirements for a duty of care in psychiatric damage cases were stated by the House of Lords to be:

1 A sufficiently close relationship of love and affection with the primary victim to make it reasonably foreseeable that the claimant might suffer nervous shock if they apprehended that the primary victim had been injured or might be injured.

   This means that the potential duty is not restricted to particular relationships such as spouses or parent–child. In spouse and parent–child cases there would appear to be a rebuttable presumption of such a relationship. In other relationships, such as siblings or engaged couples, it will be necessary for the claimant to lead evidence to prove the existence of such a relationship.

   Curiously, Lords Ackner, Keith and Oliver were not prepared to rule out even a bystander where the accident was particularly horrific and a reasonably strong-nerved person would have been affected. The example given was where a petrol tanker crashed into a school playground, caught fire and caused serious injuries to children.

   However, in *McFarlane* v *EE Caledonia Ltd* [1994] 1 All ER 1, one of the questions was whether a claimant had a claim on the basis that he was obliged to witness catastrophe at close range where 164 lives were lost after an explosion and fire on an oil rig and that it was of such a horrendous nature that even as a bystander the defendants owed him a duty of care. The Court of Appeal took a narrow view of the *Alcock* dicta and held that there must be a close tie of love and affection between claimant and victim and that courts should not extend the duty to mere bystanders unless there is a sufficient degree of proximity which requires both nearness in time and a close relationship of love and affection.

2 Proximity to the accident, or its immediate aftermath, was sufficiently close in terms of time and space.

   Sight or sound of the accident will continue to suffice. The House refused to lay down a strict definition of immediate aftermath. Lord Keith appeared to approve the Australian case of *Jaensch* v *Coffey* (1984) 54 ALR 417, where the aftermath of the accident continued as long as the victim remained in the state produced by the accident, up to and including immediate post-accident treatment. Lord Ackner viewed *McLoughlin* as being on the boundaries of what was acceptable. (See Lord Keith above.) All judges were agreed that identifying a corpse in the mortuary eight hours after the accident was not within the immediate aftermath. However, in an extempore judgment, the Court of Appeal later held that where a 16-year-old girl was killed by a car which mounted the pavement, her mother had a claim after being told that her daughter was dead and then seeing the body in the mortuary. (*Galli-Atkinson* v *Seghal* [2003] EWCA Civ 697.) It is difficult to see how this case could be distinguished from the relatives in *Alcock* who visited the mortuary. The court ruled that there was an uninterrupted sequence of events from the mother being told of the death and that the immediate aftermath extended to the mortuary.

   In *Palmer* v *Tees Health Authority* [1999] Lloyd's Rep Med 351 the claimant's 4-year-old daughter was abducted and murdered by a psychiatric patient. The body was discovered three days later and although the claimant was in the vicinity she did not see the body at the time. The claimant was held not to satisfy the immediate aftermath test.

   In *Taylor* v *A Novo (UK) Ltd* [2013] EWCA Civ 194 a claim was denied by the Court of Appeal where the claimant's mother suffered injuries as a result of the defendant's negligence and died three weeks later as a result of the injuries. The claimant witnessed the death but not the accident and was held to have insufficient proximity to be a secondary victim.

If the delay is due to the fault of the defendant in withholding information, then events a day later may constitute the immediate aftermath. (*Farrell* v *Merton, Sutton and Wandsworth Hospital* (2000) 57 BMLR 158 – mother not allowed to see her newly born and severely disabled baby for over 24 hours.)

Signs of a non-mechanical approach to immediate aftermath are apparent in *W* v *Essex County Council* [2000] 2 All ER 237. Lord Slynn, in discussing whether foster parents whose children had been abused by a child they had fostered could claim for psychiatric damage if they did not witness the abuse or come across the abuser immediately after the abuse, said that immediate aftermath had to be determined in the particular factual situation.

Developments in medical negligence cases involving psychiatric damage also show signs of a non-mechanical approach based on the trial judge's finding of fact. In *Walters* v *North Glamorgan NHS Trust* [2002] All ER (D) 87 (Dec), a woman who watched her child die over a period of 36 hours was entitled to damages for psychiatric damage. A realistic view was taken as to what constituted the necessary 'event' and there was clear medical evidence that the claimant's condition had been caused by shock.

3   They suffered nervous shock through seeing or hearing the accident or its immediate aftermath.

A person who was informed of the accident by a third party would generally have no claim. A person watching simultaneous television would normally have no claim as the broadcasting guidelines prevent the showing of suffering by recognisable individuals. If such pictures were shown, then the transmission would normally be regarded as a *novus actus interveniens*. There may be cases, however, where viewing simultaneous television may be treated as equivalent to sight and sound of the accident. An example is given of a televised hot-air balloon event with children in the balloon, which suddenly bursts into flames.

There have been developments in this area away from instantaneous communication by television or radio.

AB v *Thameside & Glossop Health Authority* [1997] 8 Med LR 91

Patients of the defendant health authority complained of the way in which they had been informed of the distressing news that a health worker had been found to be HIV positive and that they had been exposed to a remote risk of infection. The claimants alleged that they should have been informed face to face rather than by letter. Counsel conceded the existence of a duty of care but the claim failed as the Court of Appeal held that the defendants had not been negligent. It appears from the case that any duty of care owed would not be a general part of the law of negligence and so affect cases such as *Alcock*, but would be limited to where there was a pre-existing relationship between health authority and patient. (See also *Allin* v *City & Hackney Health Authority* [1996] 7 Med LR 91, where the claimant recovered damages after being incorrectly told that her baby had died. Again, the existence of a duty of care was conceded.)

Also in the area of medical negligence, damages have been awarded to the immediate family of a woman who had an unnecessary mastectomy following a misdiagnosis of breast cancer. Her husband was awarded damages for the sudden appreciation of a horrifying event at the moment that he first saw his wife undressing after the mastectomy. As the husband knew of the mastectomy before witnessing its effects, this appears difficult to match with the sudden shocking event required by *Alcock*. Her son, aged ten, was awarded damages for discovering about his mother's supposed cancer when he overheard a phone call. This appears to be a generous interpretation of unaided senses. (***Froggatt v Chesterfield & North Derbyshire Royal Hospital NHS Trust*** [2002] All ER (D) 218 (Dec).)

4 The claimant must have suffered a psychiatric injury recognised by law. This will normally be PTSD.

In ***Vernon v Bosley (No 1)*** [1997] 1 All ER 577 it was held that where the claimant's mental illness had been contributed to partly by the defendant's negligence (witnessing the death of a loved one caused by the defendant's negligence) and partly by the pathological grief attributable to the death itself, the claimant was entitled to damages for the mental illness with no discount for the consequences of the grief and the consequences of the bereavement, even though the mental illness was partly caused by the grief.

It should be noted that damages can be recovered for psychiatric damage caused by the sight of property damage such as one's house burning down as a result of the defendant's negligence. (***Attia v British Gas plc*** [1987] 3 All ER 455.)

5 In applying a foreseeability test the court will take into account the egg-shell skull principle, that the defendant must take the claimant as they find them as regards physical characteristics.

Brice v *Brown* [1984] 1 All ER 997

A 9-year-old girl and her mother were involved in an accident in the taxi in which they were travelling. The girl suffered slight injuries but the mother, who was emotionally unstable, suffered serious and long-lasting nervous shock. The court applied a test of whether the person of customary phlegm would have suffered shock in these circumstances. If not, then the claimant would have no claim. If yes, then the claimant could recover for the full extent of her shock, even if the person of customary phlegm would not have suffered shock to that extent. (But note the Court of Appeal decision in *McLoughlin v Jones*, where the parties are in a contractual relationship.)

NB. Where the claimant is a primary victim the customary phlegm test does not apply where some physical damage is foreseeable.

A cautionary note

This area of law has been primarily concerned with accidents. The primary/secondary victim distinction is specifically devised to fit with accidents. Where the case involves negligent information, has a local authority background or an employer–employee relationship to it then other tort rules come into play. In the negligent information cases the *Hedley Byrne* rules are in play and in the local authority cases the highly complex principles on statutory duties and public authorities operate. It is suggested that the primary/secondary victim divide is unhelpful in these areas as it is in the occupational stress cases where the principle does not appear to operate at all.

See Chapter 7 for public authorities.

See Chapter 5 for *Hedley Byrne.*

See Chapter 14 for occupational stress.

Conclusion

This is an area which has caused great difficulty to the courts and they appear to be no nearer to producing satisfactory rules. Lord Hoffmann in *White* said that 'the search for principle in this part of the law has been called off'. Part of the difficulty may be caused by a conception that psychiatric damage is less worthy than physical damage of compensation, and even that the prospect of compensation may delay recovery by the psychiatrically damaged claimant. The case of relational loss (secondary victims) appears to provoke a defensive stance by the judiciary and the primary/secondary divide, with the more favourable rules for primary victims, illustrates this. However, the primary/secondary divide may end up causing more problems than it solves and creating more litigation as claimants' lawyers attempt to have their clients classified as primary victims.

The issue of psychiatric damage was referred to the Law Commission, which produced recommendations for reform, including legislation (Law Commission Report No 249 (1998)). The major suggestions were as follows:

1　The requirement that the claimant be in physical proximity to the accident should be abolished where there is a sufficiently close relationship between the claimant and the person placed in danger.

2　Legislation should lay down a fixed list of relationships where a close tie of love and affection shall be deemed to exist. This would cover spouse, parent, child, sibling and cohabitant. A claimant outside this list would be allowed to prove that a sufficiently close relationship existed.

3　The requirement that the psychiatric illness be caused by shock should be abolished.

4　The courts should abandon attaching significance to whether the claimant was a primary or secondary victim.

The House of Lords decision in *White* demonstrates that the majority in that case were not in favour of the expansionist views of the Law Commission. The law therefore remains that a claimant must either satisfy the control devices in *Alcock* as a secondary victim or establish primary victim status to take advantage of the more favourable rules.

Some of the issues raised by the Law Commission were considered by the High Court of Australia, where the 'shock' and 'direct perception' requirements were abandoned. The test was whether it was reasonably foreseeable that the defendant's conduct might result in psychiatric harm to the claimant. (*Thame v New South Wales* (2002) 76 AJLR 1348.) The court also rejected the distinction between primary and secondary victims. The approach is similar to that in *McLoughlin* and leaves the question of whether English law would have been more sensible to have followed this route than the travails in which it is currently involved in this area of law.

Summary

This chapter deals with the rules on duty of care in relation to nervous shock or psychiatric damage.

● The traditional expression for this kind of damage is nervous shock but it is now referred to as psychiatric damage.

● This kind of damage raises problems because of the floodgates risk and the fear of fraudulent claims.

● No damages are given for the shock itself. Compensation is awarded for the more long-lasting effects of trauma.

● The commonest type of psychiatric damage is post-traumatic stress disorder (PTSD). This requires an external stressor of an exceptional nature to trigger it.

- Historically the common law was reluctant to compensate for psychiatric damage but rules gradually developed in the twentieth century.

- Modern claims are divided into two-party and three-party claims: in the former the claimant is a primary victim; in the latter, a secondary victim. A primary victim is a person who was directly involved in the accident.

- The law on primary victims was established by *Page* v *Smith* (1995). A duty of care is established by proving reasonable foreseeability of physical damage. No distinction is drawn between psychiatric and personal injury for the purposes of foreseeability. The secondary victim control devices do not apply.

- In *White* v *Chief Constable South Yorkshire* (1999) the police officers at Hillsborough were refused primary victim status. The fact that they were rescuers and employees of the defendant did not affect their status. They were secondary victims and unable to claim.

- The law on secondary victims was established by *Alcock* v *Chief Constable South Yorkshire* (1991). The requirements for an action are: (i) a sufficiently close relationship of love and affection with the primary victim; (ii) proximity to the accident or its immediate aftermath; and (iii) psychiatric damage suffered as a result of seeing or hearing the accident or its immediate aftermath. The defendant must take his victim as he finds him and the claimant must have suffered from a recognised psychiatric illness.

Further reading

Bailey, S. and Nolan, D. (2010), 'The *Page* v *Smith* Saga: A Tale of Inauspicious Origins and Unintended Consequences', CLJ 495.

Case, P. (2010), 'Now You See It, Now You Don't: Black Letter Reflections on the Legacies of *White* v *Chief Constable of South Yorkshire Police*', Tort Law Review 33.

Cooke, P. J. (2004), 'Primary Victims: The End of the Road?' 25(1) Liverpool LR 29.

Mullany, N. (1998), 'Liability for Careless Communication of Traumatic Information' 114 LQR 380.

Sprince, A. (1995), *Page* v *Smith*, 'Being "Primary" Colours' 11 PN 124.

Sprince, A. (1998), 'Negligently Inflicted Psychiatric Damage: A Medical Diagnosis and Prognosis' 18 LS 59.

Teff, H. (1992), 'Liability for Psychiatric Illness After Hillsborough' 12 OJLS 440.

Teff, H. (1998), 'Liability for Negligently Inflicted Psychiatric Harm: Justifications and Boundaries' CLJ 91.

Teff, H. (1998), 'Liability for Psychiatric Illness: Advancing Cautiously' 61 MLR 849.

Todd, S. (1999), 'Psychiatric Injury and Rescuers' 115 LQR 345 (on *White* v *Chief Constable of South Yorkshire Police*).

Trinidade, F. A. (1996), 'Nervous Shock and Negligent Conduct' 112 LQR 22.

5

Economic loss

Objectives

After reading this chapter you will:

1. Have a critical knowledge of the arguments for and against the recovery of economic loss in negligence.
2. Understand the legal rules which govern a claim for economic loss in negligence and the roles played by the concepts of proximity, policy and assumption of responsibility in claims for economic loss.
3. Have a critical knowledge of an alternative matrix for economic loss claims drawn from other legal jurisdictions.

Introduction

Objective 1

Economic loss unaccompanied by physical damage presents a particular problem in negligence, as negligence has traditionally operated in a protective manner to compensate people for loss caused by negligently inflicted physical damage.

Where a person has suffered economic loss, redress has traditionally been in contract law. The justification for this has been the doctrine of consideration. Where a person had entered a bargain promise and provided consideration, this would justify the court protecting their expectation interest in a breach of contract action. Damages for breach of contract are to put the claimant in the position they would have been in if the contract had been performed. Contrast this with the tortious objective of damages, to put the claimant in the position they would have been in if the tort had not been committed. This protects the status quo interest.

Example

See Chapter 3 for *Donoghue* v *Stevenson*.

Take the facts of **Donoghue v Stevenson**. The duty of care owed by the defendant was a duty not to cause physical damage, in this case personal injuries to the claimant caused by a contaminated drink. If the claimant had been sick over her clothes as a result of drinking the contaminated ginger beer, she would have had a claim for damage to property. Both the claim for personal injuries and the claim for property damage are status quo claims. But she could not have claimed for the cost of the ginger beer. This is regarded as a claim for economic loss and, as the claimant had no contract, she had no claim. In this particular area (defective products) a distinction is drawn between providing a dangerous product (tort) and a defective product (contract).

Arguments against the recovery of pure economic loss in negligence

Quality

One objection to allowing economic loss claims in negligence is that it would involve the courts in having to assess quality. Where the claim is brought in contract, the quality is fixed by the contract – in the above example, the legally required quality of the ginger beer. But this problem is somewhat exaggerated in consumer claims such as *Donoghue*. Had the purchaser of the ginger beer brought an action in contract, the quality of the drink would actually have been fixed by statute rather than by the contract. (Sale of Goods Act 1979, s 14(2), as amended by the Sale and Supply of Goods Act 1994, s 1(1).)

Undermining contract

A further argument against such recovery is that it would undermine the third-party beneficiary rule in contract. This rule states that if *A* contracts with *B* to grant a benefit to *C* and *A* fails to do so, *C* has no action for breach of contract against *A*. If *C* were entitled to sue *A* in negligence this, it is argued, would undermine the contract rule. This problem is apparent in solicitors' negligence claims involving wills. *A* (the solicitor) contracts with *B* (the testator) to confer a benefit on *C* (the beneficiary). *A* negligently fails to carry out *B*'s wishes and *C* does not receive the bequest. There is no privity of contract between *A* and *C* but does *A* owe *C* a duty of care? (See *White* v *Jones*, below.)

The question also arises where there is a chain of contracts and it becomes impossible for the claimant to sue the person with whom he has privity of contract.

Example

C contracts with *B* for *B* to construct a building for *C*. *B* contracts with *A* for *A* to do some specialised work on the building. *A* performs his contract with *B* negligently. *B* becomes insolvent. *C* has a substandard building and suffers economic loss as a result. Does *A* owe *C* a duty of care? The gist of *C*'s claim against *A* is that *A*'s failure to perform his contract with *B* properly has caused loss to *C*. This is similar to the will case, but English law has reached different conclusions in the two examples given.

One problem which could be raised in the building example is to what standard is *A* supposed to perform with regard to *C*. One way to solve this would be to look at the requirements in the *B–A* contract. English law has been prepared to do this in a negative way – in order to avoid imposing liability on *C* (see *Norwich City Council* v *Harvey* [1989] 1 All ER 1180) but not in a positive fashion, in order to create a duty.

The privity rule in contract has always been subject to a number of exceptions at common law and an important new statutory provision has been added. The Contracts (Rights of Third Parties) Act 1999 allows a person who is not a party to a contract to enforce a term of the contract if the contract expressly provides that they may or where the term purports to confer a benefit on them. The third party must be identifiable, either by name or as a member of a class, or as answering a particular description. Whether this will operate in the area of sub-contractors is uncertain. In the example given above, even if the *A–B* contract purported to confer a benefit on *C* it is probable that there would be a strong presumption against enforceability of a contract other than the one under which he (*C*) has been given specific rights (*C–B* contract).

Floodgates

See Chapter 3 for 'floodgates'.

The 'floodgates' problem is often raised as a barrier to bringing an economic loss action in negligence. Economic loss is said to have a ripple effect which is not present in physical damage claims.

> ### Example
>
> *A* negligently severs an electricity cable which leads to the business premises of *B*, *C*, *D* and *E*, who are unable to produce goods for 48 hours and suffer economic loss as a result. *B* has contracts with *F*, *G* and *H*, each of whom suffers economic loss as a result of *B*'s being unable to perform. *C*, *D* and *E* each have several further contracts which are interrupted. If liability is imposed on *A*, then where would the liability end? (See *Spartan Steel* v *Martin*, below.)

No floodgates problem exists in contract, as the doctrine of privity limits an action to those persons who have provided consideration and are therefore parties to the contract.

In order to assess the floodgates argument it is necessary to look more closely at what is meant by the expression.

One meaning is that the courts would be inundated by claims if a right of action was granted. This cannot be true, as once a right of action is established, most claims will be settled and the courts not troubled.

The major floodgates problem with economic loss could be that the defendant would incur too heavy a burden in damages because of the alleged ripple effect. Professions that deal in the provision of information could arguably be driven out of business by the imposition of liability for pure economic loss. However, other countries in western Europe do impose such liability without any apparent serious problems for the professions concerned. Also, surveyors in England and Wales who have been subjected to such liability (see *Smith* v *Bush*, below) have survived. It should be remembered that the professions would only be subjected to fault-based liability and the standard of care would effectively

See Chapter 15 for *Bolam*.

be set by their peers under the *Bolam* test. It would not be strict liability. It is important to remember that the imposition of a duty of care in negligence does not in itself impose liability; the defendant must be shown to have fallen below the required standard of care.

There is a clear argument that the physical/economic loss distinction on the ripple effect is too simplistic. There are cases of economic loss, such as beneficiaries under a will and potential purchasers of houses, where the number of potential claimants and the extent of the loss are more limited than in some physical damage cases. Principles other than duty of care, such as causation, remoteness and *novus actus interveniens* also operate to control damages.

Historical development

Objective
2

In cases of physical damage, the neighbour test provided a springboard for the development of a general principle of liability. Modern orthodoxy holds that there was no claim for economic loss. The next case is often cited to support the point.

Cattle v *Stockton Waterworks Co* (1875) LR 10 QB 453

The defendants negligently burst a water main. This added to the claimant's (formerly termed plaintiff's) expense in building a tunnel. The claimant was under contract with a third party to build the tunnel. The plaintiff was unable to recover this expense as it was pure economic loss.

This case illustrates a recurrent problem. *A* makes a contract with *B*. *C* acts negligently. This makes it more expensive for *A* to complete his contract.

Blackburn J:

...there is no pretence for saying that the defendants were malicious or had any intention to injure anyone. They were, at most, guilty of a neglect of duty, which occasioned injury to the property of Knight, but which did not injure any property of the plaintiff. The plaintiff's claim is to recover the damage which he has sustained by his contract with Knight becoming less profitable, or, it may be, a losing contract, in consequence of this injury to Knight's property. We think this does not give him any right of action.

There were cases, however, where the decision had gone in favour of recovery.

Morrison Steamship Co Ltd v *Greystoke Castle* [1947] AC 265

Ships *A* and *B* collided. There was no damage to the cargo of ship *A*. Under maritime law, the owners of the cargo on ship *A* became liable to pay a sum of money to the owners of *A*. The cargo owners successfully sued the owners of ship *B* for negligence in causing the collision although the claimants' loss was purely economic.

The recent trend against recovery of economic loss has led to this case being either ignored or explained away on the basis that it is peculiar to maritime law.

Where a person makes a negligent statement, the loss that will follow will normally be economic rather than physical. It was thought that the House of Lords decision in ***Derry* v *Peek*** (1889) 14 App Cas 337, precluded any action for negligent statements causing economic loss. Liability for statements would only arise where they were contractual, where there was a fiduciary duty or in deceit. This position was restated by the Court of Appeal.

Candler v *Crane, Christmas & Co* [1951] 2 KB 164

The defendant accountants prepared a company's accounts. They knew that these were to be given to the claimant to persuade him to invest money in the company. The claimant did invest money and suffered loss as the accounts had been negligently prepared and gave a false impression of the company. The claimant sued the defendants in negligence.

The Court of Appeal held that no duty of care arose in these circumstances in the absence of a contractual relationship.

> Denning LJ gave a powerful dissenting judgment. He argued that the defendants owed a duty of care to their:
>
> . . . employer or client; and . . . any third person to whom they themselves show the accounts, or to whom they know their employer is going to show the accounts, so as to induce him to invest money or take some other action on them. But I do not think the duty can be extended still further so as to include strangers of whom they have heard nothing and to whom their employer without their knowledge may choose to show their accounts.

A major change in the law on economic loss came with the House of Lords decision in the following case.

Hedley Byrne & Co Ltd v *Heller & Partners Ltd* [1964] AC 465

> The appellants were advertising agents who became doubtful about the financial position of one of their clients, *E* Ltd. The appellants' bankers enquired from *E* Ltd's bankers (the respondents) as to the financial position of *E* Ltd. The defendants replied that *E* Ltd was a respectably constituted company, considered good for its ordinary business engagements. The advice was given without responsibility by the respondents. Relying on this advice, the appellants lost over £17,000 when *E* Ltd went into liquidation. An action was brought alleging that the advice had been given negligently by the respondents.
>
> The appellants' action failed as the House of Lords held that the without responsibility clause amounted to a disclaimer of liability and no duty of care was owed.

The importance of the case lies in the fact that the House of Lords stated that in appropriate circumstances a duty of care could arise to give careful advice and that failure to do so could give rise to liability for economic loss caused by negligent advice.

The appellants in *Hedley Byrne* had to overcome two barriers (apart from the disclaimer clause). The first was the supposed bar on claims for negligent statements arising from *Derry* v *Peek*. It was this aspect of the law that the House of Lords concentrated on. The second barrier was the one against recovery of economic loss. This received little attention. The result was that the decision had the effect of allowing actions for economic loss caused by words but not economic loss caused by acts.

See also Chapter 23 for *Derry* v *Peek*.

Lord Reid expressed a reason for this which corresponds to an economic model of statements:

> Another obvious difference is that a negligently made article will only cause one accident, and so it is not very difficult to find the necessary degree of proximity or neighbourhood between the negligent manufacturer and the person injured. But words can be broadcast with or without the consent or the foresight of the speaker or writer. It would be one thing to say that the speaker owes a duty to a limited class, but it would be going very far to say that he owes a duty to every ultimate "consumer" who acts on these words to his detriment.

With the benefit of hindsight, it is possible to say that Lord Reid's distinction failed to take account of the fact that the type of loss in negligent misstatement cases is usually economic loss. This poses different problems to physical damage but these problems are not unique to statements cases. They also apply to cases where economic loss has been caused by a negligent act. However, one result of the case was that the law was now bedevilled by a distinction between statements and acts without any logical justification for this distinction.

Development of the *Hedley Byrne* principle

The possibility of claims for economic loss caused by negligent statements was opened up by *Hedley Byrne* v *Heller*. The House of Lords was concerned with the floodgates problem and on this basis rejected the neighbour test as being inappropriate to deal with the problems raised by negligent statements.

If a defective product is put into circulation, then any damage caused will probably be limited to a small group of people and occur on only one occasion. However, once a negligent statement is put into circulation, a large number of people could be affected for a lengthy period of time.

The special relationship

Having rejected reasonable foreseeability of damage alone as a sufficient criterion for imposing a duty, the House of Lords in *Hedley Byrne* stated that, for a duty to arise in giving advice, there had to be a 'special relationship' between the giver and the recipient of the advice.

Lord Morris stated:

> My Lords, I consider that it follows and that it should now be regarded as settled that if someone possessed of a special skill undertakes, quite irrespective of contract, to apply that skill for the assistance of another person who relies on such skill, a duty of care will arise. . . . Furthermore, if in a sphere in which a person is so placed that others could reasonably rely on his judgment or his skill or upon his ability to make careful inquiry, a person takes it upon himself to give information or advice to, or allows his information or advice to be passed on to, another person who, as he knows, or should know, will place reliance upon it, then a duty of care will arise.

Since *Hedley Byrne*, the courts have been attempting to construct a theory of liability in this area. Two major conceptual problems have not yet been resolved.

The first is whether this form of liability represents a change in the doctrine of privity of contract in cases which are 'equivalent to contract', or whether it is an expansion of the tort of negligence into the area of pure economic loss. If it is the former, then the scope of liability is relatively narrow as it would only encompass a few situations where the case cannot be brought in contract because no strict consideration has been provided by the claimant. If it is the latter, then there is scope for a massive expansion of negligence liability.

See also Chapter 3 for tests for duty of care.

The second conceptual problem is that the courts have sometimes worked outside the tripartite framework for duty of care of reasonable foreseeability, proximity and just/reasonable and used different conceptual tools such as 'assumption of responsibility'.

The expressions used have changed, but for the sake of convenience we will continue to use the expression 'special relationship' to describe the necessary ingredients of the duty. What then is required for there to be a special relationship?

Special skill

The defendant must be possessed of a special skill in giving this sort of advice.

Mutual Life & Citizens Assurance Co v Evatt [1971] AC 793

The Privy Council held by a majority of three to two that an insurance company did not owe a duty of care in giving investment advice. The majority held that a duty only arose when the defendant was in the business of giving that advice or had held himself out as competent to do so. The minority (Lords Reid and Morris) held that a duty would arise only where the claimant made it clear that he was seeking considered advice and intended to act on it in a specific way.

It is the minority view that has gained acceptance in English law. (See *Esso Petroleum Co* v *Mardon* [1976] QB 801; *Howard Marine Dredging Co* v *Ogden & Sons* [1978] QB 574; *Spring* v *Guardian Assurance plc* [1994] 3 All ER 129.)

The purpose of this requirement is to exclude liability where advice is given informally. A person will not be liable for incorrect advice given when 'somewhat the worse for wear' at a party or for a conversation with a stranger in a railway carriage. A duty will not be owed where advice is given on a social occasion.

Chaudhry v *Prabhakar* [1988] 3 All ER 718

The claimant had asked a friend who had some knowledge of cars to find a suitable one that had not been involved in an accident. The defendant found a car and recommended it. The plaintiff bought it. However, it was found to have been involved in an accident. Counsel for the defendant had conceded that his client owed a duty of care as he was a gratuitous agent. The appeal was brought on the ground of whether the defendant had been in breach of duty. The Court of Appeal found that he had and as duty had been conceded the claimant's action succeeded.

Should the duty have been conceded? (See May LJ at 725, Stuart-Smith LJ at 721 and Stocker LJ at 723.)

The present position is that provided the defendant has some special knowledge this requirement will be satisfied. The special skill point is obviously connected to reasonable reliance as if the defendant has no special knowledge why rely? There are also connections with causation as the existence of special knowledge makes it more likely that the claimant has acted in a different manner than if the advice had not been given.

Reasonable reliance

The relevance of reliance to duty of care has had a chequered history. Some cases have stated that it is vital while others have denied its relevance.

What is understood by 'reliance' varies. There is detrimental and non-detrimental reliance, although it is difficult to see how non-detrimental reliance could found an action in negligence because of the requirement of damage.

There are also concepts of specific and general reliance. Specific reliance will be present when the parties have communicated with each other, whereas general reliance will arise when the parties are more remote. The classic *Hedley Byrne* case concerned the giving of advice or information and was based on specific reliance. This version operated as a check on liability becoming too wide. For example, in the surveyor cases (see *Smith* v *Bush*, below), the surveyor or valuer will owe a duty only to the person who has paid the building society for the valuation. If that person chose to show it to someone else, who relied on it, then no duty would arise. General reliance operates in the sense that the defendant had some power which could have been exercised carefully in the claimant's favour and the claimant was aware of that fact and relied on the careful exercise of the power. An example of this is in the area of public authorities exercising statutory powers or duties in connection with building regulations. This approach has been rejected in England in this area. (See *Murphy* v *Brentwood District Council*, below.)

It should be noted that the requirement of reliance in *Hedley Byrne* cases appears to have been abandoned in *White* v *Jones* and subsumed in the assumption of responsibility test. It may well be argued that the valuers in *Smith* v *Bush* had no intention of assuming responsibility to the claimant but there appears to be a strain of liability which is based on dependence.

Outside the advice cases, specific reliance may not be necessary and the courts have struggled to define the necessary requirements of a 'special relationship'. It has been described as one 'equivalent to contract' (*Hedley Byrne* v *Heller*) or one where there has been a 'voluntary assumption of responsibility'.

Voluntary assumption of responsibility

See also Chapter 3 for assumption of responsibility.

The concept of the voluntary assumption of responsibility has given rise to considerable problems for the judiciary. Lord Reid in *Hedley Byrne* (at 486) explained that a reasonable man who knew he was being trusted to give careful advice had three courses of action open: refuse to answer, answer with a disclaimer or answer without a disclaimer. 'If he chooses the last course he must, I think, be held to have accepted some responsibility for his answer being given carefully, or to have accepted a relationship with the inquirer which requires him to exercise such care as the circumstances require.'

See also Chapter 2 for *Henderson* v *Merrett*.

Since then doubt has been expressed as to whether this criterion was necessary or useful (see, for example, *Smith* v *Bush*) but this scepticism was expressed within the context of whether the claimant was within the category of those owed a duty of care. However, in *Henderson* v *Merrett Syndicates Ltd* [1994] 3 All ER 506 at 521, Lord Goff was quite clear that in cases which were concerned with situations equivalent to contract, including negligent provision of a service, once the defendant was found to have assumed responsibility there was no problem with recovery of economic loss. What Lord Goff meant here, however, was a very broad definition of voluntary assumption, to mean voluntary assumption of a *task* not voluntary assumption of the *legal risk*.

In *White* v *Jones* [1995] 1 All ER 691 at 706, Lord Browne-Wilkinson thought that the phrase was concerned with whether some duty of care existed, not with the extent of the duty which could vary with the circumstances. He felt that the concept originated with breach of fiduciary duty, where a duty came into existence not because of any mutual dealing between the parties (the 'equivalent to contract' concept) but because the defendant had assumed a commitment to act in the claimant's affairs. A trustee is under a duty to a beneficiary whether or not he has had any dealings with him. On this basis it is not necessary that there be any reliance on the defendant. The important factor is that the defendant knows that the claimant's economic well-being depends on the careful conduct of his affairs.

Lennon v *Metropolitan Police Commissioner* [2004] 2 All ER 266

The claimant had been a member of the Metropolitan Police Force and wished to transfer to the Royal Ulster Constabulary. The arrangements for the transfer were handled by a personnel officer (*B*) who told the claimant to leave everything to her. In response to a specific enquiry from the claimant, *B* negligently informed him that his service would be continuous, whereas there was in fact a three-week break in service. This caused economic damage to the claimant. The Court of Appeal held that even where the parties were in a relationship of employer and employee (or in a situation akin to employment or equivalent to another kind of contract), there was nothing to prevent the voluntary assumption of responsibility principle applying to an omission to give advice in circumstances where, if not handled carefully, the matter for which the defendant had voluntarily assumed responsibility could result in the claimant suffering economic loss. In this case a duty of care had arisen from the express assumption of responsibility by the defendant, for a particular matter, on which the claimant had relied.

The House of Lords has previously warned against trying to find any general principle:

> circumstances may differ infinitely and . . . there can be no necessary assumption that those features which have served in one case to create the relationship between the plaintiff and the defendant on which liability depends will necessarily be determinative of liability in another case. (*Caparo Industries plc* v *Dickman* [1990] 1 All ER 568 at 587 per Lord Oliver.)

See also Chapter 3 for *Caparo* v *Dickman*.

This still leaves the question as to what is the relationship between the three-stage *Caparo* test and the voluntary assumption of responsibility test. This question was addressed by the Court of Appeal in *Merrett* v *Babb* [2001] 3 WLR 1, where it was recognised that the two tests were complementary and should produce the same result. In practice, the courts seem to prefer to use voluntary assumption of responsibility, where this is possible, in cases involving economic loss, although it remains open to the court to check the result by referring to the three-stage test. (See further *Customs and Excise Commissioners* v *Barclays Bank plc* [2006] 4 All ER 256.)

Advice given by a defendant to the claimant in the absence of a contract

This is the classic *Hedley Byrne* situation. Where the advice is given directly by *A* to *B* there would have been a contract had consideration been given for the advice.

What is the position where *A* makes a statement to *B*, who passes it on to *C* and *C* suffers loss by relying on it? In the *A–B* cases, one problem is the link between contract and tort. In the *A–B–C* cases, more familiar tortious problems such as 'floodgates' are present.

Surveyors and valuers

The problem arises where a surveyor is asked to value a house by a building society or other mortgage-lending institution. The valuation will be shown to the prospective purchaser and they may (probably will) rely on it in deciding whether to purchase the property. If the valuation was negligently carried out and the house is worth less than was paid for it, does the surveyor owe the purchaser a duty of care?

If we look at this situation in diagrammatic form, we can see that there are contracts between the surveyor and the building society and between the building society and the purchaser. Despite the fact that the purchaser pays for the valuation, there is no contract between him and the surveyor.

Surveyor _____ Building Society _____ Purchaser

The issue of whether a duty of care was owed by surveyors and the standing of the disclaimers came to the House of Lords in two linked cases.

Smith v *Eric S Bush; Harris* v *Wyre Forest District Council* [1990] 1 AC 831

In both cases valuations had been carried out for the claimants by the defendants and disclaimer clauses inserted in the valuation. For example, 'valuation is confidential and is intended solely for the information of Wyre Forest District Council in determining what advance, if any, may be made on the security and that no responsibility whatsoever is implied or accepted by the Council for the value or condition of the property by reason of such inspection and report'.

Three questions had to be answered in relation to each appeal.

1 *Was a duty of care owed to the claimant?* The House of Lords unanimously held that a surveyor or valuer was capable of owing a duty to take reasonable care to a prospective purchaser. Proximity arose from the surveyor's knowledge that the purchaser would probably rely on his valuation. It was just and reasonable to impose a duty as the advice was given in a professional rather than a social context. The extent of the duty was limited to the purchaser of the house. It did not extend to subsequent purchasers.

2 *Did the disclaimers fall within the ambit of the Unfair Contract Terms Act 1977?* Section 1(1)(b) states that 'negligence' means the breach of any common law duty to take reasonable care. One of the arguments put forward by the surveyors was that the disclaimer of liability would at common law have prevented any duty arising and the Act therefore had no application. However, s 11(3) states: 'the requirement of reasonableness under this Act is that it should be fair and reasonable to allow reliance on it, having regard to all the circumstances obtaining when the liability arose or (but for the notice) would have arisen.'

3 Section 13(1) states: 'sections 2 and 5 to 7 also prevent excluding or restricting liability by reference to terms and notices which exclude or restrict the relevant obligation or duty.' The House of Lords interpreted these sections as meaning that the existence of a common law duty of care had to be judged by considering whether it would exist 'but for' the notice excluding liability. Any other interpretation would result in removing all liability for negligent misstatements from the ambit of the Act.

4 *Did the notice satisfy the requirement of reasonableness imposed by s 2(2) of the Act?* The meaning of reasonableness is dealt with by s 11(3). The House considered that certain factors should be taken into account in determining reasonableness. Were the parties of equal bargaining power? Would it have been reasonably practicable to obtain the advice from an alternative source? How difficult is the task being undertaken for which liability is being excluded? What are the practical consequences of the decision on the question of reasonableness?

5 The conclusion was that the risk should fall on the surveyor rather than the purchaser and the disclaimer was unreasonable in the circumstances. A caveat was added to the effect that the houses in these cases were of modest value and that the risk might fall on the purchaser in cases involving the purchase of industrial property or expensive houses.

The end result of this litigation is that purchasers of a house of 'modest value' now know that they can rely on the valuation given for mortgage purposes. If this valuation is carried out negligently, then the purchaser can recover from the surveyor the difference between what the house was said to be worth and what it was actually worth. The surveyor cannot rely on a disclaimer clause in the valuation. It was forecast that the cost of such valuations would probably increase to meet the surveyor's potential liability. It appears that what has happened is that purchasers are being offered a choice of surveys, between a full structural one and a valuation.

There was an attempt to extend the application of this principle to surveys done for 'buy-to-let' mortgages.' This is where a person borrows money on the security of a property which they do not intend to live in but to let out to another person for a profit. (*Scullion* v *Bank of Scotland plc (t/a Colleys)* [2011] EWCA Civ 693.) The Court of Appeal did not think it was appropriate, for public policy reasons, to extend the scope of the duty of care owed by a valuer beyond that which already exists – namely in the context of purchases of modest properties by owner-occupiers. Also, with a buy-to-let purchase, the valuer would naturally assume that the mortgage company (for whom the valuation is being prepared) would be primarily interested in the property's capital value in order to assure itself that the amount being advanced was adequately secured. In contrast, the purchaser (although also concerned at the property's capital value) is also likely to be at least as interested in its rental potential and it is not unreasonable, therefore, for the valuer to expect that the purchaser would obtain their own independent advice on issues pertaining to rental value which will not, as a matter of course, be included in a standard mortgage valuation.

Where a surveyor carries out a valuation for their firm and signs the valuation report, there is an assumption of responsibility by the surveyor as well as by the firm. Therefore, if the firm goes bankrupt, the claimant can proceed against the individual surveyor. (*Merrett* v *Babb* [2001] 3 WLR 1.)

What if the valuation was carried out for a lender and the property was negligently over-valued? Property booms frequently result in lenders rushing to lend money on properties in a rising property market. When the market falls, a number of borrowers will default and the properties will be sold for less than the amount loaned. Where the properties have been negligently overvalued by a valuer (V), the question will arise as to the extent of V's liability in negligence to the lender (L). Was V liable for the loss which was caused by the fall in the property market?

In a complex piece of litigation, the Court of Appeal held (*Banque Bruxelles Lambert SA* v *Eagle Star Insurance Co Ltd* [1995] 2 All ER 769) that V was liable for such losses in 'no transaction' cases. These were where L would not have entered the transaction had a correct valuation been made.

However, the House of Lords reversed this decision and disapproved of the 'no transaction' concept.

South Australia Asset Management Corp v York Montague
[1996] 3 All ER 365

The *Banque Bruxelles* series of cases on negligent valuations was heard by the House of Lords which produced very different reasoning from the Court of Appeal. A single judgment was given by Lord Hoffmann.

A valuer was under a duty to take reasonable care to provide *information* on which a lender would decide on a course of action. Where the valuer had negligently overvalued the property on which the lender had secured a mortgage advance he was not responsible for all the consequences of that course of action. He was responsible only for the foreseeable consequences of the information being wrong.

The correct approach to the assessment of damages was to ascertain what element of the loss suffered as a result of the transaction going ahead was attributable to the inaccuracy of the information by comparing the valuation negligently provided and the correct property value at the time of the valuation. The valuer would *not* be liable for the amount of the lender's loss attributable to the fall in the property market, as a duty of care which imposed liability for losses which would have occurred even if the information had been correct was not fair and reasonable and therefore inappropriate as an implied term of the contract or a tortious duty.

The decision draws a distinction between giving advice and giving information. The losses recoverable for negligently giving advice will be more extensive than those for giving information. It is hard to see how the courts will draw the distinction.

The distinction between no transaction and successful transaction drawn by the Court of Appeal has been disapproved.

Example

A	Valuer (V) negligently overvalues property at	£100,000
B	Lender (L) lends 90% of valuation	£90,000
C	True value of property at date of loan	£70,000
D	Amount recovered on sale of property	£40,000

Court of Appeal approach

B (£90,000) – D (£40,000) = £50,000 (judged at date of sale).

House of Lords approach

A (£100,000) – C (£70,000) = £30,000.

Note that the House of Lords approach is based on how much security the lender would have had if the information given had been correct and how much security the lender had at the time of the loan. This approach ignores any later fluctuations in the market.

It can be seen that the judgment concentrates on the purpose of the information given by the valuer. In these cases the purpose was to enable the lender to determine how much security he would have if the loan was made. This draws on the approach in *Caparo* v *Dickman* (see below).

The distinction between information and advice was looked at again by the House of Lords in a reinsurance case.

Aneco Reinsurance Underwriting Ltd (In Liquidation) v *Johnson & Higgins* [2002] 1 Lloyd's Rep 157

The defendant insurance brokers were asked by the claimants to obtain reinsurance cover of a million dollars on an insurance risk. The defendants did obtain the cover but as a result of misrepresentations and non-disclosure by the defendants, the reinsurers were able to avoid the contract and left the claimants with a loss of $35 million. The defendants were held liable for the full loss. *SAAMCO* was explained as an exception to the general rule that a professional was liable for the foreseeable consequences of their negligence. The defendant's duty here was held to be to advise as opposed to one to give information. If they had carried out their obligations correctly they would have discovered that no reinsurer would have covered this risk and the claimants would not have entered into the insurance contract and would not have suffered the loss.

Accountants and auditors

When an accountant produces a report on the affairs of a company, to whom do they owe a duty of care? They will be in a contractual relationship with their client and a duty will accordingly be owed in contract. But the report might be seen and relied on by other people and for various purposes. The difference between these cases and the surveyor cases is that the communication of the advice is not made to an identified person (the purchaser) but to a class of persons. The position is further complicated by the fact that the company may be under a statutory duty to have an annual audit of its accounts prepared and the contents of the audit may also be laid down by statute.

JEB Fasteners v *Marks Bloom & Co* [1983] 1 All ER 583

Defendant accountants prepared accounts for their client and negligently overstated the value of the stock. The defendants were aware that the client was in financial difficulties and was seeking financial support. The claimant took over the company after seeing the accounts. He then brought an action in negligence against the defendants. It was held that a duty of care was owed to the claimant, but the action failed on the grounds of causation. The reason the claimant took over the company was to acquire the expertise of the directors. He was not concerned with the value of the stock.

In the late 1980s there was a large amount of litigation against accountants, much of it in connection with the take-over boom of this period. The question of the accountants' liability eventually arrived at the House of Lords.

See also Chapter 3 for *Caparo* v *Dickman*.

Caparo Industries plc v *Dickman* [1990] 1 All ER 568

The case involved a public company. The appellants had audited the accounts of the company. The annual audit of a public company is regulated by statute and the Companies Act 1985 laid down in detail what the statutory accounts had to contain. The respondents had owned shares in the company and in reliance on the accounts purchased further shares and made a successful take-over bid for the company. The respondents alleged that the accounts were inaccurate and negligently prepared and that they had suffered loss as a result. The issue was whether the appellants owed a duty of care to the respondents in the preparation of the accounts. The House of Lords held that in preparing the accounts a duty of care was owed to members of the company (shareholders). But this duty was a limited one. It was to enable the members to exercise proper control over the company. In this sense the interest of the member was identical to that of the company. If a director had misappropriated funds, these could be recouped by an action in the name of the company. But no duty was owed to an individual member in connection with a decision to buy additional shares based on reliance on the accounts. Whether such a duty existed in connection with a decision to sell shares was left open by the House.

Lord Jauncey:

> ... the purpose of annual accounts, so far as members are concerned, is to enable them to question the past management of the company, to exercise their voting rights, if so advised, and to influence future policy and management. Advice to individual shareholders in relation to present or future investment in the company is not part of the statutory purpose of the preparation and distribution of the accounts ...
>
> If the statutory accounts are prepared and distributed for certain limited purposes, can there nevertheless be imposed on auditors an additional common law duty to individual shareholders who choose to use them for another purpose without the prior knowledge of the auditors? The answer must be No. Use for that other purpose would no longer be ... use for the 'very transaction' which Denning

LJ in *Candler* v *Crane Christmas & Co* [1951] 2 KB 164 at 183 regarded as determinative of the scope of any duty of care. Only where the auditor was aware that the individual shareholder was likely to rely on the accounts for a particular purpose such as his present or future investment in or lending to the company would a duty of care arise. Such a situation does not obtain in the present case.

... it was argued that the relationship of the unwelcome bidder in a potential take-over situation was nearly as proximate to the auditor as was the relationship of a shareholder to whom the report was directed. Since I have concluded that the auditor owed no duty to an individual shareholder, it follows that this argument must also fail. The fact that a company may at a time when the auditor is preparing his report be vulnerable to a take-over bid cannot per se create a relationship of proximity between the auditor and the ultimate successful bidder. Not only is the auditor under no statutory duty to such a bidder but he will have reason at the material time to know neither of his identity nor of the terms of his bid.

The effect of the decision was to prevent companies contemplating a take-over bid from relying on the annual audited accounts to determine the amount of their bid. The bidder would have to make their own inquiries.

The basis of the decision was that anyone who makes an investment or lending decision in reliance on an unqualified opinion will not be able to sue the auditors for any losses suffered as a result. This applies to shareholders, investors or institutional lenders.

See Chapter 13 for breach of statutory duty.

The first ground for the House of Lords decision was based on an argument taken from breach of statutory duty. Where a statutory duty is imposed on a person then no private action for damages will be granted unless the type of harm suffered was the type which the statute was designed to prevent. It will be recalled that the House thought that the purpose of the statute in this case was to enable members of the company to raise questions about the management of the company. However, it was widely felt before the case that one of the purposes of the statutory provision was to provide investor protection and this was the reason for the requirement that the accounts be available on a public register.

This can be contrasted with a Court of Appeal decision holding that a firm of accountants retained by a firm of solicitors to prepare annual reports which the solicitors were required to deliver to the Law Society under the Solicitors Act 1974 owed a duty of care to the Law Society. This was because an adverse report from accountants could trigger intervention from the Law Society and protect the public and the Law Society compensation fund. (*Law Society* v *KPMG Peat Marwick* [2000] 4 All ER 541.)

The second ground was lack of proximity between the parties. Proximity is a notoriously difficult concept to define and apply, but helpful guidance has since been given by the Court of Appeal in *James McNaughten* (below).

James McNaughten Paper Group Ltd v *Hicks Anderson & Co* [1991] 1 All ER 134

Accountants who drew up, at short notice, draft accounts of a company for the company's chairman, owed no duty of care to a bidder who took over the company after inspecting the accounts. The accounts had been drawn up for the benefit of the chairman and not of the claimants and, as they were draft accounts and not final accounts, the auditors could not have been expected to foresee reliance on them. Certain criteria were identified by the Court of Appeal as being important in determining whether a duty of care arises:

1　The *purpose* for which the statement was made.
2　The *purpose* for which the statement was communicated. In *Caparo* the purpose of an audit report was to enable the shareholders to question the running of the company, not to enable a person to decide on share purchases.

In ***Mariola Marine Corp v Lloyd's Register of Shipping, The Morning Watch*** [1990] 1 Lloyd's Rep 547, a marine surveyor employed by Lloyd's was held not to owe a duty of care to the purchaser of a ship. The purpose of the survey was to protect life and property at sea, not to protect the economic interests of buyers of ships.

3   The relationship between the adviser, the one advised and any relevant third party.

4   The size of any class to which the person advised belonged.

5   The state of *knowledge* of the adviser. This point accounts for two cases where ***Caparo*** has been distinguished. (***Morgan Crucible v Hill Samuel Bank; Galoo v Bright Grahame Murray*** – see below.)

6   Reliance by the person advised. This must be reasonable reliance. It might be unreasonable for the claimant to rely on the defendant where he has his own independent advisers (for example, in ***James McNaughten***). But in ***Galoo*** the fact that the claimant's accountants had a right to information was not necessarily fatal to the claim.

Morgan Crucible plc v Hill Samuel Bank Ltd [1991] 1 All ER 148

Directors and financial advisers of a target company in a take-over bid had made statements regarding the accuracy of financial statements and profit forecasts, intending that a bidder should rely on those forecasts. The bidder did rely and alleged that he suffered loss as a result. The original statement of claim was drafted on the basis of a duty of care resting on reasonable foreseeability. Following ***Caparo***, the claimant applied for leave to amend the statement of claim to one based on an identified bidder. At first instance leave was refused and the claimant appealed. The Court of Appeal granted leave to amend as there was an arguable case and ***Caparo*** could be distinguished. The distinction was that here, assuming the facts pleaded were correct, express representations had been made to the claimant after it had emerged as an identified bidder.

Galoo Ltd v Bright Grahame Murray [1995] 1 All ER 16

A firm called Hillsdown had advanced loans to and purchased shares in *G* Ltd. The claim was against the auditors (BGM) of *G* Ltd during the relevant years. The Court of Appeal applied ***Caparo*** and cited four principles necessary for liability taken from Lord Oliver's judgment. An auditor will owe a duty of care to a take-over bidder if he approves a statement confirming the accuracy of accounts which he has previously audited when he has been expressly informed that the bidder will rely on the accounts for the purpose of deciding whether to make an increased bid and the bidder does so rely.

In the present case the Court of Appeal held that on the facts it was plain that the audited accounts for 1986 were to be prepared not merely for the purposes of the audit but also for the purpose of fixing the purchase consideration to be paid by Hillsdown. This took the case outside ***Caparo***. However, it was not foreseeable that any particular loan made by Hillsdown was in reliance upon a particular set of accounts and there was no duty of care owed in respect of the loans.

The *purpose* approach adopted by the Court of Appeal has been approved by the House of Lords in the negligent valuation cases. (See above.)

It is evident from recent cases that the question of an auditor's or other financial adviser's negligence is far from settled. ***Caparo*** may have been intended to impose a *caveat emptor* regime on financial advice but it may not be successful in doing so.

Development of liability for economic loss outside the *Hedley Byrne* principle

The emphasis in **Hedley Byrne** on the distinction between economic loss caused by statements and economic loss caused by acts led to two different branches of law. Outside of liability for negligent statements, the judicial approach was generally hostile to the recovery of pure economic loss.

Tripartite business arrangements

Where businesspersons embarked on a tripartite venture such as a building contract, protection was given by contract law. Problems of insolvency could give rise to attempts to circumvent the contractual chain by bringing an action in negligence.

In the case of building construction two common problems arise. The first is where the completed building is defective and the main contractor has become insolvent. The defect is due to sub-contractor *1*'s negligence. Sub-contractor *1* cannot be sued for breach of contract by the client unless the client has taken out a collateral contract or warranty with them. A similar situation would arise where the defect is due to sub-contractor *2*'s negligence and sub-contractor *1* has become insolvent. The main contractor cannot perform their contract with the client and has no contractual action against sub-contractor *2*.

Client............Main Contractor............Sub-contractor 1............Sub-contractor 2

The highpoint of recovery of economic loss was reached in 1983 when the House of Lords upheld a claim that a duty of care was owed by a sub-contractor to the client.

Junior Books Ltd v *Veitchi Co Ltd* [1983] AC 520

The claimants had contracted with the main contractors for the construction of a factory. The defendants were specialist flooring sub-contractors. They were nominated by the claimants but had no contract with them. The floor was defective and had to be re-laid. The claimants brought an action in negligence against the sub-contractors, claiming the cost of re-laying the floor and loss of profit while this was being done. The House of Lords held that because of the close proximity between the parties, a duty of care was owed to the claimants. The key factor was that the claimants had nominated the defendants as sub-contractors.

Lord Roskill:

On the facts I have just stated, I see nothing whatsoever to restrict the duty of care arising from the proximity of which I have spoken. . . . I see no reason why what was called during the argument 'damage to the pocket' simpliciter should be disallowed when 'damage to the pocket' coupled with physical damage has hitherto always been allowed. I do not think that this development, if development it be, will lead to untoward consequences.

At the time the decision was thought to mark the end of the distinction between contract and tort actions. But the decision has not proved popular with the judiciary and although it survives as a precedent on its own particular facts, it has not been followed. The following case is a single example of an action which failed. See also *Greater Nottingham Co-operative Society* v *Cementation Piling and Foundations Ltd* [1988] 2 All ER 971; *Pacific Associates Inc* v *Baxter* [1990] 1 QB 993.

Simaan General Contracting Co v Pilkington Glass Ltd [1988] QB 758

The claimants were the main contractors on a building project in Abu Dhabi. It was a term of the contract with the building owner that the curtain glass walling be a particular shade of green, as green is the colour of peace in Islam. The claimants engaged a firm to obtain and erect the glass. This firm ordered the glass from the defendants. The glass was the wrong colour and this caused extra expense to the claimants in the performance of their contract with the building owner. The glass erectors went into liquidation, which prevented a contract action against them. The claimants sued the defendants in negligence. The action failed as the claimants were unable to show that the defendants had assumed any responsibility to them. The absence of a contract between claimant and defendant was fatal. The duty in a **Hedley Byrne** type of case was said to depend on the voluntary assumption of responsibility towards a particular party giving rise to a special relationship, but in the present case the court could see nothing whatever to justify a finding that Pilkington had voluntarily assumed a direct responsibility to Simaan for the colour and quality of Pilkington's glass panels. On the contrary, all the indications were the other way and showed that a chain of contractual relationships was deliberately arranged the way it was without any direct relationship between Simaan and Pilkington. Moreover, if in principle it were to be established in this case that a main contractor or an owner has a direct claim in tort against the nominated supplier to a sub-contractor for economic loss occasioned by defects in the quality of the goods supplied, the formidable question would arise, in future cases if not in this case, as to how far exempting clauses in the contract between the nominated supplier and the sub-contractor were to be imported into the supposed duty in tort owed by the supplier to those higher up the chain.

This case demonstrates the relationship between contract and tort in the area of building contracts. Where the parties have made a contract to cover the problem of defects created by sub-contractors and the contract does not cover the method by which the loss came about, the courts are reluctant to indulge in 'gap-filling' by using the law of tort. Although the courts have not been enthusiastic about undermining the privity of contract rule when this would benefit the claimant, they have been prepared to use the contract when this would benefit the defendant.

Norwich City Council v Harvey [1989] 1 All ER 1180

The claimant employed a builder to construct an extension to a swimming pool. A sub-contractor was employed to erect the roofing on the extension. An employee of the sub-contractor negligently set fire to the pool causing property damage. The claimant sued the sub-contractor in negligence. Although this was apparently a straightforward case of negligently caused property damage the court found for the defendant as the contracts between the claimant and the builder and the builder and sub-contractor both placed liability for fire damage on the claimant.

May LJ:

> I do not think that the mere fact that there is no strict privity between the employer and the sub-contractor should prevent the latter from relying on the clear basis on which all parties contracted in relation to damage.

Acquisition of defective property

A person who acquires defective property will have a primary claim in the law of contract. The friend who purchased the ginger beer in **Donoghue v Stevenson** could have sued the café owner for the cost of the ginger beer. In such consumer cases the Sale of Goods Act

1979 implies conditions of quality into the contract. Such an action depends on a contractual relationship existing, the defendant being solvent and there being no exclusion clause in the contract. In theory, any legal problems could be solved by a chain of contract action but in practice there are problems. Insolvency by anyone in the chain could lead to the chain breaking down as it is not generally worthwhile suing an insolvent party. Attempts were therefore made to bring negligence actions to circumvent this problem.

See also Chapter 12 for defective products.

Could the purchaser sue the manufacturer in negligence for supplying a defective, as opposed to a dangerous, product? The recipient of a gift has, of course, no contractual protection as they have no contract with anyone. If the product causes physical damage then they will have a tort action against the manufacturer. But do they have any remedy if the product is simply of defective quality? Such a claim would be a claim for pure economic loss.

A logical extension of *Junior Books* would have been to apply it to the purchaser of defective property, provided there was sufficient proximity between manufacturer and purchaser. But in *Muirhead* v *Industrial Tank Specialities Ltd* [1986] QB 507, the Court of Appeal held that there was insufficient proximity between an ordinary purchaser of goods and the manufacturer of those goods to impose a duty of care in respect of economic loss.

In the case of realty, the common law historically provided little protection to the purchaser. The purchaser of a new house obtained limited contractual protection, but the financial instability of the building trade sometimes rendered this of no value. If the builder became insolvent and the damage had been caused by the negligence of a subcontractor, the purchaser has no contractual remedy. The local authority may also have a part to play in the construction by approving plans and checking the progress of buildings under construction. This work is done on the basis of statutory powers rather than contract. If the work is carried out negligently, would a person affected have a tort claim against the local authority? Purchasers of old houses obtained virtually no contractual protection because of the doctrine of 'caveat emptor'.

See also Chapter 11 for defective premises.

In the 1970s and early 1980s the common law began to provide protection in tort for the purchasers of defective realty. A duty of care would be owed by anyone involved in the building process to avoid a risk of physical damage to the health or safety of the occupier of the house. The damages in such cases were the cost of making the building safe. Actions were brought against builders and also against local authorities. No floodgates problem existed in such cases, as only a residential owner could bring a claim and the extent of the claim was reasonably foreseeable. (See generally *Anns* v *Merton London Borough Council* [1978] AC 728.)

Major statements of principle came from the House of Lords in the building cases as they tried to rein in the development unleashed by *Anns* v *Merton*.

D&F Estates Ltd v *Church Commissioners for England* [1988] 2 All ER 992

See Chapter 11 for *Murphy* v *Brentwood DC.*

The House of Lords held that a builder was not liable in negligence to a building owner for defects of quality. The builder was only liable where the defect caused personal injuries or damage to other property. Lord Bridge stated that economic loss would only be recover-able in a negligence action under the *Hedley Byrne* principles or where the unique proximity of *Junior Books* applied.

See also Chapter 11.

Murphy v *Brentwood District Council* [1990] 2 All ER 908

A seven-judge House of Lords was assembled and they overruled their own previous decision in *Anns* v *Merton*. The narrow ratio of the case was that a local authority is not liable in negligence to a building owner or occupier for the cost of remedying a dangerous defect, which resulted from the negligence of the authority in not ensuring that the building was erected in accordance with the building regulations.

The wider importance of the case is that it marks a contraction in the scope of duty of care in economic loss cases.

Any claimant arguing for a duty to be owed in respect of economic loss which does not fall within *Hedley Byrne* principles faces a difficult task.

Where did this leave *Junior Books*? In *Murphy*, the House of Lords cleared away the *Anns* v *Merton* precedent, but left *Junior Books*. A number of judicial attempts have been made to explain away the case. In *Tate & Lyle Industries Ltd* v *Greater London Council* [1983] 2 AC 509, it was treated as a case of physical damage. In *D&F Estates* Lord Bridge thought that the case rested on unique proximity. Lord Oliver was of the opinion that it rested on the *Hedley Byrne* principle of reliance.

Economic loss suffered by the claimant as a result of damage to property of a third party

Economic loss of this type occurs where the defendant negligently damages property belonging to a third party on which the claimant relied in some way. A simple example of this situation is the cable cases.

Spartan Steel & Alloys Ltd v *Martin & Co Ltd* [1973] QB 27

The defendants negligently severed an electricity cable, causing the claimant's factory to shut down. The claimant claimed damages under three heads:

(a) damage to goods in production at the time of the power cut (physical damage);
(b) loss of profit on (a) (consequential economic loss);
(c) loss of profit on goods which could not be manufactured due to the power cut (pure economic loss).

The Court of Appeal held by a majority (Edmund-Davies LJ dissenting) that (a) and (b) were recoverable but (c) was not. If such claims were allowed, then the potential losses were enormous. In this case only the claimant's factory had suffered the power cut, but an entire estate of factories could have been affected. The court thought that it was better to let the loss lie where it fell and for factories to take out insurance against interrupted production. To shift the loss to the defendant might be to impose a crippling financial burden.

Lord Denning MR:

> At bottom I think the question of recovering economic loss is one of policy. Whenever the courts draw a line to mark out the bounds of *duty*, they do it as a matter of policy so as to limit the responsibility of the defendant. Wherever courts set bounds to the *damages* recoverable – saying that they are, or are not, too remote – they do it as matter of policy so as to limit the liability of the defendant.

Subsequent cases have raised more complex factual situations in the area of shipping.

Candlewood Navigation Corp Ltd v *Mitsui OSK Lines Ltd (The Mineral Transporter)* [1986] 1 AC 1

The first claimants were the owners of a ship which was damaged by the negligence of the defendants. The first claimants had chartered the ship to the second claimants and the effect of the charter was to put the second claimants in possession of the ship. The ship was then re-let by the second claimants to the first claimants on a time charter, which does not confer possession. The first claimants claimed for the hire fees they had to pay while the ship was inoperative, and loss of profits for that period. The claim failed, as although the claimants were owners, both items of loss were suffered in their capacity as charterers, not as owners. The Privy Council refused the claim on floodgates grounds, the ripple effect which might be created if claims were allowed when a person's contractual relations had been made less profitable as a result of physical damage to the property of a third party.

Leigh & Sillavan Ltd v *Aliakmon Shipping Co Ltd (The Aliakmon)* [1986] 1 AC 785

> The claimant suffered economic loss when goods which he had contracted to purchase were damaged at sea. At the time of the damage the risk but not the ownership of the goods had passed to the claimant. The claimant claimed that he was owed a duty of care by the defendants who had damaged the goods. The loss was classified as economic loss rather than physical damage because at the time of the damage the goods belonged to a third party. There was no floodgates risk in this case but the House of Lords held that no duty was owed. Lord Brandon stated:
>
> > ... where a general rule, which is simple to understand and easy to apply, has been established by a long line of authority over many years, I do not think the law should allow special pleading in a particular case within the general rule to detract from its application. ... certainty of the law is of the utmost importance, especially but by no means only, in commercial matters. (At 816–17.)

The 'general rule' referred to by Lord Brandon is that the claimant may only sue in negligence for damage to property, or any loss consequential on that damage, if they were the owner of the property or in possession at the time of the damage. The fact that they have other contractual rights in the property which become less valuable, or a contractual obligation in respect of the property becomes more expensive, does not entitle them to sue. It was pointed out by Lord Brandon that if the law was certain, people would protect themselves by other methods, for example, contractual protection of their position.

A duty of care is also owed to a beneficial owner of property (just as much as to a legal owner of property) by a defendant who can reasonably foresee that his negligent actions would damage that property. The defendant will be liable not merely for the physical loss of that property but also for the foreseeable consequences of that loss, such as the extra expenditure to which the beneficial owner was put or the loss of profit which he incurred. Provided that the beneficial owner could join the legal owner in the proceedings, it did not matter that the beneficial owner was not himself in possession of the property. (*Shell UK Ltd* v *Total Oil* [2010] EWCA Civ 180.)

One point which is brought out by the above cases is that the key point may not be the nature of the damage, whether it is economic or physical, but the relationship between the claimant and the form of wealth in question. If this is the case, then there is an argument for applying similar rules in cases of physical damage to property and cases of 'pure' economic loss.

See also Chapter 3 for *Marc Rich & Co* v *Bishop Rock Marine*.

Marc Rich & Co v *Bishop Rock Marine (The Nicholas H)* [1995] 3 WLR 227

> The claimant was the owner of the cargo on a ship travelling from South America to Europe. During the voyage the ship developed a crack in the hull and anchored off Puerto Rico. The ship was surveyed by a surveyor for a classification society and on his recommendation put into port for repairs. Permanent repairs were going to take a long time and the ship's owners ordered temporary repairs and obtained an agreement from the surveyor that the ship should proceed to its first port of unloading and then undergo permanent repairs. The ship sank with the loss of its cargo.

> The ship's owners and the classification society were sued. The action against the owners was settled for a fixed sum of $500,000, a figure fixed by the Hague-Visby rules which govern the carriage of goods by sea. The balance of the value of the cargo was then claimed in negligence from the classification society. The loss was accepted to be physical damage and not pure economic loss.
>
> The House of Lords held (Lord Lloyd dissenting) that the classification society did not owe a duty of care to the cargo owners. The majority were prepared to accept that there was reasonable foreseeability of damage and proximity but held that it would not be fair, just and reasonable to impose a duty on the classification society, which was an independent and non-profit making body promoting the safety of lives at sea. It would also be unfair on shipowners, who would ultimately have to bear the cost, and the duty would be at variance with the Hague-Visby rules. By deciding thus they effectively held that the questions on duty of care which had previously been almost exclusively confined to cases on pure economic loss also applied to property damage cases.

The restrictive approach by English courts to what is known as relational economic loss has, in general, been followed by Commonwealth courts but they have showed willingness to extend the scope of recovery in this area. The Supreme Court of Canada recognised a claim for economic loss when the claimant railway company was deprived of the use of a railway bridge as a result of damage to the bridge caused by the negligence of the defendant's boat. The bridge was owned by a third party with whom the claimant had negotiated a contractual licence. Liability was held to arise because the claimant had engaged in a joint venture with the owner of the bridge. (***Canadian National Railway Co v Norsk Pacific Steamship Co*** [1992] 1 SCR 1021.) (For the Australian position, see ***Caltex Oil (Australia)*** v ***The Dredge Willemstad*** (1976) 136 CLR 529.)

Conclusions

The interlocking of contract and tort can clearly be seen in the above discussion and the major problem for the courts is the extent to which they should interfere with the contractual nexus by imposing a duty of care in negligence.

In some instances the claimant may have an alternative course of action in contract, in which case that course of action should be pursued. In particular, regard must be had to the contractual nexus in which it is alleged that a duty of care exists. For example, where the claimant and defendant are parties to a network of related contractual relationships, as is common in the case of the construction of a building, regard must be had to the terms of the contracts made by each of the parties. Thus, if the contract between the building owner and the main contractor clearly requires the former to insure the building against risk of fire damage, it may be unreasonable to expect a sub-contractor employed under a contract with the main contractor to owe the building owner a duty of care in respect of negligently caused fire damage when the sub-contractor is almost certainly aware of the insurance requirement in the main contract. It follows that if the terms of the relevant contracts rule out the possibility of a duty of care, any reliance on the defendant by the claimant is likely to be unreasonable.

Alternatively, the court may take the view that the claimant is well placed to insure against the risk of economic loss. This seems to have been in part the motivation behind the decision of the House of Lords in ***Murphy*** v ***Brentwood District Council***, where it was implicit in Lord Keith's view that overruling ***Anns*** v ***Merton London Borough Council*** would not significantly increase householders' insurance premiums and that he believed the householder to be the best insurer. However, it has been pointed out that the risk in ***Murphy*** was one which already existed at the time the householder took an interest in the property, in which case it would be impossible to obtain insurance. On this basis, it seems unlikely that the claimant in **Murphy** was in a position to do very much to protect himself and that regarding his reliance as unreasonable may have been mistaken.

A further policy issue is whether protection is the role of Parliament. This policy argument has been used fairly frequently in cases which have a consumer protection flavour. The argument has two consequences. First, if Parliament has already enacted legislation which protects the consumer and that legislation is intended to be exhaustive, it would be contrary to policy for the common law to go further. Second, in areas in which there has been no statutory intervention, it may be decided that proper controls are the province of the legislature rather than the courts. Where this is the case, the court may resort to the excuse that any reliance by the claimant on the act of the defendant is unreasonable.

The extended *Hedley Byrne* principle

The rejection of economic loss claims outside the **Hedley Byrne** principle led to a concentration on what the principle was based on. The emphasis on reliance-based statements causing economic loss effectively excluded negligent acts and gave very little scope for the recovery of economic loss caused by a negligently performed service. In the case of services, there could be a contract between the provider and the recipient, in which case principles of concurrent liability come into play, or liability could be purely tortious, but on what basis?

Several other problems existed, such as the extent to which a tortious solution could compensate for disappointed expectations; the basis of liability for omissions; and the issue created by cases which had succeeded but were not obviously based on reliance.

In these circumstances a reliance-based principle had little scope but one based on voluntary assumption of responsibility did. However, the concept of voluntary assumption had a mixed history. In some cases it had been rejected as a basis of liability and had been subjected to considerable academic criticism. This has not prevented the House of Lords from attempting to shape the principle to provide a basis for extended **Hedley Byrne** liability through a series of cases which bring out many of the problems involved in imposing tortious liability for negligently performed services.

References

The borderline between **Hedley Byrne** liability and negligence simpliciter is illustrated by the question of liability for references in negligence. In these cases *B* is the potential employer, *A* is the referee and *C* the subject of the reference. The position is complicated by the fact that there is a potential action for defamation, where, subject to malice, a reference will normally attract a defence of qualified privilege. The issue on this point is a variation on a familiar theme but instead of the concern being tort undermining contract rules it is one tort (negligence) undermining the rules of another tort (defamation). The issue was considered in the following case.

See Chapter 3 for the policy issues in this case.

Spring v *Guardian Assurance plc* [1994] 3 All ER 129

The House of Lords held that in certain circumstances the maker of a reference owed a duty of care to the subject of the reference. Lord Keith dissented as he felt that this would inhibit reference givers.

Was this decision based on **Hedley Byrne** principles or on basic duty of care principles? The key difference was reliance by the claimant on the defendant's advice. This was at the time apparently necessary in *Hedley Byrne*, but not necessarily so in basic negligence. Could it be argued that the subject of a reference relied on the referee? The House was split on this issue. Lord Keith was emphatic that there was no such reliance. Lord Goff, however, based his decision on *Hedley Byrne* principles, where *A* undertook responsibility towards *C* and *C* relied on *A* to exercise skill and care. The other three judges based liability on a wider principle than *Hedley Byrne*. Economic loss to *C* was clearly foreseeable if *A* failed to use reasonable care. There was clearly proximity of relationship between *A* and *C* and it was fair, just and reasonable that a duty should be imposed on *A* as the employer. These judges felt it was irrelevant whether the case was founded on basic negligence or *Hedley Byrne* lines.

Does it make any difference which line is followed? Lord Goff clearly felt that it did and was unhappy with broad negligence principles being invoked. His reasoning becomes clearer with the next case.

Liability of solicitors to third parties

White v *Jones* [1995] 1 All ER 691

A testator had quarrelled with his two daughters and instructed his solicitors, the defendants, to prepare a will cutting his daughters out of his estate. This was done. The testator was then reconciled with his daughters and instructed the defendants to prepare a fresh will leaving £9,000 to each of the daughters. The defendants did nothing for a month and then started to prepare the will. They arranged to visit the testator a month later but he died three days before the appointment.

The issue for the House of Lords was whether the defendant solicitors owed a duty of care to the daughters in respect of their lost legacies. It was held (Lords Keith and Mustill dissenting) that where a solicitor accepted instructions to draw up a will and as a result of his negligence an intended beneficiary under the will was reasonably foreseeably deprived of a legacy, the solicitor was liable for the loss of the legacy.

The first conceptual problem was the contract 'fallacy'. The solicitor had bound himself by contract to the testator and it was argued that liability for performance of the contract should be restricted to liability to the testator. While the House accepted that it was generally true that a solicitor did not owe a duty of care to third parties while performing his duties to a client (see *Gran Gelato* v *Richcliff Ltd* [1992] 1 All ER 865), this would leave the beneficiary with no claim. There is no claim in contract by a beneficiary as English law does not recognise a *ius quaesitum tertio*. There is no loss to the estate. This means that the only person who can suffer loss is the person who has no remedy, unless a negligence action is granted.

The second difficulty was that the loss suffered by the claimant was pure economic loss in the form of a lost expectation. It was argued by the appellants that this type of loss fell within the exclusive zone of contractual liability and that only Parliament could create exceptions by extending contractual rights to persons who were not parties to the contract. This point created the major difficulty for the judges. The majority judges were clearly of the opinion that the beneficiary should have an action but the existing law placed obstacles in their path. It is instructive to note how three of the judges, including a dissenting judge, dealt with the problem.

Lord Goff felt that damages for expectation losses could be recovered for contractual negligence and no relevant distinction could be drawn between the two types of action. He felt the assumption of responsibility by the solicitor to the client could be extended to the intended beneficiary. Lord Goff was mainly concerned with the just/reasonable angle of duty of care and gave no detailed analysis of proximity.

Lord Browne-Wilkinson had no problem with finding that the loss to the claimants was reasonably foreseeable and that it would be just/reasonable to find a duty of care but was concerned with whether there was proximity between the parties. It is important to note that in his speech he refers to special relationships, but he is concerned with proximity. Whether there was proximity depended on whether the solicitor had assumed a responsibility to act. This could mean either he had assumed responsibility for a task (redrafting the will) or the acceptance of a legal obligation. He felt that the expression 'assumption of responsibility' meant the former. This definition of proximity is, however, likely to cause problems as the fact that the defendant assumed responsibility for a task does not necessarily mean he assumed responsibility to the claimant.

Lord Mustill (dissenting) felt that an assumption of responsibility meant an undertaking to the claimant, not merely an undertaking to perform the task. An assumption of responsibility had to display an element of 'mutuality' between the claimant and defendant before there was sufficient evidence of proximity. This meant that both claimant and defendant must have played an active part in the transaction from which the liability arose and that there was an absence of mutuality on the facts of this case.

The third problem was that this case involved an omission to act rather than a positive act. It is generally agreed that in omissions cases there must be more than mere foreseeability of harm in order to justify the imposition of a duty of care. Lord Goff found justification for imposing a duty as *Hedley Byrne* liability was based on assumption of responsibility and within this framework a solicitor, once he had assumed responsibility for the task, was liable for negligent omissions as well as negligent acts.

See Chapter 6 for omissions.

An attempt was made to extend *White* in *Goodwill* v *British Pregnancy Advisory Service* [1996] 1 WLR 1397. The claimant had a sexual relationship with a man who had had a vasectomy several years before and told the claimant that he was permanently sterile. The vasectomy spontaneously reversed and the claimant became pregnant and sued the defendant doctor for negligence in that he had failed to warn the man of the possibility of spontaneous reversal. The action was for economic loss – the cost of bringing up an unwanted child. One argument was that the defendant was employed to confer the benefit of not getting pregnant on a class of which the claimant was a member. The Court of Appeal held that the defendant was not employed to confer a benefit on all the man's future partners and the argument failed. (See below for failed sterilisations.)

Concurrent liability

See also Chapter 2 for concurrent liability and *Henderson* v *Merrett*.

In *Henderson* v *Merrett Syndicates Ltd* [1994] 3 All ER 506 the defendants, who were managing agents, had undertaken, pursuant to a contract with a third party (the member's agents), the management of the underwriting affairs of the claimants, who were Lloyd's names. The case was to clarify some of the issues of law involved in the litigation of the Lloyd's names against their managing agents to attempt to recoup part of their losses suffered on the insurance market. The facts of the action are complex but the basic question was whether the managing agents owed a tortious duty to take reasonable care in the management of the names business.

It was necessary to resolve the controversy of the co-extensive existence of liabilities in contract and tort. The House recognised that the fact that the parties had a contractual relationship did not prevent the claimant from suing in tort.

The question of any tortious duty owed by the defendants required an examination of the *Hedley Byrne* principles and it was held that where a person assumed responsibility to perform professional or quasi-professional services for another who relied on those services, the relationship between the parties was sufficient, without more, to give rise to a duty of care. The fact that the parties were in a contractual relationship did not prevent this duty arising unless the contract prevented it from doing so.

An ethical twist

In the majority of economic loss cases the major issue is simply where the loss will lie in business transactions. However, one series of cases has introduced an ethical element where the issue is domestic life. This is the question of failed sterilisations. If a person, male or female, has a sterilisation, they will usually conclude that they cannot have any children in the future and plan their life accordingly. However, if the sterilisation is negligently performed or 'spontaneously reverses' and the person has not been warned of this possibility, can the person recover the costs of raising an unexpected/unwanted child?

The House of Lords held that the costs of raising an unwanted but healthy child were not recoverable in a negligence action. (*McFarlane* v *Tayside Health Authority* [2000] 2 AC 59.) In *Parkinson* v *St James and Seacroft University Hospital NHS Trust* [2002] QB 266, the Court of Appeal held that the additional costs of raising a disabled child after a failed sterilisation were recoverable. Then in *Rees* v *Darlington Memorial NHS Trust* [2003] 3 WLR 1091, the House of Lords overturned the Court of Appeal's decision to allow a disabled mother who had given birth to a healthy child to recover the extra costs of bringing up the baby incurred as a result of her disability. However, although special damages were denied, the House allowed a 'conventional award' of general damages of £15,000 in all cases of wrongful conception, regardless as to whether the mother or the baby is healthy or disabled.

The House stated that the award was 'not compensatory', but it is difficult to see on what basis it was awarded if not a compensatory one. The decision in *Parkinson* is left in limbo. Does a disabled mother recover the conventional sum or the extra costs of bringing up a disabled child?

The bank

This is an extremely complex area of law and one which the judiciary are far from comfortable with. One difficulty is that there are three tests, each one approved by the House of Lords. The tests are the conventional three-stage test of foreseeability/proximity/just and reasonable; the assumption of responsibility test; and the incremental test. Lower courts are faced with the problem of which test to apply and in some cases try to apply all three.

The issue arose in the following case.

Customs and Excise Commissioners v *Barclays Bank plc* [2006] 4 All ER 256

The defendant bank was served with orders from the court freezing the accounts of two companies. Several hours later the bank negligently authorised payment out of the accounts. The issue was whether a duty of care was owed by the bank to the claimants on whose behalf the orders had been made. The House of Lords held that no duty was owed. The remedy was the court's power to punish those who broke its orders and the only duty was to the court.

It could not be suggested that the customer owed a duty to the party which obtained an order, since they were opposing parties in litigation and no duty was owed by a litigating party to its opponent. The question whether in all the circumstances it was fair, just and reasonable to impose a duty of care on the defendant towards the claimant was determinative. In the instant case it was unjust and unreasonable that the bank should, on being notified of an order which it had no opportunity to resist, become exposed to a liability which was in the instant case for a few million pounds only, but might in another case be very much more.

Lord Bingham stated:

I do not think that the notion of assumption of responsibility, even on an objective approach, can aptly be applied to the situation which arose between the Commissioners and the bank on notification to it of the orders. Of course it was bound by law to comply. But it had no choice. It did not assume any responsibility towards the Commissioners as the giver of references in *Hedley Byrne* (but for the disclaimer) and *Spring*, the valuers in *Smith* v *Bush*, the solicitors in *White* v *Jones* and the agents in *Henderson* v *Merrett* may plausibly be said to have done towards the recipient or subject of the references, the purchasers, the beneficiaries and the Lloyd's names. Save for the notification of the order nothing crossed the line between the Commissioners and the bank (see *Williams* v *Natural Life Health Foods Ltd* [1998] 2 All ER 577). Nor do I think that the Commissioners can be said in any meaningful sense to have relied on the bank. The Commissioners, having obtained their orders and notified them to the bank, were no doubt confident that the bank would act promptly and effectively to comply. But reliance in the law is usually taken to mean that if A had not relied on B he would have acted differently. Here the Commissioners could not have acted differently, since they had availed themselves of the only remedy which the law provided . . .

I think it is correct to regard an assumption of responsibility as a sufficient but not a necessary condition of liability, a first test which, if answered positively, may obviate the need for further enquiry. If answered negatively, further consideration is called for.

It is common ground that the foreseeability element of the threefold test is satisfied here. The bank obviously appreciated that, since risk of dissipation has to be shown to obtain a freezing injunction, the Commissioners were liable to suffer loss if the injunction were not given effect. It was not contended otherwise. The concept of proximity in the context of pure economic loss is notoriously elusive. But it seems to me that the parties were proximate only in the sense that one served a court order on the other and that other appreciated the risk of loss to the first party if it was not obeyed. I think it is the third, policy, ingredient of the threefold test which must be determinative.

The House of Lords had clear difficulty attempting to reconcile the various tests for liability in this area and found assumption of responsibility to be of no assistance on the facts of this case, where there were no direct precedents. The bank had simply received the court order freezing the assets and had not stepped over any line which would indicate that they had assumed responsibility to the claimants. Lord Bingham's statement that assumption of responsibility is a sufficient but not necessary condition of liability means that if the objective test for assumption of responsibility is satisfied, the court does not have to go any further. If the test is not satisfied, it is necessary for the court to apply the three-stage test.

In this case it was the third stage that was conclusive against the finding of a duty of care.

Conclusions

The approach of Lord Goff, who gave judgment in *Spring*, *White* and *Henderson*, makes it clear that he is attempting to solve the economic loss riddle within the framework of the *Hedley Byrne* principles. Lord Browne-Wilkinson in both *Henderson* and *White* pursued a somewhat different course by working from analogy with fiduciary duties to create a special relationship between the parties sufficient to found a duty.

The concept of voluntary assumption of responsibility was first raised by Lord Reid in *Hedley Byrne* where he explained that a reasonable man who knew he was being trusted to give careful advice had three courses of action open: refuse to answer, answer with a disclaimer or answer without a disclaimer:

> If he chooses the last course he must, I think, be held to have accepted some responsibility for his answer being given carefully, or to have accepted a relationship with the inquirer which requires him to exercise such care as the circumstances require.

The scepticism expressed on voluntary assumption of responsibility came under attack in the above three cases. In *Henderson*, Lord Goff was clear that in that type of case, which was concerned with a situation equivalent to contract, an objective test should be applied. Once the defendant was found to have assumed responsibility there was no problem with the recovery of economic loss sustained from the negligent provision of a service. Neither was there a problem with the question of liability for negligent omissions. In *Spring*, he argued that it was clear that *Hedley Byrne* extended beyond the giving of information or advice to include the provision of other services and that where the claimant has entrusted his affairs to the defendant, the defendant may be taken to have assumed responsibility to the claimant. The example given is the professional services rendered by a solicitor to his client.

In *White* v *Jones* Lord Browne-Wilkinson gave the most extensive explanation of the concept. He explained that the phrase 'assumption of responsibility' was concerned with whether some duty of care existed, not with the extent of that duty, which would vary with the circumstances. The concept did not originate in *Hedley Byrne* but could be traced back to the cases on fiduciary duties. Such a duty came into existence not because of any mutual dealing between the parties, nor because there was a contract between them. Equity imposes the obligation because the defendant has assumed to act in the claimant's affairs. A trustee is under a duty to a beneficiary whether or not they have had any dealings with them. On this basis it is not necessary that there be reliance on the defendant, the important factor being that the defendant knows that the claimant's economic well-being depends on the defendant's careful conduct of his affairs. In the *Hedley Byrne* version of the special relationship, reliance was necessary, as damage is an essential element of the claimant's case. In cases of negligent statements, if the defendant could not foresee reliance by the claimant, there would be no cause of action. Assumption of responsibility was the key factor which gave rise to the duty, as by choosing to answer the inquiry the bank assumed to act and thereby created the special relationship. Assumption of responsibility meant assumption of responsibility for the task, not the assumption of legal responsibility. Was there a special relationship between a solicitor and an intended beneficiary which attracted a duty of care? The case did not fall within a fiduciary duty or a *Hedley Byrne*-type duty. However, adopting the incremental approach to duty of care, the category of special relationships could be increased to cover this situation.

The relevance of reliance to duty of care had as chequered a history as that of voluntary assumption of liability.

Reliance posed an acute problem in two of the cases under discussion here. In *Spring*, the specific reliance was by the potential employer on the past employer's reference. The reliance by the subject of the reference (the claimant) could more properly be described as general reliance and therefore outside the parameters of *Hedley Byrne* reliance as normally understood. This is what Lord Goff meant when he stated:

> when the employer provides a reference to a third party in respect of his employee, he does so not only for the assistance of the third party, but also, for what it is worth, for the assistance of the employee . . . Furthermore, when such a reference is provided by an employer, it

is plain that the employee relies upon him to exercise due care and skill in the preparation of the reference before making it available to the third party.

Similarly, in *Henderson* he stated:

in the case of the provision of information and advice, reliance upon it by the other party will be necessary to establish a cause of action (because otherwise the negligence will have no causative effect), nevertheless there may be other circumstances in which there will be the necessary reliance to give rise to the application of the principle. In particular, as cases concerned with solicitor and client demonstrate, where the plaintiff entrusts the defendant with the conduct of his affairs, in general or in particular, he may be held to have relied on the defendant to exercise due skill and care in such conduct.

It is clear that the House of Lords has moved away from the conservative position adopted in *Murphy* and is attempting to produce a more flexible formula to deal with the problems created by economic loss. Lord Goff saw the way forward as being through *Hedley Byrne*, albeit on an extended basis. This was done by refining the concept of 'voluntary assumption of responsibility' and broadening the concept of reliance. The major problem of this approach is the vagueness of both concepts. They can be used flexibly but it is arguable that certainty is required in this area of law, if only to guide the indemnity insurance market.

Lord Browne-Wilkinson's approach was to use an equitable formula to determine the necessary relationship. This raised a number of problems, not least of which is that negligence is not a requirement in the equitable action for breach of fiduciary duty. The rules on remoteness and limitation are also considerably different.

Both approaches, with their stress on assumption of responsibility, have the advantage that there is no problem with negligent omissions and that there appears to be no logical reason why either approach should draw the present indefensible distinction between negligent acts and negligent statements.

The law was summarised in *Natural Life Health Foods Ltd* v *Williams* [1998] 2 All ER 577. The claimant must establish that there is a special relationship within which the defendant has assumed responsibility for protecting the claimant's economic welfare and such a relationship will only arise where the claimant is identifiable as an individual or as a member of a class of persons for whom the defendant undertakes responsibility in the performance of a particular task. The role of negligence as gap-filling where contract or other torts fail to provide a solution is acknowledged. However, where the claimant suffers economic loss but is outside the extended *Hedley Byrne* principle, there is no recovery.

A new matrix for economic loss?

Objective
3

The rejection of a general principle of recovery for economic loss left a problem for English law in that cases on economic loss lacked the open textured analysis used in novel physical damage cases and, instead of analysing the substantive legal concerns for and against imposing a duty of care, the courts were concerned with factual issues which led to the use of concepts such as reliance and assumption of responsibility which tended to conceal the underlying moral, economic and other concerns relevant to the existence of tort liability.

Commonwealth courts, on the other hand, have broadly embraced the role to be played by tort law in this area and have embarked, particularly in Australia, on developing a matrix of factors which underlie recovery of economic loss and the relationship between contract and tort and markets and tort law.

The abandonment of the 'pockets of liability' approach by Commonwealth courts, and to a certain extent by English courts, has allowed the substantive themes in the courts' reasoning to be exposed and a matrix of the substantive legal concerns that govern this area to be assembled. This matrix can take account of, first, the concern that tortious intervention may impinge on the competitiveness of markets. It may also take account of the argument that the boundaries of liability be normatively justifiable and that those boundaries should be ascertainable, while also taking account of the claimant's opportunity to take appropriate forms of self-protection and the vulnerability of the claimant.

Factor 1 – Tortious intrusion into the competitiveness of markets

This argument is concerned with interference with legitimate acts of trade. English law has never accepted the proposition that a person owes a duty of care to another person because they know that their careless act may cause economic loss. Leaving aside the economic torts, a person will generally owe no duty even though they intended to cause economic loss. The trader may increase his advertising or cut his prices even though this is done with the intention of taking the market share of rivals. This principle reflects the autonomy of the individual protected by the common law and the desire to give effect to individual choices. However, assuming the other indicators of duty are present, immunity should only extend to conduct which is a legitimate pursuit of one's interests. What would not be a legitimate pursuit of one's interests? Competitive acts not prohibited by law are legitimate unless they fall within the ambit of the economic torts. At the other end of the spectrum, conduct which involves deceit, duress or intentional acts prohibited by law is seldom regarded as the legitimate pursuit of one's own interests. However, the fact that a person is in breach of the law and the other indicators of a duty are present does not in itself amount to justification for removing the immunity. This needs to be considered in conjunction with the other features in the matrix.

Factors 2 and 3 – The boundaries of liability should be normatively justifiable and ascertainable

Traditionally, this is the problem of indeterminacy of liability. The infliction of economic loss may have a ripple effect, creating indeterminacy of the class of victims and the total loss flowing from the negligence. It is now clear that this need not be fatal to a claim for economic loss provided that there is a normatively justifiable basis for who can sue and the amount which they can claim for.

These questions are clearly demonstrated in cases involving relational economic loss. Relational economic loss will occur where physical damage is caused to one person's property or person which then causes economic loss to a third person. Again, the contrast between English and Commonwealth courts is instructive.

In England the 'pockets of liability' approach has led to such loss being generally irrecoverable. Even where there is no problem of indeterminacy, the House of Lords concluded that liability would only be incurred where the claimant had a proprietary or possessory interest in the damaged property. (*Leigh & Sillivan Ltd* v *Aliakmon Shipping Co Ltd* [1986] 1 AC 785.)

The House of Lords invoked the exclusionary rule and emphasised the primacy of contract in the recovery of economic loss. If a person wanted legal protection in these circumstances then they should protect themselves through contract with the property owner.

Commonwealth courts have taken a different approach and rejected the exclusionary rule. The problems of indeterminacy and primacy of contract raised by the English courts to justify blanket exclusion have been approached by a more sophisticated route. The approach to indeterminacy is treated as one aspect of basing legal rules and drawing boundaries on principles which are normatively justifiable.

An early example of such an approach came in *Caltex Oil (Australia) Pty Ltd* v *The Dredge Willemstad* (1976) 136 CLR 529. A dredge negligently damaged an underwater pipe owned by AOR, which carried petrol from AOR's refinery to the Caltex terminal. Caltex recovered for the cost of transporting its petrol until the pipe was repaired. The High Court of Australia rejected an exclusionary rule and found that there was no indeterminacy problem. The defendants knew of the risk to Caltex as a specific individual and the claim was for expenditure necessarily incurred rather than loss of profits. Since AOR and Caltex were involved in a common venture, and, had the loss not been suffered by Caltex it would have been suffered by AOR, there was no increase in the overall damages incurred by the defendants.

In *Canadian National Railway Co* v *Norsk Pacific Steamship Co* [1992] 1 SCR 1021, a barge negligently collided with a railway bridge owned by a third party. The claimant railway company sued for economic loss incurred as a result of the non-availability of the bridge. The Supreme Court of Canada found for the claimant. There was a joint venture of the type in *Caltex*. The claimant was specifically foreseeable in terms of this loss.

In both *Caltex* and *Norsk Pacific* the court was able to offer a normatively justifiable reasoning for restricting liability to certain classes of person and excluding others. The ripple effect of economic loss necessitates a line being drawn, but not simply on the basis that the facts of the case do not sit within an established pocket of liability. If no normative justification is available for restricting and identifying meritorious claimants, then liability should be rejected.

The sophisticated reasoning which is available to the courts is apparent in some of the Australian agriculture cases. Typically, infected seed is negligently supplied, with resultant physical damage and economic loss to various parties in the chain of contracts. In *McMullin* v *ICI Australia Operations Pty Ltd* (1997) 72 FCR 1 insecticide contaminated cattle. Four classes of claimant were held by the High Court of Australia to be owed a duty of care. Graziers whose cattle were contaminated had their losses classified as physical damage. Persons who purchased already contaminated cattle and persons who owned meat which was found to be contaminated were owed a duty. Persons who incurred economic loss because of the cost of keeping contaminated cattle in their possession were classified as primary victims based on the normatively justifiable rule located in ownership/possession of contaminated meat. Other claims for economic loss were rejected as falling outside this normatively justifiable rule. In *Perre* v *Apand Pty Ltd* (1999) 198 CLR 180 infected seed was supplied to a farmer who used it to grow a crop. Legal regulation then prevented growers within a 20-mile radius from selling their crops in the Western Australian market. Claims by growers, processors and landowners were allowed as these persons were primary victims exclusively dependent on the defendant taking care. Secondary victims such as truckers would not have been successful.

Factor 4 – Self-protection and the primacy of contract

The argument that contract is the correct sphere for claims for economic loss continues to dominate English and US law. This is made apparent in actions in respect of defective products. Where a defect in a product causes physical damage, then any foreseeable victim of the defect may have a claim. Where the defect is one of quality, the supremacy of contract and the inadvisability of interfering with sales warranties are stressed.

Commonwealth courts appear on the whole to have rejected the primacy of contract approach and concentrated instead on whether contract would have provided a realistic alternative avenue of protection for the claimant. This operates in particular in cases where the claimant has suffered economic loss through the acquisition of defective property. In another contaminated seed case, **Wilkins v Dovuro Pty Ltd** (1999–2000) 169 ALR 276, the cost of weed eradication suffered by primary victims was recoverable. The damage to the claimants was reasonably foreseeable and the defendant was not legitimately protecting or pursuing its business interests. The class of victims vulnerable to lack of warning by the defendant was limited and ascertainable and there was no indeterminacy of liability. There were sound policy reasons for encouraging people to avoid or mitigate loss. The decision would not interfere with sale of goods law or interrupt any contractual matrix and it was not a situation where farmers would protect themselves with contractual warranties.

Factor 5 – Vulnerability

The final element, and one not usually considered by English courts, is the vulnerability of the claimant. It is arguable that tort law is most concerned with the protection of the vulnerable and this is supported by both rights and deterrence theories.

Where it is reasonably open to the claimant to protect himself, there will be no sound reason for imposing a duty on the defendant to protect the claimant against economic loss. This reflects the first aspect of contractual protection. The second aspect of contractual protection, that the claimant could not really have protected himself in this way, indicates that the vulnerability of the claimant is a prerequisite to imposing a duty to protect against economic loss. One important factor in determining whether the claimant is vulnerable is whether he could have protected himself by protective action such as obtaining contractual warranties. Pecuniary losses are one of the ordinary risks of commercial life and requiring a person to take steps to minimise these losses is normally more efficient than requiring another person to have regard to the risk that others might suffer economic loss. One question should be 'who is the best cost avoider?', and in the case of defective retail quality, this would be the person responsible for the defect in the goods.

It is therefore arguable that the vulnerability of the claimant may be a justifiable, but not sufficient, reason for imposing a duty of care in respect of pure economic loss when the claimant could not have protected himself in contract. A contractual assumption is that the parties will bargain to protect their position. A claimant who cannot do this in any meaningful way is vulnerable and the law of negligence may fill the gap left by contract.

The issue of vulnerability has received little attention by English courts but arose in the rather unusual facts of the following case.

Calvert v William Hill Credit Ltd [2008] EWHC 454 (Ch); [2008] EWCA Civ 1427 (CA)

> The defendant provided internet and telephone gambling services and formulated its own social responsibility policy, which provided for the exclusion of a customer in certain circumstances including when a customer requested that he be self-excluded. The claimant had been a skilful and successful gambler, with net winnings from 2000 until 2005 of about £50,000 per year. Initially his gambling was confined to greyhound racing. After a time he turned to telephone betting on a wider range of events, and began to gamble through the defendant. In June 2006, he asked the defendant

to exclude him from telephone gambling for six months as he was suffering from serious gambling problems. The defendant agreed. The employee dealing with the claimant omitted, however, to have him sign a disclaimer on liability. In the event, the defendant failed to implement its policy success-fully, and permitted the claimant to continue gambling. During the six months from June 2006, he suffered financial ruin and a deterioration in his gambling disorder. He sued for negligence.

(1) Having regard to previous authority on duty of care, exceptional circumstances might give rise to a common law duty of care to prevent or to mitigate the consequences or aggravation of self-inflicted harm. Such circumstances might include the assumption of control over a person while vulner-able to the consequences of self-inflicted harm, or the assumption of some responsibility for the care of, or the provision of assistance to, such a person. In every such case the three-stage test would be an important part of the analysis whether the circumstances were sufficiently explained.

(2) A bookmaker developing its own social responsibility policy and procedures did not thereby voluntarily assume responsibility to all its problem gambler customers, in the sense of assuming responsibility to take care, with a concomitant liability to compensate customers injured in their mind or in their pocket by any failure to take care. It might, however, assume responsibility to a particular gambler following a specific request.

In these circumstances, the defendant had assumed a sufficient voluntary assumption of responsibility to exclude the claimant from telephone gambling for six months to give rise to a duty to take care to implement that policy. The request and the response was crucial. It brought the parties into a degree of relationship akin to a contract, save for the absence of consideration. It deprived the objection that the provision of assistance might infringe the gambler's autonomy of any force, since he himself had specifically requested it. The financial and psychiatric harm was sufficiently foreseeable. There was no risk of indeterminate liability to an indeterminate class, as the claim was concerned with a specific request by a particular person. The failure to implement the policy was limited in financial terms to losses for the six-month period that the policy had intended to cover. On the facts, however, the claimant would have continued his gambling and ultimately ruined himself financially in any event, albeit at a slower rate because of the reduced scale of gambling which would have been avail-able to him. The defendant's breach was therefore not causative of any loss to the claimant.

The claimant appealed on the causation ground but the Court of Appeal held against him. The claimant's case had failed not because his continued gambling with the defendant was his own delib-erate act breaking a chain of causation, but because the scope of the defendant's duty of care did not extend to prevent him from gambling and because the quantification of his loss could not ignore other gambling losses which he would probably have sustained but for its breach of duty.

Summary

This chapter deals with the question of when a duty of care not to cause economic loss is owed in negligence.

- Economic loss presents particular problems in the tort of negligence and a number of arguments have been raised against its recovery. The major arguments are that it would undermine contract; that there is a 'floodgates problem'; and the quality of work required would be difficult to assess.

- Historically there was no liability for economic loss in negligence. (*Cattle* v *Stockton Waterworks Co* (1875).)

- The major change came with the House of Lords decision in *Hedley Byrne* v *Heller* (1964). This case stated (*obiter*) that it was possible for a person who made a negligent statement to owe duty of care to a person who relied on the statement and suffered economic loss.

- The fact that economic loss is reasonably foreseeable is not enough to establish a duty of care.

- There must be a special relationship between the parties. This requires a special skill on the part of the defendant. If advice is given in a business context then it is capable of attracting a duty of care. Advice given on a social occasion is not.

- Early cases concentrated on the requirement that there should be reasonable reliance by the claimant on the defendant. This meant specific reliance rather than general reliance.

- This gave rise to problems where there was clearly no specific reliance and the courts have now moved to asking the question of whether the defendant had 'assumed responsibility' to the claimant for his economic well-being. (*White* v *Jones* (1995).)

- The court may check its result under the above test by reference to the three-stage test.

- A surveyor or valuer will owe a duty of care to a purchaser of a house who he knows will be shown the valuation done for the lender. (*Smith* v *Bush* (1995).)

- An auditor or accountant will not owe a duty of care to a third party who has relied on the public audited accounts of a company unless there has been a specific assumption of responsibility by the auditor to the claimant. (*Caparo* v *Dickman* (1990).)

- Economic loss outside of the *Hedley Byrne* principle has been restricted.

- In tripartite business arrangements there is generally no duty of care owed outside of contract.

- Where a person acquires defective property there is usually no liability for economic loss caused by the defect. This is also the case with realty. (*Murphy* v *Brentwood District Council* (1990).)

- Economic loss suffered by the claimant as a result of damage to the property of a third party is not recoverable. (*Spartan Steel* v *Martin* (1973); *The Aliakmon* (1986).)

- The principle developed by the courts in the 1990s is known as the 'extended *Hedley Byrne* principle'. It is capable of applying to services as well as statements and is based on assumption of responsibility. The principle has been used to deal with problems of expectations and omissions.

- This principle has been applied in the case of references (*Spring* v *Guardian Assurance* (1994)); the liability of solicitors to third parties (*White* v *Jones* (1995)); the liability of a Lloyd's agent to his principal (*Henderson* v *Merrett* (1994)); the liability of a bank to the taxman (*Customs and Excise* v *Barclays Bank* (2006)).

Further reading

Barker, K. (1993), 'Unreliable Assumptions in the Modern Law of Negligence' 109 LQR 461.

Cooke, Sir R. (1991), 'An Impossible Distinction' 107 LQR 46 (*Murphy* v *Brentwood*).

Fleming, J. G. (1990), 106 LQR 349 (*Caparo*).

Markesinis, B. S. (1987), 'An Expanding Tort Law: The Price of a Rigid Contract Law' 103 LQR 354.

Murphy, J. (1996), 'Expectation Losses, Negligent Omissions and the Duty of Care' CLJ 43.

Stapleton, J. (1991), 'Duty of Care and Economic Loss' 107 LQR 249.

Whittaker, S. (1996), 'Privity of Contract and the Tort of Negligence' 16 OJLS 1.

6

Liability for omissions and third parties

Objectives

After reading this chapter you will:

1. Understand the distinction between misfeasance and nonfeasance.
2. Appreciate the problems raised for the tort of negligence by omissions.
3. Have a knowledge of the law relating to liability in negligence for the acts of third parties.

Introduction

Objective 1

One of the characteristics of a negligence action is that it is a method of compensating for wrongfully caused harm. Harm can be caused either by a positive act (*misfeasance*) or by omitting to act (*nonfeasance*). This can be expressed as making things worse and failing to make them better.

Traditionally, negligence only protected against the former. If you wanted someone to take positive action on your behalf, you had to pay them and thereby obtain contractual protection. Exceptions to this have always existed. Where there is a particular relationship between the parties, such as parent and child, then there may be a duty to act positively for the benefit of the child. The question could then be posed as to whether the parent was also liable for damage inflicted on other persons by the child.

Closely connected with liability for omissions is the question of liability for the acts of third parties. This will typically arise when a person fails to exercise control over another person who then commits a tort. This failure will, of course, usually be an omission.

Liability for omissions

Objective 2

See also Chapter 3 for *Donoghue v Stevenson*.

In *Donoghue* v *Stevenson* (1932), Lord Atkin referred to 'acts or omissions which you can reasonably foresee would be likely to injure your neighbour'. The reference to omissions here was to an omission in the course of positive conduct: for example, if a person is driving a car and omits to apply the brakes. At this time the conventional view was that there was no liability in negligence for a simple failure to act for another person's benefit.

> ### Example
>
> *X* has fallen into a river and is drowning. *X* calls out for help. *Y* is walking along the river bank and hears *X*. There is a lifebelt provided on the bank but *Y* walks past and does nothing. In these circumstances there is no liability on *Y* as he does not owe *X* a duty of care, unless there is a relationship between *X* and *Y* which gives rise to a duty to act positively.
>
> What would be the position if *Y* embarked on a rescue attempt and then withdrew, making *X*'s position worse? By embarking on a positive act, does *Y* undertake a duty? Would it be strange to say that the person who does nothing has no liability, whereas the Good Samaritan could be sued?

The principles on liability for omissions were laid down by the House of Lords in ***Smith* v *Littlewoods Organisation Ltd*** [1987] All ER 710. The case was concerned with liability for third persons inflicting damage. Lord Goff laid down a principle of no liability. This was subject to four exceptions:

1 Where there was a special relationship between the parties such as a contractual relationship (***Stansbie* v *Troman*** [1948] 1 All ER 599).

2 Where there was a special relationship between the defendant and the third party (***Home Office* v *Dorset Yacht Co Ltd*** [1970] 2 All ER 294).

3 Where the defendant negligently causes or permits a source of danger to be created which is then interfered with by third parties (***Haynes* v *Harwood*** [1935] 1 KB 146).

4 Where the defendant knew or had means of knowledge that a third party was creating a danger on his property and failed to take reasonable steps to abate it (***Goldman* v *Hargrave*** [1966] 2 All ER 989).

It should be pointed out that Lords Brandon, Griffiths and Mackay decided the case on its own facts. They did not rule out liability on the basis of any general rule of no liability. It is therefore possible that liability could be developed from these speeches.

Lord Griffiths:

> I doubt myself if any search will reveal a touchstone that can be applied as a universal test to decide when an occupier is to be held liable for a danger created on his property by the act of a trespasser for whom he is not responsible. I agree that mere foreseeability of damage is certainly not a sufficient basis to found liability. But with this warning I doubt that more can be done than to leave it to the good sense of the judges to apply realistic standards in conformity with generally accepted patterns of behaviour to determine whether in the particular circumstances of a given case there has been a breach of duty sounding in negligence.

However, the general rule against liability for pure omissions has been restated by the courts on a number of occasions.

The law on omissions is complicated by the fact that there are usually other policy issues in omissions cases. These may arise in cases involving statutory authorities such as the following one.

Stovin v *Wise* [1996] 3 All ER 801

A bank of earth on British Rail property made it difficult for drivers turning right at a junction to see traffic approaching. A number of accidents had occurred at this spot previously. *W* drove her car into *S*'s motor cycle. *W*'s insurer paid off *S* and sought a contribution from the highway authority which had failed to implement its earlier decision to remove the mound of earth, which it had the power to do. The House of Lords (by a majority) found that the highway authority was not liable. (See also *Gorringe* v *Calderdale Metropolitan Borough Council* [2004] 2 All ER 326.)

Lord Hoffmann stated:

> There are sound reasons why omissions require different treatment from positive conduct. It is one thing for the law to say that a person who undertakes some positive activity shall take reasonable care not to cause damage to others. It is another thing for the law to require that a person who is doing nothing in particular shall take steps to prevent another from suffering harm from the acts of third parties or natural causes.

Lord Hoffmann's argument was 'why pick on me?' He based it on individual freedom. Why should one person be selected for liability? He also considered the economic arguments. These are based on the efficient allocation of resources. An activity should bear its own costs and if it can impose the cost of some of its activities on others ('externalities') then this will distort the market. If a person acts negligently, causes harm and increases the cost of an activity to the community then the award of damages acts as a deterrent. However, there is no similar argument which requires a person to spend money on behalf of someone else and there is no reward for someone who voluntarily assists another without a special reason.

A further statement of the general rule came in *Sutradhar* v *National Environment Research Council* [2006] UKHL 33. The defendants had tested drinking water at a well for toxins but not for arsenic. The claimant brought an action after suffering arsenic poisoning from water from the well. The House of Lords held that the defendants were under no duty to test for arsenic. They could only be liable for what they did, not for what they did not do.

The question arose in a more complex form in the following case which involves two further twists. These are liability for the acts of third parties and the liability of public authorities. The case is further complicated as the facts arose after the Human Rights Act 1998 came into force.

For liability of public authorities see Chapter 7.

Mitchell v *Glasgow City Council* [2009] UKHL 11

The deceased and his neighbour, *D*, were tenants of the appellant local authority. *D*'s anti-social behaviour and propensity towards violence, particularly aimed at the deceased, was well documented by the local authority. On one occasion, *D*, armed with an iron bar, smashed the windows and door of the deceased's council home. The final and fatal incident of violence occurred following a meeting between local authority officials and *D* at which the latter was informed that a notice of proceedings to recover possession of his council dwelling would be served on him. *D* became verbally abusive to the officials and, after leaving the meeting, he fatally assaulted the deceased with a stick or iron bar. *D* pleaded guilty to culpable homicide. The pursuers (claimants), the mother and daughter of the deceased, brought an action against the local authority seeking damages for negligence at common law contending that, in failing to take action to evict *D* and in failing to warn the deceased after the last meeting with *D*, the local authority had acted negligently. They further contended that the local authority had acted in a way that was incompatible with the deceased's right to life under Article 2 of the European Convention on Human Rights.

Held (House of Lords): Foreseeability of harm was not of itself enough for the imposition of a duty of care. The proximity and fair, just and reasonable tests had also to be passed. The law did not normally impose a positive duty on a person to protect others. The common law did not impose liability for what, without more, might be called pure omissions. The law did not impose a duty to prevent a person from being harmed by the criminal act of a third party based simply upon foreseeability. (*Smith* v *Littlewoods Ltd* [1987] 1 All ER 710 applied.)

The question of whether it was fair, just and reasonable that the local authority should be held liable in damages for the omissions to warn the deceased, was one of fairness and public policy. As a general rule, a duty to warn another person that he was at risk of loss, injury or damage as the result of the criminal act of a third party would arise only where the person who was said to be under that duty had by his words or conduct assumed responsibility for the safety of the person who was at risk.

In the instant case, it was not suggested that the local authority had assumed a responsibility to advise the deceased of the steps that they were taking and it could not, therefore, be said that there existed a relationship of proximity or that the duty to warn was within that relationship. It followed that it would not be fair, just or reasonable to hold that the local authority were under a duty to warn the deceased of the steps that they were taking.

With regards to the Article 2 (right to life) claim, not every claimed risk to life could entail a Convention requirement to take operational measures to prevent that risk from materialising. It had to be established that the authorities knew, or ought to have known at the time, of the existence of *a real and immediate risk* to the life of an identified individual from the criminal acts of a third party and that they failed to take measures within the scope of their powers which, judged reasonably, might have been expected to avoid that risk. In the instant case, there was no basis for saying that the local authority ought to have known that, when *D* left the meeting, there was a real and immediate risk to the deceased's life.

See below and Chapters 3 and 7.

(*Osman* v *United Kingdom; Van Colle* v *Chief Constable of Hertfordshire Police; Smith* v *Chief Constable of Sussex Police* applied.)

The loss to the family was a great one but should the local authority shoulder the burden of compensation? The Lords felt that, as in the case of the police, it is desirable too that social landlords, social workers and others who seek to address the many behavioural problems that arise in local authority housing estates and elsewhere, often in very difficult circumstances, should be safeguarded from legal proceedings arising from an alleged failure to warn those who might be at risk of a criminal attack in response to their activities. Such proceedings, whether meritorious or otherwise, would involve them in a great deal of time, trouble and expense which would be more usefully devoted to their primary functions in their respective capacities.

What if the loss to the claimant was pecuniary rather than physical? This is the case where a regulatory body (frequently established by statute) fails adequately to supervise the work of a third party. This was the situation in the following case.

Yuen Kun-yeu v *Attorney-General of Hong Kong* [1987] 2 All ER 705

See also Chapter 3 for *Yuen Kun-yeu* v *AG of Hong Kong*.

The Commissioner regulated deposit-taking businesses in Hong Kong and had discretionary powers to refuse to register or to revoke the registration of an unfit company. The claimant had deposited money with a registered deposit-taking company which went into liquidation and alleged that the Commissioner should never have registered or should have revoked the company's licence.

The Privy Council held that no duty of care was owed by the Commissioner to the claimant. No such statutory duty was owed and a common law duty would not be imposed. The Commissioner's duty was towards the general public, but there was no special responsibility towards individual members of the public. A duty could not be established on the basis that the claimant had relied on the company's registration as this was neither reasonable nor justifiable.

This approach has been followed consistently by the courts in subsequent cases involving regulatory agencies, but an interesting perspective was added by the House of Lords decision in *White* v *Jones*.

White v *Jones* [1995] 1 All ER 691

See also Chapters 3 and 5 for *White* v *Jones*; the facts and decisions are analysed in Chapter 5.

The case involved an omission to act on the part of the defendant solicitors in that they failed to amend the will in accordance with the testator's wishes. Had the issue been between the testator (client) and the solicitor, there would have been no problem as there would have been an omission in the course of a positive undertaking to the client to perform a particular task. In the context of liability to a third party (the beneficiary) there was a problem as to whether the solicitor could be liable for an omission to act. In the absence of an undertaking by the solicitor to the third party, it would be expected that there would be no duty owed. However, Lord Browne-Wilkinson (with whose speech Lord Nolan agreed) thought that there was, even in the absence of an undertaking to the beneficiaries, a sufficient undertaking, in the sense of an assumption of responsibility for the task of amending the will, to found a duty of care.

The principle of assumption of responsibility can also be seen in *Barrett* v *Ministry of Defence* [1995] 3 All ER 86. Here the navy were held to owe a duty of care in respect of the death of a sailor who had drunk himself unconscious. The duty was not to prevent him drinking to that stage but once an officer had arranged for him to be taken to his room, there had been an assumption of responsibility for his welfare. (See also *Jebson* v *Ministry of Defence* [2000] 1 WLR 2055.)

Conclusion

The general rule is that there is no liability for a pure omission in English law. If a claimant wishes to succeed on the basis of an omission to act they must prove something further.

This can occur in three situations:

1 **Assumption of responsibility**

If the defendant can be said to have assumed responsibility for the claimant's wellbeing or safety then a duty of care can arise. This may occur through an employment relationship such as *Barrett* (see above). The navy were not responsible for Barrett drinking to excess. They only became responsible when they assumed responsibility for a person who was already drunk.

2 **Control**

Where the defendant exercises a high degree of control over the claimant then they may be liable for a pure omission. Where a person is arrested and placed in a police cell then the police owe a duty to take reasonable steps to assess whether the person is a suicide risk and take steps accordingly. A similar principle would apply with a mental patient.

3 **Creating or adopting risks**

Cases in nuisance where a person has adopted an existing risk and has had a duty to take positive steps imposed are an example. In cases involving the emergency services there may be a duty imposed where they encounter an existing danger and make things worse – the 'fresh damage' principle. This would apply where the fire brigade attend a fire and make it worse by turning the sprinklers off.

Liability for the acts of third parties

Objective
3

This subject is closely related to the question of liability for omissions. The question is: when will *A* be liable to *B* for the negligent act of *C*? Any question of *A*'s liability will normally concern his omission to exercise control over *C*.

Smith v Littlewoods Organisation Ltd [1987] 1 All ER 710

L bought a cinema in Dunfermline with the intention of demolishing it and building a supermarket. The cinema was empty and a fire was started by unknown children. The fire spread to the appellant's land and damaged his buildings. Fires had previously been started in the building but this fact was not known to *L*. The appellant's action in negligence against *L* failed.

Lord Goff stated that there was a general principle that no duty existed to prevent persons deliberately inflicting damage on another person. There were four exceptions to this principle.

This raises the question of what area of negligence law should be used to determine these cases. Lord Goff's approach in **Smith v Littlewoods** is to deny a general duty of care. Lord Mackay and the majority of the House of Lords concentrate on fault (breach of duty) as the determining factor. The court looks at the blameworthiness of the defendant's conduct in creating the risk. A further possibility is to argue that the damage is too remote, perhaps because of the act of the third party breaking the chain of causation. (See **Topp**, below.)

Carmarthenshire County Council v Lewis [1955] 1 All ER 565

A lorry driver was killed when he swerved to avoid a four-year-old child. The child had been left in a classroom at school while the teacher attended to another child. The child had wandered out on to the road and caused the accident. The defendants were held liable on the basis of their **vicarious liability** for the teacher's negligence. Duty was established on the basis of a reasonably foreseeable claimant. (See also **Home Office v Dorset Yacht Co**, above.)

What is noticeable in the decision is the absence of discussion on proximity and policy. In modern terms it is perhaps best regarded as a case based on the school's assumption of responsibility for controlling the child.

The exceptions

1 Special relationship between claimant and defendant. Where there was a special relationship between the parties such as a contractual relationship. An example of this arose in **Stansbie v Troman** [1948] 1 All ER 599. A decorator working on the claimant's premises was told to lock up if he went out. He did not and a thief entered the house and stole money. The decorator was held liable for the loss.

Contrast this with the following case:

P Perl (Exporters) Ltd v Camden London Borough Council [1984] QB 342

The defendant council owned adjoining premises. One (142) was let to the claimant and the other (144) was divided into flats. There was no lock on the door of 144 and thieves entered and knocked a hole in the wall into 142. Property belonging to the claimant was stolen. The Court of Appeal held that the defendants were not liable as mere foreseeability of harm was not sufficient to establish a duty. Foreseeability alone was not enough to establish proximity. (See also **Mitchell v Glasgow City Council** [2009] UKHL 11, above.)

In cases of property damage there may be a policy issue in that the court may assume that the claimant has insurance.

If there is an express or implied undertaking given by the defendant to the claimant this may suffice to establish proximity. If a person is given an assurance by the police that if they give information the police will protect their safety. If the police then negligently endanger the informant they may owe a duty of care. (*Swinney* v *Chief Constable of Northumbria Police* [1997] QB 464.) In the absence of such an undertaking there is no general duty on the police or equivalent organisations to protect specific members of the public. In *Palmer* v *Tees Health Authority* [1999] Lloyd's Rep Med 351 the claimant's four-year-old daughter was abducted and murdered by a psychiatric patient. The body was discovered three days later. The claimant alleged that the defendants had been negligent in their assessment of the patient. No duty was owed as there was no proximity. (See also *Mitchell* v *Glasgow City Council* [2009] UKHL 11, above; *K* v *Secretary of State for the Home Department* [2002] EWCA Civ 775.)

2 A special relationship between the defendant and the third party. In *Home Office* v *Dorset Yacht Co Ltd* [1970] 2 All ER 294, boys escaped from a borstal due to the negligence of the appellant's employees. The boys caused damage to the respondent's property. The appellants were responsible for controlling the third party (the boys) and were held to owe a duty of care to the respondents.

What is the difference between this decision and *Palmer*? Would it have made any difference if the court had looked at the relationship between the defendant and the third party in *Palmer*?

3 Where the defendant negligently causes or permits a source of danger to be created, which is then interfered with by third parties. In *Haynes* v *Harwood* [1935] 1 KB 146 a horse was left unattended in a busy street. Children threw stones at the horse and it bolted. A policeman was injured in attempting to stop the horse. The defendant was held to owe a duty of care to the policeman.

Topp v *London Country Buses (South West) Ltd* [1993] 3 All ER 448

The defendant bus company ran minibus services. A bus was left empty, with the keys in the ignition, waiting for a relief driver who did not turn up. This was reported to the company, which did nothing. The bus was stolen by joyriders who ran over and killed the claimant's wife. The joyriders were not traced and the claimant sued the bus company.

The Court of Appeal found that no duty of care arose. The decision was based on Lord Goff's judgment in *Smith* v *Littlewoods*. The voluntary act of another which is independent of the defendant's fault is a *novus actus interveniens* breaking the chain of causation. There was no 'special' risk giving rise to sufficient proximity.

It is certainly arguable that the law was not applied correctly in this case as it is difficult to see how the joyriders' act was independent of the defendants' fault. The trial judge had found that the defendants had been careless. The answer must lie in what Lord Goff means by independent. (See, for example, the facts and decision in *Smith* v *Littlewoods*.) This could mean 'not connected with' or it could have a meaning similar to that in vicarious liability.

4 Where the defendant knew or had means of knowledge that a third party was creating a danger on his property and failed to take reasonable steps to abate it. Examples of this

kind of liability usually arise in nuisance. See, for example, ***Goldman* v *Hargrave*** [1966] 2 All ER 989. There was no liability under this head in the present case as the defendants had no means of knowing that the building represented a fire hazard.

Where the act of a third party results in the death of a person a claimant may now invoke Article 2 of the European Convention, the 'right to life'. The courts have held in the context of public authorities such as the police and local authorities that there has to be a *real and immediate risk* and a failure to take action to safeguard the life of the third party before a public authority will be liable. (See ***Mitchell* v *Glasgow City Council*** (above); ***Osman* v *United Kingdom***; ***Van Colle* v *Chief Constable of Hertfordshire Police***; ***Smith* v *Chief Constable of Sussex Police***.)

See also Chapter 3.

Summary

This chapter deals with the special rules on omissions and liability for third parties.

- Harm can be caused either by a positive act (*misfeasance*) or by omitting to act (*nonfeasance*).

- The principles on liability for omissions were laid down in ***Smith* v *Littlewoods*** (1987). The general principle was that no duty existed to prevent persons deliberately inflicting damage on another person. The general rule of no liability for omissions has been upheld in subsequent cases.

- When will *A* be liable to *B* for the negligent act of *C*? Lord Goff's approach in ***Smith* v *Littlewoods*** is to deny a general duty of care. Lord Mackay and the majority of the House of Lords concentrate on fault (breach of duty) as the determining factor. The court looks at the blameworthiness of the defendant's conduct in creating the risk. A further possibility is to argue that the damage is too remote, perhaps because of the act of the third party breaking the chain of causation. (See ***Topp* v *London Country Buses***.)

- There are four exceptions to the general principle of no liability: (i) where there was a special relationship between the parties; (ii) where there was a special relationship between the defendant and the third party; (iii) where the defendant negligently causes or permits a source of danger to be created; (iv) where the defendant knew or had means of knowledge that a third party was creating a danger on his property and failed to take reasonable steps to abate it.

Further reading

Harris, D. (1997), 113 LQR 398 (*Stovin* v *Wise*).

7

Liability of public authorities

Introduction

Objective 1

One of the most difficult topics in tort law is the question of when a public authority will be liable. Public authorities usually operate against a background of statutory authority which may provide a mechanism for people to appeal against their decisions or failure to act and will be subject to judicial review in public law. The question here is under what circumstances will a public authority be liable in private (as opposed to public) law.

Examples

1 A public authority responsible for the highway in its area resurfaces the road but fails to reinstate the painted give way line at a road junction. A motorist pulls out without stopping and is in a collision with another vehicle. Can the public authority be held liable in negligence for its omission to act which results in a third party causing damage to the claimant?

2 A member of the public makes a complaint to the police that her life is in danger from her former partner. The police do nothing and the complainant is then murdered by her former partner. Can her estate bring an action for negligence against the police?

3 A complaint is made to Social Services that a child is being abused. Social Services investigate but carelessly concludes that there is no abuse. The abuse continues. Can the child or the parents bring an action for negligence?

> 4 A child has learning difficulties at school and is assessed to see if he needs special needs teaching. The assessment is done carelessly and the child's education suffers. Can the child sue for negligence?
>
> There are a number of actions which may possibly be brought in these circumstances.
>
> 1 An action for breach of statutory duty by the public authority.
> 2 An action for negligence on the basis that the public authority is primarily liable.
> 3 An action for negligence on the basis that the public authority is vicariously liable.
> 4 An action under the Human Rights Act 1998 for a breach of a Convention right.

Negligence actions involving public authorities are particularly complex. There are four reasons for this:

See Chapter 5 for economic loss.

1 The loss involved is generally pure economic loss, which poses particular problems for tort law.

2 The breach of duty in question is frequently an omission to act which also creates particular difficulties.

3 The breach may well take place against the background of statutory powers and raises questions of whether tort law has a role to play or whether public law remedies are appropriate.

4 As the action is against a public authority, the Human Rights Act 1998 may well have a role to play.

See Chapter 1 for human rights and tort generally.

The common law has not provided a definition of 'public authority' but the broad definition in the Human Rights Act 1998 s 6(3) states that 'it includes a court or tribunal and any person certain of whose functions are functions of a public nature'.

Typical defendants in this area are local authorities, police and other rescue services. As most of these services are publicly funded through the tax system, the emphasis is on the defendant. The courts work on the basis that there are a number of policy reasons why a public authority should be exempt from liability.

Effect of Human Rights Act 1998

It would appear that the Act may have an effect on the tortious liability of public authorities in two respects.

1 It may bolster an existing right of action against a public authority. An example of this would be the immunity debate which is taking place.

2 It may have the effect of creating new causes of action in tort as the Act provides its own independent basis for an action against a public authority. Such cases need to be heard in accordance with Strasbourg jurisprudence, such as the doctrine of proportionality. These 'constitutional torts' will be established where a claimant successfully alleges that a public authority has violated one of the constitutional rights the claimant enjoys as a result of the Act. (See *Van Colle* v *Chief Constable of the Hertfordshire Police* [2007] 3 All ER 122.)

In terms of negligence actions, the significance of the defendant being a public authority has been the allocation of resources and whether some of the scarce resources allocated to public authorities should be diverted by private law into compensating individuals for a public authority's negligence.

See Chapter 12 for the rules of this tort.

It should be remembered that many of these actions take place against a background of statute law. A claimant may invoke a claim for the tort of breach of statutory duty. The rules for this tort are separate and set out elsewhere. Alternatively, the claimant will argue that a common law duty of care can be created against the background of the provisions of the statute. These claims are argued on the usual rules of negligence. An important distinction between the two claims was made by Lord Steyn in **Gorringe v Calderdale Metropolitan Borough Council** [2004] 2 All ER 326:

> [I]n a case founded on breach of statutory duty the central question is whether from the provisions and structure of the statute an intention can be gathered to create a private law remedy? In contradistinction in a case framed in negligence, against the background of a statutory duty or power, a basic question is whether the statute excludes a private law remedy? An assimilation of the two inquiries will sometimes produce wrong results.

The framework for actions

Objective 2

The framework for actions (pre-Human Rights Act 1998) was laid down by the House of Lords.

For *Stovin v Wise* on omissions, see Chapter 6 under 'Liability for omissions'.

Stovin v Wise [1996] 3 All ER 801

A bank of earth on British Rail property made it difficult for drivers turning right at a junction to see traffic approaching. A number of accidents had occurred at this spot previously. *W* drove her car into *S*'s motor cycle. *W*'s insurer paid off *S* and sought a contribution from the highway authority which had failed to implement its earlier decision to remove the mound of earth, which it had the power to do. The allegation of negligence was therefore pure omission. The highway authority argued that it had no duty of affirmative action and therefore the relationship between it and the claimant was insufficiently proximate. A majority of the House of Lords found that the highway authority was not liable.

See also Chapter 3 for liability of emergency services.

Discussion of the very complex principles involved will occur here in two stages. The framework for actions will be set out and the law discussed primarily in the context of the emergency services cases. These have already been discussed from a different aspect. What will be described as the 'education cases' will follow.

Omissions

1 There was no liability on a public authority for a pure omission. (Lord Hoffmann.) The mere fact that a claimant's harm was foreseeable did not create a duty of care. (See also **Mitchell v Glasgow City Council** (2009).)

2 Where a statutory power was conferred, the fact that the public authority was acting under a statutory power did not generate an analogous duty to act, as an order of mandamus could only force a public authority to consider the exercise of a statutory power. It could not force it to act.

Even if the alleged negligent conduct related to a statutory duty (as opposed to a power), a private right to sue for breach of that duty did not automatically arise. That was dependent on the intention of Parliament. As Parliament had only seen fit to impose a power, this made it even more unlikely that they intended a common law duty to be recognised.

This reasoning of Lord Hoffmann in **Stovin** would appear to be at odds with the reasoning of the House of Lords in **X v Bedfordshire County Council** [1995] 3 All ER 353, which allowed actions in some of the education cases. The cases can probably only be reconciled by saying that Lord Hoffmann's reasoning for the majority represents a determination to deny a duty of care where the allegation relates to a pure omission by way of failure to exercise a statutory power.

However, some indication as to Lord Hoffmann's thinking was given in a later case:

Gorringe v Calderdale Metropolitan Borough Council [2004] 2 All ER 326

The claimant suffered severe injury driving a car when she braked and skidded into a bus just before the crest of a hill. The bus driver was not at fault and the claimant brought proceedings against the local authority alleging that their failure to place signs on the road warning motorists that they were approaching a dangerous part of the road was a breach of duty. In terms of the common law duty she alleged that the Road Traffic Act 1988, which imposed a duty on every local authority to prepare and carry out a programme of measures designed to promote and improve road safety, created a common law duty to users of the highway, in parallel with the statutory duty in the Highways Act 1980 s 41 to maintain the highway, to take reasonable steps to promote and improve road safety. This argument was rejected by the House of Lords, who held that a broad public duty did not generate a common law duty of care and thus a private law right of action.

Lord Hoffmann:

> My Lords, I must make it clear that this appeal is concerned only with an attempt to impose upon a local authority a common law duty to act based solely on the existence of a broad public law duty. We are not concerned with cases in which public authorities have actually done acts or entered into relationships or undertaken responsibilities which give rise to a common law duty of care. In such cases the fact that the public authority acted pursuant to a statutory power or public duty does not necessarily negative the existence of a duty.

This statement makes it clear that the courts will not be willing to create a common law duty where none existed before on the basis of a broad statutory power or duty. They will, however, find a duty where a local authority has acted pursuant to a statutory duty or power and the requirements of the common law duty of care are satisfied. (See **Connor v Surrey County Council** [2010] EWCA Civ 286 – below.) This would explain the difference between the 'road safety' cases and the 'education' cases.

A further example of such reluctance came in **Rowley v Secretary of State for the Department of Work and Pensions** [2007] 1 WLR 2861, where the claimant alleged that the Child Support Agency had caused her economic loss and psychiatric damage as a result of negligence in their handling of her claim for child support against her children's father. The Court of Appeal struck out her claim as there was no action for breach of statutory duty and no grounds for finding a common law duty of care. The scheme laid down by Parliament provided for judicial review and compensation for most cases where there was loss as a result of mismanagement of claims. There was no assumption of responsibility by the minister to the claimant and on the three-stage test the claim failed as it would not be fair, just and reasonable to impose a duty in these circumstances.

Exceptions to the general principle

(a) Relationship with the third party causing harm

Where the claimant suffers harm as a result of the actions of a third party over whom he alleges the defendant has carelessly failed to exercise control, proximity of relationship can be established by reference to the nature of the relationship between the defendant and the third party. For example, in *Home Office* **v** *Dorset Yacht Co* [1970] 2 All ER 294, where the defendant had responsibility to control the third party.

In practice, it is difficult for the facts of a case to provide the sort of relationship between defendant and third party that will override the omissions difficulty and create a sufficiently proximate relationship between defendant and claimant. This difficulty is evident in the cases where a person alleges that the police or a local authority have failed to take sufficient steps to avoid a third person causing them damage. (See *Mitchell* **v** *Glasgow City Council*; *Van Colle* **v** *Chief Constable of Hertfordshire Police*; *Smith* **v** *Chief Constable of Sussex Police*.)

See also Chapters 6 and 7.

(b) Undertaking and reliance

Where a public authority undertakes to exercise a power in a particular way and the claimant relied on that undertaking.

In *Stovin*, Lord Hoffmann laid down two conditions. First, that it had to have been so irrational for the public authority not to have exercised the power that there would be a duty to act under public law principles. (*Wednesbury* unreasonableness – see *Associated Provincial Picture Houses Ltd* **v** *Wednesbury Corporation* [1948] 1 KB 223.) Second, that there were exceptional grounds for holding that the policy of the statute requires compensation to be paid to persons who suffer loss because the power was not exercised. Such exceptional grounds would have to be found either in a reasonably held general reliance by the community as a whole that the discretionary service in question would be provided to all of them (general reliance) or in a similarly reasonably held particular reliance on the part of an individual that the service would be provided for him (specific reliance).

Clearly this, as Lord Hoffmann intended, would be difficult to establish. In terms of general reliance he held that the defendant's failure to act could not be described as irrational given the many other demands on its time and resources. Even if it could be deemed irrational, the second test could not be established either at a community or individual level, as the community itself, through the standard of its driving, was primarily responsible for road safety.

Specific reliance and the emergency services

See also Chapter 3 for liability of emergency services.

Actions brought against a non-local public authority are likely to fall between undertaking and reliance. Actions against the police for failing to prevent the commission of a crime, the fire brigade for failing to attend a fire and the coastguard are likely to fail. However, an action against the ambulance service, once an emergency phone call has been made and details given, may give rise to a duty. (*Kent* **v** *Griffiths* [2000] 2 WLR 1158.) This is because the ambulance service, as part of the health service, is similar to the service provided by hospitals to individual patients, whereas the police and fire brigades serve to protect the general public.

General reliance and the emergency services

The approach of the courts is that even if the public count generally on the police to investigate crime and apprehend criminals and the fire brigade to respond to emergency calls, it does not follow that it is reasonable for the public to rely on scarce resources being committed in each and every case.

It has therefore been held that the police (*Alexandrou* **v** *Oxford* [1993] 4 All ER 328), the fire brigade (*Capital & Counties* **v** *Hampshire County Council* [1997] 2 All ER 865) and coastguard (*Skinner* v *Secretary of State for Transport* (1995) Times, 3 January) owe no duty in failing to respond to an emergency call. The public apparently rely on fire insurance more than the fire brigade!

It is arguable that the Human Rights Act 1998 may provide for positive obligations which the common law has been reluctant to provide. Actions against public authorities that fail for want of a relevant affirmative obligation might succeed because of a relevant Convention obligation, such as safeguarding personal integrity, protecting property or the right to life. The courts have generally shown a reluctance to allow such actions where a common law action would not succeed. Examples can be seen in actions against the police and local authorities for breach of Article 2. (See *Mitchell* v *Glasgow City Council*; *Van Colle* v *Chief Constable of Hertfordshire Police*.)

See also Chapters 6 and 7.

 ## Carelessness in the exercise of statutory powers – proximity

This differs from what has gone before, as what the claimant is challenging is not the decision as to whether or not to exercise the statutory power, but the way in which that power has been carried out once the decision has been made to exercise it. The distinction has been expressed in a number of ways such as 'policy/operational' and 'decision making/implementation'.

In this category, it is not possible for the court to classify the alleged carelessness as a pure omission but it will still take into account the fact that the public authority was not obliged to do anything in the first place. In this sense omissions considerations still influence the court's decision. This can be done through the proximity doctrine. In the same way that a voluntary rescuer can only be held liable for any additional risks they create, the court will use the 'fresh damage' principle to limit a public authority's liability for its 'voluntary conduct'. They will only be liable if they have made the claimant's situation worse.

The fire brigade (service)

Capital and Counties plc v *Hampshire County Council* [1997] 2 All ER 865

In each of the three cases property damage to the claimant's property was found to be reasonably foreseeable as a result of the defendant's negligence. Two of the cases failed on proximity. In one (*John Monroe*) the allegation was that the fire brigade had failed to spot smouldering debris; in the second (*Church of Jesus Christ of Latter Day Saints*) it was that it had failed to maintain its hydrants. As the fire brigade is not obliged to answer an emergency call, if they do choose to answer it the same lack of proximity would bar the action. No duty is assumed to fight a fire with reasonable skill and care. In the third case (*Capital & Counties*) the allegation was that the fire brigade had turned off a sprinkler system and made the situation worse. On this fresh damage basis proximity was established.

See also Chapter 3.

The police

The police, on a similar basis, are not liable for failing to answer an emergency call (*Alexandrou* v *Oxford*) or, when answering it, for causing no more than the danger that was originally at stake. (Similar reasoning applies to the coastguard: *OLL* v *Secretary of State for Transport* [1997] 3 All ER 897.)

 ## Policy

See also Chapter 3 for policy and duty of care.

Whether a duty of care should be barred on policy grounds has troubled the courts. A distinction has been made between policy and operational decisions. In the former it would rarely be correct for a resource-allocating decision by a public authority to be challenged in a civil action for damages. In the latter it may be. The language used has now changed to decision making/implementation (*X* v *Bedfordshire County Council* [1995] 3 All ER 353) but the basic methodology is similar.

In the case of decision making, a stringent application of justiciability and public interest will be applied. A three-stage test is applied:

1 Whether the exercise of the statutory discretion in question would have involved policy considerations such as resource allocation, priority management, etc. If so, no action in negligence should lie on fundamental justiciability lines and usurping Parliament's authority.

2 Whether, exercising the (justiciable) statutory discretion, the public authority had done so in a way that took it outside the discretion Parliament was assumed to have conferred. To do so the court was to apply the *Wednesbury* unreasonableness test.

3 The court must then decide whether it was appropriate to impose a duty of care. This is the conventional third limb whereby it has to be fair, just and reasonable.

Policy and the emergency services

Assuming that a case has passed through the proximity barrier it may still fail on policy grounds. These may be on the justiciability issue, which was alluded to in *Hill* v *Chief Constable of West Yorkshire Police*, where Lord Keith felt that a court was not equipped to

See also Chapter 7.

judge the reasonableness of discretionary policing. (See also *Van Colle* v *Chief Constable of Hertfordshire Police*; *Smith* v *Chief Constable of Sussex Police*.)

There may also be general public interest factors which militate against a duty of care. These include a fear of defensive policing. (*Elguzouli-Daf* v *Commissioner of Police for the Metropolis* [1995] QB 355.) Similar fears were expressed in *Capital & Counties* with regard to the fire brigade, in that they might prioritise the protection of citizens with valuable property. The financial cost of actions, which takes money away from operations, is also raised.

None of these policy issues was found to bar a duty in the *Capital & Counties* case, which survived the proximity hurdle. The court applied a policy/operational test and concluded that it would be fair, just and reasonable to impose a duty.

Emergency services and immunity

In a number of the emergency services cases the court has concluded that the particular circumstances did give rise to broad public interest concerns and abandoned the policy/operational test in favour of a wholesale refusal to recognise a duty of care. (*Hill* v *Chief Constable of West Yorkshire Police*; *Osman* v *Ferguson* [1993] 4 All ER 344; *Alexandrou* v *Oxford* [1993] 4 All ER 328; *Ancell* v *McDermott* [1993] 4 All ER 355; *Hughes* v *National Union of Mineworkers* [1991] 4 All ER 355.) The important distinction here is that the policy/operational test balances the interests of claimant and defendant, whereas the immunity rationale subordinates the claimant's interests to a broader public interest inquiry. This may still result in a decision in the claimant's favour as in *Swinney* v *Chief Constable of Northumbria Police* [1997] QB 464, where the police were refused immunity. The public interest in granting the immunity was outweighed by the competing public interest in keeping an informant's information confidential. This decision, however, was unusual and may have been dictated by the approach of the Human Rights Act 1998. (See also *Van Colle* v *Chief Constable of Hertfordshire Police*; *Smith* v *Chief Constable of Sussex Police*.)

See also Chapters 6 and 7.

Human rights

Objective
3

See also Chapter 1
for human rights
and Chapter 3 for
Osman.

Osman v *United Kingdom* [1999] FLR 193

The European Court of Human Rights reviewed the Court of Appeal decision in *Osman*. It had been held that harm to the claimant was foreseeable and that there was proximity between the parties but that the public interest dictated that the police should not be liable for negligence in such situations. The decision was challenged on the basis that it violated an individual's right to a fair and public hearing under Article 6 of the Convention. The European Court held that the application of a generalised public interest ground for denying a duty of care amounted to a disproportionate restriction on the claimant's right of access to the courts. The Court of Appeal had failed to demonstrate that it had properly considered the scope and application of such immunity to the facts of the case by balancing out any competing public interest arguments.

The decision in *Osman* caused great difficulties to the English judiciary. (See *Barrett* v *Enfield London Borough Council* [1999] 3 All ER 193.) In essence, Article 6 was thought to confer procedural rights on a litigant rather than substantive legal rights such as whether a cause of action existed. It subsequently transpired that the European Court of Human Rights had misunderstood English tort law in *Osman*. They had failed to accept that a decision that the third limb of the test for duty of care is a part of substantive law. If a court decides that it would not be fair, just and reasonable to impose a duty of care this is different to having a procedural immunity which bars a litigant's access to the court in breach of Article 6. (*Z* v *UK* [2001] 2 FLR 612. See also *DP and another* v *United Kingdom* [2002] 3 FCR 385.)

The issues in these cases are complex and it could be argued that the decision in *Z* has settled the argument. However, it is impossible to ignore the effect that the Human Rights Act has had, and continues to have, on the fabric of substantive English tort law. The following case illustrates graphically the problems that the courts have when attempting to incorporate rights-based law into traditional English tort principles. You must remember that a claimant can now claim damages for a breach of a Convention right by a public authority as well as or in the alternative to tort damages. Even if a court determines that there is no duty of care, the claimant may still be able to sue for breach of a Convention right.

D v *East Berkshire Community Health NHS Trust*; *K and another* v *Dewsbury Healthcare NHS Trust*; *K and another* v *Oldham NHS Trust* [2003] 4 All ER 796 (CA); [2005] 2 All ER 443 (HL)

Each of three appeals before the court involved accusations of abusing a child made against a parent by the professionals concerned for the welfare of that child. All the accusations proved to be unfounded. In each case a parent claimed damages from an NHS trust for psychiatric harm alleged to have been caused by the false accusations or their consequences and in the second case, where the local authority was also a defendant, the child also claimed. The events all took place before the Human Rights Act 1998 came into force. In each case the primary case was advanced in negligence, and preliminary issues were tried, including whether any duty of care was owed to the claimant or claimants. It was common ground that the test to be applied was whether it was 'fair, just and reasonable' to impose such a duty. In each case the court of first instance held that no duty was owed to the parents, applying the principles contained in *X* that a common law duty of care could not be imposed upon a statutory duty as the observance of the common law duty of care would be inconsistent with, or have a tendency to discourage, the due performance by a local authority of its statutory duties. The claimants appealed to the Court of Appeal. The Convention rights considered included Article 3 (Article 3 provides: 'No one shall be subjected to torture or to inhuman or degrading treatment or punishment'), prohibiting torture and inhuman or degrading treatment, and Article 8 (Article 8, provides: 'Everyone has the right to respect for his private and family life, his home and correspondence . . .'), providing the right to respect for private and family life.

The Court of Appeal held:

(1) No violation of Article 6 of the Convention was involved in the procedure of determining, by way of preliminary issues, whether the test of what was 'fair, just and reasonable', applied with the required respect for case precedent, precluded the existence of a duty of care.

(2) The effect of *X* in each of the instant appeals was now restricted to the proposition that decisions by local authorities whether or not to take a child into care were not reviewable by way of a claim in negligence.

(3) The effect of the 1998 Act was that it was no longer legitimate to rule that, as a matter of law, no common duty of care was owed to a child in relation to the investigation of child abuse and the initiation and pursuit of care proceedings. Given the obligation of a local authority to respect a child's Convention rights, the recognition of a duty of care to the child on the part of those involved should not have a significantly adverse effect on the manner in which they performed their duties. In the context of suspected child abuse, breach of a duty of care in negligence would frequently also amount to a violation of Articles 3 or 8 of the Convention, although those asserting that wrongful acts or omissions occurred before the 1998 Act came into force would have no claim under that Act. The common law duty of care did not replicate the duty not to violate Articles 3 and 8. Liability for breach of that duty and entitlement to compensation could arise in circumstances where the tort of negligence was not made out. However, there were cogent reasons of public policy for concluding that, where consideration was being given to whether the suspicion of child abuse justified taking proceedings to remove a child from the parents, while a duty of care could be owed to the child, no common law duty of care was owed to the parents.

(4) In the instant appeals a concurrent duty imposed in respect of the parent would conflict with the duties owed to the child. However, in the second appeal, the judge had erred in finding that witness immunity precluded any liability on the part of those employed by the local authority.

The parents appealed to the House of Lords contending that the duty of health professionals to exercise due professional skill and care was owed to a child's primary carers, usually parents, as well as to the child himself or herself, and that there was no good policy reason to deny the existence of such a duty, which was the same duty as that owed to the child.

Held (Lord Bingham dissenting): Where the relationship between doctor and parent was confined to the fact that the parent was father or mother of the doctor's patient, the appropriate level of protection for a parent suspected of abusing his or her child was that clinical and other investigations had to be conducted in good faith. There were cogent reasons of public policy for holding that no common law duty of care should be owed to the parent and it was not fair, just and reasonable to impose such a duty. The seriousness of child abuse as a social problem demanded that health professionals, acting in good faith in what they believed were the best interests of the child, should not be subject to potentially conflicting duties when deciding whether a child might have been abused, or when deciding whether their doubts should be communicated to others, or when deciding what further investigatory or protective steps should be taken. The suggested duty owed to parents did not have the same content as the duty owed to the child, which was to exercise due skill and care in investigating the possibility of abuse. At the time when the doctor was considering the possibility of abuse by the parent, the interests of parent and child were diametrically opposed. There might, exceptionally, be circumstances where the general rule did not apply. In the instant cases there were no such special circumstances, and, accordingly, the appeals would be dismissed.

The very significant effect of this case is that children are now owed a duty of care in negligence by local authorities when they are investigating child abuse and making decisions as to whether or not to take a child into care. No duty other than one to carry out investigations in good faith is owed to the parent/carer as this would raise a conflict of interest in the circumstances of these cases.

A similar argument on conflict of interests led the House of Lords to deny a duty of care where a health authority closed down a residential home, acting under statutory powers. A claim was brought by the owners for economic loss suffered as a result of the closure. However, it was held that there was no duty as the legislation was passed to protect residents in such homes and a duty owed to avoid economic loss to the owners would conflict with this purpose.

Lord Scott stated:

> where action is taken by a state authority under statutory powers designed for the benefit or protection of a particular class of persons, a tortuous duty of care will not be held to be owed by the state authority to others whose interests may be adversely affected by an exercise of the state power.

Trent Strategic Health Authority v Jain [2009] UKHL 4

The Human Rights Act 1998 was not in force at the time of the relevant facts in this case but Lord Hope was of the opinion that damages would have been available under Article 1 of the First Protocol (peaceful enjoyment of possessions). Lord Scott and Baroness Hale were of the opinion that the procedure in the relevant legislation which allowed defective without notice closure applications to be granted *ex parte* without any mechanism to protect owners would be incompatible with Article 6 (the right to a fair hearing).

Liability of the police

The discussion on duty of care in Chapter 3 and the above discussion on the problems in imposing liability on public authorities has created a substantial area of litigation involving the police service. Many of the concepts regarding duty of care by public authorities are raised in the following discussion of the case law.

This area provides an interesting aspect to some of the developments in negligence and the impact of human rights legislation. The issue is whether the police should be exposed to litigation if they are judged to have been negligent in their investigation of a crime and a person has suffered damage as a result. The traditional approach of the English courts has been to refuse an action, either on policy grounds or because there is no proximity between the injured person and the police. The implementation of the Human Rights Act 1998 means that there is now a direct action under the legislation against the police if they are found to be in breach of one of the relevant articles. Such an action might be brought by the estate or dependants of a person who has died as a result of an alleged breach by the police of Article 2 (the right to life).

Hill v Chief Constable of West Yorkshire [1988] 2 All ER 238

The mother of the last victim of the Yorkshire Ripper alleged that the police had failed to use reasonable care in apprehending the murderer of her daughter. She claimed that had they done so the murderer would have been arrested before her daughter was killed. The question for the House of Lords was whether she was owed a duty of care by the police. Her case was held to disclose no cause of action. The policy reason was that a contrary decision might lead to police discretion being limited and exercised in a defensive frame of mind. The immunity only applies where the police fail to prevent a third party from causing damage. It does not appear to apply where the police themselves negligently cause damage.

Lord Keith stated:

> It has been said almost too frequently to require repetition that foreseeability of likely harm is not in itself a sufficient test of liability in negligence. Some further ingredient is invariably needed to establish the requisite proximity of relationship between the plaintiff and defendant, and all the circumstances of the case must be carefully considered and analysed in order to ascertain whether such an ingredient is present. The nature of the ingredient will be found to vary in a number of different categories of decided cases.
>
> It is plain that vital characteristics which were present in the *Dorset Yacht* case and which led to the imposition of liability are here lacking. Sutcliffe was never in the custody of the police force. Miss Hill was one of a vast number of the female general public who might be at risk from his activities but was at no special distinctive risk in relation to them, unlike the owners of yachts moored off Brownsea Island in relation to the foreseeable conduct of the borstal boys. It appears from the . . . speech of Lord Diplock in the *Dorset Yacht* case that in his view no liability would rest on a prison authority, which carelessly allowed the escape of an habitual criminal, for damage which he subsequently caused, not in the course of attempting to make good his getaway, to persons at special risk, but in further pursuance of his general criminal career to the person or property of members of the general public. The same rule must apply as regards failure to recapture the criminal before he had time to resume his career. In the case of an escaped criminal his identity and description are known. In the instant case the identity of the wanted criminal was at the material time unknown and it is not averred that any full or clear description of him was ever available. The alleged negligence of the police consists in a failure to discover his identity. But, if there is no general duty of care owed to individual members of the public by the responsible authorities to prevent the escape of a known criminal or to recapture him, there cannot reasonably be imposed on any police force a duty of care similarly owed to identify and apprehend an unknown one. Miss Hill cannot for this purpose be regarded as a person at special risk simply because she was young and female. Where the class of potential victims of a particular habitual criminal is a large one the precise size of it cannot in principle affect the issue. All householders are potential victims of a habitual burglar, and all females those of a habitual rapist. The conclusion must be that, although there existed reasonable foreseeability of likely harm to such as Miss Hill if Sutcliffe were not identified and apprehended, there is absent from the case any such ingredient or characteristic as led to the liability of the Home Office in the *Dorset Yacht* case. Nor is there present any additional characteristic such as might make up the deficiency. The circumstances of the case are therefore not capable of establishing a duty of care owed towards Miss Hill by the West Yorkshire police.
>
> That is sufficient for the disposal of the appeal. But in my opinion there is another reason why an action for damages in negligence should not lie against the police in circumstances such as those of the present case, and that is public policy . . . I consider that . . . the police were immune from an action of this kind on grounds similar to those which in *Rondel v Worsley* were held to render a barrister immune from actions for negligence in his conduct of proceedings in court.

Note that Lord Keith approaches the case from the point of view of proximity. The reason that the action failed was that there was no proximate relationship between the deceased and the police. The deceased was simply one of a large class who were at risk. His public policy point was to be used by the courts in later cases to deny liability on a blanket basis even where there was a specific relationship between the police and the victim. Such was the case in *Osman v Ferguson* [1993] 4 All ER 344, where the claim was struck out on public policy grounds. The decision in Strasbourg in *Osman* instigated a change of approach by

English courts as they moved towards weighing the public policy interests of claimant and defendant.

Swinney v Chief Constable of Northumberland [1997] QB 464

Numerous named references to a police informer in documentation that the police had agreed to keep confidential meant that the police had undertaken to take specific care to that person in those circumstances. The claimant was therefore able to rely on that undertaking and sue the police in negligence when they carelessly failed to prevent the documentation falling into the hands of the very person that the claimant had informed on. (On the facts it was held that the police were not in breach of duty (1999) 11 Admin LR 811.) (See also **Costello v Chief Constable of Northumbria Police** [1999] 1 All ER 550 – just as a police officer could assume a duty to a member of the public, so they could assume a duty to a fellow officer.)

The courts then moved away from using policy as a device to prevent cases proceeding, to a weighing of individual cases using the concepts of assumption of responsibility and specific reliance. However, the problem faced by a claimant against the police is that, in the absence of an assumption of responsibility by the police to a particular person, no duty of care is owed by the police to the public to protect them from criminal offences. (*Alexandrou v Oxford* [1993] 4 All ER 328. Although in *Kent v Griffiths* the Court of Appeal said that this case should be confined to its own particular facts.)

In the case of one police officer suing another for failing to assist, the issue is similar to that of employer's liability, where the Chief Constable (employer) owes a non-delegable duty to devise a safe system of work. If a police officer is injured as a result of the negligence of another officer in implementing the system then the Chief Constable can be liable. He may also be liable on the basis of vicarious liability where one officer has assumed responsibility to another, for example, by an officer who has been given the task failing to respond to calls for assistance on the radio. (*Mullaney v Chief Constable of West Midlands Police* [2001] All ER (D) 191 (May).)

See Chapter 14 for employer's liability.

Where a member of the public suffers damage they will have to prove that the police specifically assumed responsibility to them. The fact that the police turn up at the scene of a crime does not mean that they have 'assumed responsibility'. (See *Swinney*.)

The difficulties faced by a claimant in negligence against the police are illustrated by the following case, where the decision in *Hill* was challenged in the House of Lords.

Brooks v Metropolitan Police Commissioner [2005] 2 All ER 489

The claimant, a friend of Stephen Lawrence, was present when a racist and fatal attack took place in April 1993 and was himself abused and attacked. Following the findings of the Macpherson Inquiry that the police investigation was badly conducted and that the claimant was not treated as he should have been, the claimant issued proceedings against the Commissioner in April 1999 alleging negligence and seeking damages for psychiatric injury. The House of Lords, whilst reluctant to endorse the full breadth of the decision in *Hill's* case, concluded that the decision had been correct on its own facts. The facts which arose in the *Brooks* appeal had already been exhaustively investigated in the course of the inquiry, so as to render any further exploration of the facts unlikely to reveal anything new and of assistance to the claimant in establishing that a duty of care had been owed to him and had been broken. In any event, the duties alleged by the claimant, namely failing to take reasonable steps to assess whether he was a victim of crime, to afford him the protection, assistance and support commonly afforded to a key eye-witness of a serious crime, and to afford reasonable weight

> to his account of events and act upon it, were duties which could not even arguably be imposed on police officers charged in the public interest with the investigation of a very serious crime and the apprehension of those responsible. No modification of the ratio in *Hill's* case would accommodate the duties alleged in this case, which were inextricably bound up with the police function of investigating crime and therefore could not survive. The claim had rightly been struck out and the appeal was allowed.

Faced with these difficulties of suing the police in negligence, claimants have now started to utilise the Human Rights Act, invoking Article 2, the right to life. The next case is discussed at some length, as it introduces Strasbourg principles into the debate and in the final appeal to the House of Lords was heard jointly with a case pleaded on traditional common law principles.

Van Colle v *Chief Constable of the Hertfordshire Police* [2006] EWHC 360 (QB); [2007] 3 All ER 122 (CA); [2008] UKHL 50; *Smith* v *Chief Constable of Sussex Police* [2008] UKHL 50

In *Van Colle* a prosecution witness in a criminal case (*G*) was shot dead by a person charged with the offence (*B*). The police had failed to protect the witness. The witness's estate and family brought proceedings under the human rights legislation. The question was whether a police officer was under a duty to take preventive, protective measures in relation to the witness and whether the police officer breached the duty and acted incompatibly with the witness's right to life.

At first instance the judge held that the police should have taken action to protect *G* and should have known that there was a real risk to his life and that the risk was and would remain immediate until the date of *B*'s trial. The judge also ruled that where it was the conduct of the state authorities which had itself exposed an individual to the risk to his life, including, for example, where the individual was in a special category of vulnerable persons, or of persons required by the state to perform certain duties on its behalf which might expose them to risk, and who was therefore entitled to expect a reasonable level of protection as a result, the threshold expounded in the Strasbourg authorities of a real and immediate risk in such circumstances was too high. The Court of Appeal approved the judge's statement of principle. The issue which arose on appeal to the House of Lords was whether a lower test was appropriate than that set out in Strasbourg jurisprudence as to the obligation of the state in respect of *G*'s rights, in the light of his status as a witness.

Held (House of Lords): In accordance with Strasbourg jurisprudence, Article 2 might, in certain well-defined circumstances, imply a positive obligation on national authorities to take preventative measures to protect an individual whose life was at risk from the criminal acts of another. It had to be established to the court's satisfaction that the authorities had known or should have known at the time of the existence of a *real and immediate risk to life* of an identified individual or individuals from the criminal acts of a third party and that they had failed to take measures within the scope of their powers which, judged reasonably, might have been expected to avoid that risk. The test formulated by the Strasbourg court was clear and called for no judicial exegesis. It was sufficient for an applicant to show that the authorities had not done all that could *reasonably be expected* of them to avoid a real and immediate risk to life of which they had or should have had knowledge. The Strasbourg court had propounded one test. The standard was constant and not variable with the type of act in contemplation. The critical question was one which could only be answered in the light of all the circumstances of any particular case.

Where, as in the instant case, a tragic killing had occurred, it was all too easy to interpret the events which had preceded it in the light of that knowledge and not as they had appeared at the time. However, the application of the test depended not only on what the authorities had known, but also on what they should have known. Stupidity, lack of imagination and inertia did not afford an excuse to a national authority which reasonably should, in the light of what it had known or had been told, have made further enquiries or investigations. It was then to be treated as knowing what such further enquiries or investigations would have elicited.

In the instant case, the central question to be asked was whether the relevant officer, making a reasonable and informed judgement on the facts and in the circumstances known to him at the time, had appreciated that there was a real and immediate risk to the life of G. If he should, there was a breach of Article 2, since he had not taken appropriate steps to avert the risk. The judge and the Court of Appeal had erred in law by attaching undue significance to G's status as a witness and by treating the relevant test as lowered on that account. The fact that G was a witness in a forthcoming Crown Court trial was of course a relevant fact, but, in all the circumstances, not one of great weight, having regard to the minor character of the charges and the unlikelihood of a severe penalty. The test set out in the Strasbourg case law had not been met in the instant case. Judgment would be entered for the defendant.

In *Smith*, the claimant informed the police of threats to kill made against him by his estranged partner, J. He made numerous complaints and gave details of the threats made against him. J subsequently attacked him with a claw hammer, causing him serious and lasting injuries. J was arrested and was convicted of making threats to kill and causing grievous bodily harm with intent. The claimant brought a claim in negligence against the defendant Chief Constable. That claim was struck out by the judge as having no real prospect of success on the grounds that, first, the claimant's position vis-à-vis the police was that of a member of the public and not one calling for special protective measures; and that, secondly, in a situation such as the instant case, public policy was against imposing a duty of care on the police. The claimant appealed to the Court of Appeal, which found that, if the pleaded facts were established, the defendant owed the claimant a duty of care.

Held (House of Lords): There should be no retreat from the core principle that an action for damages for negligence should not lie against the police, on the ground of public policy. The positive obligations under the Convention did not justify an extension of the core principle but, rather, the alternative remedy available to claimants under the 1998 Act, applying Strasbourg jurisprudence, should sit side by side with the common law rules on liability and remedies.

If a liability principle were to be adopted, albeit confined to cases where a member of the public had furnished apparently credible evidence to the police that a third party re-presented a specific and imminent threat to his life or physical safety, that would lead to uncertainty in its application and to the detrimental effects warned against in previous authority. The balance of advantage lay in preserving the core principle in the interests of the wider community. The core principle under common law did not need to be reconsidered in the light of the Strasbourg authority as to the obligations of the state in relation to right to life under Article 2. In cases brought under ss 6 and 7 of the 1998 Act, where the Article 2 positive obligation was said to have been breached by a public authority, the relevant principle was that described in the Strasbourg case law. However, the common law, with its own system of limitation periods and remedies, should be permitted to stand on its own feet, side by side with the alternative remedy. As stated in previous authorities, a retreat from the core principle would have detrimental effects for law enforcement. Whilst focusing on investigating crime, and the arrest of suspects, police officers would, in practice, be required to ensure that in every contact with a potential witness or a potential victim time and resources were deployed to avoid the risk of causing harm or offence. Such legal duties would tend to inhibit a robust approach in assessing a person as a possible suspect, witness or victim. By placing general duties of care on the police to victims and witnesses police's ability to perform their public functions in the interests of the community, fearlessly and with despatch, would be impeded. It was clear from that authority that that principle was of public policy, to be applied generally. The principle had to be enunciated in the interests of the whole community. Replacing it with a legal principle which focused on the facts of each case would amount to a retreat from the core principle. Care should be taken not to allow the shortcomings of

> the police in individual cases to undermine that principle. A principle of public policy that applied generally might be seen to operate harshly in some cases, when they were judged by ordinary delictual principles; however, the greater public good outweighed any individual hardship. Appeal allowed. (Lord Brandon dissenting.)

These decisions illustrate the real difficulties that a claimant has in suing the police for negligence in a case where they claim that the police have failed to protect them from criminal activity after the police have been alerted to a specific danger. The House of Lords stresses the public policy aspects of denying an action against the police.

Reference is made to the 'core principle' in **Hill**. This is set out by Lord Steyn in **Brooks**:

> But the core principle of **Hill's** case has remained unchallenged in our domestic jurisprudence and in European jurisprudence for many years. If a case such as the Yorkshire Ripper case, which was before the House in **Hill's** case, arose for decision today I have no doubt that it would be decided in the same way. It is, of course, desirable that police officers should treat victims and witnesses properly and with respect: . . . But to convert that ethical value into general legal duties of care on the police towards victims and witnesses would be going too far. The prime function of the police is the preservation of the Queen's peace. The police must concentrate on preventing the commission of crime; protecting life and property; and apprehending criminals and preserving evidence: . . . A retreat from the principle in **Hill's** case would have detrimental effects for law enforcement. Whilst focusing on investigating crime, and the arrest of suspects, police officers would in practice be required to ensure that in every contact with a potential witness or a potential victim time and resources were deployed to avoid the risk of causing harm or offence. Such legal duties would tend to inhibit a robust approach in assessing a person as a possible suspect, witness or victim. By placing general duties of care on the police to victims and witnesses the police's ability to perform their public functions in the interests of the community, fearlessly and with despatch, would be impeded. It would, as was recognised in **Hill's** case, be bound to lead to an unduly defensive approach in combating crime.

Lord Brandon in his dissent in **Smith** applied a 'liability' principle. If a member of the public (*A*) furnishes a police officer (*B*) with apparently credible evidence that a third party whose identity and whereabouts are known presents a specific and imminent threat to his life or physical safety, *B* owes *A* a duty to take reasonable steps to assess such threat and, if appropriate, take reasonable steps to prevent it being executed. His Lordship gave the examples of the cases of **Osman** and **OLL** as cases where there should be a remedy. The remainder of the House of Lords disagreed and there now appears to be a rule of no liability in these circumstances.

In **Van Colle** the claimant relied on the right to life in Article 2. The **Osman** case was also litigated on this article (although it succeeded on Article 6).

Article 2 of the European Convention provides:

> Everyone's right to life shall be protected by law. No one shall be deprived of his life intentionally . . .

This provision enjoins each member state not only to refrain from the intentional and unlawful taking of life ('Thou shalt not kill') but also to take appropriate steps to safeguard the lives of those within its jurisdiction. The state's duty in this respect includes, but extends beyond, its primary duty to secure the right to life by putting in place effective criminal law provisions to deter the commission of offences against the person backed up by law enforcement machinery for the prevention, suppression and sanctioning of breaches of such provisions. Article 2 may also, 'in certain well-defined circumstances', imply a positive obligation on national authorities to take preventative measures to protect an individual whose life is at risk from the criminal acts of another. The scope of this last obligation was the subject of dispute in *Osman*.

In *Osman*, the court defined the circumstances in which the obligation arises:

> . . . it must be established to [the court's] satisfaction that the authorities knew or ought to have known at the time of the existence of a real and immediate risk to the life of an identified individual or individuals from the criminal acts of a third party and that they failed to take measures within the scope of their powers which, judged reasonably, might have been expected to avoid that risk.

This was the question at the heart of the *Van Colle* appeal and the House of Lords felt that on the facts there was no real and immediate risk. The trial judge had applied a lower threshold on the basis that the deceased was a witness but the House of Lords rejected this distinction.

What is the relationship between the common law action and the Convention action?

Lord Brandon:

> Considerable argument was devoted to exploration of the relationship between rights arising under the Convention (in particular, the Article 2 right relied on in *Van Colle*) and rights and duties arising at common law. Should these two regimes remain entirely separate, or should the common law be developed to absorb Convention rights? I do not think that there is a simple, universally applicable answer. It seems to me clear, on the one hand, that the existence of a Convention right cannot call for instant manufacture of a corresponding common law right where none exists: see *Wainwright* v *Home Office* [2003] 4 All ER 969. On the other hand, one would ordinarily be surprised if conduct which violated a fundamental right or freedom of the individual did not find a reflection in a body of law ordinarily as sensitive to human needs as the common law, and it is demonstrable that the common law in some areas has evolved in a direction signalled by the Convention: see the judgment of the Court of Appeal in *D* v *East Berkshire Community NHS Trust* [2003] 4 All ER 796. There are likely to be persisting differences between the two regimes, in relation (for example) to limitation periods and, probably, compensation. But I agree with Pill LJ in the present case that 'there is a strong case for developing the common law action for negligence in the light of Convention rights' and also with Rimer LJ that 'where a common law duty covers the same ground as a Convention right, it should, so far as practicable, develop in harmony with it'.

It therefore remains extremely difficult to bring an action for negligence against the police. The obstacles raised by the courts are substantial. The most promising routes remain undertaking and reliance on the common law route – as in *Swinney* – or if the claimant can satisfy the *real and substantial danger* test they can take the human rights route.

The 'education' cases

Objective
4

For breach of statutory duty and this aspect of the cases, see Chapter 13.

These cases are described as 'education' for shorthand purposes but cover the social work functions of local authorities as well. The principles are similar.

The cases follow broadly the same principles as those in the emergency services cases. The same problems are raised by omissions and statutory powers and cases must pass through the filter of an exception to the omissions rule based on undertaking and reliance. The claimant must also establish proximity and pass the three-part test on policy. The cases raise issues of liability for breach of statutory duty which is a separate tort with its own rules.

X (minors) v Bedfordshire County Council [1995] 3 All ER 353

This was the lead case in a series of cases which tackled the question of the liability in negligence of professionals who are responsible for taking decisions in relation to children. The central issues are whether there is an action when a child is wrongly removed from the family following negligent advice and whether there is an action if the child is not removed.

M (a minor) v Newham London Borough Council; X (minors) v Bedfordshire County Council [1995] 3 All ER 353

In the first case a child gave the first name of an abuser in an interview with a psychiatrist and a social worker. They wrongly assumed that this was the partner of the child's mother who had the same name. It was in fact the child's cousin. The child was then removed from the mother after the local authority applied for a place of safety order. The child was then made a ward of court and placed in the care of the local authority. The mother later saw a transcript of the interview and realised the mistake. The child was then returned to the mother. The child and the mother then made a claim for anxiety neurosis caused by negligence and/or breach of statutory authority.

In the second case various reports were made that the claimant children were at risk. Nothing was done for a period of years until 1992 when an order was sought by the local authority. The children then sued the local authority claiming that the local authority had failed to have due regard to their welfare as required by the Children Act 1989 and it should have acted more quickly and effectively, and this failure had caused them to suffer ill treatment, illness and impaired their health and development.

E v Dorset County Council; M v Hampshire County Council [1995] 3 All ER 353

In the first action E sued the local authority for breach of statutory duty on the ground that they had failed to diagnose a learning disability which required special provision.

E was sent to a special school at his parents' expense. A claim for common law negligence was also made as the local authority was alleged to have failed to diagnose or make proper provision for his condition.

In the second case, M sued as the headteacher had failed to refer him for assessment of his learning difficulties which were consistent with dyslexia.

House of Lords decision

1   Private law claims against public authorities for damages could be divided into four categories:
    (a) actions for breach of statutory authority;
    (b) actions based solely on the careless performance of a statutory duty in the absence of any other common law right of action;
    (c) actions based on the common law duty arising either from the imposition of the statutory duty or from the performance of it; and
    (d) misfeasance in public office.

2   In actions under (a) the breach of the statutory duty itself was not enough to give rise to any private law cause of action. (Standard rules on whether breach of the statute gives rise to an action for damages.)

3   The mere assertion of the careless exercise of a statutory power or duty (b) was not sufficient in itself to give rise to a private law cause of action. The claimant also has to show that the circumstances were such as to raise a duty of care at common law. The decision whether or not to exercise the discretion had to be distinguished from the manner in which the statutory duty was implemented in practice.

Nothing the authority did within the ambit of the discretion could be actionable at common law and the taking of decisions involving policy matters was non-justiciable. If the claim was justiciable – i.e. if the decision was so unreasonable that it fell outside the ambit of the discretion – then any action would turn on the ordinary principles of negligence.

4   In the abuse cases the claims based on (a) had been rightly struck out. The purpose of the legislation was to establish an administrative system designed to promote the social welfare of the community and this purpose was inconsistent with a private right of action against those responsible for carrying out the difficult functions under the legislation.

5   In the education cases the claims based on breach of statutory duty had also been rightly struck out as the legislation did not impose any obligation on the authority to accept a child for education in one of its schools.

6   In respect of the claims for breach of duty of care in both the abuse and education cases, assuming that the relevant authority's duty did not involve non-justiciable issues it would not be just and reasonable to impose a duty of care. Courts should be extremely reluctant to impose a duty of care in the exercise of discretionary powers conferred by Parliament for social welfare purposes.

In the abuse cases a common law duty of care would be contrary to the whole statutory system set up for the protection of children at risk. This involved many other agencies and persons connected with the child and would impinge on the delicate nature of the decisions which had to be made in child abuse cases.

7   In education cases administrative failures were best dealt with by the statutory appeals procedure.

In the education cases a local authority was under a duty of care to those using the service to exercise care in its conduct to those using the service. Educational psychologists and other members of staff of an education authority owed a duty of care in the assessment and determination of a child's educational needs and the authority was vicariously liable for any breach of such duties by their employees.

8   The claimants in abuse cases had no private law claim for damages.

In the education cases the authorities were under no liability at common law for the exercise of their statutory discretions but could be liable both directly and vicariously for negligent advice given by their employees.

None of the cases was an implementation case. The nub of the carelessness allegations in each case related to decision making. Lord Browne-Wilkinson refused to recognise a duty of care in the child care cases on the grounds that it would not be fair, just and reasonable to do so. (Statutory framework.) A similar analysis was applied to the education cases relating to careless assessment and placement of children. However, the failure to refer for advice from educational psychiatrists (*Dorset*) and the allegation relating to inadequate advice provided by the headmaster (*Hampshire*) were allowed to proceed on the grounds that the conduct in question was sufficiently distinct from the underlying statutory scheme (this was later admitted to be wrong in *Phelps*, below) and the advice in question would be provided by the educational psychiatrist and headmaster direct to the claimants. As such, it could be assumed that the local authority had assumed responsibility to the claimants.

This decision set the tone for actions against a local authority. Child abuse cases would be routinely struck out on the basis of *X* as there would be no case to answer. However, the implementation of the Human Rights Act changed the approach in these cases, culminating in the decision in *D* v *East Berkshire Community Health NHS Trust* (see above) that a duty of care was owed to children in the abuse cases and that the policy reasons given in *X* for denying a duty were no longer applicable.

A considerable amount of litigation was, however, generated in the education cases in the context of liability for special needs assessments. The European Court of Human Rights decision in *Osman* (see above) cast doubt on the legality of striking out the child abuse cases and the House of Lords had to consider *X* in the light of *Osman* in the following case.

Barrett v *Enfield London Borough Council* [1999] 3 All ER 193

The claimant was aged ten months when a care order was made in favour of the defendant local authority and he remained in care until he was 17. The claimant claimed damages for personal injuries, alleging that the defendant was in breach of its duty to act as a parent and to show the standard of care that was required of a responsible parent. A number of factual allegations were made to support the claim.

The defendant applied to strike out the claim on the grounds that it disclosed no cause of action. This was refused by the district judge but upheld by the judge and the claimant appealed to the Court of Appeal, which upheld the judge, and the claimant appealed to the House of Lords.

The House of Lords allowed the appeal against striking out. Cases should only be struck out where it was *certain* that the claim would not succeed and was inappropriate for cases where the law was uncertain and developing, such as in this area. Such developments should be on the basis of actual facts found at trial and not on hypothetical (possibly wrong) facts assumed to be true for the purpose of the strike out. Lord Browne-Wilkinson gave an example of this concern when he observed that a flood of litigation had been prompted by his dicta in *X* v *Bedfordshire*, to the effect that the court's general reluctance to impose a duty of care on a local authority might be less marked in potential actions against educational psychologists. In *Barrett*, his Lordship noted that the critical assumption of fact upon which his dicta in *X* rested actually turned out to be incorrect. This case, however, was different from *X*, as there the question was whether the decision to take a child into care was actionable in negligence, whereas here the child had been taken into care.

Lord Slynn was of the opinion that *X* did not conclude the case and that it was arguable that a duty of care was owed and was broken. On this basis causation came into play and Lord Slynn differed from the Court of Appeal who thought causation could not be established as the claimant would not be able to show that operational acts, even if negligently performed, either separately or cumulatively, caused the condition of which the claimant complained. Lord Slynn, however, stated that causation was largely a question of fact.

Further indications of the courts' reluctance to impose liability on public authorities based on a blanket policy immunity came in:

W v *Essex County Council* [1998] 3 All ER 111 (CA); [2000] 2 All ER 237 (HL)

For psychiatric damage generally see Chapter 4.

A 15-year-old boy, a known sexual abuser, was placed with a foster family without their being informed of his full history. The children of the family were sexually abused. The Court of Appeal struck out the parents' claim as it would not be just and reasonable on policy grounds to impose a duty as it would cut across the statutory arrangements for the fostering of children in care.

> However, the House of Lords refused to strike out the parents' claim for psychiatric damage allegedly suffered as a result of feeling responsible for their children's sexual abuse. It was at least arguable that the parents had a claim.

It is also now clear that a local authority is vicariously liable for the negligence of educational psychiatrists who negligently fail to diagnose learning difficulties such as dyslexia.

The following case is dealt with at some length but is crucial in understanding the changes that have taken place in this area.

Phelps v *Hillingdon Borough Council* [2000] 4 All ER 504

The claimant in the first case, who was born in 1973, was in 1985 referred by her school to the defendant local education authority's school psychological service. An educational psychologist employed by the authority reported that testing had revealed no specific weaknesses. Shortly before the claimant left school she was privately diagnosed as dyslexic. She brought an action against the authority claiming that they were vicariously liable for the psychologist's negligent assessment. The judge held that the psychologist had owed a duty of care to the claimant, that the adverse consequences of the claimant's dyslexia could have been mitigated by early diagnosis and appropriate treatment or educational provision and that, accordingly, the psychologist's negligence had caused the damage in respect of which the claimant's claim was made. He awarded her damages.

The applicant in the second case, born in 1979, was privately diagnosed in 1988 as being severely dyslexic. She contended that her severe speech and language problems had not been investigated adequately or at all by the defendant local education authority and that as a result of failure to make suitable educational provision for her she had developed, and suffered from, psychological problems.

The claimant in the third case suffered from muscular dystrophy. He was provided with a statement of special educational needs pursuant to the Education Act 1981 emphasising the need for him to have access to a computer and to be trained in its use. He contended that negligently and in breach of duty the defendant local education authority had failed to provide a proper education for him, in particular computer technology and suitable training to enable him to communicate and cope educationally and socially, and that as a result he had suffered damage in the form of lack of educational progress, social deprivation and psychiatric injury consisting of clinical depression.

The claimant in the fourth case was born in 1979. He had severe learning difficulties and his special educational needs were assessed under the 1981 Act. An educational psychologist's report did not refer to dyslexia. His mother felt that he should be placed in a unit specialising in dyslexia, but he was placed elsewhere. He issued a writ alleging, *inter alia*, negligence and breach of duty both by the psychologists for whom the local education authority was vicariously liable and by the authority itself for failing to provide competent advice through its educational psychology service.

The House of Lords considered these cases in the context of whether they should have been struck out or not as there was no cause of action disclosed.

Lord Slynn:

> It does not follow that the local authority can never be liable in common law negligence for damage resulting from acts done in the course of the performance of a statutory duty by the authority or by its servants or agents. This House decided in *Barrett* v *Enfield London Borough Council* [1993] 3 WLR 79 that the fact that acts which are claimed to be negligent are carried out within the ambit of a statutory discretion is not in itself a reason why it should be held that no claim for negligence can be brought in respect of them. It is only where what is done has involved the weighing of competing public interests or has been dictated by considerations on which Parliament could not have intended that the courts would substitute their views for the views of ministers or officials that the courts will hold that the issue is non-justiciable on the ground that the decision was made in the exercise of a statutory

discretion. In Pamela's case there is no such ground for holding that her claim is non-justiciable and therefore the question to be determined is whether the damage relied on is foreseeable and proximate and whether it is just and reasonable to recognise a duty of care: *Caparo Industries plc v Dickman* [1990]. If a duty of care would exist where advice was given other than pursuant to the exercise of statutory powers, such duty of care is not excluded because the advice is given pursuant to the exercise of statutory powers. This is particularly important where other remedies laid down by the statute (e.g. an appeals review procedure) do not in themselves provide sufficient redress for loss which has already been caused.

Where, as in Pamela's case, a person is employed by a local education authority to carry out professional services as part of the fulfilment of the authority's statutory duty, it has to be asked whether there is any overriding reason in principle why (a) that person should not owe a duty of care (the first question) and (b) why, if the duty of care is broken by that person, the authority as employer or principal should not be vicariously liable (the second question).

I accept that, as was said in *X (Minors) v Bedfordshire County Council* [1995], there may be cases where to recognise such a vicarious liability on the part of the authority may so interfere with the performance of the local education authority's duties that it would be wrong to recognise any liability on the part of the authority. It must, however, be for the local authority to establish that: it is not to be presumed and I anticipate that the circumstances where it could be established would be exceptional.

As to the first question, it is long and well-established, now elementary, that persons exercising a particular skill or profession may owe a duty of care in the performance to people who it can be foreseen will be injured if due skill and care are not exercised, and if injury or damage can be shown to have been caused by the lack of care. Such duty does not depend on the existence of any contractual relationship between the person causing and the person suffering the damage. A doctor, an accountant and an engineer are plainly such a person. So in my view is an educational psychologist or psychiatrist and a teacher including a teacher in a specialised area, such as a teacher concerned with children having special educational needs. So may be an education officer performing the functions of a local education authority in regard to children with special educational needs. There is no more justification for a blanket immunity in their cases than there was in *Capital & Counties plc v Hampshire County Council* [1997].

I fully agree with what was said by Lord Browne-Wilkinson in the *X (Minors) case* [1995] that a head teacher owes 'a duty of care to exercise the reasonable skills of a headmaster in relation to such [*sic* a child's] educational needs' and a special advisory teacher brought in to advise on the educational needs of a specific pupil, particularly if he knows that his advice will be communicated to the pupil's parents, 'owes a duty to the child to exercise the skill and care of a reasonable advisory teacher'. A similar duty on specific facts may arise for others engaged in the educational process, e.g. an educational psychologist being part of the local authority's team to provide the necessary services. The fact that the educational psychologist owes a duty to the authority to exercise skill and care in the performance of his contract of employment does not mean that no duty of care can be or is owed to the child. Nor does the fact that the educational psychologist is called in in pursuance of the performance of the local authority's statutory duties mean that no duty of care is owed by him, if in exercising his profession he would otherwise have a duty of care.

That, however, is only the beginning of the inquiry. It must still be shown that the educational psychologist is acting in relation to a particular child in a situation where the law recognises a duty of care. A casual remark, an isolated act may occur in a situation where there is no sufficient nexus between the two persons for a duty of care to exist. But where an educational psychologist is specifically called in to advise in relation to the assessment and future provision for a specific child, and it is clear that the parents acting for the child and the teachers will follow that advice, prima facie a duty of care arises. It is sometimes said that there has to be an assumption of responsibility by the person concerned. That phrase can be misleading in that it can suggest that the professional person must knowingly and deliberately accept responsibility. It is, however, clear that the test is an objective one: *Henderson v Merrett Syndicates Ltd* [1995]. The phrase means simply that the law recognises that there is a duty of care. It is not so much that responsibility is assumed as that it is recognised or imposed by the law.

> The question is thus whether in the particular circumstances the necessary nexus has been shown. The result of a failure by an educational psychologist to take care may be that the child suffers emotional or psychological harm, perhaps even physical harm. There can be no doubt that if foreseeability and causation are established, psychological injury may constitute damage for the purpose of the common law. But so in my view can a failure to diagnose a congenital condition and to take appropriate action as a result of which failure a child's level of achievement is reduced, which leads to loss of employment and wages. Questions as to causation and as to the quantum of damage, particularly if actions are brought long after the event, may be very difficult, but there is no reason in principle to rule out such claims.
>
> As to the second question, if a breach of the duty of care to the child by such an employee is established, prima facie a local or education authority is vicariously liable for the negligence of its employee. If the educational psychologist does have a duty of care on the facts is it to be held that it is not just and reasonable that the local education authority should be vicariously liable if there is a breach of that duty? Are there reasons of public policy why the courts should not recognise such a liability? I am very conscious of the need to be cautious in recognising such a duty of care where so much is discretionary in these as in other areas of social policy. As has been said, it is obviously important that those engaged in the provision of educational services under the statutes should not be hampered by the imposition of such a vicarious liability. I do not, however, see that to recognise the existence of the duties necessarily leads or is likely to lead to that result. The recognition of the duty of care does not of itself impose unreasonably high standards. The courts have long recognised that there is no negligence if a doctor 'exercises the ordinary skill of an ordinary competent man exercising that particular art'.

The change of approach by the courts is quite noticeable. At one stage they were deterred from finding negligence liability in this area because of the complex issues of social policy which are involved and their awareness that questions of private law damages could upset the complex network set up by legislation.

What is clear is that the courts are no longer deterred from finding a duty of care in operational matters where a public authority has taken steps. Omissions remain a problem as these are more likely to occur in the policy area where it is dangerous for courts to tread.

Lord Slynn's very humanitarian judgment indicates a shift away from the complex network of tests set up in *Stovin v Wise* [1996] 3 All ER 801 and a move toward more orthodox negligence principles of foreseeability, proximity and policy. Where a public authority has decided to exercise a statutory discretion then it should take reasonable care in doing so. If there is a specific nexus between the authority or its employees such as that in *Phelps*, this may serve to establish proximity based on either assumption of responsibility or specific reliance. It is, however, still open for the courts to find no duty as it would not be just and reasonable to do so after weighing up the policy considerations involved.

For occupational stress see Chapter 14.

A claimant still faces formidable obstacles in these cases. As Lord Slynn points out, the claimant still has to establish breach of duty and causation. An example of this came in a claim for occupational stress within the context of the exercise of statutory powers.

Connor v Surrey County Council [2010] EWCA Civ 286

> The claimant was a head teacher who claimed for negligence against her employers. The issue was whether there was a duty to take care in the context of the exercise of statutory powers. The local authority employed the head teacher who suffered stress due to acrimonious disputes within the governing body of the school. Under the School Standards and Framework Act 1988 and the Education Act 2002 the education authority had power to remove a governing body and replace it with an interim executive board in circumstances which included those where there was a serious breakdown in the way a school was managed or governed which was prejudicing or likely to prejudice

the standards of performance of pupils at the school. The duty of care owed by an employer to avoid negligently caused occupational stress to an employee is well established. The breach of duty was alleged to be the failure by the employer to protect the claimant by appointing an interim board at the correct time. The claimant was certified by her general practitioner as suffering from stress and depression. She spent time in hospital where she was referred for psychiatric assessment. She was diagnosed as gravely clinically depressed. She never returned to work and retired in 2006. Proceedings in negligence were issued against the authority claiming damages for personal injury in the form of psychiatric damage. Was the claim justiciable or were the actions of the education authority wholly within its public law functions? In the High Court it was held that negligence had been established. The delay in setting up an interim executive board and in setting up the independent investigation had been negligent because they had disregarded the health and welfare of the claimant and her staff when such ought to have been central considerations and that the decision to set up the investigation and to extend its scope had been made in disregard of the duty of care owed to the claimant and the staff.

The Court of Appeal upheld the first instance decision. The established principle that a discretion apparently conferred in unfettered terms had nevertheless to be exercised only for the purposes for which the statute had provided it was an important aspect of the need for conformity between private and public law duties in the instant context. The effect of the principle was to require that there be no inconsistency between the private law aim and the public law purpose, and that in exercising the public law discretion in fulfilment of the duty of care the duty-ower should not diminish or undercut his service of the public purpose; the constraints on the use of public law powers to serve an established private law duty of care were well met.

It should be noted that in this case the claimant was using a well established common law duty of care to mount the claim. She was not relying on the statute to establish an action. The issue in the case was whether the statutory provisions would preclude a private law action. The reasoning of the Court of Appeal on this issue repays reading as it deals with some of the complex issues surrounding this area.

The Court of Appeal added a warning to the effect that the result in the case offered nothing remotely resembling a *vade mecum* for others in the future to build private law claims out of what may be sensitive and difficult decisions, including policy decisions, of public authorities.

Summary

This chapter deals with the special rules on the liability of public authorities in negligence.

- Liability for the negligence of public authorities is very complex because: (i) the loss involved is generally pure economic loss; (ii) the breach of duty in question is frequently an omission to act; (iii) the breach may well take place against the background of statutory powers and raise questions of whether tort law has a role or whether public law remedies are appropriate; (iv) as the action is against a public authority, the Human Rights Act 1998 may well have a role to play.

- *Omissions* – There was no liability on a public authority for a pure omission. The mere fact that a claimant's harm was foreseeable did not create a duty of care. Where a statutory power was conferred, the fact that the public authority was acting under a statutory power did not generate an analogous duty to act.

- *Exceptions* – (i) where the claimant suffers harm as a result of the actions of a third party over whom he alleges the defendant has carelessly failed to exercise control, proximity of relationship can be established by reference to the nature of the relationship between the defendant and the third party; (ii) where a public authority undertakes to act in a particular way and the claimant relied on that undertaking. The second exception may apply to the emergency services – the Human Rights Act 1998 may impose positive obligations on the emergency services but only where there is a 'real or immediate risk'. (***Van Colle*** v ***Chief Constable of Greater Manchester Police.***) The second category of cases is where the claimant alleges carelessness in the exercise of a statutory power rather than loss caused by failure to exercise it at all. In these cases the claimant must prove the usual factors in duty of care including (i) proximity and (ii) policy – the court may find that there are policy reasons for not imposing a duty of care.

● A distinction has been made between policy and operational decisions. In the former it would rarely be correct for a resource-allocating decision by a public authority to be challenged in a civil action for damages. In the latter it may be. The language used has now changed to decision making/implementation. In the case of decision making, a stringent application of justiciability and public interest will be applied. A three-stage test is applied: (i) whether the exercise of the statutory discretion in question would have involved policy considerations such as resource allocation, priority management, etc. (if so, no action in negligence should lie on fundamental justiciability lines and usurping Parliament's authority); (ii) whether, exercising the (justiciable) statutory discretion, the public authority had done so in a way that took it outside the discretion Parliament was assumed to have conferred (to do so the court was to apply the *Wednesbury* unreasonableness test); (iii) the court must then decide whether it was appropriate to impose a duty of care. This is the conventional third limb whereby it has to be fair, just and reasonable.

● These principles are illustrated by the cases involving the emergency services and the education and child abuse cases.

Further reading

Bailey, S. (2006), 'Public Authority Liability in Negligence: The Continued Search for Coherence' 26 LS 155.

Gearty, C. (2002), 'Osman Unravels' 67 MLR 87.

Harris, D. (1997), 113 LQR 398 *(Stovin v Wise)*.

McClean, J. (1988), 'Negligent Regulatory Authorities and the Duty of Care' 8 OJLS 442.

Morgan, J. (2005), 'Slowing the Expansion of Public Authorities Liability' 121 LQR 43.

Mullender, R. (2009), 'Negligence, Neighbourliness and the Welfare State' 68 CLJ 507.

Sprince, A. and Cooke, P. J. (1999) 15 PN 228 *(Osman)*.

Steele, I. (2005), 'Public Law Liability – a Common Law Solution?' 64 CLJ 543.

8

Breach of duty and proof of negligence

Objectives

After reading this chapter you will:

1. Understand the legal rules applied by the courts to determine whether a person has been negligent.

2. Have a critical knowledge of the problems of proving negligence and appreciate the significance of the burden of proof.

3. Understand the principle of *res ipsa loquitur*.

Introduction

Objective 1

Once a claimant has shown that the defendant owed them a duty of care, it is necessary for them to prove that the defendant was in breach of that duty.

Until the last century, negligence cases were tried by jury and the question of negligence was for the jury to decide. During the nineteenth century, judges exercised increasing control over this decision and it was necessary to have a test to give to the jury to determine whether the defendant had been negligent.

Negligence cases are now tried by a judge alone. There are two questions:

1 What standard of care is expected of a particular defendant? This is the question of how the defendant ought to have behaved. The standard is usually set by law.

2 How did the defendant behave? This is the question of whether the defendant fell below that standard. This is a question of fact, to be determined by reference to all the circumstances of the case.

In cases of negligent driving, for instance, the standard of care is that of the reasonable driver, not a perfect driver or a learner driver. Whether the defendant driver in the case in question has fallen below that standard is a question for the judge to decide based on the facts proved in evidence.

As decisions in this area are usually based on findings of fact in particular cases the law on breach of duty is limited. Decided cases are more illustrations rather than authorities.

The standard set by the court may be affected by policy issues. For example, where the defendant has compulsory insurance, the court may be tempted to set a high standard as this means the claimant will be compensated. Where setting a high standard and imposing liability will affect scarce resources, the court may set a lower standard. This may be one of the factors affecting liability in medical negligence cases. To compensate one claimant may mean closing a ward and depriving a large number of patients of treatment.

See also Chapter 1 for 'compensation culture'.

Fears that the United Kingdom might be developing a 'compensation culture' have led to government scrutiny. The view of the UK government, following the conclusions in *Better Regulation Task Force in Better Routes to Redress* (Cabinet Office Publications, 2004), is that the compensation culture is a myth but that the public's erroneous belief that it exists results in real and costly burdens. This underlies the rather strange provision of s 1 of the Compensation Act 2006 which, according to the government, simply reiterates the current test for breach of duty in negligence:

> A court considering a claim in negligence or breach of statutory duty may, in determining whether the defendant should have taken particular steps to meet a standard of care (whether by taking precautions against a risk or otherwise), have regard to whether a requirement to take those steps might –
>
> (a) prevent a desirable activity from being undertaken at all, to a particular extent or in a particular way, or
> (b) discourage persons from undertaking functions in connection with a desirable activity.

Section 1 is intended to deal with the effect of negligence on social activities where people might be inhibited from involving themselves or allowing their land to be used:

> In considering a claim in negligence, a court may, in determining whether the defendant should have taken particular steps to meet the standard of care (whether by taking precautions or otherwise) have regard to whether a requirement to take those steps might prevent an activity from taking place (either at all, to a particular extent, or in a particular way), or might discourage persons from undertaking functions in connection with that activity.

See also Chapter 11 for *Tomlinson*.

It is difficult to see what this will achieve as there is stated to be no change to the common law test for breach of duty and the courts are already alert to this problem as is shown in cases such as ***Tomlinson* v *Congleton Borough Council***. (See below.)

It is up to the claimant to prove that the defendant was negligent and this may be their hardest task. The claimant may not know what happened and ascertaining the facts could be difficult and expensive. In practice, the success or failure of most negligence actions depends on the claimant's ability to prove negligence.

The reasonable man test

As a subjective inquiry by the court into each person's capabilities would be impossible, an objective test was chosen. The standard of conduct to be attained is that of the reasonable man. The classic statement was given by Alderson B in ***Blyth* v *Birmingham Waterworks Co*** (1856) 11 Ex 781:

> Negligence is the omission to do something which a reasonable man, guided upon those considerations which ordinarily regulate the conduct of human affairs, would do, or doing something which a prudent and reasonable man would not do.

The 'reasonable man' has had various descriptions over the years. 'The man on the Clapham omnibus'; 'a traveller on the London underground'; 'the anthropomorphic conception of justice.' The concept itself has been subjected to criticism and the preferred expression now is the 'reasonable person'. As it is judges who determine reasonableness the test is effectively what judges think is reasonable conduct. As the judiciary is heavily represented by white middle-aged males this could lead to a distortion which does not represent the views of the general community.

The objective standard

Because the test is objective, no account is usually taken of individual disabilities or peculiarities. Whatever a person's age, competence or experience they will be judged by the objective standard of what they ought to have done in those circumstances.

Nettleship v *Weston* [1971] 2 QB 691

The claimant gave the defendant driving lessons. The defendant had been careful but on her third lesson the car struck a lamp-post and the claimant was injured. It was held that the defendant, although a learner driver, would be judged by the standard of the average competent driver: 'The learner driver may be doing his best, but his incompetent best is not good enough. He must drive in as good a manner as a driver of skill, experience and care.'

Denning MR:

In all that I have said, I have treated Mrs Weston as the driver who was herself in control of the car. On that footing, she is plainly liable for the damage done to the lamp post. She is equally liable for the injury done to Mr Nettleship. She owed a duty of care to each. The standard of care is the same in either case. It is measured objectively by the care to be expected of an experienced, skilled and careful driver. Mr Nettleship is not defeated by the maxim volenti non fit injuria. He did not agree, expressly or impliedly, to waive any claim for damages owing to her failure to measure up to the standard. But his damages may fall to be reduced owing to his failure to correct her error quick enough. Although the judge dismissed the claim, he did (in case he was wrong) apportion responsibility. He thought it would be just and equitable to regard them as equally to blame. I would accept this apportionment. (50%)

. . . (we are) moving away from the concept: 'No liability without fault.' We are beginning to apply the test: 'On whom should the risk fall?' Morally the learner driver is not at fault; but legally she is liable because she is insured . . .

The defendant in the above case had failed to reach the standard set by the objective test and was found liable. This raises questions of the nature of 'fault' and whether it is a moral question or a loss distributing mechanism. The objective standard would seem to indicate that fault is more concerned with loss distribution but it is arguable that an objective standard is justifiable on moral grounds as it concerns responsibility. The choice here was between not compensating the victim (distributive justice) and penalising a person who could probably not have performed any better. This is contrary to corrective justice which argues that one should not be penalised for all the harm one causes but only for such harm as is caused by fault or neglect.

The following two cases deal with the difficult question of liability when a person becomes ill while driving and causes an accident.

Roberts v *Ramsbottom* [1980] 1 WLR 823

The defendant drove his car after he had unknowingly suffered a cerebral haemorrhage and was unfit to drive. He collided with a stationary van and then with a parked vehicle. It was held that he had continued to drive after he had suffered a seizure which affected his reactions and was negligent in doing so. The court stated that a person might escape liability if his actions at the relevant time were wholly beyond his control, so as to amount to automatism. The fact that his consciousness was impaired due to brain malfunction did not amount to automatism. The reasonably prudent person would have stopped driving in such circumstances.

The automatism test imported from criminal law was later disapproved by the Court of Appeal.

Mansfield v *Weetabix Ltd* [1998] 1 WLR 1263

The defendant was driving a lorry when he crashed into the claimants' shop causing extensive damage. The defendant, unknowingly, was suffering from a condition which caused a hypoglycaemic state in which the brain was starved of glucose and was unable to function properly. The judge at first instance concluded that it was highly unlikely that the defendant had completely lost consciousness before the accident occurred; his ability to drive properly was impaired because of hypoglycaemia; he was not conscious that his ability was impaired; and he would have stopped driving if he had been so conscious. The judge found the defendants negligent because the defendant had not totally lost control of the vehicle. On appeal, it was held that a driver would not be liable in negligence if a sudden disabling event affected his ability to drive, and there was no reason in principle why a driver should not escape liability where the disabling event was not sudden but gradual, provided that he was unaware of it, as distinct from a driver who knew, or ought to have known, that he was subject to a condition rendering him unfit to drive. The relevant standard of care was that which was to be expected of a reasonably competent driver unaware that he was or might be suffering from a condition that impaired his ability to drive. To imply an objective standard that did not take account of his condition would be to impose strict liability. Accordingly, the appeal would be allowed. The court observed that consideration of criminal cases could only introduce confusion, as there to escape conviction a defendant had to show that when driving he was in a state of automatism, which was not the test in a civil case.

The defendant in this case was found to have been unable to avoid the accident. This case poses difficulties for the law of negligence. The objective standard of care was set aside for someone who could not fulfil it, as otherwise strict liability would have been imposed. However, that element of strict liability is generally accepted in the law of negligence and is inherent in the objective standard.

The court in *Mansfield* did take into account subjective characteristics of the defendant. There are two other circumstances where subjective factors may be taken into account. In the case of children, the standard is still an objective one, but it is not the standard of the ordinarily prudent and reasonable adult but that of an ordinarily prudent and reasonable child of the same age.

Mullin v *Richards* [1998] 1 All ER 920

M and R, two 15-year-old schoolgirls, were fencing with plastic rulers when one of the rulers snapped and a piece of plastic entered M's eye, causing her to lose the sight in that eye. The action failed as there was insufficient evidence to prove that it was foreseeable to a normal 15-year-old. There was no evidence as to the propensity of such rulers to break and the game had not been banned in the school. (*McHale* v *Watson* [1966] ALR 513 applied.)

It is not simply foreseeability of injury that is in issue with children. That question is interlinked with the question whether conduct should be held culpable. Did the conduct fall below the standard that should objectively be expected of a child of that age. This is a separate question. (*Orchard* v *Lee* [2009] EWCA Civ 295.) It was to culpability that the majority of the High Court of Australia in *McHale* v *Watson* addressed their observations, holding that the standard of conduct in negligence had to be considered by reference not to 'the reasonable man' but to the reasonable child of the age of 12. *McHale* was approved in *Mullin* and established the correct approach.

It is perhaps worth noting that a child is unlikely to be insured and this may be a factor behind the variation of the objective standard.

The second circumstance is where a person acts in an emergency. This will be taken into account when assessing the standard of behaviour to be expected. (*Jones* v *Boyce* (1816) 171 ER 540.)

The test is that of the reasonable man placed in the defendant's position.

Glasgow Corp v *Muir* [1943] AC 448

The appellants allowed a church picnic party to use their tea room on a wet day. Members of the party had to carry the tea-urn through a passage where children were buying ice creams. For an unexplained reason, the urn was dropped and children were scalded by the tea. The House of Lords held that, judged by the standards of the reasonable man, there was no liability: 'Legal liability is limited to those consequences of our acts which a reasonable man of ordinary intelligence and experience so acting would have in contemplation "The duty to take care" . . . There was no reason why the defendants would anticipate the event happening as a result of granting permission. The urn was in the care of responsible people who took due care for the safety of the children.'

Lord Macmillan:

> The standard of foresight of the reasonable man is, in one sense, an impersonal test. It eliminates the personal equation and is independent of the idiosyncrasies of the particular person whose conduct is in question. Some persons are by nature unduly timorous and imagine every path beset with lions. Others, of more robust temperament, fail to foresee or nonchalantly disregard even the most obvious dangers. The reasonable man is presumed to be free both from over-apprehension and from over-confidence, but there is a sense in which the standard of care of the reasonable man involves in its application a subjective element. It is still left to the judge to decide what, in the circumstances of the particular case, the reasonable man would have had in contemplation, and what, accordingly, the party sought to be made liable ought to have foreseen. Here there is room for diversity of view, as, indeed is well illustrated in the present case. What to one judge may seem far-fetched may seem to another both natural and probable.

Roe v *Minister of Health* [1954] 2 QB 66

The claimant was paralysed after receiving an injection in hospital. Phenol had leaked into the syringe and caused the paralysis. At this time it was not known that phenol could get into the syringe through invisible cracks. The defendants were not negligent as, judged by the standard of the reasonable person at the time of the accident, they could not have avoided the accident. The court will not condemn a defendant with 'the benefit of hindsight'.

Factors determining negligence

The reasonable person is a fictional character and the decision as to negligence is a value judgement made by the judge.

One way of establishing negligence might be to show a failure to conform to standard practice. But it would be dangerous to use this as an infallible guideline, and it would abdicate the court's responsibility. If all drivers regularly break the speed limit on a certain road, a judge is unlikely to accept this fact as evidence that the defendant was not negligent. The test is how the defendant ought to have behaved. Similar reasoning might be applied to a factory owner who speeds up their production line to a point where it is dangerous for their employees and argues that all their competitors do the same.

See Chapter 15 for the standard demanded of the medical profession. In some areas standard practice will carry great weight and in cases of medical negligence conformity with standard practice will nearly always result in a finding of no negligence. This is also the case in emerging areas of negligence such as the liability of local government in educational special needs cases. (*Carty* v *Croydon London Borough Council* [2005] 2 All ER 517.)

Outside of the medical area, the courts have been less eager to allow common practice to defeat an action. In *Lloyds Bank* v *Savory* [1933] AC 201 it was not a defence that the defendants had followed general banking practice in their procedures for handling cheques.

In professional negligence cases, provided the defendant has complied with the required standard for that profession, there is no negligence. The court will ask what is expected of a professional according to the expertise that they hold and not demand unrealistic standards of skill and knowledge.

Luxmoore-May v *Messenger May Baverstock* [1990] 1 All ER 1067

It was alleged that the defendant auctioneers had negligently failed to identify two paintings as those of a famous painter. They were sold at auction for £840 and a few months later sold again for £88,000. The Court of Appeal likened the skill to be expected of a provincial auctioneer to that of a general medical practitioner. On the facts, the defendants had not been negligent, as differing views on the painter could have been held by experts. The auctioneer's duty was to do his job with honesty and due diligence.

Slade LJ:

I am of the opinion that the judge . . . demanded too high a standard of skill on the part of the defendants and of Mr Thomas, in concluding that no competent valuer could have missed the signs of Stubbs [a noted eighteenth-century sporting artist] potential. In my judgment, the question whether the foxhound pictures had Stubbs potential . . . was one [on] which competent valuers, and indeed competent dealers, could have held widely differing views. It has not been argued that a valuation of £30 to £40 would have been too low if these pictures were simply to be regarded as objects to be hung on a wall without Stubbs potential. For these reasons, I am of the opinion that negligence on the part of Mr Thomas has not been established, and accordingly that negligence on the part of the defendants would not have been established, even if Mrs Zarek, after taking Mr Thomas's advice, had taken no further advice in relation to the pictures.

(See also *Thomson* v *Christie Manson & Woods Ltd* [2005] All ER (D) 176 (May).)

Failure to conform with standard practice is usually good evidence that the defendant has been negligent, but this is not conclusive.

Brown v *Rolls-Royce Ltd* [1960] 1 WLR 210

The claimant contracted dermatitis at work. The defendant employers had provided washing facilities at work but did not supply a barrier cream which was supplied by other employers in the same type of work. There was conflicting evidence as to how effective this cream was. The claimant was unable to prove that if the cream had been supplied she would not have suffered dermatitis. The defendants were held not to have been negligent in failing to supply the cream.

A judge is likely to take a number of factors into account in determining negligence.

The skill which the defendant professes to have

Where a person has held themselves out as having a particular skill, they are required to show the skill normally possessed by persons doing that work. A solicitor will be required to show the skill of the average solicitor and a plumber that of the average plumber. The fact that that person is in their first day in the job is irrelevant, as the test is objective.

The standard of care expected of a doctor was laid down in the following case.

Bolam v Friern Hospital Management Committee [1957] 2 All ER 118

The allegation was that a doctor had been negligent in administering electro-convulsive therapy to a patient without a relaxant drug or restraining convulsive movements. The claimant suffered a fractured jaw.

McNair J:

I must explain what in law we mean by 'negligence'. In the ordinary case which does not involve any special skill, negligence in law means this: some failure to do some act which a reasonable man in the circumstances would do, or doing some act which a reasonable man in the circumstances would not do; and if that failure or doing of that act results in injury, then there is a cause of action. How do you test whether this act or failure is negligent? In an ordinary case it is generally said, that you judge that by the action of the man in the street. He is the ordinary man. In one case it has been said that you judge it by the conduct of the man on the top of a Clapham omnibus. He is the ordinary man. But where you get a situation which involves the use of some special skill or competence, then the test whether there has been negligence or not is not the test of the man on the top of a Clapham omnibus, because he has not got this special skill. The test is the standard of the ordinary skilled man exercising and professing to have that special skill. A man need not possess the highest expert skill at the risk of being found negligent. It is well-established law that it is sufficient if he exercises the ordinary skill of an ordinary competent man exercising that particular art. I do not think that I quarrel much with any of the submissions in law which have been put before you by counsel. Counsel for the plaintiff put it in this way, that in the case of a medical man negligence means failure to act in accordance with the standards of reasonably competent medical men at the time. That is a perfectly accurate statement, as long as it is remembered that there may be one or more perfectly proper standards; and if a medical man conforms with one of those proper standards then he is not negligent. Counsel for the plaintiff was also right, in my judgment, in saying: that a mere personal belief that a particular technique is best is no defence unless that belief is based on reasonable grounds. That again is unexceptionable.

On the facts, the defendant was found not liable, as he had conformed with a practice which was approved by a responsible body of medical opinion.

The courts therefore allowed the medical profession to set their own standard. A doctor accused of negligence by a patient can defend themselves by showing that what they did was accepted practice, provided that practice was approved by responsible opinion in the medical profession.

Bolitho v City and Hackney Health Authority [1997] 3 WLR 1151

A two-year-old with croup died after a sudden respiratory crisis. The defendant doctor urgently summoned by a nurse negligently failed to attend and could not raise her substitute, whose pager had flat batteries. Had a doctor attended and intubated the child, the child would have lived, but not all doctors would have intubated him and the defendant said she would not have done so.

The trial judge (based on evidence given by an expert in paediatric respiratory medicine called by the defence that intubation would not have been appropriate) held that, judged by the **Bolam** standard, a decision by the doctor not to intubate would have been in accordance with a body of responsible professional opinion and causation had not been proved. This was upheld by a majority of the Court of Appeal.

The House of Lords held as follows:

1 In the generality of cases the **Bolam** test had no application in deciding questions of causation; however, where the breach of duty consisted of an omission to do an act which ought to have been done, the question of what would have constituted a continuing exercise of proper care had the initial failure not taken place, so as to determine if the injuries would have been avoided, fell to be decided by that test. In applying the test, the court had to be satisfied that the exponents of a body of professional opinion relied on had demonstrated that such opinion had a logical basis and, in particular, had directed their minds to the question of comparative risks and benefits and had reached a defensible conclusion.

2 If, in a rare case, it had been demonstrated that the professional opinion was incapable of withstanding logical analysis, the judge was entitled to hold that it could not provide the benchmark by reference to which the doctor's conduct fell to be assessed. In most cases the fact that experts in the field were of a particular opinion would be a demonstration of the reasonableness of that opinion.

3 As the trial judge had directed himself correctly and there had been good reason for acceptance of the defendant's expert opinion, it had not been proved that the doctor's failure to attend had caused the injuries complained of.

See also Chapter 15 for breach of duty in medical negligence cases.

See Chapter 15 for detail of medical negligence.

The significance of the **Bolitho** decision is that it reaffirms the role of the court in assessing whether treatment has been negligent. It will rarely be necessary for a court to find that the views held by a competent medical expert are unreasonable but it is nevertheless possible. What the court will not do is to choose between two contradictory bodies of expert medical opinion.

Bolam would appear to apply to all professionals who exercise a special skill. A barrister, for example, will not be negligent unless the error they have made is one which no reasonably competent member of the profession would have made. (**Moy v Pettiman Smith** [2005] UKHL 7.)

If a layman attempts a specialised task, then all the circumstances of the case will need to be looked at.

Wells v Cooper [1958] 2 All ER 527

The defendant fixed a door handle on to a door. He did the job as well as an ordinary carpenter would do it. The handle came off in the claimant's hand and he was injured. It was held that the defendant had exercised such care as was required of him and was not liable. The degree of skill was not to be measured by the skill which the defendant actually possessed but by the skill which a reasonably competent carpenter would have.

If a person acted in an emergency, then they would be judged by the standards of a reasonable person, not a specialist. A climber who was required to treat an injured fellow climber would not be judged by the standards of a doctor. The dearth of authorities on this point perhaps suggests an inherent decency on the part of those so treated!

The degree of probability that damage will be done

Care must be taken in respect of a risk that is reasonably foreseeable. Nearly all human actions involve some risk of damage, but not every risky act will result in liability.

Bolton v *Stone* [1951] 1 All ER 1078

The claimant was injured on the highway by a cricket ball hit from the defendants' ground. The ball had been hit 100 yards and cleared a 17-foot fence which was 78 yards from the batsman. The evidence showed that the ball had only been hit out of the ground six times in the previous 30 years. The defendants were found not to have been negligent, as the risk was so small that the reasonable man would have been justified in disregarding it.

This case was also argued in nuisance, but counsel conceded that if he could not succeed in negligence, he could not succeed in nuisance.

The key question here was the degree of probability rather than the costs of prevention but in a later case (***Shine*** v ***London Borough of Tower Hamlets*** [2006] All ER (D) 79 (Jun)) it was interpreted as authority for the proposition that there has to be a balance between the likely severity of the accident and the cost of putting it right.

Hilder v *Associated Portland Cement Manufacturers Ltd* [1961] 1 WLR 1434

The claimant's husband was riding his motor cycle along a road beside a piece of open land occupied by the defendants. Children were permitted to play football on the land. A ball was kicked on to the road causing a fatal accident. As there was a strong possibility of injury to road users, the defendants were negligent, as they had taken no additional precautions to ensure the safety of road users.

It should be remembered that the test is reasonable care in all the circumstances of the case. The claimant may have characteristics which render the likelihood of harm greater and therefore increase the risk.

Haley v *London Electricity Board* [1965] AC 778

The defendants left a hammer on the pavement to warn people of excavations. The claimant, who was blind, tripped over the hammer and was injured. It was held that although the warning was adequate for sighted persons, it was inadequate for a blind person. The number of blind people was sufficiently large to make them a class which the defendants ought reasonably to have had in contemplation. The cost of prevention in this case was low.

Lord Morton:

> [The Board's duty is] to take reasonable care not to act in a way likely to endanger other persons who may reasonably be expected to walk along the pavement. That duty is owed to blind persons if the operators foresee or ought to have foreseen that blind persons may walk along the pavement and is in no way different from the duty owed to persons with sight, though the carrying out of the duty may involve extra precautions in the case of blind pedestrians. I think that everyone living in Greater London must have seen blind persons walking slowly along on the pavement and waving a white stick in front of them, so as to touch any obstruction which may be in their way, and I think that the respondents' workmen ought to have foreseen that a blind person might well come along the pavement in question.

The courts also take the view that dealings with children demand a high degree of care. In **Yachuk v Oliver Blais** [1949] AC 386 the defendants sold petrol to a 9-year-old. The claimant was burned when the child set fire to the petrol. The defendants were held liable for selling the petrol, although the child had said he needed it for his mother's car.

The magnitude of harm likely

The court will take into account not only the risk of any damage to the claimant but also the extent of the damage that is risked.

Paris v Stepney Borough Council [1951] AC 367

The claimant, who had one eye, was employed as a mechanic in the defendants' garage. Part of his job involved welding. It was not normal to supply goggles to men involved in such work. A piece of metal flew into the claimant's eye with the result that he became completely blind. The defendants were held liable, although they would not have been liable to a person with normal sight. The greater risk to the claimant meant that greater precautions than normal had to be taken.

Withers v Perry Chain Co Ltd [1961] 1 WLR 1314

The claimant was prone to dermatitis and was given the most grease-free job available. Despite this, she contracted dermatitis. The defendant employers were held not liable as they had done all that was reasonable, short of refusing to employ her at all.

The utility of the object to be achieved

The court may be called on to assess the social utility of the defendant's conduct in determining whether he was negligent. Asquith J stated in **Daborn v Bath Tramways** [1946] 2 All ER 333:

> If all the trains in this country were restricted to a speed of five miles per hour, there would be fewer accidents, but our national life would be intolerably slowed down. The purpose to be served, if sufficiently important, justifies the assumption of abnormal risk.

Watt v Hertfordshire County Council [1954] 1 WLR 835

The claimant fireman was on duty when an emergency call was received. A woman had been trapped under a car and lifting equipment was required. A heavy jack was loaded on to a lorry which was not equipped to secure it. On the way to the accident the jack moved and injured the claimant, who sued his employers. The action failed as, in the circumstances, the risk involved was not so great as to prohibit an attempt to save life.

The value of saving life is surely unarguable, but was it fair on the fireman that he should recover nothing for injuries received in the course of his employment? The Court of Appeal has expressed disquiet that members of the rescue services may go uncompensated for injuries received at work. (**King v Sussex Ambulance NHS Trust** [2002] ICR 1413.) However, as utility is a factor going to negligence, it is difficult to see how such people could be compensated by the tort system unless a form of strict liability was introduced.

Other values may not be so easy to assess. What, for example, is the value of playing cricket? Was this a factor which influenced the decision in **Bolton v Stone**? It would clearly have made a difference if the claimant's injury had been caused by an unlawful activity.

See Chapter 11 for defective premises.

The following case is taken from the area of occupier's liability of defective premises and as such was decided under the relevant statutes, the Occupiers' Liability Act 1957 and the Occupiers' Liability Act 1984. It does, however, illustrate the issues involved in a breach of duty in a particular area which has generated a considerable amount of litigation, that of an occupier of land for persons injured during leisure pursuits on the land.

Tomlinson v Congleton Borough Council [2003] 3 All ER 1122

See also Chapter 11 for *Tomlinson*.

The defendants owned, occupied and managed a public park. In the park was a lake formed from a disused sand extraction pit. The lake had sandy beaches and was a popular recreational venue where yachting, subaqua diving and other regulated activities were permitted, but swimming was not. Notices reading 'Dangerous water: no swimming' were posted but they had little or no effect. The unauthorised use of the lake and the increasing possibility of an accident was of concern to the defendants. A plan to landscape the shores and plant over the beaches from which people swam had been approved, but work had begun only shortly before 6 May 1995. On that date the claimant went to the lake. He ran into the water and dived, striking his head on the sandy bottom with sufficient force to cause him an injury which resulted in paralysis from the neck downward. He brought proceedings for damages claiming that the defendants, as occupiers, owed him the common duty of care set out in s 2(2) of the Occupiers' Liability Act 1957, which was a duty to take such care as in all the circumstances was reasonable to see that a visitor would be reasonably safe in using the premises for the purposes for which he was permitted to be there. At trial it was conceded that he had seen and ignored the warning signs, so that when he entered the water he had ceased to be at the park for purposes for which he had been invited and permitted by the defendants to be there, and had accordingly ceased to be a visitor and had become a trespasser. As such he was owed a lesser duty of care under the Occupiers' Liability Act 1984.

Lord Hoffmann:

> My Lords, it will in the circumstances be convenient to consider first the question of what the position would have been if Mr Tomlinson had been a lawful visitor owed a duty under s 2(2) of the 1957 Act. Assume, therefore, that there had been no prohibition on swimming. What was the risk of serious injury? To some extent this depends upon what one regards as the relevant risk. As I have mentioned, the judge thought it was the risk of injury through diving while the Court of Appeal thought it was any kind of injury which could happen to people in the water. Although, as I have said, I am inclined to agree with the judge, I do not want to put the basis of my decision too narrowly. So I accept that we are concerned with the steps, if any, which should have been taken to prevent any kind of water accident. According to the Royal Society for the Prevention of Accidents, about 450 people drown while swimming in the United Kingdom every year (see **Darby v National Trust** [2001] PIQR P372 at 374). About 25–35 break their necks diving and no doubt others sustain less serious injuries. So there is obviously some degree of risk in swimming and diving, as there is in climbing, cycling, fell walking and many other such activities.
>
> I turn then to the cost of taking preventative measures. Ward LJ described it [£5,000] as 'not excessive'. Perhaps it was not, although the outlay has to be seen in the context of the other items (rated 'essential' and 'highly desirable') in the borough council budget which had taken precedence over the destruction of the beaches for the previous two years.
>
> I do not, however, regard the financial cost as a significant item in the balancing exercise which the court has to undertake. There are two other related considerations which are far more important. The first is the social value of the activities which would have to be prohibited in order to reduce or eliminate the risk from swimming. And the second is the question of whether the council should be entitled to allow people of full capacity to decide for themselves whether to take the risk.

The Court of Appeal made no reference at all to the social value of the activities which were to be prohibited. The majority of people who went to the beaches to sunbathe, paddle and play with their children were enjoying themselves in a way which gave them pleasure and caused no risk to themselves or anyone else. This must be something to be taken into account in deciding whether it was reasonable to expect the council to destroy the beaches.

I have the impression that the Court of Appeal felt able to brush these matters aside because the council had already decided to do the work. But they were held liable for having failed to do so before Mr Tomlinson's accident and the question is therefore whether they were under a legal duty to do so. Ward LJ placed much emphasis upon the fact that the council had decided to destroy the beaches and that its officers thought that this was necessary to avoid being held liable for an accident to a swimmer. But the fact that the council's safety officers thought that the work was necessary does not show that there was a legal duty to do it.

... THE BALANCE OF RISK, GRAVITY OF INJURY, COST AND SOCIAL VALUE
My Lords, the majority of the Court of Appeal appear to have proceeded on the basis that if there was a foreseeable risk of serious injury, the council was under a duty to do what was necessary to prevent it. But this in my opinion is an oversimplification. Even in the case of the duty owed to a lawful visitor under s 2(2) of the 1957 Act and even if the risk had been attributable to the state of the premises rather than the acts of Mr Tomlinson, the question of what amounts to 'such care as in all the circumstances of the case is reasonable' depends upon assessing, as in the case of common law negligence, not only the likelihood that someone may be injured and the seriousness of the injury which may occur, but also the social value of the activity which gives rise to the risk and the cost of preventative measures. These factors have to be balanced against each other.

... in *Jolley v Sutton London BC* [2000] 3 All ER 409, there was no social value or cost saving to the council in creating a risk by leaving a derelict boat lying about. It was something which they ought to have removed whether it created a risk of injury or not. So they were held liable for an injury which, though foreseeable, was not particularly likely. On the other hand, in *The Wagon Mound (No 2)* [1966] 2 All ER 709 at 718, Lord Reid drew a contrast with *Bolton v Stone* [1951] AC 850 in which the House of Lords held that it was not negligent for a cricket club to do nothing about the risk of someone being injured by a cricket ball hit out of the ground. The difference was that the cricket club were carrying on a lawful and socially useful activity and would have had to stop playing cricket at that ground.

This is the kind of balance which has to be struck even in a situation in which it is clearly fair, just and reasonable that there should in principle be a duty of care or in which Parliament, as in the 1957 Act, has decreed that there should be. And it may lead to the conclusion that even though injury is foreseeable, as it was in *Bolton v Stone*, it is still in all the circumstances reasonable to do nothing about it.

See also Chapter 11 for *Tomlinson* and occupiers' liability. This is the area that the government was concerned with when it introduced the Compensation Act 2006. However, it would appear from this decision and the comments of Lord Hoffmann that the statutory intervention will add nothing to the existing common law.

The case is a warning that it will not always be the 'best insurer' who succeeds. The case illustrates that claimants retain personal responsibility for their own safety despite the defendant in this case having a deeper pocket.

The practicability of prevention

Once the court has identified a risk as reasonably foreseeable, the question is whether the defendants should have taken precautions against that risk. If the cost of eliminating the risk is out of proportion to the extent of the risk, then the defendant will not be obliged to take preventative measures. (See *Bolton v Stone*.)

Latimer v *AEC Ltd* [1953] AC 643

> After a factory was flooded, the owner did all that he could to eliminate the effects of the flooding
> by using sawdust on the floors. Some areas of floor remained uncovered. The claimant fell on one of
> these areas and was injured. He sued his employer in negligence, alleging that the factory ought to
> have been closed. It was held that it was not necessary to take such a precaution as it was out of
> proportion to the risk involved.

It is not normally necessary to eliminate the risk altogether, as this would amount to
insurance against the risk.

An economic formula?

Legal rules have been analysed by economists and tested against economic principles. It
has been suggested that a defendant should be negligent if the likelihood of the injury
multiplied by the gravity of the injury exceeds the cost of taking adequate precautions.
This is sometimes known as the 'Learned Hand' test from the name of the US judge who
laid it down in a number of cases. The test looks at three variables: the probability that
harm will result to the claimant from the defendant's act or omission (P); the gravity of the
loss or harm (L); and the cost of preventing it (B). Negligence will occur where the cost to
the defendant of taking the necessary precautions is outweighed by the magnitude of the
risk and the gravity of the possible harm.

The effect of a finding of negligence by a court is to shift the loss from the claimant to
the defendant. Economists argue that, based on efficiency, this should only happen where
the cost of avoiding the accident is less than avoiding the accident costs.

This formula omits one vital factor and that is the social utility of the defendant's
conduct. There are also severe problems in assessing what the costs of an accident are.

Proof of negligence

Introduction

Objective
2

The most difficult task that a claimant faces in a negligence action is likely to be proving
that the defendant was negligent.

The basic rule is that they who affirm must prove. It is therefore up to the claimant to
prove, on the balance of probabilities, that the defendant was negligent.

This rule is relaxed in two instances.

Proof of criminal conviction

The Civil Evidence Act 1968 s 11 provides that the fact of conviction on a criminal charge
is admissible in evidence in a civil case based on the same facts. Where the defendant has
been convicted of a criminal offence in respect of conduct which is alleged to be negligent,
a rebuttable presumption of liability is created. To escape liability the defendant must
prove that they were not negligent.

If the defendant is sued for negligent driving and has been convicted of a criminal
offence in respect of that driving, then the defendant must prove that they were not negligent. This is difficult but not impossible. To drive through a red traffic light is a criminal
offence but it does not necessarily amount to negligence.

Res ipsa loquitur

The phrase *res ipsa loquitur* means the thing speaks for itself. Where the maxim applies, the court will be prepared to infer that the defendant was negligent without hearing detailed evidence from the claimant as to what the defendant did or did not do.

The origin of the phrase lies in the following cases.

Scott v London and St Katherine's Dock Co (1865) 3 H&C 596

The claimant was standing near the door of the defendant's warehouse when some bags of sugar fell on him. The first instance judge entered a verdict for the defendant as there was no evidence that he had been negligent. The Court of Appeal directed a new trial. Erle CJ stated:

There must be reasonable evidence of negligence. But where the thing is shown to be under the management of the defendant or his servants, and the accident is such as in the ordinary course of things does not happen if those who have the management use proper care, it affords reasonable evidence, in the absence of explanation by the defendants, that the accident arose from want of care.

This maxim has since been referred to as *res ipsa loquitur*. The maxim is said to have three requirements.

1 The thing causing the damage was under the exclusive control of the defendant

This means that the very occurrence of the accident should point to negligence on the part of the defendant and to no one else. The courts have been liberal in their interpretation of control. In defective products cases, control lies in the manufacturing process, even though the damage is caused long after the product leaves the factory.

Gee v Metropolitan Railway (1873) LR 8 QB 161

The claimant leaned against the door of a train shortly after it left the station. The door opened and the claimant fell out. As the door had recently been under the control of the defendants, there was evidence of negligence on their part.

Easson v London & North Eastern Railway [1944] 1 KB 421

The claimant, a four-year-old child, fell out of the door of a train. At the time of the accident the train was seven miles from its last stopping place. It was held that *res ipsa loquitur* was not applicable in these circumstances. The defendants did not have sufficient control over the door at the time. Any passenger on the train could have interfered with the door.

2 The accident must be of the sort that does not happen in the absence of negligence

The facts in **Scott v London and St Katherine's Dock Co** illustrate this requirement. Bags of sugar do not normally fall out of the sky unless someone has been negligent.

The maxim has been invoked in medical negligence actions.

Mahon v Osborne [1939] 2 KB 14

The claimant entered hospital for an abdominal operation. He later died and a swab was found in his body. The claimant was entitled to call expert evidence to show that the accident would not have occurred without negligence.

Scott LJ:

It is difficult to see how the principle of res ipsa loquitur can apply generally to actions of negligence against a surgeon for leaving a swab in a patient, even if in certain circumstances the presumption may arise. If it applied generally, plaintiff's counsel, having, by a couple of answers to interrogatories proved that the defendant performed the operation and that a swab was left in, would be entitled to ask for judgment, unless evidence describing the operation was given by the defendant. Some positive evidence of neglect of duty is surely needed. It may be that a full description of the actual operation will disclose facts sufficiently indicative of want of skill or care to entitle a jury to find neglect of duty to the patient. It may be that expert evidence in addition will be requisite. But to treat the maxim as applying in every case where a swab is left in the patient seems to me an error of law. The very essence of the rule when applied to an action for negligence is that on the mere fact of the event happening, for example, an injury to the plaintiff, there arise two presumptions of fact, (1.) that the event was caused by a breach by somebody of the duty of care towards the plaintiff, and (2.) that the defendant was that somebody. The presumption of fact only arises because it is an inference which the reasonable man knowing the facts would naturally draw, and that is in most cases for two reasons: (1.) because the control over the happening of such an event rested solely with the defendant, and (2.) that in the ordinary experience of mankind such an event does not happen unless the person in control has failed to exercise due care.

In medical cases the claimant may not be able to show who was negligent. In such cases the maxim of *res ipsa loquitur* will be available to make the employing health authority vicariously liable. However, the complexity and difficulty of the maxim is demonstrated by its application in clinical negligence cases. The Court of Appeal has stated that it may apply in clear-cut cases, such as where a surgeon amputates the wrong foot or a patient wakes up in the middle of an operation despite a general anaesthetic. In these cases what happened is sufficient to give rise to an inference of negligence based on ordinary human experience. Most clinical negligence cases, however, depend on expert evidence and a judge summing up would decide the case on the basis of inferences he was entitled to draw from the whole of the evidence, including the expert evidence. (**Ratcliffe v Plymouth & Torbay Health Authority** (1998) PIQR P170.)

3 There must be no explanation for the accident

Res ipsa loquitur is only available where there is no explanation for the accident. If all the facts are known, then the only question is whether or not negligence can be inferred.

Barkway v South Wales Transport Co Ltd [1950] 1 All ER 392

The claimant was injured in a road accident when the bus he was travelling in burst a tyre and crashed. The reason for the burst tyre was a defect in its wall which could not have been discovered beforehand. It was held that *res ipsa loquitur* was inapplicable. The defendants were found liable because they had not instructed their drivers to report heavy blows to tyres. This was sufficient to establish negligence.

Lord Ratcliffe:

I do not think that the appellant was entitled to judgment in the action because of any special virtue in the maxim *res ipsa loquitur*. I find nothing more in that maxim than a rule of evidence, of which the

> essence is that an event which in the ordinary course of things is more likely than not to have been caused by negligence is by itself evidence of negligence. In this action much more is known than the bare fact that the omnibus mounted the pavement and fell down the bank. The true question is not whether the appellant adduced some evidence of negligence, but whether on all the evidence she proved that the respondents had been guilty of negligence in a relevant particular. In my view, the important thing is that the tyre on the respondents' omnibus was defective.

If the defendant successfully negatives any of the conditions required for *res ipsa loquitur*, the claimant must prove, by affirmative evidence, that it was the defendant's carelessness that caused their damage. (*Ng Chum Pui v Lee Chuen Tat* [1988] RTR 298.)

What is the effect of the maxim?

Once the claimant has successfully raised *res ipsa loquitur*, what the defendant has to prove to avoid liability is a matter of controversy. Do they have to prove that they were not negligent, or is it sufficient if they raise an alternative explanation for the accident which does not connote negligence on their part?

Colvilles v Devine [1969] 1 WLR 475

A pipe carrying oxygen exploded. The defendants suggested that this could have been caused by particles igniting. This would have provided a non-negligent explanation for the explosion. The court held that the defendants did not have to prove this. On the facts, the defendants were held liable, as they had not proved that filters to prevent particle entry were effective or had been checked.

Lord Donovan:

> In this state of affairs the pursuer was, in my opinion, entitled in law to say that somebody for whom Colvilles were responsible could not have exercised proper care. In other words *res ipsa loquitur*. That means that it was for the appellants to show that the accident was just as consistent with their having exercised due diligence as with their having been negligent. In that way the scales which had been tipped in the pursuer's favour by the doctrine of *res ipsa loquitur* would be once more in balance, and the pursuer would have to begin again and prove negligence in the usual way.

The result in this case appears to be consistent with the view that the defendant must prove no negligence, but some of the views expressed in the judgments appear sympathetic to the alternative explanation theory.

Ward v Tesco Stores Ltd [1976] 1 WLR 810

The claimant slipped on some yoghurt on the floor of the defendants' supermarket. This was all she could prove, except to show that three weeks later orange juice remained on the floor of the same supermarket for 15 minutes. The defendants gave evidence that the floor was brushed five or six times a day and that if staff saw a spillage they were instructed to stay there and call someone to clean it up. The Court of Appeal held that the claimant's evidence constituted a prima facie case of negligence. The floor was under the defendants' control and the accident was of the kind that does not normally happen if reasonable care is taken. The defendants were therefore obliged to take reasonable care. They had failed to do this and the claimant succeeded.

Megaw LJ:

> It is for the plaintiff to show that there has occurred an event which is unusual and which, in the absence of explanation, is more consistent with fault on the part of the defendants than the absence

of fault; and to my mind the judge was right in taking that view of the presence of this slippery liquid on the floor of the supermarket in the circumstances of this case; that is, that the defendants knew or should have known that it was a not uncommon occurrence; and that if it should happen, and should not be promptly attended to, it created a serious risk that customers would fall and injure themselves. When the plaintiff has established that, the defendants can still escape from liability. They could escape from liability if they could show that the accident must have happened, or even on balance probability would have been likely to have happened, even if there had been in existence a proper and adequate system, in relation to the circumstances, to provide for the safety of customers. But if the defendants wish to put forward such a case, it is for them to show that, on balance of probability, either by evidence or by inference from the evidence that is given or is not given, this accident would have been at least equally likely to have happened despite a proper system designed to give reasonable protection to customers. That, in this case, they wholly failed to do.

The judgments in **Ward v Tesco** did not relieve the claimant of the overall burden of proof. She had to show that the occurrence of the accident was prima facie evidence of a lack of care on the part of the defendant in failing to provide or implement a system designed to protect her from risk of accident or injury. (**Hall v Holker Estate** [2008] EWCA Civ 1422.)

Henderson v H E Jenkins & Sons [1970] AC 282

The claimant's husband was killed when the brakes on a lorry failed on a steep hill. The defendants pleaded that the failure resulted from a latent defect in a brake pipe. They advanced evidence to show that they had cleaned and visually inspected the pipe and that the cause of failure was corrosion. The corrosion could only be detected by removing the pipe, a practice which was not recommended by the manufacturers or the Ministry of Transport. The House of Lords held that the claimant had raised an inference of negligence and the defendants had failed to rebut this. They should have gone on to show that nothing in the vehicle's life would have caused abnormal corrosion or called for special inspection. Again, this case would appear to support the view that the defendant must prove that he was not negligent.

Within the cases cited above there is disagreement among the judiciary as to the precise effect that raising the maxim of *res ipsa loquitur* has. Once the claimant has satisfied the points required to raise *res ipsa loquitur*, there is an inference of negligence, which the defendant must displace. What they have to do to displace the inference will vary from case to case. In some cases they will have to prove they were not negligent. In others, raising a plausible alternative non-negligent explanation will suffice.

Summary

This chapter deals with breach of duty in negligence.

- In order to establish breach of duty the claimant must prove on the balance of probabilities that the defendant was at fault (negligent).
- This is based on case law but there is a statutory provision, s 1 of the Compensation Act 2006, which appears to add nothing to the common law.
- The test is an objective one and is based on the reasonable person in the claimant's situation.

- In general, no account will be taken of subjective factors except in the case of children and in emergencies.

- A court will take a number of factors into account in determining whether there was negligence: (i) the skill which the defendant professes to have; (ii) the degree of probability that damage will be done; (iii) the magnitude of the harm likely; (iv) the utility of the object to be achieved; (v) the practicability of precautions.

- In some cases the doctrine of *res ipsa loquitur* – the thing speaks for itself – may assist the claimant in proving negligence. The doctrine requires proof that: (i) the thing causing the damage was under the defendant's control; (ii) the accident must be of the sort that does not usually happen in the absence of negligence; (iii) there must be no explanation for the accident.

Further reading

Atiyah, P. S. (1972), '"Res Ipsa Loquitur" in England and Australia' 35 MCR 337.

Herbert, R. (2006), 'The Compensation Act 2006' *Journal of Personal Injury Law* 337.

Stapleton, J. (1988), 'The Gist of Negligence' 104 LQR 213.

9

Causation and remoteness of damage

Objectives

After reading this chapter you will:

1. Appreciate the significance of the legal rules on causation, remoteness of damage and *novus actus interveniens*.

2. Understand the basic *but for* test for causation in negligence.

3. Have a critical knowledge of the problem areas in factual causation and understand the legal rules on exposure to risk as the basis of causation and its application in the mesothelioma cases.

4. Understand the mechanisms by which the courts apply loss of chance as the basis of causation in personal injury and economic loss cases.

5. Understand the rules on remoteness of damage and the significance of policy factors in remoteness of damage cases.

6. Understand the rules on *novus actus interveniens*.

Introduction

Objective
1

The third element in the claimant's case in negligence is damage. This is an essential ingredient of the tort as it is not actionable *per se.*

The claimant must prove that their damage was caused by the defendant's breach of duty and that the damage was not too remote. The first element is sometimes called causation in fact, and the latter causation in law. This distinction can be confusing as it would appear to indicate that causation in fact is free of policy issues and is simply an evidentiary inquiry which in some cases it is clearly not. Legal causation can be a confusing expression as it has little to do with causation in the normal sense and more to do with policy issues and in particular loss shifting.

Causation in fact deals with the question of whether as a matter of fact the damage was caused by the breach of duty.

> ### Example
>
> A railway company has instructed its engine drivers that before they go over a crossing, they must sound their whistle, to give warning to anyone crossing. One morning a person is found dead on the crossing as a result of being run over by a train. During the night a train has failed to sound its whistle. All the elements of negligence are present. The railway company owes a duty of care to crossing users. There has been a breach of duty by an engine driver in failing to sound his whistle. There is damage, but, as yet, there is no negligence action. It is necessary for the claimant to establish that the train that caused the damage was the train that failed to sound its whistle.

The question of remoteness of damage arises where causation in fact is established, but the court holds that as a matter of law the damage is too remote. The court will not want the defendant to be liable indefinitely for damage and will impose a cut-off point beyond which the damage is said to be too remote.

> ### Example
>
> The defendant drove negligently on the motorway and his car swerved and left the road. The car landed on a railway line. A mainline railway train was derailed by the car. The train struck a dam, which burst, flooding a small town.
>
> In this kind of scenario the bill for damages potentially runs into millions of pounds. What the defendant has done is to set in motion a chain of events. This will establish factual causation. The court will probably wish to terminate the defendant's liability at a particular point. This may be after the damage to the train. Any damage beyond this point is too remote.

An event which occurs after the breach of duty, and which contributes to the claimant's damage, may break the chain of causation, so as to render the defendant not liable for any damage beyond this point. Where this occurs the event is known as a *novus actus interveniens*.

Factual causation

 The 'but for' test

Objective
2

The starting point for assessing whether the defendant's breach of duty is a factual cause of the claimant's damage is the 'but for' test. This basic test is whether the damage would not have occurred but for the breach of duty. The purpose of the 'but for' test is to remove irrelevant causes.

The claimant must establish *on the balance of probabilities* that the defendant's breach of duty was a cause of their damage. The civil standard of proof (balance of probabilities) is a lower one than the criminal standard of beyond reasonable doubt. The claimant must show that there was more than a 50 per cent chance that the defendant's breach of duty caused their damage.

In the example of a road accident, there may be many causes of the accident. The weather may be bad; there may be poor lighting on that stretch of road; one of the drivers involved in the accident may have been driving negligently. The purpose of the but for test is to determine whether the negligent driving is a sufficient cause to impose legal liability on the negligent driver. The policy issue here is that the driver will (or should be) insured and the imposition of liability will mean that an injured person will be guaranteed compensation by the defendant's insurer.

Barnett v *Chelsea and Kensington Hospital Management Committee* [1969] 1 QB 428

> The claimant's husband attended the defendants' hospital and complained of vomiting. The doctor in casualty refused to examine him and he was told to see his own doctor in the morning if he still felt unwell. Five hours later he died of arsenic poisoning. The defendants owed the deceased a duty of care which they had breached by failing to examine him. They were held not liable as the evidence established that, even if he had been examined, he would have died before diagnosis and treatment could have been carried out. As the deceased would have died regardless of the breach of duty, the breach was not a cause of his death.

In most cases the 'but for' test presents no difficulties. However, there are areas where the test presents problems. These are in relation to multiple causes of harm; the degree of probability of damage occurring, particularly in cases of disease and medical negligence; where the test produces unjust results; and economic loss cases. Before entering these extremely murky waters the student should be warned that these categories overlap to a significant extent.

The reason why the courts sometimes depart from 'but for' causation was explained by Lord Nicholls in *Fairchild* v *Glenhaven Funeral Services Ltd* [2002] 3 All ER 305:

> The law habitually limits the extent of the damage for which a defendant is held responsible, even when the damage passes the threshold 'but for' test. The converse is also true. On occasions the threshold 'but for' test of causal connection may be over-exclusionary. Where justice so requires, the threshold itself may be lowered. In this way the scope of the defendant's liability may be extended. The circumstances where this is appropriate will be exceptional, because of the adverse consequences which the lowering of the threshold will have for a defendant. He will be held responsible for a loss the plaintiff might have suffered even if the defendant had not been involved at all.

Problems with the 'but for' test

Objective 3

If there is uncertainty as to whether the defendant's negligence has caused the damage, it has to be determined what degree of probability of damage occurring has to be established by the claimant. The burden of proof for causation is on the claimant and he must prove that, on the balance of probabilities, the damage was caused by the breach of duty. This is the 'all or nothing' approach to proof of causation because if the claimant proves that it is probable, 51 per cent likely, that the breach caused the loss, then the claimant will succeed and recover in respect of all of their loss. If the claimant is unable to reach this standard of proof then he fails and recovers nothing. It should be stressed that this is not the only approach taken by the courts to factual causation.

Where the injury is traumatic, such as a person being struck by a car or having a hand cut off in a machine, there is usually no difficulty. The presence of the car on the road or the existence of the machine will be treated as a cause.

However, where there are several alternative explanations of the events leading to the damage, one of which may be the defendant's fault and others 'innocent' there may be a problem. An example is where a disease is contracted by the claimant. Medical science may not be able specifically to pinpoint the cause of the disease or link negligent conduct to its appearance. In industrial injury cases there may have been more than one employer who exposed the claimant to a risk. In such cases the court may take the approach of asking whether the defendant has 'materially increased the risk' of damage occurring by his negligent conduct. The case of *McGhee* (discussed below) is an example of this approach.

See Chapter 15 for *Gregg* v *Scott* and medical negligence.

Claimants have sometimes advanced the argument that the defendant's negligence has deprived them of a chance. This may be a chance of getting better if they had been treated properly. The courts have rejected this argument in cases of personal injuries involving medical negligence (see *Gregg* v *Scott* [2005] 4 All ER 812) but have accepted it in economic loss cases.

Multiple potential causes

Where there is more than one potential cause of the harm, the claimant is faced with the problem of establishing that one cause (the defendant's breach of duty) is more likely to have caused the damage than any other cause. If there are four possible causes and each is as likely to have caused the damage as the other then the claimant can only prove a 25 per cent likelihood and will therefore fail as they have not reached the balance of probabilities threshold of 51 per cent.

Wilsher v *Essex Area Health Authority* [1988] 1 All ER 871

The claimant was born prematurely and suffered from an oxygen deficiency. Due to the admitted negligence of a doctor, the claimant was given excessive oxygen. The claimant suffered from deteriorating eyesight and became almost blind. The allegation was that the excess oxygen negligently administered had caused the blindness. The medical evidence showed that excessive oxygen was a cause of blindness in premature babies, but it was not the only factor which caused blindness. The House of Lords held that the claimant had to establish, on the balance of probabilities, that the defendant's breach of duty was a cause of the injury. A retrial of the action was ordered.

The House considered the decision in *McGhee* (see below) and stated that the judgment of Lord Wilberforce in that case was a minority one and did not represent the law. The test proposed by Lord Wilberforce was that 'where a person has, by breach of duty of care, created a risk and injury occurs within the area of that risk, the loss should be borne by him unless he shows that it had some other cause.' This test effectively transferred the burden of proof to the defendant on the basis that in these cases, as a matter of justice, it is the creator of the risk who should bear the consequences.

The House held that the burden of proof of causation remained on the claimant throughout the case. The claimant had to prove that the breach of duty was at least a material contributory cause of the harm.

What is a material contributory cause? There were five possible causes of the retrolental fibroplasia (RLF) and all of these were present. The House stated that a cause was a material contributory one if either: it was more likely that the cause of the RLF was the defendant's breach of duty than any of all the other four causes put together; or the breach of duty was more likely to be the cause than any other single cause.

The House also distinguished *McGhee*, as in that case the claimant's injury was caused by the brick dust. The only question was whether earlier washing would have prevented the dermatitis. In *Wilsher* there were a number of different possible causes of the claimant's blindness and the claimant had not been able to establish the defendant's negligence as the cause. What the defendant had done was not to enhance the risk that the known factors would lead to blindness, but to add to the list of factors which might lead to blindness. The interpretation of *McGhee* was that the House of Lords had drawn a robust and pragmatic interpretation from the primary facts that the additional exposure to the dust had materially contributed to the claimant's dermatitis and that the case laid down no new principle of law whatever. (Later disapproved by the House of Lords in *Fairchild* v *Glenhaven* (2002) – see below.)

Material contribution to harm and material increase in risk

In *Wilsher* the House of Lords was effectively invited to create an exception to the 'but for' test in cases of medical negligence where the claimant was put to an impossible task of proving causation. They refused to do this but in the earlier case, an industrial disease one, a different test had been used.

Bonnington Castings Ltd v Wardlaw [1956] AC 613

> The claimant contracted pneumoconiosis as a result of inhaling dust at work. Some of the dust was 'innocent' and some was 'guilty', in the sense that it came from the defendant's breach of duty. There was no evidence as to the proportions of 'innocent' and 'guilty' dust inhaled by the claimant so the 'but for' test could not be satisfied on the balance of probabilities. The House of Lords held that the claimant does not have to prove that the defendant's breach of duty was the sole or the main cause of the damage provided that it materially contributed to the damage. An inference of fact was drawn that the 'guilty' dust was a material cause and the defendants were liable.

See also *Bailey* v *Ministry of Defence* [2008] EWCA Civ 883 and Chapter 15.

In this case the House of Lords ignored the but for test. The reasons for this are not clear but it may be that they were conscious of the employer–employee relationship and the existence of compulsory insurance taken out by the employer.

The damage in the case was caused by the cumulative exposure of the claimant to toxins. The test was whether the negligent exposure to the 'guilty dust' would materially contribute to the claimant's condition. The test was not whether the negligent exposure was the likely cause. On this test the claimant received full compensation on the all or nothing basis.

However, in diseases where the condition is a cumulative one and the extent of the defendant's contribution is known they will only be liable to that extent. (*Thompson* v *Smiths Shiprepairers (North Shields) Ltd* [1984] 1 All ER 881; *Performance Cars* v *Abraham* [1962] 1 QB 33.) It may, however, be difficult to establish the extent of the defendant's contribution.

Holtby v Brigham & Cowan (Hull) Ltd [2000] 3 All ER 421

> The claimant was exposed to asbestos dust for 40 years and developed asbestosis. He had worked for the defendants for half that time and for other employers for the rest of the time. The trial judge found the defendants liable only for the damage they had caused and the claimant appealed on the ground that once he had established material contributory cause he was entitled to recover the full extent of his loss. The Court of Appeal rejected the appeal and upheld the trial judge's deduction of 25 per cent from general damages. *McGhee* was distinguished as there the claimant had argued that he was not liable at all, not that he was only liable up to the extent of his contribution.

It is clear from *Holtby* that it is open to a defendant to argue and prove that he was only liable for a particular extent of the damage. In this case the argument was not too difficult to make as asbestosis has a linear progression and all the dust contributed to the disability. (Compare with *Fairchild* (below).) On this basis the 25 per cent deduction is generous and should have been 50 per cent.

The material contribution test in *Bonnington* was looked at again in another industrial disease case.

McGhee v National Coal Board [1973] 1 WLR 1

The claimant worked in the defendants' brick kilns. Conditions were very hot and dusty. He had to cycle home unwashed as no washing facilities were provided at work. The claimant contracted dermatitis, a skin disease. He argued that if the defendants had provided washing facilities he would not have caught the disease. The medical evidence did not establish that the claimant would not have caught the disease if washing facilities had been provided. The House of Lords held that the claimant could succeed on the ground that the defendants had materially increased the risk of the claimant contracting the disease. The defendants (who had admitted negligence) had increased the risk of particular damage occurring and that damage had occurred.

Lord Salmon:

> ... I would suggest that the true view is that, as a rule, when it is proved, on a balance of probabilities, that an employer has been negligent and that his negligence has materially increased the risk of his employee contracting an industrial disease, then he is liable in damages to that employee if he contracts the disease notwithstanding that the employer is not responsible for other factors which have materially contributed to the disease. ...
>
> In the circumstances of the present case, the possibility of a distinction existing between (a) having materially increased the risk of contracting the disease, and (b) having materially contributed to causing the disease may no doubt be a fruitful source of interesting academic discussions between students of philosophy. Such a distinction is, however, far too unreal to be recognised by the common law.

The basis on which **McGhee** was decided is controversial as the claimant never established, on the basis of the 'but for' test, that the defendants were a cause of his damage. What basis was the case decided on?

If there was a policy factor involved in the decision it could have been the superior resources of the defendant and the protective approach of the courts to employees.

This case illustrates that there is a relationship between causation and fault. (See **Bolitho v Hackney Health Authority** [1997] 3 WLR 1151.) The breach of duty was found to be a failure to provide washing facilities. But what would the situation have been if the employer was found to be negligent in allowing the employee to become covered in brick dust? There would then be no causation problem.

McGhee would therefore appear to establish a principle that where the defendant has created a risk of particular damage and that damage has occurred, the defendant should not be allowed to escape liability because the medical evidence is inconclusive.

What is the difference between **McGhee** and **Wilsher**? The argument in **McGhee** was raised in **Wilsher** and rejected by the House of Lords. They stated that **McGhee** had not established a new principle of causation. The defendant doctor had materially increased the claimant's risk of blindness but this was not sufficient to establish causation. In **McGhee** there was only one cause of the skin disease whereas in **Wilsher** there were five possible causes of the claimant's blindness. However, a more likely reason is in policy. The damages in **Wilsher** would have fallen on the National Health Service.

A further development in this area came in a specific area of damage – that of the mesothelioma cases. This saga of case law and legislation involves issues of material increase in harm and the problem of where the 'but for' test produces an unjust result.

Unjust results

(i) The mesothelioma cases

The interpretation of **McGhee** in **Wilsher** failed to gain acceptance by the House of Lords in a major consolidated appeal on cancer contracted from contact with asbestos. The problem in this case was that the claimants had worked for a number of employers. This litigation has been one of the key tests of the role of tort in disease litigation. It has involved three Supreme Court decisions and legislation in a short period of time.

The background is a form of cancer known as mesothelioma. Mesothelioma is a malignant tumour which is rare in persons not exposed to asbestos. The disease may occur after low levels of exposure but the risk increases in proportion to the dose received, though the severity of the disease does not. Therefore, successive periods of exposure each increase the risk that the disease will occur. It is for these reasons that mesothelioma is characterised as an 'indivisible' disease.

There is usually a long period between the first exposure to asbestos and the first clinical signs of mesothelioma. The latency period is more than 30 years in most cases, but intervals of as little as ten years and less in rare cases are found. There is no upper limit on the latency period. This period is not the same as the period in which the tumour grows. The tumour is thought to begin to grow on average ten years before clinical signs appear.

The number of cases of mesothelioma diagnosed in the United Kingdom is growing fast and has been characterised as an epidemic. Treasure *et al.* in 'Radical Surgery for Mesothelioma' (2004) state:

> One in every hundred men born in the [UK in the] 1940s will die of malignant Mesothelioma, which is almost exclusively a consequence of exposure to asbestos, with a lag time that is rarely less than 25 years and often more than 50 years from first exposure. Half of all cases are now aged over 70 with 80 per cent in men. For a man first exposed as a teenager, who remained in a high risk occupation, such as insulation, throughout his working life, the lifetime risk of Mesothelioma can be as high as 1 in 5. There are now over 1,800 deaths per year in Britain (that is, about 1 in 200 of all deaths in men and 1 in 1,500 in women) and the number is still increasing. As exposure in the United Kingdom continued until 1980, the peak of the epidemic is still to come. The peak of the epidemic is expected in 2015 to 2020 when the death rate is likely to be 2,000 a year in the United Kingdom.

The state of medical science is such that where a victim has been exposed to asbestos by more than one source, it cannot be said which source of exposure provided the fibre or fibres that caused the disease. This has given rise to the problem of proving causation for victims when making a claim for damages for injury or death arising from exposure by more than one employer. The problem is proving which of the employers caused the disease.

Fairchild v *Glenhaven Funeral Services Ltd* [2002] 3 All ER 305

The appellants had developed mesothelioma, a form of cancer, as a result of exposure to asbestos. The difficulty in the cases was that the appellants had been negligently exposed to asbestos by a number of employers. Mesothelioma is not a cumulative disease which meant that the appellants could not identify which employer was liable. If the appellants had developed asbestosis, which is a cumulative disease, each employer could have been held liable for a proportionate part of the disease as the severity of the condition can be related to the period of exposure. Mesothelioma can be caused by exposure to a single fibre of asbestos. If this is the case then subsequent exposure will not make the condition worse.

The Court of Appeal ([2002] 1 WLR 1052) had held the defendants (on the basis of **Wilsher**) not liable as the claimants had failed to establish causation. They could not establish on the balance of probabilities that exposure to the fibre(s) that had caused the cancer was the result of any employer's breach of duty. An injustice would have been done whichever way the decision had gone. To find the defendants not liable meant that a person who had worked for a number of negligent employers had no redress but one who had worked for a single employer did. To hold for the claimants would have meant that an employer could be liable for a person employed for a short time who could not prove that his period of employment had any causal relationship with the disease.

The House of Lords allowed the appellants' appeal and held that in the special circumstances of this type of case the normal 'but for' rule would be relaxed. A number of reasons were given for the decision.

1 In most other jurisdictions the claimants would have had a remedy, by a number of different methods. The burden of proof could be reversed; increase in risk could be treated as material contribution to damage; the ordinary approach to tortfeasors acting in concert could be enlarged; or on general policy grounds.

2 When the competing injustices were weighed in the balance the claimants should have a remedy. The defendants had been negligent and an innocent claimant had suffered a terrible disease which almost inevitably results in death. On this basis, it would be morally wrong and inconsistent with legal policy to exclude liability on the basis of causation.

3 The interpretation of *McGhee* made in *Wilsher* by Lord Bridge (see above) was disapproved. *McGhee* did decide a question of law, which was whether a claimant who could not show that the defendant's breach had probably caused the damage could succeed. The ratio of *McGhee* was said to be that in the circumstances no distinction was to be drawn between making a material contribution to causing the damage and materially increasing the risk to the claimant. In the circumstances, a material increase in the risk should be treated the same as if it had materially contributed to the risk. *Wilsher*, however, survived on its own facts as there were a number of possible agents involved. The principle only applied where there was one noxious agent involved. Under precisely what conditions could 'but for' causation be dispensed with and the principle applied? It is clear that their Lordships were not unanimous on this point.

Although all their Lordships were aware of the dangers of stating the principle too widely, their speeches leave open the precise extent of the principle. Lord Bingham limits it to the facts of the case itself. Lord Rodger states a more general principle but Lord Hoffmann limits it to employees exposed to asbestos. However, both Lords Bingham and Hoffmann acknowledged that the principle could be extended in the future.

The fact that the principle is not limited to lack of scientific knowledge appears to be acknowledged by Lord Rodger.

Fairchild left a number of problems:

1 What would be the position where the claimant is exposed to asbestos by one employer and to another cancer-causing agent by another employer? Would the case fall within *Fairchild* or *Wilsher*? The injustice that *Fairchild* was intended to prevent was the unfairness of requiring the claimant to prove the impossible where the defendant was in breach of duty. The fact that more than one noxious agent was involved should not affect the outcome and does not generally do so in other jurisdictions. However, the judges in the House of Lords appeared to be split on this. Lord Hoffmann recognised that the distinction between one agent and a number of different agents was not a principled one but Lord Bingham appeared to restrict the principle to single agents. Lord Rodger thought that where there were a number of causal agents it would be necessary to show that they all operated in substantially the same way. This would distinguish *Wilsher* where the possible causal agents operated in different ways. The question was discussed (*obiter*) by Lord Hope in *Barker v Corus* (see below):

> If the case were not one of an eventual outcome produced by a single agent but of an outcome that might have been produced by one of a number of different agents and where

the guilty agent could not be identified e.g. cases like *Wilsher* v *Essex Area Health Authority* or *Hotson* v *East Berkshire Area Health Authority* Lord Hope would not regard the *Fairchild* principle as applicable. *Fairchild* did not establish an overarching principle. It established a narrow exception to the causation requirements applicable to single agent cases. He would not extend the exception to cover multiagent cases as well. One reason is that the identification of the proportion of risk of the eventual outcome attributable to each particular agent would be well nigh impossible and highly artificial. At least in the asbestos cases it is known that asbestos was responsible for the eventual outcome and that the negligent defendants are to be held liable for subjecting the victim to a risk that has materialised.

2 What would be the position where there were two employers but only one of them had been negligent? Again, the judges were split on the issue. Lord Bingham thought the principle would not apply as it required both employers to have been negligent. Lord Rodger, though, reserved his position on this issue.

3 What would be the position if the claimant was tortiously exposed to asbestos by the defendant but there was asbestos dust in the general environment? The question was whether, in a mesothelioma case, where there is more than one source of asbestos exposure, the claimant can be required to show that the risk arising from the tortious exposure is more than twice the risk arising from the non-tortious cause or causes. Or is it sufficient, in the light of *Fairchild* and *Barker* (see below) that they need only show a material (more than minimal) increase in risk?

Sienkiewicz v *Grief* [2011] UKSC 10

Mrs Costello died of mesothelioma. She had worked at the defendant's factory for 18 years, during which time she had wrongfully been exposed to asbestos dust. However, she, along with the rest of the population of Ellesmere Port, had been subject to general environmental exposure to asbestos. It was accepted that the likely cause of the mesothelioma of which she died was exposure to asbestos dust, but on the evidence the tortious exposure increased the risk that she would contract mesothelioma by no more than 18 per cent. The trial judge held that this was insufficient to establish the crucial causal link between the defendant's negligence and the claimant's harm. The more likely cause was the 'innocent' exposure which she had experienced in the community. The Supreme Court was asked two questions:

(i) whether the *Fairchild* exception applied in cases where only one defendant was proved to have exposed the victim of mesothelioma to asbestos, but where the victim was also at risk of developing the disease from low-level exposure to asbestos in the general atmosphere;

(ii) whether there was an exception to the *Fairchild* exception where there had been only one occupational exposure to risk and that, in those circumstances, whether the 'doubles the risk' test applied in such cases. ('Double the risk' is if the 'guilty' exposure more than doubles the risk to the claimant, this will suffice to establish the causal link, otherwise not. The method, however, attempts a logical application of the normal balance of probability principle of causation, rather than the *Fairchild* exception. It seeks to establish that the 'guilty' exposure more likely than not caused the harm.)

Held. The *Fairchild* exception applied in cases where only one defendant was proved to have exposed the victim of mesothelioma to asbestos. There was no requirement for a claimant to prove that the defendant's breach of duty doubled the risk of developing the disease. Liability for mesothelioma fell on anyone who had materially increased the risk of the victim contracting the disease. In

> the instant state of knowledge about the disease, the only circumstances in which a court would be able to conclude that wrongful exposure of a mesothelioma victim to asbestos dust did not materially increase the victim's risk of contracting the disease would be where that exposure was insignificant compared to the exposure from other sources. The claimant's case succeeded.

The House of Lords attempted to provide an answer to some of these questions in a case which arose because of the insolvency of some of the former employers and insurers in the asbestos cases.

Barker v *Corus UK Ltd* [2006] 3 All ER 785

> All three claimants died of asbestos-related mesothelioma. One claimant had had three material exposures to asbestos. The first was for six weeks, the second was for six months while working for the defendants and the third was for at least three short periods working as a self-employed plasterer. The first two exposures were in consequence of breaches of duty by the employers and the last was agreed to have involved a failure by Mr Barker to take reasonable care for his own safety.
>
> The first question was whether this took the case outside the *Fairchild* exception. If it did not, the second question was whether the defendants were liable for all the damage suffered or only for its contribution to the materialised risk that he would contract mesothelioma. The first employer was insolvent and without any identified insurer, so the defendants were unable to recover any contribution.
>
> In the other two appeals, all the exposures to asbestos were in breach of duties owed by employers or occupiers and there was no dispute that the cases fell within the *Fairchild* exception. The only question was whether liability was joint and several or only several. One defendant had been regularly exposed to asbestos during his working life, in breach of duty, by four employers, two of whom were insolvent and whose insurers were also insolvent and accounted between them for 83.22 per cent of the period for which exposure took place. The first two were responsible, in roughly equal shares, for the rest. The question was whether they were nevertheless jointly and severally liable for the whole damage. In a case where there is more than one defendant and liability is joint, the claimant can sue one defendant for the whole of the damage and that defendant must then claim against the other defendants. Where liability is several, a defendant will only be liable up to the extent of the damage he caused. The other defendant spent most of his working life in the Tyne shipyards and had been exposed to asbestos, in breach of duty, by a considerable number of employers. The five joined as defendants accounted for 42.5 per cent of the period of exposure; the others were insolvent and uninsured. Again, the question was whether the solvent defendants were jointly and severally liable for the full damage.
>
> The House of Lords allowed the defendant's appeals to the extent that liability would be limited to the extent that the defendant's negligence exposed the claimant to the material risk of contracting the disease.

This marked a significant victory for the insurers, who were now only liable for a proportion of the loss. A significant number of former employers and their insurers are now insolvent.

The House accepted that the assistance which could be derived from the various formulations in *Fairchild* was limited, but instead looked at the reinterpretation of *McGhee*. Difficulties are caused because of the differing interpretations of *McGhee* given by their Lordships.

For present purposes, the importance of *McGhee* is that it was a case in which there had been two possible causes of the pursuer's dermatitis: the brick dust which adhered to his skin while he was working in the brick kilns and the dust which continued to adhere to his skin while he was on his way home. So one source of risk was tortious but the other was not. The House decided that the *Fairchild* exception allowed him to recover damages although he could not prove that the persistence of dust after he had left work was more likely to have caused the dermatitis than its original presence on his body while he was working.

It was in order to accommodate this case that Lord Rodger in *Fairchild* accepted that the exception could apply 'where, as in *McGhee*, the other possible source of the injury is a similar, but lawful, act or omission of the same defendant'.

The key factor here is that *Fairchild* did not determine that the claimant had to prove that the defendant caused the disease. Simply that the defendant, by negligently exposing the defendant to the asbestos had materially increased the risk of the claimant contracting the disease. On this basis it is irrelevant that part of the exposure was while the claimant was self-employed or exposed in a non-negligent manner by an employer.

This interpretation (or rewriting) of *McGhee* was subjected to a very strong dissent by Lord Rodger. This extract is worth reading for the insurance background it provides to the case:

> The new analysis which the House is adopting will tend to maximise the inconsistencies in the law by turning the *Fairchild* exception into an enclave where a number of rules apply which have been rejected for use elsewhere in the law of personal injuries. (See e.g. *Gregg* v *Scott*.) Inside the enclave victims recover damages for suffering the increased risk of developing mesothelioma (or suffering the loss of a chance of not developing mesothelioma) while, just outside, patients cannot recover damages for suffering the increased risk of an unfavourable outcome to medical treatment (or suffering the loss of a chance of a favourable outcome to medical treatment). On the other hand, if such a claim had been recognised outside the enclave, the patient would have been entitled to recover damages for the increased likelihood that he would suffer a premature death, whereas inside the enclave a victim who suffers an increased risk of developing mesothelioma cannot recover damages unless he actually develops it. Inside the enclave claimants whose husbands die of mesothelioma receive only, say, 60 per cent of their damages if the court considers that there is a 60 per cent chance that the defendant caused the death and no other wrongdoer is solvent or insured. Outside the enclave, claimants whose husbands are killed in an accident for which the only solvent defendant is, say, 5 per cent to blame recover the whole of their damages from that defendant.
>
> Why, then, is the House spontaneously embarking upon this adventure of redefining the nature of the damage suffered by the victims? The majority are not just on a mission to tidy up the reasoning in *McGhee* and *Fairchild*. Their aim is to open the way to making each defendant severally liable for a share of the damages, rather than liable in solidum for the whole of the damages. This is said to be a preferable, fairer, solution when the defendants are found liable for creating the risk of illness rather than for causing it.

Apportionment

The second issue that arose in all three appeals was whether, under the *Fairchild* exception, a defendant is liable, jointly and severally with any other defendants, for all the damage consequent upon the contraction of mesothelioma by the claimant or whether he is liable only for a share, apportioned according to the share of the risk created by his breach of duty.

Lord Hoffmann stated that the basis of the majority in *Fairchild* was that liability was based on an increase in a material risk that the claimant would contract the disease.

If the basis of liability is the wrongful creation of a risk or chance of causing the disease, the damage which the defendant should be regarded as having caused is the creation of such a risk or chance. If that is the right way to characterise the damage, then it does not matter that the disease as such would be indivisible damage. Treating the creation of the risk as the damage caused by the defendant would involve having to quantify the likelihood that the damage (which is known to have materialised) was caused by that particular defendant. It will then be possible to determine the share of the damage which should be attributable to him.

Lord Hoffmann stated:

> In my opinion, the attribution of liability according to the relative degree of contribution to the chance of the disease being contracted would smooth the roughness of the justice which a rule of joint and several liability creates. The defendant was a wrongdoer, it is true, and should not be allowed to escape liability altogether, but he should not be liable for more than the damage which he caused and, since this is a case in which science can deal only in probabilities, the law should accept that position and attribute liability according to probabilities. The justification for the joint and several liability rule is that if you caused harm, there is no reason why your liability should be reduced because someone else also caused the same harm. But when liability is exceptionally imposed because you may have caused harm, the same considerations do not apply and fairness suggests that if more than one person may have been responsible, liability should be divided according to the probability that one or other caused the harm.

The outcome of this case was surprising. The decision in *Fairchild* was welcomed (except by insurers) because of the justice it undeniably gave, but there were concerns that creating an exception would damage the fabric of tort law in this area.

The justice that was done to claimants in *Fairchild* created an injustice in standard tort terms to defendants. This was altered in *Barker* by making defendants and their insurers only liable to the extent to which they were responsible for negligent exposure to asbestos. This rectification was at the expense of claimants who would only have received partial compensation where a defendant/insurer had become insolvent.

In *Fairchild*, the court in effect excused the claimant in the multiple source of exposure type of case from proving which exposure caused the disease to be contracted. After *Fairchild* the courts regarded the outcome as one which imposed joint and several liability for damage on the persons who had exposed the victim in circumstances amounting to a breach of duty, on the basis set out in Lord Rodger's dissenting speech in *Barker*, that materially increasing the risk of contracting the disease in a case where it was later contracted was tantamount to causing the disease, so that the principle of the joint liability of joint tortfeasors applied.

In *Barker*, the majority rejected that analysis and explained *Fairchild* as a case that made material increase in the risk of contracting the disease through exposure in circumstances amounting to a breach of duty tortious, provided the victim contracted the disease. They held that since material increase in the risk was the basis of the tort, contribution to the risk could and should be apportioned between those who were responsible.

In theory this was fine, but it ignored the fact that, in practice, it was often impossible, in cases of exposure at work, for a claimant to identify or trace all employers and that of those that could be identified, many would be without insurance or assets. There was also a shortage of experts who could assist the court on matters of apportionment, leading to severe delays in litigation. The result was that, in the vast majority of multiple employer cases, compensation was reduced to a fraction of the full damages, for reasons totally beyond the control of the victim and at the same time the cost of investigation of a claim was increased because the burden was on the claimant to prove the apportionment.

 The Compensation Act 2006

See also Chapter 1 for Compensation Act 2006.

The decision in **Barker** was predictably unpopular with victim groups and, following adverse publicity in Parliament and the media, the decision was promptly reversed by legislation.

Section 3 of the Act does not create a free-standing statutory tort but has sought to graft the application of the section onto the law of tort in this area as it stands. Two basic principles are established which modify that law and which apply to all mesothelioma claims, as follows.

Section 3(1) provides:

(i) A person must have negligently (or in breach of statutory duty) exposed the victim to asbestos.

(ii) The victim has contracted mesothelioma.

Section 3(2) is the crucial subsection. It reverses the effect of the **Barker** decision by providing that 'the responsible person' will be liable for the whole of the damage. This applies where there is more than one responsible person; where there has been non-tortious exposure by a responsible person or by the victim himself. (Section 3 of the Compensation Act was important in the decision in **Sienkiewicz**.)

(ii) Cases outside mesothelioma

See Chapter 15 for informed consent.

The only other area where the courts appear to be prepared to depart from standard principles of causation in order to give a just result is in cases of 'informed consent' to medical treatment. Where a patient is given insufficient information on proposed treatment and a risk the patient had not been told about materialised, the question arises as to what the patient would have done if they had been informed and what they have to prove. In **Chester** v **Afshar** [2005] 1 AC 134, the House of Lords held that where, in breach of duty, a surgeon failed to warn a patient about a risk of injury inherent in an operation, and, as a result of that failure, the patient had the operation and the risk materialised, she did not have to prove, for the purposes of establishing causation, that she would never have had the operation at any time if properly warned. Rather, it was sufficient for her to prove that, if properly warned, she would not have consented to the operation which was in fact performed and which resulted in the injury. Such a conclusion could not be based on conventional causation principles because the risk was not created or increased by the failure to warn, and the chances of avoiding it were not lessened by that failure. In such a case, however, justice required the normal approach to causation to be modified. The law which imposed the duty to warn on the doctor had at its heart the right of the patient to make an informed choice as to whether, and if so when and by whom, to be operated on. Patients were entitled to have different views about those matters. For some the choice might be easy – simply to agree or to decline the operation. For many, however, the choice would be a difficult one, requiring time to think, to take advice and to weigh up the alternatives. The duty was owed as much to the patient who, if warned, would find the decision difficult as to the patient who would find it simple and could give a clear answer to the doctor one way or the other immediately. To leave the patient who would find the decision difficult without a remedy, as the normal approach to causation would indicate, would render the duty useless in the cases where it might be needed most. That would discriminate against those who could not honestly say that they would have declined the operation once and for all if they had been warned. That result was unacceptable. The function of the law was to enable rights to be vindicated and to provide remedies when the duties had been breached.

Cases involving multiple defendants

A further problem occurs where there is no 'innocent' explanation but the damage could have been caused by the fault of more than one defendant. If the 'but for' test is applied mechanically in these situations it could result in the claimant not being compensated.

Example

A and *B* simultaneously fire guns and *C* is struck by bullets from both guns. An application of the 'but for' test will mean that neither *A* nor *B* will be liable. This would be clearly unjust, so *A* and *B* will both be held liable.

Where *C* was struck by only one bullet but could not prove whose gun the bullet came from, a Canadian case has held that both *A* and *B* were liable. (*Cook* v *Lewis* [1952] 1 DLR 1.) The reason for the decision was that the burden of proof lay on the defendants to prove that they had not been negligent and they had failed to discharge this burden. How do you think an English court would decide this case? For a disease case where there was more than one negligent defendant but the claimant could not prove whose negligence caused the damage, see *Fairchild* v *Glenhaven*.

A variant on this scenario would be where the claimant was hit by two bullets fired by each of the two defendants. An application of the 'but for' test would exonerate each defendant. An example of this occurred in the context of a traffic accident in the following case.

Fitzgerald v *Lane* [1989] AC 328

The claimant stepped out into the traffic on a busy road. He was struck by a vehicle driven by the first defendant. This pushed him into the path of an oncoming vehicle driven by the second defendant. Both defendants were accepted to be negligent but it could not be established that the second accident contributed to the injury. The second defendant therefore argued that there was no causal link between his negligence and the claimant's injuries. The Court of Appeal held both defendants liable on Lord Wilberforce's principle in *McGhee*. Each defendant had materially increased the risk of that injury by his negligence and therefore had the burden of disproving a causal link.

A radical approach to this problem was taken in the USA in *Sindell* v *Abbott Laboratories* 607 P 2d 924 (1980). The case concerned a design defect in a pregnancy drug which was made by several hundred manufacturers. Any of the manufacturers could have been liable in each case. The court held each manufacturer liable according to its market share. The approach has been criticised as departing from the idea of tort as a system of individual responsibility.

Supervening or overtaking causes

Where the causal effect of the defendant's fault is overtaken by a later event or by the emergence of a latent condition, neither of which is related to the original tort, the 'but for' test may not provide an answer.

What is the position when the first defendant is sued and the second defendant has caused similar or greater damage?

Baker v Willoughby [1970] AC 467

The claimant suffered injuries to his left leg as a result of the defendant's negligence. The claimant went to work in a new job after the accident and while at work he was shot in the left leg during an armed robbery. As a result, the claimant's leg had to be amputated. The armed robbers, needless to say, did not stay around to be sued. The defendant argued that any liability which he had extended only from his breach of duty until the armed robbery. At this point, the effects of his negligence were overtaken by the effects of the second tort (the armed robbery). Applying the 'but for' test would have produced this result. But the House of Lords refused to apply the 'but for' test. First, the claimant was compensated for the loss he suffered as a result of the injury, not for the injury itself. The second tort had not reduced the claimant's suffering or his reduction in earning capacity. Second, even if the claimant could have sued the armed robbers, they would only have been liable for depriving the claimant of a damaged left leg. So if the defendant's argument succeeded, the claimant would be left under-compensated.

The clear injustice that would have been caused by denying liability to the claimant in this case was avoided by the House of Lords abandoning the 'but for' test in order to do justice. This is an approach which has subsequently been taken in other areas. (See e.g. *Fairchild* v *Glenhaven* and *Chester* v *Afshar*.)

Where the claimant has already suffered damage as a result of the first tort, the second tortfeasor is only liable for the additional damage they have caused on the basis of the 'but for' test.

Performance Cars v Abraham [1962] 1 QB 33

The second defendant negligently collided with the claimant's Rolls-Royce. The car had previously been in a collision caused by the negligence of the first defendant. The second defendant damaged the same part of the car as the first defendant. The court held that the second defendant was not liable for the cost of a respray, as at the time of the accident the car was already in need of one. (Affirmed by the Court of Appeal in *Halsey* v *Milton Keynes General NHS Trust* [2004] EWCA Civ 576.)

In *Baker* the court decided that the causal effect of the first tort continued despite the fact that the leg would have been lost as a result of the second tort. The situation is apparently different where the tort is followed by a supervening illness.

Jobling v Associated Dairies Ltd [1982] AC 794

The claimant suffered an injury to his back at work in 1973, caused by the defendant's breach of duty. The injury reduced the claimant's earning capacity by 50 per cent. Before the trial of the action in 1979 the claimant was discovered to be suffering from a back disease, unrelated to the injury, which rendered him totally unfit for work by 1976. The House of Lords applied the 'but for' test to restrict the defendant's liability for loss of earnings to the period before the onset of the disease.

The House of Lords criticised the reasoning in *Baker*, but the decision survives. Where there are two successive torts, the first tortfeasor's liability is unaffected by the second tort. Where the tort is followed by a disabling illness, this must be taken into account in assessing the tortfeasor's liability.

Lord Wilberforce:

We do not live in a world governed by the pure common law and its logical rules. We live in a mixed world where a man is protected against injury and misfortune by a whole web of rules and dispositions, with a number of timid legislative interventions. To attempt to compensate him upon the basis of selected rules without regard to the whole must lead either to logical inconsistencies, or to over – or under – compensation. As my noble and learned friend, Lord Edmund-Davies, has pointed out, no account was taken, in *Baker v Willoughby* [1970] AC 467 of the very real possibility that the plaintiff might obtain compensation from the Criminal Injuries Compensation Board. If he did in fact obtain this compensation he would, on the ultimate decision, be over-compensated.

In the present case, and in other industrial injury cases, there seems to me no justification for disregarding the fact that the injured man's employer is insured – indeed since 1972 compulsorily insured – against liability to his employees. The state has decided, in other words, on a spreading of risk. There seems to me no more justification for disregarding the fact that the plaintiff – presumably, we have not been told otherwise – is entitled to sickness and invalidity benefit in respect of his myelopathy the amount of which may depend on his contribution record, which in turn may have been affected by his accident. So we have no means of knowing whether the plaintiff would be over-compensated if he were, in addition, to receive the assessed damages from his employer, or whether he would be under-compensated if left to his benefit. It is not easy to accept a solution by which a partially incapacitated man becomes worse off in terms of damages and benefit through a greater degree of incapacity. Many other ingredients, of weight in either direction, may enter into individual cases. Without any satisfaction I draw from this the conclusion that no general, logical, or universally fair rules can be stated which will cover, in a manner consistent with justice, cases of supervening events, whether due to tortious, partially tortious, non-culpable or wholly accidental events. . . .

If rationalisation is needed, I am willing to accept the 'vicissitudes' argument as the best available. I should be more firmly convinced of the merits of the conclusion if the whole pattern of benefits had been considered, in however general a way. The result of the present case may be lacking in precision and rational justification, but so long as we are content to live in a mansion of so many different architectures, this is inevitable.

Both the above cases are personal injury cases and tort damages are not the only form of compensation available. *Baker* is based on a policy of not under-compensating the claimant. *Jobling* is based on not over-compensating the claimant. The House of Lords pointed out in *Jobling* that the claimant in *Baker* would have been entitled to compensation from the Criminal Injuries Compensation Scheme and there was therefore a danger of over-compensation. This is not entirely correct, as the only compensation would have been for the damage caused by the armed robbery. Had the defendant been found not liable in *Baker*, the claimant would still have remained uncompensated for his original injuries.

In *Jobling*, the claimant might have been able to claim social security benefits partially to compensate for his losses. But it is still possible to fall between tort damages and entitlement to social security.

The distinctions between the two cases are not convincing and the apparent conflict and the difficulties posed by causation in the industrial disease and medical negligence cases show the drawbacks of using the tort system as a method of compensating for personal injuries.

The court was satisfied in *Jobling* that the tort and the onset of the disease were unrelated and the claimant would have suffered the loss despite the defendant's negligence. The test applied was on the balance of probabilities: but for the defendant's negligence, would the damage have occurred? An Australian decision took a different approach to future hypothetical events. In *Malec v JC Hutton Ltd* (1990) 64 ALJR 316 the Australian High Court stated that in these cases the balance of probabilities test should be modified. The claimant had suffered an occupational disease for which his employer was liable but it was found that it was more likely than not that he would have contracted the disease anyway. Instead of applying a cut-off point beyond which no damages could be recovered, the court awarded damages subject to a reduction for the chance that he would have suffered the disease anyway.

Loss of chance

Objective 4

Cases such as *McGhee* and *Wilsher* deal with uncertainties. What would have happened if . . . ? These uncertainties also arise in assessing damages for future loss, such as loss of income. The court has to speculate as to how much a claimant would have earned and in doing so takes into account the vicissitudes of life, such as illness or redundancy. The damages awarded thus include a discount for uncertainty but at this stage the court has already held that the *damage* was caused by the defendant's negligence. What the court is assessing is the quantum – how much – the claimant actually gets in damages. The question on causation is whether the court can use the same process to determine whether the claimant can recover anything at all when there is doubt about causation.

If the claimant cannot establish that the breach of duty was a material contributory cause of their harm, could the question be approached on the basis of loss of chance?

Chance in this sense means the chance of avoiding the loss which has actually occurred. Instead of taking an all-or-nothing approach based on causation, look at the question in terms of measure of damages and award a percentage. This approach was taken by the Court of Appeal in the following case but failed on the facts in the House of Lords.

Hotson v East Berkshire Area Health Authority [1987] 2 All ER 909

See Chapter 15 for *Hotson* and medical negligence.

The claimant fell and was taken to hospital, where his knee was X-rayed. A hip injury was not diagnosed. Five days later he returned to hospital, when the hip injury was discovered. By this time the hip injury had resulted in a deformity of the hip joint. The defendants argued that deformity would have occurred as a result of the injury, whether or not it had been properly diagnosed on the first trip to hospital. The trial judge found that the delay denied the claimant a 25 per cent chance of avoiding the hip deformity and awarded 25 per cent of the damages he would have awarded had the injury been solely caused by the delayed diagnosis. This approach was approved by the Court of Appeal. The claimant's claim was for loss of the benefit of timely treatment rather than the chance of successful treatment. The House of Lords held that the issue was one of causation, not quantification of damage. As the claimant had failed on the balance of probabilities to prove that the delayed treatment had at least been a material contributory cause of the deformity, the claimant's action failed. The House did not, unfortunately, deal with the question of whether a claim framed as a loss of chance claim was acceptable.

The burden of proof to establish causation therefore rests on the claimant throughout the case. If they fail to establish, on the balance of probabilities, that the defendant's negligence was a material contributory cause of their damage, their action fails. Where there is only one possible cause of the damage and the defendant's breach of duty has exposed the claimant to the risk of damage which has materialised, then causation is established.

The major argument for recovery for loss of chance is that the claimant has been deprived of something tangible. Before the defendant's breach of duty he had a prospect of recovery. This may have been indeterminate but it was real. Whether there should be recovery for loss of a chance of *physical* recovery is highly controversial. Opponents argue that it would give rise to a multiplicity of claims (floodgates) and give rise to evidential difficulties.

In the following case it was argued that the approach in *Fairchild* to causation justified a policy-based approach to loss of chance claims in personal injury actions.

Gregg v *Scott* [2005] 2 AC 176

See Chapter 15 for *Gregg* v *Scott*.

In November 1994, the claimant developed a lump under his left arm. He visited the defendant, his general practitioner, who wrongly diagnosed it as lipoma and failed to refer him to a specialist for confirmation or otherwise of his diagnosis. In 1995, the claimant moved to another area. He visited his then general practitioner and complained, again, of the lump. That practitioner referred him on a non-urgent basis to the local hospital for an investigation. The surgeon who examined him arranged for an urgent biopsy which revealed that the claimant had a lymphoma. On 13 January 1996, the claimant was admitted to hospital with acute and intense chest pain which was a result of the lymphoma having spread. The claimant underwent a course of treatment and eventually was told in 1998, after suffering a relapse, that he could not be cured. The effects on the claimant and his life both as a result of the treatment and the fact that he believed he was living on borrowed time were devastating. He brought an action for negligence. The judge concluded that the failure of the defendant to refer the claimant for a specialist opinion in November 1994 delayed treatment by about nine months and reduced the claimant's chances of survival to 25 per cent. Nevertheless, relying on *Hotson*, he dismissed the claim for damages on the grounds that the claimant had not established on the balance of probabilities that the negligence had had a material effect on the outcome of the disease. He did so on the basis that the evidence before him established that it was more probable than not that he would have been in his present position even if treatment had commenced at the proper time. The claimant's appeal to the Court of Appeal was dismissed.

There was evident disquiet even amongst the majority in the Court of Appeal about the fact that a person who has suffered in the manner of the claimant in this case has no action. This disquiet was further echoed in an economic loss case on loss of chance in the Court of Appeal (*Normans Bay Ltd v Coudert Brothers* [2004] All ER (D) 458).

On appeal to the House of Lords, the appeal was dismissed, Lord Nicholls and Lord Hope dissenting. The key factor in the approach of the majority in rejecting loss of chance is contained in the judgment of Lord Hoffmann:

> In *Fairchild*'s case [2003] 1 AC 32, 68, Lord Nicholls of Birkenhead said of new departures in the law:
>> To be acceptable the law must be coherent. It must be principled. The basis on which one case, or one type of case, is distinguished from another should be transparent and capable of identification. When a decision departs from principles normally applied, the basis for doing so must be rational and justifiable if the decision is to avoid the reproach that hard cases make bad law.
>
> I respectfully agree. And in my opinion, the various control mechanisms proposed to confine liability for loss of a chance within artificial limits do not pass this test. But a wholesale adoption of possible rather than probable causation as the criterion of liability would be so radical a change in our law as to amount to a legislative act. It would have enormous consequences for insurance companies and the National Health Service. In company with my noble and learned friends, Lord Phillips of Worth Matravers and Baroness Hale of Richmond, I think that any such change should be left to Parliament.

The main argument before the House of Lords was that the *Fairchild* exception should be extended to this case. The majority refused to take this step, as there was a distinction in that this case involved a choice between the defendant and natural causes, whereas *Fairchild* involved choosing between defendants, both of whom were negligent. The majority dismissed the claim on the basis that introducing loss of chance claims would disturb the structure of tort law and impose an excessive burden on medical professionals.

Lord Nicholls (dissenting) thought that a patient should have an appropriate remedy when he lost the very thing it was the doctor's duty to protect, a correct diagnosis. The law should therefore recognise the existence and loss of poor and indifferent prospects as well as those that are more favourable.

One further point is worth noting. The case is concerned with a diminished chance rather than a lost chance. In **Hotson** and the economic loss of chance cases (see below) the chance had gone but in **Gregg** (at the time of judgment) the claimant still had a chance of survival but this chance had been diminished rather than lost, it was in the future rather than the past.

The House of Lords took this opportunity to reject loss of chance in personal injury cases; however, the relationship between causation and quantum in loss of chance cases is raised in actions for economic loss where the claimant has been deprived of a chance by the defendant's negligent advice or omission to give advice. (See below.)

See also Bailey v Ministry of Defence [2008] EWCA Civ 883 and Chapter 15.

 ## Economic loss

See Chapter 5 for duty of care and economic loss.

The expansion of negligence to cover possible recovery of pure economic loss has also led to causation problems. As with personal injury actions a 'but for' test is normally applied but this test will be modified where it would cause injustice.

The typical negligence action is concerned with a careless act which directly causes physical damage to the claimant. Where the damage is financial, however, the defendant's carelessness may be a direct cause of financial loss to the claimant or may simply provide the opportunity for the claimant to suffer loss. A simple application of the 'but for' test may establish liability on the defendant where they have simply created an opportunity for the claimant to suffer loss.

Galoo Ltd v *Bright Grahame Murray* [1995] 1 All ER 16

An action was brought by Galoo Ltd and Gamine Ltd (which owned all the shares in Galoo) against BGM, a firm of chartered accountants who had audited the accounts of Galoo and Gamine during the relevant periods.

The claim was in contract and tort, in that BGM were negligent in failing to discover substantial inaccuracies in the audited accounts of Galoo. The Court of Appeal ruled that the same principles of causation applied to both the contract and tort actions.

The claimants claimed for:

(a) an obligation to repay loans made to Galoo; and
(b) trading losses incurred as a result of relying on the negligent auditing and continuing to trade when, had they known the true position, the company would have ceased trading.

In respect of item (a), it was held that accepting a loan with a simple obligation to repay it could not be described as damage.

In respect of item (b) the defendants had submitted that the appropriate test was 'but for'. The Court of Appeal drew on the few strands of contract causation law which establish that the breach of contract must be the effective cause of the loss and not simply the occasion for the loss. Australian cases were also drawn on which suggested that 'but for' was not the definitive test for causation and determining whether the breach of duty was the cause of, or the occasion for, the loss was difficult to determine but was a question of common sense. Applying this to the facts, the court held that BGM's breach of duty merely gave the opportunity to the company to continue trading and did not cause the losses in the sense in which cause is used in law.

Contrast with the following case where the court of first instance had no difficulty in finding that the breach of duty was an effective cause of the claimant's loss.

Brown v KMR Services [1995] 4 All ER 598

The claimant, who was a Lloyd's name, sued his agent for failing to warn him of the danger of placing 49 per cent of premium income with excess of loss syndicates, despite requests by the claimant for a review of his premium allocations and advice on the balance of his portfolio. The claimant had been underwriting since 1977 but suffered losses for the years 1987–90. The action was brought for breach of contract and negligence.

The Court of Appeal held that there was a breach of duty on the part of the agent in failing to warn the name of the dangers of placing a high percentage of his premium limit on high-risk syndicates.

The causation issue was what advice the name should have received and what would have been the consequence had he received it. At first instance the court had held that the breach did not simply provide the opportunity for loss to be suffered; it was an effective cause of the loss.

The Court of Appeal was concerned with what (hypothetically) the name would have done if given the warning. The claimant was independently minded and it was held that he would not necessarily have followed the agent's advice and would have placed 22 per cent of his money in high-risk syndicates. The quantum would therefore be the difference in losses between that figure and 49 per cent.

The causation problems caused by cases of economic loss in tort demonstrated by *Galoo* and *Brown* appeared in a series of cases brought against solicitors. The background to the cases was the rise and fall of the property market in the late 1980s and the subsequent losses suffered by lenders in the property market. These, of course, are the same facts that gave rise to the litigation against valuers which culminated in the *South Australia* case. The difficulties for the courts were similar in that the question was the extent of a negligent solicitor's liability when the lender's losses had been caused by a drop in the property market.

See Chapter 5 for South Australia Asset Management Corp. case

All the cases in the series involved the solicitor acting for both the lender and the borrower, and the actions were brought by the lender for breach of contract, negligence and breach of fiduciary duty. Initially, the lenders attempted to obtain summary judgment in a number of cases on the basis that there was no case to answer. The issue of whether the cases were suitable for summary judgment or whether it was incumbent on the lender to prove a causative link was heard by the Court of Appeal in *Bristol & West*, below.

Bristol & West Building Society v Mothew [1996] 4 All ER 698

A loan was made on condition that the balance of the purchase price was provided personally by the borrower with no resort to further borrowing and that there was no second mortgage. Both these conditions were broken by the borrower, but the solicitor carelessly (but not fraudulently) reported that everything was in order and the lenders released the mortgage cheque. The purchasers defaulted and the property was repossessed at a loss to the lenders of £6,000. The lenders sued the solicitor for breach of fiduciary duty, breach of contract and negligence.

In the action for breach of fiduciary duty, the Court of Appeal held that something more than mere carelessness was required in these circumstances. The solicitor had to act in bad faith in deliberately preferring one client's interests to the other. This was not the case here.

In the common law actions the court distinguished between misfeasance and nonfeasance. If the action was for failure to give the correct advice (nonfeasance), it was necessary for the lender to show what advice he should have been given and that he would have acted differently if it had been given. If the breach of duty was misfeasance, it was sufficient for the lender to show that he relied on the information. However, the Court of Appeal purported to base its decision on the fraud case of *Downs v Chappell* [1996] 3 All ER 344, and in the later case of *Swindle v Harrison* [1997] 4 All ER 705 the Court of Appeal found that 'but for' causation had to be established in misfeasance as well as nonfeasance cases.

What this means is that lenders will find it difficult to obtain summary judgment and, except in cases of bad faith or a combination of breaches of duty, will come within the *South Australia* regime for assessing the scope of the duty owed and the quantum of damages.

What *South Australia* did was to concentrate on the duty owed (advice or information) in order to define the potential scope of the defendant's liability. What a lender will have to prove post *Mothew* and *Swindle* is that the solicitor was under a duty to give the lender information, and that with that information the lender would not have entered into that loan. This proved an insuperable burden in most of the cases litigated to a conclusion in *Bristol & West Building Society* v *Fancy & Jackson* [1997] 4 All ER 582.

In contrast to actions for personal injuries, the courts have been prepared to allow an action for loss of chance in cases where economic loss is the damage. Such cases frequently arise in cases of solicitor's negligence.

Example

P retains *X* as his solicitor to bring negligence proceedings against *D* (*P*'s employer). *X* negligently misses the limitation period for the action and *P* is unable to proceed with the action. *P* then sues *X* for negligence. What is *P*'s damage? He has been deprived of the chance of recovering damages against *D*. In order to assess these damages, the court has effectively to try the *P* v *D* action and determine *P*'s chances of success. If the action is valued at £100,000 and was almost bound to succeed, then *P* recovers the £100,000. If the action was almost inevitably doomed to failure, then *P* recovers nothing. Anywhere in between and the court must assess the chance of success. If this is put at 60 per cent, then *P* recovers £60,000 against *X*.

A more complex situation arose in *Allied Maples Group* v *Simmons & Simmons*.

Allied Maples Group v *Simmons & Simmons* [1995] 1 WLR 1602

The claimants wished to acquire a business and properties of *G*. In order to acquire the properties the claimants were advised to buy *K* (a subsidiary of *G*), which was the first tenant of the properties, the leases on which were assigned. *K* had first tenant liability, which meant that any default on the part of the assignees had to be met by *K*. By acquiring *K*, the claimants also acquired the first tenant liability. A warranty against such liability was included in the original contract between the claimants and *G* but this warranty did not appear in the final contract. The assignees defaulted and the claimants were obliged to meet the losses and sued their solicitors for negligence.

The breach of duty lay in the failure to advise the claimants that a warranty or indemnity against first party liability should be included in the contract.

The Court of Appeal held that where the claimant's loss depends on the actions of an independent third party (in this case whether *G* would have given an indemnity or warranty in the original terms), it has to be considered what, as a matter of law, is necessary to establish causation, where causation ends and quantum begins.

1 If the loss sustained by the claimant depends on a positive act then causation is a question of historical fact, on the balance of probabilities. (See, for example, *Wilsher*.) If this hurdle is overcome then it is a question of quantum. Quantum questions are on the basis of the risk eventuating, for example, arthritis or promotion.

2 Where the claimant's loss depends on the defendant's omission – the failure to provide safety equipment (see *McWilliams* v *Arrol*, below) or the failure to give the correct advice

– causation is not based on historical fact but on the answer to a hypothetical question 'what would . . .'? This is a matter of inference from the evidence. The claimant must show on balance that had precautions been available they would have used them or that had the correct advice been given they would have taken a particular course of action.

3 Where the outcome depends on the hypothetical action of a third party (whether *G* would have given a warranty or indemnity) either in addition to action by the claimant or independent of it, does the claimant have to show that: (a) the third party would have acted so as to confer the benefit or avoid the risk or (b) there was a substantial chance (not a speculative one) that the third party would have so acted? If (b) then the matter is not one of all or nothing but a question of quantification. Was the chance great or small?

See Chapter 5 for *Spring* v *Guardian Assurance*.
The court held (b) to be the law. ***Spring* v *Guardian Assurance*** was cited in support. Once duty and breach have been established the claimant only has to show that by reason of that negligence they lost a reasonable chance (of obtaining employment or obtaining a warranty). Millett LJ dissented on the application of the test as he did not feel that there was a substantial chance that G would have granted the warranty.

See Chapter 23 for *4 Eng Ltd*.
Damages for loss of chance are also available in the tort of deceit. (*4 Eng Ltd* v *Harper* [2008] EWHC 915.)

Conclusions on causation

This is an extremely complex area of law. There are two reasons for this. One is that cases are determined on a factual basis and the second is that it is increasingly policy driven, as can be seen from the discussion above on the mesothelioma cases.

The starting point is that claimants usually need to satisfy the 'but for' test, which operates as a filter to exclude hopeless claims. The burden of proof is on the claimant and he needs to prove 'but for' on the balance of probability. Most cases of traumatic injury are dealt with satisfactorily by this basic test.

The major problem areas are where the claimant has contracted a disease and the medical evidence is inconclusive. In these circumstances the courts have shown that they are prepared to assist claimants by relaxing the 'but for' test and not insisting that the claimant prove on the balance of probabilities that the breach of duty caused the damage. In certain cases the claimant will succeed if he can prove that the breach of duty 'materially increased the risk' of damage to the claimant and that risk materialised. The problem is, when will this approach be permitted? On the present state of the law it is clear that where there is one causal agent (e.g. brick dust or asbestos) and the claimant was negligently exposed to the risk by more than one defendant, the claimant does not have to prove which defendant was responsible for the actual damage. However, if there is more than one causal agent (e.g. as in ***Wilsher***) then the claimant may have to satisfy standard causation principles unless the causal agents work in substantially the same way. The distinction is not a principled one and it is difficult to state when the 'material increase in risk' might be permitted in other cases. This will depend on policy factors but at present we do not know what those policy factors are. It is becoming clear that one of the policy factors will be the type of defendant involved. The House of Lords were invited effectively to extend ***Fairchild*** to cases of medical negligence in ***Gregg* v *Scott*** but declined to do so. However, in ***Bailey* v *Ministry of Defence*** [2008] EWCA Civ 883 the Court of Appeal allowed the material increase in risk approach in a medical negligence case, a decision which has caused some controversy.

See Chapter 15 for *Bailey*.
Where the contribution made by a particular defendant is known then the principle will have no application. (***Holtby* v *Brigham & Cowan*.**)

Remoteness of damage

Introduction

Objective
5

Damages may be denied even where the claimant is able to establish a factual link between the breach of duty and their damage. This will be on the ground that the breach of duty was not the legal cause of the damage and will be expressed by saying that the damage was too remote. This area of law is affected by policy considerations, as the court will not wish to impose too heavy a burden on the defendant or their insurers.

The basic test for remoteness of damage remained the same until 1961 and was then changed by a Privy Council decision. The earlier test will be considered here for reasons of comparison and because it still provides the basis of the remoteness test in some other torts.

The direct consequence test

This is the test for remoteness of damage that held sway until 1961. It was laid down by the Court of Appeal in the following case.

Re Polemis and Furness, Withy & Co Ltd [1921] 3 KB 560

Charterers of a ship loaded it with benzene. The benzene leaked and this caused the ship's hold to fill with vapour. A stevedore negligently dropped a wooden plank into the hold of the ship. This caused a spark, which ignited the vapour, causing an explosion which destroyed the ship. The Court of Appeal held that the stevedore's employers were vicariously liable for the stevedore's negligence and that the damage was not too remote. The test for remoteness of damage in negligence actions was stated to be whether the damage was a direct consequence of the breach of duty. An indirect consequence was damage due to the operation of independent causes having no connection with the negligent act, except that they could not avoid its results.

It is important to note that in order for the defendant to be liable at all, he must owe the claimant a duty of care. For a duty to arise, some damage to the claimant must be reasonably foreseeable. In *Polemis* some damage was foreseeable as a result of the plank being dropped. Duty was therefore established. The explosion was a direct consequence of the breach of duty; therefore the damage was not too remote, although the kind of property damage that occurred could not have been foreseen.

Reasonable foreseeability test

The test for remoteness of damage was changed by the Privy Council in 1961.

Overseas Tankship (UK) Ltd v *Morts Dock & Engineering Co (The Wagon Mound No 1)* [1961] AC 388 *(hereafter Wagon Mound No 1)*

The defendants negligently discharged fuel oil into Sydney Harbour. The oil spread to the claimants' wharf where welding was taking place. The claimants were assured that there was no danger of the oil catching fire on water and continued welding. Two days later the oil caught fire and the wharf and ships being repaired there were damaged by the fire. There was also some damage by fouling to the wharf. The trial judge found that it was not foreseeable that fuel oil on water would catch fire, but there was some foreseeable damage in the fouling. This was sufficient to establish duty and, as the fire damage was a direct consequence of the breach of duty, the defendants were also liable for the fire damage.

On appeal, the Privy Council held that the defendants were not liable for the fire damage. The test for remoteness of damage was whether the kind of damage suffered by the claimant was reasonably foreseeable by the defendant at the time of the breach of duty.

Viscount Simonds:

> It is a principle of civil liability, subject only to qualifications which have no present relevance, that a man must be considered to be responsible for the probable consequences of his act. To demand more of him is too harsh a rule, to demand less is to ignore that civilised order requires the observance of a minimum standard of behaviour.
>
> This concept applied to the slowly developing law of negligence has led to a great variety of expressions which can, as it appears to their Lordships, be harmonised with little difficulty with the single exception of the so-called rule in *Polemis*. For, if it is asked why a man should be responsible for the natural or necessary or probable consequences of his act (or any other similar description of them) the answer is that it is not because they are natural or necessary or probable, but because, since they have this quality, it is judged by the standard of the reasonable man that he ought to have foreseen them. Thus it is that over and over again it has happened that in different judgments in the case, and sometimes in a single judgment, liability for a consequence has been imposed on the ground that it was reasonably foreseeable or, alternatively, on the ground that it was natural or necessary or probable. The two grounds have been treated as coterminous and so they largely are. But, where they are not, the question arises to which the wrong answer was given in *Polemis*. For, if some limitation must be imposed on the consequences for which the negligent actor is to be held responsible – and all are agreed that some limitation there must be – why should that test (reasonable foreseeability) be rejected which, since he is judged by what the reasonable man ought to foresee, corresponds with the common conscience of mankind, and a test (the 'direct' consequence) be substituted which leads to no-where but the never-ending and insoluble problems of causation.

Is there any difference between *Polemis* and *Wagon Mound No 1*? Reasonable foreseeability is always a necessary ingredient of a negligence action as it is required to establish duty of care. What needs to be reasonably foreseeable for this purpose is a broad type of damage such as personal injuries or property damage. The key to the *Wagon Mound* test is what is meant by a *kind of damage*. If this is taken in a very broad sense, then there is no difference between the direct consequence and the reasonable foreseeability test. But if kind is interpreted more narrowly, then it will have the effect of limiting the defendant's liability. In *Wagon Mound No 1* the kind of damage that needed to be foreseeable was fire damage. This is clearly narrower than property damage. Had the reasonable foreseeability test been used in *Polemis*, it is likely that the defendants would have been not liable. Damage by explosion was probably not a foreseeable kind of damage.

It is now necessary to see how the courts have interpreted the reasonable foreseeability test.

Kind of damage

A number of principles have emerged on remoteness of damage.

If the kind of damage suffered is reasonably foreseeable, it does not matter that the damage came about in an unforeseeable way

Hughes v Lord Advocate [1963] AC 837

The defendants' employees erected a tent over a manhole and surrounded the tent with paraffin lamps. The hole was left unguarded while the men were on a tea break. The ten-year-old claimant dropped one of the paraffin lamps down the hole and due to an unusual combination of circumstances there was an explosion and the claimant was badly burned. The defendants argued that they were not liable, as the way in which the damage came about was not foreseeable and the damage was therefore too remote. This was rejected by the House of Lords. Their Lordships asked what kind of damage was foreseeable as a result of the breach of duty. The answer was burns. What kind of damage had occurred? The answer was burns. The damage was therefore not too remote. The fact that the burns had come about in an unforeseeable way did not render the damage too remote.

However, the claimant-friendly approach in *Hughes* can be contrasted with the approach in the next three cases.

Doughty v Turner Manufacturing Co Ltd [1964] 1 QB 518

A workman at the defendants' factory dropped an asbestos cover into some molten liquid. The asbestos reacted with the liquid; there was an eruption and the claimant was burned. The court held that the damage to the claimant was too remote. Damage by eruption was not foreseeable in the circumstances, but damage by splashing was.

Harman LJ:

We ought, in my opinion, to start with the premise that the criterion in English law is foreseeability. I take it that whether Overseas Tankship (UK) Ltd v Morts Dock and Engineering Co Ltd (*The Wagon Mound*) is or is not binding on this court we ought to treat it as the law. Our inquiry must, therefore, be whether the result of this hard-board cover slipping into the cauldron, which we know now to be inevitably an explosion, was a thing reasonably foreseeable at the time when it happened. It is acknowledged by the plaintiff that no one in the defendant's service knew of the likelihood of such an event, and it is clear that no one in the room at the time thought of any dangerous result. There was a striking piece of evidence of the two men who went and looked over the edge of the cauldron to see where the piece of board had gone. Neither they, nor anyone else, thought that they were doing anything risky.

The plaintiff's argument most persuasively urged by Mr James rested, as I understood it, on admissions made that, if this lid had been dropped into the cauldron with sufficient force to cause the molten material to splash over the edge, that would have been an act of negligence or carelessness for which the defendants might be vicariously responsible. Reliance was put on *Hughes v Lord Advocate*, where the exact consequences of the lamp overturning were not foreseen, but it was foreseeable that, if the manhole were left unguarded, boys would enter and tamper with the lamp, and it was not unlikely that serious burns might ensue for the boys. Their Lordships' House distinguished *The Wagon Mound* case on the ground that the damage which ensued, though differing in degree, was the same in kind as that which was foreseeable. So it is said here that a splash causing burns was foreseeable and that this explosion was really only a magnified splash which also caused burns and that, therefore, we ought to follow *Hughes v Lord Advocate* and hold the defendants liable. I cannot accept this. In my opinion, the damage here was of an entirely different kind from the foreseeable splash. Indeed, the evidence showed that any disturbance of the material resulting from the immersion of the hard-board was past an appreciable time before the explosion happened. This latter was caused by the disintegration of the hard-board under the great heat to which it was subjected and the consequent release of the moisture enclosed within it. This had nothing to do with the agitation caused by the dropping of the board into the cyanide. I am of opinion that it would be wrong on these facts to make another inroad on the doctrine of foreseeability which seems to me to be a satisfactory solvent of this type of difficulty.

Did the court ask the right question on kind of damage here? Or should the kind of damage have been burns? Does this case contradict *Hughes*? One view of this case is that no damage to the claimant was foreseeable because of the angle at which the cover fell into the molten liquid. The decision could be supported on this basis.

Tremain v Pike [1969] 1 WLR 1556

The claimant was employed by the defendant as a herdsman. He contracted Weil's disease, a rare disease contracted from rat's urine. The defendant had allowed the rat population on his farm to grow too large. The court held that the damage suffered by the claimant was too remote as Weil's disease was unforeseeable, although it was foreseeable that the claimant would have suffered damage from rats.

It is thought that this decision is doubtful in view of the Court of Appeal's decision in *Parsons* v *Uttley Ingham* & *Co* [1978] QB 791.

Some of the difficulties in applying the *Hughes* test and the differing judicial approaches can be seen in the following case.

Jolley v Sutton London Borough Council [1998] 3 All ER 559 (CA); [2000] 3 All ER 409 (HL)

See also Chapter 11 for *Jolley* v *Sutton*.

The council owned a piece of amenity land near a block of flats on which a boat had been left lying for at least two years. The claimant, a 14-year-old, and a friend decided to repair it. They jacked up the boat, which fell and caused severe spinal injuries to the claimant, who sued under the Occupiers' Liability Act 1957. At first instance the judge held that the boat was an attraction to children of the claimant's age and that it was reasonably foreseeable that it would be meddled with, and that there was a foreseeable risk of physical injury.

The Court of Appeal held that the defendant was not liable for breach of a duty of care if the accident which caused the claimant's injuries was of a different type and kind from anything he could have foreseen. Although the boat was both an allurement and a trap and the council had been negligent in failing to remove it, the attractiveness of the boat and its dangerous condition had not been established to be part of the causes of the accident. The immediate cause of the accident had been the two boys jacking it up. This was an activity very different from normal play.

The court applied *Hughes*, but was this a correct application and was it even the correct doctrine? Lord Woolf considered various speeches from *Hughes* and chose to apply that of Lord Pearce on the basis that the accident was of a different type and kind from anything the defendant could have foreseen. Consider the following extracts from *Hughes* and see if you agree with the conclusion.

Lord Reid (at 845):

So we have (first) a duty owed by the workmen, (secondly) the fact that if they had done as they ought to have done there would have been no accident, and (thirdly) the fact that the injuries suffered by the appellant, though perhaps different in degree, did not differ in kind from injuries which might have resulted from an accident of a foreseeable nature. *The ground on which this case has been decided against the appellant is that the accident was of an unforeseeable type. Of course, the pursuer has to prove that the defender's fault caused the accident, and there could be a case where the intrusion of a new and unexpected factor could be regarded as the cause of the accident rather than the fault of the defender. But that is not this case. The cause of this accident was a known source of danger, the lamp, but it behaved in an unpredictable way.* (Emphasis added.)

Lord Guest (at 856):

Was the igniting of paraffin outside the lamp by the flame a foreseeable consequence of the breach of duty? In the circumstances, there was a combination of potentially dangerous circumstances against which the Post Office had to protect the appellant. If these formed an allurement to children it might have been foreseen that they would play with the lamp, that it might tip over, that it might be broken, and that when broken the paraffin might spill and be ignited by the flame. All these steps in the chain of causation seem to have been accepted by all the judges in the courts below as foreseeable. But because the explosion was the agent which caused the burning and was unforeseeable, therefore the accident, according to them, was not reasonably foreseeable. In my opinion, this reasoning is fallacious. An explosion is only one way in which burning can be caused. Burning can also be caused by the contact between liquid paraffin and a naked flame. In the one case paraffin vapour and in the other case liquid paraffin is ignited by fire. I cannot see that these are two different types of accident. They are both burning accidents and in both cases the injuries would be burning injuries. Upon this view the explosion was an immaterial event in the chain of causation. It was simply one way in which burning might be caused by the potentially dangerous paraffin lamp. I adopt, with respect, Lord Carmont's observation in the present case (1961 SC 310 at 331): 'The defender cannot, I think, escape liability by contending that he did not foresee all the possibilities of the manner in which allurements – the manhole and the lantern – would act upon the childish mind.'

Lord Pearce (at 857):

The defenders are therefore liable for all the foreseeable consequences of their neglect. When an accident is of a different type and kind from anything that a defender could have foreseen he is not liable for it (see *The Wagon Mound*). But to demand too great precision in the test of foreseeability would be unfair . . . since the facets of misadventure are innumerable . . .

The allurement in this case was the combination of a red paraffin lamp, a ladder, a partially closed tent, and a cavernous hole within it, a setting well fitted to inspire some juvenile adventure that might end in calamity. The obvious risks were burning and conflagration and a fall. All these in fact occurred, but unexpectedly the mishandled lamp instead of causing an ordinary conflagration produced a violent explosion. Did the explosion create an accident and damage of a different type from the misadventure and damage that could be foreseen? In my judgment it did not. The accident was but a variant of the foreseeable.

The House of Lords, however, reversed the Court of Appeal and upheld the trial judge who had been correct to identify the risk as one that the children would meddle with the boat at the risk of some physical injury. The accident that occurred was of a type that was reasonably foreseeable.

Lord Hoffmann (at 419):

In the Court of Appeal, Lord Woolf MR observed that there seemed to be no case of which counsel were aware 'where want of care on the part of a defendant was established but a plaintiff, who was a child, has failed to succeed because the circumstances of the accident were not foreseeable'. I would suggest that this is for a combination of three reasons: first, because a finding or admission of want of care on the part of the defendant establishes that it would have cost the defendant no more trouble to avoid the injury which happened than he should in any case have taken; secondly, because in such circumstances the defendants will be liable for the materialisation of even relatively small risks of a different kind, and thirdly, because it has been repeatedly said in cases about children that their ingenuity in finding unexpected ways of doing mischief to themselves and others should never be underestimated. For these reasons, I think that the judge's broad description of the risk as being that children would 'meddle with the boat at the risk of some physical injury' was the correct one to adopt on the facts of this case. The actual injury fell within that description and I would therefore allow the appeal.

Counsel for the Borough made the concession (regarded as rightly made by Lord Steyn) that if the Borough could not succeed on this point then they could not succeed in a *novus actus interveniens* plea.

Provided that the kind of damage is reasonably foreseeable, it does not matter that it is more extensive than could have been foreseen

Vacwell Engineering Co Ltd v *BDH Chemicals Ltd* [1971] 1 QB 88

The defendants supplied a chemical to the claimants but failed to warn that it was liable to explode on contact with water. A scientist working for the claimants placed the chemical in water. This caused a violent explosion resulting in extensive damage. The defendants were held liable. Some property damage was foreseeable and the fact that it was more extensive than might have been foreseen did not matter.

In terms of economic loss the extent rule is illustrated by ***Brown* v *KMR Services*** [1995] 4 All ER 598. (For facts see above.) The action was brought in contract and negligence and one of the issues was whether the defendant agent was liable for the full extent of the loss suffered by the Lloyd's name. This loss was greater than anyone could have foreseen due to an unusually high number of serious claims falling on the Lloyd's market due to hurricane damage in the USA and the Piper Alpha oil rig explosion. The problem was compounded by the system of reinsurance at Lloyd's. The Court of Appeal held that the extent rule applied in both contract and tort and that market movements did not affect the tortfeasor's liability. In support of this it cited ***Banque Bruxelles Lambert SA* v *Eagle Star Insurance Co*** [1995] 2 All ER 769, which held that a surveyor's liability for a negligent over-valuation of a property extended to losses caused by a drop in the price of property which meant that a lender who had relied on the valuation was unable to recoup losses on a default sale.

Since this decision, the House of Lords, in the negligent valuation cases, has held that losses caused by market falls are not generally recoverable. (***South Australia Asset Management Corp* v *York Montague*** [1996] 3 All ER 365.) Would this analysis apply to the Lloyd's cases? This would depend on the 'purpose' of the statement made by the agent to the name. Was the agent giving information (which would enable the name to decide what course of action to take) or giving advice on what course of action to take? At present, the latter seems more likely so market falls would still be recoverable.

See also Chapter 5 for South Australia Asset Management Corp. case.

The extent of damage principle is also illustrated by the 'egg-shell skull rule'. This states that the defendant must take the claimant as they find them, as regards their physical characteristics.

Smith v *Leech Brain & Co* [1962] 2 QB 405

The claimant suffered a burn on his lip as a result of the defendants' negligence. The burn caused the claimant to contract cancer, as the tissues of his lips were in a premalignant state. He died three years after the accident. The defendants argued that they were not responsible for his death, as it could not have been foreseen. The court stated that they had to take the claimant as they found him. The question for remoteness was whether the defendants could have foreseen a burn, not whether they could have foreseen cancer. The defendants were held liable.

Lord Parker CJ:

> The test is not whether these employers could reasonably have foreseen that a burn would cause cancer and that he [Mr Smith] would die. The question is employers these employers could reasonably foresee the type of injury which he suffered, namely, the burn. What, in the particular case, is the amount of damage which he suffers as a result of that burn, depends on the characteristics and constitution of the victim.

The principle also applies where the claimant's damage is a combination of the defendant's negligence and medical treatment to which they were allergic.

Robinson v Post Office [1974] 1 WLR 1176

> The claimant was employed by the defendants. He fell down a ladder as a result of the defendants' negligence and cut his leg. The doctor gave him an anti-tetanus injection to which the claimant was allergic. As a result he contracted encephalitis, an inflammation of the brain. The defendants were held liable for both the original injury and the encephalitis, as it was foreseeable that the claimant would be given an anti-tetanus injection.

If the medical treatment was given negligently, i.e. if the doctor should have been aware that the claimant was allergic, then it is likely that the court would treat the medical negligence as a *novus actus interveniens* which broke the chain of causation.

There is no case in civil law which extends the egg-shell skull rule beyond physical characteristics. This could arise if the claimant suffered negligently inflicted injuries and then refused to have a blood transfusion because of their religious beliefs. If the claimant died, the court would then have to determine whether the defendant was liable for the death.

Degree of probability of damage

There has been little discussion on the necessary degree of probability of a kind of damage occurring.

In cases of personal injury, it has been seen that the courts generally take a broad view of the question of kind of damage and also of the degree of foreseeability necessary. The egg-shell skull rule and the rule on extent of damage make the remoteness rules claimant-friendly where personal injuries are suffered. Broadly speaking, provided the claimant can establish that personal injury was reasonably foreseeable as a real risk, the damage is not too remote.

In property damage cases, the courts have generally been more restrictive. We have seen that in the **Wagon Mound No 1** they did not define the kind of damage necessary as property damage but distinguished between damage by fouling and fire damage.

Overseas Tankship (UK) Ltd v Miller Steamship Co Pty Ltd (The Wagon Mound No 2) [1967] 1 AC 617

> This case was concerned with the same facts as the **Wagon Mound No 1** and the same defendants. The action was brought by the owners of the two ships which were being repaired at the time of the fire and were damaged. The action was brought in negligence and nuisance. The trial judge found that there was a bare possibility of fire damage, but that this was so remote it could be ignored. The Privy Council reversed the decision, stating that provided fire damage was foreseeable as a kind of damage, the degree of likelihood was irrelevant to the question of kind of damage suffered. The reason for the different decisions in the two cases was the different finding of fact at first instance.
>
> The Privy Council held that the test for remoteness of damage in nuisance was the same as that in negligence.

For nuisance see Chapter 17.

The narrower approach to remoteness of damage in property damage cases could be explained on the grounds that the claimant is likely to be insured against such damage and that the extent of the damage in such cases could be great.

Impecuniosity

The claimant's initial loss may be made greater by their financial inability to take steps to minimise their loss. Is such loss too remote or not?

The Liesbosch Dredger v *SS Edison* [1933] AC 448

A dredger was sunk due to the defendant's negligence. The owners of the dredger required it to complete a contract which contained an onerous penalty clause. The claimants could not afford to buy a new dredger and had to hire one. The question was whether the cost of hire was recoverable or was too remote. The House of Lords held that the cost of hire was an indirect consequence (note the date of the case) and therefore too remote.

This decision has not proved popular and has now been disapproved.

Lagden v *O'Connor* [2004] 1 All ER 277

The defendant negligently drove her motor car into the claimant's parked car and damaged it. The claimant's car required repair and he took it to a garage. He wanted the use of a vehicle while his car was being repaired but could not afford to pay ordinary commercial car hire charges. He therefore entered into agreements with a credit hire company under which, by a combination of credit facility and insurance cover, a substitute car was made available to him and the credit hire company sought to recover its charges from the defendant's insurers. The total cost of the credit hire company scheme was greater than the cost of ordinary car hire. The claimant brought proceedings against the defendant claiming the total cost of the credit hire scheme as damages for loss of use of his car. The judge held that the rule that a claimant could not recover the additional fee charged by credit hire companies, damages for loss of use being limited to the ordinary rate quoted by car hirers, did not apply to the claimant as he was too poor to be able to afford to hire a replacement car at commercial rates and therefore had had no other choice but to obtain a credit hire agreement package. The judge accordingly held that the claimant should be able to recover in damages the cost of taking that package. The Court of Appeal agreed with that decision, ruling that a wrongdoer had to take his victim as he found him. The defendant appealed.

Held (House of Lords) (Lord Scott and Lord Walker dissenting): The damages payable for the loss of use of a damaged car included the reasonable costs of a credit hire company if an innocent claimant could not afford to pay car hire charges, so that, left to himself, he would be unable to obtain a replacement car to meet the need created by the negligent driver. In measuring the loss suffered by an impecunious innocent claimant by loss of use of his own car, the law recognised that, because of his lack of financial means, the timely provision of a replacement vehicle for him cost more than it did in the case of his more affluent neighbour, in that someone had to provide him with credit, by incurring the expense of providing a car without receiving immediate payment, and then incur the administrative expense involved in pursuing the defendant's insurers for payment. Lack of financial means was, almost always, a question of priorities. In the instant case the innocent claimant had no choice, without making sacrifices he could not reasonably be expected to make, but to use the services of the credit hire company. Accordingly, the appeal would be dismissed.

Lord Hope:

> The Judicial Committee did not go so far in the *Alcoa Minerals* case as to say that the *Liesbosch* case was wrongly decided. As it was a decision of the House of Lords, it was for the House and not the Board to decide whether the rule that was laid down in that case should now be departed from. The opportunity for the House to take that step has now come. It is not necessary for us to say that

> the *Liesbosch* case was wrongly decided. But it is clear that the law has moved on, and that the correct test of remoteness today is whether the loss was reasonably foreseeable. The wrongdoer must take his victim as he finds him: *talem qualem* . . . This rule applies to the economic state of the victim in the same way as it applies to his physical and mental vulnerability. It requires the wrongdoer to bear the consequences if it was reasonably foreseeable that the injured party would have to borrow money or incur some other kind of expenditure to mitigate his damages.

Torts where *Wagon Mound* does not apply

The *Wagon Mound* test is now established as the remoteness test for negligence and nuisance. There are torts where a different test is used.

See Chapter 17 for nuisance.

See Chapter 20 for trespass.

See Chapter 23 for deceit.

If the defendant intends to do harm, for example, in trespass, then liability will be more extensive than where they are negligent. Policy factors which restrict liability in negligence cases do not apply in intentional torts. The defendant will generally be liable for all damage flowing from the tort once factual causation has been established. In deceit cases the defendant will be held liable for all the loss flowing from the fraudulent statement. (*Doyle v Olby (Ironmongers) Ltd* [1969] 2 QB 158.)

Novus actus interveniens

Introduction

Objective 6

The defendant's breach of duty may be a cause of the claimant's damage in the sense that it satisfies the 'but for' test, but some other factual cause, intervening after the breach, may be regarded as the sole cause of some, or all, of the claimant's damage. Where this happens the intervening cause is known as a *novus actus interveniens* and breaks the chain of causation between the defendant and claimant. Any damage occurring after the *novus actus interveniens* will be regarded as being too remote.

> ### Example
>
> *A* negligently runs over *B*, who is then run over by *C*. *C*'s action is unlikely to break the chain of causation, as this is a risk to which *A*'s negligence exposed *B*. But if *C* stole *B*'s wallet, the court would be unlikely to find *A* liable, as this was not a risk to which *A* had exposed *B*.

The law in this area is far from clear. One of the difficulties is created by the courts obscuring policy factors with legalistic reasoning. The problem is not unique to this area, but is particularly acute here. The key policy factor is the court's determination of where the loss should lie. The legal (formalistic) tests used can be demonstrated by two cases.

Home Office v Dorset Yacht Co Ltd [1970] 2 All ER 294

> Due to the negligence of the defendant's employees, borstal trainees escaped and caused damage to neighbouring property. The majority of the House of Lords treated the case as being concerned with duty of care. Lord Reid considered that the case was one of remoteness of damage. He considered whether the boys' acts broke the chain of causation. In order to do this they had to be something very unlikely to happen or they would not be regarded as a *novus actus interveniens*. As it was very likely that if the boys escaped, nearby property would be damaged, the boys' acts did not break

the chain of causation. The escape took place in Dorset and the damage occurred nearby. Had the boys boarded a train to Carlisle and caused damage there, this might have been regarded as too remote.

Lord Reid:

> The cases show that, where human action forms one of the links between the original wrongdoing of the defendant and the loss suffered by the plaintiff, the action must at least have been something very likely to happen if it is not to be regarded as a *novus actus interveniens* breaking the chain of causation. I do not think that a mere foreseeable possibility is or should be sufficient, for then the intervening human action can more properly be regarded as a new cause than as a consequence of the original wrongdoing. But if the intervening action was likely to happen I do not think that it can matter whether that action was innocent, tortious or criminal.

Lamb v *Camden Borough Council* [1981] QB 625

The defendants negligently broke a water main. The water damaged the claimant's house and caused it to be left empty. Squatters broke in and caused damage. The question was whether the defendants were liable for the damage caused by the squatters or whether the squatters' actions amounted to a *novus actus interveniens*.

Lord Oliver took up and modified Lord Reid's test. If the act should have been foreseen by a reasonable man as likely, it would not break the chain of causation. He found that the squatters' actions were not foreseeable in this sense and therefore did amount to a *novus actus interveniens*.

Oliver LJ:

> Few things are less certainly predictable than human behaviour and if one is asked whether in any given situation a human being may behave idiotically, irrationally, or even criminally, the answer must always be that that is a possibility, for every society has its proportion of idiots and criminals. It cannot be said that you cannot foresee the possibility that people will do stupid or criminal acts, because people are constantly doing stupid or criminal acts. But the question is not what is foreseeable merely as a possibility but what would the reasonable man actually foresee if he thought about it . . . If the instant case is approached as a case of negligence and one asks the question, did the defendants owe a duty not to break a waterpipe so as to cause the plaintiffs' house to be invaded by squatters a year later, the tenuousness of the linkage between act and result becomes apparent. I confess that I find it inconceivable that the reasonable man wielding his pick in the road in 1973 could be said reasonably to foresee that his puncturing of a water main would fill the plaintiffs' house with uninvited guests in 1974.

Lord Denning decided the case on the basis of policy. He thought that as the claimant was more likely to be insured against the risk, then the loss should lie with the claimant. This illustrates one of the problems of judges making policy decisions. In fact, the defendants were more likely to be insured on an all risks policy for council employees. As the claimant had ceased to occupy the house, it was likely that she was not covered by insurance.

A *novus actus interveniens* may take one of three forms.

A natural event

The courts will generally be reluctant to find that a natural event breaks the chain of causation as the claimant has no one else to sue if the defendant is exonerated. If the defendant negligently starts a fire and strong winds then cause the flames to spread to the claimant's property, the court will not find that the winds break the chain of causation.

However, if the natural event causes damage simply because the breach of duty has placed the claimant or their property in a position where the damage can be caused, the chain of causation will be broken, unless the natural event was likely to happen.

> ### Example
>
> The claimant is injured in a road accident caused by the defendant's negligence. An ambulance is called to take the claimant to hospital. On the way, a strong wind gets up and blows a tree down. The tree lands on the ambulance and causes further injuries to the claimant. The defendant will not be liable for the injuries caused by the tree. This will be treated as a *novus actus interveniens* which breaks the chain of causation.
>
> What would the position be if there was an exceptionally strong gale blowing at the time of the original road accident? Should the defendant have foreseen damage caused by a falling tree?

This principle is illustrated in relation to property damage by the following case.

Carslogie Steamship Co v *Royal Norwegian Government* [1952] AC 292

> The claimant's ship was damaged in a collision for which the defendant's ship was responsible. After temporary repairs the ship set out for the United States on a voyage it would not have made had the collision not occurred. The ship suffered damage due to heavy weather conditions. The storm damage was not treated as a consequence of the collision but as an intervening event in the course of an ordinary voyage. It is important that the decision of the ship's owners to put to sea was voluntary.

Intervening act of a third party

Where the defendant's breach of duty is followed by a third-party act which is also a cause of the claimant's damage, the court has to determine the extent of the defendant's liability. If the third-party act is held to be a *novus actus interveniens*, then the defendant is not liable for any damage occurring after the act.

Where the defendant's duty was to guard the claimant or their property from a third party, then the third-party act will not relieve the defendant from the consequences of their negligence.

Stansbie v *Troman* [1948] 1 All ER 599

> The defendant was employed as a decorator by the claimant. He was told to lock the door if he went out. He failed to do this and a thief (third party) entered the house and stole property belonging to the claimant. The defendant was held liable for the loss, as the thief's act did not break the chain of causation.

Neither, apparently, will an act of the claimant. (*Reeves* v *Commissioner of Police of the Metropolis* [1999] 3 WLR 363.)

See Chapter 6.

Recent cases in this area have tended to concentrate on the aspect of duty rather than remoteness.

Where there is no duty to guard the claimant or their property, the situation is more difficult. In order to break the chain of causation the third-party act must be independent of the breach of duty.

The Oropesa [1943] P 32

A collision at sea was caused by the negligence of *The Oropesa*. The captain of the other ship put out a boat to discuss salvage. At the time there were very heavy seas. The boat overturned and a sailor was drowned. The question was whether the captain's decision to put out the boat amounted to a *novus actus interveniens*. The court held that the action of sending the boat out was caused by and flowed from the collision. As this act was not independent of the defendants' negligence it did not break the chain of causation and the defendants were liable for the sailor's death.

Lord Wright:

> In all these cases the question is not whether there was what one may call negligence or not. Negligence involves a breach of duty as between the plaintiff and the defendant. The captain or Lord, or whoever was deciding what to do, were not then owing a duty to anybody except, possibly, a duty to minimise damage so far as they could; but that is not a point which is relevant here. They were acting in an emergency. If they did something which was outside the exigencies of the emergency, whether it was from miscalculation or from error, or, if you like, from mere wilfulness, they would be debarred from saying that there had not intervened a new cause. The question is not whether there was new negligence, but whether there was a new cause. It must always be shown that there is something which I will call ultroneous, something unwarrantable, a new cause coming in disturbing the sequence of events, something that can be described as either unreasonable or extraneous or extrinsic.

The third-party act must be voluntary in order to amount to a *novus actus interveniens*. The captain's action in **The Oropesa** was not voluntary in this sense. Where the third-party act is negligent, it may or may not break the chain of causation.

Rouse v Squires [1973] QB 889

The negligence of the first defendant caused an accident. The second defendant also drove negligently and collided with the vehicles that had been involved in the first accident, killing the claimant. The court held that the first defendant's negligence was a cause of the death and he was held 25 per cent responsible. The second accident did not break the chain of causation as it was a natural consequence of the first accident.

Cairns LJ:

> If a driver so negligently manages his vehicle as to cause it to obstruct the highway and constitute a danger to other road users, including those who are driving too fast or not keeping a proper lookout, but not those who deliberately or recklessly drive into the obstruction, then the first driver's negligence may be held to have contributed to the causation of an accident of which the immediate cause was the negligent driving of the vehicle which because of the presence of the obstruction collides with it or with some other vehicle or some other person. Accordingly, I would hold in this case that the third party driver's [Mr Allen] negligence did contribute to the death of Mr Rouse.

Knightley v Johns [1982] 1 All ER 851

The negligent driving of the defendant caused an accident and blocked a road tunnel. A police officer negligently sent the claimant, another police officer, into the tunnel, against the traffic flow. The defendant was held not liable for the injury to the claimant. The court stated that 'negligent conduct is more likely to break the chain of causation than conduct which is not'. Stephenson LJ stated that the courts sought refuge in 'common sense rather than logic on the facts and circumstances of each case'.

Negligent medical treatment which intervenes between the breach and the damage will be treated as *novus actus* if it is serious and amounts to a completely inappropriate response to the patient's condition. (**Rahman v Arearose Ltd** [2001] QB 351.) Medical negligence may not sever the chain of causation and the defendant may remain liable for the damage on the basis that there was some risk that medical treatment might be negligent.

Where the third-party act consists of deliberate wrongful conduct, the courts will use the tests set out in **Home Office v Dorset Yacht** and **Lamb v Camden BC** (see above).

Act of the claimant

Cases where the claimant's conduct is called into question are normally concerned with contributory negligence. Where the claimant has been found to have been contributorily negligent, their damages will be reduced by the proportion that they are found to be to blame for their damage. However, the defendant may allege that the claimant's conduct breaks the chain of causation, so as to render the defendant not liable for some, or all, of the claimant's damage.

The test applied by the courts in these cases is whether the claimant was acting reasonably in the circumstances.

McKew v Holland & Hannen & Cubbitts (Scotland) Ltd [1969] 3 All ER 1621

The claimant injured his leg as a result of the defendants' negligence. Because of his injury he sometimes lost control of his leg. He attempted to descend a steep staircase which had no handrail, while holding a small child by the hand. His leg gave way and he pushed the child to safety. He then jumped to avoid falling and broke his ankle. The defendants were held not liable for this injury, as the claimant's unreasonable conduct broke the chain of causation. It was not the decision to jump that was unreasonable, it was placing himself unnecessarily in a position where he might be confronted with such an emergency.

Weiland v Cyril Lord Carpets Ltd [1969] 3 All ER 1006

The claimant was unable to adjust her bifocal spectacles as a result of a neck injury inflicted by the defendant's negligence. She was worried about catching public transport in such a condition and went to her son's office to ask him to drive her home. On the way into the office she fell down a flight of stairs and was injured. On these facts the claimant was held to have acted reasonably and the defendant was liable for her injuries.

Conclusion

It can be seen that this area raises many difficult issues for the courts to decide. The factual circumstances that can arise are infinite and the judges rely on a mixture of legal principle, policy and common sense to guide them through the maze.

Illustrations of the problems and possible solutions are provided by the following examples. These also highlight the way in which a court may choose from a number of doctrines in coming to a solution.

Example

Fred received head injuries at work as a result of his employer's negligence. As a result of his injuries, Fred became depressed and two years after the accident committed suicide as a result of his depression. The medical evidence establishes that, but for the accident, Fred would probably not have committed suicide.

Legally there are a number of ways in which the court could approach this, but the basic question is whether the court wishes to compensate the estate and dependants of a suicide. This is the policy issue. Factual causation based on the 'but for' test is established.

The court could determine that the death was too remote.

Pigney v *Pointer's Transport Services Ltd* [1957] 1 WLR 1121

The claimant's husband was injured in an accident at work. The injuries led to anxiety neurosis and depression, as a result of which the husband hanged himself. The claim by the widow was allowed by the court applying the direct consequence test for remoteness.

This case was decided under the *Polemis* test. Would the death be reasonably foreseeable or need it be reasonably foreseeable? If the deceased was prone to depression, the court could treat it as an example of the egg-shell skull rule.

Corr v *IBC Vehicles Ltd* [2008] UKHL 13; [2008] 2 WLR 499

In 1996 the claimant's husband was employed by the defendant as a maintenance engineer when he suffered severe head injuries caused by malfunctioning machinery. Following lengthy reconstructive surgery, he began to suffer post-traumatic stress disorder causing him to lapse into depression. Prior to the accident he had been a happily married man of equable temperament. In February 2002 he was admitted to hospital after taking a drug overdose; by March he was diagnosed as being at significant risk of suicide; in May he was further diagnosed as suffering from severe anxiety and depression, and three days later he committed suicide by jumping from the top of a multi-storey car park. Proceedings were brought by his widow and the defendant admitted that the accident had been caused by his negligence and/or breach of statutory duty, but denied liability under s 1(1) of the Fatal Accidents Act 1976 for the deceased's suicide and also pleaded contributory negligence. The judge awarded damages to the estate but dismissed the Fatal Accidents Act claim, holding that the defendant's duty of care to the deceased had not extended to a duty to take care to prevent his suicide and that the suicide had not been reasonably foreseeable by the defendant. He made no finding as to contributory negligence. The Court of Appeal allowed the claimant's appeal against the judge's dismissal of her claim under the Fatal Accidents Act.

On appeal by the defendant –

Held, dismissing the appeal, that an employer owed his employee a duty to take reasonable care to avoid causing him personal, including psychiatric, injury, and foreseeability of risk of physical injury was sufficient to establish liability; that the depressive illness from which the deceased had suffered had been the direct and foreseeable consequence of the accident for which the defendant had been responsible; that his suicide, although his own deliberate, conscious act, had been the direct result of that depressive illness at a time when his capacity to make reasoned and informed judgments about his future had been impaired by it, and, accordingly, the chain of causal consequences for which the defendant was liable had not been broken by the suicide as a *novus actus interveniens*; and that (Lord Scott of Foscote dissenting) it would be inappropriate to reduce the damages to be awarded to the claimant on the basis of the deceased's contributory negligence in the absence of satisfactory material on which to decide whether such a reduction should be made, and in what amount.

The case showed clearly the difference between factual causation, and so-called 'legal' causation, also known as remoteness of damage. The employer conceded that, but for its breaches of duty, Mr Corr would not have developed the serious depression which led to his suicide: before the accident he was a contented husband and father with no history of psychiatric illness. However, just because a defendant's conduct is a 'but for' cause of harm does not necessarily mean that the law will attribute responsibility for the harm to the defendant.

The issue of suicide has also arisen in cases where a person has committed suicide whilst in police custody.

Kirkham v *Chief Constable of the Greater Manchester Police* [1990] 3 All ER 246

The action was brought against the police on the grounds that they failed to inform the prison authorities of the deceased's suicidal tendencies. The deceased had committed suicide at a remand centre.

1 When the police took the deceased into custody they assumed certain responsibilities, including that of passing on information which might affect his well-being when he was transferred to the prison authorities.
2 As the deceased had been suffering from clinical depression which impaired his judgement, his act had not been voluntary and the defence of *volenti* failed.
3 The defence of *ex turpi causa* would not apply having regard to the changing public opinion of suicide.
4 Suicide was not too remote a consequence of the breach of duty.
5 The suicide did not amount to a *novus actus interveniens.*

There are apparently 70 or so suicides in police custody every year. If the dependants of the deceased can claim damages for the death, this will impose a considerable burden on police finances and there is, therefore, a policy issue involved. In **Kirkham** the Court of Appeal distinguished between sane and insane suicide. The deceased in the case was clinically depressed and, therefore, insane for this purpose. What, however, would the position be if the deceased was sane? How would this affect the defences and causation? This situation arose in the next case.

Reeves v *Commissioner of Police of the Metropolis* [1999] 3 WLR 363

The deceased hung himself in a police cell. The police were aware that he was a suicide risk and conceded that they owed him a duty of care. Liability was denied on the basis that the suicide constituted a *novus actus interveniens* breaking the chain of causation. The trial judge had found that the deceased was of sound mind.

The House of Lords held that the suicide did not constitute a *novus actus interveniens* as this was the very act that they were under a duty to guard against.

Lord Hoffmann (at 367):

> ... once it is admitted that this is the rare case in which such a duty is owed, it seems to me self-contradictory to say that the breach could not have been a cause of the harm because the victim caused it to himself. ... It would make nonsense of the existence of such a duty if the law were to hold that the occurrence of the very act which ought to have been prevented negatived causal connection between the breach of duty and the loss.

Remember that the key to these cases is that the defendant is under a duty to guard. Outside of the police custody cases, a claimant who is of sane mind and commits suicide will break any causative link between the breach of duty and the death.

Reeves complies with the United Kingdom's obligations under the European Convention on Human Rights. In *Keenan* v *UK* (2001) 10 BHRC 319 it was held by the European Court of Human Rights that, under Article 2, once a person has been taken into custody by the state and identified as a suicide risk, irrespective of their mental state there is a duty to take reasonable steps to prevent that suicide.

This principle was applied in the following case.

Savage v *South Essex Partnership NHS Foundation Trust* [2008] UKHL 74

S absconded from an open acute psychiatric ward at an NHS hospital, where she had been detained under the Mental Health Act and committed suicide. The inquest concluded that the precautions in place at the hospital to prevent S from absconding had been inadequate. The claim included damages under the Human Rights Act 1998 for a breach of Article 2 of the European Convention (the right to life).

Held: Where there was a real and immediate risk of a detained patient committing suicide, Article 2 of the Convention imposed an operational obligation on the medical authorities to do all that could reasonably be expected of them to prevent it. There was no basis in the jurisprudence of the Court of Human Rights for the proposition that medical staff could never be subject to such an operational duty; Article 2 imposed on the authorities and their staff an obligation to adopt a framework of general measures to protect detained patients from the risk of suicide and there was no reason why they should not be under the complementary distinct operational obligation to try to prevent a particular suicide in the appropriate circumstances.

Example

M is a passenger in O's car. O is drunk and due to his negligent driving the car crashes and M suffers injuries including brain damage. This results in a complete transformation in M's personality, who then becomes aggressive, violent, dangerous and commits violent sexual assaults on women for which he is sentenced to life imprisonment.

There is no problem with *M* recovering damages for his original injuries, but can he recover for his life imprisonment? Assume that but for (see 'Factual causation' above) the injuries *M* would not have attacked the women and ended up in prison. Is the damage too remote – in the sense that the crimes were deliberately committed by *M* – and is the decision of the court to imprison a *novus actus interveniens*?

These were the facts in *Meah* v *McCreamer (No 1)* [1985] 1 All ER 367, but counsel did not argue either remoteness or *novus actus,* and Meah recovered substantial damages.

M's victims then sued *M* for assault (*W and D* v *Meah* [1986] 1 All ER 935) and *M* claimed a contribution from *O* (*Meah* v *McCreamer (No 2)* [1986] 1 All ER 943). It was held that the type of loss was foreseeable and that the defendant must take the victim as he finds him. (*M* was particularly susceptible to personality change.) However, the judge was unable to hold that the crimes were a *novus actus*, as he had not held this in relation to *M*'s own claim for damages. He therefore held that the injuries to the victims were not the direct consequence of *O*'s negligent driving. Had the previous case been argued and decided on the basis of *novus actus*, it would have been more logical and doctrinally correct to find that the crimes broke the chain of causation in the second case.

Counsel in *Meah* did not argue a public policy rule such as *ex turpi causa* and the decision may not be followed as a result of the decisions in *Clunis* and *Gray*.

Clunis v Camden and Islington Health Authority [1998] 3 All ER 180

See Chapter 10 for *ex turpi causa*.

The claimant, who had a long history of mental disorder, stabbed a man to death and was convicted of manslaughter on the ground of diminished responsibility. He sued the defendants for failure to provide proper care for him after his discharge from hospital. The Court of Appeal struck out the claim on the ground of *ex turpi causa* and that the statutory obligation to provide aftercare did not give rise to a duty of care at common law.

Gray v Thames Trains [2009] UKHL 33

See Chapter 10 for *ex turpi causa*.

The claimant was a victim of the Ladbroke Grove rail crash. He suffered relatively minor physical injuries, but the accident had a major psychological impact upon him, in the form of post-traumatic stress disorder (PTSD). Two years later he stabbed a stranger to death. He pleaded guilty to manslaughter on the grounds of diminished responsibility. He was ordered to be detained in a hospital under s 37 of the Mental Health Act 1983. The defendants admitted duty of care, breach of duty and causation (including his PTSD). They also admitted that they were liable in respect of his losses, including loss of earnings, incurred before the stabbing. However, they denied liability in respect of losses incurred after that date on the basis that *ex turpi causa* applied. The House of Lords accepted this argument.

Summary

This chapter deals with the issues of causation and remoteness of damage:

- The claimant in a negligence action must prove that the damage was caused by the defendant's breach of duty (factual causation). Any damage which is too remote is not recoverable (legal causation). The chain of causation may be broken by a *novus actus interveniens*.

- Factual causation is usually determined by the 'but for' test. The claimant must prove, on the balance of probabilities, that, but for the breach of duty, he would not have suffered the damage.

- The 'but for' test raises problems in a number of areas.

- Where medical science is unable specifically to pinpoint the cause of a disease the court may apply a test of whether the defendant 'materially increased the risk' of damage. (**McGhee v NCB.**) However, this approach will not be used where there are a number of possible causes, none more likely than the other. (**Wilsher v Essex AHA.**)

- In cases where the damage is mesothelioma, where the defendant worked for a number of different employers, the 'but for' test is not applied and the claimant can succeed on material contribution to the risk. (**Fairchild v Glenhaven.**) Liability in these circumstances is joint and several. (Compensation Act 2006 s 3.)

- Where there is a supervening or overtaking cause the first defendant will not be exonerated by a subsequent tort causing the same or greater damage. (**Baker v Willoughby.**) Where the second tortfeasor is sued, he will only be liable for the additional damage he has caused. Where the effects of a tort are overtaken by the effects of a disease, the tortfeasor is liable only up to that point. (***Jobling v Associated Dairies.***)

- In personal injuries cases the claimant cannot succeed on the basis of loss of chance. (*Gregg* v *Scott*.)

- Causation in economic loss cases has differing principles. The 'but for' test is used and the claimant must prove causation on the balance of probabilities. However, there is a claim for loss of chance. (*Simmons* v *Simmons*.) In some cases the courts distinguish between negligence causing the damage and negligence simply providing the opportunity for damage to be suffered. (*Galoo*.)

- The test for remoteness of damage is whether the type or kind of damage suffered by the claimant was reasonably foreseeable. (*Wagon Mound (No 1)*.)

- The way in which the damage came about does not have to be foreseeable. (*Hughes* v *Lord Advocate*.)

- The extent of the damage does not have to be foreseeable.

- The defendant must take the claimant as he finds him. (The egg-shell skull rule.)

- An act occurring after the defendant's breach of duty may break the chain of causation, rendering any damage beyond that point too remote. Such an act is known as a *novus actus interveniens*.

- The chain of causation may be broken by a natural act (*The Carslogie*); by the act of a third party where the act is voluntary and unlikely to happen; or by the act of the claimant where the claimant's behaviour after the breach of duty is unreasonable.

Further reading

Dias, R. W. M. (1962), 'Remoteness of Liability and Legal Policy' CLJ 178 (*Wagon Mound*).

Hill, M. (1991), 'A Lost Chance for Compensation in the Tort of Negligence by the House of Lords' 54 MLR 511 (*Hotson*).

Hoffmann, L. (2005), 'Causation' 121 LQR 592.

Laleng P. (2010), 'Causal Responsibility for Uncertainty and Risk in Toxic Torts', 18(2) *Tort Law Review* 102 (*Fairchild* etc.).

Merkin R. and Steele J., (2011) 'Compensating Mesothelioma Victims' 27 LQR 329 (*Fairchild*).

Morgan, J. (2003), 'Lost Causes in the House of Lords' 66 MLR 277 (*Fairchild*).

Mullany, N. J. (1992), 'Common Sense Causation – An Australian View' 12 OJLS 431.

Peel, E. (2005), 'Loss of a Chance in Medical Negligence' 121 LQR 364 (*Gregg* v *Scott*).

Reece, H. (1996), 'Losses of Chances in the Law' 59 MLR 188.

Stapleton, J. (1988), 'Law, Causation and Common Sense' 8 OJLS 111.

Stapleton, J. (1988), 'The Gist of Negligence' 104 LQR 389.

Stapleton, J. (1997), 'Negligent Valuers and Falls in the Property Market' 113 LQR 1.

Stapleton, J. (2002), 'Lords a'leaping Evidentiary Gaps' 10 Tort LJ 276 (*Fairchild*).

Treasure, T. *et al.* (2004), 'Radical Surgery for Mesothelioma' *British Medical Journal*, 31 January.

Wellington K. (2013), 'Beyond Causative Agents: The Scope of the *Fairchild* exception Post-*Sienkiewicz*' 20(3) Torts LJ 208 (*Fairchild*).

10

Defences to negligence

Objectives

After reading this chapter you will:

1. Understand the legal rules applying to the defence of *volenti non fit injuria* in negligence.
2. Appreciate the significance of agreement in establishing the defence of *volenti*.
3. Understand the legal rules applying to the defence of contributory negligence.
4. Understand the mechanisms of the Contributory Negligence Act 1945.
5. Understand the elements of a contributory negligence defence.
6. Understand the use of apportionment.
7. Have a critical knowledge of the effect of illegality on claims in negligence.
8. Appreciate the application of the defences in the 'rescue cases'.

Introduction

It is traditional to find a chapter on defences at the end of a tort textbook. However, the development of negligence doctrines means that it is convenient to consider certain defences which have particular relevance to negligence at this stage.

There are three defences to a negligence action. *Volenti non fit injuria* means that the claimant voluntarily agrees to undertake the legal risk of harm at his own expense. This is a complete defence to an action. Contributory negligence is where the claimant's fault has contributed to their damage and the damages awarded are reduced in pro-portion to their fault. *Ex turpi causa* means that from a bad cause no action arises. A person who is involved in a criminal act at the time they are injured may be denied an action.

Example

John and Brian had been drinking together. John offered Brian a lift home and Brian accepted. Due to John's negligent driving the car crashed and Brian was injured. Brian was not wearing a seat belt, was thrown forward and hit his head on the windscreen.

If Brian sued John for negligence he could be met with the defences of *volenti non fit injuria* and contributory negligence. The defence of *volenti* would fail as Brian may be aware that John is drunk but he did not consent to him driving negligently. Knowledge of a risk does not equal consent to run that risk. There is also a statutory provision which prevents *volenti* operating in these circumstances. Brian would have his damages reduced for contributory negligence in riding with a driver who he knew was drunk and in failing to wear a seat belt.

If Brian and John were engaged in a get-away from the scene of a crime at the time of the accident, John could also raise the defence of *ex turpi causa* (illegality) to the action.

Volenti non fit injuria

Introduction

Objective 1

The requirements for a defence of *volenti non fit injuria* in a negligence action are a matter for some controversy. It must be shown that the claimant acted voluntarily in the sense that they could exercise a free choice. Some judges are of the opinion that there must be an express or implied agreement between the parties before the defence can operate. The other view is that where the claimant comes across a danger which has already been created by the defendant the defence can operate. If the defence is successful, then the claimant will recover no damages at all. This was also the case where contributory negligence was established before 1945. In cases before that date there was no practical difference for the claimant in being found to be *volenti* or contributorily negligent. The pre-1945 cases must be read with this in mind.

Before this defence has any role to play, it must be shown that the defendant has committed a tort.

Wooldridge v *Sumner* [1963] 2 QB 43

The claimant was a professional photographer. During a horse show he positioned himself at the edge of the arena. He was knocked down and injured by a horse when the rider lost control while riding too fast. The Court of Appeal held that the defendant rider's failure to control his horse was simply an error of judgement which did not amount to negligence. The standard of care owed by a competitor to a spectator was not to act with reckless disregard for the spectator's safety. As this duty had not been broken there was no room for the defence of *volenti non fit injuria* to operate.

Diplock LJ:

'A person attending a game or competition takes the risk of any damage caused to him by any act of a participant done in the course of and for the purposes of the game or competition notwithstanding that such an act may involve an error of judgment or a lapse of skill, unless the participant's conduct is such as to evince a reckless disregard of the spectator's safety.'

The spectator takes the risk because such an act involves no breach of the duty of care owed by the participant to him. He does not take the risk by virtue of the doctrine expressed or obscured by the maxim volenti non fit injuria. The maxim states a principle of estoppel applicable originally to a Roman citizen who consented to being sold as a slave. Although pleaded and argued below it was only faintly relied upon by Mr Everett [counsel for the first defendant] in this court. In my view, the maxim in the absence of express contract has no application to negligence simpliciter where the duty of care is based solely on proximity or 'neighbourship' in the Atkinian sense. The maxim in English law presupposes a tortious act by the defendant. The consent that is relevant is not consent to the risk of injury but consent to the

> lack of reasonable care that may produce that risk . . . and requires on the part of the plaintiff at the time at which he gives his consent full knowledge of the nature and extent of the risk that he ran. . . . In **Dann v Hamilton**, Asquith J expressed doubts as to whether the maxim ever could apply to license in advance a subsequent act of negligence, for if the consent precedes the act of negligence the plaintiff cannot at that time have full knowledge of the extent as well as the nature of the risk which he will run.

The standard of care laid down in this case has been doubted in subsequent cases. In **Condon v Basi** [1985] 2 All ER 453 a standard of reasonable care was applied to participants in a football match. In **Blake v Galloway** [2004] 3 All ER 315 a number of people were involved in horseplay involving throwing pieces of bark at one another and a participant was struck in the eye. The Court of Appeal set the standard of care in these circumstances as recklessness or a very high degree of carelessness.

The defence applies in cases of intentional and negligent infliction of harm, although it operates in different ways.

In intentional torts the defence operates in the form of consent. Where the claimant has consented to the defendant's act they will have no action. So a boxer who is struck by their opponent cannot sue them for battery. A patient who signs a consent form for a surgical operation cannot later sue the surgeon for battery.

Where the harm was negligently inflicted, the defence gives rise to greater difficulties. The defendant has to show that the claimant assumed the legal risk of injury in circumstances where the defendant's act would otherwise amount to negligence. The effect of the defence is that the claimant consents to exempt the defendant from a duty of care which would otherwise have been owed.

There are certain requirements before the defence will apply.

Voluntary

The claimant must have had a genuine freedom of choice before the defence can be successfully raised against them.

> . . . a man cannot be said to be truly 'willing' unless he is in a position to choose freely, and freedom of choice predicates, not only full knowledge of the circumstances on which the exercise of choice is conditioned, so that he may be able to choose wisely, but the absence from his mind of any feeling of constraint so that nothing shall interfere with the freedom of his will. (Scott LJ in **Bowater v Rowley Regis Corp** [1944] KB 476.)

The approach to this point in employer–employee cases has changed. In the early part of the nineteenth century, employees were assumed to consent to the risks in the work that they did. The courts did not accept that the employer–employee relationship was not an equal one and that an employee might have continued to work in the face of danger for fear of losing their job. At the end of the nineteenth century, judicial attitudes changed.

Smith v Baker [1891] AC 325

> The claimant was employed by the defendants on the construction of a railway. While he was working, a crane moved rocks over his head. Both he and his employers knew there was a risk of a stone falling on him and he had complained to them about this. A stone fell and injured the claimant and he sued his employers for negligence. The employers pleaded *volenti non fit injuria* but this was rejected by the court. Although the claimant knew of the risk and continued to work, there was no evidence that he had voluntarily undertaken to run the risk of injury. Merely continuing to work did not indicate *volens*.

The approach in this case has been continued by the courts and it is very rare for a *volenti* plea to succeed in an employee–employer case. Such a plea might be successful where the employee had been paid danger money to undertake precisely that risk. The defence has also succeeded where the employee was under no pressure to take a particular risk but deliberately chose a dangerous method of working.

ICI Ltd v *Shatwell* [1965] AC 656

The claimant and his brother were both experienced shotfirers employed by the defendants. They jointly chose to ignore their employer's orders and statutory safety regulations by testing detonators without taking shelter. There was an explosion and the claimant was injured. He sued the defendants on the grounds of their vicarious liability for his brother's negligence and breach of statutory duty. The question for the House of Lords was whether an employer who was under no statutory duty could be vicariously liable for an employee's breach of statutory duty to another employee. Had the claimant acted on his own, rather than in combination with his brother, no action would have lain. The House held that the claimant was *volens* to the risk of harm and his action therefore failed. Had the claimant sued his brother then the action would have failed on the grounds of *volenti*. There had been no pressure brought by the employers to adopt that method of working. Therefore, there was no reason why *volenti* should not succeed for the employer.

There is a difficult problem posed by a person who commits suicide. Are they acting voluntarily or not? It was held that *volenti* would provide a complete defence in actions against the police or hospital authorities where the deceased was of sound mind. If the deceased's judgement was impaired by mental illness and they were incapable of coming to a balanced decision, their act was not voluntary and *volenti* would not apply. (***Kirkham* v *Chief Constable of the Greater Manchester Police*** [1990] 3 All ER 246.) However, in ***Reeves* v *Commissioner of Police of the Metropolis*** [1999] 3 WLR 363, the House of Lords held that the defence of *volenti* was inappropriate where the act of the defendant relied on to raise the defence was the act the defendant was under a duty to prevent. On this basis, a plea of *volenti* on a suicide in custody could not succeed, even where the deceased was of sound mind.

See also Chapter 9 for suicide.

The concept of voluntariness implies that the claimant should take responsibility for their own actions, and tortious liability will not lie where the claimant was the author of their own misfortunes. Thus, in ***Barrett* v *Ministry of Defence*** [1995] 3 All ER 86 a member of the armed forces, who died after choking on his own vomit when drunk, was held not to be owed a duty of care by his employers to prevent him from consuming an excessive amount of alcohol. They were, however, held to be in breach of a duty of care in not taking sufficient care of him when they assumed responsibility for him after his collapse.

See also Chapter 7 for *Barrett v MoD*.

The issue of voluntariness also arises in the rescue cases. A rescuer who acts to save a person in danger and is injured cannot be said to exercise the free choice which is necessary for *volenti*. (See under 'The Rescue cases' below.)

Agreement

Objective 2

Where the parties have reached an express agreement that the claimant will voluntarily assume the risk of harm and this agreement is made before the negligent act, then the defence will operate.

This point is subject to any statutory restriction which is placed on the parties' freedom to agree. If the agreement is subject to the Unfair Contract Terms Act 1977, then it is important that it does not contravene its provisions: for example, in certain circumstances it is not possible to exclude liability for death or personal injuries at all. The defendant will not be allowed to get round the Act by saying that the claimant was *volenti*. (See s 2(1) and (3).)

In limited circumstances the courts may be prepared to imply the agreement to run the risk (for example, *ICI* v *Shatwell*). The reluctance of the courts to imply an agreement can be seen in the cases where the claimant has accepted a lift with the defendant who is incapable of driving.

Dann v Hamilton [1939] 1 KB 509

The defendant drove the claimant and her mother to London to see the Coronation lights. They visited several public houses and the defendant's ability to drive was clearly impaired. One passenger decided that the driver was drunk and got out of the car. The claimant said she would take the risk of an accident happening. A few minutes later there was an accident and the claimant was injured. It was held that *volenti* did not apply on these facts as the claimant had not consented to or absolved the defendant from subsequent negligence on his part.

Asquith J stated that the defence of *volenti* was applicable where the claimant came to a situation where the danger had already been created by the defendant's negligence.

Nettleship v Weston [1971] 2 QB 691

The claimant gave the defendant driving lessons. On the third lesson the defendant drove negligently and hit a lamp-post. The claimant was injured and sued in negligence. The action was successful and the defence of *volenti* failed. The claimant had not consented to run the risk of injury as he had checked on whether the car was covered for passenger's insurance.

Lord Denning stated: 'Nothing will suffice short of an agreement to waive any claim for negligence. The plaintiff must agree, expressly or impliedly, to waive any claim for any injury that may befall him due to the lack of reasonable care by the defendant.'

Owens v Brimmell [1977] 2 WLR 943

The claimant and defendant spent the evening on a pub crawl together. The claimant accepted a lift home with the defendant although he knew the defendant was drunk. The defendant drove negligently and the claimant received serious injuries in a crash. The defence of *volenti* was held to be inappropriate, but the claimant's damages were reduced for his contributory negligence in riding with a drunken driver and failing to wear a seat belt.

In these cases the claimant is aware of the risk but does not consent to the act of negligence that causes their injury. It was pointed out in **Dann v Hamilton** that the defence could apply in cases where:

> . . . the drunkenness of the driver at the material time is so extreme and so glaring that to accept a lift from him is like engaging in an intrinsically and obviously dangerous occupation, intermeddling with an unexploded bomb or walking on the edge of an unfenced cliff.

Morris v Murray [1990] 3 All ER 801

The claimant went for a ride in a private plane piloted by the defendant, despite the fact that he knew the defendant was drunk. The plane crashed and the claimant was injured. It was held by the Court of Appeal that the pilot's drunkenness was so extreme and obvious that participating in the flight was like engaging in an intrinsically and obviously dangerous occupation. The defence of *volenti* succeeded. Accepting lifts with drunken pilots is more dangerous than with drunken drivers.

The position with drunken drivers is affected by a statutory provision. The Road Traffic Act 1988 s 149 provides that *volenti* is not available where a passenger in a car sues the driver in circumstances where insurance is compulsory. At one time it was thought that the section applied only to express agreements and not to an implied agreement. This view has now been rejected by the Court of Appeal.

Pitts v *Hunt* [1990] 3 All ER 344

The claimant was a pillion passenger on a motor bike driven by the defendant. The defendant was drunk, had never passed a driving test, was uninsured and drove dangerously. The claimant encouraged him in this behaviour. The statutory provision was held to prevent the defendant from relying on any form of the *volenti* defence. Had it not been for the section, the court was of the view that the claim would have been defeated by *volenti*.

The claimant's case was held to have been defeated by the maxim of *ex turpi causa*. This would appear to defeat the intention of the statutory provision.

Problem

Is it necessary for the defendant to prove that the claimant agreed to waive their legal rights in order to succeed in a *volenti* plea?

Judicial views on whether an agreement that the claimant will waive any claim against the defendant is necessary, are mixed. At one extreme Diplock LJ stated in **Wooldridge v Sumner**: '[The defence of *volenti*] in the absence of express contract has no application to negligence simpliciter where the duty of care is based solely on proximity or "neighbourship" in the Atkinian sense.'

Where there is an express agreement to such effect there is little difficulty. Whether the agreement takes the form of a contract term or notice, it will be regulated by statute. Such waivers are probably covered by the Unfair Contract Terms Act 1977. An express agreement by a passenger in a car to waive their rights to sue the driver for negligently inflicted injuries is, as we have seen, negated by statute.

Slightly less extreme was Lord Denning's view in **Nettleship v Weston**: 'Nothing will suffice short of an agreement to waive any claim for negligence. The plaintiff must agree, expressly or impliedly, to waive any claim for any injury that may befall him due to the lack of reasonable care by the defendant.'

The courts are understandably reluctant to imply an agreement. It is necessary that there should be some kind of previous relationship between the parties. We have seen this in cases such as **Dann v Hamilton**. However, in **Morris v Murray** the Court of Appeal held that the defence of *volenti* should have succeeded. This was on the basis that the act of the claimant relied on as consent preceded, and licensed in advance, a possible subsequent act of negligence. The claimant had waived the defendant's duty to take care. A similar view may be taken where the parties embark on a criminal act together and the claimant is injured as a result of the defendant's negligence. The trend in such cases is, however, to apply the maxim *ex turpi causa*.

Can *volenti* be raised where the claimant encounters a risk which has already been created by the defendant's negligence?

Baker v *T E Hopkins & Son Ltd* [1959] 1 WLR 966

The defendant's employees had been placed in danger by being required to work in a confined space with a petrol-driven engine producing poisonous fumes. A doctor attempted to rescue the men and was killed by the fumes. He was aware of the danger at the time he attempted the rescue. *Volenti* was held to be inapplicable as the doctor could not be said to have agreed to the risk. He had only become involved after the defendant's negligent act.

This case can perhaps be explained on policy grounds as the claimant was a rescuer and the courts do not wish to deter rescue. It could also be argued that the doctor was not acting voluntarily.

Judicial support for the view that *volenti* can be raised in these circumstances exists in ***Dann v Hamilton***, ***Morris v Murray*** and ***Pitts v Hunt***. This presents certain problems. The fact that the claimant chose to run the risk should not give rise to *volenti*, as knowledge of the risk is not sufficient. In these circumstances the claimant's conduct amounts to contributory negligence as they acted negligently. This confuses the two defences, which have different outcomes. *Volenti* operates to defeat the claim completely. Contributory negligence reduces the claimant's damages.

Statutory provisions also exist which suggest that a *volenti* plea can succeed in the absence of agreement. These provisions are the Occupiers' Liability Act 1957 s 2(5), the Animals Act 1971 s 5(2) and the Unfair Contract Terms Act 1977 s 2(3). However, these provisions could be viewed as one-off examples of voluntary acceptance of risk.

Knowledge

In order for *volenti* to operate, the claimant must have knowledge of the existence of the risk and its nature and extent. The test for knowledge is subjective. If the claimant should have been aware of the risk but was not, the defence will fail. (***Smith v Austin Lifts Ltd*** [1959] 1 WLR 100.) This raises problems where the claimant was drunk at the time. If they were so drunk that they could not appreciate the nature of the risk, they will not be *volenti*.

The relationship between *volenti* and exclusion clauses

In cases where *volenti* is based on agreement, that agreement may amount to an exclusion clause. If it does, then it will be subject to the provisions of the Unfair Contract Terms Act 1977. Attempts to exclude liability for negligence are governed by s 2. This section operates where the clause attempts to exclude or restrict business liability as defined in s 1(3).

Section 2(1) will operate to defeat any attempt to exclude or restrict liability for death or personal injuries caused by negligence.

Section 2(2) applies a test of reasonableness to other types of damage caused by negligence.

Section 2(3) states: 'Where a contract term or notice purports to exclude or restrict liability for negligence a person's agreement to or awareness of it is not of itself to be taken as indicating his voluntary acceptance of any risk.'

As any agreement between the parties will be covered by the rest of the section, this subsection will only apply where there is no agreement between the parties and the claimant comes upon an already existing risk.

Contributory negligence

Introduction

Objective
3

This defence will apply where the damage which the claimant has suffered was caused partly by their own fault and partly by the fault of the defendant. In order to establish the defence, the defendant must prove that the claimant failed to take reasonable care for their own safety and that this failure was a cause of their damage. If contributory negligence is established, the modern position is that the claimant will have their damages reduced by the court in proportion to their fault. If they would have received £10,000 but were found to be 25 per cent contributorily negligent, their damages will be reduced to £7,500.

This was not always the case. At common law, if the court found that the claimant was partially to blame for their injuries, they received nothing at all. Contributory negligence operated as a complete defence.

Butterfield v *Forrester* (1809) 11 East 60

The claimant rode his horse violently and collided with a pole which the defendant had negligently left in the road. It was held that if the claimant had used ordinary care the accident would not have happened. The claimant was therefore guilty of contributory negligence and could recover nothing.

This rule proved too severe for the courts and exceptions were developed to it. One of these was the rule of last opportunity or effective last chance.

Davies v *Mann* (1842) 10 M&W 546

The claimant negligently fastened his ass up on the highway. The defendant drove his wagon too fast and collided with the ass, which was killed. The defendant was held liable as, if he had driven more slowly, he could have avoided the accident.

After this the law became increasingly convoluted as the courts tried to escape the rigours of a rule which meant that the court had to make a finding in favour of one party or the other. The rule was all or nothing.

In 1911 courts were given a statutory power to apportion damages in cases of collision at sea (Maritime Conventions Act 1911). In 1945 a general power to apportion damages was given to the courts by the Law Reform (Contributory Negligence) Act 1945. Section 1(1) provides:

> Where any person suffers damage as the result partly of his own fault and partly of the fault of any other person or persons, a claim in respect of that damage shall not be defeated by reason of the fault of the person suffering the damage, but the damages recoverable in respect thereof shall be reduced to such an extent as the court thinks just and equitable having regard to the claimant's share in the responsibility for the damage.

The scope of the 1945 Act

Objective
4

The Act will apply only where a person has suffered damage. Damage is defined by s 4 as including loss of life and personal injury. Property damage would appear to be included as this was the case before the Act was passed.

The Act will apply only where the damage was caused partly by the fault of the defendant and partly by the fault of the claimant. In the absence of fault, the court therefore has no power under the Act to apportion damages.

Fault is defined by s 4: 'negligence, breach of statutory duty or other act or omission which gives rise to a liability in tort or would, apart from this Act, give rise to the defence of contributory negligence.'

It must be remembered that fault is referred to in two contexts: the fault of the defendant and the fault of the claimant. Fault of the defendant means negligence, breach of statutory duty or other act or omission which gives rise to a liability in tort. This causes no problem, as the defendant can be said to be at fault whenever they commit a tort. The fault of the claimant means an act or omission which would, apart from the Act, give rise to the defence of contributory negligence. This causes problems of interpretation.

A narrow view would be that if contributory negligence was not a defence at common law, then it will not be available under the Act. This would mean that the defence was not available for torts such as deceit and intentional trespass to the person. This view was applied by the House of Lords in a deceit case. (*Standard Chartered Bank* v *Pakistan National Shipping Corp (No 2)* [2002] UKHL 43.)

The other view is that where the conduct of the claimant would have given rise to the defence at common law if they were suing for negligence, the defence is applicable.

What is clear is that the Act does not apply to conversion or intentional torts against goods by virtue of the Torts (Interference with Goods) Act 1977 s 11.

The Act does apply in negligence, nuisance, and actions under the rule in *Rylands* v *Fletcher*. The Act does not apply to actions in deceit.

Whether the Act applied to trespass to the person was formerly a matter of dispute although it is difficult to see why fault is a defence to an intentional tort concerned with a person's integrity rather than a compensatory tort concerned with apportionment of loss. The issue was considered by the Court of Appeal in *Co-operative Group (CWS) Ltd* v *Pritchard* [2011] EWCA Civ 669. It was held that the 1945 Act would not allow damages to be reduced by virtue of a party's alleged contributory negligence in cases where claims were based on the tort of assault and battery.

Where there is concurrent liability and the claim in contract is co-extensive with an independent tort claim, the defence of contributory negligence will apply in a contract action. (*Barclays Bank plc* v *Fairclough Building Ltd* [1995] 1 All ER 289.) This means that the claimant cannot avoid the defence by bringing proceedings in contract which could have been brought in negligence.

This issue has been clarified by the litigation which arose from the rise and fall of the property market in the late 1980s. Numerous actions were brought against valuers and solicitors who had acted on the transactions. The courts held that the imprudent lending policies of the time would amount to contributory negligence, whether the proceedings were brought in contract or tort. (See *Bristol & West Building Society* v *Fancy & Jackson* [1997] 4 All ER 582 – solicitors; *Platform Home Loans Ltd* v *Oyston Shipways Ltd* [1999] 2 WLR 518 – valuers.)

See Chapter 5 for negligence of valuers and lawyers in conveyancing.

Elements of contributory negligence

Objective
5

The defendant must prove that the claimant failed to take reasonable care for their own safety and that this failure was a cause of their damage.

It is not necessary for the claimant to owe the defendant a duty of care:

Although contributory negligence does not depend on a duty of care, it does depend on foreseeability. Just as actionable negligence requires the foreseeability of harm to others, so contributory negligence requires the foreseeability of harm to oneself. A person is guilty of contributory negligence if he ought reasonably to have foreseen that, if he did not act as a reasonable, prudent man, he might be hurt himself; and in his reckonings he must take into account the possibility of others being careless. (Denning LJ in *Jones* v *Livox Quarries Ltd* [1952] 2 QB 608.)

A motorcyclist does not owe a duty to other road users to wear a crash helmet, but in failing to do so they are guilty of contributory negligence if they suffer head injuries in an accident. They should foresee harm to themselves, although there is no risk of harm to anyone else. A person who smokes should foresee that they are likely to develop lung cancer and, where they are exposed to cancer causing material such as asbestos and also smoke, their damages will be reduced for contributory negligence. (*Badger* v *Ministry of Defence* [2006] 3 All ER 173.)

The claimant's conduct

In considering whether the claimant was contributorily negligent, the court will take into account factors similar to those which would render the defendant negligent. The test is basically an objective one, although subjective factors are introduced when looking at child defendants and persons under a disability.

The claimant's failure to take care for their own safety may be a cause of the accident which results in their damage. This occurs where two motorists are held to be equally to blame for a collision and the claimant is injured. A person who plies a driver with drinks and then accepts a lift and is injured will also be liable under this head.

Alternatively, a person may place themselves in a dangerous position which exposes them to the risk of involvement in the accident in which they are harmed.

Davies v *Swan Motor Co (Swansea) Ltd* [1949] 2 KB 291

The claimant's husband rode on the offside step of a dust-cart. He was aware of the danger of such a practice. The dust-cart was being overtaken by one of the defendant's buses when a collision occurred; the husband was killed. The driver of the dust-cart, the driver of the bus and the husband were all held to have been negligent, the husband because of the dangerous manner in which he was riding on the dust-cart. He was therefore held to have been guilty of contributory negligence and the widow's damages were reduced.

Jones v *Livox Quarries Ltd* [1952] 2 QB 608

The claimant was riding on the tow bar at the back of a traxcavator on his way back to the canteen. Another vehicle was driven negligently into the back of the traxcavator, causing injury to the claimant. The claimant's damages were reduced on the grounds of his contributory negligence. Lord Denning said that the result would have been otherwise if the claimant had been, for example, hit in the eye by a shot from a negligent sportsman.

Similar reasoning could be applied where the claimant puts themselves in a position which is not dangerous in itself but they are aware of circumstances which make it more likely that they will suffer harm. This would explain the cases where the claimant accepts a lift with a driver who they know is drunk. In these circumstances the courts will find that the claimant was guilty of contributory negligence but not *volens* to the risk. (*Owens* v *Brimmell* [1977] 2 WLR 943.)

The third possibility is that the claimant may take up a position which is not in itself dangerous but where their failure to take precautions increases the risk of the extent of harm which they may suffer.

Froom v *Butcher* [1976] QB 286

> The claimant's car was in a collision with the defendant's car caused by the defendant's negligence. At the time of the accident the claimant was not wearing a seat belt. His injuries were worse than they would have been if he had been wearing a seat belt. It was held by the Court of Appeal that his damages should be reduced by 20 per cent. The standard of care was to be judged objectively and the prudent man would wear a seat belt unless there were exceptional circumstances.
>
> Lord Denning MR:
>
> > The question is not what was the cause of the accident. It is rather what was the cause of the damage. In most accidents on the road the bad driving, which causes the accident, also causes the ensuing damage. But in seat belt cases the cause of the accident is one thing. The cause of the damage is another. The *accident* is caused by the bad driving. The *damage* is caused in part by the bad driving of the defendant, and in part by the failure of the plaintiff to wear a seat belt. If the plaintiff was to blame in not wearing a seat belt, the damage is in part the result of his own fault. He must bear some share in the responsibility for the damage: and his damages fall to be reduced to such extent as the court thinks just and equitable.

Since this case, it has been made a criminal offence not to wear a seat belt in the front seat of a car. There are certain exceptions to this, such as pregnant women.

There are a number of areas where problems are caused in trying to ascertain the appropriate standard of care for the claimant.

Children

The traditional view is that there is no age below which a child cannot be held to be guilty of contributory negligence. This view has been challenged by Lord Denning.

Gough v *Thorne* [1966] 1 WLR 1387

> The claimant was aged 13 years. A lorry driver signalled to her to cross the road. She did so without stopping to see if the road was clear. She was run over by a car travelling at excessive speed and overtaking on the wrong side. It was held that the claimant was not guilty of contributory negligence. If she had been an adult the position would have been different. Lord Denning stated:
>
> > A very young child cannot be guilty of contributory negligence. An older child may be. But it depends on the circumstances. A judge should only find a child guilty of contributory negligence if he or she is of such an age as reasonably to be expected to take precautions for his or her own safety: and then he or she is only to be found guilty if blame should be attached to him or her.

(See also **Mullin v Richards** [1998] 1 All ER 920.)

Yachuk v *Oliver Blais* [1949] AC 386

> A nine-year-old child bought petrol from the defendants after falsely stating that his mother needed it for her car. The child used the petrol for a game in which he was burned. The defendants were held to have been negligent in selling the child the petrol but the child was not contributorily negligent. He did not know and could not have been expected to know the qualities of petrol.

Dilemma

When assessing the claimant's conduct, the court will make allowance for the fact that the defendant's negligence has placed the claimant in a dilemma. If the claimant chooses a course which carries a risk of harm in order to avoid a reasonably perceived greater danger, they will not be contributorily negligent.

Jones v *Boyce* (1816) 171 ER 540

The claimant was a passenger on the defendant's coach. A coupling rein broke loose and, thinking that the coach was about to crash, the claimant jumped out and broke his leg. The coach did not in fact crash and if he had remained on it he would have suffered no harm. As his actions were those of a prudent and reasonable man, he was not contributorily negligent.

Where the defendant's negligence has placed a person in danger and the claimant has attempted a rescue, the court will be slow to find the rescuer contributorily negligent. (See 'The Rescue cases' below.)

Workers

In cases where an employee sues their employer for breach of statutory duty, the court will be slow to find that the employee was guilty of contributory negligence. Regard must be had to the fact that the employee's sense of danger will have been dulled by familiarity, repetition, noise, confusion, fatigue and preoccupation with work. (***Caswell* v *Powell Duffryn Associated Collieries Ltd*** [1940] AC 152.) The reason for this lenient approach is that the court will not want to undermine the statutory regulations which are often designed to protect workers from the consequences of their own carelessness.

The courts will hold employees liable for their contributory negligence, however.

Jayes v *IMI (Kynoch) Ltd* [1985] ICR 155

The claimant, an experienced workman, was cleaning a machine when his hand was pulled into the machine and he lost the tip of a finger. The machine had had its safety guard removed. The claimant, in an action under the Factories Act 1961 s 14, was held to have been 100 per cent contributorily negligent after he admitted that what he had done had been extremely foolish.

This decision can be criticised on a number of grounds. The defence is one of contributory negligence, which indicates that there must be fault on the part of both parties. Second, a finding of 100 per cent contributory negligence has the same effect as a finding of *volenti* and would undermine the principle in ***Smith* v *Baker*** that such a finding should not usually be made in employer–employee cases. Finally, the Law Reform (Contributory Negligence) Act 1945 s 1, which comes into operation only where there is fault on the part of both parties, provides that a claim shall not be defeated by the fault of the claimant.

The Court of Appeal held, without reference to *Jayes*, that a finding of 100 per cent contributory negligence is logically indefensible. (***Pitts* v *Hunt*.**)

In ***Anderson* v *Newham College of Further Education*** [2003] ICR 212 it was suggested that *Jayes* had been decided *per incuriam* and that it should not be followed. Where the fault lies entirely on the part of the claimant, there can be no fault by the defendant. The claimant's contributory negligence could reduce the defendant's liability but it could not nullify it.

None of this is intended to suggest that actions of this kind should not be defensible by the employer, but the argument should be on causation grounds, not those of contributory negligence.

Causation

See Chapter 9 for causation generally. In order for contributory negligence to constitute a defence, the claimant's fault must be a legal and factual cause of the harm suffered. It is not necessary that the claimant's fault be a cause of the accident itself.

In *Jones* v *Livox Quarries*, the claimant's position on the traxcavator was held to be one of the causes of his damage, although the most obvious risk to the claimant was that he would fall off. His action in riding on the tow bar had sufficient causal potency to be regarded as a cause of his injuries. Factual causation was established and the damage was not too remote. Had the claimant been shot, then this would have been too remote a consequence and causation not established.

In the seat belt cases the claimant's failure to take precautions for their own safety is regarded as a contributing cause of their injuries, but it is necessary for the defendant to prove that the failure to wear a seat belt was a cause of the injuries. If the claimant was thrown forwards and injured, then clearly failure to wear a seat belt is contributory negligence. But for the failure, either the claimant would not have been injured or their injuries would not have been so severe. However, if something enters the vehicle and crushes the claimant backwards against the seat, the failure to wear the seat belt would appear to be irrelevant and fail the test of causation. The claimant would have suffered the injuries even if they had been wearing a seat belt.

The first test that must be passed is the 'but for' test for factual causation. Would the alleged consequence have occurred but for the negligent cause? If the claimant's alleged contributory negligence fails this test it is not necessary to go any further.

The Act itself does not change the rules on causation, so it is still necessary to use common law rules. This can give rise to some difficult problems.

Stapley v *Gypsum Mines Ltd* [1953] AC 663

Two miners had been instructed to bring down an unsafe part of the roof which presented a danger to the miners. They disobeyed instructions by continuing to work when they had failed to do this. The roof collapsed and one of the men was killed. His widow sued the defendants for negligence. The court had to decide whether the damage was solely as a result of the negligence of the claimant's husband or whether the negligence of his workmate was also a factor. The House of Lords approached the question in a common-sense manner and held the actions of both workmen were causes. The claimant's action succeeded but his damages were reduced by 80 per cent on the ground of contributory negligence.

Lord Reid:

> One must discriminate between those faults which must be discarded as being too remote and those which must not. Sometimes it is proper to discard all but one and to regard that one as the sole cause, but in other cases it is proper to regard two or more as having jointly caused the accident. I doubt whether any test can be applied generally. It may often be dangerous to apply to this kind of case tests which have been used in traffic accidents by land or sea, but in this case I think it useful to adopt phrases from Lord Birkenhead's speech in **Admiralty Comrs** v **SS Volute**, and to ask was Dale's fault 'so much mixed up with the state of things brought about' by Stapley that 'in the ordinary plain common sense of this business' it must be regarded as having contributed to the accident. I can only say that I think it was and there was no 'sufficient separation of time, place or circumstance' between them to justify its being excluded. Dale's fault was one of omission rather than commission, and it may often be impossible to say that, if a man had done what he omitted to do, the accident would certainly have been prevented. It is enough, in my judgment, if there is a sufficiently high degree of probability that the accident would have been prevented. I have already stated my view of the probabilities in this case, and I think that it must lead to the conclusion that Dale's fault ought to be regarded as having contributed to the accident.

A different slant on causation and 'blameworthiness' is provided by the next case which involves 'lifestyle' issues.

St George v Home Office [2008] EWCA Civ 1068

The claimant, an abuser of drugs and alcohol for 13 years, was imprisoned for theft. The prison was aware of his problems, which included withdrawal seizures. He was assigned to sleep on a top bunk and suffered a withdrawal seizure which led him to fall from his top bunk and to sustain a head wound, leading to severe brain damage and the claimant becoming severely disabled. The judge found that there had been contributory negligence on the part of the claimant, the fault lying in his addiction to benzodiazepine and alcohol, which had been the result of his own lifestyle decisions.

The Court of Appeal held that, in applying the test in s 1(1) of the Act (see below for s 1(1)), it was necessary to have regard both to blameworthiness and to what was sometimes called causal potency. Whilst it was true that, but for his addiction, the claimant would not have suffered a withdrawal seizure and would not, therefore, have fallen from the top bunk and suffered the head injury which had triggered the status – and whilst in that sense the injury was the result partly of his addiction – the addiction was not a potent cause of the injury. The claimant's fault in becoming addicted to drugs and alcohol in his mid-teens was not a potent cause of the status and consequent brain injury which were triggered by the fall. It was too remote in time, place and circumstances and had not been sufficiently connected with the negligence of the prison staff – or not sufficiently mixed up with the state of things brought about by the prison staff – to be properly regarded as a cause of the injury.

It is important to remember that if one act is held to be the sole cause of the damage and that act is one of the claimant, then the claimant will recover nothing. The act could be regarded as a *novus actus interveniens*. (See, for example, *McKew v Holland & Hannen & Cubitts*.)

Apportionment

Objective
6

The Law Reform (Contributory Negligence) Act 1945 s 1(1) directs the court to reduce the claimant's damages to the extent that the court thinks just and equitable having regard to the claimant's share in the responsibility for the damage.

There are two possible ways of assessing the claimant's share in the responsibility for the damage: causation and blameworthiness. (See *St George v Home Office*.)

If a test of causative potency is used, then logically every case should end with a 50/50 apportionment, as the conduct of both the claimant and the defendant is a cause. The courts, however, take a common-sense view, rather than a philosophical view, and arrive at apportionments other than 50/50. (See *Stapley v Gypsum Mines Ltd*.)

Where the comparative blameworthiness or culpability of the parties is taken into account, then the test is an objective one of deviating from the standard of behaviour of the reasonable person. It is not a moral test. The reasonable person, for example, would wear a seat belt.

The requirement that the reduction should be just and equitable means that there is no single test for determining the level of reduction of damages. The courts treat it as a question of fact and take an *ad hoc* approach.

Reeves v Commissioner of Police of the Metropolis [1999] 3 WLR 363

See also Chapter 9
for *Reeves*.

Lord Hoffmann:

. . . what section 1 requires the court to apportion is not merely degrees of carelessness but 'responsibility' and . . . an assessment of responsibility must take into account the policy of the rule . . . A person may be responsible although he has not been careless at all, as in the case of breach of an absolute statutory duty. And he may have been careless without being responsible, as in the case of 'acts of inattention' by workmen.

Can there be a 100 per cent reduction for contributory negligence? If there can be then there is no practical difference between this defence and *volenti*, as the claimant receives no damages. In **Pitts v Hunt** [1990] 3 All ER 344, the trial judge felt he was unable to apply *volenti non fit injuria* because of the statutory provision. However, he held the claimant to be 100 per cent contributorily negligent. The Court of Appeal stated that it was impermissible to make a finding of 100 per cent contributory negligence, as the Act states that the claimant must suffer damage partly as a result of their own fault and partly as a result of the defendant's fault. The trial judge must therefore apportion blame between the parties. A finding of 100 per cent contributory negligence does not do this. (But see **Jayes v IMI (Kynoch) Ltd**, and discussion above.)

That the argument on 100 per cent reduction is not over is shown by the case of suicide in police custody of **Reeves v Commissioner of Police** [1998] 2 WLR 401. The trial judge had held the deceased to be 100 per cent contributorily negligent, with which Morritt LJ (dissenting) agreed in the Court of Appeal. The majority were hesitant. Buxton LJ held that a claim which was not susceptible to attack on the grounds of *volenti* or *novus actus interveniens*, could not be defeated on the ground of contributory negligence. Lord Bingham MR would have held the deceased to be 50 per cent contributorily negligent, but, in order to avoid all three judges disagreeing, he concurred with Buxton LJ.

In the House of Lords it was held that where the deceased was of sound mind he bore at least partial responsibility for killing himself and damages were reduced by 50 per cent ([1999] 3 WLR 363). Could the damages of an insane suicide be reduced? Lord Hoffmann was of the opinion that they could not and drew an analogy with children who were not of full understanding.

Multiple defendants

Difficulties arise where there is more than one defendant. In cases where the claimant was not at fault, they can recover their full loss against any of the defendants. That person will then have to seek a contribution from the other defendants under the Civil Liability (Contribution) Act 1978.

Where the claimant was at fault and contributed to their own injuries, is it necessary to balance the claimant's contributory negligence against each defendant separately?

Fitzgerald v Lane [1989] AC 328

The claimant stepped out into the traffic on a busy road. He was struck by a vehicle driven by the first defendant. This pushed him into the path of an oncoming vehicle driven by the second defendant. Both defendants were accepted to be negligent and the claimant was contributorily negligent. At first instance the three parties were held equally to blame and the claimant's damages were therefore reduced by one-third. This was held to be the wrong approach by the House of Lords. It was necessary to distinguish two questions: first, the contributory negligence of the claimant and the amount by which his damages should be reduced; second, the amount of contribution recoverable between the two defendants. The claimant's culpability was in setting the scene for the accident. The response of the defendants then had to be looked at. The claimant's conduct and the totality of the tortious conduct of the defendants were compared. As the claimant was as much to blame for his injuries as the defendants, his damages were reduced by 50 per cent.

Lord Ackner:

It is axiomatic that whether the plaintiff is suing one or more defendants, for damages for personal injuries, the first question which the judge has to determine is whether the plaintiff has established liability against one or other or all the defendants, i.e. that they, or one or more of them, were negligent (or in breach of statutory duty) and that that negligence (or breach of statutory duty) caused or materially contributed to his injuries. The next step, of course, once liability has been established, is to assess what is the total of the damage that the plaintiff has sustained as a result of the established negligence. It is only after these two decisions have been made that the next question arises, namely, whether the defendant or defendants have established (for the onus is upon them) that the plaintiff, by his own negligence, contributed to the damage which he suffered. If, and only if, contributory negligence is established does the court then have to decide, pursuant to section 1 of the Law Reform (Contributory Negligence) Act 1945, to what extent it is just and equitable to reduce the damages which would otherwise be recoverable by the plaintiff, having regard to his 'share in the responsibility for the damage'.

All the decisions referred to above are made in the main action. Apportionment of liability in a case of contributory negligence between plaintiff and defendants must be kept separate from apportionment of *contribution between the defendants inter se*. Although the defendants are each liable to the plaintiff for the whole amount for which he has obtained judgment, the proportions in which, as between themselves the defendants must meet the plaintiff's claim, do not have any direct relationship to the extent to which the total damages have been reduced by the contributory negligence, although the facts of any given case may justify the proportions being the same.

Once the questions referred to above in the main action have been determined in favour of the plaintiff to the extent that he has obtained a judgment against two or more defendants, then and only then should the court focus its attention on the claims which may be made between those defendants for contribution pursuant to the Civil Liability (Contribution) Act 1978, re-enacting and extending the court's powers under section 6 of the Law Reform (Married Women and Tortfeasors) Act 1935. In the contribution proceedings, whether or not they are heard during the trial of the main action or by separate proceedings, the court is concerned to discover what contribution is just and equitable, having regard to the responsibility between the tortfeasors inter se, for the damage which the plaintiff has been adjudged entitled to recover. That damage may, of course, have been subject to a reduction as a result of the decision in the main action that the plaintiff, by his own negligence, contributed to the damage which he sustained.

Thus, where the plaintiff successfully sues more than one defendant for damages for personal injuries, and there is a claim between co-defendants for contribution, there are two distinct and different stages in the decision-making process – the one in the main action and the other in the contribution proceedings.

One final point to be remembered about contributory negligence is that it differs in effect from a finding of negligence. The latter does not usually directly affect the defendant's pocket, as they will be insured. A finding of contributory negligence, on the other hand, has a direct financial effect on the claimant. They get less in damages.

Ex turpi causa

Objective 7

The court may deny an action to a claimant who suffered damage while participating in a criminal activity. In negligence actions the court may find that no duty of care was owed in the circumstances. The defence may be referred to as illegality or *ex turpi causa non oritur actio*. This means that an action cannot be founded on a bad cause.

The formulation of an appropriate test has caused serious problems for the court because of the wide range of circumstances in which the issue can arise. The mere fact that the claimant's conduct is illegal is not sufficient. There must be some connection between the illegality and the damage suffered by the claimant.

Examples

1 Two safebreakers are on their way to open a safe and they have a fight. One is injured. *Ex turpi causa* would not provide a defence. (But see *Murphy v Culhane* [1977] QB 94 for a case involving a criminal affray where the claimant got more than he bargained for and it was stated that the defence could apply.) If the safebreakers were actually trying to open the safe and one was injured by the other's negligent use of explosives, then the defence could apply.
2 The claimant is injured as a result of the defendant's negligent driving. The car contains dangerous drugs which the pair intended to sell. The defence will not apply. (*Delaney v Pickett* [2012] 1 WLR 2149.)
3 Two men steal a set of ladders. They put them in the back of a van and drive away from the scene of the crime at speed. One man falls out of the back of the van as the doors are open to accommodate the ladders. The defence will apply. (*Joyce v O'Brien* [2013] EWCA Civ 546.)

A major problem is the type of conduct by the claimant which will give rise to the defence. This issue has arisen in the case of suicide by the claimant which is linked to the defendant's breach of duty. For example, in *Kirkham v Chief Constable of the Greater Manchester Police* [1990] 3 All ER 246, the court refused to bar the claim on the ground of suicide. This was no longer an affront to the public conscience, where the suicide resulted from mental instability. However, in *Reeves v Commissioner of Police of the Metropolis* [1999] 3 WLR 363, the House of Lords preferred the approach that neither *ex turpi* nor *volenti* could be raised as a defence when they were based on the very act that the defendant was under a duty to prevent (in this case, to prevent suicide in custody).

The House of Lords has laid down two rules for *ex turpi*. The first (narrow rule) is relatively clear-cut but the wider rule still leaves severe problems for judges in determining whether there is sufficient connection between the illegality and the claimant's damage.

Gray v Thames Trains [2009] UKHL 33

The claimant was a victim of the Ladbroke Grove rail crash. He suffered relatively minor physical injuries, but the accident had a major psychological impact upon him, in the form of post-traumatic stress disorder (PTSD). Two years later he stabbed a stranger to death. He pleaded guilty to manslaughter on the grounds of diminished responsibility. He was ordered to be detained in a hospital under s 37 of the Mental Health Act 1983. The claimant brought a claim in negligence against the defendants. The defendants admitted that they owed the claimant a duty of care and that they had been in breach of that duty; and admitted that his injuries, including his PTSD, were caused by their negligence. They also admitted that they were liable in respect of his losses, including loss of earnings, incurred before the stabbing. However, they denied liability in respect of losses incurred after that date on the basis that *ex turpi causa* applied.

The Court of Appeal held that they were bound by authority to hold that the *ex turpi causa* principle precluded the claim for general damages but not for loss of earnings.

Held (House of Lords): The issue was whether the intervention of the claimant's criminal act in the causal relationship between the defendants' breaches of duty and the damage of which he complained prevented him from recovering that part of his loss caused by the criminal act.

The appeal would be allowed and the claim for loss of earnings after the killing barred.

Orders made by the criminal courts were necessary for the protection of the public from serious harm in cases involving a violent claimant. For as long as the orders were in force, the claimant's earning capacity was removed, and therefore the civil court should not award compensation where the criminal act of the claimant eliminated his earning capacity.

> Causation was clear. The mere fact that the killing had been the claimant's own voluntary and deliberate act was not in itself a reason for excluding the defendants' liability. However, the matter had to be approached on the basis that, even though the claimant's responsibility for killing the victim had been diminished by his PTSD, he knew what he had been doing when he had killed the victim and he had been responsible for what he had done. The claimant's claims for loss of earnings after his arrest and for general damages for his detention, conviction and damage to reputation were all claims for damage caused by the lawful sentence imposed upon him for manslaughter and therefore fell within the narrower version of the rule. However, the wider rule covered the remaining heads of damage in the instant case. The claimant's liability to compensate the dependants of the victim was an immediate inextricable consequence of his having intentionally killed him.

The narrow version

In its narrower form, the *ex turpi* rule is that you cannot recover for damage which is the consequence of a sentence imposed upon you for a criminal act.

In **Gray**, the defendants argued that after the homicide any lost earnings arose *ex turpi causa* and so could not be recovered. The claimant sought to evade the application of the illegality defence on the basis that his earning capacity had already been destroyed before the killing. He contended that his loss of earnings was caused by the PTSD, not the manslaughter. Although the act of manslaughter did not break the chain of causation from the defendants' negligence to the claimant's lost earnings (**Corr v IBC Vehicles Ltd** [2008] UKHL 13), the defendants argued that the claimant's voluntary and deliberate crime clearly did have an impact upon his ability to earn, and that he should bear the consequences of his illegal act. The House of Lords held that the defence did apply.

The Lords agreed that the principle of 'consistency' was a satisfactory reason for the claim to be barred. The civil law must be consistent with any criminal sentence already imposed. They cited the passage of the Law Commission: 'it would be quite inconsistent to imprison or detain someone on the grounds that he was responsible for a serious offence and then to compensate him for the detention' (CP No 160, *The Illegality Defence in Tort* (2001), para 4.100).

> Mr Gray's claims for loss of earnings after his arrest and for general damages for his detention, conviction and damage to reputation were all claims for damage caused by the lawful sentence imposed upon him for manslaughter and therefore fell within the narrower version of the rule.

The narrow version of the rule is illustrated by the following case.

Clunis v Camden and Islington Health Authority [1998] 3 All ER 180

The claimant sued the defendants for negligence on the ground that he had been released prematurely from their care and had then killed a stranger. The claimant had been charged with murder, reduced to manslaughter on the ground of diminished responsibility. No private law duty of care was held to be owed (see **X v Bedfordshire County Council** [1995] 2 AC 633), but the Court of Appeal stated that *ex turpi* would only be inappropriate where the claimant did not know the nature and quality of his acts, i.e. where a plea of insanity would have been successful in a murder case.

Clunis was followed by the Court of Appeal in **Worrall v British Railways Board** [1999] CA Transcript No 684, in which the claimant alleged that an injury which he had suffered as a result of his employer's negligence had changed his personality. As a result, he had on two occasions committed sexual assaults on prostitutes, for which offences he had been sentenced to imprisonment for six years. He claimed loss of earnings while in prison and thereafter. The Court of Appeal struck out this claim. Mummery LJ said: 'It would be inconsistent with his criminal conviction to attribute to the negligent Defendant in this action any legal responsibility for the financial consequences of crimes which he has been found guilty of having deliberately committed.'

The *Clunis* decision was approved by the Law Commission in its Consultation Paper *The Illegality Defence in Tort* (No 160, 2001) on the same narrow ground as that of Mummery LJ in *Worrall*'s case: '*Clunis* v *Camden and Islington Health Authority* . . . seems entirely justifiable if the rationale of consistency is accepted: it would be quite inconsistent to imprison or detain someone on the grounds that he was responsible for a serious offence and then to compensate him for the detention.' (Paragraph 4.100.)

Mr Gray's claims for loss of earnings after his arrest and for general damages for his detention, conviction and damage to reputation were all claims for damage caused by the lawful sentence imposed upon him for manslaughter and therefore fell within the narrower version of the rule.

The wider version

In its wider form, the rule is that a party cannot recover compensation for loss which had been suffered in consequence of his or her own criminal act. It differs from the narrower version in at least two respects: first, it cannot be justified on the grounds of inconsistency in the same way as the narrower rule. Instead, the wider rule has to be justified on the ground that it is offensive to public notions of the fair distribution of resources that a claimant should be compensated (usually out of public funds) for the consequences of his own criminal conduct. Secondly, the wider rule may raise problems of causation which cannot arise in connection with the narrower rule. The sentence of the court is a consequence of the criminality for which the claimant was responsible.

Some of Mr Gray's claims fell within the wider principle, such as the claim for an indemnity against any claims which might be brought by dependants of the dead pedestrian and the claim for general damages for feelings of guilt and remorse consequent upon the killing. Neither of these was a consequence of the sentence of the criminal court but the House of Lords barred these claims under the wider principle.

The wider principle had been applied by the Court of Appeal in the following case.

Vellino v *Chief Constable of the Greater Manchester Police* [2002] 1 WLR 218

The claimant was injured when he jumped from a second-floor window in order to avoid arrest by the police. He alleged that the police owed a duty of care not negligently to let him escape after they arrested him. The Court of Appeal (by a majority) held that there was no duty of care in these circumstances, rather than applying the defence. The dissenting judge (Sedley LJ) felt that the power to apportion responsibility in contributory negligence was a more appropriate method of doing justice.

Sir Murray Stuart-Smith:

The operation of the principle arises where the claimant's claim is founded upon his own criminal or immoral act. The facts which give rise to the claim must be inextricably linked with the criminal activity. It is not sufficient if the criminal activity merely gives occasion for tortious conduct of the defendant.

If the claimant suffers damage in the course of a joint criminal enterprise the court may apply an automatic bar to the claim or in some cases has set a much lower standard of care than would normally be applied.

Example

Where two criminals are engaged in attempting a getaway from the scene of the crime, the car is driven negligently at speed and the passenger is injured. The court would be unwilling or unable to determine what speed would be expected from a competent getaway driver. (See *Ashton v Turner* [1981] QB 137.)

Pitts v *Hunt* [1990] 3 All ER 344

(For facts see *'Volenti non fit injuria'*.) Beldam LJ argued that the test should be whether there had been any illegality of which the court should take note and would it be an affront to the public conscience to allow the claimant to recover? The fact that there had been unlawfulness should not mean that a remedy should be denied. Taking account of the view of drunk driving, the claimant should be precluded on grounds of public policy from recovering compensation.

Dillon LJ dismissed the conscience approach as it would be difficult to apply and would inevitably be affected by emotional factors. This would lead to a graph of illegalities graded according to moral turpitude. Dillon and Balcombe LJJ agreed that a preferable approach would be to deny a duty of care in certain cases of joint illegal enterprises. The defence would have this effect where, first, the claimant's action is directly connected with the joint illegal enterprise and not merely incidental to it. Secondly, the circumstances of the illegal venture must be such that the court cannot determine the standard of care to be observed.

An objection to the use of the defence in this case was that it enabled the court to evade the statutory prohibition on applying *volenti non fit injuria*. This cannot have been the intention of Parliament when it prevented drivers from contracting out of their liability to a passenger.

The test of difficulty in setting the appropriate standard of care poses problems. One is that the defence applies in torts other than negligence and also applies in contract. A second is that cases arise where there is no doubt about the appropriate standard.

Rance v *Mid-Downs Health Authority* [1991] 1 All ER 801

The allegation of negligence was that the defendant had failed to observe a foetal abnormality during pregnancy and the claimant had been denied the possibility of an abortion. Such an abortion would have been illegal under the then existing law. There would have been no difficulty in establishing the appropriate standard of care for the medical defendant. It was held that there had been no negligence, but on grounds of public policy the court would not award compensation where the claimant would have had to have broken the law.

The public conscience test was rejected by the House of Lords in a trusts case in favour of a test of whether the claimant had to rely on illegality to found the claim. (*Tinsley* v *Milligan* [1994] 1 AC 340; see also *Stone & Rolls Ltd* v *Moore Stephens* [2009] UKHL 39.) It is doubtful whether this approach is useful in the context of most tort cases as, in, for example, the car passenger cases, the claimant will usually be able to found the claim on negligent driving without mentioning any criminal context. However, in the following case the test was used to deny part of a claim for damages for personal injuries.

Hewison v Meridian Shipping PTE [2002] EWCA Civ 1821

The claimant suffered serious personal injuries while employed by the defendant as a crane operator on a ship. One of the heads of damages claimed was for loss of future earnings for a period of 27 years. However, the claimant had lied to obtain the job by stating falsely that he had never suffered from epilepsy. This amounted to the criminal offence of obtaining a pecuniary advantage by deception. The Court of Appeal held that he was unable to base any loss of earnings claim on earnings he would have made as a seaman. This was on the basis that the claimant's future employment had been dependent on his continuing deceit of his employers. The deceit was therefore not collateral, but essential to establish that part of his claim. The test was not whether an award of damages would be acceptable to public conscience. It was based on the rule of public policy that the court would not lend its aid to a man who founded his cause of action on an illegal or immoral act.

See Chapter 11 for trespass.

It is not clear what kind of conduct will bar an action. The fact that a tort was committed is not sufficient. A duty of care can be owed to a trespasser. The conduct does not even have to be illegal. The conduct will usually be criminal, but not all crimes will be sufficient to raise the defence. For example, a breach of statutory duty will not bar a claim.

The Law Commission have looked at the illegality defence on a number of occasions. The Law Commission Consultation Paper No 160 (2001) proposed that the present law should be replaced by a structured discretion to bar a claim where the claim arises from or is connected to an illegal act on the part of the claimant. However, they doubted whether the defence should ever apply in personal injury actions. This is on the grounds that damages for personal injury are compensatory rather than profit-making and that the claimant could lose a lot of money and have to rely on other sources such as state benefits. Neither of these grounds was particularly compelling as virtually all tort damages are compensatory and the second ground has not been raised in other areas of negligence such as causation. The claimant in *Ashton v Turner* did lose £75,000 as a result of stealing three radios, but to suggest that this should give him a claim appears equivalent to saying that claims should be allowed where there is a clear-cut case of *volenti*.

The Law Commission Consultation Paper No 189 (2009) has recommended greater transparency and consistency through judicial reform in tort law rather than legislation. Has the decision in *Gray* set the illegality defence in tort law on a more transparent, comprehensible footing? The decision explicitly recognises the need to identify the policy justifications for the illegality defence and signals that a discretionary approach, taking into account a range of factors, is appropriate. Lord Rodger stated that the result might have been different had the offence been trivial. Lord Phillips had reservations about what the outcome might have been had Mr Gray not shown any turpitude – for example, if he had been found not guilty by reason of insanity but still detained under the Mental Health Act 1983. Thus the seriousness of the illegality must be considered. However, what other factors underpin the public policy behind the defence remains unclear. The 2009 Law Commission Consultation Paper also refers to: furthering the purpose of the rule which the illegal conduct has infringed; preventing a claimant from profiting from his wrong; deterrence; proportionality. Such policy rationales may well be crucial when deciding subsequent cases; unfortunately, they were not referred to in *Gray*.

The rescue cases

Objective
8

We have seen that issues of causation and blameworthiness raise problems for the courts when deciding whether the claimant's conduct was sufficiently serious to deserve a reduction in their entitlement to damages, or to deserve no damages at all. Public policy plays a part in a number of these decisions and a student could be forgiven for confusion at the complexity of the area and the number of legal doctrines used. This chapter will be concluded by looking at the so-called 'rescue cases' and seeing how the various doctrines apply.

See also Chapter 4 for rescuers and psychiatric damage. The public policy issue in these cases is that the courts do not want to deter rescue and it has been held that a duty of care is owed to rescuers. (***Chadwick v British Railways Board*** [1967] 1 WLR 912.)

Example

A's negligence has placed *B* in danger and *C* is injured in attempting a rescue of *B*. *C* sues *A* in negligence. Assume that a duty of care is owed by *A* to *C* as a rescue was reasonably foreseeable in the circumstances.

There are three possible 'defences' that *A* can raise to *C*'s action.

He could argue that *C*'s action in attempting a rescue was a *novus actus interveniens* of the claimant which broke the chain of causation. *A*'s negligence would not then be a cause of *C*'s injuries. The court will apply a test of whether the claimant's rescue attempt was likely as a result of the breach of duty and whether the claimant acted reasonably.

Alternatively, *A* could argue that, in attempting a rescue, *C* was volens to the risk of injury. Because of the nature of rescue cases, the danger will usually have been created by the defendant's negligence before the claimant comes on the scene. If the view is taken (see '*Volenti*') that an agreement is necessary for *volenti*, then it will usually be inapplicable in rescue cases. The courts do not always take this view.

Finally, A could attempt to prove that *C* was contributorily negligent in that his fault was a cause of his injuries.

The courts will generally be reluctant to invoke any of these defences to deny the rescuer compensation.

Haynes v *Harwood* [1935] 1 KB 146

A horse van was left unattended by the driver in an area with three schools. There were always a number of children in the street. A child threw a stone at the horse, which bolted. The claimant, a police officer, saw that highway users were in danger and tried to stop the horse. He suffered personal injuries. The court held that *volenti non fit injuria* did not succeed as a defence as the claimant did not exercise the freedom of choice which was necessary. (There is also a problem as to whether the defence applies where the claimant encounters an already existing danger.) There was no *novus actus interveniens* as what occurred was a likely result of the original breach of duty by the defendants.

Contrast this case with ***Cutler v United Dairies*** [1933] 2 KB 297. Here a horse had bolted into a field. Nobody was in any danger from the horse but the claimant entered the field and tried to calm the horse and was injured. The claimant was *volenti* as he had freedom of choice as to whether to attempt a rescue and there was a *novus actus interveniens* as the danger had passed.

Harrison v British Rail Board [1981] 3 All ER 679

The defendant attempted to board a moving train. The claimant guard saw the defendant on the outside of the train and gave the incorrect signal to the driver. It should have been a signal to stop but was the accelerate signal. The guard attempted to pull the defendant into the train but both fell out and the guard was injured. The court held that where a person places himself in danger and it is foreseeable that another person may attempt a rescue, the rescued person owes a duty of care to the rescuer. However, the claimant was found to have been contributorily negligent in pressing the wrong signal and his damages were reduced by 20 per cent.

The court pointed out that it was rare that a rescuer would be found to be contributorily negligent.

This case supports the view expressed in **Baker v Hopkins** that a person who places himself in danger may owe a duty of care to a rescuer. If a climber ignores safety advice and a member of the mountain rescue team is injured attempting a rescue, that person could sue the climber for negligence.

Would a rescuer be denied an action on the ground of *ex turpi causa*, for example, if one burglar was injured attempting to assist another who had been placed in danger by the dangerous condition of the house they were breaking into? (See **Pitts v Hunt** for possible tests.)

Summary

This chapter deals with the defences to negligence.

- There are three common law defences to negligence: *volenti non fit injuria*; contributory negligence; and *ex turpi causa*.

- In the defence of *volenti* the defendant must assume the legal risk of injury in circumstances in which the defendant's act would otherwise amount to negligence.

- The defence requires that the claimant acted voluntarily. The courts are reluctant to apply the defence in employer–employee cases for this reason. (**Smith v Baker**.) Where a person commits suicide in police custody they are not acting voluntarily. (**Reeves v Commissioner of Police**.)

- Where there is an express agreement made before the negligent act, this is sufficient to raise the defence in the absence of statutory prohibition. The defence may not be raised in cases of drunk drivers (Road Traffic Act 1988 s 149) but can operate against drunken pilots.

- The courts are reluctant to imply an agreement.

- In order for *volenti* to operate the claimant must have knowledge of the existence of the risk and its nature and extent.

- Contributory negligence can act as a defence where the damage was suffered partly as a result of the claimant's fault. Fault is defined by the Law Reform (Contributory Negligence) Act 1945 s 4.

- The defendant must prove that the claimant failed to take reasonable care for his own safety and this failure was a cause of his damage. It is not necessary for the claimant to owe the defendant a duty of care. The standard of care is the usual objective standard used in negligence with allowances made for children, people who act in a dilemma and workmen.

- The claimant's fault must be a legal and factual cause of the harm suffered.
- Where the defence is established, the court will reduce damages to the extent that is just and equitable under s 1(1) of the 1945 Act.
- *Ex turpi causa* enables the court to deny a duty of care to a person who suffered damage while participating in a criminal activity. (*Pitts v Hunt*.) There is some controversy as to the basis of the defence. Some judges base it on public conscience and some on joint illegal activity.
- Modern case law in *Gray v Thames Trains* (2009) divides the rule into a narrow version that you cannot recover for damage which is the consequence of a sentence imposed on you for a criminal act; and a wide version based on public notions of a fair distribution of resources.

Further reading

Davies, P. S. (2009), 'The Illegality Defence and Public Policy' LQR 125, 556–60 (*ex turpi – Gray*.)

Glofcheski, R. (1999), 'Plaintiff's Illegality as a Bar to Recovery of Personal Injury Damages' 19 LS 6.

Jaffey, A. J. E. (1985), '*Volenti Non Fit Injuria*' CLJ 87.

Law Commission (2001), *The Illegality Defence in Tort* (Consultation Paper No 160).

Law Commission (2009), *The Illegality Defence: A Consultative Report* (Consultation Paper No 189).

Law Commission (2010), *The Illegality Defence* (Law Com No 320).

Tan, K. (1995), '*Volenti Non Fit Injuria*: An Alternative Framework' 3 Tort L Rev 208.

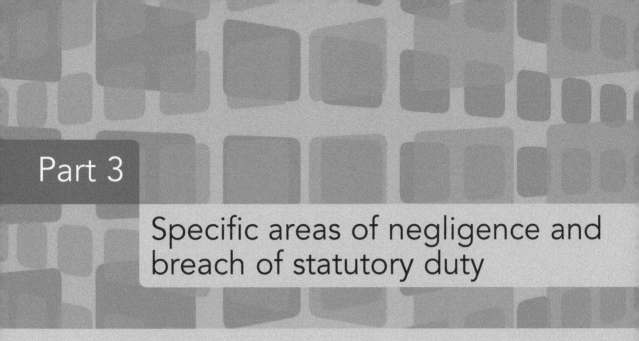

Part 3

Specific areas of negligence and breach of statutory duty

11

Defective premises

Objectives

After reading this chapter you will:

1. Understand the distinction between lawful visitors to land and trespassers, the legal rules which apply to lawful visitors to land and the provisions of the Occupiers' Liability Act 1957.
2. Appreciate the socio-economic factors relating to claims against the occupiers of land and have a critical knowledge of the law on child visitors.
3. Have a knowledge of the legal rules relating to trespassers to land.
4. Understand the provisions of the Occupiers' Liability Act 1984.
5. Have a knowledge of the statutory and common law rules applying to claims against landlords for defective premises.
6. Understand the statutory and common law rules which apply to builders of premises.

Introduction

A specialised area of negligence is provided by liability for defective premises. This chapter is divided into three parts. It considers, first, the liability of an occupier of the premises to a **visitor** or **trespasser** to the premises; secondly, the liability of a landlord for defects in the premises; and finally, the liability of a person involved in the construction process.

Occupiers' liability

Introduction

Objective
1

Liability in this area is governed by two statutes. Where the claimant was a visitor to the premises, the Occupiers' Liability Act 1957 applies. Where the claimant was a trespasser, the Occupiers' Liability Act 1984 will be applied. The fact that the law is statute-based means that attention must be paid to the wording of the relevant sections in answering questions.

A common factor in either action is the defendant, who will be the occupier of the premises. There is no statutory definition of occupier so it is necessary to turn to the common law. The term 'occupier' is rather misleading, as it is the person who controls the premises, rather than the physical occupier, who is responsible.

Wheat v E Lacon & Co Ltd [1966] AC 522

The defendants were the owners of a public house which was run by a manager and his wife, who had a licence to live on the first floor and to take in paying guests. The manager occupied the premises on the basis of being an employee rather than a tenant. A paying guest was killed when he tried to get to the bar on the first floor by an emergency staircase. The House of Lords considered who was the occupier. They held that it was both the manager and the owners. Lord Denning stated:

> ... wherever a person has a sufficient degree of control over premises that he ought to realise that any failure on his part to use care may result in injury to a person coming lawfully there, then he is an 'occupier' and the person coming lawfully there is his 'visitor'. . . .

Lord Denning identified four categories of occupier:

1. A landlord who lets premises. The landlord has parted with control of the premises so the tenant will be the occupier.
2. The landlord lets part of a building but retains other parts such as a common staircase. The landlord remains as occupier for the parts of the building he has retained.
3. Where a landowner licenses a person to use premises and the owner has a right to enter on the premises to do repairs, the owner retains control and is the occupier.
4. Where independent contractors are employed to do work on premises, the owner will generally retain sufficient control to be an occupier. It is possible that the contractors will also be occupiers. This will depend on the amount of control which they have while the work is in progress.

In the event, neither the manager nor the owners were held to be in breach of duty. There had been a bulb on the staircase but this had been removed by a stranger, for whose actions the defendants were not responsible.

The case established that there can be more than one occupier of the same premises, although the duty required of each might be different: for example, a seaside promenade might be under the control of a local authority and the water authority as part of the sea defences. If a person was injured by broken glass left there, the relevant occupier would be the local authority. If the injury was due to the state of repair of the structure, the water authority would be the relevant occupier.

An estate in land is not necessary in order to be an occupier and neither is physical possession. The key factor is whether a person exercised a sufficient degree of control.

Harris v Birkenhead Corporation [1976] 1 WLR 279

A local authority issued a compulsory purchase order on a house and a notice of entry which enabled them to take over the premises after 14 days. The house was not vacated for several months. When it was vacated no steps were taken by the local authority to have it boarded up. The claimant, a four-year-old child, entered the house through an unsecured door and fell from a second-floor window. The Court of Appeal held that actual physical possession was not necessary for there to be control. The fact that the local authority had the legal right to control the premises made them occupiers to the exclusion of the previous owners of the house. The local authority were in the best position to avoid accidents.

Once the relevant occupier or occupiers have been identified, the next stage is to ascertain the status of the claimant. If they are a lawful visitor, it is necessary to go to the 1957 Act. If the claimant was a trespasser, then the 1984 Act is appropriate.

Occupiers' liability to visitors

The scope of the Occupiers' Liability Act 1957

At this stage it is necessary to make three points about the scope of the Act.

1 A claimant may claim for personal injuries and damage to property. The scope of property includes property of persons who are not themselves visitors (s 1(3)(b)).

2 Before the Act, the courts had drawn a distinction between the occupancy duty and the activity duty. The former was concerned with dangers due to the state of the premises, the latter with dangers created by the occupier's activities on his premises, such as driving a vehicle. In cases of occupancy duty, the special rules on occupiers' liability applied. For activity duty, the ordinary rules of negligence applied.

For negligence, see Chapters 2–10.

It is not clear whether this distinction has survived the Act. Section 1(1) refers to dangers due to the state of the premises or things done or omitted to be done on them. This could be interpreted as meaning that the Act applies to the activity duty. However, s 1(2) refers to harm suffered, in consequence of a person's occupation or control of premises. This appears to include only the occupancy duty. There is no conclusive case on the point but in **Ogwo v Taylor** [1988] AC 431, Brown LJ (*obiter*) was of the opinion that where a fireman was injured fighting a fire at the defendant's premises, which was not due to a defect in the premises, the Act had no application.

The distinction is unlikely to make much difference as, once a duty has been found to exist, the standard of care will be the same: reasonable care in all the circumstances of the case.

See Chapter 9 for Fairchild.

It may, of course, make a difference in respect of whether a duty exists or not. In the case of **Fairchild v Glenhaven Funeral Services Ltd** [2002] 1 WLR 1052 the Court of Appeal held that the claimants' contact with asbestos dust at work was a result of an activity carried on on the premises rather than their static state. This meant that the claimants had to establish a duty of care at common law. This point is not affected by the subsequent House of Lords decision.

3 The Act applies not only to land and buildings but also to fixed and movable structures, including any vehicle or aircraft (s 1(3)(a)). The Act has been held to apply to a digging machine used to construct a tunnel. (**Bunker v Charles Brand & Son Ltd** [1969] 2 QB 480.)

Who is a visitor?

The duty of care under the 1957 Act is owed to visitors (s 1(2)). All lawful visitors to the premises are covered by this term. It includes invitees and licensees and those who have a contractual right to enter, where there is no express contractual duty of care (s 5(1)). Where a person enters under a contractual right, the common duty of care under the Act will be implied into the contract, unless the contract expressly provides for a higher standard of care. The court will not imply a higher duty of care into the contract. (**Maguire v Sefton Metropolitan Borough Council** [2006] 1 WLR 2550.)

A person who enters under a right conferred by law is treated as a visitor, whether or not they have the occupier's express permission to enter (s 2(6)). Police officers, firefighters and employees of public utility companies may come into such a category provided they do not exceed their power of entry.

Four problem areas arise with visitors, as follows.

1 Rights of way

Persons who lawfully exercise a private right of way are not treated as visitors and are therefore not covered by the 1957 Act. (*Holden* v *White* **[1982]** 2 WLR 1030.) Such people are now covered by the Occupiers' Liability Act 1984 s 1(1)(a) and will be owed a duty of care under that Act.

Persons exercising a public right of way are not treated as visitors. (*Greenhalgh* v *British Railways Board* [1969] 2 QB 286.) Neither are they covered by the 1984 Act, as s 1(7) of that Act specifically excludes them. Any duty owed to such a person would therefore have to be at common law. The owner of land over which a public right of way passes is under no liability for negligent nonfeasance towards members of the public using it. (*McGeown* v *NI Housing Executive* [1994] 3 All ER 53.)

2 Implied permission

A person who claims that they had implied permission to enter premises must prove that there was such permission.

There is implied permission for a person to enter premises and state their business to the occupier. If the occupier then asks them to leave, they must be allowed a reasonable time to leave, after which they will become trespassers. Reasonable force may then be used to eject them. This presumption can be rebutted by the occupier putting up a notice specifically excluding certain types of person, such as salesmen and politicians.

When the occupier's duty to a trespasser was a limited one of not intentionally or recklessly injuring the trespasser, the concept of implied permission was an important one. The success or failure of the action would depend on whether the claimant was classed as a trespasser or not. In deserving cases the courts would sometimes find implied permission.

Lowery v *Walker* [1911] AC 10

People regularly used the defendant's unfenced land to take a short cut. The defendant had taken no serious steps to prevent them as most were his customers. The defendant then allowed a wild horse on his land, which attacked the claimant. The claimant was held to have implied permission and therefore was not a trespasser.

The court's willingness to find an implied licence or permission was particularly strong in the case of children, especially where there was something attractive to children on the land.

The passing of the Occupiers' Liability Act 1984 means that there should now be an insignificant number of cases where the court is asked to find implied permission. There is little difference, for example, between the position of a child trespasser whom the occupier knows to be present and a child visitor.

3 Limitations on permission

The occupier may place limitations on the permission to enter. A person who is allowed to enter one part of a building only will become a trespasser if they enter another part: 'When you invite a person into your house to use the stairs you do not invite him to slide down the banisters.' (*The Calgarth* [1927] P 93 per Scrutton LJ.) However, any usage incidental to that permitted will be covered. A person entering a public house will be allowed to enter the toilet.

If a person is given permission to enter a building at a particular time, then entry at another time may render them a trespasser. This is a question of interpretation. A visitor to a public house who is asked to stay on for a private party by the landlord will remain a visitor.

Finally, a person who is given permission to enter for a particular purpose will be a trespasser if they enter for a different purpose. The decorator who is given the keys for the purpose of working will be a trespasser if they let themselves in during the middle of the night to watch a video.

4 It is possible for a person to be a visitor in relation to one occupier and a trespasser to another

Ferguson v Welsh [1987] 3 All ER 777

The council owned land and employed demolition contractors to do work there. The contractors sub-contracted the work to another firm. An employee of the sub-contractors was injured during the demolition work. The cause of the accident was held to be the unsafe system of work used by the claimant's employers rather than use of the premises. As the sub-contracting was unauthorised, the claimant could have been a trespasser to the council.

Lord Keith of Kinkel:

It would not ordinarily be reasonable to expect an occupier of premises having engaged a contractor whom he has reasonable grounds for regarding as competent, to supervise the contractor's activities in order to ensure that he was discharging his duty to his employees to observe a safe system of work. In special circumstances, on the other hand, where the occupier knows or has reason to suspect that the contractor is using an unsafe system of work, it might well be reasonable for the occupier to take steps to see that the system was made safe.

The crux of the present case therefore, is whether the council knew or had reason to suspect that Mr Spence, in contravention of the terms of his contract, was bringing in cowboy operators who would proceed to demolish the building in a thoroughly unsafe way. The thrust of the affidavit evidence admitted by the Court of Appeal was that Mr Spence had long been in the habit of sub-contracting his demolition work to persons who proceeded to execute it by the unsafe method of working from the bottom up. If the evidence went the length of indicating that the council knew or ought to have known that this was Mr Spence's usual practice, there would be much to be said for the view that they should be liable to Mr Ferguson. No responsible council should countenance the unsafe working methods of cowboy operators. It should be clearly foreseeable that such methods exposed the employees of such operators to very serious dangers. It is entirely reasonable that a council occupying premises where demolition work is to be executed should take steps to see that the work is carried out by reputable and careful contractors. Here, however, the council did contract with Mr Spence subject to the condition that sub-contracting without their consent was prohibited. The fresh evidence sought to be adduced by Mr Ferguson does not go the length of supporting any inference that the council or their responsible officers knew or ought to have known that Mr Spence was likely to contravene this prohibition.

What is the duty?

Objective 2

The occupier of the premises owes a common duty of care to all lawful visitors to the premises. The duty is in s 2(2) of the Act:

The common duty of care is a duty to take such care as in all the circumstances of the case is reasonable to see that the visitor will be reasonably safe in using the premises for the purposes for which he is invited or permitted to be there.

Whether the duty has been broken is a question of fact in each case. The factors which are applicable to the standard of care in common law negligence are applicable. However, the section makes two things clear.

For breach of duty in negligence see Chapter 8.

It is the visitor and not the premises that have to be reasonably safe. The circumstances of the particular visitor have to be taken into account.

The duty extends only to the purpose for which the visitor was allowed entry.

Tomlinson v *Congleton Borough Council* [2003] 3 All ER 1122

The defendants owned, occupied and managed a public park. In the park was a lake formed from a disused sand extraction pit. The lake had sandy beaches and was a popular recreational venue where yachting, sub-aqua diving and other regulated activities were permitted, but swimming was not. Notices reading 'Dangerous water: no swimming' were posted but they had little or no effect. The unauthorised use of the lake and the increasing possibility of an accident was of concern to the defendants. A plan to landscape the shores and plant over the beaches from which people swam had been approved, but work had begun only shortly before 6 May 1995. On that date the claimant went to the lake. He ran into the water and dived, striking his head on the sandy bottom with sufficient force to cause him an injury which resulted in paralysis from the neck downward. He brought proceedings for damages claiming that the defendants, as occupiers, owed him the common duty of care set out in s 2(2) of the Occupiers' Liability Act 1957, which was a duty to take such care as in all the circumstances was reasonable to see that a visitor would be reasonably safe in using the premises for the purposes for which he was permitted to be there. At trial it was conceded that he had seen and ignored the warning signs so that when he entered the water he had ceased to be at the park for purposes for which he had been invited and permitted by the defendants to be there, and had accordingly ceased to be a visitor and had become a trespasser. As such he was owed a lesser duty of care under the Occupiers' Liability Act 1984.

Lord Hoffmann:

My Lords, it will in the circumstances be convenient to consider first the question of what the position would have been if Mr Tomlinson had been a lawful visitor owed a duty under s 2(2) of the 1957 Act. Assume, therefore, that there had been no prohibition on swimming. What was the risk of serious injury? To some extent this depends upon what one regards as the relevant risk. As I have mentioned, the judge thought it was the risk of injury through diving while the Court of Appeal thought it was any kind of injury which could happen to people in the water. Although, as I have said, I am inclined to agree with the judge, I do not want to put the basis of my decision too narrowly. So I accept that we are concerned with the steps, if any, which should have been taken to prevent any kind of water accident. According to the Royal Society for the Prevention of Accidents, about 450 people drown while swimming in the United Kingdom every year (see *Darby* v *National Trust* [2001] PIQR P372 at 374). About 25–35 break their necks diving and no doubt others sustain less serious injuries. So there is obviously some degree of risk in swimming and diving, as there is in climbing, cycling, fell walking and many other such activities.

I turn then to the cost of taking preventative measures. Ward LJ described it [£5,000] as 'not excessive'. Perhaps it was not, although the outlay has to be seen in the context of the other items (rated 'essential' and 'highly desirable') in the borough council budget which had taken precedence over the destruction of the beaches for the previous two years.

I do not, however, regard the financial cost as a significant item in the balancing exercise which the court has to undertake. There are two other related considerations which are far more important. The first is the social value of the activities which would have to be prohibited in order to reduce or eliminate the risk from swimming. And the second is the question of whether the council should be entitled to allow people of full capacity to decide for themselves whether to take the risk.

The Court of Appeal made no reference at all to the social value of the activities which were to be prohibited. The majority of people who went to the beaches to sunbathe, paddle and play with their children were enjoying themselves in a way which gave them pleasure and caused no risk to themselves or anyone else. This must be something to be taken into account in deciding whether it was reasonable to expect the council to destroy the beaches.

I have the impression that the Court of Appeal felt able to brush these matters aside because the council had already decided to do the work. But they were held liable for having failed to do so before Mr Tomlinson's accident and the question is therefore whether they were under a legal duty to do so. Ward LJ placed much emphasis upon the fact that the council had decided to destroy the beaches and that its officers thought that this was necessary to avoid being held liable for an accident to a swimmer. But the fact that the council's safety officers thought that the work was necessary does not show that there was a legal duty to do it.

See also Chapter 8 for *Tomlinson*.

Although ***Tomlinson*** was decided on the basis that the claimant was a trespasser, the case is indicative of a trend in a series of cases involving leisure pursuits on land frequently owned by local authorities. The cases are a good illustration of two principles which frequently conflict in tort cases, those of autonomy and paternalism. The council had decided to destroy the beaches as they had been advised that there was a risk of legal action against them should an accident occur. The House of Lords has sent out a clear message that such actions are not necessary and that adults who are given suitable warning should take responsibility for their own safety.

This principle has also been applied in a holiday contract case. (***Evans*** v ***Kosmar Villa Holidays plc*** [2008] 1 All ER 530.) A holidaymaker suffered personal injuries when he dived into the shallow end of a pool in a holiday complex. The Court of Appeal held that, although the extent of the duty owed by occupiers of land to trespassers and even to lawful visitors might be affected by policy considerations, that had no parallel in the context of a holiday contract; there was no reason not to apply the core of the reasoning in the leading authority on occupiers' liability, namely that people should accept responsibility for the risks they chose to run; and that there should be no duty to protect them against obvious risks.

The Act gives specific guidance on certain points in relation to the duty of care.

1 Children

Section 2(3)(a) states: 'An occupier must be prepared for children to be less careful than adults. If the occupier allows a child to enter the premises then the premises must be reasonably safe for a child of that age.'

Glasgow Corp v *Taylor* [1922] 1 AC 44

The claimant, aged seven, died after eating poisonous berries from a tree in a public park. The tree was not fenced and no warning was given. The defendants were held liable. The danger was not obvious to a child of that age.

Lord Atkinson:

The liability of defendants in cases of this kind rests, I think, in the last resort upon their knowledge that by their action they may bring children of tender years, unable to take care of themselves, yet inquisitive

> and easily tempted, into contact, in a place in which they, the children, have a right to be, with things alluring or tempting to them, and possibly in appearance harmless, but which, unknown to them and well known to the defendants, are hurtful or dangerous if meddled with. . . . I think, in the latter case, as in the former, the defendant would be bound, by notice or warning or some other adequate means, to protect the children from injury. In this case the averments are that the appellants did nothing of the kind. If that be true, they were, in my view, guilty of negligence, giving the pursuer a right of action.

Very young children present a problem in that there may be a question as to whether their parents should have exercised supervision over them. In such cases it may come down to allocating liability between the parents and the occupier.

Phipps v *Rochester Corp* [1955] 1 QB 450

The five-year-old claimant was injured while out with his seven-year-old sister. He fell into a trench on land which was used by children as a play area. The defendants were aware of this but took no steps to keep the children out. The defendants were held not liable on the facts. The court stated that reasonable parents will not send their children into danger without protection and that both the parents and the occupier must act reasonably.

Devlin J:

> . . . the responsibility for the safety of little children must rest primarily upon the parents; it is their duty to see that such children are not allowed to wander about by themselves, or at least to satisfy them-selves that the places to which they do allow their children to go unaccompanied are safe for them to go to. It would not be socially desirable if parents were, as a matter of course, able to shift the burden of looking after their children from their own shoulders to those of persons who happen to have acces-sible bits of land. Different considerations may well apply to public parks or to recognized playing grounds where parents allow their children to go unaccompanied in the reasonable belief that they are safe.

There had been a tendency, in cases involving children, that once a duty and breach were established and ensuing damage shown, that liability was established. Questions of remoteness were dealt with under *Hughes* **v** *Lord Advocate* [1963] AC 837 and the question of foreseeable risk to a child widely interpreted. This appeared to have been stemmed by the Court of Appeal in the following case, but orthodoxy was restored by the House of Lords.

See Chapter 9 for *Hughes* v *Lord Advocate* and *Jolley*.

Jolley v *Sutton London Borough Council* [1998] 3 All ER 559 (CA); [2000] 3 All ER 409 (HL)

The council owned a piece of amenity land near a block of flats on which a boat had been left lying for at least two years. The claimant, a 14-year-old, and a friend decided to repair it. They jacked up the boat, which fell and caused severe spinal injuries to the claimant, who sued under the Occupiers' Liability Act 1957. At first instance the judge held that the boat was an attraction to children of the claimant's age and that it was reasonably foreseeable that it would be meddled with and that there was a foreseeable risk of physical injury.

The Court of Appeal held that the defendant was not liable for breach of a duty of care if the accident which caused the claimant's injuries was of a different type and kind from anything he could have foreseen. Although the boat was both an allurement and a trap and the council had been negligent in failing to remove it, the attractiveness of the boat and its dangerous condition had not been established to be part of the causes of the accident. The immediate cause of the accident had been the two boys jacking it up. This was an activity very different from normal play.

However, the House of Lords upheld the view of the trial judge that the foreseeable risk was that children would meddle with the boat with a risk of foreseeable physical injury. Defining the foreseeable risk in broad terms meant that the damage was not too remote.

2 Persons entering in the exercise of a calling

Section 2(3)(b) states: 'An occupier may expect that a person, in the exercise of his calling, will appreciate and guard against any special risks ordinarily incident to it, so far as the occupier leaves him free to do so.'

Roles v *Nathan* [1963] 1 WLR 1117

Two chimney sweeps were killed by carbon monoxide gas while attempting to seal a sweep hole in the chimney of a boiler. The defendant occupiers were held not liable, as they could assume that sweeps would be aware of this particular danger and also because the sweeps had been warned of the danger. Lord Denning stated that the position would have been different if the stairs leading to the basement had given way. That would not have been a risk incidental to the trade of chimney sweep.

General Cleaning Contractors v *Christmas* [1953] AC 180

See Chapter 14 for *General Cleaning Contractors*.

The occupier was held not liable to a window cleaner who was injured when a defective window closed suddenly, causing him to fall. Defective windows were a risk which window cleaners should guard against.

The claimant did recover against his employer for using an unsafe system of work.

The fact that the visitor has a specific skill is not in itself sufficient to absolve the occupier where they have not exercised the requisite degree of care. Firemen who exercise reasonable care in attempting to extinguish a negligently started fire will be able to recover against the occupier if they are injured in the process of extinguishing the fire. (*Salmon* v *Seafarers Restaurant* [1983] 1 WLR 1264; *Ogwo* v *Taylor* [1988] AC 431.)

3 Independent contractors

Section 2(4)(b) states:

> Where damage is caused to a visitor by a danger due to the faulty execution of any work of construction, maintenance or repair by an independent contractor employed by the occupier, the occupier is not to be treated without more as answerable for the danger if in all the circumstances he had acted reasonably in entrusting the work to an independent contractor and had taken such steps (if any) as he reasonably ought in order to satisfy himself that the contractor was competent and that the work had been properly done.

A number of points need to be made about this section, which was passed to reverse a common law rule, which placed an occupier under a non-delegable duty to certain types of entrant. This duty could not be discharged by entrusting the work to an independent contractor.

1 The facts of the case must come within the section, which only applies to the 'faulty execution of…construction, maintenance or repair…' Where a case falls outside the section the common law rule will apply.

2 It must be reasonable for the occupier to entrust the work to an independent contractor. The more technical the work is, the more likely it will be reasonable to do so. The occupier must also be looked at. If the occupier is a layman with no technical skill then most jobs will be reasonably entrusted to contractors. The situation might be different with occupiers such as local authorities.

3 The occupier must take reasonable steps to check that the contractor was competent to carry out the work. A lay person would appear to be able to do little in this direction, except perhaps check with local trade associations. Large corporate bodies and local authorities may have to take more exhaustive steps.

4 The occupier must take reasonable steps to check that the work has been properly done. With technical work, the appointment of a competent contractor may be sufficient to discharge the duty.

5 It would appear that the occupier is also under a duty to check that the independent contractor is adequately insured to cover any risks. An inquiry coupled with an assurance from the contractor would appear to be enough to satisfy this requirement. (***Gwilliam* v *West Hertfordshire Hospital NHS Trust*** [2002] 3 WLR 1425.)

Haseldine v *Daw* [1941] 2 KB 343

The claimant was killed when a lift fell to the bottom of its shaft. The occupiers had appointed a normally competent firm of engineers to maintain the lift. In doing so they had discharged their duty of care. The technical nature of the work meant that they could not be expected to check it had been satisfactorily done.

Woodward v *Mayor of Hastings* [1945] KB 174

The claimant child slipped on a snow-covered step at a school. The step had been negligently cleaned by a cleaner. There was some doubt as to whether the cleaner was an independent contractor, but the occupiers were held liable as they had failed to take reasonable steps to check that the work had been reasonably done: 'The craft of the charwoman may have its mysteries but there is no esoteric quality in the nature of the work which the cleaning of a snow covered step demands.'

If the section bars the claimant from suing the occupier, they may still be able to proceed against the contractor, either as an occupier or under the common law negligence rules.

4 Warnings

Section 2(4)(a) states:

> Where damage is caused to a visitor by a danger of which he has been warned by the occupier, the warning is not to be treated without more as absolving the occupier from liability, unless in all the circumstances it was enough to enable the visitor to be reasonably safe.

The legal effect of a sufficient warning under this section is to discharge any duty of care which might have been owed by the occupier.

The mere fact that a warning has been given will not be sufficient to absolve the occupier. The warning must enable the visitor to take reasonable care for their own safety.

An example was given by Lord Denning in **Roles v Nathan**. Where a house has a river in front of it and a bridge across the river with a sign saying the bridge is dangerous, this is not an adequate warning, as any visitor has no choice as to whether to use the bridge. If there were two bridges and one of them said 'Danger, use other bridge', then a person injured using the dangerous bridge would have no claim.

If the danger is obvious, then no warning need be given. There is no need to warn an adult that it is dangerous to go near the edge of a cliff. (**Cotton v Derbyshire Dales District Council** (1994) *Times*, 20 June.)

Where the danger is not obvious, then the warning must indicate its nature in sufficient detail for the visitor to take reasonable care for their own safety. A simple notice saying 'Danger' will not discharge the duty. However, in **Tomlinson v Congleton Borough Council** [2003] 3 All ER 1122 (see below), the placing of signs on a beach stating 'Dangerous water: no swimming', which had been seen and ignored by the claimant, was sufficient to turn the claimant from a visitor into a trespasser.

Defences

1 Volenti

See Chapter 10 for *volenti*.

A defence of *volenti non fit injuria* is provided by s 2(5). 'The common duty of care does not impose upon an occupier any obligation willingly accepted as his by the visitor.'

This defence is covered by the general principles of *volenti*. The claimant must act voluntarily, so any person who has no choice as to whether they enter premises is not *volenti*.

Knowledge of the danger does not amount to the defence.

2 Contributory negligence

See Chapter 10 for contributory negligence.

This defence will apply in actions under the Act; a visitor who has failed to use reasonable care for their own safety, and that failure was a cause of their damage, will have their damages reduced. Section 2(3) provides that, in considering the common duty of care, the circumstances include the degree of care and want of care which would ordinarily be looked for in such a visitor.

3 Exclusion

Section 2(1) states:

> An occupier of premises owes the same duty, the 'common duty of care', to all his visitors, except in so far as he is free to and does extend, restrict, modify or exclude his duty to any visitor or visitors by agreement or otherwise.

The reference to agreement or otherwise means that the duty can be excluded, etc. by means of a contract term or by a notice communicated to the visitor.

There are certain restrictions on the occupier's freedom to exclude, etc.

1 The Unfair Contract Terms Act 1977. The Act will apply where the premises are being used for business purposes as defined in s 1(3). It is the purpose that the premises are being used for, rather than the purpose of the visitor, that is important. Business will include professions, government and local authority activities. It does not include the granting of access for recreational or educational purposes, unless the granting of such access falls within the business purposes of the occupier. (Occupiers' Liability Act 1984 s 2.)

The occupier cannot exclude liability for death or personal injuries caused by negligence (s 2(1)). Any attempt to exclude liability for property damage will be subjected to a test of reasonableness (s 2(2)).

The fact that a person was aware of an exclusionary term or notice does not in itself mean that he has voluntarily accepted the risk (s 2(3)).

Example

Alan is a sales representative for a company. As part of his job he is required to visit building sites. He enters a site occupied by Bob. There is a notice on the gate which says: 'Danger, building sites are dangerous places. The occupier accepts no liability for injuries suffered by visitors or for damage to their property.' While on the site, a wall collapses on Alan, causing him injuries and damaging his car.

This notice could take effect in three ways. First, as a warning discharging the duty of care. As it fails to enable Alan to take reasonable care for his own safety, it will not have this effect.

Secondly, to exclude the common duty of care. As Bob is using the premises for business purposes, the Unfair Contract Terms Act 1977 will apply. Section 2(1) means that the notice will fail to exclude Bob's liability for Alan's personal injuries. As regards Bob's liability for the damage to Alan's car, the exclusionary notice would be subjected to a reasonableness test.

Finally, if Bob claims that Alan was *volenti* to the risk. The Unfair Contract Terms Act 1977 s 2(3) will prevent any claim that Alan's awareness of the attempted exclusion rendered him *volens* to the risk. As Alan had to enter the site as part of his job, he lacked the necessary degree of voluntariness necessary for the defence.

2 It may not be possible for the occupier to exclude liability to a person who enters under a right conferred by law.

3 If it is correct that the duty owed to trespassers is a minimum standard which cannot be excluded, then this minimum standard cannot be excluded against visitors. (See 'Liability to trespassers' below.)

4 Section 3(1) provides that where an occupier is bound by contract to permit strangers to the contract to enter or use the premises, the duty of care owed to the stranger as a visitor cannot be restricted or excluded by the contract. A landlord who retains control over common parts of a building such as the stairs, and puts an exclusion clause in the lease, cannot exclude liability to the tenant's visitors by virtue of this clause.

Liability to trespassers

Introduction

Objective
3

A trespasser is a person who goes on to land without an invitation of any sort and whose presence there either is unknown to the occupier, or, if known, is objected to.

The common law was traditionally hostile to trespassers. The original duty owed was the basic one of not intentionally or recklessly injuring a trespasser known to be present. (*Addie v Dumbreck Collieries* [1929] AC 358.) This remained the law until 1972. The judiciary were forced to resort to legal fictions such as implied licences and allurements to turn trespassers into visitors in deserving cases, mainly involving children.

In *British Railways Board v Herrington* [1972] AC 877, the House of Lords introduced a new duty. The occupier owed a duty of common humanity to a trespasser known to be present. The duty was a subjective one as, in considering whether it had been broken, the court had to take account of the resources of the occupier.

The ***Herrington*** decision was subjected to a certain amount of criticism and was referred to the Law Commission, whose report (Law Commission Report No 75, Cmnd 6428) formed the basis of the Occupiers' Liability Act 1984.

The law on trespassers presents certain difficulties. To what extent should the occupier be aware of the presence of the trespasser? How can a distinction be made between trespassers of differing degrees of culpability, such as burglars and stray children? What standard of care should be owed and which defences should be applied? The Act attempts to answer these problems.

Scope of the Occupiers' Liability Act 1984

Objective 4

The Act will apply to persons other than visitors (s 1(1)(a)). This covers trespassers; persons entering land under an access agreement or order under the National Parks and Access to the Countryside Act 1949; persons lawfully exercising a private right of way. The rest of this section will concentrate on the occupier's liability to trespassers.

The Act will apply in respect of any risk of their suffering injury on the premises by reason of any danger due to the state of the premises or to things done or omitted to be done on them (s 1(1)(a)).

Keown v Coventry Healthcare NHS Trust [2006] 1 WLR 953

A property owned and occupied by the defendants was used as student accommodation and a day clinic. The grounds were used by the public as a means of going between the streets on either side and as a place where children liked to play. A fire escape with cross-bars on its outside was climbable and thus an attraction to adventurous children. The claimant, who was 11 years old, fell from a height of about 30 feet, fracturing his arm and suffering a significant brain injury which led to loss of intellectual functioning and a personality change which allegedly caused him to be subsequently convicted of various sexual offences. The parties accepted that he must be treated as a trespasser while climbing the fire escape. This was apparently on the basis that children playing in the grounds were not lawful visitors but it could also have been because this case must be the closest one will come to in real life to the example of a trespasser given by Scrutton LJ in ***The Carlgarth*** [1927] P 93 at 110: 'When you invite a person into your house to use the staircase, you do not invite him to slide down the banisters, you invite him to use the staircase in the ordinary way in which it is used.' Had the claimant been an adult, the decision would have been straightforward. Any danger was due to the claimant's activity on the premises and was not due to the state of the premises. If an adult chose to create danger by climbing them, any such danger was due to such person's activity not the state of the premises. Did it make any difference that the claimant was a child?

Held (Court of Appeal): The answer was that premises which are not dangerous from the point of view of an adult can be dangerous for a child, but it must be a question of fact and degree. It would not be right to ignore a child's choice to indulge in a dangerous activity in every case merely because he was a child. The claimant was 11 at the time he decided to climb the fire escape; the judge's finding was that he appreciated not only that there was a risk of falling but also that what he was doing was dangerous and that he should not have been climbing the exterior of the fire escape. In these circumstances it could not be said that Mr Keown did not recognise the danger and it was not seriously arguable that the risk arose out of the state of the premises, rather it arose out of what the claimant chose to do. There was no suggestion that the fire escape was fragile or had anything wrong with it as a fire escape and it could not be said that the claimant had suffered his injury by reason of any danger due to the state of the premises and had therefore not passed the threshold requirement contained in s 1(1)(a) of the 1984 Act.

When is a duty owed?

Once the relationship of occupier and visitor is established, the occupier owes the common duty of care to the visitor. Once the relationship of occupier and trespasser is established, there is not automatically a duty. It is necessary to apply s 1(3), which states:

> An occupier of premises owes a duty to another (not being his visitor) in respect of any such risk as is referred to in subsection (1) if –
>
> (a) he is aware of the danger or has reasonable grounds to believe it exists;
> (b) he knows or has reasonable grounds to believe that the other is in the vicinity of the danger concerned or that he may come into the vicinity of the danger (in either case whether the other has lawful authority for being in that vicinity or not); and
> (c) the risk is one against which, in all the circumstances of the case, he may reasonably be expected to offer the other some protection.

This section poses some problems: (c) is objective but (a) and (b) may be subjective. If the test is objective, then it is based on the beliefs of the reasonable occupier. If it is subjective, then it is based on the beliefs of the defendant.

Section 1(3)(a) requires actual knowledge of the actual risk or of the primary facts from which an inference could be drawn. Such knowledge includes 'shut-eye' knowledge, but not constructive knowledge. The distinction is that with the former the occupier deliberately shuts their eyes to the relevant facts, and with the latter they negligently do so. (*Swain v Natui Ram Puri* [1996] PIQR 442.)

The fact that the occupier took precautions to prevent people getting on to the land does not mean they had reason to believe that someone was likely to come into the vicinity of the danger for the purposes of s 1(3)(b).

A likely interpretation is that knowledge of the primary facts is subjective. Once it is established what the defendant knew, then the inference to be drawn from these primary facts is objective. Would a reasonable occupier have drawn the inference that there was a danger and that the presence of the trespasser was likely? This would mean that there is no duty on the occupier to inspect their premises for dangers or trespassers.

Tomlinson v Congleton Borough Council [2003] 3 All ER 1122

See also Chapter 8 for *Tomlinson*.

Lord Hoffmann:

> ... in my opinion, there was no risk to Mr Tomlinson due to the state of the premises or anything done or omitted upon the premises. That means that there was no risk of a kind which gave rise to a duty under the 1957 or 1984 Acts. I shall nevertheless go on to consider the matter on the assumption that there was.
>
> THE CONDITIONS FOR THE EXISTENCE OF A DUTY
> (i) Knowledge or foresight of the danger
> Section 1(3) of the 1984 Act has three conditions which must be satisfied. First, under para (a), the occupier must be aware of the danger or have reasonable grounds to believe that it exists. For this purpose, it is necessary to say what the relevant danger was. The judge thought it was the risk of suffering an injury through diving and said that the council was aware of this danger because two men had suffered minor head injuries from diving in May 1992. In the Court of Appeal, Ward LJ described the relevant risk much more broadly. He regarded all the swimming incidents as indicative of the council's knowledge that a danger existed. I am inclined to think that this is too wide a description. The risk of injury from diving off the beach was in my opinion different from the risk of drowning in the deep water. For example, the council might have fenced off the deep water or marked it with buoys and left people to paddle in

the shallows. That would have reduced the risk of drowning but would not have prevented the injury to Mr Tomlinson. We know very little about the circumstances in which two men suffered minor cuts to their heads in 1992 and I am not sure that they really provide much support for an inference that there was knowledge, or reasonable grounds to believe, that the beach posed a risk of serious diving injury.

(ii) Knowledge or foresight of the presence of the trespasser

Once it is found that the risk of a swimmer injuring himself by diving was something of which the council knew or which they had reasonable grounds to believe to exist, para (b) presents no difficulty. The council plainly knew that swimmers came to the lake and Mr Tomlinson fell within that class.

(iii) Reasonable to expect protection

That leaves para (c). Was the risk one against which the council might reasonably be expected to offer Mr Tomlinson some protection? The judge found that 'the danger and risk of injury from diving in the lake where it was shallow were obvious'. In such a case the judge held, both as a matter of common sense and following consistent authority (**Staples v West Dorset District Council** (1995) 93 LGR 536, **Ratcliff v McConnell** [1999] 1 WLR 670, **Darby v National Trust** [2001] PIQR P372), that there was no duty to warn against the danger. A warning would not tell a swimmer anything he did not already know. Nor was it necessary to do anything else. 'I do not think', said the judge, 'that the defendants' legal duty to the claimant in the circumstances required them to take the extreme measures which were completed after the accident'. Even if Mr Tomlinson had been owed a duty under the 1957 Act as a lawful visitor, the council would not have been obliged to do more than they did.

The Court of Appeal disagreed. Ward LJ said that the council was obliged to do something more. The gravity of the risk, the number of people who regularly incurred it and the attractive-ness of the beach created a duty. The prohibition on swimming was obviously ineffectual and therefore it was necessary to take additional steps to prevent or discourage people from getting into the water. Sedley LJ said ([2003] 3 All ER 1122 at [45]): '. . . it is only where the risk is so obvious that the occupier can safely assume that nobody will take it that there will be no liability.'

The House of Lords held that the risk of the claimant suffering injury had not arisen within the scope of s 1(1)(a) but had arisen from the claimant's own actions in diving into the water. The risk was therefore not one that the defendants had any duty to offer him protection against.

The content of the duty

Section 1(4) states that the duty is 'to take such care as is reasonable in all the circumstances of the case to see that he does not suffer injury on the premises by reason of the danger concerned'.

This is the usual objective negligence standard. Unfortunately, the division of the test into whether a duty exists and whether it has been broken means that the court will have to consider similar factors for both. The factors will be the age of the entrant, the nature of the premises, the extent of the risk and the practicability of precautions. As the test is an objective one, factors which are personal to the occupier, such as skill and resources, are not considered and do not come within the expression 'all the circumstances'.

Tomlinson v *Congleton Borough Council* [2003] 3 All ER 1122

See Chapter 8 for *Tomlinson*.

Lord Hoffmann:

THE BALANCE OF RISK, GRAVITY OF INJURY, COST AND SOCIAL VALUE

My Lords, the majority of the Court of Appeal appear to have proceeded on the basis that if there was a foreseeable risk of serious injury, the council was under a duty to do what was necessary to prevent it. But this in my opinion is an oversimplification. Even in the case of the duty owed to a lawful visitor under s 2(2) of the 1957 Act and even if the risk had been attributable to the state of the premises was rather than the acts of Mr Tomlinson, the question of what amounts to 'such care as in all the circumstances of the case is reasonable' depends upon assessing, as in the case of common law negligence, not only the likelihood that someone may be injured and the seriousness of the injury which may occur, but also the social value of the activity which gives rise to the risk and the cost of preventative measures. These factors have to be balanced against each other.

... in *Jolley* v *Sutton London BC* [2000] 3 All ER 409, [2000] 1 WLR 1082 there was no social value or cost saving to the council in creating a risk by leaving a derelict boat lying about. It was something which they ought to have removed whether it created a risk of injury or not. So they were held liable for an injury which, though foreseeable, was not particularly likely. On the other hand, in *The Wagon Mound (No 2)* [1966] 2 All ER 709 at 718, [1967] 1 AC 617 at 642 Lord Reid drew a contrast with *Bolton* v *Stone* [1951] 1 All ER 1078, [1951] AC 850 in which the House of Lords held that it was not negligent for a cricket club to do nothing about the risk of someone being injured by a cricket ball hit out of the ground. The difference was that the cricket club were carrying on a lawful and socially useful activity and would have had to stop playing cricket at that ground.

This is the kind of balance which has to be struck even in a situation in which it is clearly fair, just and reasonable that there should in principle be a duty of care or in which Parliament, as in the 1957 Act, has decreed that there should be. And it may lead to the conclusion that even though injury is foreseeable, as it was in *Bolton* v *Stone*, it is still in all the circumstances reasonable to do nothing about it.

THE 1957 AND 1984 ACTS CONTRASTED

In the case of the 1984 Act, there is the additional consideration that unless in all the circumstances it is reasonable to expect the occupier to do something, that is to say, to 'offer the other some protection', there is no duty at all. One may ask what difference there is between the case in which the claimant is a lawful visitor and there is in principle a duty under the 1957 Act but on the particular facts no duty to do anything, and the case in which he is a trespasser and there is on the particular facts no duty under the 1984 Act. Of course in such a case the result is the same. But Parliament has made it clear that in the case of a lawful visitor, one starts from the assumption that there is a duty whereas in the case of a trespasser one starts from the assumption that there is none.

FREE WILL

The second consideration, namely the question of whether people should accept responsibility for the risks they choose to run, is the point made by Lord Phillips MR in *Donoghue* v *Folkestone Properties Ltd* [2003] 3 All ER 1101 at [53] and which I said was central to this appeal. Mr Tomlinson was freely and voluntarily undertaking an activity which inherently involved some risk. By contrast, Miss Bessie Stone, to whom the House of Lords held that no duty was owed, was innocently standing on the pavement outside her garden gate at 10 Beckenham Road, Cheetham when she was struck by a ball hit for six out of the Cheetham Cricket Club ground. She was certainly not engaging in any activity which involved an inherent risk of such injury. So compared with *Bolton* v *Stone*, this is an a fortiori case.

I think it will be extremely rare for an occupier of land to be under a duty to prevent people from taking risks which are inherent in the activities they freely choose to undertake upon the land. If people want to climb mountains, go hang gliding or swim or dive in ponds or lakes, that is their affair. Of course the landowner may for his own reasons wish to prohibit such activities. He may think that they are a danger or inconvenience to himself or others. Or he may take a paternalist view and prefer people not to undertake risky activities on his land. He is entitled to impose such conditions, as the council did by prohibiting swimming. But the law does not require him to do so.

My Lords, as will be clear from what I have just said, I think that there is an important question of freedom at stake. It is unjust that the harmless recreation of responsible parents and children with buckets and spades on the beaches should be prohibited in order to comply with what is thought to be a legal duty to safeguard irresponsible visitors against dangers which are perfectly obvious. The fact that such people take no notice of warnings cannot create a duty to take other steps to protect them. I find it difficult to express with appropriate moderation my disagreement with the proposition of Sedley LJ ([2003] 3 All ER 1122 at [45]) that it is 'only where the risk is so obvious that the occupier can safely assume that nobody will take it that there will be no liability'. A duty to protect against obvious risks or self-inflicted harm exists only in cases in which there is no genuine and informed choice, or in the case of employees, or some lack of capacity, such as the inability of children to recognise danger (see *British Railways Board* v *Herrington* [1972] 1 All ER 749, [1972] AC 877) or the despair of prisoners which may lead them to inflict injury on themselves (see *Reeves* v *Metropolitan Police Comr* [1999] 3 All ER 897, [2000] 1 AC 360).

. . . But the balance between risk on the one hand and individual autonomy on the other is not a matter of expert opinion. It is a judgment which the courts must make and which in England reflects the individualist values of the common law. As for the council officers, they were obviously motivated by the view that it was necessary to take defensive measures to prevent the council from being held liable to pay compensation. The borough leisure officer said that he regretted the need to destroy the beaches but saw no alternative if the council was not to be held liable for an accident to a swimmer. So this appeal gives your Lordships the opportunity to say clearly that local authorities and other occupiers of land are ordinarily under no duty to incur such social and financial costs to protect a minority (or even a majority) against obvious dangers. On the other hand, if the decision of the Court of Appeal were left standing, every such occupier would feel obliged to take similar defensive measures. Sedley LJ was able to say that if the logic of the Court of Appeal's decision was that other public lakes and ponds required similar precautions, 'so be it'. But I cannot view this prospect with the same equanimity. In my opinion it would damage the quality of many people's lives.

See also *Rhind* v *Astbury Water Park* [2004] EWCA Civ 756.

See Chapter 1 for the 'compensation culture' debate.

The social cost involved in a decision which would have resulted in the beach being closed to the public was taken into account in finding that there was no duty. This is part of the 'compensation culture' debate which is currently taking place.

An occupier may well expect the presence of visitors but is unlikely to expect the presence of a trespasser. However, all trespassers do not neatly fit into the category of 'Burglar Bill'.

Higgs v *Foster* [2004] EWCA Civ 843

The appellant was a serving police officer. In the early hours of the 29 April 1999, he was investigating a suspected stolen trailer which had been parked in the service yard of a supermarket in the centre of Glastonbury. He entered the respondents' property, which adjoined the service area, in order, eventually, to take up a position overlooking the service yard. In doing so he fell into an uncovered inspection pit and suffered serious knee injuries as a result of which he was unable to continue working as a police officer. The appellants' claim against the respondent was brought under the Occupiers' Liability Act 1957 on the basis that the appellant was a visitor, alternatively under the Occupiers' Liability Act 1984 in the event that the Recorder concluded that he was a trespasser. The Recorder found that he was a trespasser, and accordingly considered his claim under the provisions of that Act. The claim failed on the grounds that the defendant would have been unaware of the presence of a trespasser. This decision was upheld by the Court of Appeal.

The Occupiers' Liability (Scotland) Act 1960 took the approach of imposing a duty of care on occupiers to all entrants. The standard of care varied according to the nature of the entrant. When Parliament was considering the 1984 Act it was only concerned with trespassers. The decision to split the test may have been a political one. The word trespasser has anti-social connotations, and to say that a duty was automatically owed to a trespasser, but qualified by the standard, may have been too sophisticated.

The duty owed was tested under rather bizarre circumstances in the following case.

Revill v *Newbery* [1996] 1 All ER 291

The 76-year-old defendant was asleep in his garden shed where he was guarding valuable articles. The claimant attempted to break into the shed and the defendant fired his shotgun through a small hole in the door without being able to see whether there was anyone in the way. The claimant was wounded and later pleaded guilty to certain criminal offences committed that night. The defendant was charged with wounding but later acquitted. The claimant then sued the defendant for breach of the duty of care under s 1 and for negligence.

It was held that the fact that a claimant in a personal injuries case was a trespasser and engaged in criminal activities was not a bar to recovery in an action against the occupier under the 1984 Act or against persons other than the occupier at common law. On the facts the trial judge had been justified in finding that some duty of care was owed and the defendant had used greater violence than was justified in self-defence and was in breach of that duty. Damages were reduced by two-thirds because of the claimant's contributory negligence. The defence of *ex turpi causa* was rejected.

The decision of the Court of Appeal is useful in a number of respects.

1 What is the scope of the duty owed under s 1 of the Act? The court concluded that the duty was imposed on the occupier as occupier and was concerned with things done or omitted to be done on the premises. Therefore, in considering whether the defendant was liable on the facts of the case, the fact that they were an occupier was irrelevant and rested on the same basis as if a friend of the defendant had been in the hut and had shot the claimant.

2 If the defendant is not liable as occupier, can the factors in s 1 be taken into account? Neill LJ (at 298) found that the factors in s 1(3) and (4) could be taken into account when considering a case decided at common law. In this case the court took into account s 1(3)(b) and found that the defendant had reasonable grounds for believing that the claimant was in the vicinity of the danger. The danger in this case was that the gun was about to be discharged. A distinction was drawn between what actually happened in the case and the hypothetical instance of the occupier firing a warning shot in the air and accidentally hitting a burglar on the roof.

See Chapter 10 for *ex turpi causa non oritur actio.*

3 What part does the maxim *ex turpi causa non oritur actio* play in such actions? The court felt that it was unnecessary to consider the application of the maxim in other areas of tort. In cases of this nature Parliament, by enacting s 1 of the 1984 Act, had decided that an occupier could not treat a burglar as an outlaw and that the test applicable was that set out in s 1(4). There was no room to take the approach of considering whether there had been a breach of duty and then considering whether the claimant was barred by the fact that he had been engaged in a crime.

Warnings

Section 1(5) states:

Any duty owed by virtue of this section in respect of a risk may, in an appropriate case, be discharged by taking such steps as are reasonable in all the circumstances of the case to give warning of the danger concerned or to discourage persons from incurring the risk.

Whether such a warning will discharge the duty of care will depend on the age of the entrant. In the case of an adult, a warning notice will normally discharge the duty. (See ***Tomlinson* v *Congleton Borough Council*** [2003] 3 All ER 1122.) Almost any notice will be sufficient. With children there is a problem of their not appreciating the danger, or not being able to read. If the occupier has reason to anticipate the presence of a child trespasser he would do well to erect an obstacle to entry that is not in itself dangerous.

Volenti non fit injuria

See also Chapter 10 for *volenti*.
Section 1(6) states:

> No duty is owed by virtue of this section to any person in respect of risks willingly accepted as his by that person (the question of whether a risk was so accepted to be decided on the same principles as in other cases in which one person owes a duty of care to another).

A warning at the shallow end of a swimming pool stating: 'Deep end shallow dive' was a factor that led the Court of Appeal to reject the claim of a trespasser who had been injured diving into the shallow end of the pool. The pool was kept locked after hours and the claimant knew that access was prohibited. The claimant was aware of the risk and had clearly accepted it. (*Ratcliffe* v *McConnell* [1999] 1 WLR 670.)

In the case of trespassers, the courts have adopted an objective rather than a subjective test of agreement. Where the claimant is an adult, then knowledge of the risk accompanied by entry on the land will render the claimant *volenti*. (***Titchener* v *British Railways Board*** [1983] 3 All ER 770.)

If this principle applies to the 1984 Act then it would mean that the defence of *volenti* will vary according to the category of entry. In the case of visitors, knowledge of risk plus entry is not sufficient to amount to *volenti*. The visitor must know enough to be reasonably safe.

Exclusion

The 1984 Act is silent on the question of exclusion, which means that any duty owed may or may not be excludable. There are three points in favour of any duty being unexcludable.

The Unfair Contract Terms Act 1977 does not apply to the 1984 Act as it only has application to common law duties and the statutory duty under the 1957 Act.

It was thought that the common law duty to trespassers was unexcludable as a minimum standard below which the law would not go. If this was the case and that principle was carried forward to the Act then the duty under the Act would be unexcludable. Against this is the fact that the standard under the Act is reasonable care, the normal negligence standard, whereas the common law duty was a lower one of common humanity.

The 1957 Act has specific provisions on its excludability whereas the 1984 Act is silent. If the duty were held to be unexcludable, this would have the odd effect that a trespasser to premises not in business use could be better off than a visitor. The occupier could exclude their duty to the visitor but not to the trespasser.

Example

Charles is the owner of a piece of waste ground adjacent to his house. He has used the waste ground to dump old cars, which he intends to renovate. The waste ground is separated from a park by some old fencing which is in need of repair. Charles, who has just failed the first year of a law degree and is hard up, put up a notice on the fence: 'Danger – Keep Out – No Liability Accepted.'

Damian, an adult, entered the waste ground through a hole in the fence, intending to burgle Charles' house. On his way across the waste ground he tripped over some rusty car parts and was injured. His action would be determined by whether a duty was owed. One does not normally anticipate the presence of a burglar. If a duty was held to be owed, then it would probably be discharged by the warning notice. In any event Damian would probably be *volenti*.

Elvis, an 8-year-old, entered the waste ground by a hole in the fence to explore. He was injured by drinking petrol from a can left in the boot of one of the cars. The court would have to consider whether a duty was owed. The key factor would be whether the presence of the trespasser should have been anticipated by Charles. Warning and *volenti* would not appear to have any chance of success in this case. If the duty is unexcludable Elvis would appear to have a good chance of success.

Floella, the child of an ex-friend of Charles, was left in Charles' care. She wandered into the waste ground to play and was injured by rusty metal. Floella is a visitor and would be owed the common duty of care. It appears likely on the facts that the duty would be broken. But if Floella's parents were aware of the notice, would Charles have succeeded in excluding liability?

Landlord's liability

Introduction

Objective
5

The liability of a landlord to a person injured as a result of defective premises is complex. The tenant may have a remedy in contract based on the lease if they are injured and the landlord has broken a covenant to repair.

The landlord could be an occupier of part of the premises and be liable under the Occupiers' Liability Acts. (See above, for the test for occupier.)

Normally, the landlord will part with control of the premises after the lease and no occupier's liability action will be possible against them.

The common law was opposed to actions in tort and the landlord was immune from a tort action in respect of dangerous premises. (*Cavalier v Pope* [1906] AC 428.)

Liability in negligence

The immunity of a landlord from actions in negligence was confirmed by the Court of Appeal in 1984.

Rimmer v Liverpool City Council [1984] 1 All ER 930

The claimant was a tenant in a council flat designed and built by the defendants. He put his hand through a glass panel and was injured. He sued the council for letting a flat with a dangerous feature. It was held that there was no duty of care on landlords to ensure that premises were reasonably safe at the time of the letting.

It was held that the defendants owed a duty of care as designers and builders of the flat and were liable under that head.

Statutory liability

The Defective Premises Act 1972 contains two provisions in relation to the landlord's position.

Section 3

Section 3 states:

> Where work of construction, repair, maintenance or demolition or any other work is done on or in relation to premises, any duty of care owed, because of the doing of the work, to persons who might reasonably be expected to be affected by defects in the state of the premises created by the doing of the work shall not be abated by subsequent disposal of the premises by the person who owed the duty.

This section does no more than restate the common law position and could be considered superfluous. It does not apply to a failure to do work or to work carried out after the letting.

Section 4

Of more practical importance is s 4:

1 Where premises are let under a tenancy which puts on the landlord an obligation to the tenant for the maintenance or repair of the premises, the landlord owes to all persons who might reasonably be expected to be affected by defects in the state of the premises a duty to take such care as is reasonable in all the circumstances to see that they are reasonably safe from personal injury or from damage to their property caused by a relevant defect.

2 The said duty is owed if the landlord knows (whether as the result of being notified by the tenant or otherwise) or if he ought in all the circumstances to have known of the relevant defect.

For this section to apply, the landlord must be under an obligation to the tenant for the maintenance or repair of the premises, or they must have an express or implied right or power to enter the premises to carry out any description of maintenance or repair. The obligation may arise from an express term in the lease or may be implied by statute: for example, the Landlord and Tenant Act 1985 ss 11 and 12, which require the landlord to repair the exterior and structure of premises, where the lease of a dwelling house is for less than seven years. This provision cannot be contracted out of.

The duty will be owed where the landlord knows, or ought to have known, of a defect which would constitute a breach of their obligation to the tenant to repair the premises. It is not necessary that the landlord knows the precise defect provided that he has failed to take reasonable care in all the circumstances of the case to see that the tenant was reasonably safe.

Sykes v *Harry* [2001] 3 WLR 62

The landlord failed to have a gas fire serviced for eight years. He was not aware of the actual defect as the tenant had not told him but should have been aware of the dangers of carbon monoxide poisoning if a gas fire is not regularly serviced.

The duty is no longer than the reach of the covenant to repair and maintain owed by the landlord in any particular case. There is no warrant for equating a duty to maintain and repair with a duty to make safe. Moreover, a duty to keep in good condition, even if it encompassed a duty to put in good condition, does not encompass a duty to put in safe condition. (*Alker* v *Collingwood Housing Association* [2007] 1 WLR 2230.)

The duty will be owed to the tenant, residents, neighbours and passers-by on the highway. Whether a trespasser would be a foreseeable claimant is not known.

See Chapter 17 for the law of nuisance. It should be noted that in the case of injury to neighbours and highway users there is an overlap between this section and the law of nuisance.

> ### Example
>
> Albert let a dwelling house on a monthly tenancy to Brenda. Due to high winds the chimney stack became unsafe. Brenda pointed this out to Albert, who took no remedial action. The chimney collapsed and fell to the ground.
>
> Part of the chimney fell through the roof and injured Carol, Brenda's daughter. Albert is under a statutory obligation to repair the structure. He was aware of the need for repair and did nothing. He is therefore in breach of s 4 and Carol would have an action under this section.
>
> Donald was sitting in a deck-chair in his garden next door, when part of the chimney fell on him. He would have an action under s 4 and in private nuisance.
>
> Edith was walking on the highway outside the house when she was injured. Edith would have an action under s 4 and an action in public nuisance.

Builder's liability

Introduction

Objective 6

The expression 'builder' is used in the sense of all persons involved in the construction and sale of buildings. This includes developers, builders, sub-contractors, architects, surveyors, civil engineers and local authorities.

In a typical example, the land will be bought by a development company; a geological survey done by surveyors; plans drawn up by architects; the plans submitted to the local authority for approval and to check that they comply with the Building Regulations, which lay down minimum standards for public health and safety; a builder engaged to construct the houses, who may sub-contract certain aspects of the work to specialist firms. The builder and the development company may be the same entity. Each house will then be sold to a purchaser (*P1*), who after a number of years may sell it to another purchaser (*P2*).

The house may show a defect a number of years after construction. A recurring problem is cracks caused by the fact that the foundations were of the wrong depth or made from the wrong materials. The house needs remedial action to make it safe, but who has to bear the cost of this work? If no work is done, then the house will eventually collapse and may cause personal injuries to the occupants.

Take an example. The house was built by *B* and completed in 2009. The plans were approved and work in progress inspected by the local authority. In 2009 the house was sold to *P1*. In 2011 *P1* sold the house to *P2*. In 2012 a crack appeared in one of the walls. An engineer's report states that the foundations are defective and that the house will need underpinning and the foundations repaired. The cost of this work is £50,000.

What category does the damage fall into: physical damage or economic loss? The courts have taken the view that this is economic loss. If, for example, the house had collapsed and damaged an adjacent property, the damage to the adjacent property would be classed as physical damage, damage to *other* property.

In practical terms, *P2*'s most important protection would be the National House Building Council (NHBC) Scheme. This scheme applies to registered builders and developers. A purchaser of such a house obtains a House Purchaser's Agreement from the vendor. This provides that the house will be built in an efficient and workmanlike manner, with proper materials, and be fit for human habitation. The vendor agrees to remedy any defects at their own expense in the first two years, where the defect arises from a breach of NHBC standards. Any major damage to the building which occurs within ten years is covered by an insurance policy. The agreement can be transferred with the house. If the house is covered by the scheme, then *P2* may be able to have the work done on this basis.

If not, what legal remedies does *P2* have? The diagram sets out the situation.

B—Contract—*P1*—Contract—*P2*

It can be seen that any contractual remedy that *P2* has would be against *P1*. However, private sales of houses are subject to the doctrine of *caveat emptor* (let the buyer beware). *P1* is not under a contractual duty to tell *P2* of any defects he is aware of, unless *P2* specifically asks. The defect in any case may not have been known at the time of the sale. The chances are that *P2* will have no contract action against *P1*.

As *P2* is not in privity of contract with *B*, and has no contract action against *B*, this leaves two possibilities.

Statutory liability

Parliament created a limited form of protection from builders with the Defective Premises Act 1972.

Section 1(1) imposes on builders, sub-contractors, architects and other professional persons a three-part duty: that the work will be done in a workmanlike manner, proper materials will be used, and the house will be fit for human habitation.

The duty applies only in respect of dwellings and does not apply to commercial or industrial properties.

The duty is owed to the person to whose order the building is provided and to every person who acquires an interest in the dwelling. This means that the doctrine of privity of contract does not apply, and *P2* in the example would have a theoretical claim against *B*.

Liability under the section is strict, in the sense that fault does not have to be proved against the builder. The duty cannot be excluded.

This statutory provision received relatively little attention while the courts were creating a more extensive common law liability (see below). The virtual elimination of common law liability by the appellate courts has led lawyers to focus more on it and its defects.

A major problem is the limitation period, which is six years from the date on which the dwelling was completed. In many cases of defective buildings, however, the defect does not become apparent until many years after the building was completed. By the time the occupier realises that there is an action, he is statute barred as there is no provision for latent damage in the statute.

A further problem was thought to be s 2 of the Act which provides that s 1 does not apply where the dwelling is protected by an 'approved scheme'. In practice, this has meant the NHBC scheme (see above) but it appears that since 1988 this 'approved scheme' has not been effective and the fact that a dwelling was built under the scheme does not preclude the owner from taking action under s 1.

Yet another problem is with the scope of s 1 and whether it includes quality defects or is limited to ensuring that the dwelling is fit for human habitation.

In *Andrews* v *Schooling* [1991] 3 All ER 723, the Court of Appeal held that the section applied to nonfeasance as well as to misfeasance and that a failure to carry out necessary work would give rise to liability. If the dwelling was without some necessary attribute such as a damp course or a roof, then it would be unfit for human habitation, even though the problems resulting from the lack of the attribute had not then become apparent. However, the effectiveness of the section will be limited in terms of quality defects if a first instance decision (*Thompson* v *Alexander* (1992) 59 BLR 77), which held that the defects must render the dwelling unfit for human habitation, prevails.

In *Bayoumi* v *Protim Services Ltd* [1996] EGCS 187 the test for causation was held to be whether the defendant's breach was a significant cause of or factor in the dwelling's unfitness. It need not be the sole cause. The measure of damages is all losses naturally consequent on the breach, not just the cost of repair or diminution in value.

Negligence liability

See Chapter 5 for liability for economic loss.

In the 1970s the courts embarked on a massive extension of the builder's liability in negligence. They created a duty of care imposed on builders and owed to foreseeable victims of their negligence. As the loss to an owner-occupier was economic loss, the courts sidestepped the problems this presented by framing the duty in terms of not constructing a building which was a danger to the health and safety of the occupier. (*Anns* v *Merton London Borough Council* [1978] AC 728.)

In the example, *P2* would have had a negligence action against *B*. The measure of damages would have been the amount required to make the house safe for occupation, i.e. £50,000. As the building trade is notoriously unstable financially and *B* might have gone out of business, many actions were brought against local authorities for negligently approving plans or negligent inspection of houses under construction.

From about 1983 the courts started to rein back the development they had unleashed. The specific reasons for this are not known but are connected with the wider trend of not allowing claims for economic loss in negligence actions. The courts may also have been influenced by the rising premiums which had to be paid by anyone involved in the construction of buildings. This rise was a result of successful actions being brought under the negligence principle.

The retrenchment by the courts took place in two House of Lords cases but it is unlikely that the problem has been solved.

D&F Estates Ltd v *Church Commissioners for England* [1988] 2 All ER 992

A company of builders undertook construction work on a block of flats and sub-contracted the plastering work, which was carried out negligently. The result was that 15 years later the plaster was loose and needed replacement. The claimants, who were lessees and occupiers of a flat in the block, sued the builders for the cost of remedial work already performed and the cost of future remedial work.

The House of Lords held that, in the absence of a contractual relationship between the parties, the cost of repairing a defect in the structure, which was discovered before the defect had caused personal injury or physical damage to other property, was not recoverable in a negligence action. The cost of doing the repairs was economic loss which was not recoverable in a negligence action, except within the **Hedley Byrne** principle, or on the unique proximity of **Junior Books** v **Veitchi**.

A number of doubts were left by this decision. The idea of a complex structure was introduced. If the building is regarded as a complex structure, then damage to one part of the structure, caused by a hidden defect in another part, could be treated as damage to the other property. The position of local authorities was also left unclear until the next case, which represents the present law.

Murphy v *Brentwood District Council* [1990] 2 All ER 908

See also Chapter 5 for *Murphy*.

The claimant purchased a pair of semi-detached houses from a construction company. The houses had been built on a concrete raft on an infilled site. The raft was defective and settlement occurred causing serious cracks to appear in the houses. It was alleged that the defendant council had negligently approved plans for the construction of the raft. The claimant's case was based on the argument that repair was necessary in order to avert a present or imminent danger to the health or safety of the occupant. Gas and drainage pipes had broken as a result of the settlement and there was a risk of further breaks.

The House of Lords held that the council was not liable for the claimant's loss, which was economic and not within the accepted categories.

Lord Bridge:

> . . . these considerations lead inevitably to the conclusion that a building owner can only recover the cost of repairing a defective building on the ground of the authority's negligence in performing its statutory function of approving plans or inspecting buildings in the course of construction if the scope of the authority's duty of care is wide enough to embrace purely economic loss. The House has already held in *D&F Estates* that a builder, in the absence of any contractual duty or of a special relationship of proximity introducing the *Hedley Byrne* principle of reliance, owes no duty of care in tort in respect of the quality of his work. As I pointed out in *D&F Estates*, to hold that the builder owed such a duty of care to any person acquiring an interest in the product of the builder's work would be to impose on him the obligations of an indefinitely transmissible warranty of quality.
>
> By s 1 of the Defective Premises Act 1972 Parliament has in fact imposed on builders and others undertaking work in the provision of dwellings the obligations of a transmissible warranty of the quality of their work and of the fitness for habitation of the completed dwelling. But, besides being limited to dwellings, liability under that Act is subject to a limitation period of six years from the completion of the work and to the exclusion provided for by s 2. It would be remarkable to find that similar obligations in the nature of a transmissible warranty of quality, applicable to buildings of every kind and subject to no such limitations or exclusions as are imposed by the 1972 Act, could be derived from the builder's common law duty of care or from the duty imposed by building byelaws or regulations. In *Anns* Lord Wilberforce expressed the opinion that a builder could be held liable for a breach of statutory duty in respect of buildings which do not comply with the byelaws. But he cannot, I think, have meant that the statutory obligation to build in conformity with the byelaws by itself gives rise to obligations in the nature of transmissible warranties of quality. If he did mean that, I must respectfully disagree. I find it impossible to suppose that anything less than clear express language such as is used in s 1 of the 1972 Act would suffice to impose such a statutory obligation.
>
> As I have already said, since the function of a local authority in approving plans or inspecting buildings in the course of construction is directed to ensuring that the builder complies with building byelaws or regulations, I cannot see how, in principle, the scope of the liability of the authority for a negligent failure to ensure compliance can exceed that of the liability of the builder for his negligent failure to comply. There may, of course, be situations where, even in the absence of contract, there is a special relationship of proximity between builder and building owner which is sufficiently akin to contract to introduce the element of reliance so that the scope of the duty of care owed by the builder to the owner is wide enough to embrace purely economic loss. The decision in *Junior Books Ltd* v *Veitchi Co Ltd* [1983] 1 AC 520 can, I believe, only be understood on this basis.

The decision is logical, in the sense that it places local authorities in the same position as other builders. They are not liable in negligence for the cost of remedial measures caused by a defect in the building's construction.

The House considered the complex structure point in *D&F Estates*. They considered that a building or product cannot be regarded as a complex structure if it has been wholly constructed or manufactured by one person, so as to form a single indivisible unit. The idea of a complex structure can be applied to equipment manufactured by different suppliers: for example, central heating boilers.

A number of points remained unclear after the decision:

1 whether a local authority is liable for breach of statutory duty and, if so, to what extent;

2 whether the local authority will be liable for personal injury or property damage suffered by occupiers of houses which have been inspected and the Building Regulations not complied with.

In *Targett* v *Torfaen Borough Council* [1992] 3 All ER 27, it was held that the claimant tenant of a council house built and designed by the defendant council could recover for personal injuries suffered as a result of a design defect consisting of unlit stairs with no handrail. The Court of Appeal applied *Rimmer* v *Liverpool City Council* [1984] 1 All ER 930 in reaching the decision, but it appears to stretch *Murphy* as the claimant was aware of the defect before the injuries were suffered. The court's interpretation of *Murphy* was that no damages could be recovered for a latent defect which had not yet caused physical damage, but they could be awarded where physical damage was suffered even where the claimant was aware of the defect. A comparison could usefully be drawn with common law liability for defective products and when an intermediate examination by the claimant will exonerate the defendant.

In *Tesco Stores Ltd* v *Wards Construction (Investment) Ltd* (1995) 76 BLR 94 the claimants alleged that the spread of a fire at a new shopping centre was caused by defects in the design and construction and that the local authority was in breach of duty in respect of its approval of drawings and inspection of construction. It was held that the local authority did not owe a duty with respect to damage to property as the building regulations were concerned with the health and safety of persons and not property. Alternatively, it would not be fair, just or reasonable to impose a duty of care (applying *Marc Rich & Co* v *Bishop Rock Marine (The Nicholas H)* [1995] 3 WLR 227). The question of personal injuries was left open.

In the example, neither *B* nor the local authority would be liable in negligence for the cost of repair to *P2*'s house. The cost of remedying the defect is economic loss and neither party owes a duty of care to *P2* in that respect.

The *Murphy* decision has been attacked from various quarters and academic commentary has been generally hostile. There are now signs that the lower courts are interpreting the case in, perhaps, a way their Lordships did not intend.

In *Targett* v *Torfaen* (above) there is an indication that the courts may be generous in terms of personal injury actions against builders and a further case has indicated flexibility relating to property damage.

Nitrigin Eireann Teoranta v *Inco Alloys Ltd* [1992] 1 All ER 854

Cracks in steel alloy tubing which formed part of a refinery caused an explosion. The explosion damaged the refinery. The claimants were aware of the cracks but were allowed to recover. It was held that the limitation period ran from the date of the explosion rather than from the date of the appearance of the cracks.

The case provides an example of the complex structure concept. The defendants had supplied the tubing which formed part of the refinery. No damages could be recovered by the claimants in respect of repair of the tubing as this was a quality defect and would therefore constitute pure economic loss. However, the defendants would be liable for any damage caused by the defect to the rest of the refinery which would constitute 'other property'. This assumes that the defect was latent and could not have been discovered by the claimants using all due care. The claimants were aware of the cracks, but not their cause, and had tried to repair them. The court held that the claimants were therefore not aware of the defect which caused the physical damage. It was added (*obiter*) that if the claimants had been negligent in failing to discover the cause of the cracks they would still have had a cause of action, with damages reduced for contributory negligence.

? Question

Peabody Park is owned and maintained by the Peabody Trust. Admission to the public is granted on payment of 50 pence; this is done by placing a 50-pence piece in a ticket-dispensing machine. Each ticket bears the words: 'For conditions of entry see notice in Park office.' The conditions referred to include the clause: 'The Trust shall not be liable for damage to visitors or their property whether caused by negligence or otherwise.'

Bertram paid his 50 pence and entered the park. He was badly injured when a rowing boat, which he took on the lake, sank because it had not been properly maintained by the Trust.

Clarence entered the park at the request of the Trust to repair the gas cooker in the cafeteria. He suffered personal injuries when the cooker exploded.

Dick, an eight-year-old boy, entered the park through a hole in the fence, after the park had closed. He was attracted by some bright red berries on a bush. The berries were poisonous and a notice to this effect was attached to the bush. Dick suffered personal injuries after eating the berries.

Advise Bertram, Clarence and Dick as to their legal position.

Suggested approach

This question is on occupiers' liability for defective premises. Although an area of negligence, liability is governed by statute, the Occupiers' Liability Acts 1957 and 1984.

Liability in such case falls on the occupier of the premises. This term is not defined by either Act and was considered by the House of Lords in *Wheat* v *Lacon* (1966). In order to be an occupier a person has to have sufficient control over the premises. In this case the Peabody Trust will be the occupier.

In order to determine which Act is applicable it is necessary to determine the status of the claimant. If the claimant is a visitor, then the 1957 Act will apply. If the claimant is a trespasser, the 1984 Act will apply. Bertram and Clarence would be classed as visitors as they came lawfully on to the land. Dick is a trespasser, as the occupier was unaware of his presence and, if he had known of his presence, would have objected to it.

As Bertram is a visitor, the Trust will owe him the common duty of care under the 1957 Act s 2(2). This is a duty to take reasonable care for the visitor's safety for the purposes for which he was permitted to be there. Bertram is also a contractual entrant. If the contract is silent as to the duty owed to the visitor, then the common duty of care in the Act will apply.

Prior to the Act, the courts had drawn a distinction between the occupancy duty, which was concerned with dangers due to the state of the premises, and the activity duty, which was concerned with the occupier's activities on his premises. Is a rowing boat within the occupancy or the activity duty? There is no clear case as to whether the Act applies to the activity duty. However, s 1(3)(a) states that the Act applies to fixed and movable structures, and this could include a rowing boat. Bertram might be well advised to bring his action in the alternative, under the Act and in common law negligence.

What effect would the notice on the ticket have? As Bertram is a contractual entrant, any terms of the contract would have to be brought to his attention at or before the time when the contract is made. This would be when the money was placed in the ticket machine. It would appear that the Trust have failed to include the notice in the machine as a term of the contract. (*Thornton* v *Shoe Lane Parking* [1971] 2 QB 163.) If they have, what is the effect of the term? It attempts to exclude liability. Would the Unfair Contract Terms Act 1977 apply? This would depend on an interpretation of s 1(3). Are the premises being used for business purposes? If they are, then the Act will apply. Under s 2(1), liability for death or personal injuries caused by negligence cannot be excluded. The notice does not appear to operate as a warning and neither could it raise the defence of *volenti non fit injuria*. (Unfair Contract Terms Act 1977 s 2(3).)

As Bertram is owed a duty of care, the Trust would appear to be in breach of duty by failing to maintain the boat, and Bertram has suffered damage as a result. Bertram would appear to have an action.

Clarence is also a visitor to the premises and is owed the common duty of care. Section 2(3)(a) of the 1957 Act provides that where a person enters in the exercise of his calling, the occupier may expect that that person will appreciate and guard against risks which are ordinarily incident to that calling. (*Roles* v *Nathan* and *General Cleaning Contractors* v *Christmas*.) However, the fact that a person has a specific skill will not absolve an occupier who has not exercised a sufficient degree of care. (*Ogwo* v *Taylor*.) Liability in this case would depend on why the cooker exploded. If Clarence had lit a cigarette and that caused the explosion, then the Trust would be under no liability. But if Clarence had exercised reasonable care, the court would have to decide whether the Trust were at fault.

Dick is a trespasser and any duty owed would be under the 1984 Act. The fact that the relationship of occupier–trespasser is established does not establish a duty of care. It is necessary to pass the threshold of s 1(1) (*Keown* v *Coventry Healthcare NHS Trust*) and apply s 1(3) of the Act. If the claimant satisfies these three requirements then a duty will be owed. (NB: in an examination a student would be expected to set out and apply these requirements.) If a duty is owed, the court would have to determine whether there had been a breach. The standard of care is the usual negligence one of reasonable care (s 1(4)).

Would the notice displayed next to the berries suffice as a warning within s 1(5)? This would appear to depend upon the age of the trespasser. If a duty had been held to be owed to Dick, then the occupier had cause to appreciate the presence of the child and the premises would have to be reasonably safe for a child trespasser and an obstacle to entry erected. Although the case is similar on the facts to (*Glasgow Corp* v *Taylor*, the approach of the statute might be different from the old common law approach. What may be important is how Dick got into the park and whether reasonable steps were taken to prevent this.

Summary

This chapter deals with the specific rules of negligence on defective premises.

- Occupiers' liability for defective premises is dealt with by statute.
- An occupier is defined as a person who has 'control' of the premises. (*Wheat* v *Lacon*.) There may be more than one occupier.
- An occupiers' liability to visitors is dealt with by the Occupiers' Liability Act 1957. A visitor may claim for personal injuries or damage to property and a distinction is drawn between the 'occupancy duty' and the 'activity duty'.
- The duty of care under the Act is owed to visitors (s 1(2)).
- The duty owed to a visitor is the common duty of care (s 2(2)). It is a duty of reasonable care in all the circumstances of the case and extends to the purposes for which the

visitor was permitted to enter. The occupier must be prepared for children to be less careful than adults (s 2(3)(a)). Persons entering in the exercise of a calling are expected to guard against risks inherent to that calling (s 2(3)(b)). Where an independent contractor has been appointed to do work this will discharge the occupiers' duty of care (s 2(4) (b)) provided it was reasonable to use an independent contractor and steps were taken to check the contractor was competent. With non-technical work the occupier must check the work. A sufficient warning will discharge the duty of care (s 2(4)(a)).

- The defences of *volenti* (s 2(5)), contributory negligence (s 2(3)) and exclusion (s 2(1)) are available to the occupier but there are statutory restrictions on when the duty may be excluded.

- Liability to trespassers is governed by the Occupiers' Liability Act 1984. The Act applies to persons other than visitors.

- A duty is owed where the occupier knows or ought to know of the danger, the presence of the trespasser and ought to have offered some protection to the trespasser (s 1(3)). The leading authority is *Tomlinson* v *Congleton BC* (2003).

- The duty is to take such care as is reasonable in the circumstances (s 1(4)). This is the usual objective negligence standard. The social costs of a finding of negligence have to be taken into consideration. (*Tomlinson.*) The duty can be discharged by taking reasonable steps to give a warning (s 1(5)). The defence of *volenti* is available to the defendant (s 1(6)) but the Act is silent on the question of exclusion.

- A landlord was not liable at common law in respect of dangerous premises. (*Cavalier* v *Pope* (1906).) There is now a statutory liability on a landlord of reasonable care where the landlord is under a duty to maintain or repair. (Defective Premises Act 1972 s 4.)

- A builder is under a statutory liability in respect of dwellings. (Defective Premises Act 1972 s 1.) The duty is strict but has limited value because of the strict limitation period and does not apply where the dwelling is covered by an 'approved scheme'.

- There is now no liability on a builder (*D&F Estates* v *Church Commissioners* (1988)) or local authority (*Murphy* v *Brentwood DC* (1990)) at common law for negligence leading to economic loss. It is possible for such losses to be recovered if the building is a complex structure.

Further reading

Occupiers' liability

Buckley, R. (1984), 'The Occupiers' Liability Act 1984 – Has Herrington Survived?' Conv 413.

Jones, M. (1984), 'The Occupiers' Liability Act 1984' 47 MLR 713.

Mesher, J. (1979), 'Occupiers, Trespassers and the Unfair Contract Terms Act 1977' Conv 58.

Builder's liability

Cooke, R. (1991), 'An Impossible Distinction' 107 LQR 46.

Spencer, J. (1974–75), 'Defective Premises Act' (1974) CLJ 307; (1975) CLJ 48.

Stapleton, J. (1991), 'Duty of Care and Economic Loss' 107 LQR 249.

Wallace, I. D. (1991), '*Anns* Beyond Repair' 107 LQR 228.

Weir, T. (1991) CLJ 24 (*Murphy*).

12

Defective products

Objectives

After reading this chapter you will:

1. Have a knowledge of the legal problems and the common law negligence rules relating to defective products.

2. Understand the 'narrow rule' in *Donogue* v *Stevenson*.

3. Have a critical knowledge of the provisions of the Consumer Protection Act 1987.

Introduction

Objective 1

After a product is manufactured and put into circulation, liability is governed primarily by the chain of contracts between the manufacturer and the ultimate user.

Manufacturer —— Wholesaler —— Retailer —— Purchaser........Donee

Example

Alice bought a hot-water bottle from a retailer which did not give off any heat. The product is defective in the sense that it is not of the standard that Alice expected. Alice would have an action for breach of contract against the retailer and could utilise the Sale of Goods Act 1979 s 14(2) and (3) (as amended by the Sale and Supply of Goods Act 1994). The product is not of satisfactory quality and it is not fit for the purpose for which it was sold.

The retailer in turn would have an action for breach of contract against the wholesaler and the wholesaler against the manufacturer. The loss would then be carried by the person responsible for the defect.

This theory has two problems which arise when the chain of contracts breaks down.

First, if the retailer became insolvent, then Alice would have no contractual remedy. Similarly, any insolvency along the chain would destroy the particular contract action. Further up the chain there may be an exclusion clause which would prevent any contract action. The manufacturer may have sold to the wholesaler on the basis that they would not be responsible for any claims for defective quality.

Second, if Alice gave the hot-water bottle to Bert as a present, then Bert would be a donee and have no contract with anyone. This was the position of the claimant in *Donoghue* v *Stevenson*.

So far we have looked at the defectiveness of the product. What would be the position if the product was dangerous rather then merely defective? If Alice or Bert filled it with hot water and it leaked causing injury, would either of them have an action? The modern position is that they may have an action for negligence, or under the Consumer Protection Act 1987.

Let us look at the claims in terms of types of damage. A claim that the product is not as good as the purchaser expected is a claim for economic loss, which traditionally should be brought in contract. A claim that the product is dangerous and has caused personal injuries or damage to other property (i.e. other than the product itself) is a claim for physical damage and can be brought in contract or tort or under statute.

Liability in contract

Although this a book on tort law there are some instances where it is difficult to understand the law without a knowledge of another legal subject. In the case of defective products this is contract law.

In the example above Alice has a contract with the retailer of the hot-water bottle. This claim is for poor quality and Alice has a right to the cost of replacing or repairing the goods. If the hot water bottle leaked and caused her personal injuries or damaged her bed, then Alice would have a claim for these items of loss. These claims are known as her 'statutory rights'. They arise under the Sale of Goods Act 1979, s 14(2) (satisfactory quality) and s 14(3) (fitness for purpose). The statutory rights cannot be excluded or limited in a consumer contract (Unfair Contract Terms Act 1977, s 6(2)). The consumer has a right to repair, refund or replacement.

A consumer who has a contract is therefore very well protected but contract law has limitations. The first is if the consumer does not have a contract. If Alice bought the hot-water bottle as a present for Bert, then Bert has no contractual protection as there is no privity of contract between Bert and the retailer. The second is if the sale is not made in the course of a business. If it is a private sale then the implied terms in the Sale of Goods Act will not apply and in the absence of an express term or misrepresentation there would be severe difficulties with a contractual claim. Thirdly, the retailer may have become insolvent or the claimant may not wish to sue them as they are a small local company.

In these circumstances the claimant will have to make a claim in tort against a person further up the supply chain.

The negligence action

Prior to 1932 the courts refused to allow the chain of contracts to be disturbed by tort actions. The view was that people ordered their affairs on the basis of their contractual liability and to allow a third party to sue in tort would upset this arrangement. This was the privity fallacy. Developments before 1932 were limited to where the product was dangerous in itself or where the danger was actually known to the transferor. In *Donoghue* v *Stevenson* in 1932 the House of Lords shaped a general theory of manufacturer's liability in tort for products. This is known as the narrow rule.

See also Chapter 3 for 'privity fallacy' and Donoghue.

The tortious principle gives protection to the ultimate consumer of a product where the product has caused physical damage. The action lies against the manufacturer of the product where they have been negligent. Generally speaking, there is no tort action where the product is merely defective and has not caused any physical damage.

In the example, no claim in tort would lie if the hot-water bottle did not give off enough heat. A claim would lie for scalded feet. Either Alice or Bert could bring such a claim if they suffered damage.

The common law was perceived to have certain defects and there was pressure from the then EEC to harmonise consumer safety law across the Community. This resulted in the passing of the Consumer Protection Act 1987, which introduces a strict liability regime for defective products (see below).

A consumer who suffers physical damage from a defective product now has a choice between the common law and the statutory actions.

The narrow rule in *Donoghue* v *Stevenson*

Introduction

Objective 2

See also Chapter 3 for *Donoghue* v *Stevenson*.

Lord Atkin laid down the narrow rule in ***Donoghue* v *Stevenson*** [1932] AC 562:

> . . . a manufacturer of products, which he sells in such a form as to show that he intends them to reach the ultimate consumer in the form in which they left him with no reasonable possibility of intermediate examination, and with the knowledge that the absence of reasonable care in the preparation or putting up of the products will result in an injury to the consumer's life or property, owes a duty to the consumer to take that reasonable care.

This quotation sets out all the points required for an action. The relevant points will be looked at in turn.

Who owes the duty?

The duty is owed by manufacturers. This expression has been widely interpreted by the courts as meaning anyone responsible for putting into circulation a product which is not reasonably safe. It has therefore been applied to manufacturers in the conventional sense: retailers, wholesalers, repairers of products (such as garages), assemblers and those who hire and lease goods. It might appear strange to classify a retailer as a manufacturer but this will only happen where they are under a duty to inspect the goods and fail to do so.

It would also appear that the rule applies to realty and could be applied to the builder of a house and possibly a local authority building inspector.

A duty to whom?

See also Chapter 3 for duty of care.

The duty is owed to consumers. The consumer is anyone whom the manufacturer should foresee would be affected by the product. This will include purchasers, donees, borrowers, employees of a purchaser and bystanders who happen to be injured.

Stennett v *Hancock* [1939] 2 All ER 578

The claimant pedestrian was struck on the leg by a part of the wheel of the defendants' lorry, which came off as it was being driven along the road. The defendants had repaired the wheel shortly before the accident and were held to be manufacturers. As the repair had been carried out negligently and the claimant was a consumer, the action succeeded.

Products

The original rule applied to food and drink but has now been extended to cover all manufactured products. It has been held to cover motor vehicles, lifts, clothes, cleaning fluids and buildings. The rule extends to the packaging in which the goods are supplied.

Breach of duty

See Chapter 8 for reasonable care.

The claimant must prove that the manufacturer failed to take reasonable care in the preparation or putting up of the product.

In practice this will mean identifying a breakdown in the production process, failure to give adequate instructions for use or a defective design. Problems with the production process may be demonstrated by showing an impurity which should have been removed before the product was put into circulation.

Grant v *Australian Knitting Mills Ltd* [1936] AC 85

The claimant contracted dermatitis because of excessive sulphites in underwear manufactured by the defendants. The sulphites had been negligently left in the underwear by the defendants during the manufacturing process, although they could not have been detected by any reasonable examination. The defendants were held liable in negligence. It was important that the underwear was intended to be worn as supplied and no instructions to wash before using were given.

Alternatively, the claimant may complain that the product was in itself inadequately constructed. If a car manufacturer becomes aware of a significant number of a particular fault on one of its models, then a failure to recall the cars for a check may amount to negligence. (*Walton* v *British Leyland UK Ltd* (1978) unreported.)

Design defects may pose more serious problems. If the manufacturer is producing at the limits of scientific knowledge, then they may not be able to foresee injury being caused by their product. This is particularly acute with the development of new drugs, as adverse side effects may not be foreseeable.

The product must be supplied with instructions for use and adequate warning of any known danger. If a warning has been given, then on causation grounds this may mean some other person is liable. Typical examples of instructions and warnings can be found on household paints. The consumer will be informed to keep the product away from their eyes but if it does get in the eyes, to wash it out and seek medical advice.

It may be important to determine whether a warning discharges the duty of care or is an attempt to exclude liability. If it is the latter or an attempt to prevent a duty arising then it would be subject to the Unfair Contract Terms Act 1977. In *Hurley* v *Dyke* [1979] RTR 265, a second-hand car was sold 'as seen and with all its faults'. The House of Lords held that this was sufficient to protect the previous owner who knew that the car was potentially dangerous. If this statement was an attempt to exclude liability it could be struck down by the Act.

Proof of negligence

The burden of proof is on the claimant to establish that the product was defective, that the injury was caused by that defect, and that the injury was caused by the manufacturer's lack of reasonable care.

This may appear to place a heavy burden on the claimant but it has been held that they do not have to identify the exact person responsible for the defect. (**Grant v Australian Knitting Mills**.) Negligence may be inferred from the fact that the product left the manufacturer in a defective state. This leaves the manufacturer with the problem of proving that their employees were not negligent and that they were using a safe system. This appears to be very close to the doctrine of *res ipsa loquitur*.

See Chapter 8 for *res ipsa loquitur*.

 ## Causation

See also Chapter 9 for causation.

Causation in defective product cases works on the basis of showing that the goods were intended to reach the consumer in the form in which they left the manufacturer (alternative cause) and that there was no reasonable possibility of intermediate examination.

Alternative cause

The manufacturer is only liable for damage caused by their own negligence. If another person in the chain of distribution or natural wear and tear has caused the defect, then the manufacturer will be not liable.

It is important that the product reaches the claimant in the same form that it left the manufacturer. This is not to be taken literally. The product does not have to remain in the packaging and the mere possibility of someone having tampered with the goods is not sufficient to exonerate the defendant. If the product has been assembled, checked or altered, then this may provide an alternative explanation for the defect.

Evans v Triplex Glass Co Ltd [1936] 1 All ER 283

> The claimant bought a car fitted with a windscreen made by the defendants. One year later the windscreen shattered and injured passengers in the car. It was held that the claimant had to show it was more probable than not that the injury was due to faulty manufacture. He was unable to do this as it was possible that the cause of the defect was faulty fitting.

Intermediate examination

Where it is reasonable to expect someone to inspect the goods before they are used, the manufacturer may not be regarded as the cause of the damage. If the goods were examined and the defect was negligently not identified, this makes the examiner a cause of the damage. It is not sufficient that someone had an opportunity to examine the goods; it must be shown that the manufacturer could reasonably expect that person to make an examination. For example, it would not be reasonable for a manufacturer to expect that a person would wash underwear before using it.

Griffiths v Arch Engineering Co [1968] 3 All ER 217

> The first defendants lent a grinding tool owned by the second defendants to the claimant. An employee of the second defendants had fitted an incorrect part to the tool and the claimant was injured. The first defendants were liable because they had an opportunity to examine the tool. The second defendants were liable because they could not rely on such an examination taking place.

Where the manufacturer has issued a warning that tests should be carried out before use, it is reasonable to expect an examination.

Kubach v *Hollands* [1937] 3 All ER 907

The manufacturers sold chemicals to the second defendants with a warning that they should be tested before use. The second defendants sold the chemicals to a teacher without the warning. The claimant child was injured when the chemical exploded during a school experiment. Her action against the school (the first defendants) failed but she recovered from the second defendants. Their claim for an indemnity from the manufacturers failed as they had been given an adequate warning and ignored it.

The intermediate examination could be by the claimant or by a third party. If the claimant is at fault then the court could find no liability on the basis that the damage was caused by the claimant; or a reduction could be made for contributory negligence. Where a third party is responsible the principle can be used to exonerate a person in the chain (*Kubach*) or, where more than one person is at fault (*Griffiths*), the principle of apportionment between defendants can be used.

Damage

The narrow rule states that the manufacturer's negligence must result in damage to the consumer's life or property. A claim under the rule will therefore be for physical damage, consisting of personal injuries or damage to the consumer's property. It would also appear that any consequential economic loss may be recovered.

The claimant cannot recover damages if their claim is that the product is not worth as much as they expected. This is classed as economic loss and, subject to *Junior Books* v *Veitchi*, is only recoverable in a contract action.

Muirhead v *Industrial Tank Specialities Ltd* [1986] QB 507

The claimant's lobsters died after the failure of a pump to oxygenate the water where they were kept. The pump manufacturer was held liable for the value of the lobsters (property damage) but not for the costs of buying and attempting to repair the pumps. Neither was there any liability for loss of profit on the sale of the lobsters.

Nourse LJ:

> In his analysis of *Junior Books Ltd* v *Veitchi Co Ltd* Robert Goff LJ has identified the three features of that case on which the decision that the nominated sub-contractor had voluntarily assumed a direct responsibility to the building owner was founded. The first two of these were very close proximity between the subcontractor and the building owner and reliance by the building owner on the subcontractor. Having been so decided, that case cannot, in my respectful opinion, be taken to be authority for the proposition that where those features are absent a defendant is liable in tort in respect of economic loss which is not consequent upon physical damage to the person or property of the plaintiff. Where those features are absent, I agree with O'Connor LJ that we remain bound by the decision of this court in *Spartan Steel and Alloys Ltd* v *Martin & Co (Contractors) Ltd*.

See also Chapter 5 for economic loss.

See Chapter 11 for Murphy v Brentwood District Council.

Although the claimant cannot recover for a quality defect in the goods, they can recover if the defect causes damage to 'other property'. This raises the problem of what is 'other property'.

Aswan Engineering Establishment Co v *Lupdine Ltd* [1987] 1 All ER 135

The claimants bought some waterproofing material from the first defendants and stored it in buckets supplied by the second defendants. The buckets were stacked awaiting shipment and burst, causing some of the material to be lost. The second defendants were unsuccessfully sued on the basis that they owed a duty to provide buckets that were suitable for the journey and would preserve the material. Damage was held to be unforeseeable. Was the material 'other property'? The material had been bought in the buckets and property in both passed simultaneously. However, Lloyd LJ was of the opinion that there was damage to 'other property' (without deciding the issue).

If this view was to be followed, then the narrow rule would be available in a wider range of circumstances. If a person buys a defective tyre for his car and the tyre bursts causing damage to the car, then the tyre manufacturer is liable for the damage to the car. What if the car was new and the tyre had been supplied with the car? Would the car be other property? On Lloyd LJ's view it would be.

Problems with the common law

The common law on defective products was subjected to a number of criticisms. Most of the claims under the narrow rule are for defects in the manufacturing process. Where the problem is with the design of the product, the classic negligence action has problems. By their nature design defects are liable to be more serious than manufacturing defects as they are more difficult to discover by examination and are likely to affect all end users of the product. The difficulty with proving a design defect is in breach of duty and causation. This problem is clearly shown in the difficulties in litigating against a drug manufacturer.

A.-G. v *Times Newspapers* [1973] QB 710

Per Lord Denning MR:

Nearly 12 years ago an overwhelming tragedy befell hundreds of families in this country. Mothers when pregnant had taken thalidomide as a sedative to help them rest. All believed it was safe. The manufacturers had proclaimed it to be so. The doctors had accepted their assurances. But, unknown to anyone, if a pregnant woman took it between the fourth and 12th weeks it would affect the limbs of the foetus in the womb. In consequence some 451 babies were born deformed. Some without arms or legs. Others with gross distortions.

The claimants in this litigation faced three major problems. At that time there was a question as to whether a duty of care was owed to a foetus. This has now been established by statute (Congenital Disabilities (Civil Liability) Act 1976). The second problem was whether Distillers had actually been negligent. This was a design defect in the drug not a flaw in the manufacturing process. The cases were eventually settled following intense media pressure on Distillers but it would have been extremely difficult for the children to prove that Distillers had been negligent in designing the drug. The third problem was causation. At this time there were fewer restrictions on what pregnant women took during pregnancy and to prove that the cause of the disabilities was thalidomide would have been extremely difficult.

The story of the thalidomide children led to calls for reform in the law and in particular for the introduction of strict liability on defective products.

As the manufacturer created the hazard in pursuit of profit and was best placed to insure against the risk it was reasonable to expect the manufacturer to accept liability. Imposing such liability would give the manufacturer greater incentive to take safety precautions. The counter argument to this is that it might dissuade a manufacturer from placing a product on the market which has social benefits but also has risks. This is particularly applicable in the case of drugs.

The then European Economic Community produced a Directive on product liability in 1985 (Directive 85/374/EEC) and member states were given three years to introduce national laws which complied with the Directive.

In 1987 the Consumer Protection Act was passed with the intention of bringing English law into line with the provisions of the Directive.

Consumer Protection Act 1987

Introduction

Objective 3

Liability for defective products is covered by Part I of the Act. Its purpose is to introduce a strict liability regime on producers of defective products. The intention is that the producer should insure the product against its potential for causing harm.

The basic principle of the Act is in s 2(1): 'Where any damage is caused wholly or partly by a defect in a product, every person to whom subsection (2) . . . applies shall be liable for the damage.'

This is liability without proof of fault and therefore imposes a form of strict liability on manufacturers for defective products. There are a number of defences given to manufacturers under the Act.

The Directive allowed a margin of discretion in introducing national laws but where problems arise over interpretation of the Act reference may be made to the Directive. There are differences between the Directive and the Act and it has been stated that it is simpler to go straight to the Directive. (*A* v *National Blood Authority* [2001] 3 All ER 289 at 297 per Burton J.)

Who can be sued?

Section 2(2) provides a list of those who can be sued under the Act.

Producers

A producer is defined by s 1(2) as:

(a) the manufacturer;

(b) the person who wins or abstracts products;

(c) the person who carries out an industrial or other process which adds an essential characteristic to a product which has not been won, abstracted or manufactured. An example of this would be the freezing of vegetables.

A problem arises with a product finished by one producer but defective because of parts supplied by another. The supplier of the finished product will normally be liable for the supply, provided the finished product is covered by the Act. Where the finished product is exempt from the Act, then the manufacturer is not liable where the defectiveness arises solely from the component part (s 1(3)). An important exception to this principle exists in the case of buildings. The builder is not liable in respect of supply of the building but is liable for defective components used to construct the building (s 46(3)).

Suppliers and importers

In order to make the claimant's task easier, the Act makes provision for them to sue own-branders, suppliers and importers in certain circumstances.

1 *Own-branders.* A person who puts their own name on a product, thereby holding himself out as a producer, will be treated as a producer. This would apply to supermarket chains that sell goods under their own name which are manufactured by someone else (s 2(2)(b)).

2 *Importers.* A person who, in the course of a business, imports a product into the European Union from outside, is deemed to be a producer (s 2(2)(c)).

3 *Suppliers.* If it is not possible to identify the producer or importer of a product, the Act provides for liability on the part of another supplier (s 2(3)). This is likely to be the person who supplies the consumer.

It is necessary that a person supplied a defective product for there to be liability and this supply must be in the course of a business. The supply does not need to be to the ultimate consumer.

For a supplier (as opposed to a manufacturer) to be liable, four requirements have to be satisfied:

1 the consumer must have asked the supplier to identify the producer (s 2(3)(a));

2 the request by the consumer must have occurred within a reasonable time of the occurrence of the damage (s 2(3)(b));

3 it must have become impracticable for the consumer to identify the actual producer (s 2(3)(b));

4 the supplier must have failed within a reasonable time of the request to comply with it or to identify the person who supplied him with the product (s 2(3)(c)).

> ### Example
>
> James purchases a tin of baked beans from Megastores. The beans contain an impurity which causes James to become violently ill. The beans were sold as Megabeans but were manufactured for Megastores by Beaneasy. Megastores will be liable under the Act to James as suppliers/own-branders unless they comply with the four conditions. Compliance with the conditions means that Megastores are not liable, even if Beaneasy is insolvent and James has no effective remedy against Beaneasy.

Products

Products are defined in s 1(2): 'any goods or electricity and . . . includes a product which is comprised in another product, whether by virtue of being a component part or raw material or otherwise.'

Further definition is provided by s 45(1) to include substances, growing crops, things comprised in land by virtue of being attached to it, ships, aircraft and vehicles.

Certain things are specifically exempted:

1 A building supplied by way of a creation or disposal of an interest in land is exempt (s 46(4)).

2 Nuclear power is also exempt (s 6(8)).

3 Agricultural produce which had not undergone an industrial process was exempt (s 2(4)). This covered processes such as packaging, canning and possibly freezing. The Act required that the process change the essential characteristics of the product. Whether freezing does so is questionable. Following food scares involving salmonella and BSE, the agricultural exception has now been abolished (EC Directive 99/34/EC) with regard to products put into the market after 4 December 2000 and from that date liability will apply to primary agricultural produce. Where a process has been undertaken, then the producer is liable for pre-existing defects in the product, as well as those they introduce themselves.

It was uncertain whether human blood and organs were products but it has now been held that human blood is a product within the Act. (*A* v *National Blood Authority* [2001] 3 All ER 289.)

Defectiveness

Section 3(1) provides: 'there is a defect in a product . . . if the safety of the product is not such as persons generally are entitled to expect.'

In considering what is meant by 'safety', s 3(2) provides that all the circumstances shall be taken into account including:

(a) the manner in which, and purposes for which, the product has been marketed, its get-up, the use of any mark in relation to the product and any instructions for, or warnings with respect to, doing or refraining from doing anything in relation to the product;

(b) what might reasonably be expected to be done with or in relation to the product; and

(c) the time when the product was supplied by its producer to another.

The gist of the section is that the product must be safe but the Act has no application if it is useless. Consumers may have a natural expectation that a condom will not fail but this is not something that persons are generally entitled to expect. (*Richardson* v *LRC Products Ltd* [2000] Lloyd's Rep Med 280.) This case could be viewed as a 'wrongful birth' case rather than a product liability case. At the time it was decided there was no action for the costs of bringing up an unwanted child.

The fault-based reasoning in *Richardson* was criticised in *Abouzaid* v *Mothercare (UK) Ltd* [2000] EWCA Civ 348. A 12-year-old child was injured trying to fasten a sleeping bag to the back of a pushchair. The buckle sprang back injuring his eye and causing a significant loss of vision. The court considered the severe consequences of the injury and it was irrelevant whether this defect should reasonably have come to the attention of the manufacturer. The ease with which the manufacturer could have avoided the risk of injury was taken into account. The test was that the product must be judged against the expectations of people generally in all the circumstances of the case. Did the product have a level of safety which the general public would have of such a product at the time the injury occurred. The public would not expect injury to be caused by such a product and therefore the product was defective. The court found that the defendants would not have been liable in negligence. (See also *A* v *National Blood Authority* below.)

Pollard v Tesco Stores Ltd [2006] EWCA Civ 393

When the claimant was 13 months old, he ingested dishwasher powder from a plastic bottle and in consequence became seriously ill. Thereafter, he sought damages for personal injury from the first defendant, from whom the bottle of dishwasher powder had been bought, and the second defendant, who had manufactured the bottle. The factual case against those defendants was that the neck of the bottle and the cap, which had a 'child resistant closure' (CRC), had been defective, so that the cap had been easier to detach than it should have been; and that the claimant had managed to detach it and so ingest some of the contents. The judge accepted evidence that the bottle had less than the proper minimum torque required for a British Standard certificate, but that although the bottle was easier to open (without squeezing) than it should have been, it still had some 'child resistance' effect. The judge also accepted the mother's evidence that she had closed the bottle of dishwasher powder properly and placed it on a worktop in the kitchen out of the claimant's reach. He concluded that what had most probably happened was that the claimant had reached the bottle by standing on a pile of washing and knocked it to the floor. The judge then turned to the question how, or whether, the claimant could actually have opened the bottle, and concluded that there was bound to have been some squeezing, pulling, twisting and pushing, and that the defective CRC was causative of the claimant obtaining access to the bottle's contents. The judge exonerated the third defendant of any negligence. The judge therefore held the first and second defendants liable of the basis, *inter alia*, of breach of statutory duty, contrary to s 3(1) of the Consumer Protection Act 1987. The first and second defendants appealed against that decision.

Held: the appeal would be allowed. In the circumstances, persons were generally entitled to expect that the bottle would be more difficult to open than if it had an ordinary screwtop. The bottle in the instant case had been more difficult to open than an ordinary screwtop, though not as difficult as it would have been if the British Standard torque measure had been complied with. That was, however, enough to ensure that there had been no breach of the 1987 Act.

Laws LJ:

[Counsel] at first submitted that the public were entitled to expect that the product in question would function in accordance with whatever safety standard might in the particular case be imposed by any relevant public authority. I apprehend that he appreciated this was a step too far, since there is no trace of any reference to the British Standard on the bottle, packaging or get up of this product . . . [U]ltimately his argument was that under the statute the public are entitled to expect that the product will function to the full extent of the design standard to which it was manufactured.

If [counsel] is right, it means that every producer of a product whose use causes injury effectively warrants to the general public that the product fulfils its design standards. Now, the producer may have no contract with any member of the public, as here, the appellants did not. Members of the public are unlikely to have the faintest idea to what safety standard the product they are buying has been designed, if it has been designed to any. In my judgment [counsel's] arguments in truth demand a radical rewriting of the statute. They are an attempt to confer on purchasers and users of everyday products a right to sue the product's producers as if there were a contractual warranty as to the safety standard to which the product had been designed. It is quite impossible to get such a result out of the terms of the 1987 Act.

What, on the facts here, were 'persons generally entitled to expect' of the safety features of this cap and bottle? In my judgment they were entitled to expect that the bottle would be more difficult to open than if it had an ordinary screwtop. Anything more specific, as a test of public expectation, runs into the difficulties which I have just described. Here, the bottle was more difficult to open than an ordinary screwtop, though not as difficult as it would have been if the British Standard torque measure had been complied with. There was, in my judgment, no breach of the 1987 Act.

Marketing and get-up, etc.

The court will have to consider a number of factors. What was the market that the product was aimed at and what sort of advertising was used? If the product is a child's toy then the target market will clearly be important. The instructions supplied with the product will need to be taken into account.

A more controversial point is the court taking into account the purposes for which the product has been marketed. Does this enable the court to take into account the comparative social utility of the product and apply a cost–benefit analysis? In the case of drugs, would the court be able to say that the risk was worthwhile given the benefits that the drug would bring?

It is clear from the section that the producer can negative their liability by providing a suitable warning of any danger, and the warning enables the consumer to avoid the danger.

Reasonable expectations as to use

Where the defect arises from a production defect which renders the product unsafe, then liability will attach under the Act.

If the defect is in design then greater difficulties are created. The court may have to balance the risk against the benefits in deciding whether the decision to market the product was justified.

The conduct of the consumer may also be relevant where they have put the product to a use for which it was not intended. A producer of microwave ovens would not be liable where the consumer used the oven to dry a poodle and the dog died. The question of warnings may be relevant here. A failure to warn that a product is not suitable for a particular purpose may give rise to liability: for example, that fireworks are not suitable for indoor use. If the use of the product is clearly out of line with reasonable expectations (for example, the poodle) then failure to give a warning will not be fatal.

Time of supply

Safety is to be judged in terms of the time when the product was supplied. Developments in safety after that time will not make the producer liable if their product has not conformed to them. If furniture was supplied by a producer in 2014 with a certain type of filling and in 2016 a series of fires involving that filling gave rise to new safety features, the producer would be judged by safety standards in 2014 not 2016. This, of course, is subject to the question of whether the producer should have recalled the furniture if the risk was great, or issued warnings to retailers to pass on to consumers.

Cost of precautions

Can a producer argue that the cost of taking precautions should be weighed against the risk of injury to the consumer? This is probably the crucial point in the Act and the Act is silent on the issue. If the answer to the question is yes, then taken to its logical conclusion there would be no difference between liability under the Act and negligence. For example, a producer could argue that incorporation of the relevant safety factor would make the product so expensive that no one would want to buy it.

It is therefore necessary for courts to interpret the Act as meaning that any private costs to the producer of making the product safe for the purposes for which it might reasonably be used by the consumer are not to be set off against consumer safety. On the other hand, a court can set off consumer safety for some against a greater public benefit for others.

A drug company is not allowed to argue that to cure a defect in one dose of drugs in 10,000 would raise the costs of production. It can argue that even if one person in 10,000 will be adversely affected by the drug, the benefit to the rest outweighs the dangers to the one.

It can be seen that there are clear parallels with negligence and that most of the factors above could come into the equation as to whether or not there was common law negligence. So is there any difference between defectiveness and negligence?

A v National Blood Authority [2001] 3 All ER 289

Blood taken from infected donors resulted in the claimants being infected with the Hepatitis C virus. The risk of Hepatitis C was known, but was impossible to avoid, as either the virus had not been discovered or there was no test for the virus in blood products. Although the claimants accepted that liability was strict, they argued that the fact that it was impossible to detect should be taken into account when determining whether it was defective. As blood was an inherently risky product, the infected blood should not be treated as a non-standard product which fell below the standards of safety to be expected from a standard product. It was held that the infected blood was defective under the Product Liability Directive, Article 6. This Article states that a product is defective if it does not provide the level of safety which a person is entitled to expect, irrespective of whether that lack of safety could have been avoided by the manufacturer. The consumer expectation was that the blood used in transfusions would be 100 per cent safe and the consumer was entitled to that expectation. The argument on reasonable precautions was rejected. Whether the defendants could have avoided the damage to the claimants was not one of the factors to be taken into account in Article 6. Neither were the costs or difficulty of taking precautions or the social utility of the product.

The gist of this decision is that there is a difference between liability under the Act and negligence and that without the exclusion of matters such as cost and social utility from the defectiveness formula the purpose of the Directive would be lost and the Act would be toothless. The judge also cast doubt on the decision in **Richardson v LRC Products**.

In reaching his decision on the meaning of defect he looked at the Directive rather than the provisions of the Act. The court had to look at:

1 What harmful characteristic in the product caused the injury?

2 Was the product standard or non-standard?

3 What are the consumer's legitimate expectations as to the product?

A consumer does not have the right to expect that a condom will not burst but does have the right to expect that blood used in transfusions will not be contaminated. Public knowledge of the risk and whether it is socially acceptable would appear to be factors.

Causation

The claimant must prove that the producer has put the product into circulation, that the product was defective and that the defect has caused damage within the meaning of the Act.

Actions under the Act differ from those at common law in that the consumer does not have to prove fault, but causation still needs to be established and the burden of proof is on the consumer.

See also Chapter 9 for causation.

The defect need not be the sole cause of the damage. It is sufficient that it was partly responsible for the damage. Where the damage results partly from a defect in the finished product and partly from a defective component, this will be sufficient to make the producer liable. In some cases it may be the consumer's conduct that is regarded as the sole cause of the damage: for example, the poodle in the microwave oven.

Damage

Losses which can be claimed for under the Act are death, personal injuries and any loss of or damage to property (s 5(1)).

Certain limitations are placed on property damage:

1 no award may be made where the amount is less than £275;

2 the property must have been intended for private use, occupation or consumption (there is no liability under the Act for damage to business property); and

3 the claim may not include damages for damage to the defective product itself.

Defences

The defences are contained in s 4.

1 If the product complies with a mandatory European or statutory obligation, this is a defence if the defect was an inevitable result of compliance (s 4(1)(a)).

2 The defendants did not at any time supply the product to another. This could apply if the product has been stolen and marketed before it was fully tested (s 4(1)(b)).

3 Supply by the defendants was not in the course of their business and either: (a) s 2(2) does not apply (they are only suppliers); or (b) they are within s 2(2) but are not acting at the time with a view to profit (s 4(1)(c)).

4 If the producer can prove that the defect came about after the time of supply by them, this will provide a defence (s 4(1)(d)). To establish this defence, the producer must prove that the defect was not present at the time of supply by them.

5 Where the defendant can show that 'the state of scientific and technical knowledge at the relevant time was not such that a producer of products of the same description as the product in question might be expected to have discovered the defect if it had existed in his products while they were under his control', this is a defence (s 4(1)(e)).

Member states were allowed a discretion as to whether to include a state of the art defence and its inclusion is controversial, as states which do have the defence could become testing grounds for new products.

The inclusion of the defence was justified on the grounds that to omit it would stifle innovation, increase insurance costs and place UK businesses at a competitive disadvantage with countries which did not have the defence. The United States, however, does not have such a defence and this does not appear to have stifled innovation. The decision to include the defence means that business rather than consumer protection interests are advanced.

Some commentators have argued that even without the defence similar considerations would have to be taken into account in a defective products regime which is based on defectiveness. However, the absence of the defence might have improved testing of new products.

The wording of the defence has also attracted criticism as being too wide and diverging from the wording of Article 7(e) of the Directive. This states that it is a defence if the defendant proves 'that the state of scientific and technical knowledge at the time when he put the product into circulation was not such as to enable the existence of the defect to be discovered'.

The difference between this and the Act is the standard of knowledge which will suffice in order for the defence to succeed. With the Act it is the standard of knowledge within that industry which is arguably an industry-set standard. With the Directive it is the standard of knowledge inside and outside the industry and whether it was sufficient to enable the defect to be discovered.

The key point is clearly what is meant by scientific and technical knowledge. At what point must an industry take note of evidence? When it is a hypothesis? When there is evidence, however disputed this evidence is? Or when there is conclusive proof?

Commission of the European Communities v UK [1997] All ER (EC) 481

The discrepancy was referred to the European Commission, which took the issue to the European Court and the court concluded that there was no conflict between s 4(1)(e) and Article 7(e) of the Directive. In the court's opinion, what was necessary was that the relevant knowledge must have been accessible at the time the product was put into circulation. This leaves the question of how accessible? If it is a standard of reasonable accessibility this would amount to a negligence standard.

In the blood transfusion case (*A v National Blood Authority* [2001] 3 All ER 289) it was held that the defence in Article 7(e) of the Directive (s 4(1)(e) is based on this Article) does not apply where the existence of a generic defect was known or should have been known in the light of accessible information. Once the existence of the defect was known, there was a risk of that defect materialising in any particular product and it was immaterial that the known risk was unavoidable. A risk could be 'unknown' where it was only known to scientists 'in Manchuria'. If it was only known to persons in an inaccessible laboratory it would continue to be a development risk.

Most discussion on the defence has centred on the producer's knowledge that the defect might exist ('design' defect). However, it is possible that the defence might apply to a 'construction' defect which is known to occur but cannot be eliminated by a quality control system. This was not the view taken in *Richardson v LRC Products Ltd* [2000] Lloyd's Rep Med 280, where it was stated that the defence did not apply in the case of a 'defect of a known character merely because there is no test which is able to reveal its existence in every case'.

The defence was raised in *Abouzaid v Mothercare*, where it was argued that, as the defendants were unaware of the potential problems with the buckle and there was no record of any comparable accident, the state of scientific and technical knowledge did not indicate a problem. The Court of Appeal stated that the defence was present to deal with technical advances, not to deal with problems that no one had thought about.

It would appear that the effect of the section will be to apply a fault-based regime to new products. The producer will only be liable where they knew or ought reasonably to have known of the defect. The burden of proof will, however, rest on the defendant.

Example

Dracula Labs have been developing a new 'blood substitute' for use by hospitals and blood transfusion services. The product has been subjected to testing on animals but not on humans. The tests show no adverse reaction to the product but it has a 0.1 per cent impurity introduced in the manufacturing process, which it is impossible to eliminate. There is a very profitable market for the product and a competitor is thought to be close to marketing a rival product when a scientific journal publishes a report which purports to show that blood substitutes of the type proposed by Dracula Labs could have fatal effects on people of certain blood groups. If Dracula Labs went ahead and marketed the product, would it be defective under the Act and/or would they have a defence under s 4 in the event of: (a) damage caused as a result of an impurity introduced in the manufacturing process; (b) damage caused as a result of the 'design' of the product?

6 Contributory negligence. The Law Reform (Contributory Negligence) Act 1945 applies (s 6(4)). The court therefore has the power to apportion damages where the claimant has been partly to blame for the harm suffered.

Limitation

See Chapter 26 for limitation.

The limitation period for actions under the Act runs for three years from the date on which the damage was caused by the defective product, or the date on which the damage could have reasonably been discovered. (Limitation Act 1980 s 11A(4).)

There is a long-stop provision which prevents any action against the producer more than ten years from the date on which the product was first put into circulation (s 11A(3)).

Compensation culture

See Chapter 1 for 'compensation culture'.

The area of consumer protection would appear to be a likely one for any signs of 'compensation culture.'

There have been very few cases decided under the Consumer Protection Act. No one knows the reasons for this. It could be that the high costs of litigation deter people; that the idea of strict liability may encourage more defendants to settle out of court; that products have actually become safer as a result of the legislation; or simply that there is very little benefit in bringing an action under the Act rather than in negligence.

A brief comparison between an English case and a US case may help in the compensation culture debate. In **Bogle v McDonald's Restaurants Ltd** [2002] EWHC 490, customers in the defendant's restaurant were scalded by hot coffee. The court dismissed the claim that the product was defective as it was too hot and the lids came off too easily. Had there been negligence in the serving of the coffee then this would have established a claim.

In contrast in **Liebeck v McDonald's Restaurants** (1994), a US court awarded a claimant $3 million (the jury award) where she was burned by hot coffee bought at a drive-through window.

This was later reduced to $640,000 by the trial judge.

Mrs Liebeck suffered very serious burns and was found 20 per cent contributorily negligent. One of the reasons why the jury award was so high was that the defendants had initially offered only $800 in compensation and had refused offers from the claimant to settle.

? Question

Pyro buys from Dynamight Ltd a box of fireworks manufactured by Sparky Ltd. Pyro asks whether any of the fireworks can be used indoors. Harriet, the shop assistant, says 'I don't suppose the sparklers would cause any harm inside'.

On Bonfire Night, Pyro puts on a firework display. He reads the instructions on a firework called a roman candle. These state, incorrectly, that the firework can be held in the hand. As a result of this Pyro and his daughter Nancy, who is standing beside him, are both badly injured.

At the same time Harry, Pyro's son, takes a lighted sparkler into the house. A spark from this firework starts a fire in Pyro's kitchen which causes considerable damage.

Dynamight Ltd has now gone into liquidation.

Advise Pyro and Nancy.

Suggested approach

The primary remedy of the purchaser of a defective product lies in contract against the retailer. Pyro has a contract with Dynamight Ltd and terms of satisfactory quality and fitness for the purpose would be implied into the contract under the Sale of Goods Act 1979 (as amended by the Sale and Supply of Goods Act 1994). However, any contract action against Dynamight would be pointless as the judgment could probably not be enforced.

Does Pyro have an action against Sparky Ltd? There are two possibilities: an action under the Consumer Protection Act 1987 or under the 'narrow rule' in *Donoghue* v *Stevenson* in negligence.

The purpose of the Consumer Protection Act 1987 was to introduce a strict liability regime on producers of defective products. The basic principle of the Act is in s 2(2). Where any damage is caused wholly or partly by a defect in a product, any person to whom subs (2) applies shall be liable.

The action is brought against producers of defective products. A producer is defined by s 2(2) as the manufacturer. Sparky Ltd are the manufacturers of the product and therefore the defendants.

The producer will be liable for any defect in the product which causes damage. A defect is defined by s 3(1). There is a defect if the safety of the product is not such as persons generally are entitled to expect. Section 3(2) states that all the circumstances are to be taken into account. These include the purposes for which the product has been manufactured and any instructions or warnings with respect to doing or refraining from doing anything in relation to the product. What might reasonably be expected to be done with the product?

Pyro has suffered two items of damage. As regards his personal injuries there is no warning that the firework cannot be held in the hand. This could amount to a defect. If so, Pyro has an action under the Act as personal injuries are covered by the Act (s 5(1)) and none of the defences would appear to be relevant, unless Pyro is held to be contributorily negligent, when his damages would be reduced.

The damage to the kitchen is more difficult. Again, the case would turn on whether the sparklers were defective. Should a warning have been included that they were not suitable for indoor use? Probably it should have been, as this is a use which the producer should expect the product to be put to. A failure to give the warning may amount to a defect. Provided Pyro's loss exceeds £275, Pyro would have a claim.

If Pyro has a claim under the Act for his personal injuries, then Nancy will also be successful. The Act does not define consumer, but Nancy definitely falls into this category.

Both Pyro and Nancy may have a claim in negligence for their injuries under the narrow rule in *Donoghue* v *Stevenson*. Pyro may also have a claim for his property damage. Sparky is a manufacturer within the rule and Pyro and Nancy are consumers. A consumer is anyone that the manufacturer should foresee would be affected by the product. The fireworks are products within the rule. The difference between an action under the Act and a negligence action is that in the latter the claimant must show that the defendant was negligent, i.e. that they failed to take reasonable care in the preparation and putting up of the product. This covers instructions for use and warnings. The defendant may escape liability if there is an alternative cause for the defect, or the damage could have been avoided by intermediate examination. Would the retailer's failure to warn of the dangers amount to reasonable examination?

Summary

This chapter deals with liability for defective products.

- After a product is manufactured and put into circulation, liability is primarily governed by the chain of contracts.

- The 'narrow rule' in *Donoghue* v *Stevenson* lays down the circumstances where a person who suffers damage as a result of the defect may sue in negligence.

- The duty of care is owed by manufacturers to the ultimate consumer of the product. The claimant must prove that the manufacturer failed to take reasonable care in the preparation or putting up of the product. The claimant does not have to identify the exact person responsible for the defect. Causation works on the basis that there was no alternative cause and no possibility of intermediate examination.

- The claimant can recover for personal injuries or property damage but not for pure economic loss.

- The Consumer Protection Act 1987 has the purpose of introducing a strict liability regime for defective products because of the problem in establishing negligence.

- The claimant can sue the manufacturer, supplier or importer of the product (s 2).

- The product must be defective (s 3(1)). The gist of this is that the product must be safe. The court will also look at the marketing and get-up of the product; what uses the product could reasonably be put to; the time when the product was supplied; and the cost of precautions.

- Damages can be claimed for personal injuries and loss or damage to property.

- There are a number of defences (s 4), of which the most important is developmental knowledge (s 4(1)(e)).

Further reading

Guide to the Consumer Protection Act 1987 (2001), HMSO.

Hodges, C. (1998), 'Development Risks: Unanswered Questions' 61 MLR 560.

Hodges, C. (2001), '*A v National Blood Authority*' 117 LQR 528.

Howells, G. and Mildred, M. (2005), '*A v National Blood Authority*' 65 MLR 95.

Law Commission Report No 82, Cmnd 6831 (1977).

Newdick, C. (1988), 'The Development Risks Defence of the Consumer Protection Act 1987' 47 CLJ 455.

Report of the Royal Commission on Civil Liability and Compensation for Personal Injury (The Pearson Report) Cmnd 7054 (1978) Vol. 1, Ch 22.

13

Breach of statutory duty

Objectives

After reading this chapter you will:

1. Understand the concept of a statutory duty.
2. Have a critical knowledge of when a breach of statutory duty gives rise to an action for damages at common law.
3. Appreciate the variety of standards of care that can be imposed by statute and understand the legal rules which govern an action for breach of statutory duty.
4. Appreciate the distinction between an action for common law negligence and an action for breach of statutory duty.

Introduction

Objective 1

For standard of care in negligence, see Chapter 8.

Where a statute imposes a duty on a person, breach of that duty may give rise to an action for damages by a person injured as a result. This is known as the tort of breach of statutory duty.

The tort is sometimes referred to as statutory negligence, but it is preferable to treat the action as separate from negligence, as the standard of care owed may differ.

The action has played a strong part in industrial safety, but attempts to introduce it into other areas have been less successful.

Example

Alan employs Brian as a machine operator. Statutory regulations applying to the industry state that all machines must be fitted with a guard. The guard on Alan's machine was removed for cleaning and inadvertently not replaced before the machine was used. Brian put his hand into the machine and lost a finger.

Brian would have an action for breach of statutory duty against Alan. He could also sue Alan for negligence. The difference in the actions would be that in the former the absence of the guard establishes breach of duty, whereas in negligence Brian would have to prove that Alan had failed to exercise reasonable care.

It is normal for actions in such cases to be pleaded in the alternative. The action for breach of statutory duty is advantageous to the claimant when the statutory duty is strict or absolute. However, statutory duties have a limited sphere of operation. If a piece of metal had flown out of the machine and blinded Brian, the court could hold that the purpose of the statute was to keep the employee out, not the machine in. The action would then fail. In a negligence action, the damage has to be a foreseeable risk. The negligence action could therefore succeed where the statutory action failed.

In an action for breach of statutory duty the claimant must prove the following points:

1 that the statutory duty in question gives rise to an action for damages;

2 that the duty was owed to the claimant;

3 that the duty was broken; and

4 that the damage was caused by the breach of duty.

The defendant can raise the defences of *volenti non fit injuria* or contributory negligence to the action.

Does the statute give rise to an action for damages?

Introduction

Objective 2

Not all breaches of statutory duty will give rise to an action for damages by a person injured as a result. The court must first determine whether the particular statute gave rise to the right to sue for damages.

This is said to depend on the intention of Parliament. The intention is to be discovered by interpretation of the statute. Sometimes the statute will give guidance on this question. The wording, 'nothing in the Act shall be construed as conferring a right of action in any civil proceedings', is conclusive that no action exists.

Alternatively, the statute may create an action by specific wording such as the Financial Services and Markets Act 2000 s 150; such an action may be either as a substitute for a common law action (Nuclear Installations Act 1965), or in addition (Mineral Workings (Offshore Installations) Act 1971 s 11).

In many cases the statute will be silent on the question and the search for Parliamentary intention will be illusory as Parliament never considered the question.

The whole area of health and safety at work was transformed as a result of the EC Framework Directive on Health and Safety (Council Directive 89/391/EEC). This was implemented through the Management of Health and Safety at Work Regulations 1999. The regulations establish a framework of procedures and establish general principles for employers and employees.

Tests

The leading modern statement on the test used was given by Lord Diplock.

Lonrho Ltd v Shell Petroleum Co (No 2) [1982] AC 173

Lord Diplock laid down a presumptions approach to the question:

... one starts with the presumption ... that 'where an Act creates an obligation, and enforces the performance in a specified manner ... that performance cannot be enforced in any other manner' ...

> ... there are two classes of exception to this general rule.
>
> The first is where upon the true construction of the Act it is apparent that the obligation or prohibition was imposed for the benefit or protection of a particular class of individuals, as in the case of the Factories Acts and similar legislation ...
>
> The second exception is where the statute creates a public right ... and a particular member of the public suffers ... 'particular, direct and substantial' damage 'other and different from that which was common to all the rest of the public'.

His Lordship added that where the presumptions created a result which was contrary to the intention of Parliament then the presumptions had to give way.

Groves v Lord Wimborne [1898] 2 QB 402

> The defendants were subject to a fine of £100 for breach of statutory duty in failing to fence factory machinery. Part of the fine was payable to the claimant at the discretion of the Secretary of State. The claimant was held to have an action for breach of statutory duty when he was injured as the result of no fencing.
>
> Smith LJ:
>
> > The Act ... is not in the nature of a private legislative bargain between employers and workmen ... but is a public Act passed in favour of the workers in factories and workshops to compel their employers to do certain things for their protection and benefit.

The decision is justified on the grounds that there was no guarantee that the claimant would receive any of the fine and that Parliament could not have intended a workman to be deprived of the chance to seek compensation for his injuries. In terms of presumptions, the Act did enforce performance in a specified manner (a fine) but this gives way to the first exception, that the obligation was imposed for the benefit of a class of people, factory employees.

Atkinson v Newcastle Waterworks Co (1877) 2 ExD 441

> The defendants supplied water to Newcastle. They were required by statute to keep their pipes at a certain pressure level. Failure to do this could result in a £10 fine. The claimant's premises caught fire and, as there was insufficient pressure in the pipes, the premises were burned down. In an action for breach of statutory duty it was held that the penalty imposed by the statute was an exclusive one. No action for damages lay. The fact that no part of the fine was payable to an individual damaged was regarded as evidence that Parliament did not intend the statute to give rise to an action.

This case could be regarded as an example of the first presumption applying and neither of the exceptions being relevant. The manner of enforcement was laid down by the statute. Alternatively, it could be regarded as an attempt by the courts to avoid the floodgates problem in the area of utilities by shifting the burden onto householders through private insurance.

Wentworth v Wiltshire County Council [1993] 2 WLR 175

> Breach of the Highways (Miscellaneous Provisions) Act 1961 s 1 (failure to repair the highway) did not give an action for pure economic loss as the Highways Act 1959 s 59 provided a mechanism for enforcement of the highway authority's obligation.

The courts have had difficulty with enforcement mechanisms. Two Court of Appeal cases (*Todd* v *Adam* [2002] 2 All ER (Comm) 97 (*T*) and *Ziemniak* v *ETPM Deep Sea Ltd* [2003] 2 All ER (Comm) 283 (*Z*)) dealt with breaches of safety rules under the Merchant Shipping Act 1995. In *T* the court found that breaches of the rules which led to the total loss of life of a fishing boat crew did not give rise to a civil action because of the criminal sanctions and penalties applied. In *Z* a breach of the rules in a different part of the Act did provide a civil remedy for a claimant seriously injured by a lifeboat test in a harbour. The distinction was that in *Z* the claim was treated as one of safety in the workplace.

It is rare to find a statute that provides no mechanism for its enforcement and it is arguable that where this occurs there should be no action, as it will probably be to provide a discretionary framework for administrative authorities.

In *Cocks* v *Thanet District Council* [1983] 2 AC 286 it was held that challenges to administrative decisions made by local authorities must be made by application for judicial review, rather than by actions for breach of statutory duty.

This is supported by *O'Rourke* v *Camden London Borough Council* [1997] 3 WLR 86, where the House of Lords held that the duty of a housing authority to provide temporary accommodation under the Housing Act 1985 did not confer any additional rights in private law to sue for damages. The Act was enforceable solely by way of judicial review.

The recognisable class of claimants test has proved to be difficult to apply in practice.

Phillips v *Britannia Hygienic Laundry Co Ltd* [1923] 2 KB 832

The defendant's vehicle was in breach of the Construction and Use Regulations for motor vehicles. The vehicle was involved in an accident in which the claimant's van was damaged. The claimant sued for breach of statutory duty. The enforcement method for the regulations was a criminal penalty. It was held that the regulations did not give rise to an action for damages. The public using the highway was held not to be a class. It was the public itself and not a class of the public.

A suggested reason for this decision is that to grant an action would have subverted the common law negligence action which lay in these circumstances. An action for breach of statutory duty would have given a strict liability action in many cases of road traffic accidents. This would have subverted the fault-based negligence action.

If the action would reinforce the common law action it may be allowed.

Monk v *Warbey* [1935] 1 KB 75

The defendant gave permission to an uninsured driver to use his vehicle. This was in breach of the Road Traffic Act 1930. The driver's negligence caused an accident in which the claimant was injured. It was not worth the claimant suing the driver as he was uninsured and had no money. The court allowed an action for breach of statutory duty against the defendant. In this case the action did not subvert the common law but supplemented it.

A case on these facts would now be covered by the Motor Insurance Bureau Scheme, whereby motor insurers provide a fund to meet claims against uninsured drivers.

The unpredictable nature of decisions in this area is illustrated by the next case which, on the face of it, is similar to *Monk* v *Warbey*, which was distinguished on the grounds of 'technical reasons'.

Richardson v *Pitt-Stanley* [1995] ICR 303

The claimant was unable to recover damages against his former employer as the company which employed him had gone into liquidation, and in breach of the Employer's Liability (Compulsory Insurance) Act 1969 had not taken out insurance against its liability to employees. The claimant brought an action for breach of statutory duty against the directors and secretary of the former company on the basis that it was their omission which had led him to be unable to recover for his personal injuries.

The Court of Appeal held that the statute did not create any civil liability in addition to its criminal sanctions, despite the fact that a decision in favour of the claimant would have supplemented the underlying policy of the Act. They gave the following reasons:

1   as the Act did not indicate that the company itself could be civilly liable, it would be strange if its officers could be;
2   the claim was for economic loss;
3   there was a severe criminal penalty for breach of the Act; and
4   the Act was not purely for the protection of employees, but also for small employers who might be bankrupted unless insured. In this case why would Parliament wish to protect employers from financial ruin but not employees?

Benefit of a class

This was a controversial issue before the *Lonrho* case. Atkin LJ criticised the idea in *Phillips* v *Britannia*: 'it would be strange if a less important duty which is owed to a section of the public may be enforced by an action, while a more important duty which is owed to the public at large cannot be so enforced.'

The *Lonrho* case establishes this as an exception but leaves the court with the problem of determining what is meant by an ascertainable class.

In industrial safety cases there is a well-established jurisprudence and unless the statute specifically excludes liability the court will hold that an industrial safety statute gives rise to an action. Employees are an ascertainable class.

In other areas, the test has been less successful. The Court of Appeal held that residential occupiers were not a class for the purpose of the offence of harassment created by the Rent Act 1956. (*McCall* v *Abelesz* [1976] QB 585.) The House of Lords held that a provision in the Betting and Lotteries Act 1934, that required track owners to provide available space for bookmakers on the track, was passed for the benefit of the race-going public rather than bookmakers. (*Cutler* v *Wandsworth Stadium* [1949] AC 398.)

In *R* v *Deputy Governor of Parkhurst Prison ex p Hague* [1992] 1 AC 58, the House of Lords held that a breach of the Prison Rules 1964 did not give a prisoner any private law claim to damages. The Rules had been passed to deal with the administration of prisons and the management of prisoners.

In a complex series of actions reported as *X* v *Bedfordshire County Council* [1995] 3 All ER 353, the House of Lords had to rule on two groups of cases. The first group (the 'child abuse' cases) involved actions against local authorities for decisions made by psychiatrists and social workers as to whether to take a child into care or not. In some cases the child had been taken into care where there was no need and in others children at risk had not been taken into care. The second group (the 'education cases') involved decisions by local authorities as to whether a child had learning disabilities and therefore needed special provision. In some cases this had not been diagnosed and the claim was that it should have been and in other cases the claim was that the child had been diagnosed as having learning difficulties when they did not.

Actions were brought for breach of statutory duty and common law negligence against the defendant local authorities.

The House decided that:

1 breach of the statutory duty itself was not enough to give rise to a private law cause of action;

2 the mere assertion of the careless exercise of a statutory power or duty was not sufficient in itself to give rise to a private law cause of action. The claimant has to show that the circumstances were such as to raise a duty of care at common law; and

3 the decision as to whether or not to exercise a statutory discretion had to be distinguished from the manner in which the statutory duty was implemented in practice.

Nothing an authority did within the ambit of the discretion could be actionable at common law and the taking of policy decisions was non-justiciable. If the claim was justiciable – i.e. if the decision was so unreasonable that it fell outside the ambit of the discretion – then any action would turn on the ordinary principles of negligence.

This complex litigation illustrates the difficulties of modern social legislation which frequently involves a number of agencies seeking a solution to a particular problem, and the House was probably correct in rejecting the action for breach of statutory duty as a remedy for failure. The decision not to impose liability for negligence was questionable, however, as the reluctance to impose a duty ignored the valuable and deterrent function of negligence and the fact that imposition of a duty does not equate with liability.

This point was probably answered when the case reached the European Court of Human Rights. (*Z* v *UK* [2001] 2 FLR 612.) The court found that there was a breach of Article 3 of the Convention because of the failure of the local authority to intervene where there was serious long-term neglect and abuse of children. There was also a breach of Article 13 as there were no means to determine the applicants' allegations that they had been subjected to degrading and inhumane treatment. This issue has now been addressed by the Human Rights Act 1998, which allows Convention rights to be dealt with in domestic courts.

See Chapters 3 and 7 for 'child abuse' cases.

The House of Lords has now held that a common law duty of care may be owed to a child in the 'child abuse' cases. See Chapter 7 for *D* v *East Berkshire Community Health NHS Trust* [2005] 2 All ER 443.

This does not change the position with regard to the action for breach of statutory duty as is shown by the following case.

Phelps v *Hillingdon Borough Council* [2000] 4 All ER 504

This case involved breaches by educational psychiatrists, employed by local authorities, which led to children failing to be diagnosed as having learning difficulties.

The children had not been treated in accordance with the statutory intent of the 1944 and 1981 Education Acts but this did not lead to the conclusion that Parliament had intended there to be a remedy in damages for breach of statutory duty.

Lord Slynn:

These statutory duties laid on local education authorities are of the greatest importance; the authorities must provide the facilities which Parliament intended should be available for children with learning difficulties. A failure to fulfil the duties by an authority either generally or in a particular case can have a serious effect on a child's education, his well-being and his future life.

It is clear from the legislative provisions to which I have referred that Parliament intended that various stages of the process were to be monitored by an appeals procedure. Moreover, there can be no doubt that some of the acts of the authority may be examined by way of judicial review, even if in other areas the extent of the discretion conferred on the authority with its particular expertise is likely to lead to a court refusing to interfere even by way of judicial review (see e.g. *A v Liverpool City Council* [1981] 2 All ER 385 at 388–389, [1982] AC 363 at 373 per Lord Wilberforce).

There is, however, no express indication that a failure to carry out these duties, even in respect of a particular individual, should lead to an award of monetary compensation if damage can be shown. That still leaves the question whether, having regard to the purpose of the legislation, Parliament is to be taken to have intended that there should be a right to damages.

It is clear that the loss suffered by a child who has not been treated in accordance with the statutory intent can often be said to be foreseeable, proximate and serious. The damage may be physical or psychological, emotional or economic. This does not, however, in itself lead necessarily to the conclusion that Parliament intended there to be a remedy in damages for breach of statutory duty.

. . .

In the present case, although the duties were intended to benefit a particular group, mainly children with special educational needs, the 1981 Act is essentially providing a general structure for all local education authorities in respect of all children who fall within its provision. The general nature of the duties imposed on local authorities in the context of a national system of education and the remedies available by way of appeal and judicial review indicate that Parliament did not intend to create a statutory remedy by way of damages. Much of the 1981 Act is concerned with conferring discretionary powers or administrative duties in an area of social welfare where normally damages have not been awarded when there has been a failure to perform a statutory duty. The situation is quite different from that concerning the maintenance of factory premises as in *Groves v Wimborne (Lord)* [1898] 2 QB 402.

Taking all these factors into account, it does not seem to me that it can be said that Parliament intended that there should be a remedy by way of damages for breach of statutory duty in respect of the matters complained of here.

See also Chapter 7 for *Phelps*.

See also *Morrison Sports Ltd* v *Scottish Power UK plc* [2010] UKSC 37.

Public right and special damage

See Chapter 17 for nuisance.

The second exception in Lord Diplock's statement has close analogies with public nuisance. There must be a public right, the breach of which will constitute a public nuisance and a member of the public must suffer special damage. In the ***Lonrho*** case, there was a breach of the sanctions order which prevented the supply of oil to Southern Rhodesia. This was held not to create a public right to be enjoyed by all Her Majesty's citizens. It was an instrument of state policy which prevented members of the public from doing what had previously been lawful.

The distinction between a statute creating a public right and a statute prohibiting what had previously been lawful is not a satisfactory one as it does not appear to be based on any particular principle. At present, some criminal legislation will give rise to an action on proof of special damage and some will not. How the distinction is to be made is unclear.

Conclusion

The present position outside of industrial safety legislation is clearly unsatisfactory in terms of certainty. It is far from clear, even using the Diplock test, which statutes will give rise to civil liability.

The test of benefit of a class leaves the courts considerable discretion as to how to define the class.

Other tests have been suggested. The Law Commission suggested that if the statute provided no remedy for its enforcement, there should be a presumption of an action (Law

Commission Report No 21 (1969) para 38 and Appendix A(4)). This was not adopted and is unlikely to be, as it conflicts with the court's ability to take into account policy factors and whether the civil action furthers the aims of the legislation. The same criticism, though, could be directed at the presumptions approach. The court's decision as to what constitutes a class conceals the policy issues in the decision.

In the United States and Canada the action for breach of statutory duty is regarded as a species of negligence called statutory negligence. This has two versions. The first is negligence *per se*. This is that a breach of a statutory requirement constitutes negligence where the statute was passed to prevent a mischief in respect of which the defendant was already under a duty at common law. The standard of care is set by the statute. The second approach is that breach of the statute provides only prima facie evidence of negligence. The statutory negligence approach has not been adopted in England and this is probably a good thing. It would restrict actions to existing tort law and would reproduce the problems which have been encountered with liability for omissions and economic loss.

Perhaps the most honest judicial statement in this area came from Lord Denning:

> The truth is that in many of these statutes the legislature has left the point open . . . The dividing line between the pro-cases and the contra-cases is so blurred and ill-defined that you might as well toss a coin to decide it. (*Ex parte Island Records* [1978] Ch 122.)

Was the duty owed to the claimant?

Objective 3

For duty of care in negligence, see Chapter 3.

The claimant must show that the duty was owed to them. Industrial safety legislation will normally confer a right on persons employed. It follows, therefore, that a firefighter fighting a fire at a factory which is not their place of employment will not be able to sue for breach of such a statutory duty. (*Hartley v Mayoh & Co* [1954] 1 QB 383.)

The claimant must also show that the type of injury that they suffered was the type the legislation sought to prevent.

Gorris v Scott (1874) 9 LR Exch 125

The defendant shipowner was under a statutory duty to provide pens for cattle on board his ship. The purpose of the statute was to lessen the risk of cattle catching a contagious disease while in transit. The defendant was held not liable for breach of statutory duty when the claimant's sheep were swept overboard when not in pens. The purpose of the statute was not to protect the animals from the perils of the seas.

Breach of duty

For breach of duty in negligence, see Chapter 8.

This is a question of statutory interpretation. There is no single standard of care. The court must look at the words used in the statute, which may impose an absolute, strict or fault-based standard.

It is possible that the statute may create absolute liability on the defendant, although the court will be wary of creating a strict liability criminal offence in the absence of clear language.

John Summers and Sons Ltd v Frost [1955] AC 740

The Factories Act 1961 s 14(1) requires every dangerous part of any machinery to be securely fenced. The claimant's hand came into contact with a moving grinding-wheel which was not fenced. The defendants argued that if the machine was securely fenced it would be unusable. This was rejected by the court, which refused to read the words 'so far as reasonably practical' into the statute. According to Lord Reid, as the statute only required the fencing of machinery that was 'dangerous', this meant reasonably foreseeably dangerous. Once the machinery was classified as 'dangerous' in this sense it meant that the employer had either to fence it or to not use it. The principal difference between this and a test of negligence is that the court will not take the cost of taking precautions into account.

In the above case the word 'dangerous' in the statute meant 'reasonably foreseeably dangerous'. In **Robb v Salamis Ltd** [2007] 2 All ER 97 the House of Lords had to consider the Provision and Use of Work Equipment Regulations 1998 when the pursuer (claimant) was injured on an oil rig when a ladder he was using to descend from a bunk bed gave way. The question was whether the ladder was suitable and suitable meant 'suitable in any respect which it is reasonably foreseeable would affect the health and safety of any person'. The ladders had to be moved and reattached at intervals. The aim of the relevant regulations was to ensure that work equipment which was made available to workers could be used by them without impairment to their safety or health. It was in that context that the issue of foreseeability became relevant; the obligation was to anticipate situations which might give rise to accidents. Carelessness in the replacement was one of the risks that had to be anticipated and addressed before the defenders could be satisfied that the suspended ladders were suitable. Accordingly, the accident had been caused by the defenders' breaches of the regulations but a deduction was made for contributory negligence.

Some statutes are so specific that there can be no qualification.

Chipchase v British Titan Products Co Ltd [1956] 1 QB 545

The statutory regulations provided that any working platform from which a person is likely to fall more than 6 ft 6 in had to be at least 34 in in width. The defendants were not liable for breach of statutory duty when the claimant fell from a 9 in wide platform 6 ft above the ground.

A form of strict liability may be created by wording that allows for the practicability of precautions. This means that the employer must prove the impracticability of precautions. This may not be easy to prove, as if the precaution is possible it must be taken, even if the risks involved in taking it outweigh the benefits.

Alternatively, the statute may provide for the reasonable practicability of precautions. This wording allows the court to balance the time and expense involved in taking the precaution against the risk of injury. This is similar to a negligence test, but in the statutory action the burden of proof is on the employer.

A difficult problem was posed to the House of Lords by the next case.

Fytche v Wincanton Logistics plc [2004] 4 All ER 221

The claimant was employed by the defendant company to drive a milk tanker. The Personal Protective Equipment at Work Regulations 1992 imposed an obligation on employers to supply employees, who might be exposed to a risk to their health or safety while at work, with suitable 'personal protective equipment'. The claimant was supplied by the company with boots which had steel toe caps in order to protect his toes from impact injuries from, for instance, falling milk churns. In exceptionally wintry weather the claimant's tanker became stuck on an icy country road. The company's standard instructions in such a case were for the driver to use the telephone in the cab to call for help and then wait to be rescued. The claimant, however, decided to dig himself out. One of his boots had a tiny hole and the effect of the penetration of water in freezing conditions was a mild frostbite in the claimant's little toe, which kept him away from work for some months and left him with a permanent sensitivity to cold in that toe. The claimant argued that, as the boots were personal protective equipment, his employer had been under a duty under the 1992 Regulations to maintain them in an efficient state, in efficient working order and in good repair; and that the existence of the hole meant that the boots were not in good repair and that, as liability under the 1992 Regulations was strict, the company was liable for the damage caused.

Held (Lord Hope of Craighead of Richmond and Baroness Hale dissenting): The concept of personal protective equipment being in an 'efficient state, in efficient working order and in good repair' was not an absolute one but had to be construed in relation to what made equipment 'personal protective equipment'. It had to be efficient for the purpose of protecting against the relevant risk. The employer had a duty to maintain personal protective equipment so that it continued to be suitable personal protective equipment, but he did not have a duty to do repairs and maintenance which had nothing to do with its function as personal protective equipment. In the instant case, the boots had been adequate for the claimant's ordinary conditions of work, and the continuing existence of the tiny hole had not, therefore, been a breach of the employer's obligation.

The dissentients in this case stressed the purpose of the regulations which was that prevention was better than cure. Unlike the majority, they were not impressed by the argument that there was no action on the facts and that there was an absolute obligation on the employer to keep the boots in good repair.

Causation

For causation generally, see Chapter 9.

It is necessary for the claimant to prove that the defendant's breach of statutory duty was a cause of their injuries. Generally speaking, there is no difference between actions for breach of statutory duty and actions for common law negligence. The claimant must prove that but for the breach of statutory duty they would not have suffered the injury.

McWilliams v *Sir William Arrol & Co Ltd* [1962] 1 WLR 295

The defendant employer was in breach of statutory duty in removing safety belts from a building site. The claimant scaffolder was injured when he fell and was not wearing a safety belt. The action failed, as the defendant proved that, even if the safety belt had been provided, the claimant would not have worn it.

The action for breach of statutory duty raises one specialised issue of causation. The statute may impose a duty on an employer to provide safety equipment and ensure that it is used. If the equipment is provided but the employee does not use it, this may have the effect of placing both the claimant and the defendant in breach of statutory duty.

Ginty v Belmont Building Supplies Ltd [1959] 1 All ER 414

The claimant was an experienced workman employed by the defendant roofing contractors. Statutory regulations binding on both parties required crawling boards to be used on fragile roofs. The defendant provided the boards but the claimant did not use them. The claimant fell through a roof and was injured. The claim failed as the defendant had done everything possible to ensure that the statutory duty was complied with. The sole reason for the breach was the claimant's omission to use the equipment.

This decision was somewhat controversial and a gloss was placed on it in *Boyle* v *Kodak* [1969] 1 WLR 661. If any causal responsibility rests with the employer, they will be liable. Proving the breach of statutory duty establishes a prima facie case. The defendant can escape liability if they prove that the only act or default which caused the breach was that of the claimant. But if any blame can be attached to the defendant, they will be liable. This could occur if the claimant was asked to do a job beyond their competence, the equipment was not easily accessible, or pressure was brought to bear on the claimant not to use the equipment.

Defences

For *volenti* and contributory negligence, see Chapter 10.

Volenti non fit injuria is not usually available as a defence in the industrial safety cases. The exception is where an employee is in breach of their statutory duty and this has the effect of making the employer vicariously liable. If the defence of *volenti* would have been available against the employee, it will be available against the employer. (*ICI Ltd* v *Shatwell* [1965] AC 656.)

Contributory negligence is a defence and the Law Reform (Contributory Negligence) Act 1945 will apply. The courts are usually slow to attribute contributory negligence to an employee where the employer is in breach of statutory duty.

A person who is subject to a statutory duty cannot discharge that duty by entrusting responsibility for its performance to someone else.

Breach of statutory duty and negligence

Objective 4

The two actions should be treated separately. In a breach of statutory duty action the duty is imposed by the statute. In negligence actions the courts must determine whether a duty is owed. In negligence actions the standard of care is reasonable care in all the circumstances of the case. In breach of statutory duty, the standard of performance is fixed by the statute and may be strict.

It is normally easier for the claimant to succeed in an action for breach of statutory duty, but not always.

Rux v Slough Metals Ltd [1974] 1 All ER 262

The employer was under a statutory duty to provide safety goggles, which he did. The claimant employee did not wear them and was injured. The action for breach of statutory duty failed, but the negligence action succeeded. The evidence showed that the claimant would have worn the goggles if he had been firmly instructed to do so and supervised.

European legislation

If there is a breach of a European Treaty or a Council of Ministers' regulation which results in an individual suffering loss, do they have a claim?

Under the European Communities Act 1972 s 2(1) the state has an obligation to ensure that national law is consistent with EU law. If the state acts in breach of Treaty provisions, it will breach the duty.

There is a right to a remedy in national law for certain breaches of European law and such remedies will arise in the tort of breach of statutory duty. (*Garden Cottage Foods Ltd v Milk Marketing Board* [1984] AC 130.)

The right to damages in this area is wider than that in the national action for breach of statutory duty and these are referred to as 'Eurotorts'.

The scope of the right to damages in national law was laid down in the following case.

R v Secretary of State for Transport ex parte Factortame (No 4) [1996] QB 404

A private individual is entitled to damages where a member state fails properly to implement European Union legislation and the following conditions are satisfied:

1 the rule of Community law breached was intended to confer rights on individuals;
2 the breach was sufficiently serious; and
3 there is a direct causal link between the breach and the damage suffered.

The difference between the traditional action for breach of statutory duty and the 'Eurotort' lies in the second condition. This is not a fault-based test but looks at whether the state has shown a manifest and grave disregard to the limits of its discretion. It is for the national courts to find the facts and decide whether the breach of Community law is sufficiently serious and whether there is a causal link.

It is not yet settled as to how this links with the tort of breach of statutory duty. The most likely solution is that a breach of European legislation should be treated as a separate category of liability within breach of statutory duty. (*R v Secretary of State for Transport ex p Factortame (No 7)* [2001] 1 WLR 942.)

Summary

This chapter deals with the tort of breach of statutory duty.

- Breach of statutory duty is a tort in its own right and should be kept separate from negligence.
- The statute must give rise to an action for damages. This is said to depend on the intention of Parliament but in practice policy factors may shape the court's decision. Where Parliament has created an obligation and enforced performance in a specified manner, there is a presumption that performance cannot be enforced in any other manner. However, if the obligation is for the benefit or protection of a particular class and the claimant is a member of that class, the claimant may have an action. (*Lonrho v Shell Petroleum (No 2)* (1982).)

- If the statute does give rise to an action for damages then the claimant must show that the duty was owed to him, that there was a breach of that duty and the damage was caused by the breach of duty.
- The duty must be owed to the claimant and must be of a type that the statute sought to prevent.
- There is no single standard of care. Liability may be strict, absolute or fault based. The standard is set by the statute.
- The defendant's breach of statutory duty must be a cause of the claimant's injuries. The 'but for' test is generally used. Problems arise where the statutory duty is imposed on the claimant and defendant.
- Contributory negligence is available as a defence but *volenti* is usually not available in an industrial safety case.
- In some cases there may be an action for a breach of EU legislation.

Further reading

Buckley, R. A. (1984), 'Liability in Tort for Breach of Statutory Duty' 100 LQR 204.

Stanton, K. (2004), 'New Forms of the Tort of Breach of Statutory Duty' 120 LQR 324.

Williams, G. (1960), 'The Effect of Penal Legislation in Tort' 3 MLR 233.

14

Employer's liability

Objectives

After reading this chapter you will:

1. Appreciate the historical background to claims for tort damages by employees against employers and understand the distinction between the primary or personal liability of the employers and their **vicarious liability**.

2. Understand the legal rules governing an action by an employee against an employer for breach of their personal duty of care.

3. Understand the defences available to the employer and have a critical knowledge of the law relating to claims by employees for negligently caused stress at work.

Introduction

Objective 1

For *volenti* and contributory negligence, see Chapter 10.

During the nineteenth century the response of the courts to claims by employees injured at work tended to be hostile. Liability was seen in terms of contractual duties. As the employer dictated the contract of employment there was usually little or no liability.

To counter claims in tort, the courts erected the unholy trinity of defences of common employment, *volenti non fit injuria* and contributory negligence.

A claim for negligence by an employee injured by the negligence of a fellow employee would be met by the defence of common employment. If the risk had been created by the employer, a defence of *volenti* could usually be mounted by the employer, if the employee was aware of the danger and continued to work. Any contributory negligence on the part of the employee would be fatal to their claim.

From the end of the nineteenth century a change in approach is noticeable. The decision in **Smith v Baker** (1891) made it difficult for employers to rely on a *volenti* defence. An action for breach of statutory duty on the part of the employee was created by **Groves v Lord Wimborne** (1898). In 1945 contributory negligence ceased to be a complete defence and became grounds for apportioning liability. The defence of common employment was finally abolished in 1948 by the Law Reform (Personal Injuries) Act 1948. By this time it had lost most of its effect because of the introduction of a personal, non-delegable duty on the employer in **Wilsons & Clyde Coal Co Ltd v English** [1938] AC 57. Where the employer was in breach of this duty they could not rely on the defence of common employment. This resulted in a strict demarcation between the employer's personal duty and their vicarious liability.

It should be observed that the most significant contribution to compensation for injured workers has been through insurance rather than the tort system. The Pearson Commission found that only 10–15 per cent of industrial injuries are compensated through the tort damages system (Vol 1, Table 13.5).

Insurance compensation started with the Workmen's Compensation Act 1897. The Act enabled workers to recover compensation without the necessity of proving fault on the part of the employer. The employer became an insurer for injuries received out of and in the course of employment. This scheme was replaced in 1946 by a state scheme for victims of industrial accidents and prescribed industrial diseases. It is not possible to consider this scheme in a tort book and students should consult a specialist work for detail.

At present, an employer's tortious liability for the safety of their employees may take one of three forms.

For vicarious liability, see Chapter 24.

1 The employer may be vicariously liable for the negligence of an employee which leads to the claimant employee being injured. The employer's liability here is strict, in the sense that there need be no fault on their part.

For breach of statutory duty, see Chapter 13.

2 The employer may be in breach of statutory duty and the employee suffers injury as a result.

3 The employer may be in breach of their personal duty of care owed to the employee. This is a particular example of negligence liability but is owed only to employees and not to independent contractors.

The system is backed up by the Employers' Liability (Compulsory Insurance) Act 1969, which makes it compulsory for employers to take out insurance cover for liability for bodily injury, including death and disease, for their employees. Any employee who can establish a claim in tort is therefore guaranteed to have the judgment met and not be defeated by an insolvent employer.

The employer's personal duty of care

Objective 2

The duty is to take reasonable care for the safety of employees in the course of their employment. The duty is personal as it cannot be delegated and is discharged by the exercise of due skill and care.

For duty of care generally, see Chapter 3.

This duty does not generally extend to protecting the economic welfare of the employee. Not taking out insurance or warning them of the need for insurance cover is not actionable. In *Reid v Rush & Tompkins Group plc* [1989] 3 All ER 228 the claimant was injured in a road accident while working in Ethiopia. He could not obtain compensation from the person who had caused the accident and sued his employer for failing to provide insurance or advising him of the need to take out insurance. The court held that the employer owed no such duty in tort. If such a duty was to be owed it would have to be based on an express or implied term in the contract of employment.

This decision must be now be read in the light of cases which provide actions in negligence where an employer gives a negligent reference leading to economic loss (*Spring v Guardian Assurance*) and fails to give advice on valuable pension rights (*Scally v Southern Health*). In the latter case, liability was in contract and not tort.

The classic exposition of the duty was given by Lord Wright in *Wilsons & Clyde Coal Co Ltd* v *English* (1938). The employer must provide a competent staff, adequate material, a proper system and effective supervision.

It is probably not accurate to regard the employer's duty as a series of separate obligations, but rather as a single duty to take reasonable care for the safety of employees. For the sake of exposition, the duty will be analysed here in four parts. However, when the courts are considering new situations, they will not be constrained by trying to fit them into existing categories.

Competent staff

The employer may be liable when using an employee with insufficient experience or training for a particular job and a fellow employee is injured as a result.

The employer may also be liable for a practical joker whom they know about and fail to take steps to deal with. (*Hudson* v *Ridge Manufacturing Co Ltd* [1957] 2 QB 348.)

The abolition of the doctrine of common employment has rendered this area of comparatively little importance, as in most cases the employer will be vicariously liable for the torts of their employees. However, where the employee was acting outside the course of their employment, then the employer would not be vicariously liable, but could be personally liable.

The duty will extend to a personal duty on the employer not to expose their employees to bullying, victimisation or harassment by their fellow employees. (*Waters* v *Commissioner of Police for the Metropolis* [2000] UKHL 50.)

Adequate material

The duty is to provide the necessary plant and equipment and take reasonable care to maintain it in proper condition.

At common law the employer did not guarantee the safety of the equipment and could not be held liable for latent defects in the equipment which could not be discovered with reasonable care. This placed the employee at a disadvantage. If injured as a result of equipment having such a defect, they had the onerous task of suing the manufacturer of the equipment under the defective products rule.

The Employer's Liability (Defective Equipment) Act 1969 s 1(1) now provides:

> Where . . . an employee suffers personal injury in the course of his employment in consequence of a defect in equipment provided by his employer for the purposes of the employer's business and the defect is attributable wholly or partly to the fault of a third party (whether identified or not) the injury shall be deemed to be also attributable to negligence on the part of the employer.

This section has the effect of imposing a form of strict liability on the employer for defective equipment. This relieves the employee of the need to identify and sue the manufacturer of the defective equipment. The employer will have a contract with the person who sold them the equipment and will probably be able to recoup their losses through a contract action.

Equipment is defined by s 1(3) as including any plant and machinery, vehicle, aircraft and clothing. It has been held that a ship is equipment. It comes within the definition of machinery or plant.

Coltman v *Bibby Tankers Ltd* [1988] AC 276

Lord Oliver:

My Lords, it is common ground that the Act of 1969 was introduced with a view to rectifying what was felt to be the possible hardship to an employee resulting from the decision of this House in ***Davie*** v ***New Merton Board Mills Ltd*** [1959] AC 604. In that case an employee was injured by a defective drift supplied to him by his employers for the purpose of his work. The defect resulted from a fault in manufacture but the article had been purchased by the employers without knowledge of the defect from a reputable supplier and without any negligence on their part. It was held that the employers' duty was only to take reasonable care to provide a reasonably safe tool and that that duty had been discharged by purchasing from a reputable source an article whose latent defect they had no means of discovering. Thus the action against them failed although judgment was recovered against the manufacturer. Clearly this opened the door to the possibility that an employee required to work with, on or in equipment furnished by his employer and injured as a result of some negligent failure in design or manufacture might find himself without remedy in a case where the manufacturer and the employer were, to use the words of Viscount Simonds ... 'divided in time and space by decades and continents' so that the person actually responsible was no longer traceable or, perhaps, was insolvent or had ceased to carry on business. Parliament accordingly met this by imposing on employers a vicarious liability and providing, in a case where injury was due to a defect caused by the fault of the third party, that the employer should, regardless of his own conduct, be liable to his employee as if he had been responsible for the defect, leaving it to him to pursue against the third party such remedies as he might have whether original or by way of contribution.

Further consideration was given to the question of 'equipment' in **Knowles** v **Liverpool City Council** [1993] 4 All ER 321. The claimant was employed by the defendants and suffered personal injury when a flagstone he was handling broke. The House of Lords held that a broad approach to construction was required and held that the flagstone was 'equipment'. Every article of whatever kind furnished by the employer to the employee for the purposes of his business was equipment. This interpretation was used by the House of Lords in **Spencer-Franks** v **Kellogg Brown & Root Ltd** [2009] 1 All ER 269 where a door closer on an oil platform was held to be equipment when it was being repaired.

However, where a wheelchair ramp was installed by the NHS outside a person's home and a carer/driver employed by the local authority stumbled on the ramp while pushing the wheelchair, there was held to be no liability on the employer for breach of the statutory regulations on maintenance as there was no underlying responsibility on the employer to maintain. (**Smith** v **Northampton County Council** [2008] EWCA Civ 181.)

Safe place of work

See *Latimer* v *AEC Ltd* [1953] AC 643 in Chapter 8.

Where the employee is working on the employer's premises, the employer must act in the same manner as a reasonably prudent employer. Reasonable care must be taken for the employee's safety. There is no guarantee that the premises are safe.

Safe system of work

The employer must devise a suitable system, instruct employees what to do and supply any implements they may require. In doing this the employer must take care to see that the system is complied with and bear in mind that employees are often careless for their own safety.

General Cleaning Contractors v Christmas [1953] AC 180

The claimant window cleaner was instructed by his employers in the sill method of cleaning windows. He was to hold on to the window sash while cleaning. A window fell on his fingers and he fell to the ground. It was held that the employers were in breach of their personal duty of care, as they should have told the claimant to test the sashes to see if they were loose and provided him with wedges. They had failed to provide a safe system.

McDermid v Nash Dredging and Reclamation Co Ltd [1987] AC 906

The defendants employed the 18-year-old claimant as a deckhand, a job in which the claimant had no experience. While the claimant was working under the control of an associated company he was injured. The House of Lords stated that the employer had to devise a safe system and operate it. On the facts, a safe system had been devised but when the operation of the system was delegated to the other company it was not operated properly.

Certain factors were relevant in determining whether reasonable care had been taken. These were: the skill and experience of the employee; the nature of the work on which he was employed; the place where the employee was employed; the degree of control exercised over him by the tortfeasor; the relationship between the tortfeasor (associated company) and the employee; and the relationship between the employer and the tortfeasor.

It was held that as the employer's duty was a personal one it could not be discharged by delegation. Performance of the duty was not discharged by delegation.

Lord Brandon:

> A statement of the relevant principle of law can be divided into three parts. First, an employer owes to his employee a duty to exercise reasonable care to ensure that the system of work provided for him is a safe one. Secondly, the provision of a safe system of work has two aspects: (a) the devising of such a system and (b) the operation of it. Thirdly, the duty concerned has been described alternatively as either personal or non-delegable. The meaning of these expressions is not self-evident and needs explaining. The essential characteristic of the duty is that, if it is not performed, it is no defence for the employer to show that he delegated its performance to a person, whether his servant or not his servant, whom he reasonably believed to be competent to perform it. Despite such delegation the employer is liable for the non-performance of the duty.

The relevance of the place and the requirement of reasonable care is illustrated by *Cook* v *Square D Ltd* [1992] ICR 262. The claimant was injured in Saudi Arabia by a small hole in the floor. As the site occupiers and contractors were reliable companies and bearing in mind the distance between the UK-based employers and the site of the accident, the Court of Appeal held that there had been no breach of duty.

The number of UK citizens working in the building trade in Germany at one point raised questions of who the employer is. *McDermid* was clear that a person could only be liable if they remained the employer. Most work of this variety is arranged through employment agencies and this was the case in *Johnson* v *Coventry Churchill International Ltd* [1992] 3 All ER 14. The claimant fell and was seriously injured on a building site in Germany and it was held that in the absence of clear and cogent evidence to the contrary, which was not present, the agency would remain the employer.

Defences

Objective 3

For *volenti* and contributory negligence, see Chapter 10.

The defences of *volenti non fit injuria* and contributory negligence are available to the employer. *Volenti* will rarely succeed and the courts are generally slow to find contributory negligence.

Stress at work

For psychiatric damage generally, see Chapter 4.

Historically, claims against employers were for physical injury. Many actions arose out of heavy manufacturing industry, which has now declined in the UK. Claims still arise from occupations such as building and construction, but most employees now face different problems at work which have raised different issues for the courts. One of these is the question of negligently caused stress in the workplace. The scope of the employer's duty is illustrated by *Walker* v *Northumberland County Council*, where it was held that the concept of safe system included avoiding unnecessary stress to employees.

Walker v *Northumberland County Council* [1995] 1 All ER 737

The claimant was employed by the defendant council as an area social services officer from 1970–87 and was responsible for managing teams of social workers in an area which had a high proportion of child-care problems. In 1986 the claimant suffered a nervous breakdown because of stress of work and was off work for three months. His superior agreed before he returned to work that some assistance should be given to relieve his burden. Only limited assistance was given and he had to clear up the backlog of cases. Six months later he had another breakdown and had to stop work permanently. In 1988 he was dismissed on the ground of permanent ill health.

The action was for the breach of duty by the employer to avoid exposing him to a health-endangering workload.

Is there a duty to take steps to protect an employee against the risk of psychiatric damage?

Colman J:

There is no logical reason why risk of psychiatric damage should be excluded from the scope of an employer's duty of care or from the co-extensive implied term in the contract of employment . . . the circumstances in which claims based on such damage are likely to arise will often give rise to extremely difficult evidential problems of foreseeability and causation . . . at what point is the employer's duty to take protective steps engaged? . . . what assumption is he entitled to make about the employee's resilience, mental toughness and stability of character . . . the mental illness and the lasting impairment of his personality . . . in consequence of the 1987 breakdown was so substantial and damaging that the magnitude of the risk to which he was exposed must be regarded as relatively large . . . by 1985 at latest it was reasonably foreseeable . . . there was in general some risk that Mr Walker might sustain a mental breakdown of some sort in consequence of his work . . . before the 1986 illness it was not reasonably foreseeable to the council that the workload . . . gave rise to a material risk of mental illness . . . in 1987 Mr Walker was exposed in his job to a reasonably foreseeable risk to his mental health which exceeded the risk to be anticipated in the ordinary course of an area officer's job . . . the standard of care to be expected of a reasonable local authority required that additional assistance should be provided.

The defendants were found to be in breach of the common law duty of care owed to the claimant.

The decision in *Walker* triggered a considerable amount of litigation, particularly from public sector employees. The Court of Appeal then laid down the principles to be applied where occupational stress leads to a psychiatric illness.

Hatton v Sutherland [2002] 2 All ER 1

1 There are no jobs which are inherently dangerous in terms of mental stress as it is the interaction between the individual and the job which causes the harm rather than the job itself.

2 Stress in itself is a subjective concept in the sense that it is an individual response to pressures which he feels he may not be able to meet. The reaction to stress is also subjective as it ranges from minor physical symptoms to major mental illness.

3 As the employer's duty is owed to the individual employee the question is whether this harm was reasonably foreseeable to this particular individual. It is not a question of 'ordinary fortitude'.

4 Issues which go to the foreseeability of psychiatric harm to the employee include:
   (a) The nature and extent of the work being done by the employee. Is the employer putting pressure on the employee and are other employees demonstrating signs of stress?
   (b) Signs from the employee. A distinction is drawn between signs of stress and signs of impending damage to mental health.
   (c) Unless the employer knows of some particular problem or vulnerability he is usually entitled to assume that the employee is up to the normal stresses of the job. The employer is entitled to take what he has been told by or on behalf of the employee at face value.

5 When assessing the precautions that an employer should take to avoid the risk of psychiatric harm to an employee the court should take into account:
   (a) The size and scope of the employer's operation.
   (b) The employer's resources.
   (c) Whether the job is in the public or private sector.
   (d) Other demands placed on the employer, including the interests of other employees. It would not be reasonable for an employer to be expected to rearrange the work for one employee to the detriment of all other employees.

Barber v Somerset County Council [2004] 2 All ER 385

This was one of the joined hearings in **Hatton**. The claimant was a teacher employed by the defendant council. The post he held as head of a department was abolished in a restructuring of staffing and the claimant reapplied for a new post in his subject. In order to maintain his salary level he also applied to be the school's project manager for public and media relations. He worked long hours in discharging his new responsibilities and began to suffer from stress. In February 1996 he spoke of 'work overload' to one of the senior management team. He was away from work in May 1996 for three weeks, returning with sick notes signed by his doctor recording his condition as 'overstressed/ depression'. He completed his employer's form of sickness declaration stating his trouble as 'overstressed/depression'. That form was signed by the claimant and countersigned by another of the senior management team. During June and July he had meetings with the senior management team about his workload and his health but no steps were taken to investigate or remedy the situation. In November the claimant suffered a mental breakdown at school and he took early retirement at the end of March 1997, when he was 52 years old. He was unable to work as a teacher, or to do any work other than undemanding part-time work. The claimant brought proceedings against the council, claiming damages for personal injuries, principally in the form of serious depressive illness. The trial judge gave judgment for the claimant, holding that a prudent employer, with the knowledge that the senior management team had had, would have investigated the claimant's situation to see how his difficulties might have been improved, and that the response of the senior management team to the claimant's difficulties had been inadequate. The council appealed. The Court of Appeal concluded that the judge had been wrong in finding a breach of the council's duty of care to the claimant. The claimant appealed. The House of Lords held that the judge had been entitled to form the view that the school's senior management team, measured by the general principle of the conduct of a

> reasonable and prudent employer taking positive thought for the safety of its workers in the light of what it knew or ought to have known, was in a position of continuing breach of the employer's duty of care, and that that had caused the claimant's serious nervous breakdown. It was not a clear case of a flagrant breach of duty any more than it was an obviously hopeless claim. But the judge had seen and heard the witnesses, and there was insufficient reason for the Court of Appeal to set aside his finding.

These cases raise a number of problems.

See Chapter 4 for control tests.

1 What is the relationship between these claims and claims for psychiatric damage? Do the same control tests that were discussed elsewhere also apply to employee stress claims? The approach taken in **Hatton** was not to apply the **White/Alcock** control mechanisms where the harm was a reasonably foreseeable product of specific breaches of a contractual duty of care between the defendant and the claimant. It should be noted that when an employee suffers psychiatric harm as a result of witnessing a single shocking event for which their employer is responsible, they must bring themselves within the normal rules which apply to claims for psychiatric damage. The claimant must either be a primary victim or satisfy the rules of secondary victims.

See *White v Chief Constable of South Yorkshire Police* [1999] 1 All ER 1 in Chapter 4.

In *French v Chief Constable of Sussex* [2006] EWCA Civ 312 a number of police officers were involved in events leading up to an armed raid resulting in a fatal shooting. They made claims against their employer for stress at work. The Court of Appeal held that these were not stress at work cases. An employer had to know that a particular employee was at risk of psychiatric injury by reason of stress.

2 The employer will only be liable if he knows or should know of some particular problem or vulnerability in that particular employee. The question is then what the 'threshold' is. Mrs Hatton had not complained and received no compensation. Many employees may take the view that they do not wish to complain for fear of losing their job or a promotion opportunity. Mr Barber also lost in the Court of Appeal because of the time lag between his complaints and his breakdown. The House of Lords took a more employee friendly approach with a simpler test. The *Hatton* guidelines were not appealed and were said by the House of Lords to provide valuable practical assistance.

3 What must be foreseeable in these cases is psychiatric harm. It is not enough to show that the employer had been in breach of its general duty to the employee and that psychiatric injury had then ensued. (*Hartman v South Essex Mental Health and Community Care NHS Trust* [2005] IRLR 293.)

4 It would appear that employees who are exposed as a part of their work to a high risk of psychiatric illness may have a claim if the employer has accepted the need for a counselling service but then does not implement it. (*Hartman.*) Can the duty be discharged by the employer by providing counselling services? In *Daw v Intel* [2007] 2 All ER 126 the Court of Appeal held that the approach the court should adopt to allegations of psychiatric illness caused by stress at work did not render the availability of counselling services a panacea by which employers could discharge their duty of care in all cases. The consequences of the management's failure to take action were not avoided by the provision of counsellors who might have been able to bring home to the defendant that action was required.

In practice, it is very difficult to bring a successful stress claim. Even if the employee establishes a duty and breach, he still has to prove causation. Where a person has a stress-related breakdown, there will often be a number of causes, including non-negligent stress at work. The employee must show that the employer's breach of duty was a material contributory cause to the damage. In *Hatton* only one of the four claimants succeeded. She had complained to her employer, who had acknowledged the problem and promised to do something about it but did not.

The Court of Appeal considered the issue of causation in stress at work cases in the following.

Dickins v O2 plc [2008] EWCA Civ 1144

The claimant worked for the defendant for a number of years. She claimed that the defendant had been negligent in failing to act on her complaints of stress. In April 2002, she had expressly warned her line manager that she was not coping with some aspects of her job and that she was 'at the end of her tether'. However, she alleged that, in breach of duty, the defendant had failed to relieve her situation so that she had carried on working. She had been told to use the defendant's internal counselling service. She had repeated her concerns at her annual appraisal in May. A few days later, she had felt unable to come to work. She never returned to work and her employment was terminated in November 2003.

It was common ground that her personality rendered her psychologically vulnerable. The psychiatric evidence was to the effect that the perceived work problems, in combination with the prior psychological vulnerability, had resulted in the deterioration in the claimant's mental health. The judge awarded the claimant 50 per cent of the total damages.

The Court of Appeal upheld the judge's decision:

1 In the present case, the evidence had been quite strong enough for the judge to conclude that the employer had received a clear indication of impending illness.

2 In the present case, the claimant had not been afraid to tell her line manager that she was 'at the end of her tether'. Given the situation where the claimant was describing severe symptoms, alleging that they were due to stress at work and was warning that she did not know for how long she could carry on, a mere suggestion that she seek counselling could not be regarded as an adequate response.

3 The test of causation, according to *Hatton*, is whether the breach has made a *material contribution to the claimant's ill health*. The judge had not applied the correct test. Instead of asking whether the breach had made a material contribution to the onset of illness, he had spoken of the claimant losing the chance of a swift recovery and the chance of not plummeting to the depths of her subsequent illness. In doing so, he had entered unnecessarily into the difficult area of damages for 'loss of a chance'. It was not a 'loss of a chance' case but a case where more than one factor had *causative potency* in the development of the illness.

It was clear that the identified breach had made a material contribution to the claimant's severe illness.

In *Pakenham-Walsh* v *Connell Residential* [2006] All ER (D) 275 (Feb), the Court of Appeal refused to overturn the trial judge's verdict that there had been no breach of duty where a housing saleswoman suffered psychiatric damage. The claimant had not complained or sought medical assistance and had a number of other problems in her life. The defendant's conduct had not crossed the threshold. In contrast, in *Hone* v *Six Continents Retail Ltd* [2006] IRLR 49, the Court of Appeal upheld the claim of a public house manager who had worked a 90-hour week, complained of his hours and refused to sign an opt-out of the Working Time Directive.

Question

Arthur, Bert and Charlie are employed by Chartist plc as welders. The Welding Regulations 1970 impose a statutory duty on employers and employees that 'safety goggles must as far as is practicable be worn at all times when welding operations are being carried out'.

Arthur developed a skin complaint, unrelated to his employment, which made the wearing of goggles painful. He stopped wearing the goggles and was struck and blinded in one eye by a piece of metal.

Bert was told by Arthur, who was known in the firm as a practical joker, that wearing goggles could result in loss of libido. Bert took this seriously, stopped wearing his goggles and suffered partial blindness caused by the glare from the welding torch.

Charlie was wearing his goggles when a piece of molten metal struck them, shattering the protective glass and causing him eye injuries.

Advise Arthur, Bert and Charlie as to any rights of action they might have in tort against Chartist plc and as to any defences with which they might be met.

(*NB*: The Welding Regulations 1970 are fictitious.)

 Suggested approach

An employer can incur tortious liability in respect of his employees in one of three ways. The employer may be in breach of statutory duty, in breach of his personal duty of care or vicariously liable for the tort of one of the other employees.

Arthur may have an action for breach of statutory duty. He must establish that the statute in question gave rise to an action for damages. This is said to depend on the intention of Parliament, but the test is fictitious as Parliament frequently gives no thought to the question. The most generally accepted test is that put forward by Lord Diplock in *Lonrho* v *Shell Petroleum*, based on presumptions. If the statute provides a means of enforcement then it can only be enforced in this manner, unless the obligation is imposed for the benefit of a class and the claimant is a member of that class.

This is used with industrial safety statutes such as the Welding Regulations to give employees injured by a breach of statutory duty an action in damages. Arthur is a member of the class (employees) for whose benefit the statute was passed. It is necessary to prove that there was a breach of the statutory duty. This depends on interpretation of the statute. The duty imposed may be strict or fault based. This duty is neither absolute nor negligence based. It is a form of strict liability.

The word practicable means that the employer must prove the impracticability of precautions. The word has been interpreted as meaning that the precaution must be taken even if the risk involved in taking it outweighs the benefit. (*Boyton* v *Willment Bros Ltd* (1971).) It would appear that Chartist are in breach of statutory duty. It is also necessary for the claimant to prove causation. The normal causation rule of 'but for' applies unless the sole reason the employer is in breach was the claimant's omission to use the safety equipment. (*Ginty* v *Belmont Building Supplies* (1959).)

As Arthur is in breach of his duty by omitting to wear the goggles, it may be that the court will find that causation is not established. If it is, then Chartist may attempt to raise *volenti* non *fit injuria* or contributory negligence as defences. *Volenti* would not appear to be applicable, but the court might hold that Arthur has been contributorily negligent in respect of his injury and reduce damages accordingly.

Arthur may also have an action in negligence under the employer's personal duty of care. This is a duty to provide competent staff, adequate material, a safe place of work and a safe system of work. (*Wilsons & Clyde Coal* v *English* (1938).) On the facts of the problem he is more likely to succeed in the action for breach of statutory duty as that duty on the employer is stricter.

Bert may have an action for breach of statutory duty but may fail for the same reason as Arthur. The damage was caused by Bert not wearing the glasses. Applying the *Ginty* test, the cause of the damage was Bert's breach of statutory duty.

Bert's best chance of success is the personal duty of care, under the head of competent staff. An employer has been held liable where he failed to take steps to deal with a practical joker whom he knew about. (*Hudson* v *Ridge Manufacturing* (1957).) Alternatively, the employer could be vicariously liable if Arthur was negligent in respect of his statement to Bert. Arthur would probably be outside the course of his employment though. Again, the question could be raised as to whether Bert was volenti or contributorily negligent.

Charlie's case raises the question of the employer's personal duty of care and the duty to provide adequate equipment. At common law the employer did not guarantee the safety of the equipment and could not be held liable for a latent defect in it. The Employer's Liability (Defective Equipment) Act 1969 imposes a form of strict liability on the employer. Charlie could sue the employer for his injury and the employer would then have to recover from the manufacturer/supplier of the goggles. No defence is available in this action on these facts.

Summary

This chapter deals with an employer's liability in tort to his employees.

- Liability by an employer to an employee can arise through an employer's personal liability; through breach of a statutory duty imposed on an employer; or through the employer's vicarious liability.

- An employer may be liable under his personal duty of care to an employee. This duty is a specialised aspect of negligence and usually applies only to an employee's physical well-being. There is usually no duty on an employer in respect of an employee's economic well-being, although this situation may be changing.

- The duty is to provide a competent staff, adequate materials and a safe system of work. In respect of materials, legislation imposes strict liability on the employer for supplying injury-causing defective equipment. The system is underpinned by compulsory insurance cover.

- The defence of contributory negligence applies but *volenti* will rarely be successful.

- There is now an action by an employee for negligently caused stress at work.

Further reading

Lang, B. (1984), 'The Employer's Liability (Defective Equipment) Act: Lion or Mouse?' 47 MLR 48.

McKendrick, E. (1990), 'Vicarious Liability and Independent Contractors' 53 MLR 770.

Mullaney, N. J. (2002), 'Containing Claims for Workplace Mental Illness' 118 LQR 373 (stress claims).

Mullender, R. (1996), 'Law Labour and Mental Harm' 59 MLR 296.

Njoya, W. (2005), 'Employment, Implicit Contracts and the Duty of Care' 121 LQR 33.

Sprince, A. (1995), 'Recovering Damages for Occupational Stress: *Walker* v *Northumberland County Council*' 17 Liverpool LR 189.

15

Medical negligence and related issues

Objectives

After reading this chapter you will:

1. Have a critical knowledge of the background to tort claims against the medical profession.

2. Understand the legal application of battery to medical practice and the legal rules on consent in a battery action.

3. Understand the legal rules relating to a negligence action against the medical profession.

Introduction

Objective 1

See Chapter 20 for trespass to the person.

See Chapters 2–10 for negligence.

See also Chapter 1 for cost of claims.

This chapter is designed to include the relevant tort materials on one area of litigation which has its own peculiarities. The chapter includes material which is covered generally in trespass to the person; negligence; defences to battery and negligence. Tort litigation against members of the medical profession is said to have raised problems for the financing of health care and medical practice. There have been claims that England is suffering a medical malpractice crisis similar to the United States. Doctors claim that the threat of litigation leads to 'defensive medicine': i.e. carrying out procedures in order to avoid being sued, rather than for the benefit of the patient. The rise in the Caesarean section rate is often pointed to as an example of defensive medicine. However, recent research shows that the number of claims for clinical negligence is dropping but the overall cost of claims is rising due to changes in the way in which damages are calculated and legal costs. The number of claims dropped from 10,980 in 2000–01 to 7,196 in 2004–05. The cost of claims, however, rose from £415 million in 2000–01 to £503 million in 2004–05. (R. Lewis, A. Morris and K. Oliphant (2006).) The amount paid out by the NHS Litigation Authority for 2009–10 was £787 million. Only 4 per cent of cases went to court. The remainder were settled or abandoned.

Victims of medical accidents are not happy with the negligence system. Numerous problems stand in the way of a person who wishes to sue for medical negligence. The action is expensive and legal aid is not easily available; lawyers with the necessary skills in this specialised area are not always easy to find; the system leads to a closing of ranks on the part of the medical profession, which makes it difficult for the patient to find out what went wrong; even if the victim does obtain compensation, this may be many years after the event.

Disenchantment with the system on the part of both doctors and patients led to calls for medical negligence to be replaced by a no-fault scheme of compensation. This was supported by the medical insurers, doctors, professional bodies and victim support agencies but the cost of such a scheme was estimated at £4 billion.

Evidence shows that family doctors are less likely to be sued than hospital doctors, as the former are more likely to have a relationship of trust with their patients than the more anonymous hospital doctors. The more complex procedures which are likely to lead to medical misadventures will be carried out in hospitals and, except in minor cases, patients are referred to specialists in hospitals.

For breach of duty, see Chapter 8.

From the point of view of the doctor, even an unsuccessful action can have negative effects on a career, and the action will be time consuming.

For causation, see Chapter 9.

The claimant in such an action will be faced with a difficult task in establishing matters such as breach of duty and causation, but the action may be the only way in which any compensation for the injury can be obtained. Research shows that many injured patients simply want to find out what went wrong. Ironically, the system means that they are unlikely to be told, in case they use the information as evidence in an action.

The question of taking medical 'accidents' out of the legal system has been discussed for a number of years, but the option of a comprehensive no-fault scheme was dismissed in 2003, when the cost was estimated at £4 billion per annum. An alternative to tort law was

See also Chapter 1 for NHS Redress Act.

introduced in the NHS Redress Act 2006, which establishes an NHS redress scheme to enable the settlement of certain low-value claims arising after adverse incidents without the need for court proceedings.

The scheme applies only to claims under £20,000 and will apply where the claim is by the estate or dependants of a deceased patient. It is not a 'no-fault scheme' as it applies only to claims in tort but it is hoped that it will remove the need for patients to go to court on low-cost claims.

The aim of the Act was to introduce a low-cost, quick and just procedure. It will apply where, in providing 'qualifying services', a person has incurred a qualifying liability in tort. In its initial phase it will apply to hospitals but not to general practitioners or dentists. The current clinical negligence litigation system will apply – this has been criticised because it retains some of the problems inherent in the present system and these may even be exacerbated by the fact that the NHS Litigation Authority (the current defender of NHS interests in litigation) will be the scheme manager. Further criticisms of the scheme are that it does not safeguard protections available to the patient with regard to accessing medico-legal advice and does not provide for any independent mechanism of appeal on facts. An advantage is that it will provide greater access for patients pursuing low-value claims.

Implementation of the scheme has been delayed as a result of the criticisms, the compensation culture debate and a long running inquiry as to how it fits with complaints against the NHS.

In legal terms, actions against doctors are likely to be brought in either battery (trespass to the person) or negligence. The battery action protects personal integrity and guards against treatment without consent. The negligence action acts as a form of compensation for a negligently injured patient and as a deterrent to doctors. A doctor's duty of care can be divided into three areas: advice, diagnosis and treatment.

> ### Example
>
> Nancy has gone to the Accident and Emergency Department of her local hospital. She has fallen from her bicycle and lost a lot of blood. She is seen by Doctor White who states that she needs a blood transfusion. Nancy refuses a blood transfusion because of her religious beliefs. Nancy then becomes unconscious and Dr White performs the blood transfusion. Due to negligence on the part of the hospital Nancy is given the wrong type of blood and dies.
>
> The issues here are whether Dr White has committed a battery to Nancy. This will involve issues of consent to treatment. Also, whether the hospital is liable in negligence for Nancy's death.

The battery action

Objective 2

For battery, see Chapter 20.

Consent is central to the idea of medical treatment and to the doctor–patient relationship. There is a general principle that a person cannot complain of that which they have consented to. A battery is the infliction of unlawful force on another person. A doctor who treats without consent may be guilty of a battery on the patient. The classic definition was given in a United States case by Cardozo J (*Schloendorff* v *Society of New York Hospitals* 105 NE 92 (NY 1914)):

> Every human being of adult years and sound mind has a right to determine what shall be done with his own body; a surgeon who performs an operation without the patient's consent commits an assault.

The issue of consent is an extremely complex one and raises a number of legal and ethical issues. The courts may be faced with a choice between individual autonomy (the right to choose) and paternalism (a court taking a decision in the patient's best interests).

The tests for consent were laid down common law but are now in statutory form. There is no difference between the common law and statutory tests. This test is now in statutory form. The Mental Capacity Act 2005 states:

Section 1

(2) A person must be assumed to have capacity unless it is established that he lacks capacity.

(3) A person is not to be treated as unable to make a decision unless all practicable steps to help do so have been taken without success.

(4) A person is not to be treated as unable to make a decision merely because he makes an unwise decision.

(5) An act done, or decision made, under this Act for or on behalf of a person who lacks capacity must be done, or made, in his best interests.

Sections 2, 3 and 5

A person will be considered to lack capacity if:

(i) the person is suffering from an impairment of or a disturbance in the functioning of the mind or brain which means they are unable to make a decision for themselves. This may be long term or temporary.

(ii) The person will be considered unable to make a decision if the doctor reasonably believes and takes reasonable steps to ensure that the patient is unable;

    (a) To understand the information relevant to the decision

    (b) To retain that information

    (c) To use or weigh that information as part of the process of making that decision, or

    (d) To communicate his decision.

If the test is satisfied then the doctor will not be liable in battery provided that he reasonably believes that the treatment is in the patient's best interests.

(Analysis of the Act taken from S. Pattinson, *Medical Law and Ethics* (2nd edition, Sweet and Maxwell, 2009.)

Nature of consent

The patient may give express consent, for example, by signing a consent form for a surgical operation, or there may be an implied consent, for example, by holding out an arm for an injection.

The patient's consent must be real. Once the patient has been informed in broad terms of the nature of the intended procedure and gives consent, then that consent is real.

Chatterton v Gerson [1981] QB 432

The claimant suffered a trapped nerve after a hernia operation. She consulted the defendant specialist who performed an operation to free the trapped nerve. As a result of the operation, the claimant lost all feeling in her leg. She sued the defendant in battery, on the ground that she had not truly consented to the operation, as its effect had not been properly explained to her. The claim failed. A battery action could only succeed where her consent was not real. As the defendant had explained the nature of the operation in general terms, her consent was real for the purposes of battery.

NB: Any alleged failure by the doctor to disclose risks about the treatment, which might have enabled the patient to give an informed consent, does not invalidate the consent. Any such action must be brought in negligence. (See 'Informed consent' below.)

Certain types of patients present particular problems.

Coma patients and the ending of life

What is the position where a person is in a coma and is unable to give or refuse consent and is unlikely to recover?

Airedale NHS Trust v Bland [1993] 1 All ER 821

The patient was in a persistent vegetative state (PVS), which meant that he was permanently unconscious. He had been in this state for three years and was kept alive by feeding tubes and the medical advice was that he would never recover. His doctor and parents agreed that it would be best for the patient if his tubes were withdrawn and the House of Lords granted a declaration that it would be lawful to do so, holding that an adult has an absolute right to refuse treatment, even if the consequence is that they will die. The doctor had a duty of care to the patient that required him to act in the patient's best interests. As the patient had no hope of recovery it would not be in his best interests to continue and it would therefore be lawful to withdraw the life support.

Lord Goff stated that there was no absolute rule that a patient's life had to be prolonged by treatment or care regardless of the circumstances. The patient's right of self-determination qualified the principle of sanctity of life. It was inconsistent with self-determination that no means should be provided for treatment to be withheld in a case where the patient was incapable of indicating whether or not he consented to treatment. A distinction was drawn between a case where a doctor sought to bring life to an end by an act of commission, such as a fatal overdose, and one where life-saving treatment was discontinued. The test was what was in the patient's best interests. (See also *Wyatt v Portsmouth NHS Trust* [2005] 1 WLR 3995.)

Re AK (adult patient) (medical treatment: consent) [2001] 1 FLR 129

A patient who suffered from motor neurone disease was being kept alive on a ventilator. He lost the ability to communicate and two weeks later asked the doctors to remove the ventilator. This would inevitably result in his death. A declaration was given that in withdrawing treatment at the patient's request the doctors would not be acting unlawfully. If they continued to treat they would be acting unlawfully. (See also *Re B (adult: refusal of medical treatment)* [2002] 2 All ER 449.)

In these cases the courts drew a distinction between a doctor taking positive steps actively to end life (euthanasia) and an omission where the doctor discontinues life-saving treatment. The former is illegal and the court's permission should be sought on the latter in virtually all cases.

The withdrawal of treatment in these circumstances will not amount to a breach of Article 2 (right to life) or Article 3 (right not to suffer degrading treatment) of the European Convention on Human Rights. (*NHS Trust A v M; NHS Trust B v H* [2001] 2 WLR 942.) Article 2 requires a deliberate act rather than an omission, by someone acting on behalf of the state, which results in death. Where treatment has been discontinued in the best interests of the patient following the views of a respectable body of medical opinion (the *Bolam* test), the state's positive obligations under Article 2 have been discharged.

Pregnancy

A further problem is in the case of pregnant women where the interests of the mother and the interests of the foetus may conflict.

St George's Healthcare Trust v S [1999] Fam 26

The Court of Appeal confirmed that an adult of sound mind had the right to refuse medical treatment even though this would result in the death of a foetus. A pregnant woman was refusing medical treatment for a life-threatening condition. The fact of pregnancy does not take away the mother's right to decide whether or not to have medical treatment. Neither can the Mental Health Act 1983 be used to detain and treat a person because their thought processes are regarded as bizarre, irrational and contrary to the views of the majority of the population.

Judge LJ:

> . . . while pregnancy increases the personal responsibilities of a woman it does not diminish her entitlement to decide whether or not to undergo medical treatment. Although human . . . an unborn child is not a separate person from its mother. Its need for medical assistance does not prevail over her rights. She is entitled not to be forced to submit to an invasion of her body against her will, whether her own life or that of her unborn child depends on it. Her right is not reduced or diminished merely because her decision to exercise it may appear morally repugnant.

The unconscious

Where a patient is unconscious and therefore incapable of giving a consent, the doctor will be entitled to give treatment on the basis of necessity.

F v West Berkshire Health Authority [1989] 2 All ER 545

The test for whether treatment is necessary is whether it is in the best interests of the patient. What is in the best interests of the patient will be judged by the standards of a responsible body of medical opinion. The decision would appear to give the medical profession considerable latitude in deciding what is necessary.

Lord Goff stated that where the unconsciousness was temporary, the doctor may not proceed contrary to the stated interests of the patient, provided the patient was rationally capable of forming such a wish. Neither should the doctor do more than is reasonably necessary in the interests of the patient.

Lord Brandon stated that an operation or treatment would be in the patient's best interests if it was carried out to save the patient's life, ensure improvement, or prevent physical or mental deterioration.

Lord Bridge stated:

> The issues canvassed in argument before your Lordships revealed the paucity of clearly defined principles in the common law which may be applied to determine the lawfulness of medical or surgical treatment given to a patient who for any reason, temporary or permanent, lacks the capacity to give or to communicate consent to that treatment. It seems to me to be axiomatic that treatment which is necessary to preserve the life, health or well-being of the patient may lawfully be given without consent. But, if a rigid criterion of necessity were to be applied to determine what is and what is not lawful in the treatment of the unconscious and the incompetent, many of those unfortunate enough to be deprived of the capacity to make or communicate rational decisions by accident, illness or unsoundness of mind might be deprived of treatment which it would be entirely beneficial for them to receive.
>
> Moreover, it seems to me of first importance that the common law should be readily intelligible to and applicable by all those who undertake the care of persons lacking the capacity to consent to treatment. It would be intolerable for members of the medical, nursing and other professions devoted to the care of the sick that, in caring for those lacking the capacity to consent to treatment, they should be put in the dilemma that, if they administer the treatment which they believe to be in the patient's best interests, acting with due skill and care, they run the risk of being held guilty of trespass to the person, but, if they withhold that treatment, they may be in breach of a duty of care owed to the patient. If those who undertake responsibility for the care of incompetent or unconscious patients administer curative or prophylactic [tending to prevent disease] treatment which they believe to be appropriate to the patient's existing condition of disease, injury or bodily malfunction or susceptibility to such a condition in the future, the lawfulness of that treatment should be judged by one standard, not two. It follows that if the professionals in question have acted with due skill and care, judged by the well-known test laid down in **Bolam v Friern Hospital Management Committee** [1957] 1 WLR 582, they should be immune from liability in trespass, just as they are immune from liability in negligence. The special considerations which apply in the case of sterilisation of a woman who is physically perfectly healthy or of an operation on an organ transplant donor arise only because such treatment cannot be considered either curative or prophylactic.

If a patient is in a persistent vegetative state (permanently unconscious) it is not in the patient's best interests that they continue to receive medication or nourishment which is futile. The justification for continuing treatment does not apply and it is not unlawful to discontinue medical treatment or nourishment for such a patient even though the inevitable outcome is that the patient will die. This will not be an act done by someone acting on behalf of the state but a responsible decision by a medical team based on clinical judgement that it is no longer in the patient's best interests to continue treatment. As this is an omission it cannot amount to intentional deprivation of life contrary to Article 2 of the European Convention on Human Rights. (**NHS Trust A v M; NHS Trust B v H** [2001] 2 WLR 942.)

Advance directives

Difficulties can arise where a patient has indicated their wishes in advance. The following case is one where the claimant sought judicial review of the legality of guidance to doctors issued by the General Medical Council.

R (on the application of Burke) v *General Medical Council* [2006] QB 273

The claimant suffered from a congenital degenerative brain condition which would at some time in the future inevitably result in his needing to receive nutrition and hydration by artificial means. It was expected that he would remain competent until the final stages of his condition. He was concerned that, before those final stages, a decision might be taken by medical practitioners responsible for his care to withdraw artificial nutrition and hydration from him when he wished to continue to receive it, regardless of his pain or suffering. In order to obtain clarification as to the circumstances in which treatment might lawfully be withdrawn, he claimed judicial review of guidance issued by the General Medical Council by way of declarations to the effect that it was incompatible with his rights at common law and under Articles 2, 3 and 8 of the Convention for the Protection of Human Rights. The judge held the guidance to be amenable to judicial review and made declarations to the effect.

The Court of Appeal held, allowing the appeal, that once a patient was accepted into hospital, the medical staff came under a positive common law duty to care for him, a fundamental aspect of which was a duty to take reasonable steps to keep the patient alive; that where that necessitated artificial nutrition and hydration the duty of care would normally require it to be supplied; that, although the duty to keep a patient alive by administering artificial nutrition and hydration or other life-prolonging treatment did not apply where a competent patient refused such treatment or where it was not considered to be in the best interests of an incompetent patient for him to be artificially kept alive, where a competent patient made it clear that, regardless of pain, suffering or indignity, he wished to be kept alive, the positive duty to take reasonable steps to do so persisted; that deliberately to bring about the death of a competent patient by withdrawing life-prolonging treatment contrary to the patient's wishes would infringe the patient's rights under Articles 2, 3 and 8 of the Convention; that, accordingly, the doctor with care of the claimant would be obliged, so long as the treatment was prolonging the claimant's life, to provide artificial nutrition and hydration in accordance with his expressed wish; and that, since the General Medical Council's guidance in relation to the withdrawal of such treatment did not provide otherwise, there were no grounds for declaring it to be unlawful.

Per curiam. (i) For a doctor deliberately to interrupt life-prolonging treatment in the face of a competent patient's expressed wish to be kept alive, with the intention thereby of terminating the patient's life, would leave the doctor with no answer to a charge of murder.

(ii) Where in the last stage of life the provision of artificial nutrition and hydration would not prolong life but might hasten death, the patient's wish to continue to receive it would not be determinative, since a patient cannot demand that a doctor administer treatment which the doctor considers is adverse to the patient's clinical needs.

(iii) Where the legality of a proposed treatment or the withdrawal of treatment is in doubt, good practice may require a medical practitioner to seek a declaration as to its lawfulness but he is not required to do so as a matter of law.

(See also *Practice Note (Official Solicitor: Declaratory Proceedings: Medical and Welfare Decisions for Adults who Lack Capacity)* [2006] 2 FLR 373.)

Religious beliefs

Another problem in this area is that of the patient who for religious reasons objects to a blood transfusion. If the patient is conscious and capable, then the doctor must observe their wishes or be liable in battery. If the patient is unconscious and the doctor is unaware of the objection, then provided the best interests of the patient test is satisfied, no liability attaches. It is clear that a patient's next of kin has no legal right to consent or refuse consent in the case of an adult patient. (*Re T (an adult)* [1992] 4 All ER 649.) However, it is fairly common for doctors to obtain the consent of the next of kin as this makes litigation less likely. If the doctor is aware of the objection, then it would appear from Lord Goff's judgment that the doctor may be liable if he goes ahead with the transfusion.

Minors

In order to give a valid consent, it is necessary that the patient had the capacity to do so. At what age will a child be capable of giving a valid consent? There are two possibilities: status or understanding. If a status test is used, then a particular age is fixed at which consent may be given. This has the advantage for the medical profession of certainty, but does not allow for children maturing at different ages.

The consent of a minor aged 16 years or more is effective and there is no need for parental consent. (Family Law Reform Act 1969 s 8(1).)

In the case of children under 16 years, the courts have adopted a test of understanding. (*Gillick* v *West Norfolk& Wisbech Area Health Authority* [1986] AC 112.) The case was concerned with whether a child under the age of 16 years could be given contraceptive advice without the consent of her parents. The House of Lords ruled that she could, provided she had sufficient understanding. The problem with this test is what is meant by *understanding*. In *Gillick*, a high test of understanding was set, but it is not clear whether this applies to all forms of medical treatment.

Where the child is incapable of giving a valid consent, it is standard practice to seek parental consent where this is possible. If such consent is withheld, then the doctor could seek to initiate care proceedings (*Re R (a minor)* [1993] 2 FCR 544) or invite the High Court to exercise its inherent jurisdiction (*Re O (a minor)* [1993] 2 FLR 149). The former is a statutory jurisdiction, but in either case the court was willing to order a blood transfusion contrary to the parent's wishes where the medical arguments showed the need. The court can then give consent to the proposed treatment or withholding of treatment, if it thinks this is in the best interests of the child. Parental objections to HIV testing of a baby when the mother was HIV positive were overruled as the welfare of the child was of paramount concern. (*Re C (a child) (HIV testing)* [2000] Fam 48.) Parental objection to the separation of conjoined twins was also overruled, even though the inevitable result of the separation was that one of the twins would die. (*Re A (children) (conjoined twins: surgical separation)* [2001] Fam 147.) This case demonstrates the importance of necessity in medical treatment.

See also Chapter 1 and Chapter 22 on Article 9.

Where there is no application to the court, there may be a breach of Article 8 of the European Convention on Human Rights.

Glass v *United Kingdom* [2004] 39 EHRR 15

The first applicant was a severely mentally and physically disabled child requiring 24-hour care. The second applicant was his mother. The child had been particularly unwell and required ventilation. The mother opposed the use of morphine or drugs to relieve distress in the future treatment of her son and expected him to receive resuscitation should his heart stop. The treating doctors did not agree and an application to court was considered. Eventually the mother agreed to morphine in therapeutic doses only. The child's condition deteriorated and the doctors wanted to administer diamorphine as pain relief as they believed he was dying. The mother and her family did not agree. The mother wished to take her son home but was told she would be arrested if she removed him and she was unable to contact her solicitor. A 'do not resuscitate' (DNR) order was put on the child's case notes without the mother's consent. The doctors agreed to cease diamorphine if the family agreed not to resuscitate. The mother believed that her son was being covertly euthanased and a fight broke out between the doctors and the family. The mother successfully resuscitated her son who later improved and was discharged home. The applicants alleged, amongst other matters, that domestic law and practice failed to ensure effective respect for the first applicant's right to physical and moral integrity within the meaning of 'private life' under Article 8. The European Court of Human Rights found a violation of Article 8 and awarded non-pecuniary damage and costs. The decision to impose treatment in defiance of the parent's objections gave rise to an interference with the child's right to respect for his private life and in particular his right to physical integrity. The fact that doctors are regularly confronted with an emergency and have to act quickly does not detract from the fact of interference, but goes to the question of necessity. Earlier discussions on treatment in the event of an emergency highlighted disagreement and the NHS Trust should have sought the intervention of the court at that time and should not have engaged in insensitive attempts to overcome the parent's opposition.

Where the treatment is urgent in order to save life and the parents refuse consent, the doctor will probably be protected at common law if the treatment is in the child's best interests. (*F v West Berkshire Health Authority* [1989] 2 All ER 545.)

Mental disorder

The fact that a person is suffering from a mental disorder within the Mental Health Act 1983 does not preclude a legally effective consent (ss 57 and 58). The question in each case is whether the person was capable of understanding.

Where a person was not capable of understanding, the doctor must apply the best interests of the patient test. In *F v West Berkshire Health Authority*, Lord Goff stated:

> where the state of affairs is permanent or semi-permanent, as . . . in the case of a mentally disordered person . . . there is no point in waiting to obtain the patient's consent . . . the doctor must act in the best interests of his patient, just as if he had received his patient's consent so to do . . . the lawfulness of the doctor's action is to be found in the principle of necessity . . . the doctor must act in accordance with a responsible and competent body of relevant professional opinion . . . it may be good practice to consult relatives and others who are concerned with the care of the patient.

Refusal of treatment

A series of Court of Appeal decisions has attempted to lay down guidelines for minors and adults as to when a refusal to be treated can be overridden by a parent or by the court. The cases bring into stark contrast the difficulties of attempting to balance personal autonomy, what is in the patient's best interests and what is in the state's best interests.

Each case, however, has to be determined on its own facts. The welfare of the patient is the paramount consideration. In the case of a child, the parent's wishes will be taken into consideration but are not decisive.

Children present particular difficulties in terms of consent and we have already seen in *Gillick* that in the case of a child under 16 years the court adopts a test of understanding. However, what happens when the child does understand and refuses treatment which the parent or person *in loco parentis* feels they should have?

Re R (a minor) [1991] 4 All ER 177

The patient was a 15-year-old girl who suffered phases of disturbed behaviour for which she was given sedative treatment. She refused the treatment and wardship proceedings were instituted by the local authority. The Court of Appeal held that the court had wider powers than a parent in these matters and the refusal or consent to treatment by a ward could be overridden by the court if that was in the ward's best interests.

This may seem inconsistent with the *Gillick* decision, which gave autonomy to a competent child. The court stated that *Gillick* was concerned with normal children and that *R* was not competent to make the decision.

Of more far-reaching consequence, the court stated that while a '*Gillick* competent' child could consent to treatment, the refusal of such a child to have treatment did not have the same force and could be overridden, certainly by the court and possibly by the parents. This point does not seem to be consistent with *Gillick*, although it is perhaps defensible on the grounds that where a child consents to treatment, medical opinion must be in favour of the treatment, whereas a refusal could be contrary to the child's best interests and the opinion of the medical profession.

Persons over the age of 16 years have a statutory right to give consent to medical treatment under the Family Law Reform Act 1969 s 8(1). Do they have a right to refuse treatment?

Re W (a minor) [1992] 4 All ER 627

The 16-year-old patient suffered from anorexia nervosa and refused treatment. The Court of Appeal held that she should be treated on the basis that her illness had destroyed her capacity to make an informed choice.

It was also held that the court had powers in wardship irrespective of the Family Law Reform Act 1969 s 8(1). This section gives minors who have reached the age of 16 the right to consent to medical treatment. Lord Donaldson MR stated that this right could be overridden by those with parental responsibility for the child.

Any minor who was '*Gillick* competent' had the right to consent to treatment to which that competence extended. This right could be overridden by the court.

No minor had the power, by refusing treatment, to override the consent by someone who had parental responsibility. However, such a refusal was a very important consideration to be taken into account when making clinical judgements, and the importance of the refusal increased with the age and maturity of the minor.

Does a court have the power to override a refusal of treatment by an adult?

Re T (an adult) [1992] 4 All ER 649

The patient was injured in a crash and refused to sign a consent form for a blood transfusion after speaking to her mother who was a Jehovah's Witness.

A declaration that she should be given a blood transfusion was upheld by the Court of Appeal as it was in her best interests. The absolute right of an adult to consent or refuse treatment was upheld by the court and the decision was justified on the grounds that her mental condition had deteriorated to the state where she was incapable of making the choice and that her decision was swayed by her mother's influence.

> The court upheld the principle that a competent adult Jehovah's Witness had the right to refuse a blood transfusion, even though the refusal was life-threatening, and even where the refusal was expressed prior to the patient becoming incompetent to make a decision. Three conditions were required. The patient had to be competent at the time the decision was made. The decision had to cover a situation that was life-threatening. The decision to refuse was not to be made under the undue influence of another.

The decision in *Re T* does not mean that an adult suffering from some mental disability cannot refuse consent. The question is always one of the patient's capacity. Does the patient have the capacity to comprehend and retain the information given, believe it and make a choice? (*Re JT (adult: refusal of medical treatment)* [1998] 1 FLR 48.)

The decision in *Re W* and that in *Re S (adult: refusal of medical treatment)* [1992] 4 All ER 671 cast some doubt on whether English courts are willing to uphold the autonomy of the patient. Does the *Re W* decision mean that a court would be prepared to order a teen-aged girl to have an abortion against her wishes? *Re S* was concerned with the difficulty created where doctors wished to carry out a Caesarean section on a competent pregnant woman whose refusal was based on her religious beliefs. The court held that it would be lawful to carry out the operation contrary to her wishes as the well-being of her baby took priority.

That the courts are no nearer to solving this dilemma is illustrated by *Re MB* (below).

Re MB (medical treatment) [1997] 2 FLR 426

> The patient refused to consent to a Caesarean section because of her needle phobia, and the risk to the foetus would have been greatly enhanced in the absence of this procedure. The Court of Appeal restated the absolute right to refuse medical treatment of an adult competent patient. The doctors could not intervene unless the patient lacked capacity and the treatment was in the patient's best interests. The court had no capacity to take into account the interests of the unborn child. (*Re S* was said to be out of line with other decisions and explained as having been made under pressure of time.) Despite this, the court found that, at the critical point, the needle phobia put the patient in such a state of panic that she was incapable of making a decision and was, therefore, incompetent. (See also *St George's Healthcare Trust v S* [1999] Fam 26.)

A different problem is created where there is a conflict of opinion between medical staff and a minor's parents as to whether or not the minor should be given medical treatment. The Court of Appeal in an earlier case (*Re J (a minor)* [1992] 2 FLR 165) stated that there is no right to demand medical treatment and that the medical profession cannot be ordered to undertake treatment contrary to their judgement. This decision was consistent with the policy that the allocation of scarce health care resources is generally a question for the health services and not for the courts. The principles in these difficult cases were considered in the following case where the medical staff wished to withdraw treatment from a child and the patient's parents wanted invasive surgery.

An NHS Trust v MB [2006] 2 FLR 319

> The claimant NHS trust (*N*) sought a declaration in respect of the first defendant (*M*) that it should be lawful and in *M*'s best interests for *N* to withdraw all forms of ventilation from him, and *M*'s parents applied for a declaration that it should be lawful and in *M*'s best interests for a tracheostomy to be performed to enable long-term ventilation to be carried out. *M* had been in hospital since the age of

seven weeks. He suffered from spinal muscular atrophy of the severest type. The condition was progressive and degenerative. Even with the continuation of treatment, death was inevitable. *M* could survive even for a small number of years or could die suddenly and soon. It was very difficult to assess how much discomfort or distress *M* experienced, but it was inevitable that some interventions were uncomfortable for him. *N* considered that the quality of life for *M* was so low, and the burdens of living so great, that it was unethical to continue artificially to keep him alive.

Held: Both applications were rejected. (1) *M*'s welfare was the paramount consideration. Considerable weight had to be attached to the prolongation of life but it was not absolute or necessarily decisive. (***Wyatt v Portsmouth NHS Trust*** [2005] 1 WLR 3995 applied.) The views of both the doctors and the parents had to be carefully considered, but the latter's wishes were irrelevant to consideration of the objective best interests of the child save to the extent that they illuminated the quality and value to the child of the child-parent relationship.

(2) It was probable and had to be assumed that *M* continued to see and to hear and to feel touch; to have an awareness of his surroundings, in particular of the people who were closest to him; and to have the normal thoughts and thought processes of a small child of 18 months, with the proviso that, because he had never left hospital, he had not experienced the same range of stimuli and experiences as a more normal 18-month-old.

(3) It was not in *M*'s best interests to discontinue ventilation with the inevitable result that he would die. *M* had age-appropriate cognition, a relationship of value with his family, and other pleasures from sight, touch and sound. Those benefits were precious and real and the routine discomfort, distress and pain that *M* suffered did not outweigh those benefits.

(4) However, it would not be in *M*'s best interests to undergo procedures that went beyond maintaining ventilation, required the positive infliction of pain and would mean, if they became necessary, that *M* had moved naturally towards death, despite the ventilation.

The negligence action

Introduction

Objective 3

For negligence, see Chapters 2–10.

For vicarious liability, see Chapter 24.

If the patient has been referred to a hospital or has sought emergency treatment at a hospital, then they may proceed against the negligent individual, the relevant health authority, or both.

The individual will be primarily liable and the health authority vicariously liable for its employees' negligence. The vicarious liability of hospitals for all their full-time staff was finally established in ***Cassidy v Ministry of Health*** [1951] 2 KB 343.

There is some doubt as to whether a health authority is primarily liable, i.e. that it owes a non-delegable duty to its patients; there is no direct authority in English law, but the Court of Appeal has remarked, *obiter*, that it 'can see no reason why, in principle, the health authority should not be [directly] liable if its organisation is at fault'. (***Wilsher v Essex Area Health Authority*** [1987] 2 All ER 909.) This could occur where a mistake is made by a junior doctor who has been required to work long hours because of his contract of employment and made the mistake through exhaustion. (See also ***Bull v Devon AHA*** [1993] 4 Med LR 117.)

Until 1990, an agreement between the Ministry of Health and the medical defence societies (who provide indemnity insurance for doctors) allowed for the costs of any action to be shared between the two parties. Since January 1990, however, the entire cost of a negligence action has been borne by the National Health Service.

In structure, the negligence action against a doctor is no different to any other negligence case. The claimant must prove that a duty of care was owed to them, that this was broken and that reasonably foreseeable damage was caused as a result.

The duty of care

For duty of care generally, see Chapter 3.

Duty of care presents few problems in this area. The question of whether a duty of care exists is not in dispute. The only problem is what the duty is, i.e. what did the doctor undertake to do, and when did the duty come into existence? A doctor owes a duty of care in respect of advice, diagnosis and treatment.

One problem area is the primary liability of health authorities (see above). One point is clear on this. If the authority can show that a lack of sufficiently qualified staff is due to overall financial problems, then an action would be unlikely to succeed. The issue has, to date, arisen in the context of public law cases alleging misuse of statutory powers.

R v Secretary of State for Social Services ex p Hincks (1979) 123 Sol Jo 436

Patients sought a declaration that the Secretary of State and health authorities were in breach of duty as they had had to wait an unreasonable time because of a decision not to build a new block for a hospital on grounds of cost. The application failed, as the decision could only be challenged if the decision was thoroughly unreasonable.

Similar decisions were reached in the cases involving hole-in-the-heart babies who had to wait for treatment because of a shortage of trained specialist nursing staff. It is thought that these cases were brought more for publicity, to force the health authority to act, than in the hope of legal success. Courts will interfere with a spending decision of a public authority only in the most unusual circumstances. However, in *R (on the application of Rogers)* v *Swindon NHS Primary Care Trust* [2006] 1 WLR 2649, the Court of Appeal held that a health authority's policy on treatment for breast cancer was irrational. However, in this case the trust had decided to fund a drug for some patients and not others.

Breach of duty

See also Chapter 8 for breach of duty generally.

As this is a negligence action, liability is based on proof of fault. The claimant must prove that the defendant fell below the relevant standard of care. The doctor does not guarantee a cure, only undertakes to use reasonable care.

The standard of care expected of a doctor was laid down in the following case.

Bolam v Friern Hospital Management Committee [1957] 2 All ER 118

The allegation was that a doctor had been negligent in administering electro-convulsive therapy to a patient without a relaxant drug or restraining convulsive movements. The claimant suffered a fractured jaw.

McNair J stated:

I must explain what in law we mean by 'negligence'. In the ordinary case which does not involve any special skill, negligence in law means this: some failure to do some act which a reasonable man in the circumstances would do, or doing some act which a reasonable man in the circumstances would not do; and if that failure or doing of that act results in injury, then there is a cause of action. How do you test whether this act or failure is negligent? In an ordinary case it is generally said, that you judge that by the action of the man in the street. He is the ordinary man. In one case it has been said that you judge it by the conduct of the man on the top of a Clapham omnibus. He is the ordinary man. But where you get a situation which involves the use of some special skill or competence, then the test whether there has been negligence or not is not the test of the man on the top of a Clapham omnibus, because he has not got this special skill. The test is the standard of the ordinary skilled man exercising and professing to have that special skill. A man need not possess the highest expert skill at the risk of being found negligent. It is well-established law that it is sufficient if he exercises the ordinary skill of an ordinary competent man exercising that particular art. I do not think that I quarrel much with any of the submissions in law which have been put before you by counsel. Counsel for the plaintiff put it in this way, that in the case of a medical man negligence means failure to act in accordance with the standards of reasonably competent medical men at the time. That is a perfectly accurate statement, as long as it is remembered that there may be one or more perfectly proper standards; and if a medical man conforms with one of those proper standards then he is not negligent. Counsel for the plaintiff was also right, in my judgment, in saying: that a mere personal belief that a particular technique is best is no defence unless that belief is based on reasonable grounds. That again is unexceptionable.

On the facts, the defendant was found not liable, as he had conformed with a practice which was approved by a responsible body of medical opinion.

The test for medical negligence is therefore the standard of the ordinary skilled doctor and the question is whether what the defendant did is something that no medical practitioner using due care would do. The courts therefore allowed the medical profession to set their own standard. A doctor accused of negligence by a patient can defend themselves by showing that what they did was accepted practice, provided that practice was approved by responsible opinion in the medical profession. (See *Bolitho* below.)

The *Bolam* test has come under criticism (not least because it allows the profession to set its own standard) but has survived virtually intact. (But see *Bolitho* below.)

Whitehouse v *Jordan* [1981] 1 All ER 267

Negligence was alleged on the part of a senior registrar in charge of a childbirth. It was claimed that he had pulled too long and too hard in a trial of forceps delivery and this had caused the claimant's head to become wedged or stuck, resulting in asphyxia and brain damage. At the trial the mother gave evidence that when the forceps were applied she was lifted off the bed. The questions for decision were: (a) In what manner did the defendant use the forceps? (b) Was that manner consistent with the degree of skill which a member of his profession is obliged by law to exercise? On (a) the evidence was held not to establish the allegation. On (b) the House of Lords restated the *Bolam* test and rejected any test based on errors of clinical judgement.

In the Court of Appeal Lord Denning had attempted to qualify *Bolam* by saying that an error of clinical judgement was not necessarily negligence.

Lord Edmund-Davies:

To say that a surgeon committed an error of clinical judgment is wholly ambiguous, for, while some such errors may be completely consistent with the due exercise of professional skill, other acts or omissions in the course of exercising 'clinical judgment' may be so glaringly below proper standards as to make a finding of negligence inevitable. Indeed, I should have regarded this as a truism were it not that, despite the exposure of the 'false antithesis' by Donaldson LJ in his dissenting judgment in the Court of Appeal, counsel for the defendants adhered to it before your Lordships. But doctors and surgeons fall into no special category, and, to avoid any future disputation of a similar kind, I would have it accepted that the

> true doctrine was enunciated, and by no means for the first time, by McNair J in **Bolam v Friern Hospital Management Committee** [1957] 1 WLR 582 at 586 in the following words:
>
> > . . . where you get a situation which involves the use of some special skill or competence, then the test as to whether there has been negligence or not is not the test of the man on the top of a Clapham omnibus, because he has not got this special skill. The test is the standard of the ordinary skilled man exercising and professing to have that special skill.
> >
> > If a surgeon fails to measure up to that standard in any respect ('clinical judgement' or otherwise), he has been negligent and should be so adjudged.

Maynard v West Midland Regional Health Authority [1985] 1 All ER 635

Two consultants believed that the claimant was suffering from pulmonary tuberculosis, but also considered the possibility that she might have Hodgkin's disease. She was in fact suffering from tuberculosis. Tests were carried out but it was decided to operate before the results of the tests were known. The claimant sued for damage to the vocal cords as a result of the operation. It was held by the House of Lords that the defendants were not negligent as they had conformed to a practice approved by one responsible body of medical opinion. Where there are conflicting practices (as there were in this case), negligence is not established by proving that the defendant has not followed one practice.

What constitutes a 'responsible body of medical opinion' was considered by the Court of Appeal in **Defreitas v O'Brien** [1995] 6 Med LR 108. The claimant's action alleged medical negligence against a consultant orthopaedic surgeon and a consultant neurosurgeon. The Court of Appeal considered the claimant's contention that the court had to be satisfied that the standard accorded with that upheld by a 'substantial body of medical opinion' and that *substantial* had to be viewed in a quantitative sense. Otton LJ, however, observed that:

> the issue could not be determined by counting heads. It was open to the judge to find as a fact that a small number of specialists constituted a responsible body and that body would have considered the surgeon's decision justified, or, more simply, that the plaintiff had failed to discharge the burden of proof that the surgeon had been negligent.

The **Bolam** test applies to advice, diagnosis and treatment. (But see 'Informed consent' on advice.) The degree of skill will vary according to the post held by the doctor, rather than the experience of the individual. A consultant will be expected to show the degree of skill normally exhibited by a consultant in that field. A novice is expected to show the degree of skill exhibited by a junior doctor, even if it is the first day on the job. The inexperienced should be able to call on the advice of their superiors. Where there is a failure in supervision, then the superior could be negligent. If the system does not provide for supervision, then the health authority could be primarily liable because it is well established that doctors need to do their training on the job.

The duty of care is imposed by law but the standard is a matter of medical practice. Where there is only one accepted practice, then following this practice will not amount to negligence. In exceptional cases the courts may take the view that established practice is unsatisfactory and find negligence. However, there appears to be only one reported case since **Bolam** where this has occurred. (**Hucks v Cole** (1968) 112 Sol Jo 483.)

Where there is more than one accepted practice, then following a practice approved by a responsible body of medical opinion will exonerate the doctor.

The issue of who sets the standard of care and the relationship between standard of care and causation was considered by the House of Lords in **Bolitho** (below).

Bolitho v City and Hackney Health Authority [1997] 3 WLR 1151

See also Chapter 8 for *Bolitho*.

A two-year-old with croup died after a sudden respiratory crisis. The defendant doctor urgently summoned by a nurse negligently failed to attend and could not raise her substitute, whose pager had flat batteries. Had a doctor attended and intubated the child, the child would have lived, but not all doctors would have intubated him and the defendant said she would not have done so.

The trial judge (based on evidence given by an expert in paediatric respiratory medicine called by the defence that intubation would not have been appropriate) held that, judged by the **Bolam** standard, a decision by the doctor not to intubate would have been in accordance with a body of responsible professional opinion and causation had not been proved. This was upheld by a majority of the Court of Appeal.

The House of Lords held as follows:

1 In the generality of cases the **Bolam** test had no application in deciding questions of causation; however, where the breach of duty consisted of an omission to do an act which ought to have been done, the question of what would have constituted a continuing exercise of proper care had the initial failure not taken place, so as to determine if the injuries would have been avoided, fell to be decided by that test. In applying the test, the court had to be satisfied that the exponents of a body of professional opinion relied on had demonstrated that such opinion had a logical basis and, in particular, had directed their minds to the question of comparative risks and benefits and had reached a defensible conclusion.

2 If, in a rare case, it had been demonstrated that the professional opinion was incapable of withstanding logical analysis, the judge was entitled to hold that it could not provide the benchmark by reference to which the doctor's conduct fell to be assessed. In most cases the fact that experts in the field were of a particular opinion would be a demonstration of the reasonableness of that opinion.

3 As the trial judge had directed himself correctly and there had been good reason for acceptance of the defendant's expert opinion, it had not been proved that the doctor's failure to attend had caused the injuries complained of.

The significance of the **Bolitho** decision is that it reaffirms the role of the court in assessing whether treatment has been negligent. It will rarely be necessary for a court to find that the views held by a competent medical expert are unreasonable but it is nevertheless possible.

The standard of care owed by medical professionals can be summarised as follows:

1 Has the defendant acted in accordance with a medical practice accepted as correct by a respectable body of medical opinion? (**Bolam.**)

2 Was this practice logical and reasonable? (**Bolitho.**)

3 The courts will not choose between two contrary bodies of respectable medical opinion. (**Ministry of Justice v Carter** [2010] EWCA Civ 694.)

Proof of negligence

See also Chapter 8 for proof of negligence and *res ipsa loquitur*.

The burden of proof is on the claimant to prove negligence and this may be difficult as they may not know what happened.

The courts may allow the claimant to rely on the doctrine of *res ipsa loquitur*. The precise nature of the negligence must be unknown and no explanation of the way in which the injury was inflicted offered by the defendant. The injury must be of the kind that does not normally happen unless there is negligence. If the injury sustained was an inherent risk of the procedure, then the doctrine will be inapplicable.

In general, the courts are reluctant to allow the doctrine to be used in medical negligence cases unless there is a clear inference of negligence from the known facts.

The Court of Appeal has stated that it may apply in clear-cut cases, such as where a surgeon amputates the wrong foot or a patient wakes up in the middle of an operation despite a general anaesthetic. In these cases what happened is sufficient to give rise to an inference of negligence based on ordinary human experience. Most clinical negligence cases, however, depend on expert evidence and a judge summing up would decide the case on the basis of inferences he was entitled to draw from the whole of the evidence, including the expert evidence. The Court of Appeal suggested that the phrase '*res ipsa loquitur*' should be dropped from the litigators' phrasebook and replaced with the expression '*prima facie* case'. (*Ratcliffe* v *Plymouth & Torbay Health Authority* (1998) PIQR P170.)

Cassidy v Ministry of Health [1951] 2 KB 343

The claimant went into hospital with two stiff fingers and came out with four stiff fingers. The court held that this should not have happened if due care had been used and the doctrine was applied. As the defendants were unable to rebut the inference of negligence, they were liable.

The doctrine has also been used in cases where swabs have been left in patients after operations (*Mahon* v *Osborne* [1939] 2 KB 14) and where the heart of a healthy man went into cardiac arrest under general anaesthesia. (*Glass* v *Cambridge Health Authority* [1995] 6 Med LR 91.) In the latter case the defendants escaped liability by proving that they were not negligent.

Informed consent

The concept of informed consent originates in the United States and requires that the doctor not only obtain the patient's consent to the treatment, but also must give the patient sufficient information to enable the patient to make an informed choice as to whether to undertake the treatment or not. Typically, this will involve warnings as to the dangers inherent in the treatment and the alternatives available.

Informed consent involves a fascinating tension between the right of personal autonomy and the right to compensation. Originally, the idea was to broaden the scope of compensation for medical accidents in the United States and extend compensation to more victims. However, this created a problem as the right which is violated is the right of self-determination (autonomy) and the remedy is compensation for personal injuries. The harm suffered by the patient is not the direct result of infringement of the right to personal autonomy, but of the medical treatment itself.

Example

Patient *A* is referred to consultant *B* suffering from pains in the leg. *B* correctly diagnoses this as a problem with a nerve in *A*'s leg. There are three methods of treating this, but *B* wishes to undertake one of these methods as he is preparing to do research on this method of treatment. He therefore explains to *A* that he proposes to operate and carry out a certain procedure. *A* signs a consent form for the operation which is carried out with all reasonable care by *B*. However, the operation carries with it a 3 per cent risk that the patient's leg will be paralysed. This happens to *A* and he sues *B*.

The right which has been infringed by B is A's right of self-determination. A was not told that the risk existed or that other methods of treatment existed and was therefore unable to make an informed choice. However, the harm in this case has been caused by the medical treatment itself (which is non-negligent) rather than the infringement of A's right of self-determination.

In the United States, a doctor will not avoid litigation by simply informing the patient of the nature of the treatment in broad terms. They will be under a duty to warn of dangers in the proposed treatment and to give the information which the patient has the right to expect. The duty is one of reasonable disclosure of the choices available. This duty to disclose is not limited by medical practice; it is set by law. The view is that a consent is not valid unless the patient has enough information to make an informed choice. Any information material to the patient's decision should therefore be revealed. The doctor may exercise therapeutic privilege if they think that revealing a particular risk would be adverse to the patient's health. (*Canterbury* v *Spence* (1972) 464 F 2d 772.)

Is there such a doctrine in England? This will depend on whether the *Bolam* test applies to the giving of information as well as diagnosis and treatment. The key decision in England was the following.

Sidaway v *Board of Governors of the Bethlem Royal Hospital* [1985] AC 871

The claimant had pain in her neck, shoulder and arms. A neurosurgeon examined her and recommended an operation. What the claimant was told is not clear, as the surgeon had died by the time of the trial. The operation carried with it a 1 per cent risk of damage to the spinal cord and a 1–2 per cent risk of damage to the nerve roots. The surgeon had apparently told the claimant about the risk of damage to the nerve roots, but not of that to the spinal cord. The operation was carried out without negligence by the surgeon, but the claimant was severely disabled as a result of damage to her spinal cord.

The House of Lords held that the surgeon had followed approved practice of neuro-surgeons in not disclosing the risk of damage to the spinal cord and was not negligent.

The majority of the House (Lord Scarman dissenting) was prepared to accept a modified version of the *Bolam* test for the giving of information. The major modification was that where the judge thought that disclosure of a particular risk was obviously necessary but it was not medical practice to disclose, then following standard practice would not avoid liability. The example given was a 10 per cent risk of a stroke. If medical practice was not to disclose the risk, then a court would probably declare practice to be wrong.

Lord Bridge:

> . . . I can see no reasonable ground on which the judge could properly reject the conclusion to which the unchallenged medical evidence led in the application of the *Bolam* test. The trial judge's assessment of the risk at one per cent or two per cent covered both nerve root and spinal cord damage and covered a spectrum of possible ill effects 'ranging from the mild to the catastrophic'. In so far as it is possible and appropriate to measure such risks in percentage terms – some of the expert medical witnesses called expressed a marked and understandable reluctance to do so – the risk of damage to the spinal cord of such severity as the appellant in fact suffered was, it would appear, certainly less than one per cent. But there is no yardstick either in the judge's findings or in the evidence to measure what

fraction of one per cent that risk represented. In these circumstances, the appellant's expert witness's agreement that the non-disclosure complained of accorded with a practice accepted as proper by a responsible body of neuro-surgical opinion afforded the respondents a complete defence to the appellant's claim.

Lord Scarman rejected current medical practice as the test for what a patient needs to know and asserted the patient's right to know based on self-determination. He thought the doctor should be liable where the risk is such that a prudent person, in the patient's position, would have regarded it as significant. A doctor would have a defence of therapeutic privilege if disclosure would have posed a serious threat of psychological detriment to the patient.

The principle in *Sidaway* applies to both therapeutic and non-therapeutic treatment. (*Gold* v *Haringey Health Authority* [1987] 2 All ER 888.)

A change in the law relating to breach of duty by medical professionals came about in the House of Lords decision in *Bolitho*. (See above.) Has this change affected the way in which courts approach the question of the advice which should be given to a patient in order to validate consent?

The relationship between the decisions in *Sidaway* and *Bolitho* was considered in the following case.

Pearce v United Bristol Healthcare NHS Trust (1998) 48 BMLR 118

The claimant was expecting her sixth child and was overdue. She wanted an induced labour or a Caesarean section and was in a distressed condition. The consultant wanted a natural birth and told her it would be risky to be induced and take her longer to recover from a Caesarean section. The baby died *in utero*. Should the consultant have told her that there was an increased risk of stillbirth as a result of being overdue and, if he had so advised, would the claimant have changed her decision?

The Court of Appeal held, applying the tests in *Bolam* and *Bolitho*: In a case in which the claimant complains of being deprived of the opportunity to make a proper decision about treatment, if there is a 'significant risk' attached to a particular treatment or course of action, which would affect the judgment of a reasonable patient, then, in the ordinary course, the doctor is responsible for informing the patient of that risk. The doctor has to take into account all the relevant considerations when deciding how much to tell a patient, including the patient's physical and emotional state at the time, and his or her ability to comprehend information.

The risk in this case was 0.1–0.2 per cent, which was not significant.

The approach in *Pearce* was interesting. There is now one legal standard, whether the case is concerned with diagnosis, advice or treatment. There are not two separate lines of authority based on *Sidaway* and *Bolitho*. It is not for the medical profession to set the standard of disclosure, as that is for the court. The standard of disclosure was said to be that of 'a significant risk which would affect the judgement of a reasonable patient'. This appears to move very close to the Australian decision of *Rogers* v *Whittaker* (1992) 175 CLR 479 where the Australian High Court rejected *Bolam* and *Sidaway*.

The position where the patient specifically asks questions is not clear. In *Sidaway*, Lord Bridge said there was a duty to answer as truthfully and fully as the questioner requires. In *Pearce* Lord Woolf MR said that counsel for the claimant correctly submits that it is clear that, if a patient asks a doctor about the risk, then the doctor is required to give an honest answer. However, in *Blyth* v *Bloomsbury Health Authority* (1987) 5 PN 167, the Court of

Appeal said there was no duty to pass on all the information available to the hospital. The reply would be satisfactory if it conformed to standard practice.

In *Chester* v *Afshar* [2005] 1 AC 134, the claimant, who was considering an operation on her spine, specifically asked her consultant about the risks inherent in the operation. The defendant failed to explain that the operation carried a small but inherent risk and responded: 'I have never crippled anyone yet'. The defendant was held to be in breach of duty.

Finally, it should be noted that even if the claimant manages to overcome the hurdle of proving a duty existed to give them the information, they must still establish causation (see below). The important question here is if the claimant had been told of the risk would they have consented to the medical procedure.

Causation

See also Chapter 9 for causation.

The claimant must prove that their damage would not have occurred, but for the defendant's breach of duty.

In practice, medical negligence cases present problems in causation, as medical science may not be able to identify the precise cause of the claimant's damage.

Wilsher v Essex Area Health Authority [1988] 1 All ER 871

The claimant was born three months prematurely. He suffered from retrolental fibroplasia (RLF). This is an incurable condition of the retina which caused almost total blindness. He sued the defendants on the ground that his RLF was caused by an excess of oxygen in his bloodstream, due to lack of proper skill and care in the management of his oxygen supply. The first allegation was that a misplaced catheter gave misleading readings of oxygen pressure. The trial judge found this amounted to negligence. The second allegation was that medical staff allowed the oxygen level to remain above the accepted safety level. The trial judge relied on the causation test in *McGhee* v *NCB* (1973).

See also Chapter 9 for *Wilsher*.

The House of Lords allowed the defendants' appeal with the result that the case had to go back for a retrial 11 years after the claimant had suffered damage. The problem was in the conflict of medical evidence as to the cause of RLF. It can be caused by a high level of oxygen in premature babies, but it can occur without artificial administration of oxygen. The trial judge had found that the claimant's exposure to high levels of oxygen had materially increased the risk of suffering RLF and the defendants had to show on the balance of probabilities that the exposure did not cause the RLF. The House of Lords held that the onus of proving causation lies on the claimant. Where the claimant is unable to establish what the cause of their injuries was, then the action will fail.

The principle of material contribution to the damage does apply in medical negligence cases.

Bailey v Ministry of Defence [2008] EWCA Civ 883

The claimant was admitted to the defendant's hospital to deal with a suspected gallstone in her bile duct. Following the procedure her condition began to deteriorate rapidly and dramatically, and, despite a number of further interventions, her condition became critical. She was then moved to another hospital. Urgent surgery was performed and her condition then improved through the next two weeks to a point where she was safe, but severely weakened, and it was established that she had developed pancreatitis. Late in the night while unattended, the claimant vomited. Due to her condition of extreme weakness she was unable to expel the vomit as a person normally would, and the aspirated vomit caused her cardiac arrest. She was resuscitated but left with permanent brain damage. The claimant's case in negligence against the first hospital was that had proper professional diagnosis and care been there provided, she would not, whilst in the second hospital, have been in such a poor physical condition that she could not evacuate the vomit. The immediate cause of her heart failure and consequent brain damage was her natural response in vomiting due to nausea, and her physical inability to cope with the vomit, not any negligent failures on the part of the first, defendant, hospital, in terms of the surgery and other treatment they had provided prior to her transfer. In law, then, was there the necessary causal link between the defendant's negligence and the claimant's damage? Was it the earlier lack of care at the defendant hospital which was responsible for her critically weakened state, or would the pancreatitis, which would have developed anyway, alone be sufficient to induce that? The medical evidence was incapable of establishing it one way or the other. On the conventional 'but for' approach to causation, the claimant's action must fail.

Held: The trial judge had found that the critically weak condition to which the claimant succumbed at the time of her death was the product of two factors, closely interlinked. One was the pancreatitis. The other was the consequence of the negligent failures of the defendants during the period when she was in their care. The Court of Appeal upheld the judge's finding that she had not recovered from the effects of the second of these and that this was sufficient to establish a causal link as a material contribution.

The Court of Appeal distinguished *Hotson* and *Wilsher*. In *Hotson* the House of Lords had held that the cause of the boy's damage was the fall from the tree. This was not due to any negligence on the defendant's part; it was a distinct cause. In *Wilsher* it was simply not possible to establish what the cause of the baby's blindness was.

In the case of consecutive causes, then, the causal link is established if the defendant is responsible for a material contribution to the claimant's harm. The answer to the question as to what is 'material', considering the facts of the precedent cases, cannot be clear. However, the consensus of opinion appears to be that it must be something sufficient to be regarded as substantial. The Court of Appeal in *Bailey* expressly preferred the opinion of Lord Rodger in *Fairchild*. Conceptually, 'substantial' is meant to connote a level of contribution to risk which goes considerably beyond something minimal or trivial.

The position in relation to cumulative cause cases could be summarised as follows: If the evidence demonstrated on a balance of probabilities that the injury would have occurred as a result of the non-tortious cause or causes in any event, the claimant would have failed to establish that the tortious cause contributed. *Hotson v East Berkshire Area Health Authority* ([1987] AC 750) exemplified such a situation. If the evidence demonstrated that but for the contribution of the tortious cause the injury would probably not have occurred, the claimant would have discharged the burden. Where medical science could not establish the probability that but for an act of negligence the injury would not have happened but could establish that the contribution of the negligent cause was more than negligible, the 'but for' test was modified, and the claimant would succeed.

There would have been no room for the principle to apply in *Wilsher* as in that case there were alternative rather than cumulative causes.

Attempts to make it easier for claimants to establish causation by proving a loss of chance have so far not been accepted by English courts. (See *Hotson v East Berkshire Area Health Authority* [1987] 2 All ER 909; *Gregg v Scott* [2005] 2 AC 176.)

See also Chapter 9.

For the overlap between breach of duty and causation, see *Bolitho v City and Hackney Health Authority* (above).

In informed consent cases the claimant must prove that, if the information had been given, their decision as to treatment would have been different.

Chester v *Afshar* [2002] 3 All ER 552 (CA); [2005] 1 AC 134 (HL)

The claimant suffered from back pain and was advised by the defendant surgeon to undergo an operation, although she had been anxious to avoid surgery. The operation carried a risk of nerve damage resulting in paralysis. The risk was 0.9 per cent. The defendant did not inform the claimant of the risk. The operation was properly carried out, but the claimant suffered paralysis. She sued the surgeon for negligence, alleging that if she had been informed of the risk she would not have had the operation carried out when she did. The Court of Appeal held that where a patient had an operation which they would not otherwise have had at the time and the risk materialised and caused her injury, the causal connection between the negligence and the injury was not broken merely because the patient was unable to show that she would never, at any time in the future, have had an operation of that kind.

Held (House of Lords) (Lord Bingham and Lord Hoffmann dissenting): Where, in breach of duty, a surgeon failed to warn a patient about a risk of injury inherent in an operation, and, as a result of that failure, the patient had the operation and the risk materialised, she did not have to prove, for the purposes of establishing causation, that she would never have had the operation at any time if properly warned. Rather, it was sufficient for her to prove that, if properly warned, she would not have consented to the operation which was in fact performed and which resulted in the injury. Such a conclusion could not be based on conventional causation principles because the risk was not created or increased by the failure to warn, and the chances of avoiding it were not lessened by that failure. In such a case, however, justice required the normal approach to causation to be modified. The law which imposed the duty to warn on the doctor had at its heart the right of the patient to make an informed choice as to whether, and if so when and by whom, to be operated on. Patients were entitled to have different views about those matters. For some the choice might be easy – simply to agree or to decline the operation. For many, however, the choice would be a difficult one, requiring time to think, to take advice and to weigh up the alternatives. The duty was owed as much to the patient who, if warned, would find the decision difficult as to the patient who would find it simple and could give a clear answer to the doctor one way or the other immediately. To leave the patient who would find the decision difficult without a remedy, as the normal approach to causation would indicate, would render the duty useless in the cases where it might be needed most. That would discriminate against those who could not honestly say that they would have declined the operation once and for all if they had been warned. That result was unacceptable. The function of the law was to enable rights to be vindicated and to provide remedies when the duties had been breached. Unless that was done, the duty was a hollow one, stripped of all practical force and devoid of all content. It would have lost its ability to protect the patient and thus to fulfil the only purpose which brought it into existence. It followed that, on policy grounds, the test of causation was satisfied in the instant case. The injury was the product of the very risk that the patient should have been warned about when she gave her consent, and it could therefore be regarded as having been caused, in the legal sense, by the breach of the duty to warn. Accordingly, the appeal would be dismissed.

See also Chapter 9 for *Fairchild*. This majority decision of the House of Lords is in the same mould as the ***Fairchild*** decision. Conventional causation rules have been discarded in order to do justice where there is a right and damage. In this case the right was that of the patient to make an informed decision on whether and when to have treatment.

The decision has been controversial because of the way in which conventional causation rules were discarded. Could the court have reached the same decision by applying 'but for' causation and remoteness? (See J. Stapleton (2006) 122 LQR 427.)

Summary

This chapter deals with the rules of negligence applying in medical cases and the law of battery applying to medical actions.

- There does not appear to be a medical malpractice crisis in the United Kingdom leading to defensive medicine. Research shows that the number of claims has dropped but that the total amount of damages has risen.

- There have been calls for medical accidents to be taken out of the litigation system. A new NHS redress scheme for low-value claims is being introduced but has been heavily criticised.

- Before a patient can be treated they must consent to the treatment otherwise a battery is committed. Battery raises conflicts between autonomy and paternalism.

- Where a patient is in a coma and the doctors wish to discontinue treatment the test is what is in the best interests of the patient. (*Bland.*) There is a distinction between taking positive steps to end life and discontinuing life-saving treatment. The latter can be done with the court's permission and does not breach the European Convention on Human Rights.

- Consent to treatment can be express or implied but it must be real. The patient must be informed of the nature and purpose of the treatment. Where a patient is unconscious, treatment may be given on the basis of necessity. (*F* v *West Berkshire.*) The next of kin have no legal right to give or refuse consent.

- In the case of minors, a child over the age of 16 can give a valid consent. In the case of a child under 16 years the test is *Gillick* understanding. If the child is incapable of giving consent, the consent of a parent should be obtained or an application to the court made.

- Problems arise with minors who refuse treatment. In these cases the doctor should apply to the court and the court will determine what is in the best interests of the minor, even if this means overriding the minor's refusal.

- In a negligence action the patient must prove duty, breach and damage. Actions are usually brought against the hospital on the basis of their vicarious liability but a doctor or (exceptionally) a hospital may be primarily liable.

- Duty of care rarely presents a problem in these cases. The duty relates to advice, diagnosis and treatment.

- The test for breach of duty is the *Bolam* test: that of a reasonably skilled doctor in the defendant's position. This test has been criticised on the basis that it allows the medical profession to set its own standards. In *Bolitho* the House of Lords stated that in rare cases the court would intervene where it felt that medical practice was not adequate.

- The burden of proof of negligence is on the claimant. The courts may allow the claimant to rely on the doctrine of *res ipsa loquitur*.

- Where the case relates to advice, the claimant must have given an informed consent to the treatment. The nature of the procedure, the alternatives and the risks (if sufficiently severe) should be explained. The leading case is *Sidaway*, which applied a modified *Bolam* test. The courts appear to have relaxed their approach in recent years. A claimant must also establish causation in such cases. (*Chester* v *Afshar.*)

- The principle of *material contribution to the damage* test for causation does apply in medical negligence cases. (*Bailey* v *Ministry of Defence* (2008).)

Further reading

Brazier, M. (2007), *Medicine, Patients and the Law* (4th edn), Penguin.

Farrell, A. M. and Devaney, S. (2007), 'Making Amends or Making Things Worse? Clinical Negligence Reform and Patient Redress in England' 27(4) LS 630.

Grubb, A. (1998), 6 Med L Rev 120.

Gurnham, D. (2006), 'Losing the Wood for the Trees: Burke and the Court of Appeal' 14 Med L Rev 253.

Keown, J. (2000), 'Beyond *Bland*: a Critique of the BMA Guidance on Withholding and Withdrawing Treatment' 20(1) LS 66.

Lewis, R., Morris, A. and Oliphant, K. (2006), 'Tort Personal Injury Claims Statistics: Is There a Compensation Culture in the United Kingdom?' 2 JPIL 87.

Mulheron, R. (2010), 'Trumping *Bolam*: A Critical Legal Analysis of *Bolitho's* "Gloss"', *Cambridge Law Journal* 609.

Robertson, G. (1981), 'Informed Consent to Medical Treatment' 97 LQR 102.

Stapleton, J. (2006), 'Occam's Razor Reveals an Orthodox Basis for *Chester* v *Afshar*' 122 LQR 426.

Teff, H. (1985), 'Consent to Medical Proceedings' 101 LQR 432.

Part 4

Torts based on land

16

Trespass to land

Objectives

After reading this chapter you will:

1. Understand the concept of possession of land and the legal rules relating to trespass to land.
2. Understand the forms of trespass to land.
3. Appreciate the effects of the title of the claimant in trespass to land cases.
4. Have a knowledge of the defences and remedies applicable to trespass to land.

Introduction

Objective 1

Trespass to land is an *unjustifiable interference with the possession of land*. It is important to note that, for historical reasons, the tort is committed against possession and not ownership of land.

For nuisance, see Chapter 17.

As this is a form of trespass, the injury must be *direct* rather than consequential. The latter form of interference may give rise to liability in nuisance.

If a person throws stones onto the land of another he commits trespass but if he allows tree branches to grow over his neighbour's land this is a nuisance and damage must be proved.

Esso Petroleum Co Ltd v Southport Corp [1956] AC 218

The captain of an oil tanker ran the ship aground and, in order to save the ship and the crew, large quantities of oil were discharged. The oil was carried by the tide on to the shore. The court held that necessity was a defence to the claim in trespass and nuisance. Two judges in the House of Lords thought that the damage was consequential, not direct, and therefore not capable of constituting a trespass.

See Chapter 1 for torts actionable *per se*.

The tort is actionable *per se* and the claimant need not show any damage to the land as a result of the defendant's act. The remedy sought will in any case often be an injunction to prevent any repetition of the trespass. (For the award of an injunction see ***Secretary of State for the Environment, Food and Rural Affairs v Meier*** [2009] UKSC 11.)

As most trespasses are self-evidently intentional because the defendant intends to be there, the question of the state of mind of the defendant is not often of importance. Two points may be noted at this stage. First, if the claimant did not intend to be on the land, i.e. if they were thrown there, no trespass is committed. (*Basely v Clarkson* (1681) 3 Lev 37.) Second, the fact that the defendant thought that the land was their own will not be a defence. (*Smith v Stone* (1647) Sty 65.) The fact that the defendant was lost is not a defence to trespass.

It has been clear for a long time that where land adjoining the highway is unintentionally entered, i.e. as a result of a car accident, the claimant must prove negligence. (*River Wear Commissioners v Adamson* (1877) 2 App Cas 743.)

League Against Cruel Sports v *Scott* [1986] QB 240

It was held that where a hunt entered land after permission to enter had been refused, then the master would be liable if he intended the hounds to enter; or, if the entry was caused by his failure to exercise proper control over them, when there was a real risk of entry. If this decision is correct, it means that the tort may be committed negligently.

Forms of trespass to land

Objective 2

The tort may be committed by entry on land, remaining on land or by placing objects on land.

Trespass by wrongful entry

This is the commonest form of trespass and consists of a personal entry on the claimant's land by the defendant. The slightest crossing of the boundary will be sufficient, such as putting a hand through a window.

Entick v *Carrington* (1765) 19 State Trials 1029

The claimant alleged that officers of the king broke into his house and searched and took documents. The defendants said that they were authorised by a warrant granted by the Secretary of State. The court held that the Secretary of State had no jurisdiction to grant a warrant and the defendants were guilty of trespass.

This form of trespass may also be committed by abuse of right of entry. A person who used the highway for any purpose other than that of passage became a trespasser against the owners of the subsoil.

Hickman v *Maisey* [1900] 1 QB 752

Where the highway across land in the possession of the claimant was used by a racing tout for the purpose of taking notes on the form of a racehorse, a trespass was committed.

However, the House of Lords has now decided that lawful use of the highway also includes those reasonable and usual activities which are consistent with the public's right to use the highway for the purpose of passage.

DPP v *Jones* [1999] 2 All ER 257

> Under the Public Order Act 1986 s 14A, an order was in force banning trespassory assemblies around Stonehenge. The intention was to protect the ancient monument from possible damage from groups gathered there for the summer solstice. A prosecution ensued after a protest against the ban took place on the grass verge of the highway next to Stonehenge. The prosecution argued that the protest was caught by the ban and the case therefore turned on whether the assembly on the highway amounted to a trespass. The test is reasonable use of the highway. Therefore, a peaceful assembly would not constitute a trespass provided that the highway was not blocked or a nuisance committed. What is reasonable use is a question of fact. It is therefore possible that *Hickman* could still be decided the same way.

Trespass by remaining on land

A person commits trespass if they remain on land when their right of entry has ceased. To refuse or to omit to leave is as much a trespass as to enter originally without any right.

A person who holds over at the end of a lease is not a trespasser until demand is made, as only the person in possession can be trespassed against. (*Hey* v *Moorhouse* (1839) 6 Bing NC 52.)

Trespass by placing objects on land

It is a trespass to place any chattel on the claimant's land. This form of trespass is known as continuing trespass, as the trespass continues as long as the offending article remains on the land. Successive actions will lie from day to day until the article is removed.

Holmes v *Wilson* (1839) 10 A & E 503

> The defendants erected buttresses to support a sinking road. To do this they had to trespass on the claimant's land. The claimant sued and recovered damages. The defendants failed to remove the buttresses and the claimant sued again. The defence was that the action was time barred. This was rejected as it was a case of continuing trespass which continued as long as the buttresses were on the land.

Trespass *ab initio*

Where the defendant's entry is by authority of law as opposed to the claimant's authority and the defendant subsequently abuses that right, then they become a trespasser *ab initio* (from the moment of entry). In the *Six Carpenters Case* (1610) 8 Co Rep 146A, the defendants entered a tavern and, after consuming food and drink, refused to pay. As failure to pay was an omission as opposed to an act, they were not trespassers *ab initio*. The rule only applies where the subsequent abuse is a positive wrongful act as opposed to an omission.

The modern application of this doctrine lies in the use of police search warrants. The usefulness has been removed by modern cases, which have held that partial abuse of an authority does not render everything done under it unlawful. (*Elias* v *Pasmore* [1934] 2 KB 164.)

Chic Fashions (West Wales) Ltd v Jones [1968] 2 QB 299

> Police searching the claimant's premises for stolen goods seized goods which they mistakenly thought to be stolen. The seizure was held to be lawful as police entering premises with a warrant had authority to remove anything which they believed to have been stolen. The Court of Appeal doubted the validity of trespass *ab initio*, as it meant that lawful acts could be made unlawful by subsequent events and the lawfulness of an act should be judged at the time it took place.

Despite this criticism, the doctrine was applied without criticism in the later case of *Cinnamond v British Airports Authority* [1980] 2 All ER 368 to mini-cab drivers who were unlawfully touting for business.

Trespass above and beneath the surface

The person who owns the land also owns the sky above and the subsoil beneath. Trespass can therefore be committed by a person who digs a tunnel under land or who abuses the airspace. Intrusion into airspace at any height, however high, is not automatically wrongful, but it is a wrong where such airspace is necessary for the full use of the land below. A distinction is drawn between the area of ordinary user and outside it.

Kelsen v Imperial Tobacco Co [1957] 2 QB 334

> The defendants erected an advertising sign which projected into the claimant's airspace by eight inches. This was held to be trespass to land as it was an invasion of the airspace necessary for the ordinary use of the land.

This principle could clearly cause severe difficulties to aircraft. The Civil Aviation Act 1982 s 76(1) and (2) therefore make special provision for civil aircraft. No trespass is committed where the aircraft flies at a reasonable height, having regard to wind, weather and all the circumstances of the case. A form of strict liability is also created for damage caused by articles falling from an aircraft while in flight.

The position of aircraft has also been clarified at common law.

Lord Bernstein of Leigh v Skyviews & General Ltd [1978] QB 479

> The defendants took an aerial photograph of the claimant's house and were sued for trespass to land. The court held that trespass to airspace was not committed where the flight took place at a height which did not affect the use of the land. The claimant was in any case prevented from bringing an action by the statutory provision, which is not limited to a bare right of passage and is not lost by the taking of a photograph.

A distinction has since been drawn between aircraft and a structure which over-hangs land. In the latter case a trespass is committed even if the structure (a crane) was at a height which did not affect the claimant's use of the land. (*Anchor Brewhouse Developments Ltd v Berkley House (Docklands Developments) Ltd* (1987) 38 BLR 82.)

Trespass to the subsoil is illustrated by the following case which involves drilling for oil.

Bocardo SA v Star Energy UK Onshore Ltd and another [2010] UKSC 35

The defendant held a petroleum production licence authorising it to search and bore for and obtain petroleum from a naturally occurring oilfield, part of which extended beneath the claimant's land. Pipelines were drilled diagonally under the substrata of the claimant's land and oil extracted of about £10 million in value. The claimant suffered no physical or other actual damage. The pipelines were at least 800 ft below sea level. The claimant sued for damages for trespass to land, contending that it owned all the earth beneath the land down to the centre of the earth and the laying of the pipes underneath the surface of its land amounted to trespass as the defendants had failed to negotiate rights of access.

Held: The well-known saying, *cuius est solum, eius est usque ad coelum et ad inferos,* expressed by the statement that the owner of the surface was entitled to the surface itself and everything below it to the centre of the earth, had value in English law as encapsulating, in simple language, a proposition of law which had commanded general acceptance. It was an imperfect guide, as it had ceased to apply to the use of airspace above a height which might interfere with the ordinary use of the land. The better view was that the owner of the surface was the owner of the strata beneath it, including the minerals that were to be found there, unless there had been an alienation of it by a conveyance at common law or by statute to someone else. There would obviously be some stopping point where one reached the point at which physical features such as pressure and temperature rendered the concept of the strata belonging to anybody so absurd as to be not worth arguing about. Where a party had paper title to land, in the absence of evidence to the contrary, that was enough for it to be deemed to be in possession of the land.

The claimant's title, as freehold owner of the estate, extended down to the strata through which the three wells passed. Although the claimant had done nothing to reduce those strata into its actual possession, as the paper title owner to the strata, it had the prima facie right to possession of those subsurface strata too, so as to be deemed to be in factual possession of them.

NB. There are now proposals to change the law in this area because of the development of 'fracking.' This is a new method of extracting oil and gas which involves inserting pipes into the ground and pumping water and chemicals through them.

Title of the claimant

Objective 3

Trespass to land is normally actionable only by the person who is in possession of the land. This includes a person who is entitled to immediate and exclusive possession. Licence rights for access to land, e.g. for building work, will not be sufficient evidence of possession to give standing to sue protestors occupying the land in trespass. (*Manchester Airport plc v Dutton* [2000] QB 133.)

A landlord cannot normally bring an action for trespass as the tenant is the person who has possession. The landlord may sue if they can prove that actual harm has been caused to the reversion or in the circumstances illustrated in the next case.

Portland Management Ltd v Harte [1977] QB 306

A landlord brought an action against persons who were alleged to be squatters. It was held that where an absolute owner brings an action for trespass he must prove title and an intention to regain possession. The slightest act by the owner indicating an intention will be sufficient. The defendant must then show title or a right to possession consistent with the claimant's ownership.

The mere use of land without exclusive possession is not sufficient. A lodger or boarder will generally not be able to sue.

Trespass by relation

At one time actual possession was more favoured than property or the right to possession. Where, at the time of the commission of a trespass, the owner was out of possession, he had no remedy for trespass. A legal fiction called trespass by relation was developed to deal with this problem. A person who has the right to immediate possession of the land, and enters in exercise of that right, is then deemed to have been in possession ever since the accrual of the right of entry. That person may sue for any trespass committed since the accrual of the right of entry.

This doctrine enables a lessee to sue for any trespass committed between the granting of the lease and their entering in pursuance of it. A landlord who is entitled to enter on the determination of a lease may, on re-entry, sue for any trespass since the lease determined.

Co-owners

A tenant in common or joint tenant of land cannot sue his co-tenant in trespass, unless the defendant's act amounts to the total exclusion or ouster of the claimant or destructive waste of the common property. Each of the co-tenants is entitled to possession of the land.

Defences

Licence

Objective
4

A licence is that consent which, without passing any interest in the property to which it relates, merely prevents the acts for which consent is given from being wrongful. Trespass is therefore not committed when the defendant enters with the authority of a licence. This is unless they exceed the terms of the licence or the claimant has legally revoked the licence.

A bare licence, which is one granted other than for valuable consideration, may be revoked at any time on the giving of reasonable notice. A contractual licence may also be revoked at any time, but this may involve the grantor in an action for breach of contract. This appears to be subject to an exception where the licence was granted for a limited period of time and for a specific purpose. If a person bought a ticket for the cinema then they would probably have an irrevocable licence for the period of the film. (*Hurst v Picture Theatres Ltd* [1915] 1 KB 1.) The person ejected could then mount an action for battery and the defence of reasonable force to eject a trespasser would fail.

A licence coupled with an interest, for example, a profit, is irrevocable, as although the licence itself is only a right *in personam*, it confers a right *in rem* to do something once an entry has been made.

Justification by law

Acts which would otherwise be trespass are not so when justification is provided by law. For example, the police have powers to enter premises and to search them.

One problem was the situation where householders needed access to neighbouring land to undertake repairs to their property. The Access to Neighbouring Land Act 1992 now provides that a court may grant an order allowing access to land for the purpose of carrying out works which are reasonably necessary for the preservation of adjoining or adjacent land and which cannot be carried out or would be substantially more difficult to carry out without entry on the land. The court cannot make such an order if it would cause unreasonable interference with the neighbour's enjoyment of the land or unreasonable hardship.

Necessity

See also Chapter 27 for necessity.

It is a defence to show that it was necessary for the defendant to enter the claimant's land. It is for the defendant to prove that the necessity arose without negligence on their part. (*Rigby* v *Chief Constable of Northamptonshire* [1985] 2 All ER 985.)

The House of Lords has identified three situations where the defence might apply (*F* v *West Berkshire Health Authority* [1989] 2 All ER 545 at 564):

1 Cases of public necessity such as the destruction of property to prevent the spread of fire.

2 Cases of private necessity.

Cope v *Sharp* [1912] 1 KB 496

Fire broke out on *X*'s land. *X*'s servants attempted to put the fire out and *Z*'s gamekeeper set fire to land between the fire and some of *Z*'s nesting pheasants. The gamekeeper was sued for trespass. He was held not liable as there was a real and imminent danger and he had done what was reasonably necessary. The necessity depends on the state of things when the trespass takes place and not upon the inference as to necessity to be drawn from the event.

3 Where action is taken as a matter of necessity to come to the aid of another whose property or person is in imminent danger. There must be a necessity to act when it is not practicable to communicate with the assisted person and the action must be such as a reasonable person would take, acting in the best interests of the assisted person. The courts are reluctant to apply this defence and it was rejected by the Court of Appeal where squatters argued that their occupation of an empty house was justified by their need to find shelter for homeless families. (*Southwark London Borough Council* v *Williams* [1971] Ch 734.) Lord Denning stated:

> If homelessness were once admitted as a defence to trespass, no one's house could be safe. Necessity would open a door which no man could shut. It would not only be those in extreme need who would enter. There would be others who would imagine that they were in need, or would invent a need, so as to gain entry.

The decision appears harsh but the courts were applying a policy that the social problems cannot be cured by tinkering with the rules of private law but have to be dealt with by society.

This approach and the immediacy of the danger were stressed in a case involving trespassory protests against genetically modified crops. The danger faced by others had to be so immediate as to amount to an emergency and changes to government policy had to be brought about through lawful means in a democratic society. The real purpose of the campaign was held to attract publicity for their cause. The Court of Appeal stressed that the defence of necessity should not be used to justify all sorts of wrongdoing. (*Monsanto plc* v *Tilly* [2000] Env LR 313.)

Although necessity is a defence to trespass it may not be a defence to another tort such as negligence.

Rigby v Chief Constable of Northamptonshire [1985] 2 All ER 985

Police fired CS gas into a shop in an attempt to force a psychopath out. As a result, the claimant's shop was burned down. The court held that necessity was a defence to trespass provided there was no negligence on the part of the defendant. On the facts of the case, the police were held liable in negligence as they had no fire-fighting equipment present when the CS gas was fired. The defence of necessity succeeded in the trespass action as the police had not been negligent in creating the emergency.

Remedies

Re-entry

A person who is entitled to possession can enter or re-enter the premises. By the Criminal Law Act 1977 s 6, it is a crime to use or threaten violence for the purposes of securing entry to any premises occupied by another, except by a displaced residential occupier. At civil law reasonable force may be used to evict a trespasser.

Hemmings v Stoke Poges Golf Club [1920] 1 KB 720

The claimant, a tenant of the defendants, was served with a notice to quit and refused to leave. The defendants entered the claimant's cottage and removed the claimant and his furniture using reasonable force. The defendants were found not liable in trespass.

Ejectment

A person who has been dispossessed may bring an action for ejectment where he can establish an immediate right to possession. A claimant can only recover on the strength of their own title and not on the weakness of the defendant's. The defendant only needs to assert that they are in possession and the claimant must then show that their title is better than the defendant's.

Mesne profits

An action lies for damage which the claimant has suffered through being out of possession of land. This includes profits taken by the defendant during the occupation and damages for deterioration and the reasonable costs of getting possession. The basis for calculating damages is known as the user principle and the defendant is required to pay a reasonable rent for the period in which he was in adverse possession. (*Inverugie Investments Ltd* v *Hackett* [1995] 1 WLR 713 (HL).)

In the *Hackett* case the defendants had unlawfully ejected the tenant of a hotel complex and run the hotel at an occupancy rate of 35–40 per cent. The House of Lords held that the claimant was entitled to compensation based on a reasonable rent for all the apartments in the complex, not just those that the defendant had managed to rent.

When considering mesne profits the person entitled to possession of land can make a claim against a person who had been in occupation without his consent on two alternative bases:

1 the loss which they had suffered in consequence of the defendant's trespass which was the normal measure of damages in the law of tort;

2 a claim for restitution of the value of the benefit which the occupier had received. In a case of permanent expropriation, it would be unrealistic to measure the claimant's loss on the basis of a hypothetical licence fee, since in reality if the trespasser had negotiated with the owner for the use of the land there would have been no licence. Instead, the trespasser would have bought the land outright, and the owner would have received its capital value sooner. (**Ramzan v Brookwide** [2011] 2 All ER 38.)

Distress damage feasant

Where a chattel is unlawfully on the claimant's land and has caused actual damage, the claimant may retain the chattel until the damage has been paid for. If a football is kicked through a window, then the football can be retained until the window is paid for.

The principle used to have particular importance in relation to damage caused by straying livestock, but there is now a specific statutory rule in the Animals Act 1971 s 7.

The remedy is generally only available where the chattel is unattended and must be made while the chattel is trespassing. This is an alternative to an action and no action can be maintained while there is distraint of the chattel.

A modern application of the doctrine can be seen in the following case.

Arthur v Anker [1996] 2 WLR 602

Lessees of a private car park employed the defendants to clamp the wheels of cars parked there without permission. Notices were placed on the land saying that cars would only be released on payment of a fee. The Court of Appeal held that distress damage feasant could only be invoked in a case such as this if the unauthorised vehicles were causing damage. The argument that the cost of towing away the car could be regarded as damage was rejected. The court was still able to find in the defendants' favour by the application of the doctrine of *volenti* because of the clearly worded notices.

Injunction

See also Chapter 28 for remedies.

Where a trespass is threatened or where the trespass is of a continuing nature, then the claimant may seek an injunction. The claimant is prima facie entitled to the injunction but it may be refused where the interference is trivial.

Llandudno UDC v Woods [1889] 2 Ch 705

The council sought an injunction to prevent a clergyman from trespassing by holding services on the claimant's seashore. The application was rejected on the ground of triviality.

Secretary of State for the Environment, Food and Rural Affairs v Meier [2009] UKSC 11

The case concerned travelling people who had illegally camped on Forestry Commission land and moved from area to area. The claimants sought a possession order for land which the defendant travellers might move to and an injunction restraining the defendants from trespassing.

> The Supreme Court held: (1) A court had no power to grant an order for possession in respect of land not yet occupied or possessed by a defendant. There was no legitimate basis for making a wider or precautionary order for possession; if there was, it would require a defendant to do something which he could not do, namely to deliver up possession of land he did not occupy, and would purport a return to a claimant of something which he had not lost, namely possession of land of which already he had possession.
>
> (2) The decision whether an injunction should be granted restraining a defendant from trespassing on land of which he was not in possession or occupation would have to turn on the facts of each individual case. Where a trespass to property was threatened, and particularly where a trespass was being committed, and had been committed in the past, an injunction to restrain the threatened trespass (or continuing trespass) would, in the absence of good reasons to the contrary, be appropriate.

Where a person has been displaced from their property then in assessing damages in lieu of reinstatement (injunction), in determining the value of the land, the court would have regard to the amount the claimant could reasonably have sought from the defendant as the price of the property taking into account the value to the defendant of the property. (*Ramzan v Brookwide* [2011] 2 All ER 38.)

Damages

See also Chapter 28 for damages.

Where the trespass is trivial, the damages will be nominal, but where the trespass involves some beneficial use of the land, the claimant is entitled to a reasonable remuneration for the use of the land, as if the use had been made under an agreement, such as a lease or a contract. (See also 'Mesne profits' above.)

Ramzan v Brookwide [2011] 2 All ER 38

See Chapter 28 for exemplary damages.

> The defendant expropriated property belonging to the claimant and incorporated it into his own property without warning. The defendant was part of a group of property companies and the claimant was a small business owner. The first instance court was asked: (i) whether an award of exemplary damages was appropriate ; (ii) if an injunction was refused, whether determination of damages in lieu of an injunction was to be on the basis of value of lost land or value of land to defendant (see Injunctions above); (iii) where the defendant expropriated the claimant's store room to create a new flat, whether the measure of damages for mesne profits was loss in tort or in restitution for the value of the benefit received by the occupier and whether the loss was to be calculated on the basis of the property's previous use as a store room or as part of new flat (see Mesne profits above).
>
> *Held*: The court was not persuaded that an award of exemplary damages was simply designed to operate as an indirect method for extracting profits tortiously obtained by the defendant and thus to prevent his unjust enrichment. The object of such an award was to act as a deterrent, and the question whether requiring the defendant to repay the profits would satisfy that objective would depend on the facts of the individual case. Among the matters to be taken into consideration when determining the amount of any exemplary damages were: (i) the means of the parties; (ii) the conduct of the defendant who had not shown any contrition or apologised for its conduct. Whilst the award of damages was not insubstantial and the defendant had had to disgorge its gross profits, it was the court's view that that was not sufficient to deter the defendant from repeating its behaviour. Exemplary damages were assessed at £60,000. (Reduced to £20,000 on appeal.)

Summary

This chapter deals with the rules on the tort of trespass to land.

- The tort is an unjustifiable interference with the possession of land.
- The tort is committed against possession not ownership.
- The injury must be direct rather than consequential.
- The tort is actionable *per se*.
- The tort may be committed by entry on to land, by remaining on land or by placing objects on land.
- Trespass by wrongful entry may be committed by crossing the boundary without permission or by abuse of the purpose for which one was allowed entry. Use of the highway for a purpose other than passage may be trespass against the highway owner.
- Remaining on land after permission to be there has ceased is trespass.
- Placing objects on land is trespass.
- Where a person enters by authority of law and then abuses that right he becomes a trespasser *ab initio*.
- Trespass can be committed against the subsoil and the sky above land. Special provision is made for aircraft.
- To sue in trespass a person must have possession of the land. A landlord cannot normally sue.
- Entry with a licence is normally a defence.
- Entry under justification of law is a defence.
- Necessity may be a defence in limited circumstances.
- The remedies for the tort are re-entry to the land, ejectment, mesne profits, distress damage feasant and/or an injunction.

Further reading

Weir, T. (2008), *Casebook on Tort* (11th edn), Sweet & Maxwell, chs 8 and 9.

17

Nuisance

Objectives

After reading this chapter you will:

1. Understand the distinction between statutory nuisance, public nuisance and private nuisance.
2. Have a knowledge of the rules relating to public nuisance.
3. Have a critical knowledge of the legal rules relating to who can sue and be sued in private nuisance and understand the legal rules applying to an action in private nuisance.
4. Appreciate the concept of interference with use and enjoyment.
5. Understand the role played by fault in a nuisance action.
6. Understand the legal rules relating to defences and remedies in a nuisance action.
7. Appreciate the role played by human rights in a nuisance action.

Introduction

Objective 1

See Chapter 18 for *Rylands v Fletcher*.

In any society, there are bound to be disputes between adjacent landowners. English law deals with these by means of the tort of nuisance and the rule in *Rylands* v *Fletcher*. It might seem more appropriate to deal with this issue through the medium of property law, as is the case in most civil systems, but English law has tended to concentrate on providing remedies rather than upon conferring property rights. This emphasis serves to explain why the law of tort has been employed in this respect.

The tort of nuisance is of ancient origin, and has three roots. The first was the assize of nuisance which allowed an action for loss of profit arising from the defendant's interference with incorporeal rights, such as rights to water and rights of way. The second was common or public nuisance, which constituted an interference with the neighbourhood, usually interference with the highway. Thirdly, gaps in the law were filled by the action on the case in the fifteenth and sixteenth centuries. A remedy was given to non-freeholders who could not proceed under the assize. This was done by extending the meaning of interferences with enjoyment from disseisin to those involving noxious trades. A remedy was also given to those who suffered special damage as a result of common or public nuisance.

During the sixteenth and seventeenth centuries, the action on the case supplanted the assize and covered three very different kinds of loss. The confusion caused by this development is still evident in modern law.

The modern law of nuisance was shaped in the nineteenth century, and was influenced by two factors. In legal procedure, jury influence declined, and the court acquired greater power to shape the law. Secondly, the nature of land changed with the Industrial Revolution. Nuisance acquired a public law function. In the absence of detailed planning law and environmental protection legislation, the courts used private law as an instrument for zoning land for particular purposes such as industrial or residential, and to set permissible standards of noise and air and water pollution. The drawback with this technique was that the courts had to wait for litigants to proceed. As a method of environmental control, nuisance law has largely been supplanted by legislation and, in any case, is an inefficient method of achieving such control.

Nuisance retains importance in dealing with the innumerable problems that arise between neighbouring landowners. Apart from problems caused by the unfortunately named public nuisance, the subject is best understood if it is realised that nuisance is concerned with invasions of a person's interest in the use or enjoyment of their land. The gist of a nuisance lies in the kind of harm caused, not in the type of conduct used in causing it. Conduct may be relevant in determining whether a particular kind of damage amounts to a nuisance.

There are three types of nuisance: public, private and statutory. Although the same conduct by the defendant may give rise to liability in any of these, the attachment of the word nuisance to public nuisance is confusing as it originates in criminal law.

Public nuisance is primarily a criminal offence, but may give rise to an action in tort where the claimant has suffered special damage. The commonest example is probably interferences with the highway.

Private nuisance is a tort that deals with disputes between adjacent landowners. It involves drawing a balance between the right of one person to use their land in whatever way they wish and the right of their neighbour not to be interfered with. Private nuisance was left with the task of dealing with disputes between neighbouring landowners and the gist of the subject is an unreasonable interference with a person's use or enjoyment of land.

One important point to make at this stage is that nuisance is concerned with the type of harm caused and the interest invaded, rather than the defendant's conduct. Students who have become obsessed with negligence should take note! The distinction between nuisance and trespass to land is that the latter is concerned with direct interferences with land whereas nuisance is concerned with indirect and unreasonable interferences.

Nuisance is a difficult tort and has been described as uncertain and lacking definition or any coherent goals or purpose. It is a useful source for historians as it illustrates the issues that have been of concern at various times in history. The tort is based on land and therefore reflects the interests of the landed classes.

Does common law nuisance have a role to play in the modern world?

The modern law of nuisance exists against a background of statutory provisions which include planning permission and specific permissions given to companies to carry out particular activities. Does common law nuisance have a role to play in the modern world?

The Supreme Court gave a positive answer in the case below. The issues in this case cover much of this chapter and will be dealt with as they come up.

Lawrence and another v Fen Tigers Ltd [2014] UKSC 13

The appellants claimed damages and an injunction in respect of nuisance by noise emanating from a site used for speedway and stock car racing, motocross and greyhound racing, and other events. The respondents had planning permission (granted in 1975) and a Certificate of Lawfulness of Existing Use or Development (CLEUD), a retrospective permit (granted in 1997) in respect of the racing activities. The appellants moved into an adjoining property in 2006. At first instance the court concluded that the activities constituted a nuisance. The Court of Appeal reversed that decision, on the ground that use of the stadium and track over a number of years, with planning permission, or a CLEUD, should be taken into account in determining the character of the locality. There was an appeal to the Supreme Court who held in the appellants' favour.

The case raises a number of issues in relation to nuisance but the central concept is the conflict between private rights, defended by nuisance, and public interest where an activity infringes private rights but is arguably for the greater good of the community.

Statutory nuisances

The increasing concern of central government for public health and the environment has led to a mass of legislation concerned with noise, run-down premises, clean air and accumulations. Although statutory nuisances are the most important in terms of the environment, they are not dealt with in any detail in a tort course as they are enforced by public bodies.

From the claimant's point of view, the most significant point about statutory nuisance is that enforcement is in the hands of the local authorities. This saves a person who is affected from the time and expense of having to bring a private action. The normal method of enforcement is for the local authority to serve an abatement order on the offender.

Public nuisance

Objective 2

Every public nuisance is a crime. It acquires its tortious characteristic by virtue of the rule that a person who suffers special damage may bring an action in tort. The classic definition of public nuisance was given in the following case.

Attorney General v PYA Quarries [1957] 2 QB 169

Quarrying operations were conducted in such a way that local residents were affected by dust and vibrations from explosions. The court defined public nuisance as 'one which materially affects the reasonable comfort and convenience of life of a class of Her Majesty's subjects'. The defendant's activities were held to amount to a public nuisance.

The very existence of the crime of public nuisance has become controversial as many acts which would formerly have been charged as public nuisance are now statutory offences and an attempt was made to challenge the offence as being contrary to the Human Rights Act. (*R v Rimmington; R v Goldstein* [2006] 1 AC 459.) The House of Lords held that the common law offence of causing a public nuisance was committed when a person did an act not warranted by law, or omitted to discharge a legal duty, and the effect of the act or omission was to endanger the life, health, property or comfort of the public, or to obstruct the public in the exercise of rights common to everyone. The definition of the offence was clear, precise, adequate and based on a rational discernible principle so that it had the certainty and predictability necessary to meet the requirements of the common law and of Article 7 of the Convention on Human Rights, that the citizen should be able to foresee, if need be with appropriate advice, the consequences which a given course of action might entail. It was an offence which still existed in law, and power to abolish an existing offence lay only with Parliament and not with the courts.

Whether the number of persons affected amounts to a class is a question of fact in each case. Where the nuisance is interference with the highway, then the class affected will be highway users. Acts which will amount to a public nuisance are a mixed bag and difficult to define precisely. Two distinct groups can be identified: these are abuses of the highway and carrying on trades which cause discomfort to others. A third group consists of an unclassifiable group of acts such as making a hoax bomb alarm call, keeping a brothel and holding a badly organised pop festival.

The issue of whether acts could become a public nuisance if they were a series was considered by the House of Lords in the next case.

R v *Rimmington; R* v *Goldstein* [2006] 1 AC 459

An individual act of causing a private nuisance such as making an offensive telephone call or sending an offensive communication by post could not become a criminal public nuisance merely by reason of the fact that the act was one of a series; that individual acts causing injury to several different people, rather than to the community as a whole, or a significant section of it, could not amount to the offence of causing a public nuisance, however persistent or objectionable the acts might be; that the sending of racially offensive material by post to different individuals lacked an essential ingredient of the offence of causing a public nuisance in that it did not cause common injury to a section of the public and that, accordingly, a defendant could not be charged with causing a public nuisance.

In order to sue in the tort of public nuisance, the claimant must prove that they suffered special damage. For this purpose, special damage means damage over and above that suffered by the class of persons affected. It can consist of any significant interference with an individual's commercial operations or the enjoyment of private rights. The damage must be substantial and direct rather than consequential.

Castle v *St Augustine's Links* (1922) 38 TLR 615

The claimant car driver was struck by a golf ball hit from the thirteenth tee of the defendants' golf course as he was driving on the highway. Balls frequently went over the highway. The siting of the tee amounted to a nuisance. The class of persons affected were highway users. The claimant had suffered special damage, so the defendants were liable in public nuisance.

NB: If the claimant had been on his own land the action would have been in private nuisance.

Could interference with television reception to a large group of people by the erection of a large building constitute a public nuisance? In **Hunter v Canary Wharf Ltd** [1996] 1 All ER 482, Pill LJ stated:

The judge answered this question 'Yes, in the case only of plaintiffs who can show that they have suffered particular damage beyond that suffered by the relevant public generally' . . . The plaintiffs indicated an amendment to the . . . statement of claim . . . to bring them within the category of persons who can sue in public nuisance. It reads:

> In the whole of the shadow area more than 100,000 people suffered some impairment but in only about 30,000 did television pictures fall below an acceptable standard. The severity of disruption varied. In broad terms, the closer to Canary Wharf the disruption was so severe that in a great many cases, including those of the plaintiffs, it was impossible to receive a coherent picture . . .

That proposed amendment serves in my judgment only to show the extreme difficulty which I expect the plaintiffs to have in establishing on the evidence any right to sue in public nuisance.

The House of Lords upheld the Court of Appeal on the point that interference with television reception was incapable of amounting to an actionable nuisance where it emanated from a physical obstruction on the defendant's land. (***Hunter*** v ***Canary Wharf Ltd*** [1997] 2 All ER 426.)

Bolton v *Stone* [1951] 1 All ER 1078

See also Chapter 8 for *Bolton* v *Stone*.

> The claimant was hit by a cricket ball struck over a high fence from a distance of 100 yards. The evidence showed that a ball had been hit out of the ground only six times in the last 30 years. The action in nuisance failed as the likelihood of injury would not have been anticipated by the reasonable man.

In a public nuisance action it appears that damages may be recovered for personal injuries (***Claimants appearing on the Register of the Corby Group Litigation*** v ***Corby Borough Council*** [2008] EWCA Civ 463), property damage and economic loss. Economic loss has been recovered where the highway was obstructed and business losses incurred. (See ***Fritz*** v ***Hobson*** (1880) 14 ChD 542; ***Benjamin*** v ***Storr*** (1874) LRCP 400.)

See also Chapter 5 for economic loss.

One distinction between public and private nuisance is that the claimant does not need to have an interest in land to sue in public nuisance. They must, however, have suffered special damage.

Tate & Lyle Industries Ltd v *Greater London Council* [1983] 2 AC 509

> The defendants constructed ferry terminals in the River Thames. These caused silting which obstructed the access of vessels to the claimants' jetty. The claimants had to spend money on dredging. No action lay in private nuisance as the jetty was not affected. The claimants had no private rights of property in the river bed which was affected. The public right of navigation for river users had been interfered with and the claimants were able to bring an action in public nuisance for their expenditure.

The highway

Many public nuisance cases are concerned with the highway. The usual action is concerned with obstructing the highway. If the highway is unreasonably obstructed this will amount to a public nuisance. The following case brings out the distinct nature of public nuisance.

Dymond v *Pearce* [1972] 1 QB 497

The defendant left his lorry parked on the highway with its parking lights on and it was visible from a distance of 200 yards. The claimant motor cyclist ran into the lorry. It was held that the defendant had committed a public nuisance but was not liable for the claimant's injuries, as these were caused entirely by the claimant's negligence.

It is also possible to cause a nuisance by creating a danger close to the highway. Occupiers of premises adjacent to the highway are under a duty to keep them in reasonable repair.

Tarry v *Ashton* (1876) 1 QBD 314

A lamp on the defendant's premises fell and injured the claimant. The defendant had employed a contractor to keep the lamp in good repair and argued that this discharged his duty to highway users. It was held that the duty in such cases was to keep the lamp in good repair and that the duty was non-delegable; the defendant was liable.

Wringe v *Cohen* [1940] 1 KB 229

The Court of Appeal held that the occupier of premises on the highway was under a duty to keep premises in repair whether they knew of a danger or not. This apparent strict liability is somewhat undermined by two exceptions. The defendant will not be liable where the damage resulted from a secret and unobservable operation of nature or from the unforeseeable act of a trespasser, unless he knew or ought to have known of the danger.

Highway authorities are under a statutory duty to maintain highways. (Highways Act 1980 s 41.) A defence is provided where they have taken reasonable care in all the circumstances to ensure that the part of the highway to which the action relates was not dangerous for traffic. What constitutes reasonable care will include, among other things, the character of the highway, the appropriate standard of maintenance and what amounts to a reasonable standard of repair. (Highways Act 1980 s 58.)

Private nuisance

Introduction

Objective 3

Private nuisance is an unlawful interference with a person's use or enjoyment of land, or some right over, or in connection with it. A nuisance which consists of an interference with a right in land is dealt with in land law under the heading of servitudes. This chapter will look at interferences with use and enjoyment. Some idea of private nuisance can be given by looking at the parties to a nuisance action.

Claimants

Private nuisance is historically concerned with the regulation of land use between neighbours. This is reflected in the rule that the claimant in an action for private nuisance has to have an interest in the land or exclusive possession of the land which is affected in order to be able to sue. This has been confirmed by the House of Lords in **Hunter v Canary Wharf Ltd** [1997] 2 All ER 426, where an action was denied to spouses and children of tenants of a property affected by dust and interference with television reception.

The rule can be traced to the case of **Malone** (below).

Malone v Lasky [1907] 2 KB 141

> The wife of a tenant of premises was injured when a cistern was dislodged by vibrations caused by the defendant. The wife had no claim in private nuisance, as she had no proprietary or possessory interest in the land.

The rule came under attack and in **Khorasandjian v Bush** [1993] 3 WLR 476 the Court of Appeal held an injunction to prevent pestering telephone calls could be granted to the daughter of the owner of the house to which the calls were made. This approach was adopted by the Court of Appeal in **Hunter v Canary Wharf Ltd** [1996] 1 All ER 482.

Pill LJ:

> A substantial link between the person enjoying the use and the land on which he or she is enjoying it is essential but, in my judgment, occupation of property, as a home, does confer upon the occupant a capacity to sue in private nuisance.
>
> There has been a trend in the law to give additional protection to occupiers in some circumstances. Given that trend and the basis of the law of nuisance in this context, it is no longer tenable to limit the sufficiency of that link by reference to proprietary or possessory interests in land. I regard satisfying the test of occupation of property as a home provides a sufficient link with the property to enable the occupier to sue in private nuisance.

However, both cases were overruled by the House of Lords on the question of who had the right to sue in private nuisance.

Hunter v Canary Wharf Ltd [1997] 2 All ER 426

> Two separate group actions were brought arising out of the redevelopment of the London Docklands. Damages were claimed in nuisance for interference with television signals caused by the building of the Canary Wharf tower and in negligence/nuisance for dust created by the construction of the Limehouse link road. The Court of Appeal dismissed the television action as, on the facts, the interference was not capable of amounting to a nuisance, but it allowed the dust action to proceed.
>
> The House of Lords considered two questions on appeal: (i) whether interference with television reception is capable of amounting to an actionable nuisance (see 'Sensitivity', below on this point); and (ii) whether it is necessary to have an interest in the property affected to claim in private nuisance and, if so, what interest.
>
> A majority of the House (Lord Cooke dissenting) held that it was necessary for the claimant in a nuisance action to prove an interest in the land affected, and thus established that it was a tort against land. The article by Professor Newark ((1949) 65 LQR 480) arguing that the boundaries of nuisance had become blurred by the failure to recognise that it was a tort to land and not to be used as a remedy for personal injuries was cited with approval. Lord Goff stated (at 688) that it 'should be nailed to the doors of the law courts and defended against all comers'.
>
> Occupation of the property as a home was not sufficient. An action may be brought by the owner or by the tenant or by a person who enjoyed exclusive possession but lacked any proprietary interest. No action can be brought by a licensee without exclusive possession. Any rights which are granted

by the Matrimonial Homes Act 1983, by which a spouse who lacks any proprietary interest may apply to the court to be granted exclusive possession of the property, remain contingent until they are recognised by a court and only at that point give *locus standi* for a nuisance action.

Lord Goff:

> [A]ny such departure from the established law on this subject, such as that adopted by the Court of Appeal in the present case, faces the problem of defining the category of persons who would have the right to sue. The Court of Appeal adopted the not easily identifiable category of those who have a 'substantial link' with the land, regarding a person who occupied the premises 'as a home' as having a sufficient link for this purpose. But who is to be included in this category? It was plainly intended to include husbands and wives, or partners, and their children, and even other relatives living with them. But is the category also to include the lodger upstairs, or the au pair girl or resident nurse caring for an invalid who makes her home in the house while she works there? If the latter, it seems strange that the category should not extend to include places where people work as well as places where they live, where nuisances such as noise can be just as unpleasant or distracting. In any event, the extension of the tort in this way would transform it from a tort to land into a tort to the person, in which damages could be recovered in respect of something less serious than personal injury and the criteria for liability were founded not upon negligence but upon striking a balance between the interests of neighbours in the use of their land. This is, in my opinion, not an acceptable way in which to develop the law.

Lord Hoffmann:

> Finally, there is the position of spouses. It is said to be contrary to modern ways of thinking that a wife should not be able to sue for interference with the enjoyment of the matrimonial home merely because she has no proprietary right in the property. To some extent, this argument is based upon the fallacy which I have already discussed, namely that the action in nuisance lies for inconvenience or annoyance caused to people who happen to be in possession or occupation of land. But so far as it is thought desirable that the wife should be able to sue for injury to a proprietary or possessory interest in the home, the answer, in my view, lies in the law of property, not the law of tort. The courts today will readily assume that a wife has acquired a beneficial interest in the matrimonial home. If so, she will be entitled to sue for damage to that interest. On the other hand, if she has no such interest, I think it would be wrong to create a quasi-proprietary interest only for the purposes of giving her locus standi to sue for nuisance. What would she be suing for? Mr Brennan QC, who appeared for the plaintiffs, drew our attention to the rights conferred on a wife with no proprietary interest by the Matrimonial Homes Act 1983. The effect of these provisions is that a spouse may, by virtue of an order of the court upon a break-up of the marriage, become entitled to exclusive possession of the home. If so, she will become entitled to sue for nuisance. Until then, her interest is analogous to a contingent reversion. It cannot be affected by a nuisance which merely damages the amenity of the property while she has no right to possession.
>
> I would therefore allow the appeal of the defendants in the dust case and their cross-appeal in the television case and restore the declaration made on this point by the judge.

Lord Cooke gave a strong dissenting judgment on this point. He thought it strange that people should be excluded from an action in nuisance when they had sufficient status to qualify for protection under English legislation and under international treaties. The House of Lords clearly believed that giving non-owners the right to sue would turn the tort into one to the person rather than to land. The decision may be open to challenge under the Human Rights Act 1998. No distinction is made under Article 8(1) of the Convention (providing that everyone has the right to respect for his home) between applicants with a proprietary interest in land and those without. The distinction made is a factual one, namely the existence of sufficient and continuous links. (***Khatun* v *United Kingdom*** (1998) EHRR CD 212.)

In ***McKenna* v *British Aluminium Ltd*** (2002) Times, 25 April, the defendant applied to strike out actions in nuisance and ***Rylands* v *Fletcher*** alleging that emissions and noise from the defendant's factory had caused them distress, physical damage and invasion of privacy, as the claimant had no proprietary interest in the affected land. The judge accepted that prior to the Human Rights Act only those with a proprietary interest could sue but refused to strike out as it was arguable that this restriction was incompatible with Convention rights under the Human Rights Act.

Neuburger J:

> There is obviously a powerful case for saying that effect has not been properly given to Article 8(1) if a person with no interest in the home, but who has lived in the house for some time and had his enjoyment of the home, is the only person who can bring proceedings.

The question of proprietary interest and Article 8 was also raised in a Court of Appeal decision. It is important to note that this decision was made upon assumed facts, i.e. there had not been a trial and determination of the facts of the case.

Dobson v *Thames Water Utilities Ltd* [2009] EWCA Civ 28

Odours from a sewage works had affected persons in nearby houses. The major issue in the case was the relationship between common law damages for private nuisance and damages under the Human Rights Act 1998. (See below for damages for nuisance.)

Some of the claimants had no proprietary interest in land and were therefore unable to claim in private nuisance. Could they claim damages under the Human Rights Act or were they covered by an award to the proprietary owners? An example would be a child who had suffered amenity damage from the smells and an award had been made to its parents. The judge at first instance had ruled that the award to the parents would cover the child. The Court of Appeal reversed the ruling and made the following points:

(a) An award of damages in nuisance to a person or persons with a proprietary interest in a property would be relevant to the question whether an award of damages was necessary to afford just satisfaction under Article 8 to a person who lived in the same household but had no proprietary interest in the property.

(b) *Canary Wharf* clearly established that damages in nuisance were for injury to the property and not to the sensibilities of the occupier or occupiers. On ordinary principles, it was clear that a claimant had to show that he had in truth suffered a loss of amenity before substantial damages could be awarded.

(c) *Canary Wharf* provided no support for the view that the person who had the right to sue in nuisance was recovering damages on behalf of other occupiers of the property.

See Chapter 1 and Chapter 22 for Article 8.

It remains to be seen whether the courts will change the characteristic of nuisance on the basis of Article 8.

The rule laid down in ***Hunter*** was that the claimant must have an interest in land or exclusive possession. Exclusive possession was held to include a secure tenant against whom an order for possession had been obtained and suspended and continued to occupy the property and pay rent as a 'tolerated trespasser'. (***Pemberton* v *Southwark LBC*** [2000] 3 All ER 924.)

Defendants

The law concerning defendants in private nuisance actions is complex and will be divided into three categories of defendant.

Creators

The creator of a nuisance may always be sued even though they are no longer in occupation of the land from which the nuisance originates.

This rule must be read in the light of the House of Lords decision in *Cambridge Water Co v Eastern Counties Leather plc* [1994] 1 All ER 53. It is necessary that the defendant should have been able to foresee damage of the relevant type when the act alleged to be a nuisance occurred. The defendant (creator) will not be liable for continuing damage when they are unable to rectify the situation (see Lord Goff at 81).

See Chapter 18 for facts of Cambridge Water Co.

Occupiers

In most nuisance cases it will be the occupier of the land from which the nuisance originates who is sued. The occupier is liable for nuisances created by themselves, and by their servants (on the basis of vicarious liability), but not for nuisances created by an independent contractor, unless the occupier is under a non-delegable duty or the contractor is working on the highway and creates a danger to highway users.

Bower v *Peate* (1876) 1 QBD 321

The parties owned adjoining houses. The defendant employed a contractor to work on his house. During the course of the work the support of the claimant's house was undermined. The defendant was held liable as he was under a non-delegable duty.

Historically, an occupier was not liable for nuisances created by trespassers or acts of nature. This was in line with the view that ownership of land was a source of rights rather than duties. Recent case law has changed this view, imposing duties of affirmative action on landowners for dangers emanating from their land.

Sedleigh-Denfield v *O'Callaghan* [1940] AC 880

A trespasser installed piping in a ditch on the respondent's land. Three years later the pipe became blocked and the appellant's land was flooded. One of the respondent's servants had cleaned out the ditch twice a year. As the respondents were presumed to know of the danger and had done nothing to abate it they were liable in nuisance. Liability in these circumstances would arise where the occupier, with knowledge of the existence of the nuisance, adopted it for his own purposes or continued it by failing to take steps to avoid it.

Goldman v *Hargrave* [1966] 2 All ER 989

A redgum tree on the appellant's land was struck by lightning and caught fire. The appellant had the tree cut down and left the fire to burn out. A strong wind got up and the fire spread and damaged the respondent's property. The Privy Council held that where an occupier becomes aware of the existence of a nuisance, he is under a duty to take positive action. The standard of care imposed on the occupier is subjective rather than the normal objective standard. In determining the occupier's liability, the court must take into account the cost of abatement and balance it against the occupier's resources. In this context resources means financial and physical resources. The appellant was held liable for failing to abate the nuisance.

Leakey v National Trust for Places of Historic Interest or Natural Beauty [1980] QB 485

The defendants occupied a hill which was known to crack and slip as a result of weathering. Debris fell on the claimant's land and the claimants asked the defendants to remove it. The defendants denied responsibility but were found liable in nuisance. The Court of Appeal held that the principle in **Goldman** applied in English law and extended to nuisances caused by the state of the land itself. The court also held that the action had been correctly brought in nuisance.

Holbeck Hall Hotel v Scarborough Borough Council [2000] 2 All ER 705

The claimant's hotel was on a cliff close to the sea. The land between the hotel and the sea was owned by the local authority and had been gradually eroded. In 1993 there had been a landslip, the third in three years, resulting in the hotel being undermined and having to be demolished. The claimants argued the case on the ground that the defendants were liable on the basis of withdrawal of support. However, the Court of Appeal held that there was no difference between withdrawal of support and any other claim in nuisance which resulted from natural forces. These depended on the negligence of the defendant when he had knowledge of the danger. The defendants did not have actual knowledge of the danger of a major landslip and such knowledge could not be presumed from the minor landslips which had previously occurred. Where the defendant has done nothing to create the danger, which arises solely from the operation of nature, the scope of the duty is restricted and does not extend to damage which, although of the same type that is foreseeable, is much more extensive than could have been foreseen.

The modern law can be stated as being that an occupier is liable for nuisances caused by a trespasser or act of nature, where the occupier is or should be aware of the presence of the nuisance on their premises and has failed to take reasonable steps to abate the nuisance. The standard of reasonableness is a subjective one. However, the duty is limited by the occupier's ability (physical and financial) to abate the nuisance and by its foreseeable extent. In the case of a latent defect (as in **Holbeck Hall Hotel**) the occupier is not liable for failure to make further investigations which would have revealed the defect.

It appears that the courts are careful about imposing unreasonable and unacceptable burdens on local authorities. This has occurred with encroaching tree roots and the possibility of imposing large bills for the underpinning of buildings affected by them. Usually the defendant is entitled to notice of the damage and the opportunity to abate by removing the tree before liability for repairing the building can be imposed. (**Delaware Mansions Ltd v Westminster City Council** [2001] 1 AC 321.)

The duty of affirmative action on landowners in the **Sedleigh-Denfield** line of cases may be enhanced by the Human Rights Act 1998. The relevant provisions are Article 8 of the European Convention and Article 1 of the First Protocol. These were considered in a case where the nuisance was caused by structure or activity which initially did not constitute a nuisance but became one as a result of increased usage. The first question was whether the defendant's activities constituted a nuisance on the **Sedleigh-Denfield** line of cases authority.

Marcic v Thames Water Utilities Ltd [2002] 2 All ER 55 (CA); [2004] 1 All ER 135 (HL)

Sewers which were originally adequate had become inadequate as a result of increased use, resulting in flooding which affected the claimant's property. Remedial work could have been carried out but under the defendant's scheme of prioritising work this would not be done in future. The Court of Appeal held the defendant liable in nuisance. On appeal to the House of Lords it was held that the defendant's conduct did not constitute a nuisance.

Lord Hoffmann:

> If *Sedleigh-Denfield's* case lays down a general principle that an owner of land has a duty to take reasonable steps to prevent a nuisance arising from a known source of hazard, even though he did not himself create it, why should that not require him to construct new sewers if the court thinks it would have been reasonable to do so?
>
> The difference in my opinion is that *Sedleigh-Denfield's* case, *Goldman's* case and *Leakey's* case were dealing with disputes between neighbouring land owners simply in their capacity as individual landowners. In such cases it is fair and efficient to impose reciprocal duties upon each landowner to take whatever steps are reasonable to prevent his land becoming a source of injury to his neighbour. Even then, the question of what measures should reasonably have been taken may not be uncomplicated. As Lord Wilberforce said in *Goldman's* case . . . the court must (unusually) have regard to the individual circumstances of the defendant. In *Leakey's* case . . . Megaw LJ recoiled from the prospect of a detailed examination of the defendant's financial resources and said it should be done 'on a broad basis'.
>
> Nevertheless, whatever the difficulties, the court in such cases is performing its usual function of deciding what is reasonable as between the two parties to the action. But the exercise becomes very different when one is dealing with the capital expenditure of a statutory undertaking providing public utilities on a large scale. The matter is no longer confined to the parties to the action. If one customer is given a certain level of services, everyone in the same circumstances should receive the same level of services. So the effect of a decision about what it would be reasonable to expect a sewerage undertaker to do for the plaintiff is extrapolated across the country. This in turn raises questions of public interest. Capital expenditure on new sewers has to be financed; interest must be paid on borrowings and privatised undertakers must earn a reasonable return. This expenditure can be met only by charges paid by consumers. Is it in the public interest that they should have to pay more? And does expenditure on the particular improvements with which the plaintiff is concerned represent the best order of priorities?
>
> These are decisions which courts are not equipped to make in ordinary litigation. It is therefore not surprising that for more than a century the question of whether more or better sewers should be constructed has been entrusted by Parliament to administrators rather than judges . . .
>
> It is plain that the Court of Appeal, in deciding that better sewers should have been laid to serve Mr Marcic's property, was in no position to take into account the wider issues which Parliament requires the Director to consider. The judge, who heard fairly detailed evidence about what the cost of such improvements would be, confessed himself unable to decide whether the priorities laid down by the Director were fair or not . . .
>
> The system of priorities used by the defendant may be entirely fair, and I have no reason to doubt that it is intended to be. But its fairness in balancing the competing interests of the defendant's various customers must depend in part on the numbers in each class, the total costs involved in relation to each class, and the resources of the defendant. The answers to the questions raised above as matters for consideration might depend on the figures. If the exercise of assessing the fairness of the system were carried out, it might lead to the conclusion that for all its apparent faults, the system fell within the wide margin of discretion open to the defendant and the director. But on the limited evidence available to me, it is not possible to carry out such an exercise . . .
>
> The 1991 Act makes it even clearer than the earlier legislation that Parliament did not intend the fairness of priorities to be decided by a judge. It intended the decision to rest with the Director, subject only to judicial review. It would subvert the scheme of the 1991 Act if the courts were to impose upon the sewerage undertakers, on a case-by-case basis, a system of priorities which is different from that which the Director considers appropriate.

The gist of the House of Lords decision here is that the line of cases starting with *Sedleigh-Denfield* had no effect on the older line of cases which precluded liability in nuisance for failing to build more sewers. In doing so, their Lordships did not deal with the Court of Appeal's decision to place the onus of proving that reasonable steps had been taken on the defendant. The House of Lords differed from the Court of Appeal on the categorisation of the complaint. Mr Marcic was treated as a dissatisfied customer complaining of a failure to drain his property rather than as a person harmed by positive interference for which Thames Water was responsible. What the claim boiled down to was a demand that Thames build more sewers. By the time of the appeal to the House of Lords the remedial work had actually been carried out, perhaps prompted by the court action.

? Question

What are these cases really based on? Are they negligence cases in disguise? Are they *Rylands* cases? In *Leakey* the Court of Appeal said that the two actions (negligence and nuisance) were essentially the same. Given that most of the cases involve an 'escape' then they could be brought in *Rylands* except for the 'non-natural user' requirement. The claims continue to be brought in nuisance, probably because this is where the precedents lie.

Landlords

The law on whether a landlord is liable for a nuisance is complex. The basic principle is that the landlord will not be liable as they have parted with control of the land. There are a number of exceptions to this principle.

Where a nuisance existed at the time of the letting the landlord will be liable if they knew or ought to have known of the nuisance before letting. They will also be liable if they can be said to have authorised the nuisance.

Harris v *James* (1876) 45 LJQB 545

A field was let by S to J for J to work it as a lime quarry and to set up lime kilns. The claimant complained of smoke from the kilns and nuisance caused by blasting in the quarrying. J was liable as occupier and S for authorising the commission of a nuisance.

Tetley v *Chitty* [1986] 1 All ER 653

The defendant council allowed a go-cart club to use its land. An action in nuisance was brought by nearby residents on the ground of noise. The council's defence that it was not liable as it had neither created the nuisance nor permitted one to occur was rejected. The noise was an ordinary and necessary consequence of the go-carts and the defendant had therefore expressly or impliedly consented to the nuisance.

Southwark London Borough Council v *Mills* [1999] 4 All ER 449

The landlords let flats in a communal block which had very poor soundproofing resulting in the noises of everyday living being audible through the walls. It was held by the House of Lords that the normal use of a residential flat cannot be a nuisance and as the tenants were not liable for nuisance the landlord could not be liable for authorising a nuisance.

If the landlord has taken a covenant in the lease from the tenant that the tenant will not cause a nuisance and the nuisance is not an inevitable consequence of the letting (as in *Tetley* v *Chitty*), the landlord is not liable. So where a local authority let a house to a problem family who had covenanted not to cause a nuisance, the local authority was not liable for the family's behaviour. (*Smith* v *Scott* [1973] Ch 314.) However, a considerable amount of litigation has surrounded local authorities as landlords. In *Page Motors Ltd* v *Epsom & Ewell Borough Council* (1982) 80 LGR 337, the authority was held liable for failing to take steps to halt the activities of gypsies camped on their land when the gypsies' activities interfered with the claimant's business. However, where the acts complained of do not involve the use of the tenant's land, such as racial harassment and intimidation, they do not fall within the scope of the tort of nuisance (*Hussain* v *Lancaster City Council* [1999] 4 All ER 125) and there had been no adoption by the council of the tenant's nuisance as in *Page*. The defendant's standard tenancy agreement included an anti-discriminatory clause and the defendant could not be said to have authorised the relevant acts. (See also *Mowan* v *London Borough of Wandsworth* [2000] All ER (D) 2411 (Dec).) The problems raised by the local authority cases are serious social problems and the courts view nuisance as an unsatisfactory forum with which to deal with these problems. (For the position in negligence see *Mitchell* v *Glasgow City Council* [2009] UKHL 11.

See Chapters 6 and 7 for detail of *Mitchell*.

However, where travellers occupied council land and their activities interfered with the claimant's land, it was held that there was at least an arguable case that there was a nuisance action. (*Lippiatt* v *South Gloucestershire Council* [1999] 4 All ER 149.) *Hussain* was distinguished as in *Lippiatt* the travellers had been allowed to congregate on the defendant's land and use it as a base for their unlawful activities against the claimants. The licensor, unlike the landlord, retains control of the premises and licensees can be moved more easily than tenants. It is submitted that the distinction between this case and *Hussain* is not particularly convincing.

The landlord may also be liable for nuisances arising after the demise, where they have reserved the right to enter and repair in the lease or have the implied right to do so. The landlord will be liable whether they knew of the defect or not (*Wringe* v *Cohen*), unless the defect was due to the act of a trespasser or an act of nature (*Leakey* v *National Trust*).

In the case of residential tenancies for less than seven years, there is a statutory obligation on the landlord to repair the structure and exterior, which they cannot contract out of. (Landlord and Tenant Act 1985 ss 11–14.)

See also Chapter 11 for s 4.

There is also a form of statutory liability on landlords. The Defective Premises Act 1972 s 4 imposes a duty on landlords of premises after their demise. The section applies where the landlord is under an obligation to the tenant for maintenance or repair of the premises. Where the landlord knows or ought to know of the relevant defect, they owe a duty to all persons who might reasonably be expected to be affected by the defects in the state of the premises.

Therefore, if *L* leases premises to *T* and reserves a right to enter and carry out repairs and the premises develop a defect which *L* knows about and damage is caused to *N*, an adjacent property owner, *N* may have a statutory action by virtue of s 4, or may be able to bring themselves within one of the common law exceptional rules on landlords, so as to be able to sue in private nuisance.

Interference with use and enjoyment

Objective 4

Private nuisance is a balancing act between the defendant's right to use their land as they wish and the claimant's right to enjoy their land without interference. The claimant must establish that the defendant has caused a substantial interference with their use or enjoyment of their land. No account is taken of trivialities. The interference may take a number of forms but some of the commonest are: physical damage to the claimant's land; substantial interference with enjoyment of land through smells, vibrations, noise, dust and other emissions; encroachment onto land by roots or branches.

Whether the interference amounts to a nuisance is a question for the court. Normally this will be determined by applying a reasonableness test, but where the interference causes *material damage* to the claimant's land, the defendant will be liable unless the claimant is over-sensitive or one of the defences to nuisance applies.

St Helens Smelting Co v Tipping (1865) 11 HL Cas 642

> The claimant bought an estate near to the defendant's copper smelting works. Fumes from the works damaged the claimant's trees and crops. The court drew a distinction between nuisances causing material damage to the land and those which caused sensible personal discomfort. In the latter case the question of locality was relevant. As the claimant's land had suffered material damage, the fact that the locality was a manufacturing area was irrelevant and an injunction was granted.

The problem with this decision is that it is difficult to determine what is meant by material damage. Any substantial interference with residential land may lower its value, but unless the land itself is damaged the locality factor may defeat the claimant's action.

The reasonableness test

Where the interference causes sensible personal discomfort the court will apply a reasonableness test to determine whether it amounts to a nuisance. A number of factors may be taken into account, either in isolation or in conjunction to determine whether the defendant's conduct was reasonable.

It is important to note the effect of **Hunter v Canary Wharf Ltd** [1997] 2 All ER 426 on this point. The House of Lords' stress on nuisance being a tort to land and not a separate tort of causing discomfort to people is a reference to the distinction between nuisances causing material damage to the property and those causing sensible personal discomfort. Smells and noise would normally come into the latter category. One of the main thrusts in *Hunter* was a desire to prevent the distinction from becoming one of a distinction between property and personal damage. This means that in future cases the court will concentrate on the land itself rather than on the landowner, and the landowner must find a way of identifying how their land has been affected, whether this is in a reduction in its capital value or in its amenity.

Lord Hoffmann:

> *St Helens Smelting Co v Tipping* was a landmark case. It drew the line beyond which rural and landed England did not have to accept external costs imposed upon it by industrial pollution. But there has been, I think, some inclination to treat it as having divided nuisance into two torts, one of causing 'material injury to the property', such as flooding or depositing poisonous substances on crops, and the other of causing 'sensible personal discomfort', such as excessive noise or smells. In cases in the first category, there has never been any doubt that the remedy, whether by way of injunction or damages, is for causing damage to the land. It is plain that in such a case only a person with an interest in the land can sue. But there has been a tendency to regard cases in the second category as actions in respect of the discomfort

or even personal injury which the plaintiff has suffered or is likely to suffer. On this view, the plaintiff's interest in the land becomes no more than a qualifying condition or springboard which entitles him to sue for injury to himself.

If this were the case, the need for the plaintiff to have an interest in land would indeed be hard to justify . . . But the premise is quite mistaken. In the case of nuisances 'productive of sensible personal discomfort', the action is not for causing discomfort to the person but, as in the case of the first category, for causing injury to the land. True it is that the land has not suffered 'sensible' injury, but its utility has been diminished by the existence of the nuisance. It is for an unlawful threat to the utility of his land that the possessor or occupier is entitled to an injunction and it is for the diminution in such utility that he is entitled to compensation.

The effect of the majority view is that a claimant in a nuisance action claims on behalf of the land, whether their action falls on the material damage or amenity side. This means that in order to establish damage they must show damage to the land in capital or amenity value. This will prove very difficult to apply and was intended by the majority as an exclusionary rule.

Locality

Sturges v Bridgman (1879) 11 Ch D 852

A confectioner had for more than 20 years used industrial pestles and mortars. This caused no interference until the claimant doctor built an extension consulting room in his garden, adjacent to the confectioner's premises. At this stage the noise and vibration were alleged to be a nuisance. The doctor's action succeeded. The court took into account the fact that the area consisted largely of doctors' consulting rooms and stated that that which would be a nuisance in Belgrave Square would not necessarily be so in Bermondsey.

The effect of this rule is to make it difficult for those who live in industrial areas to succeed. The distinction made in the *St Helens* case between material damage to the land and sensible personal discomfort combined with the locality rule seriously limited the liability of industrialists for amenity damage. People who were most subject to environmental degradation were held to be those least deserving of any protection. For a successful case see the following:

Rushmer v Polsue & Alfieri Ltd [1906] 1 Ch 234

The claimant milkman lived in an area of London which contained a large number of printing companies. He found it difficult to sleep at night and sought an injunction for nuisance by noise. The injunction was granted although the claimant was the only resident, as the noise went beyond the boundaries of what was acceptable.

It is possible for the nature of a locality to change with time. When this happens the change is normally dealt with by planning permission but what is the relationship between planning law and nuisance?

Lawrence v Fen Tigers [2014] UKSC 13

(For the facts, see above.)

The extent to which planning permission should be taken into account in assessing the character of a locality, was a key issue in the conflicting Court of Appeal decisions in *Fen* itself and *Barr v Biffa Waste Services Ltd* [2012] EWCA Civ 312.

The grant of planning permission for a particular use is potentially relevant to a nuisance claim in that:

(a) the grant or terms of the planning permission may permit the very noise (or other disturbance) which is alleged to constitute the nuisance;

(b) the planning permission may provide evidence that the permitted activity is part of a pattern of use of land, so as to define or change the character of the locality; and

(c) the terms and conditions of the planning permission may provide a useful benchmark as to the noise or disturbance that would be considered to be reasonable on an objective basis.

However, the Supreme Court clarified that although the implementation of planning permission can give rise to a change in the character of the locality, it has no special status over any other change of use which does not require planning permission.

Lord Neuberger approved the analysis by Carnwath LJ in *Barr v Biffa Waste Services Ltd*:

> The common law of nuisance has co-existed with statutory controls, albeit less sophisticated, since the nineteenth century. There is no principle that the common law should 'march with' a statutory scheme covering similar subject matter. Short of express or implied statutory authority to commit a nuisance . . . there is no basis, in principle or authority, for using such a statutory scheme to cut down private law rights.

Lord Sumption considered this issue in the context of legal policy as to how one could reconcile public and private law in the domain of land use and stated (at [156]):

> I agree with Lord Neuberger that the existence of planning permission for a given use is of very limited relevance to the question whether that use constitutes a private nuisance. It may at best provide some evidence of the reasonableness of the particular use of land in question. But planning authorities are concerned with the public interest in development and land use, as that interest is defined in the planning legislation and any relevant development plans and policies. Planning powers do not exist to enforce or override private rights in respect of land use, whether arising from restrictive covenants, contracts, or the law of tort. Likewise, the question whether a neighbouring landowner has a right of action in nuisance in respect of some use of land has to be decided by the courts regardless of any public interest engaged.

Lord Carnwath (at [183]):

> After more than 60 years of modern planning and environmental controls, it is not unreasonable to start from the presumption that the established pattern of uses generally represents society's view of the appropriate balance of uses in a particular area, taking account both of the social needs of the area and of the maintenance of an acceptable environment for its occupants. The common law of nuisance is there to provide a residual control to ensure that new or intensified activities do not need lead to conditions which, within that pattern, go beyond what a normal person should be expected to put up with.

Lord Carnwath (at [222]) stated the fundamental difference between planning law and the law of nuisance. The purpose of planning law is to protect and promote the public interest, whereas the law of nuisance protects the rights of individuals. Although planning decisions may result in an interference with the interests of individuals for the benefit of the wider public, it is generally no defence to a claim of nuisance that the activity in question is of benefit to the public:

> I think there should be a strong presumption against allowing private rights to be overridden by administrative decisions without compensation.

Duration

The longer the interference continues, the more likely it is to be unreasonable. The question frequently arises in connection with building works. The courts have laid down a principle that provided these are carried on with reasonable skill and care and interference is minimised, then no nuisance is committed. (*Andreae* v *Selfridge & Co Ltd* [1938] Ch 1.)

The duration principle raises difficulties with one-off nuisances where there is an isolated or single escape. These occur where there is a state of affairs on the defendant's land which causes damage on one occasion to the claimant.

Spicer v *Smee* [1946] 1 All ER 480

Defective electrical wiring was installed in the defendant's premises. This caused a fire which destroyed the claimant's adjacent house. The defendant was held liable in nuisance. The nuisance was the state of affairs on the defendant's land which foreseeably exposed his neighbour's property to danger.

See Chapter 8 for *Bolton*.

The cases on isolated escape illustrate a connection between nuisance and negligence. In *Bolton* v *Stone* [1951] 1 All ER 1078, the isolated escape of a cricket ball from the ground was held not to be a nuisance. Whether there is a state of affairs on the land sufficient to give rise to liability in nuisance will depend on the frequency with which balls escape. This is also a factor in determining negligence.

Sensitivity

If the damage is due more to the sensitivity of the claimant's property than to the defendant's conduct then no nuisance is committed.

Robinson v *Kilvert* (1889) 41 ChD 88

The claimant occupied the ground floor of the defendant's premises and used it to store brown paper. Heat created by the defendant's manufacturing process damaged the paper. It was held that the damage was due more to the sensitivity of the paper than to the defendant's activities and there was no nuisance.

The issue of television reception has also arisen for decision under the sensitivity point. An early case raised two issues on this point.

Bridlington Relay Co v *Yorkshire Electricity Board* [1965] Ch 436

The defendant's overhead power cables interfered with the transmissions from the claimant's television booster mast. The claimant's action failed as their activity was held to be sensitive and television reception, as a leisure activity of little value to its users, was not protected by nuisance.

NB: Subsequent Commonwealth decisions on the latter point failed to follow the English view and found that television reception was protected. The sensitivity point is still valid and the issue arose for decision in a different context in *Hunter* v *Canary Wharf Ltd*.

Hunter v *Canary Wharf Ltd* [1996] 1 All ER 482 (CA); [1997] 2 All ER 426 (HL)

The claimant (and others) claimed damages in nuisance for interference caused by the defendants with their television reception by the erection of a tall building in an enterprise zone where planning restrictions had been eased. It was held that this was not capable of constituting an actionable public or private nuisance since, as with a loss of visual prospect caused by a tall building, the erection or presence of a building in the line of sight between a TV transmitter and other properties was not actionable as interference with use and enjoyment of land.

Pill LJ:

> the erection or presence of a building in the line of sight between a television transmitter and other properties is not actionable as an interference with use and enjoyment of land. The analogy with loss of prospect is compelling. The loss of a view, which may be of the greatest importance to many householders, is not actionable and neither is the mere presence of a building in the sightline to the television transmitter.

The House of Lords ([1997] 2 All ER 426) held that interference with television reception was not capable of constituting an actionable nuisance on the facts of the case. This was based on the general rule which entitled a building owner to do what they liked on their land and in the refusal to impose liability where a building blocked a neighbour's air or light, unless an easement had been acquired. The House doubted whether an easement in respect of unimpaired television signals would be granted. Two possible exceptions to the principle of no liability where signals were blocked by a building were put forward by Lord Cooke. The first was where the building was erected in contravention of planning law and the second where the defendant was actuated by malice. (The second example, however, appears to conflict with *Bradford Corp v Pickles* [1895] AC 587, unless the defendant's action was independently unlawful by building in breach of planning law.)

Aside from the facts of the case, the House did not completely rule out the possibility of an action where television reception was interfered with, for example, if the interference was by electrical signals. Lord Goff (at 432) did not approve of Buckley J's reasoning in *Bridlington Relay* and recognised that the importance of television had changed and transcended the function of mere entertainment. Lord Cooke (at 463) thought that in appropriate cases television and radio reception could and should be protected by the law of nuisance and Lord Hoffmann (at 455) thought that in principle this was the correct approach.

Given the property-based approach to the tort of the majority, it appears unlikely that television interference will be actionable, as it lacks the necessary proprietary characteristics. One commentator has suggested that the effect of *Hunter* is that nuisance might be better viewed as an adjunct to the law of property rather than a part of the framework of the law of obligations. (P. Cane (1998) 113 LQR 515.)

The Court of Appeal has, however, recognised that electromagnetic interference by a railway signalling system with electric guitars in an adjacent recording studio could be protected by the law of nuisance but that on the facts the defendants could not have foreseen the interference. The Court recognised that the use of electronic equipment was now a feature of modern life. (*Morris (t/a Soundstar studio)* v *Network Rail Infrastructure Ltd* [2004] EWCA Civ 172.)

As in psychiatric damage cases, the courts will grant protection in sensitivity cases if it can be shown that the breach of duty would have affected non-sensitive interests.

McKinnon Industries Ltd v *Walker* [1951] 3 DLR 577

> The defendant's factory emitted sulphur dioxide which damaged the claimant's commercially grown orchids. As the interference would have damaged non-sensitive plants, the claimant was able to recover the full extent of the loss, including the damage to the sensitive orchids.

Public utility

Can the defendant advance the argument that although their activity may be causing damage to the claimant, it is in the public interest that they be allowed to continue? The traditional view is that public interest is irrelevant to the question of private rights and will be ignored. This is dramatically illustrated by a case where Ireland's only cement factory was closed down for causing a nuisance at a time when building was an urgent public necessity. (*Bellew* v *Cement Co Ltd* [1948] IR 61.) Confirmation was given to this view where the claimant's estate was subjected to 'fearsome noise' by Royal Air Force jets flying over it. (*Dennis* v *Ministry of Defence* [2003] EWHC 793.)

The modern view would appear to turn on what remedy is being sought. In deciding whether or not to grant an injunction, the court may take into account public utility.

Miller v *Jackson* [1977] QB 966

> Cricket balls frequently entered the claimant's garden from the adjacent cricket club, despite the attempts of the club to prevent this. The Court of Appeal held by 2–1 that a nuisance had been committed, but refused by 2–1 to grant an injunction on the grounds of public utility. The court felt that the utility of the club to the community outweighed the claimant's interest.

The argument on public benefit is essentially who should bear the losses. This was vividly illustrated in *Marcic* v *Thames Water Utilities Ltd* [2002] 2 All ER 55 (for facts, see above), where the damage to the claimant's land caused by flooding had to be weighed against the public interest in the sewage system. The Court of Appeal felt that on the facts of the case it was unjust that the householder should receive no compensation. The flooding was a consequence of the benefit that was provided to the public and that it would be just to require those benefiting to pay to cover the cost of the damage to the minority who suffered as a result of the operation of the system. However, the House of Lords ruled ([2004] 2 All ER 385) that the statutory scheme set up by Parliament had to be used and that this prevented a common law remedy.

NB: See also 'Remedies' below, for the grounds for granting an injunction. One method of taking into account public utility is for Parliament to grant statutory authority to the defendant for their activity. On this, see 'Defences' below.

Malice

See also Chapter 1 for malice generally. The bad motive or malice of the defendant may make what would otherwise have been reasonable conduct, unreasonable and a nuisance.

Christie v *Davey* [1893] 1 Ch 316

> The claimant and defendant lived in adjoining houses. The claimant gave music lessons in the house. This annoyed the defendant who responded by banging trays on the wall and shouting while the lessons were in progress. The claimant was held entitled to an injunction. The defendant's malice made his conduct unreasonable and a nuisance.

Hollywood Silver Fox Farm v Emmett [1936] 2 KB 468

> The claimant bred silver foxes. The defendant, after an argument, ordered guns to be fired on his own land but close to the claimant's land. His intention was that the noise would prevent the foxes from breeding. An injunction was granted to restrain the defendant. What would otherwise have been a reasonable act was a nuisance because of his malice.

Nuisance and fault

Objective 5

See Chapters 1 and 8 for fault.

Is it necessary for the claimant to prove that the defendant was negligent in order to succeed in a nuisance action? If this was the case, the tort of nuisance would become redundant, as all actions would be brought in negligence.

There is a distinction between nuisance and negligence. In negligence the court will look at the way the defendant did something, whereas in nuisance the court is looking at a protected interest of the claimant and balancing it against what the defendant did.

> ### Example
>
> Take a factory which is built with the latest state of the art pollution control machinery. Despite this, the factory still emits foul smells which nearby residents allege amount to a nuisance and/or negligence. In the negligence action the court will have to ask whether the defendant took all reasonable care. If they used the best available equipment and maintained it properly, then the negligence action will fail. In the nuisance action the court will have to balance the interests of the two parties using the tests set out above. The question is whether the defendant acted reasonably, not whether they used all reasonable care. The court could find that the defendant's activity was unreasonable and grant an injunction in nuisance.

See also Chapter 9 for *Wagon Mound No 2*.

The law in this area was confused by dicta of Lord Reid in ***Wagon Mound No 2*** [1967] 1 AC 617:

> . . . negligence is not an essential element in nuisance. Nuisance is a term used to cover a wide variety of tortious acts or omissions and in many negligence in the narrow sense is not essential. . . . And although negligence may not be necessary, fault of some kind is almost always necessary and fault generally involves foreseeability. . . .

Negligence in the narrow sense means breach of duty in negligence, i.e. that the defendant failed to act with reasonable care.

Where the application is for an injunction then 'consideration of the strictness of the duty is out of place – all that the court is concerned with is the question, "Should the defendant be told to stop this interference with the claimant's rights?" Whether or not the defendant knew of the noise or smell or the like when it first began to annoy the claimant does not matter; he becomes aware of it at the latest when the claimant brings his claim before the court.' (Law Commission Report No 32, 'Civil Liability for Dangerous Things & Activities', p. 25.)

Where the nuisance was due to the act of a trespasser or an act of nature, negligence (in the narrow sense) is necessary, albeit with a subjective rather than an objective test.

If the damage is due to an isolated escape, the claimant probably needs to establish facts which would establish negligence in order to succeed in nuisance.

See Chapter 18 for
*Cambridge Water
Co.*
In any claim for damages in nuisance it is necessary that interference of the kind which occurs should have been reasonably foreseen by the defendant. (***Cambridge Water Co* v *Eastern Counties Leather plc*** [1994] 1 All ER 53.) This case establishes a fault-based test for remoteness of damage, but it is submitted that there may still be actions for damages in nuisance where negligence 'in the narrow sense' is not necessary. In the ***Cambridge Water*** case it was stated (*obiter*) that the fact that the defendant has used all reasonable care will not exonerate them from liability.

Confusing as all this may sound, the student needs to remember that in a nuisance case the court is looking at essentially something different from that in a negligence action. In negligence, the court looks at the way the defendant was performing the activity complained of. In nuisance, the court is looking at what the defendant was doing and how it impinges on a neighbour's use of their land. Control devices such as remoteness of damage are still necessary to prevent the defendant from being held too widely liable, especially in an era of judicial caution where considerable legislative effort has gone into environmental law.

Remedies

Injunction

See also Chapter 28
for injunctions.
The injunction is the primary remedy in nuisance actions and its objective is to force the defendant to cease their activities. The injunction may be perpetual and terminate the activity or limit it to certain times. It is possible for the court to suspend the injunction and give the defendant the opportunity to eliminate the source of the complaint.

Injunctions are equitable remedies and as such are not available as of right. The question of when the court should exercise its discretion to refuse an injunction was considered in the following case.

Shelfer v *City of London Electric Lighting Co* [1895] 1 Ch 287

> Vibration and noise were caused by the defendant's activities. The defendant claimed that the claimant should be limited to damages as the award of an injunction would deprive many Londoners of electricity. The court held that the discretion not to award the injunction should be exercised only in exceptional circumstances:
>
> (a) where the injury to the claimant's legal right is small; and
> (b) is capable of being estimated in money terms; and
> (c) is one which can be adequately compensated by a small money payment; and
> (d) it would be oppressive to the defendant to grant an injunction.

These tests were applied in a number of cases, however, for present purposes the following two are sufficient examples.

Examples

In ***Miller* v *Jackson*** (see above) the Court of Appeal did refuse the injunction in the public interest of the playing of cricket. However, in ***Kennaway* v *Thompson*** ([1981] QB 88 an injunction was granted in the following case concerning a sporting event. The claimant lived by Lake Windermere, which was used by the defendants for power boat racing. The noise from the boats amounted to a nuisance and an injunction was granted to restrain the number of events and the noise level of boats. The social utility argument of the defendants was rejected as not compatible with the ***Shelfer*** principle.

In *Lawrence* **v** *Fen Tigers* [2014] UKSC 13 the Supreme Court approved the test but with modifications. The court was critical of the mechanical application of the tests but had not heard full argument on the issue and was reluctant to make a major jurisprudential statement.

Lord Neuberger accepted the appropriateness of that test but subject to the following modifications (at [123]):

> First, the application of the four tests must not be such as 'to be a fetter on the exercise of the court's discretion'. Secondly, it would, in the absence of additional relevant circumstances pointing the other way, normally be right to refuse an injunction if those four tests were satisfied. Thirdly, the fact that those tests are not all satisfied does not mean that an injunction should be granted.

Lord Neuberger considered that the grant of planning permission for an activity of benefit to the public would be relevant to the question of whether or not to grant an injunction. In particular, where the activity could not be carried out without causing the nuisance complained of and an injunction would involve a loss to the public or a waste of resources, or the financial implications of an injunction would be disproportionate to the damage to the claimant, an injunction may well not be the appropriate remedy.

Lord Sumption, with whom Lord Clarke agreed, went further and considered that the test in *Shelfer* was no longer appropriate, although he did not go so far as to overrule it. The tension between the rights of the individual and the wider public could be resolved by a greater use of damages in lieu of an injunction (at [161]):

> The whole jurisprudence in this area will need one day to be reviewed in this court. There is much to be said for the view that damages are ordinarily an adequate remedy for nuisance and that an injunction should not usually be granted in a case where it is likely that conflicting interests are engaged other than the parties' interests. In particular, it may well be that an injunction should as a matter of principle not be granted in a case where a use of land to which objection is taken requires and has received planning permission.

Lord Carnwath was more cautious as to whether there should be any presumption of damages, rather than an injunction, where there was planning permission for the use of property giving rise to the nuisance (at [247]):

> The judge is not asked to bring the defendant's activity to an end altogether, but to set reasonable limits for its continuation. In so doing he should take into account not only the claimant's environment but also the viability of the defendant's business. In some cases it may be appropriate to combine an injunction with an award of damages. (See *Watson* **v** *Croft Promosport Ltd* [2009] 3 All ER 249.) I also agree with Lord Mance that special importance should attach to the right to enjoy one's home without disturbance, independently of financial considerations.

The issues concerning the tensions between public interest and private right therefore await full consideration by the Supreme Court.

 ## Damages

See also Chapter 28 for damages. In public nuisance actions the claimant must prove special damage in order to succeed. Damage must usually be proved in a private nuisance action but may be presumed.

It is normal for the claimant to seek damages for past losses and an injunction to prevent future losses. It is possible that the change in approach to the tort which may be brought about by the Human Rights Act 1998 could require the courts to rethink their views on damages for prospective future losses. A building such as a nuclear power station, which is for the public benefit, could hardly be removed as a result of an injunction in private nuisance but might give rise to damages on the part of those damaged as a result of its operation. In such cases it is the protection of the value of the land which is important, coupled with an amenity award. (**Dennis v Ministry of Defence** [2003] EWHC 793.)

See also Chapter 9 for *Wagon Mound No 2*.

The remoteness of damage test in nuisance is the same as that in negligence: the defendant must have been able reasonably to foresee the kind of damage which occurred. (**Wagon Mound No 2** [1967] 1 AC 617.)

Where the nuisance causes damage to the land, the measure of damages will usually be the depreciation in value of the land. Where the nuisance consists of interference with use and enjoyment, then assessment of damages presents problems.

Bone v Seale [1975] 1 All ER 787

The defendant's pig farm was adjacent to the claimant's land. The claimant sought an injunction and damages in nuisance in respect of smells caused by pig manure and the boiling of pig swill. The court held that there was no damage to the claimant's property or his health and awarded damages of £1,000 based on the amount that would have been awarded in a personal injuries action for loss of sense of smell.

Lord Hoffmann in **Hunter v Canary Wharf Ltd** [1997] 2 All ER 426 at 451 expressly disapproved of this approach to quantifying damages in private nuisance cases, as nuisance is a tort against land and not against the person. He suggested that damages should be fixed by the diminution in capital value of the land as a result of the amenity damage.

The approach of the House of Lords will affect both the interests protected and the quantum of damage. Damages may be awarded for damage to the land itself, but damages for personal injury and damage to the landowner's property may be excluded completely. Lord Lloyd and Lord Hoffmann stated that an action could not lie in private nuisance for personal injury, although Lord Cooke pointed out that it was anomalous for personal injuries to be recoverable in public nuisance but not in private nuisance.

Where the land itself is damaged, damages will be assessed by the diminution in the capital value of the land. Where the damage is amenity damage and transitory, Lord Hoffmann said he would quantify damage by reference to the diminution in value during the period in which the nuisance persists (at 451).

Lord Hoffmann:

I cannot therefore agree with Stephenson LJ in **Bone v Seale** [1975] 1 All ER 787 at 793–794, [1975] 1 WLR 797 at 803–804, when he said that damages in an action for nuisance caused by smells from a pigsty should be fixed by analogy with damages for loss of amenity in an action for personal injury. In that case it was said that 'efforts to prove diminution in the value of the property as a result of this persistent smell over the years failed'. I take this to mean that it had not been shown that the property would sell for less. But diminution in capital value is not the only measure of loss. It seems to me that the value of the right to occupy a house which smells of pigs must be less than the value of the occupation of an equivalent house which does not. In the case of a transitory nuisance, the capital value of the property will seldom be reduced. But the owner or occupier is entitled to compensation for the diminution in the amenity value of the property during the period for which the nuisance persisted. To some extent this involves placing a value on intangibles. But estate agents do this all the time. The law of damages is sufficiently flexible to be able to do justice in such a case (cf. **Ruxley Electronics and Construction Ltd v Forsyth, Laddington Enclosures Ltd v Forsyth** [1995] 3 All ER 268, [1996] AC 344).

There may of course be cases in which, in addition to damages for injury to his land, the owner or occupier is able to recover damages for consequential loss. He may use the land for the purposes of his business. Or if the land is flooded, he may also be able to recover damages for chattels or livestock lost as a result. But inconvenience, annoyance or even illness suffered by persons on land as a result of smells or dust are not damage consequential upon the injury to the land. It is rather the other way about: the injury to the amenity of the land consists in the fact that the persons on it are liable to suffer inconvenience, annoyance or illness.

In *Dobson* v *Thames Water Utilities Ltd (Water Services Regulation Authority (Ofwat) intervening)* [2008] 2 All ER 362, where odours from a sewage works had affected persons in nearby houses, it was held that where the nuisance had not caused permanent loss, the loss of rental value was the prima facie measure of damages. Where this could not be assessed, loss of amenity may be the correct measure.

On appeal (*Dobson* v *Thames Water Utilities Ltd* [2009] EWCA Civ 28) the major issue was the relationship between common law damages for private nuisance and damages under the Human Rights Act 1998. (See the section 'Nuisance and human rights' below.)

If the action is in public nuisance, then the claimant can recover damages for economic loss. There is little authority on economic loss in private nuisance, but as the claimant must have had a property interest damaged before they can sue, the same problems are not present as in negligence. The Court of Appeal allowed a Wildlife Trust to recover £100,000 for an investigation into silting of feeding grounds on an estuary. The cost of the survey was held to be consequential on physical interference with the claimant's property rights. (*Jan de Nul (UK) Ltd* v *AXA Royale Belge SA* [2002] 1 All ER (Comm) 767.)

Abatement

See also Chapter 27 for abatement.

This remedy of abatement is a form of self-help and consists of the claimant taking steps to stop the nuisance, for example, by cutting off the branches of overhanging trees or unblocking drains.

Where the exercise of the remedy requires the claimant to enter another person's land, then notice must be given, otherwise the abator will become a trespasser.

It is fair to say that the law does not usually favour this remedy and in most cases it is not advisable. (*Delaware Mansions Ltd* v *Westminster City Council* [2002] 1 AC 321.)

Defences

Objective 6

There are a number of issues which might be thought to be defences but which are generally not. These will be dealt with first, followed by the established defences to nuisance.

Coming to the nuisance

Coming to the nuisance is not a defence. The defendant cannot argue that the claimant was aware of the nuisance when they moved to the area.

Sturges v *Bridgman* (1879) 11 Ch D 852

(For facts, see above under 'Locality'.) The confectioner argued that when the doctor built his extended consulting room he was aware of the noise and had therefore come to the nuisance. The court rejected this argument as this was not a recognised defence in nuisance.

Miller v Jackson [1977] QB 966

> (For facts, see 'Public utility' above.) Lord Denning argued that as the claimants had bought a house next to a cricket field they could not be heard to complain about interference by cricket balls. This was rejected by the rest of the Court of Appeal so far as establishing a nuisance was concerned, but it was a factor in the decision of the majority not to grant an injunction.

In *Lawrence* v *Fen Tigers* [2014] UKSC 13 the Supreme Court held that it is well established that it is not a defence to a claim in nuisance to show that the claimant acquired, or started to occupy, the affected property after the nuisance had started. However, Lord Neuberger indicated that where a claimant built on, or changed the use of, his or her land, it might well be wrong to hold that a defendant's pre-existing activity gave rise to a nuisance provided that: (i) it could only be said to be a nuisance because it affected the senses of those on the claimant's land; (ii) it was not a nuisance before the building or change of use of the claimant's land; (iii) it was, and had been, a reasonable and otherwise lawful use of the defendant's land; (iv) it was carried out in a reasonable way; and (v) it caused no greater nuisance than when the claimant first carried out the building or changed the use.

Lord Neuberger stated (at [58]):

> Accordingly, it appears clear to me that it is no defence for a defendant who is sued in nuisance to contend that the claimant came to the nuisance, although it may well be a defence, at least in some circumstances, for a defendant to contend that, as it is only because the claimant has changed the use of, or built on, her land that the defendant's pre-existing activity is claimed to have become a nuisance, the claim should fail.

? Question

Where does this leave *Sturges*? See Lord Neuberger at 53.

Usefulness

Usefulness is simply the question of public utility as a defence, rather than a factor going towards reasonableness. The fact that the defendant's activity is a useful one is not a defence.

Nuisance due to many

Where the nuisance is caused by a number of persons, it is not a defence for the defendant to prove that their contribution alone would not have amounted to a nuisance.

Prescription

In actions for private (but not public) nuisance it will be a defence to show that the nuisance has been actionable for a period of 20 years and the claimant was aware that it affected his interests during the relevant period.

Sturges v Bridgman (1879) 11 Ch D 852

(For facts, see 'Locality' above.) The defence of prescription failed, as the noise from the confectioner's activities only became a nuisance when the doctor had his extended consulting room built. Only from this time did the 20 years start to run.

In *Lawrence* v *Fen Tigers* [2014] UKSC 13 at [89]), Lord Neuberger accepted that a right to emit noise could be characterised as an easement, namely, the right to transmit sound waves over the servient land. However, in order to establish such a right by prescription, it would not be sufficient to show that the activity had been carried on for 20 years, or even that the activity had created a noise for 20 years. What must be established is that the activity had created a nuisance over 20 years. Otherwise, it could not be said that the putative servient owner had the opportunity to object to the nuisance, or could be said notionally to have agreed to it.

Statutory authority

In the light of what has been said about nuisance, a person would be justified in looking quizzically at certain parts of the industrial landscape of England and Wales. The answer lies in the defence of statutory authority. During the nineteenth century it became common for industrial operators to obtain the passing of a private Act of Parliament to give them authority to commit a nuisance, provided that there was no negligence on their part. This was done by the railway companies, as the operation of steam trains would cause a nuisance by smoke, noise and vibration.

Where a statute orders something to be done, there will be no liability in nuisance for doing this and for any inevitable consequences. An inevitable consequence is one which cannot be avoided by the use of due skill and care.

In the absence of negligence, most cases will involve the interpretation of the statute and the court may take into account the national interest.

Metropolitan Asylum District v Hill (1881) 6 App Cas 193

A local authority was given statutory power to build a smallpox hospital. It was restrained from erecting it in a place which would have been a source of danger to the local community. In this case the power could have been carried out without committing a nuisance, by siting it in a less populated area.

Allen v Gulf Oil Refining Ltd [1981] 1 All ER 353

The defendants were given statutory power to compulsorily purchase land and build an oil refinery and associated works. The claimant complained of nuisance caused by smell, noise and vibration. On a preliminary point the House of Lords held that statutory authority was available as a defence. The claimant had argued that the statute empowered the construction of the refinery but not its use. The court took into account the preamble to the statute and the public demand for oil and that Parliament would not have authorised the construction of the refinery without also authorising its use.

The problem created by statutory authority, taking away private rights in the public interest, could be avoided if Lord Denning's suggestion in the Court of Appeal had been taken up. He suggested that although the injunction could not be granted the claimant should be entitled to damages. The House of Lords did not agree. The advent of the Human Rights

Act and the possible effect of Article 8 giving a right to a private and family life may yet prove Lord Denning right. The onus of attempting to prove the justifiability of an intrusion on this right would fall on those seeking to intrude.

Contributory negligence

See also Chapter 10 for contributory negligence.

There is little authority on whether contributory negligence is available as a defence to nuisance. There is dictum in *Trevett* v *Lee* [1955] QB 966 to the effect that it operates as a defence in public nuisance cases.

Nuisance and human rights

Objective 7

The Human Rights Act 1998 has the scope for affecting nuisance law. Article 8 of the European Convention protects privacy, which includes a right to respect for a person's home and private life. The First Protocol confers a right to the peaceful enjoyment of possessions.

See Chapter 1 for tort law and human rights.

A number of nuisance rules have been challenged as private nuisance is a tort based on interference with property rights, rather than a physical nexus with a home. However, there are as yet no clear-cut answers. (See *Marcic* v *Thames Water Utilities*; *Dobson* v *Thames Water*; *Watson* v *Croft Promo-Sport*.)

The relevant issues are:

1 Challenges to statutory schemes to see if they are 'Convention compliant'.
In the following case the House of Lords had denied that a common law nuisance had been committed. The second question was whether Mr Marcic's human rights had been infringed.

Marcic v *Thames Water Utilities* [2004] 1 All ER 135

The [Water Industry Act] 1991 provided for a regulator of the water industry in England and Wales. The regulator was required to exercise and perform his statutory powers and duties in the manner he considered best calculated to secure that the functions of water undertakers and sewerage undertakers were properly carried out. He was required to protect the interests of customers of sewerage undertakers. The regulator had power to enforce the obligations of a sewerage undertaker by means of enforcement orders. Where a contravention of a statutory requirement was enforceable, the 1991 Act limited the availability of other remedies so that a person who sustained loss or damage as a result of a sewerage undertaker's contravention of his general duty had no direct remedy under the 1991 Act; such a person could, however, bring proceedings against a sewerage undertaker in respect of its failure to comply with an enforcement order, if one had been made. The claimant relied on a common law cause of action in nuisance (see above) and on two pro-visions of the European Convention, namely the right to respect for a person's home under Article 8(1). Article 8, so far as material, provides: 'Everyone has the right to respect for his private and family life, his home and his correspondence . . . and the right to peaceful enjoyment of possessions under Article 1'. Article 1, so far as material, provides: 'Every . . . person is entitled to the peaceful enjoyment of his possessions . . .'. The second issue before the House of Lords was whether the statutory scheme of the 1991 Act as a whole complied with the Convention.

The scheme of the 1991 Act was not unreasonable in its impact on householders whose properties were periodically subject to sewer flooding. A fair balance had to be struck between the interests of the individual and of the community as a whole. The balance struck by the statutory scheme was to impose a general drainage obligation on a sewerage undertaker but to entrust enforcement of that obligation to an independent regulator who had regard to all the different interests involved and whose decisions were subject to judicial review. While, in the instant case, matters had plainly gone awry, and it had not been acceptable that several years after the sewerage undertaker knew of the claimant's serious problems, there had still been in the foreseeable future no prospect of the necessary work being carried out, the malfunctioning of the statutory scheme on that occasion did not cast doubt on its overall fairness as a scheme. Accordingly, the scheme set up by the 1991 Act complied with the Convention and the company's appeal would therefore be allowed.

Lord Nicholls:

> THE CLAIM UNDER THE HUMAN RIGHTS ACT 1998
> I turn to Mr Marcic's claim under the 1998 Act. His claim is that as a public authority within the meaning of s 6 of the 1998 Act Thames Water has acted unlawfully. Thames Water has conducted itself in a way which is incompatible with Mr Marcic's convention rights under art 8 of the convention and art 1 of the First Protocol to the convention . . . The flooding of Mr Marcic's property falls within the first paragraph of art 8 and also within art 1 of the First Protocol. That was common ground between the parties. Direct and serious interference of this nature with a person's home is prima facie a violation of a person's right to respect for his private and family life (art 8) and of his entitlement to the peaceful enjoyment of his possessions (art 1 of the First Protocol) . . .

So the claim based on the 1998 Act raises a broader issue: is the statutory scheme as a whole, of which this enforcement procedure is part, Convention-compliant? Stated more specifically and at the risk of over-simplification, is the statutory scheme unreasonable in its impact on Mr Marcic and other householders whose properties are periodically subjected to sewer flooding?

The recent decision of the European Court of Human Rights, sitting as a Grand Chamber, in *Hatton v UK* [2003] All ER (D) 122 (Jul) confirms how courts should approach questions such as these. In *Hatton's* case the applicants lived near Heathrow airport. They claimed that the government's policy on night flights at Heathrow violated their rights under Article 8. The court emphasised 'the fundamentally subsidiary nature' of the convention. National authorities have 'direct democratic legitimation' and are in principle better placed than an international court to evaluate local needs and conditions. In matters of general policy, on which opinions within a democratic society may reasonably differ widely, 'the role of the domestic policy maker should be given special weight'. A fair balance must be struck between the interests of the individual and of the community as a whole.

In the present case the interests Parliament had to balance included, on the one hand, the interests of customers of a company whose properties are prone to sewer flooding and, on the other hand, all the other customers of the company whose properties are drained through the company's sewers. The interests of the first group conflict with the interests of the company's customers as a whole in that only a minority of customers suffer sewer flooding but the company's customers as a whole meet the cost of building more sewers. As already noted, the balance struck by the statutory scheme is to impose a general drainage obligation on a sewerage undertaker but to entrust enforcement of this obligation to an independent regulator who has regard to all the different interests involved. Decisions of the Director are of course subject to an appropriately penetrating degree of judicial review by the courts.

In principle this scheme seems to me to strike a reasonable balance. Parliament acted well within its bounds as policy maker. In Mr Marcic's case matters plainly went awry. It cannot be acceptable that in 2001, several years after Thames Water knew of Mr Marcic's serious problems, there was still no prospect of the necessary work being carried out for the foreseeable future. At times Thames Water handled Mr Marcic's complaint in a tardy and insensitive fashion. But the malfunctioning of the statutory scheme on this occasion does not cast doubt on its overall fairness as a scheme. A complaint by an individual about his particular case can, and should, be pursued with the Director pursuant to the statutory scheme, with the long stop availability of judicial review. That remedial avenue was not taken in this case.

The flooding did amount to a prima facie breach of Mr Marcic's rights under the European Convention. However, these rights are subject to justifiable limitations requiring the defendant to show that a fair balance has been struck between individual and community interests. The lower courts found that Thames Water's system of priorities for remedial work did not strike a fair balance. The House of Lords felt that the fairness of such a scheme was not for the courts to assess, as the matter was not justiciable and Parliament had assigned their responsibility to the Director. The scheme provided for a person to make a complaint to the Director, who could then make an enforcement order against the utility company. This decision would be subject to judicial review. If the enforcement order was not complied with then compensation was payable. The scheme as a whole was felt to be Convention-compliant. Mr Marcic should have taken advantage of the statutory scheme but did not.

That the statutory scheme did not provide an answer to all complaints was established in the next case.

Dobson v *Thames Water Utilities Ltd (Water Services Regulation Authority (Ofwat) intervening)* [2008] 2 All ER 362

The claimants, who were a large group, lived in Isleworth and Twickenham in the vicinity of the Mogden Sewage Treatment Works. They complained of odours and mosquitoes. Some of the claimants were owners or lessees of properties in the area; others lived in the area but had no property interest. The claimants sought damages in nuisance, negligence and under the Human Rights Act 1998. Thames Water raised various defences arising primarily from the Water Industry Act 1991 and the decision of the House of Lords in *Marcic*. It was held that the claimants could not bring a claim in nuisance absent any negligence. Some causes of action in nuisance based on negligence could co-exist with the duties under the Water Industry Act 1991. Similar considerations would apply to actions under the Human Rights Act 1998. This category was likely to include some cases of physical operation and/or operational management of the works. The *Marcic* principle would not preclude a claim based on Thames Water's failure to press for capital funding for odour-related expenditure within the asset management plan prior to 2000. In general, inability to fund an expense would not provide a defence in an action in negligence.

The judge held that the authority's obligation under s 94(1)(b) of the Water Industry Act was not limited to a duty to empty the contents of the sewers but extended to a duty to reduce the harmful and polluting effects of the sewerage. Therefore, if, and to the extent that, the residents claimed damages in respect of the authority's failure to treat the sewerage adequately, they were precluded by the decision in *Marcic* from framing the claim in nuisance based on the principle in *Leakey* v *National Trust for Places of Historic Interest or Natural Beauty* [1980] QB 485, i.e. in the absence of negligence.

However, the residents were not precluded from bringing a claim in nuisance based on negligence (as in the case of *Allen* v *Gulf Oil Refining Ltd* [1981] 1 All ER 353), a claim in negligence or a claim based on negligence under the Human Rights Act 1998.

2 The approach to compensation when statutory authority is pleaded as a defence.

3 The principles on assessment of damages.

4 The rule that only a person with a property interest can sue in private nuisance. (See 'Claimants' above.)

Dobson v *Thames Water Utilities Ltd* [2009] EWCA Civ 28

(For facts see above.) The major issue was the relationship between common law damages for private nuisance and damages under the Human Rights Act 1998. This involved two issues:

1 The first concerned claimants with no proprietary interest in land and therefore unable to claim in private nuisance. Could they claim damages under the Human Rights Act or were they covered by an award to the proprietary owners? An example would be a child who had suffered amenity damage from the smells and an award had been made to its parents. The Court of Appeal made the following points:

(a) An award of damages in nuisance to a person or persons with a proprietary interest in a property would be relevant to the question whether an award of damages was necessary to afford just satisfaction under Article 8 to a person who lived in the same household but had no proprietary interest in the property.

(b) Canary Wharf clearly established that damages in nuisance were for injury to the property and not to the sensibilities of the occupier or occupiers. On ordinary principles, it was clear that a claimant had to show that he had in truth suffered a loss of amenity before substantial damages could be awarded.

(c) Canary Wharf provided no support for the view that the person who had the right to sue in nuisance was recovering damages on behalf of other occupiers of the property.

2 On the question of damages at common law and damages under the Human Rights Act:

(a) The vital question would be whether it was necessary to award damages to another member of the household or whether the remedy of a declaration that Article 8 rights had been infringed sufficed, alongside the award to the landowner, especially when no pecuniary loss had been suffered. In the instant case, in the state of the law it was not possible to give an answer at the preliminary stage. It was not possible to say, until the case had been tried, whether it was just, appropriate and necessary to award some damages to B if he was to have just satisfaction, pursuant to Article 41 of the Convention.

(b) The second issue was whether those persons with a proprietary interest in the land affected who had been awarded damages in private nuisance had a right to have their damages 'topped up' under the Human Rights Act. The award of damages would normally constitute 'just satisfaction' under s 8(3) of the Human Rights Act and no additional compensation would be necessary.

For damages under the Human Rights Act, see Chapter 28.

Dobson represents an attempt to get round the restrictive rules in **Canary Wharf** on the award of damages for interference with amenities in private nuisance. The claimants had limited success as, although the door to damages under the human rights legislation was not completely closed, the Court of Appeal made it clear that they thought there was little chance, in a fully litigated case, of obtaining anything other than a declaration or nominal damages.

The case illustrates the difficulties with nuisance claims which arise out of smells or noise. Claims are for the benefit of the owners only, yet assessment of damages in relation to the loss of amenity value of the property proceeds at least in part by reference to the actual discomfort experienced by all the occupants. This leads to some interesting results. An owner who is absent from his property during the time of the nuisance can presumably recover damages in nuisance according to the discomfort experienced by the occupiers. An owner of a property which is wholly unoccupied can recover no more than nominal damages.

The Court of Appeal was clear in stating that damages for nuisance were not to be increased by any detriment caused to other family members. What happens where in two adjoining three-bedroom properties one is occupied by a family of five and the other by a single person? Should the owner of the home occupied by the family of five recover more by way of nuisance damages than the single person? *Hunter* would suggest that damages should not be increased according to the number of those occupying the house. At the same time, if, as the Court of Appeal found, the experience of the family members is likely to be the best evidence available of how the amenity has been affected in practical terms, that is very close to saying that the combined discomfort of all five family members should lead to an increased award in nuisance over the award to the single person.

What is the position of co-owners? The Court of Appeal found that co-owners were highly unlikely to require Article 8 top-up damages because their Article 8 entitlement would be satisfied by their nuisance claim. If that is right, it surely can only be on the basis that co-owners of a one-bedroom property would, all things being equal, recover twice as much as the single owner of an adjoining one-bedroom property.

If a child living in the affected property has received no damages in nuisance and the award is only for the owners then, unless he receives damages under Article 8, he will have received no compensation for smells and mosquitoes suffered over a period of six years.

? Question

An unidentified person entered the premises of the Cosmetic Photography Co and dropped a burning cigar into a pile of leaves, which began to smoulder.

The managing director of the company noticed the smoke but took no steps to extinguish the fire, even though there were inflammable chemicals nearby. He now states that he took no action as the wind was blowing the smoke away from the chemicals.

The wind direction changed, the fire spread to the chemicals and there was an explosion.

A pedestrian on a nearby road was injured. A customer's car in the company's yard was destroyed. Prize ferrets on a nearby farm stopped breeding as a result of the noise of the explosion.

Advise the Cosmetic Photography Co as to its potential liability in tort.

Suggested approach

In any question of this nature it is necessary to see where each claimant suffered their damage in order to assess which tort each claimant may be able to use. The question clearly points to nuisance, but there may be actions in negligence or *Rylands* v *Fletcher* as well.

What would the company's liability in nuisance be? It has not created the nuisance so any liability would stem from its occupation of land on which the nuisance occurred. Is an occupier liable for nuisances created by trespassers? To determine this, it is necessary to consider the law developed in the trilogy of cases of *Sedleigh-Denfield* v *O'Callaghan; Goldman* v *Hargrave; Leakey* v *National Trust.*

The principle that emerges from the cases is that an occupier is liable if they knew or should have known of such a nuisance and failed to take reasonable steps to abate the nuisance. The company is clearly aware of the potential nuisance. What amounts to reasonable steps? The test is similar to that for negligence with the exception that it is subjective rather than objective. The court will look at the cost/effort required to abate and will balance this against the occupier's financial/physical resources.

On this basis there would appear to have been a breach of duty. Given that a state of affairs existed on the defendant's land which amounted to a potential nuisance, for what damage is the occupier liable? The test for remoteness of damage in nuisance is whether the kind of damage was reasonably foreseeable. (*Wagon Mound No 2; Cambridge Water Co v Eastern Counties Leatherwork plc.*) However, in order to sue in private nuisance, a person must have a proprietary interest in the property affected. (*Hunter v Canary Wharf.*) In order to sue in public nuisance, it is necessary to show that the claimant suffered special damage. (*Castle v St Augustine's Links.*)

The pedestrian on the road does not have a sufficient interest and therefore has no action in private nuisance. Could they sue in public nuisance? The nuisance must affect a class of Her Majesty's subjects. (*Attorney General* v *PYA Quarries*.) The class would be highway users. The claimant must have suffered special damage. The pedestrian satisfies this criterion as he was injured by the explosion. Personal injuries can be compensated by a public nuisance action. The pedestrian could also sue the company in negligence if he could establish that it owed him a duty of care.

Would an action lie under *Rylands* v *Fletcher?* The problem points in such an action would be whether there had been a non-natural user of land and whether personal injuries can be compensated by the tort. Where industrial material is stored on land and there is an escape causing damage, the courts may use the test in *Mason* v *Levy Auto Parts*. Look at the nature of the area, the quantity of the goods and the way in which they are stored. As this virtually amounts to a negligence test, it is unlikely that the claimant would succeed in *Rylands* if they were to fail in negligence. However, in the *Cambridge Water* case the House of Lords stated (*per curiam*) that the storage of substantial quantities of chemicals on industrial premises is an almost classical case of non-natural use. It is doubtful whether a claim for personal injuries can now be made *Rylands* as recent decisions of the House of Lords have confirmed that the tort is to protect interests in land. (*Hunter* v *Canary Wharf; Transco* v *Stockport* [2004] 2 AC 1.) The correct view may be that if the claimant has an interest in land and there has been damage to the land then such damages are recoverable. This approach would rule out the pedestrian.

An action in respect of damage to the car could not be brought in private nuisance (no interest) or in *Rylands* (no escape). A public nuisance action is doubtful and the best course of action would be to sue in negligence under the Occupiers' Liability Act 1957. The claimant is a visitor to the premises and is owed the common duty of care under s 2(2). The failure to extinguish the fire may amount to a breach of the duty and reasonably foreseeable damage has been caused.

The owner of the prize ferrets may have an action in private nuisance as he has an interest in the land affected. The difficulty here would be with sensitivity. If normal animals would have been affected by the noise, then an action will lie for the full extent of the damage, even to sensitive property. (*Robinson* v *Kilvert; McKinnon Industries* v *Walker.*) A *Rylands* action could be prevented on the ground of non-natural user or on a defence of act of a third party. There may also be difficulties with the issue of damage following *Hunter*. The intention of the majority was to remove claims for personal injuries from nuisance and also claims for damage to property other than land. If the damage to the ferrets can be connected to land – perhaps in the sense that the land is used for ferret breeding, then an action may succeed.

Summary

This chapter deals with the tort of nuisance.

- There are three types of nuisance: statutory, public and private.

- Statutory nuisances are enforced by local authorities serving an abatement order.

- Public nuisances are criminal offences. In order to amount to a tort they must affect a class of Her Majesty's subjects. What is a class is a question of fact in each case. Most public nuisances consist of abuses of the highway, carrying on offensive trades and an unclassifiable class. In order to sue in tort the claimant must prove that they have suffered damage over and above that suffered by the class of persons affected. The claimant does not need an interest in land to sue in public nuisance.

- Private nuisance is an unlawful interference with a person's use or enjoyment of land.

- In order to sue in private nuisance the claimant must have an interest in land. (*Hunter* v *Canary Wharf*.) This rule may be challengeable under the Human Rights Act.

- The creator of a nuisance may always be sued in private nuisance unless they are unable to rectify the situation.

- An occupier of the land from which the nuisance emanates can be sued. The law has moved from a situation where ownership of land was viewed as a source of rights to one of affirmative duties. Hence an occupier may be liable for a nuisance created by a trespasser (*Sedleigh-Denfield*), an act of nature (*Goldman* v *Hargrave*), nuisances caused by the state of the land itself (*Leakey*) but not for nuisances where the owner had no actual knowledge of the danger (*Holbeck Hall*). In these cases, which are close to negligence, the standard of care is failing to take reasonable steps to abate the nuisance. The standard is a subjective one and is limited by the occupier's ability to abate the nuisance. In the case of major sewerage works where a statutory scheme is laid down to protect consumers there is no action in private nuisance and the question is whether the scheme is 'Convention compliant'. (*Marcic.*)

- A landlord is not liable for a nuisance unless: the nuisance existed at the time of the letting and they knew or ought to have known of it; they have authorised the nuisance; nuisances arising after the demise where they have reserved the right to enter and repair or have an implied right to do so; there are statutory obligations on landlords.

- In order to establish the tort, the claimant must prove that there has been a substantial interference with their use and enjoyment of land. The court will apply a reasonableness test. Where there is material damage to the land, the interference will be unreasonable. Where there is amenity damage the question is more difficult. (*St Helens Smelting Co* v *Tipping.*) A claimant claims on behalf of the land and whether there has been amenity damage or material damage there must be damage to the capital value of the land.

- The court will take a number of factors into account in determining whether the interference is unreasonable. These will include: the locality; the duration of the interference; the sensitivity of the claimant's property; the public utility of the defendant's activity; whether there was malice on the part of the defendant.

- The primary remedy in nuisance is an injunction. The principles on which an injunction is awarded were laid down in *Shelfer*. Whether an injunction can be refused in the public interest is arguable. The claimant can seek damages for past losses. These are based on the capital diminution of the land. (*Hunter* v *Canary Wharf.*) The test for remoteness of damage is reasonable foreseeability of damage. (*The Wagon Mound No 2.*)

- Abatement of the nuisance is also a remedy but not one favoured by the courts.

- Coming to the nuisance is not a defence. The fact that the defendant's activity is a useful one is not a defence. If the nuisance is due to many this is not a defence.

- Prescription is a defence. Statutory authority is a defence. (*Allen* v *Gulf Oil.*)

Further reading

Buxton, R. J. (1966), 'Nuisance and Nuisance Again' 29 MLR 676 (*Wagon Mound No 2*).

Cane, P. (1997), 113 LQR 515 (*Hunter*).

Dias, R. W. M. (1967), CLJ 61 (*Wagon Mound*).

Gearty, C. (1989), 'The Place of Nuisance in the Modern Law of Torts' CLJ 214.

Kodilinye, G. (1986), 'Public Nuisance and Particular Damage in the Modern World' 6 LS 182.

Lee, M. (2003), 'What is Private Nuisance?' 119 LQR 298.

Markesinis, B. (1989), 'Negligence, Nuisance and Affirmative Duties of Action' 105 LQR 104.

McLaren, J. P. S. (1983), 'Nuisance Law and the Industrial Revolution' 3 OJLS 155.

Newark, F. H. (1949), 'The Boundaries of Nuisance' 65 LQR 480.

Ogus, A. I. and Richardson, G. M. (1977), 'Economics and the Environment: A Study of Private Nuisance' 36 CLJ 284.

O'Sullivan, J. (2000), 'Nuisance, Local Authorities and Neighbours from Hell' 59 CLJ 11.

Spencer, J. (1989), 'Public Nuisance: A Critical Examination' 48 CLJ 55.

Steele, J. (1995), 'Private Law and the Environment: Nuisance in Context' 15 LS 236.

Tromans, S. (1982), 'Nuisance: Prevention or Payment' 41 CLJ 87.

Wightman, J. (1998), 'Nuisance – the Environmental Tort' 61 MLR 870.

18

Rylands v *Fletcher* and liability for fire

Objectives

After reading this chapter you will:

1. Appreciate the concept and history of strict liability in tort law.

2. Understand the legal rules relating to an action in the rule in *Rylands* v *Fletcher*.

3. Have a critical knowledge of the possible future of the rule in *Rylands* v *Fletcher*.

4. Understand the legal rules relating to liability for fire.

Introduction

Objective 1

For fault, see Chapter 1.

The rule in ***Rylands* v *Fletcher*** arose as a result of the Industrial Revolution in the nineteenth century. As land was put to industrial use, damage was frequently inflicted on neighbouring landowners. The rule represented a judicial attempt to impose strict liability on industrialists who did this. This was on the basis that if a person exploited land for profit and imposed costs on a neighbour as a result, then those costs should be met by the profit taker, without the need for the loss maker to prove fault.

The rule has had a rather unhappy history and has been treated with hostility by some of the judiciary who were obsessed by the fault principle. A further obstacle to its development was the fact that it was misunderstood by some judges and applied to inappropriate circumstances, such as falling flagpoles and escaping caravanners. This wider application increased judicial hostility, as it was perceived as strict liability undermining the fault-based tort system.

For nuisance, see Chapter 17.

The gist of the tort is that it governs liability for escapes from land, used for a non-natural purpose, which cause damage. It overlaps with nuisance and liability may lie in the alternative. In the ***Cambridge Water*** case ([1994] 1 All ER 53) the House of Lords accepted the view advanced by Professor Newark ('The Boundaries of Nuisance' (1949) 65 LQR 480) that the rule simply extended strict liability in nuisance to cases where there was an isolated escape.

Rylands v Fletcher (1865) 3 H&C 774; (1868) LR 3 HL 330 (HL)

The defendant had employed contractors to build a reservoir on his land to supply water for his factory. The contractors negligently failed to block a disused mine shaft and, when the reservoir was filled, the claimants adjoining mine was flooded. At first instance, Blackburn J laid down the following rule:

> A person who, for his own purposes, brings on his land, and collects and keeps there anything likely to do mischief if it escapes, must keep it at his peril, and, if he does not do so, he is prima facie answerable for all the damage which is the natural consequence of its escape.

The House of Lords approved the decision, subject to the addition of the requirement that the defendant's user of his land should be non-natural.

No existing action would have been possible. There was no trespass as the damage was not direct and immediate. At this time no nuisance action would lie for an isolated escape, and an employer was not liable for the negligence of their independent contractor. The rule has been examined by the House of Lords and the statements in the *Cambridge Water* case are likely to have a wide-ranging effect on the rule. The House of Lords stressed the close relationship with nuisance and negated the idea that there was any general principle of strict liability for ultra-hazardous activities, feeling that this was best dealt with by legislation.

Cambridge Water Company v Eastern Counties Leatherwork plc [1994] 1 All ER 53

The claimant brought an action for injunctive relief and damages in respect of the pollution of groundwater. This pollution had prevented the claimant from using water pumped from his borehole for the purpose of public water supply. An investigation in 1983 showed that a chemical called PCE had entered the water supply and the claimant therefore ceased pumping for public supply as the level of PCE contravened legislation. The source of the chemical was traced to the defendant's premises where a tanning business using the chemical was in operation. The loss to the claimant in terms of finding alternative supply was calculated at £900,000.

At first instance the *Rylands v Fletcher* claim was dismissed as there was no non-natural user. The nuisance action failed as the damage was unforeseeable.

The Court of Appeal took the view that in some areas of nuisance negligence played no part. In this instance the claimant alleged interference with a right enjoyed as an incident of the ownership of land. This right was one to naturally occurring water which comes beneath the land by percolation in undefined underground channels. It was irrelevant that the chemical was spilt by accident by the defendant.

The House of Lords, however, held that foreseeability of damage was a prerequisite of liability in *Rylands*. Liability arose only if the defendant knew or ought reasonably to have foreseen that those things might, if they escaped, cause damage. The same test applies in nuisance.

The defendant could not have reasonably foreseen that the seepage of the solvent through the tannery floor could have caused the pollution of the claimant's borehole and was therefore not liable under the rule in *Rylands v Fletcher*.

It was noted, *per curiam*, that the storage of substantial quantities of chemicals on industrial premises is an almost classical case of non-natural use, even in an industrial complex.

The House of Lords was faced with a problem here. The loss had to be placed somewhere and there was a choice between distributive and corrective justice. If the loss was placed on Cambridge Water this favoured distributive justice as they would have to raise their water rates in order to recoup their losses. If the loss was placed on the defendants then this favoured corrective justice and the 'polluter pays' principle. The defendants were regarded as a 'model company' and a damages bill of £1,000,000 would have threatened their entire future. But why did the House of Lords come down on the side of the defendants? Lord Goff considered that the environmental question of protecting society from the problems of pollution was better left to Parliament and was more a question of public rather than private law.

In *Rylands* itself the defendants could not have foreseen the flooding but were held strictly liable.

However, when the House of Lords was invited to abolish *Rylands* in *Transco plc* v *Stockport Metropolitan Borough Council* [2004] 2 AC 1, they refused to do so on the basis that this would leave a lacuna in the law and confirmed the view that it was a sub-species of nuisance. They rejected the view taken in Australia (*Burnie Port Authority* v *General Jones* (1994) 120 ALR 42) that it should be absorbed into negligence and held that only those with rights in land could sue. The rule itself was confined to narrow circumstances.

For negligence and breach of duty, see Chapter 8.

The claimant's case

Things likely to do mischief if they escape

Objective 2

The rule was concerned with the accumulation of things likely to do damage if they escaped and a considerable amount of case law built up on what were 'things' within the rule. Water, electricity, fire, chemicals, explosives, slag heaps, chair-o-planes and caravan dwellers were all held to be 'things' within the rule.

The *Cambridge Water* and *Transco* cases stressed the connection of *Rylands* v *Fletcher* with nuisance and the House of Lords rejected any general principle of liability for ultra-hazardous activities. This probably means that any future litigation will be concerned with whether the thing was likely to cause damage if it escaped, based on a remoteness test of reasonable foreseeability.

Lord Bingham (in *Transco*):

> I do not think the mischief or danger test should be at all easily satisfied. It must be shown that the defendant has done something which he recognised, or judged by the standards appropriate at the relevant place and time, he ought reasonably to have recognised, as giving rise to an exceptionally high risk of danger or mischief if there should be an escape . . .

Accumulation

The thing must have been accumulated or brought on to the defendant's land. The rule therefore only applies to things which are artificially brought or kept on the defendant's land and does not apply to things which are naturally on the land. In such cases the claimant must look to nuisance or negligence. (See, for example, *Goldman* v *Hargrave*; *Leakey* v *National Trust*.)

In the case of water, the defendant will not be liable for escape where the water was naturally on the land and the defendant was not responsible for its presence there (*Smith* v *Kenrick* (1849) 137 ER 205), or for flooding (*Ellison* v *Ministry of Defence* (1997) 81 BLR 101).

In the case of trees which are naturally there or self-grown, these would appear to be outside the rule.

Where the defendant accumulates a slag heap and there is an escape, then there will be liability under the rule. But where the land itself cracks and weathers, causing an escape, liability will lie in nuisance rather than *Rylands*. (See *Leakey* v *National Trust*.)

Transco plc v *Stockport Metropolitan Borough Council* [2004] 2 AC 1

Lord Bingham:

It has from the beginning been a necessary condition of liability under the rule in *Rylands* v *Fletcher* that the thing which the defendant has brought on his land should be 'something which . . . will naturally do mischief if it escape out of his land' (per Blackburn J), 'something dangerous . . .', 'anything likely to do mischief if it escapes', 'something . . . harmless to others so long as it is confined to his own property, but which he knows to be mischievous if it gets on his neighbour's', . . . 'anything which, if it should escape, may cause damage to his neighbour' (per Lord Cranworth). The practical problem is of course to decide whether in any given case the thing which has escaped satisfies this mischief or danger test, a problem exacerbated by the fact that many things not ordinarily regarded as sources of mischief or danger may none the less be capable of proving to be such if they escape. I do not think this condition can be viewed in complete isolation from the non-natural user condition to which I shall shortly turn, but I think the cases decided by the House give a valuable pointer. In *Rylands* v *Fletcher* itself the courts were dealing with what Lord Cranworth . . . called 'a large accumulated mass of water' stored up in a reservoir, . . . *Rainham Chemical Works* v *Belvedere Fish Guano Co Ltd* [1921] 2 AC 465, 471, involved the storage of chemicals, for the purpose of making munitions, which 'exploded with terrific violence'. In *Attorney General* v *Cory Bros & Co Ltd* [1921] 1 AC 521 . . . the landslide in question was of what counsel described as an 'enormous mass of rubbish', some 500,000 tons of mineral waste tipped on a steep hillside. In *Cambridge Water* [1994] 2 AC 264 the industrial solvents being used by the tannery were bound to cause mischief in the event, unforeseen on the facts, that they percolated down to the water table. These cases are in sharp contrast with those arising out of escape from a domestic water supply (such as *Carstairs* v *Taylor* (1871) LR 6 Ex 217, *Ross* v *Fedden* (1872) 26 LT 966 or *Anderson* v *Oppenheimer* (1880) 5 QBD 602) which, although decided on other grounds, would seem to me to fail the mischief or danger test. Bearing in mind the historical origin of the rule, and also that its effect is to impose liability in the absence of negligence for an isolated occurrence, I do not think the mischief or danger test should be at all easily satisfied. It must be shown that the defendant has done something which he recognised, or judged by the standards appropriate at the relevant place and time, he ought reasonably to have recognised, as giving rise to an exceptionally high risk of danger or mischief if there should be an escape, however unlikely an escape may have been thought to be.

Non-natural user

At first instance Blackburn J said that the rule applied only to a thing which was not naturally there. In the House of Lords, Lord Cairns said that the rule applied when the accumulation was a non-natural use of the land.

At first it was uncertain whether natural meant non-artificial or ordinary and usual. It has since been given the latter and narrower meaning.

Rickards v *Lothian* [1913] AC 263

A tap in part of a building which was leased to the defendant was turned on by an unknown person and caused a flood which damaged the claimant's stock on the floor below. There was held to be no liability under the rule, as the defendant was making an ordinary and proper use of the building. Lord Moulton defined non-natural use as: 'some special use bringing with it increased danger to others and [which] must not merely be the ordinary use of the land or such use as is proper for the general benefit of mankind.'

This is not an objective test as was shown when the use of land as a munitions factory in wartime was held to be a natural use (***Read*** v *J Lyons & Co Ltd* [1947] AC 156), when in peacetime it had been held to be non-natural. (***Rainham Chemical Works Ltd*** v ***Belvedere Fish Guano Co Ltd*** [1921] 2 AC 465.) The use of land for military-related purposes can be natural in peacetime. (***Ellison*** v ***Ministry of Defence*** (1997) 81 BLR 101.)

At one stage the courts used the idea of non-natural user to remove the strict liability aspect of the rule and there was a tendency to interpret it almost as a negligence test.

Mason v Levy Auto Parts of England Ltd [1967] 2 QB 530

The defendant stored quantities of combustible materials on his land. These caught fire under mysterious circumstances and burnt the claimant's ornamental hedge. In determining whether there had been a non-natural user, regard had to be had to: (a) the quantities of materials stored; (b) the way in which they were stored; and (c) the character of the neighbourhood. The court recognised that satisfaction of these requirements would also justify a finding of negligence.

British Celanese v A H Hunt [1969] 1 WLR 959

The defendants manufactured electrical components on an industrial estate. The claimants alleged that metal foil strips had escaped and caused a power failure at their electricity substation. On the ***Rylands*** action it was held that the defendants were not liable as there was no non-natural user of the defendants' land. The defendants were held liable in negligence and nuisance. This suggests, in contrast to ***Mason***, that there is a difference between negligence and ***Rylands***. However, Lawton J took a different approach to non-natural use. The use of land in the vicinity had to be looked at and as it was an industrial estate the land was being used for the purpose for which it was designed. There were no special risks attached to the storage of foil and the use was beneficial to the community.

In terms of the original rule, ***British Celanese*** is probably correct. Equating ***Rylands*** with negligence is the wrong approach. ***Rylands*** is to deal with extraordinary or special risks where the use of reasonable care should not excuse the defendant. The concept of non-natural user should enable the court to distinguish between hazardous operations and those which are part and parcel of everyday life. Some support was given to this in the ***Cambridge Water*** case where the storage of large amounts of chemicals on industrial premises was stated to be 'an almost classic example of non-natural use'.

A further example of water supply being a natural user is given in the next case.

Transco plc v Stockport Metropolitan Borough Council [2004] 2 AC 1

In 1966 the claimant was granted a right to install a gas main along a stretch of disused railway line which included an embankment in Stockport. On a nearby site owned by the defendant local authority lay a tower block of flats which was supplied with water by means of a water pipe which the authority had constructed between the tower block and the water main. In 1972 part of the disused line, including the embankment, was purchased by the authority, with the claimant continuing to have an easement of support in respect of its gas main. In 1992, without any negligence on the part of the authority, the water pipe leading to the block of flats fractured. As a result, large quantities of water escaped underground and caused the collapse of the embankment, leaving the gas main exposed and unsupported. The claimant, having been compelled to carry out emergency repair work to its gas main, brought an action in the High Court to recover the cost of the remedial work on the ground. The House of Lords dismissed the claim, holding that the rule in *Rylands v Fletcher* required that an occupier of land, acting other than under statutory authority, had brought on to his land or was keeping there some dangerous thing which posed an exceptionally high risk to neighbouring property should it escape and which amounted to an extra-ordinary and unusual use of the land, that there had been an escape on to some other property otherwise than by Act of God or the intervention of a third party and that the damage claimed for had been to that other property and was a foreseeable consequence of the escape; that the provision of a water supply to a block of flats by means of a connecting pipe from the water main, though capable of causing damage in the event of an escape, did not amount to the creation of a special hazard constituting an extraordinary use of land.

Lord Bingham:

> No ingredient of *Rylands v Fletcher* liability has provoked more discussion than the requirement of Blackburn J (LR 1 Ex 265, 280) that the thing brought on to the defendant's land should be something 'not naturally there', an expression elaborated by Lord Cairns (LR 3 HL 330, 339) when he referred to the putting of land to a 'non-natural use': . . . Read literally, the expressions used by Blackburn J and Lord Cairns might be thought to exclude nothing which has reached the land otherwise than through operation of the laws of nature. But such an interpretation has been fairly described as 'redolent of a different age' (*Cambridge Water* [1994] 2 AC 264, 308), and in *Read v J Lyons & Co Ltd* [1947] AC 156 . . . and *Cambridge Water*, at p. 308, the House gave its imprimatur to Lord Moulton's statement, giving the advice of the Privy Council in *Rickards v Lothian* [1913] AC 263, 280:
>
>> 'It is not every use to which land is put that brings into play that principle. It must be some special use bringing with it increased danger to others, and must not merely be the ordinary use of the land or such a use as is proper for the general benefit of the community.'
>
> I think it clear that ordinary user is a preferable test to natural user, making it clear that the rule in *Rylands v Fletcher* is engaged only where the defendant's use is shown to be extraordinary and unusual. This is not a test to be inflexibly applied: a use may be extra-ordinary and unusual at one time or in one place but not so at another time or in another place (although I would question whether, even in wartime, the manufacture of explosives could ever be regarded as an ordinary user of land, as contemplated by Viscount Simon, Lord Macmillan, Lord Porter and Lord Uthwatt in *Read v J Lyons & Co Ltd* [1947] AC 156. . . . I also doubt whether a test of reasonable user is helpful, since a user may well be quite out of the ordinary but not unreasonable, as was that of *Rylands*, *Rainham Chemical Works* or the tannery in *Cambridge Water*. Again, as it seems to me, the question is whether the defendant has done something which he recognises, or ought to recognise, as being quite out of the ordinary in the place and at the time when he does it. In answering that question, I respectfully think that little help is gained (and unnecessary confusion perhaps caused) by considering whether the use is proper for the general benefit of the community. In *Rickards v Lothian* itself, the claim arose because the outflow from a wash-basin on the top floor of premises was maliciously blocked and the tap left running, with the result that damage was caused to stock on a floor below: not surprisingly, the provision of a domestic water supply to the premises was held to be a wholly ordinary use of the land. An occupier of land who can show that another occupier of land has brought or kept on his land an exceptionally dangerous or mischievous thing in extraordinary or unusual circumstances is in my opinion entitled to recover compensation from that occupier for any damage caused to his property interest by the escape of that thing, subject to defences of Act of God or of a stranger, without the need to prove negligence. . . .
>
> . . . By the end of the hearing before the House, the dispute between the parties had narrowed down to two questions: had the council brought on to its land at Hollow End Towers something likely to cause danger or mischief if it escaped? and was that an ordinary user of its land? Applying the principles I have tried to outline, I think it quite clear that the first question must be answered negatively and the second affirmatively, as the Court of Appeal did: [2001] EWCA Civ 212.

> . . . It is of course true that water in quantity is almost always capable of causing damage if it escapes. But the piping of a water supply from the mains to the storage tanks in the block was a routine function which would not have struck anyone as raising any special hazard. In truth, the council did not accumulate any water, it merely arranged a supply adequate to meet the residents' needs. The situation cannot stand comparison with the making by Mr Rylands of a substantial reservoir. Nor can the use by the council of its land be seen as in any way extraordinary or unusual. It was entirely normal and routine. Despite the attractive argument of Mr Ian Leeming for Transco, I am satisfied that the conditions to be met before strict liability could be imposed on the council were far from being met on the facts here.

The requirements of non-natural user and dangerousness were seen as interlinked in this case and were to be tested by ordinary contemporary standards. There has to be an 'exceptionally high risk of danger' and the activity must be highly unusual or special to warrant strict liability. Whether an activity is dangerous or unusual is to be tested by reasonable foreseeability.

Again this case raises the question of who is to bear the loss in these cases. The choice here was between a profit making company and a local authority. The decision in this case meant that the loss fell on council tax payers.

Should it matter whether either party was insured? Lord Hoffmann thought that it should but his economic analysis was rejected by the other Law Lords.

Escape

There must be an escape from the land of which the defendant is in occupation or control.

Read v *J Lyons & Co Ltd* [1947] AC 156

> The claimant was employed in the defendant's munitions factory and was injured when a shell exploded in the factory. It was held that the ***Rylands*** principle was not applicable, as there had been no escape of the thing causing injury from the defendant's land. In the absence of negligence, the claimant could not succeed.

This rule creates an unfortunate distinction between those outside the premises and those inside. This is illustrated by the Abbeystead pumping station disaster. The North West Water Authority invited a group of local residents to tour the pumping station. A build-up of methane gas caused an explosion while they were on the premises. The victims had to prove negligence, but had they been outside the premises they might have been able to rely on the strict liability rule.

The harm which is caused need not be immediately caused by the thing which is accumulated. If explosives are stored on land and used to blast rocks which are blown on to adjacent land and cause damage, then an action may lie.

It is necessary that the escape takes place from land of which the defendant is in control.

Smith v *Scott* [1973] Ch 314

> A local authority let a house to a homeless family who covenanted not to commit a nuisance. The claimant lived next door and found the anti-social behaviour of the family intolerable. It was held that the rule in ***Rylands*** could not be applied to a landlord, as he no longer had the control over the tenant which the rule required.

> *NB*: It was also held that there is no duty of care owed by a landowner to their neighbour in respect of persons to whom they let their property. The action in nuisance also failed as the landlord had expressly forbidden the commission of a nuisance.

The normal action will be where there is an escape from land under the defendant's control to the claimant's adjacent land. The courts have also had to consider cases where an escape occurred on the highway. This can arise where two companies use the highway for utility purposes. Where water escapes and damages adjacent electricity cables, then liability may lie. There may also be liability where a dangerous thing is brought on to the highway.

Rigby v *Chief Constable of Northamptonshire* [1985] 2 All ER 985

See also Chapter 27 for *Rigby*.

> Police fired CS gas into a shop in an attempt to flush out a dangerous psychopath. There were no fire-fighting appliances standing by. The shop was set on fire by the gas. It was held that the rule applied to the escape of things from the highway. But it probably does not apply to the intentional or voluntary release of a dangerous thing. If it does apply to a voluntary release, then the defence of necessity will apply.
>
> *NB*: The court also held that the defence of necessity was available in a trespass action, provided that there was no negligence on the part of the defendant.

Damage

The tort is not actionable *per se*, so damage must be proved.

See also Chapter 1 for torts actionable *per se*.

The remoteness rule was stated in *Cambridge Water Co* v *Eastern Counties Leatherwork plc* [1994] 1 All ER 53. The House of Lords held that foreseeability of damage was a prerequisite of liability. The defendant must have known or ought reasonably to have foreseen that those things might, if they escaped, cause damage of the relevant kind.

Prior to this case there was some doubt as to what the relevant rule was. When the House of Lords aligned *Rylands* v *Fletcher* with nuisance it was inevitable that foreseeability had to be the guiding principle.

Damages are recoverable where there is damage to the land or to chattels on the land.

The position with regard to damages for personal injuries was not clear. The difficulty stemmed from *obiter dicta* in *Read* v *Lyons*, where it was stated that negligence must be proved in order for damages for personal injuries to be recovered. If *Rylands* was regarded as a tort of strict liability, then such damages would appear not to be recoverable. There are cases before *Read* v *Lyons* where damages for personal injuries were recoverable, but these could technically be regarded as incorrect. But in some subsequent cases such damages were stated to be recoverable. (*Perry* v *Kendricks Transport Ltd* [1956] 1 WLR 85; *Rigby* v *Chief Constable of Northamptonshire*.) The view taken by the House of Lords in *Hunter* v *Canary Wharf Ltd* [1997] 2 All ER 426 of the non-recovery of damages for personal injury in a nuisance action would appear to support the views expressed in *Read* v *Lyons*. The point on *locus standi* in *Hunter* applies to *Rylands* actions (*Transco plc* v *Stockport Metropolitan Borough Council* [2004] 2 AC 1), so *only* a person with a proprietary interest in land is able to sue. The courts are faced with the same problem as they face in nuisance as to where the line is to be drawn between personal injury and consequential damage. (But see *McKenna* v *British Aluminium Ltd* (2002) Times, 25 April.) The House of Lords has now ruled that the rule does not apply to personal injuries.

Transco plc v *Stockport Metropolitan Borough Council* [2004] 2 AC 1

Lord Bingham:

. . . The rule in *Rylands* v *Fletcher* is a sub-species of nuisance, which is itself a tort based on the inter-ference by one occupier of land with the right in or enjoyment of land by another occupier of land as such. From this simple proposition two consequences at once flow. First, as very clearly decided by the House in *Read* v *J Lyons & Co Ltd* [1947] AC 156, no claim in nuisance or under the rule can arise if the events complained of take place wholly on the land of a single occupier. There must, in other words, be an escape from one tenement to another. Second, the claim cannot include a claim for death or personal injury, since such a claim does not relate to any right in or enjoyment of land. This proposition has not been authoritatively affirmed by any decision at the highest level. It was left open by Parker LJ in *Perry* v *Kendricks Transport Ltd* [1956] 1 WLR 85, 92, and is inconsistent with decisions such as *Shiffman* v *Order of the Hospital of St John of Jerusalem* [1936] 1 All ER 557 and *Miles* v *Forest Rock Granite Co (Leicestershire) Ltd* (1918) 34 TLR 500. It is however clear from Lord Macmillan's opinion in *Read* [1947] AC 156, 170–171 that he regarded a personal injury claim as outside the scope of the rule, and his approach is in my opinion strongly fortified by the decisions of the House in *Cambridge Water* [1994] 2 AC 264 and *Hunter* v *Canary Wharf Ltd* [1997] AC 655, in each of which nuisance was identified as a tort directed, and directed only, to the protection of interests in land.

This ruling is strange in that the examples of disasters given by their Lordships, such as Flixborough, which justified retention of the rule, were disasters involving personal injuries. Equally, many of the statutes referred to in the judgments were enacted on the basis that the rule existed also to cover personal injuries.

It is equally unclear whether damages for economic loss may be recovered.

Weller v *Foot and Mouth Disease Research Institute* [1966] 1 QB 569

A virus escaped from the defendant's premises and caused a ban on the movement of livestock. The claimant cattle auctioneers sued for loss of income. It was held that they had no action under *Rylands* as they had no interest in any land to which the virus escaped.

Whether developments in negligence have affected this position is unknown. But given the courts' tendency to equate *Rylands* and nuisance with property interests, it is unlikely. However, in *D Pride & Partners (a firm)* v *Institute for Animal Health* [2009] EWHC 1617 the court excluded claims for pure economic loss from claims in both nuisance and *Rylands*.

Defences

Liability in *Rylands* is said to be strict. This means that the absence of negligence on the part of the defendant is not a defence. However, as liability is strict and not absolute, there are certain defences to the action.

Consent of the claimant

For consent (*volenti*) generally, see Chapter 10.

If the claimant expressly or impliedly consents to the presence of the thing on the defend-ant's property, then the defendant is not liable for damage caused by the escape unless they have been negligent.

Peters v *Prince of Wales Theatre (Birmingham) Ltd* [1943] 1 KB 73

The claimant had leased a shop from the owners of an adjoining theatre. The claimant's shop was flooded when pipes for a sprinkler system in the theatre burst during cold weather. There was held to be implied consent on the part of the claimant to the existence of the sprinkler system, which existed at the time he took his lease.

Where the consent of the claimant is relevant, it is an illustration of the general defence of *volenti non fit injuria*.

Common benefit

The defence of consent of the claimant overlaps with a defence called common benefit. The basis of the defence is that no action will lie when the source of the danger is maintained for the benefit of both parties to the action: for example, a box for water collection which leaks.

Could this defence be maintained by utility companies?

Dunne v *North Western Gas Board* [1964] 2 QB 806

A gas mains exploded without any negligence on the part of the defendants. The court considered common benefit and the judge doubted whether the defendants, as a nationalised industry, could be said to accumulate the gas for their own purposes.

Act of a stranger

Where the escape is caused by the act of a stranger over whom the defendant has no control, this will be a defence.

Perry v *Kendricks Transport Ltd* [1956] 1 WLR 85

The defendants parked their coach on their car park. The petrol tank had been drained. The child claimant was crossing waste land adjacent to the car park, when he was injured by an explosion caused by a small boy throwing a lighted match into the petrol tank. An unknown person had removed the cap from the petrol tank. The defendants were held not liable, as the explosion was caused by the act of a stranger over whom they had no control.

The basis of the defence is the absence of control by the defendant over the act of a stranger on his land. If the act was foreseeable and could have been guarded against, then there can be liability.

Hale v *Jennings Bros* [1938] 1 All ER 579

The mountings on a chair-o-plane at a fairground were tampered with by an unknown person. The chair-o-plane became detached and landed on a tombola stall, causing injury to the occupant. The defendant was held to have had sufficient control to prevent this from happening.

Once the defendant has successfully shown that the escape was caused by the act of a stranger, then the action effectively becomes one of negligence. The claimant must show that the defendant should have foreseen this risk and guarded against it. This tends to undermine the original purpose of the rule, which was intended to place liability for exceptional risks on the person creating the risk. This defence has the effect of making liability dependent on a negligent failure to control the risk.

Note that a proprietary interest in land is necessary for *locus standi* in a **Rylands** action therefore both **Perry** and **Hale** would now be decided differently.

Two points are in doubt on this defence. The first is whether the act of the stranger has to be intentional or whether it can be negligent. Logically, it should apply to negligent acts as the emphasis should be on whether the defendant negligently failed to deal with the acts of the third party. The second is whether these cases belong in **Rylands** at all or are cases of negligence. Some writers now take the view that these are negligence cases.

Act of God

This is a defence which is remembered by students but which has little application. It is available when the escape is caused by natural forces, in circumstances which no human foresight can provide against and of which human prudence is not bound to recognise the possibility.

Nichols v *Marsland* (1876) 2 Ex D 1

> The defendant had three artificial lakes made on his land by damming a natural stream. A heavy thunderstorm accompanied by unprecedented rain caused the banks of the lakes to burst and water to destroy four bridges on the claimant's land. It was held that the flooding was caused by an Act of God for which the defendant was not liable.

This decision has since been criticised (***Greenock Corp* v *Caledonian Railway*** [1917] AC 556) and its application is extremely limited. It may apply in the case of earthquakes, lightning or tornadoes. In principle, it should not be a defence, as it is the defendant who has created the risk. The effect of Act of God is to shift attention to whether the defendant ought to have foreseen the event. Again, this brings negligence principles into strict liability.

Default of the claimant

Where the escape is due to the default of the claimant they will have no action.

Eastern and SA Telegraph Co Ltd v *Cape Town Tramways Co Ltd* [1902] AC 381

For contributory negligence, see Chapter 10.

> The defendants stored electricity to run their tramways. Electricity escaped and interfered with the claimant' cable, which was used for sending messages. The claimants were unable to recover, as the damage was caused by the sensitivity of their equipment.

Where the claimant's default amounts to contributory negligence they will have their damages reduced in proportion to their responsibility for the damage suffered.

Statutory authority

Whether a statute confers a defence under **Rylands** is a question of construction of the statute.

Green v *Chelsea Waterworks Co* (1894) 70 LT 547

The defendants' water main burst and flooded the claimant's premises. The defendants were obliged by statute to maintain a water supply. The court held that bursts were in-evitable from time to time and in the absence of negligence there was no liability.

Charing Cross Electricity Co v *Hydraulic Co* [1914] 3 KB 772

On similar facts to the above case the defendants were held not to have a defence of statutory authority, as they only had a power to supply water and were not under a duty to do so.

NB: A statute may expressly impose strict liability for the escape of dangerous things: for example, the Reservoirs Act 1975. Not even express statutory authority to construct the reservoir will exonerate the defendant.

The future of *Rylands* v *Fletcher*

**Objective
3**

Whether the original purpose of the rule was to impose strict liability for extra hazardous activities, or simply to extend nuisance, the courts view ***Rylands*** now as simply an extension of nuisance. There are now few differences between the torts, except that in nuisance the claimant need not show an accumulation or non-natural user.

The dominance of the fault principle in the twentieth century succeeded in eradicating virtually any claims the tort may have had to being strict liability and distinct from nuisance or negligence. This is apparent in non-natural user and the defences of act of a stranger, common benefit, Act of God and statutory authority. In most cases, an action in negligence would succeed on the same facts as a successful ***Rylands*** action. For this reason, and the problem posed by the requirement of escape, there are very few successful actions.

The vexed question of strict liability has been examined by the Law Commission (Law Commission Report No 23 (1970)), which made proposals based on dangerous things and dangerous activities. However, it made no recommendation for change until the entire fault principle had been examined. The Pearson Report (1978) is the nearest that England has come to such an examination. The report, almost as an afterthought, put forward a scheme limited to death and personal injuries (Vol 1, Ch 31) but this was not well thought through and, like so much else of Pearson, nothing has come of it.

Transco plc v *Stockport Metropolitan Borough Council* [2004] 2 AC 1

Lord Bingham:

The future development of ***Rylands*** v ***Fletcher***.

. . . In the course of his excellent argument for the council, Mr Mark Turner canvassed various ways in which the rule in ***Rylands*** v ***Fletcher*** might be applied and developed in future, without however judging it necessary to press the House to accept any one of them. The boldest of these courses was to follow the trail blazed by a majority of the High Court of Australia in ***Burnie Port Authority*** v ***General Jones Pty Ltd*** (1994) 120 ALR 42 by treating the rule in ***Rylands*** v ***Fletcher*** as absorbed by the principles of ordinary negligence. In reaching this decision the majority were influenced by the difficulties of interpretation and application to which the rule has undoubtedly given rise . . . , by the progressive weakening of the rule by judicial decision . . . , by recognition that the law of negligence has been very greatly developed and expanded since *Rylands* v *Fletcher* was decided . . . and by a belief that most claimants entitled to succeed under the rule would succeed in a claim for negligence anyway. . . .

. . . Coming from such a quarter these comments of course command respect, and they are matched by expressions of opinion here. Megaw LJ observed in *Leakey* v *National Trust for Places of Historic Interest or Natural Beauty* [1980] QB 485, 519 that application of the decision and of the dicta in *Rylands* v *Fletcher* had given rise to continual trouble in the law of England. In its report on Civil Liability for Dangerous Things and Activities (1970) (Law Com No 32), p 12, para 20(a) the Law Commission described the relevant law as 'complex, uncertain and inconsistent in principle'. There is a theoretical attraction in bringing this somewhat anomalous ground of liability within the broad and familiar rules governing liability in negligence. This would have the incidental advantage of bringing the law of England and Wales more closely into line with what I understand to be the law of Scotland (see *RHM Bakeries (Scotland) Ltd* v *Strathclyde Regional Council* 1985 SLT 214, 217, where Lord Fraser of Tullybelton described the suggestion that the decision in *Rylands* v *Fletcher* had any place in Scots law as 'a heresy which ought to be extirpated'). Consideration of the reported English case law over the past 60 years suggests that few if any claimants have succeeded in reliance on the rule in *Rylands* v *Fletcher* alone.

. . . I would be willing to suppress an instinctive resistance to treating a nuisance-based tort as if it were governed by the law of negligence if I were persuaded that it would serve the interests of justice to discard the rule in *Rylands* v *Fletcher* and treat the cases in which it might have been relied on as governed by the ordinary rules of negligence. But I hesitate to adopt that solution for four main reasons. First, there is in my opinion a category of case, however small it may be, in which it seems just to impose liability even in the absence of fault. In the context of then recent catastrophes *Rylands* v *Fletcher* itself was understandably seen as such a case. With memories of the tragedy at Aberfan still green, the same view might now be taken of *Attorney General* v *Cory Bros & Co Ltd* [1921] 1 AC 521 even if the claimants had failed to prove negligence, as on the facts they were able to do. I would regard *Rainham Chemical Works Ltd* v *Belvedere Fish Guano Co Ltd* [1921] 2 AC 465, and *Cambridge Water Co* v *Eastern Counties Leather plc* [1994] 2 AC 264 (had there been foreseeability of damage), as similarly falling within that category. Second, it must be remembered that common law rules do not exist in a vacuum, least of all rules which have stood for over a century during which there has been detailed statutory regulation of matters to which they might potentially relate. With reference to water, section 209 of the Water Industry Act 1991 imposes strict liability (subject to certain exemptions) on water undertakers and Schedule 2 to the Reservoirs Act 1975 appears to assume that on facts such as those of *Rylands* v *Fletcher* strict liability would attach. If the law were changed so as to require proof of negligence by those previously thought to be entitled to recover under the rule in *Rylands* v *Fletcher* without proving negligence, the effect might be (one does not know) to falsify the assumption on which Parliament has legislated, by significantly modifying rights which Parliament may have assumed would continue to exist. Third, although in *Cambridge Water* [1994] 2 AC 264, 283–285, the possibility was ventilated that the House might depart from *Rylands* v *Fletcher* in its entirety, it is plain that this suggestion was not accepted. Instead, the House looked forward to a more principled and better controlled application of the existing rule: see, for example, p 309. While this is not a conclusive bar to acceptance of the detailed argument presented to the House on this occasion, 'stop-go' is in general as bad an approach to legal development as to economic management. Fourth, while replacement of strict *Rylands* v *Fletcher* liability by a fault-based rule would tend to assimilate the law of England and Wales with that of Scotland, it would tend to increase the disparity between it and the laws of France and Germany. Having reviewed comparable provisions of French and German law, van Gerven, Lever and Larouche (*Cases, Materials and Text on National, Supranational and International Tort Law* (2000), p 205) observe: 'Even if the contours of the respective regimes may differ, all systems studied here therefore afford a form of strict liability protection in disputes between neighbouring landowners.' The authors indeed suggest (p 205) that the English rule as laid down in *Rylands* v *Fletcher* is 'the most developed of these regimes'.

> . . . Should, then, the rule be generously applied and the scope of strict liability extended? There are certainly respected commentators who favour such a course and regret judicial restrictions on the operation of the rule . . . But there is to my mind a compelling objection to such a course, articulated by Lord Goff of Chieveley in *Cambridge Water* [1994] 2 AC 264, 305:
>
>> Like the judge in the present case, I incline to the opinion that, as a general rule, it is more appropriate for strict liability in respect of operations of high risk to be imposed by Parliament, than by the courts. If such liability is imposed by statute, the relevant activities can be identified, and those concerned can know where they stand. Furthermore, statute can where appropriate lay down precise criteria establishing the incidence and scope of such liability.
>>
>> It may be added that statutory regulation, particularly when informed by the work of the Law Commission, may take such account as is judged appropriate of the comparative law considerations on which I have briefly touched.
>>
>> . . . There remains a third option, which I would myself favour: to retain the rule, while insisting upon its essential nature and purpose; and to restate it so as to achieve as much certainty and clarity as is attainable, recognising that new factual situations are bound to arise posing difficult questions on the boundary of the rule, wherever that is drawn.

In *Transco* the House of Lords decided:

See Chapter 17 for nuisance.

1 The rule in *Rylands* was a sub-species of private nuisance. Compare the cases on the continuing or adopting of a nuisance and the role played by fault in those cases.

2 To reject the argument that the rule should be abolished and absorbed into negligence as has happened in Australia.

3 Only those with interests in land can sue and that there is no action for personal injuries. This has the effect of bringing it into line with the rules in nuisance.

4 To confine the rule to exceptional circumstances. See the extract above for the reasons why the House of Lords did not want to extend the rule but did not want to abolish it either.

The rule was initially introduced to deal with the conflict between landowners and the dangers posed by industrialisation, particularly large reservoirs which were built to service industry. By the time of *Cambridge Water* the area which we now know as environmental law had developed, primarily through legislation. Development of protection through the common law was regarded as too uncertain and slow. The influence of landowners has now decreased and the emphasis is on business and job creation. The tort of negligence has now fully developed and the influence of fault based liability is now virtually all pervasive.

Liability for fire

Objective 4

Most of the cases which now come before the courts fall under the Fires Prevention (Metropolis) Act 1774 s 86. Despite its title, the operation of the Act is not confined to London.

No one will be liable for a fire which begins on his premises, unless he has been negligent in respect of it. But if the fire arises by accident, then the occupier may be liable if they are negligent in allowing it to spread.

The gist of an action is that there has to be some fault or other established basis of legal liability in allowing the fire to spread. (*Johnson v BJW Property Developments Ltd* [2002] 3 All ER 574.)

Musgrove v *Pandelis* [1919] 2 KB 43

A fire accidentally started in the carburettor of the defendant's car. The defendant's employee negligently failed to turn off the petrol tap and the fire spread. The defendant was held liable not for the original fire, but for the spreading of the fire.

As the Act confers immunity for the original fire where it accidentally begins, then if the fire was produced by negligence or nuisance it is actionable.

Could there be an action under the rule in *Rylands*?

Gore v *Stannard* [2012] EWCA Civ 1248

A fire which broke out in the defendant's business premises ignited some 3,000 rubber composite motor vehicle tyres stored there. The tyres were stored in racks inside a building and in piles outside. The fire spread with great rapidity and intensity. The claimant's adjoining premises were destroyed. He brought proceedings in negligence and in strict liability. The claim in negligence failed; the judge held that the fire was accidental. However, the judge held that the defendant was liable under the rule in *Rylands*. The defendant appealed.

The Court of Appeal considered whether there was a special or different rule under *Rylands* v *Fletcher* to deal with damage caused by the spread of fire. The appeal was allowed.

There was no special category of fire damage outside the general rule in *Rylands* v *Fletcher*; however, cases of fire damage were likely to be difficult to bring within the rule because (i) it was the 'thing' brought onto the land which must escape, not the fire started or increased by the 'thing'; (ii) while fire could be a dangerous thing, the occasions when fire as such was brought onto the land might be limited to cases where the fire had been deliberately or negligently started by the occupier or someone for whom he was responsible; and (iii) starting a fire on one's land could well be an ordinary use of the land. In the instant case, liability under the rule was not established; the 'thing' brought onto the defendant's premises was not exceptionally dangerous. Keeping a large stock of tyres on the premises of a tyre-fitting business was not an extraordinary or unusual use of the land.

If the circumstances of the fire come within the rule in *Rylands*, then there will be liability: for example, if a person brings on to land a highly explosive article which amounts to a non-natural use.

Where liability is for the spread of the fire, this may lie in negligence, nuisance or *Rylands*.

Summary

This chapter deals with the rule in *Rylands* v *Fletcher* and liability for fire.

● This tort governs liability for escapes from land used for a non-natural purpose which cause damage. It overlaps with nuisance and liability may lie in the alternative. Liability is strict. The rule has been severely confined by recent House of Lords cases (*Cambridge Water* and *Transco*) but still survives in a reduced form.

● The claimant must prove that a thing likely to cause damage was accumulated on the defendant's land. This must amount to a non-natural user of the land. There must be an escape from the land of which the defendant is in occupation or control. Damage must be caused as the tort is not actionable *per se*. The damage must have been foreseeable by the defendant. (*Cambridge Water*.) Damages can be recovered for damage to the land or to chattels on the land. Damages are not recoverable for personal injuries and only a person with an interest in land can sue.

● A number of defences exist. These are: consent of the claimant; common benefit; act of a stranger over whom the defendant had no control; Act of God; default of the claimant; statutory authority.

● The rule is now viewed as an extension of nuisance and there is no general principle imposing strict liability for ultra-hazardous activities. The House of Lords in *Transco* refused to follow the Australian example and abolish the rule.

● Where a fire starts on a person's land and spreads, causing damage, there has to be fault or some other established basis of legal liability in allowing the fire to spread.

Further reading

Rylands

Bagshaw, R. (2004), '*Rylands* Confined' 120 LQR 388.

Law Commission Report No 32 (1970).

Layard, F. (1997), 'Balancing Environmental Considerations' 113 LQR 254.

McBride, N. J. (2004), 120 LQR 711 (*Marcic*).

Murphy, J. (2004), 'The Merits of *Rylands* v *Fletcher*' 24 OJLS 643.

Newark, F. H. (1961), 'Non-Natural User and *Rylands* v *Fletcher*' 24 MLR 557.

Nolan, D. (2005), 'The Distinctiveness of *Rylands* v *Fletcher*' 121 LQR 421.

Report of the Royal Commission on Civil Liability and Compensation for Personal Injury (The Pearson Report) Cmnd 7054 (1978) Vol 1, ch 31.

Fire

Ogus, I. A. (1969), 'Vagaries in Liability for the Escape of Fire' CLJ 104.

Part 5

Miscellaneous torts

19

Liability for animals

Objectives

After reading this chapter you will:

1. Have a knowledge of the common law rules relating to animals.

2. Understand the provisions of the Animals Act 1971 and appreciate the distinction between dangerous and non-dangerous animals.

3. Have a critical knowledge of strict liability applied to animals.

Introduction

Objective 1

For negligence, see Chapters 2–10.

For nuisance, see Chapter 17.

Liability for damage caused by animals falls under two heads. There are specific statutory rules contained in the Animals Act 1971 and a person may also be liable at common law in a number of torts. It is the former that we will be concerned with here, but brief mention will be given of the common law rules.

Where an action is brought in a tort such as negligence or nuisance, for damage caused by animals, the usual rules of that tort will apply and can be found in the appropriate chapter.

Pitcher v *Martin* [1937] 3 All ER 918

The defendant was walking his dog on a long lead. The dog broke away and the claimant pedestrian became entangled in the lead, fell and was injured. The defendant was held liable in both negligence and nuisance.

Draper v *Hodder* [1972] 2 QB 556

The infant claimant was savaged by a pack of Jack Russell terriers which had rushed out from the defendant's adjacent premises. The dogs had not previously misbehaved so they had no dangerous propensity for the purposes of strict liability. But the owner was held liable in negligence for allowing the dogs to escape. Jack Russells in a pack have a tendency to attack moving persons or objects. The defendant as an experienced breeder should have known this and, given the dogs' tendency to dash next door, some damage (although not the extent or precise manner of its infliction) was foreseeable to the claimant. The failure to secure the dogs was a breach of duty.

Historically, there had been examples of stricter forms of liability for animals, such as the scienter rule and liability for cattle trespass. These were replaced by the Animals Act 1971, which also contains provisions about dogs and animals on the highway.

Dangerous and non-dangerous animals

Objective 2

The Animals Act 1971 replaced the common law rules which had divided animals into fierce and docile categories for the purpose of establishing liability. The Act divides animals into dangerous and non-dangerous species. Some of the old case law may still be relevant, but the fact that an animal was classed as docile at common law does not mean that it will be a non-dangerous species under the Act. Camels were treated as docile, but are now a dangerous species.

A dangerous animal is defined by s 6(2):

(a) a species not commonly domesticated in the British Isles; and
(b) whose fully grown animals normally have such characteristics that they are likely, unless restrained, to cause severe damage or that any damage that they may cause is likely to be severe.

Dangerous animals

Clearly, only a limited number of British animals will fall into this category: for example, wild stags, foxes and wild cats.

No distinction is made between individual animals within a species.

Behrens v *Bertram Mills Circus* [1957] 2 QB 1

The claimants were injured by the defendant's Indian elephant. Although the elephant in question was 'no more dangerous than a cow', it was held to be *ferae naturae* (dangerous).

If the animal is not commonly domesticated in the British Isles, then it must meet one of two criteria before it is classified as dangerous: it must be likely to cause severe damage, for example, snakes or tigers; or any damage which it does cause, even if this is unlikely, is likely to be severe, for example, elephants on account of their bulk.

Liability for dangerous animals is governed by s 2(1):

where any damage is caused by an animal which belongs to a dangerous species, any person who is a keeper of the animal is liable for the damage, except as otherwise provided by this Act.

Liability under this section is therefore strict, unless the defendant can bring themselves within one of the defences in s 5.

Keeper is defined by s 6(3):

a person is a keeper of an animal if–

(a) he owns the animal or has it in his possession; or
(b) he is the head of a household of which a member under the age of sixteen owns the animal or has it in his possession.

The second part of the definition deals with the problem of an animal which is in theory owned by a child.

Non-dangerous animals

Liability for non-dangerous animals is governed by s 2(2):

> Where damage is caused by an animal which does not belong to a dangerous species, a keeper of the animal is liable for the damage . . . if–
>
> (a) the damage is of a kind which the animal, unless restrained, was likely to cause or which, if caused by the animal, was likely to be severe; and
> (b) the likelihood of the damage or of its being severe was due to characteristics of the animal which are not normally so found in animals of the same species or are not normally found except at particular times or in particular circumstances; and
> (c) those characteristics were known to that keeper or were at any time known to a person who at that time had charge of the animal as that keeper's servant or, where that keeper is the head of a household, were known to another keeper of the animal who is a member of that household and under the age of sixteen.

Each of the three requirements in the subsection must be proved by the claimant and it is clear that the keeper will not be strictly liable unless he was aware of the animal's dangerous characteristics. Beyond this there is much uncertainty about what is a badly drafted section.

Conditions (a) and (b) lay down an objective test. The first condition is whether the type of damage was foreseeable. In order to be foreseeable the damage has to be likely. This has been stated to mean, 'to be reasonably expected'. (*Mirvahedy* v *Henley* [2003] 2 All ER 401.) The test therefore lies between probability and possibility. The second objective condition is that the likelihood of damage has to be as a result of a characteristic of the animal causing the damage. The third condition is subjective and requires actual knowledge of the potential danger by the keeper.

This section has caused the courts considerable problems as a result of its rather tortuous wording. Subsection (a) does not present any particular difficulties as the keeper will be liable if the animal has a characteristic which other animals of that species do not have. These are referred to as 'permanent characteristics'. (*Curtis* v *Betts* [1990] 1 WLR 459.) The main problem lies with subsection (b), which deals with 'temporary characteristics'. The problem is a result of the double negative in the subsection – 'characteristics not normally found except at particular times'. There are two possibilities here. It could mean normal characteristics which arise at particular times or circumstances, or abnormal characteristics which only arise at particular times. The House of Lords has decided that it bears the former meaning (*Mirvahedy* v *Henley* [2003] 2 All ER 401 – see below), as it is preferable to place the burden on keepers of animals rather than expose the public to the risk of injury.

What is clear is that the keeper will not be strictly liable unless he was aware of the animal's dangerous characteristics.

Wallace v *Newton* [1982] 1 WLR 375

The claimant was the defendant's groom and had charge of a horse which was known to be nervous. The horse was being loaded on a trailer when it became aggressive, jumped forward and caused the claimant to injure her arm. It was held that in order to succeed the claimant did not have to prove that the horse had a vicious tendency to attack people, merely that it exhibited a tendency not found in horses generally.

For a relatively straightforward example of the application of s 2(2), see the next case.

Cummings v *Granger* [1977] 1 All ER 104

The claimant was bitten by the defendant's Alsatian which was used as a guard dog in a scrap yard occupied by the defendant. The dog was allowed to run around loose in the yard. The claimant had entered the yard with a friend who had a licence to be there. A notice on the gates stated 'Beware of the Dog'.

On the question of whether s 2(2) was satisfied, Lord Denning said:

Section 2(2)(a): this animal was a dog of the Alsatian breed. If it did bite anyone, the damage was likely to be severe. Section 2(2)(b): this animal was a guard dog kept so as to scare intruders and frighten them off. On the owner's own evidence, it used to bark and run round in circles . . . Those characteristics – barking and running around to guard its territory – are not normally found in Alsatian dogs except in the circumstances where used as guard dogs. Those circumstances are particular circumstances within s 2(2)(b). It was due to those circumstances that the damage was likely to be severe if an intruder did enter on its territory. Section 2(2)(c): those characteristics were known to the keeper.

NB: The claimant's case failed on the grounds of defences under s 5. (See below.)

The Court of Appeal was called on to interpret a more complex example.

Curtis v *Betts* [1990] 1 WLR 459

While it was being taken to a car to go to the park for exercise, a bull mastiff attacked a 10-year-old child in the street. At first instance the judge found that bull mastiffs have a tendency to react fiercely at particular times and in particular circumstances (usually when defending their own territory). The Court of Appeal stated that the mere fact that the dog shared its characteristics with other animals of the same species would not preclude s 2(2)(b) being satisfied if the likelihood of damage was attributable to characteristics normally found in bull mastiffs at times or in circumstances similar to those in which the damage occurred.

However, in deciding the case this way, the Court of Appeal had ruled that there could be liability for a characteristic of an animal which was normal in the circumstances in question (bull mastiffs defending their own territory) even if this was not in the usual course of events.

The fact that an Alsatian dog is trained by the police to attack under certain circumstances does not amount to an abnormal characteristic. The relevant characteristic is the ability of the dog to respond to training and instructions, which is a characteristic of Alsatians. There was therefore no liability when the Alsatian mistakenly attacked the claimant in reaction to instructions. (*Gloster* v *Chief Constable of Greater Manchester Police* [2000] PIQR 114.) In this case Pill LJ thought the section was not concerned with animals behaving in a normal way for animals of that species or sub-species. Hale LJ, however, did not agree and it was her view that prevailed in the House of Lords in the next case.

Mirvahedy v *Henley* [2003] 2 All ER 401

The claimant suffered personal injuries when the car he was driving was in collision with the defendants' horse, which had panicked due to some unknown event and escaped with two others from its field. On his claim for damages the judge found that the field had been adequately fenced so that the defendants had not been negligent and concluded that, although the horse had displayed characteristics normal for its species in the particular circumstances within the second limb of s 2(2)(b) of the Animals Act 1971, those characteristics had not caused the damage. The Court of Appeal allowed an appeal by the claimant.

On appeal by the defendants:

Held, dismissing the appeal (Lord Slynn of Hadley and Lord Scott of Foscote dissenting): Under s 2(2)(b) of the 1971 Act the keeper of a non-dangerous animal was strictly liable for damage or injury caused by it while it was behaving in a way that, although not normal behaviour generally for animals of that species, was nevertheless normal behaviour for the species in the particular circumstances, such as a horse bolting when sufficiently alarmed; and, since the accident to the claimant had been caused by the defendants' horses behaving in an unusual way caused by their panic, they were liable to him.

Lord Walker:

That leads to the central problem on this appeal. It is agreed that section 2(2)(b) contains two limbs, linked by the word 'or'. The second limb contains what is akin to a double negative ('not . . . except . . .') and this (coupled with the cumbersome words at the beginning of paragraph (b), the feature which has so far attracted most of the adverse judicial comment) makes it difficult to see what paragraph (b) as a whole is getting at. The cumbersome words at the beginning appear to me to reflect the simple proposition . . . that risk is a product of two factors, the likelihood of injury and the severity of the possible injury. So the subsection could be set out in a simplified form (using the abbreviation 'risk' and some other simplifications) as follows: 'the [risk] was due to characteristics of the [horse] which are not normally found in [horses] or are not normally . . . found [in horses] except [on particular occasions].'

If paragraph (b) is simplified in this way, it is easier to see that there are two possible interpretations of the second limb. Each is permissible (although not necessarily equally acceptable) as a matter of language. Which is to be preferred depends on the legislative context and purpose, and in particular, on what appears to be the essential purpose of the second limb as a whole. This can be illustrated by the example (based on ***Barnes v Lucille Ltd*** (1907) 96 LT 680 and discussed both by the Law Commission and in later authorities) of the bitch which acts fiercely and bites in defence of her pups. Suppose that a labrador bitch (which is not nursing pups and is not subjected to any other provocation) bites a pedestrian in the park. That would on the face of things be abnormal behaviour for a labrador, and the first limb of paragraph (b) would apply. The only function of the second limb (one argument goes) is to forestall the owner's excuse, 'but all labrador bitches have a propensity to bite sometimes' in a case where that excuse cannot, on the facts, make any difference.

The competing explanation of the second limb is that it adds a further possible head of liability where the particular circumstances are actually present (in the example, where the bitch is nursing pups). In such a case the animal's normal behaviour in abnormal circumstances is equated with a more vicious dog's abnormal behaviour in normal circumstances. Either is to be treated as introducing the element of abnormal, dangerous behaviour which goes towards the establishment of strict liability, if the other elements (in paragraphs (a) and (c) of section 2(2)) are also present.

That is the explanation which was preferred by the Court of Appeal in ***Cummings v Granger*** [1977] QB 397 and ***Curtis v Betts*** [1990] 1 WLR 459 . . .

The weight of authority favours the view taken by the Court of Appeal in ***Curtis v Betts*** (with dicta of two members of the Court of Appeal in ***Breeden v Lampard*** (unreported) 21 March 1985 going the other way). But Mr Lissack (for the defendants) has strenuously argued that the current of authority is wrong, because (contrary to Parliament's general purpose) it treats normal animal behaviour as if it were abnormal . . .

In my view the crux of the matter is this. Both sides agree that Parliament intended to impose strict liability only for animals which are (in some sense) dangerous. Subsections (1) and (2) of section 2 mark the first subdivision which Parliament has made in identifying one (very limited) class of dangerous animals. This rather crude subdivision has contributed to the difficulties which have arisen, since it implies (but does not clearly spell out) that entirely normal behaviour of an animal of a non-dangerous species can never give rise to strict liability (this is the basis of the first anomaly relied on by the defendants). Domesticated animals are to be the subject of strict liability only if their behavioural characteristics are (in some sense) abnormal (and so dangerous). Did Parliament contemplate that the generality of animals in a domesticated species might in some circumstances show dangerous behavioural characteristics so as to be liable to be treated, in those circumstances, as dangerous? Or is there a presumption underlying the Act (and providing guidance as to the correct construction of section 2) that an animal of a domesticated species behaving in a way that is (in particular circumstances) normal and natural for its species cannot be treated as dangerous?

In my view the scheme and language of the Act do not yield any such underlying presumption. I consider that the claimant's proposed construction of the second limb of section 2(2)(b) is more natural as a matter of language, and that it is not inconsistent with Parliament's general intention to impose strict liability only for animals known to present special dangers. The suggested anomalies, although far from insignificant, could be matched by comparable anomalies arising from the alternative construction. Moreover the claimant's proposed construction is in my view closer to . . . the common experience of everyday life.

It is common knowledge (and was known to the defendants in this case) that horses, if exposed to a very frightening stimulus, will panic and stampede, knocking down obstacles in their path (in this case an electric fence, a post and barbed wire fence behind that, and then high undergrowth) and may continue their flight for a considerable distance. Horses loose in that state, either by day or by night, are an obvious danger on a road carrying fast-moving traffic. The defendants knew these facts; they could decide whether to run the unavoidable risks involved in keeping horses; they could decide whether or not to insure against those risks. Although I feel sympathy for the defendants, who were held not to have been negligent in the fencing of the field, I see nothing unjust or unreasonable in the appellants having to bear the loss resulting from their horses' escape rather than the claimant (who suffered very serious and painful injuries in the accident, although he was wearing a seatbelt and slowed down as soon as he saw the first horse in his headlights).

On the other principal issue in the appeal, the issue of causation . . . the essential point is that in order to recover the claimant had to show that the damage which he had suffered was caused, not merely by the horses escaping and being on the main road, but by the characteristics which are capable of founding strict liability under section 2(2) – in short, a frightened horse's propensity to bolt, to continue to flee, and to ignore obstacles in its path. The trial judge (following the Court of Appeal in *Jaundrill v Gillett* Times, 30 January 1996) thought that the damage was caused by the presence of the horses on the highway, rather than by any relevant characteristic. Hale LJ and the other members of the Court of Appeal took a different view. Hale LJ [2002] QB 769, 776, para 16 said:

> . . . In this case, however, it is indeed difficult to conclude that it was anything other than the particular characteristics of these horses once they had been terrified which led to their escape and to this accident taking place. They were still not behaving in the ordinary way in which they would behave when taken on the road. One witness referred to them bolting; another to them trotting across the road in front of the vehicles; they crashed into the vehicles rather than the other way about. It is precisely because they were behaving in the unusual way caused by their panic that the accident took place.

I consider that that was the correct approach. I think that the Court of Appeal reached the right conclusion on both issues. I would therefore dismiss this appeal.

Damage in the subsection means damage due to the abnormal characteristic. If a dog is known to be vicious, the keeper will not be liable if it accidentally trips someone up.

The connection between s 2(2)(a) and s 2(2)(b) is shown in **Bowlt v Clark** [2006] All ER (D) 295 (Jun). A very heavy horse collided with a car, injuring the passengers. The judge held that, for the purposes of s 2(2)(a), any damage caused by the horse would be likely to be severe, since the horse was a heavy animal, weighing 600 lb. For the purposes of s 2(2)(b), he identified the relevant characteristic as a propensity occasionally to move otherwise than as directed. On that basis, he found that the requirements of s 2(2) had been made out, and that the defendant was liable under s 2(2) of the Animals Act 1971. On appeal the Court of Appeal held that the appeal would be allowed as the judge had erred in not considering whether the damage caused by the horse was damage which the horse, unless restrained, was likely to cause. Instead, he had concluded that the alternative limb of s 2(2)(a) was satisfied, namely that if the horse caused damage, it was likely to be severe, due to the horse's weight. That conclusion could not be quarrelled with, but the judge, in addressing the requirement under s 2(2)(b), ought to have asked himself whether the likelihood of the damage being severe was due to characteristics of the animal not normally found in animals of the same species. The relevant characteristic was the weight of the animal. Had the judge asked that question, he would have concluded that the horse's weight was a normal characteristic of its species, so that requirement (b) was not satisfied. However, instead of identifying the horse's weight as the relevant characteristic, the judge had identified the propensity of a horse in particular times and in particular circumstances to 'assert an inclination to move otherwise than as directed'. It was doubtful whether such a propensity could be described as a characteristic of an animal, and, even if it could, the judge's assertion that it was one that was not normally found in horses 'except at particular times and in particular circumstances' was questionable. The judge had failed to identify either the particular times or the particular circumstances when that characteristic manifested itself. Moreover, in saying that that was a characteristic of horses generally, the judge had come close to accepting that propensity was a normal characteristic of a horse, not one that only arose at a particular time or in particular circumstances. Furthermore, the judge had failed to recognise that the characteristic that he was considering was one relevant to the first limb of requirement (a), namely, that it was relevant to the likelihood of the horse causing the damage that had occurred. It only became relevant to consider that characteristic if the judge had first given an affirmative answer to the question in s 2(2)(a) that the damage which the horse had caused was of a kind which the horse, unless restrained, had been likely to cause, but the judge had never addressed that question. If he had, he would have concluded that the horse, unless restrained, had not been likely to have caused the damage which it had. It followed that the claimant had failed to establish that the linked requirements of either limb of s 2(2)(a) and s 2(2)(b) were satisfied. The accident was an unlikely mischance for which no one had been to blame, and which attracted no liability under the provisions of s 2 of the Animals Act 1971.

The application of the majority decision in *Mirvahedy* can be seen in the following two cases.

Welsh v *Stokes* [2008] 1 All ER 921

The claimant, aged 17 at the relevant time, worked as a trainee at the defendant's yard. The defendants were experienced in keeping horses. On the day of the accident, she was riding a horse which was said to have been sensible with no history of misbehaviour or vice of any kind. However, the horse reared up and the claimant fell, seriously injuring herself. As to the defendant's knowledge, for the purposes s 2(2)(c), the judge held that the defendants, as experienced keepers of horses, would have known that the horse, like any horse of his kind, was capable of rearing. The judge held that strict liability was established under s 2(2).

On appeal it was held that once the judge had found that damage caused was likely to be severe and that the horse had the characteristic of rearing, it was inevitable that he would find that the likelihood of the damage being severe was due to that characteristic. The core meaning of 'normal' was 'conforming to type'. If a characteristic of an animal was usual, then it would certainly be normal.

It was difficult to see why Parliament should have intended to exclude from the ambit of s 2(2)(b) cases where the relevant characteristic was natural, although unusual, in the animal which had caused the damage. If s 2(2)(b) was interpreted in that way, there was nothing unjust or unreasonable, as between the keeper, who could decide whether to run the unavoidable risks involved in keeping horses, and whether or not to insure against those risks, and the victim of the horse's behaviour, in requiring the keeper to bear the loss.

McKenny v *Foster (trading as Foster Partnership)* [2008] EWCA Civ 173

The defendant's cow had her third calf, which was six to seven months old. The cow was known to be of good temperament. The cow was put into a properly enclosed and properly gated field suitable for containing the defendant's cows. The cow had showed no sign of distress when separated from its calf. The cow climbed over a six-barred livestock gate, and crossed a 12-foot cattle grid. The cow strayed onto an A road. A vehicle driven by the first claimant collided with the cow. The first claimant's passenger, and partner, was killed, as was the cow. Agreed expert evidence was that what had driven the cow to climb over the gate and jump the cattle grid was her extreme agitation and her desire to try to return to her recently weaned calf. Expert evidence also indicated that the cow was quite capable of judging the length of the cattle grid, but was only likely to do so in the particular and unusual circumstances of her supposed excitement; and that it was not normal for a recently weaned suckler cow to jump or otherwise negotiate such a gate. The judge stated that the defendant could not have possibly foreseen the instant events which led to the accident; and that the cow had never previously given any warning or indication of abnormal propensities. The judge summarily rejected the defendant's allegation.

On appeal it was held that the causative characteristic had to be a dangerous behavioural characteristic, even though it might be limited to particular times or circumstances. The cow in the instant case had no known propensity to act as she had. There was a clear distinction between an attack by a newly calved cow and the facts of the present case, where the cow's exceptional behaviour could not properly be described as normal in any circumstance. The strict liability claim had to fail because the behavioural characteristic relied on by the claimants, agitation resulting from the cow's normal maternal instinct upon being separated from her calf, was neither dangerous nor causative; whereas the dangerous and causative behaviour, exceptional and exaggerated agitation resulting from her maternal instinct, so that she was in the state of an excited, wild animal, was not normal and had not been known to the defendants. Neither the cow, nor the breed generally, were known to exhibit their maternal instinct with such excited and exaggerated anxiety as had been inferred for whatever abnormal reason in the instant case.

Defences

For contributory negligence, see Chapter 10.

Defences to actions brought under s 2 are provided by s 5(1)–(3):

(1) A person is not liable under sections 2 to 4 of this Act for any damage which is due wholly to the fault of the person suffering it.

(2) A person is not liable under section 2 of this Act for any damage suffered by a person who has voluntarily accepted the risk thereof.

(3) A person is not liable under section 2 of this Act for any damage caused by an animal kept on any premises or structure to a person trespassing there, if it is proved either–

(a) that the animal was not kept there for the protection of persons or property; or

For volenti, see Chapter 10.

(b) (if the animal was kept there for the protection of persons or property) that keeping it there for that purpose was not unreasonable.

The operation of these defences can be seen in the following case.

Cummings v *Granger* [1977] 1 All ER 104

(For facts see above.)

Lord Denning:

> It follows that the keeper of the dog is strictly liable unless he can bring himself within one of the exceptions in s 5. Obviously s 5(1) does not avail. The bite was not *wholly* due to the fault of the [plaintiff] but only *partly* so. Section 5(3) may, however, avail the keeper. It shows that if someone trespasses on property and is bitten or injured by a guard dog, the keeper of the guard dog is exempt from liability if it is proved that keeping it there for that purpose was not unreasonable. [Lord Denning went on to hold that it was not unreasonable to keep a guard dog because of the nature of the area (East End of London) and the fact that the yard contained scrap metal.]

Ormrod LJ [after agreeing with Lord Denning on s 5(3)]:

> The other defence which is open to him is under s 5(2) . . . They are, to my mind, fairly simple English words . . . I do not think it is open to any doubt . . . she accepted the risk. No doubt she knew about the dog, she said that she was frightened of the dog. For whatever reason she went in . . . I would myself come to the conclusion that she accepted the risk, and it is no answer to say that she had Mr Hobson with her.

NB: Since this decision, the Guard Dogs Act 1975 has made it a criminal offence to use or permit the use of a guard dog on premises without the guard dog being at all times under the control of a handler. Although the Act provides for no civil penalty, it may be that contravention of the Act would mean that use of a guard dog was unreasonable for the purposes of s 5(3).

Trespassing livestock

Objective 3

For strict liability, see Chapter 1.

Strict liability for trespassing livestock is of ancient origin and was one of the strands of precedent drawn on in creating the rule in **Rylands v Fletcher**. The present law is in the Animals Act 1971.

Livestock is defined by s 11 and includes cattle, horses, asses, mules, hinnies, sheep, goats, poultry and deer not in a wild state. The definition does not include dogs and cats.

Livestock trespassing on to land

Liability is governed by s 4:

(1) Where livestock belonging to any person strays on to land in the ownership or occupation of another and–
    (a) damage is done by the livestock to the land or to any property on it which is in the ownership or possession of the other person; or
    (b) any expenses are reasonably incurred by that other person in keeping the livestock while it cannot be restored to the person to whom it belongs or while it is being detained in pursuance of section 7 of this Act, or in ascertaining to whom it belongs;

the person to whom the livestock belongs is liable for the damage or expenses, except as otherwise provided by this Act.

Two points should be noted on this section. First, that liability is strict. The claimant does not have to show that the keeper was aware of a tendency by the livestock to stray.

Secondly, that there is no liability under the section for personal injuries or for damage to the property of a third party. In such cases the claimant would need to rely on s 2(2) or the common law.

Defences

The only defences to an action under s 4 are provided by s 5(5)–(6):

> (5) A person is not liable under section 4 of this Act where the livestock strayed from a highway and its presence there was a lawful use of the highway.
>
> (6) ... the damage shall not be treated as due to the fault of the person suffering it by reason only that he could have prevented it by fencing; but a person is not liable under that section where it is proved that the straying of the livestock on to the land would not have occurred but for a breach by any other person, being a person having an interest in the land, of a duty to fence.

The s 5(5) defence is of ancient common law origin, based on the idea that a person driving livestock on the highway should only be liable where there was negligence involved.

Matthews v Wicks (1987) Times, 25 May

> The defendant's sheep were left to graze on common land and were also left free to wander on to the highway. The sheep entered the claimant's garden and caused damage. The Court of Appeal held that s 5(5) had no application as letting the sheep wander on the highway did not constitute a lawful use.

Section 5(6) should be read with s 5(1). In general, the fact that the claimant could have prevented the livestock entering by fencing their land will not be a defence. This is because there is no general duty in English law to fence out. But where there is a duty to fence out imposed on the claimant, who is in breach of the duty, and the defendant's animals stray on to their land, there will be a defence under s 5(6).

Detention of trespassing livestock

Section 7 of the Act provides a partial remedy in the case of trespassing livestock. This replaces the old common law remedy of distress damage feasant. A person may detain the livestock until the damage is paid for. If the right of detention is exercised, then notice must be given to the police and the owner (if known) within 48 hours. If an offer is made to pay for the damage, then the livestock must be released to the owner. The detainer must feed the livestock during the detention. After 14 days the livestock may be sold at market or auction. After deducting the costs of the sale, keeping the livestock and compensation for any damage caused, any surplus must be returned to the owner.

Animals escaping on to the highway

At common law there was no liability where an animal escaped from land on to the highway and caused damage to highway users. This immunity from liability existed before modern traffic conditions and was abolished by s 8 of the Act:

> (1) So much of the rules of the common law relating to liability for negligence as excludes or restricts the duty which a person might owe to others to take such care as is reasonable to see that damage is not caused by animals straying on to a highway is hereby abolished.

(2) Where damage is caused by animals straying from unfenced land to a highway a person who placed them on the land shall not be regarded as having committed a breach of the duty to take care by reason only of placing them there if-
  (a) the land is common land, or is land situated in an area where fencing is not customary, or is a town or village green; and
  (b) he had a right to place the animals on that land.

Liability under the Act is therefore based on negligence and the court will consider all relevant matters on the question of reasonableness, such as the possibility of fencing, the nature of the animal, the amount of traffic on the highway and whether there is a local custom of fencing. There is no general duty imposed on landowners to fence animals in. This is a question of local custom except where s 8(2) specifically applies.

Davies v Davies [1975] QB 172

> The defendant worked on a farm owned by his mother. He owned sheep which he kept on the farm. His mother was entitled to graze cattle and sheep on adjacent common land and the defendant also grazed his sheep there. The claimant collided with the sheep on the highway as he was driving past the common land. It was held that s 8(2) protected persons with a legal right to place animals on the common land and anyone licensed by the owner to place his animals there. The defendant was therefore not liable for the damage to the claimant.

Special liability for dogs

Two sections of the Act provide special liability in the case of dogs.

Section 3 provides that where a dog causes damage by killing or injuring livestock, then the keeper of the dog is liable for the damage unless he can bring himself within one of the defences provided by the Act. The relevant defences would be fault of the claimant (s 5(1)), assumption of risk (s 5(2)), and contributory negligence (ss 10 and 11). There is also a specific defence in s 5(4), where the livestock had strayed on to land and the dog belonged to the occupier of the land or its presence on the land was authorised by the occupier.

Section 9(3) provides that it is lawful for a person to kill or injure a dog which:

(a) is worrying or is about to worry livestock, and there are no other reasonable means of ending or preventing the worrying; or
(b) the dog has been worrying livestock, has not left the vicinity, is not under the control of any person and there are no practicable means of ascertaining to whom it belongs.

The person harming the dog must also show:

1 that he was a person entitled to act for the protection of livestock (i.e. he owns either the livestock or the land on which it is, or is authorised by either owner); and
2 that he gives notice to the police within 48 hours. (Section 9(1).)

Remoteness of damage

For remoteness of damage generally, see Chapter 9.

The Act is silent on the question of remoteness; it might be assumed that the remoteness test for the strict liability provisions under the Act is directness.

For s 2(2) to apply, the keeper of the animal has to be aware of a particular characteristic of the animal to be liable. If damage is of a kind likely to be caused by this characteristic, then the keeper will be liable. But if the damage is not of such a kind, then the keeper will not be liable: for example, if a dog has a tendency to bite people, the keeper will be liable for bites. But if a child who does not know the dog runs away and falls over, it is unlikely that the keeper would be liable under the section for this kind of damage.

Summary

This chapter deals with the rules on liability for animals.

- There is liability for animals under a number of torts and also a specific statutory regime under the Animals Act 1971. A person can be sued in torts such as negligence and nuisance for damage caused by animals.

- The Animals Act 1971 divides animals into dangerous and non-dangerous species.

- A dangerous species is defined by s 6(2). The keeper of a dangerous animal is strictly liable for damage caused. Keeper is defined by s 6(3).

- Liability for non-dangerous animals is defined by s 2(2): the damage caused must be of a kind the animal was likely to cause or likely to be severe; the likelihood of the damage being severe must be due to characteristics of the animal not normally found in animals of that species or not normally found except at particular times or in particular circumstances; and those characteristics must be known to the keeper.

- This section has caused considerable problems for the courts. The House of Lords in *Mirvahedy* v *Henley* has held that a keeper is liable for behaviour which is not normal for an animal of that species but was normal for the species in the particular circumstances, such as a horse bolting when alarmed.

- Defences to actions under s 2 are in s 5. These are: that the damage was due to the fault of the person suffering it; *volenti*; and trespassing where keeping the animal in those circumstances was reasonable.

- There is strict liability for trespassing livestock under s 4. Defences are provided by s 5(5) and (6).

- Under s 7 a person can detain livestock under certain circumstances where it has caused damage.

Further reading

Amirthalingam, K. (2003), 'Animal Liability: Equine, Canine and Asinine' 119 LQR 563 (*Mirvahedy*).

Howarth, D. (2003), 'The House of Lords and the Animals Act: Closing the Stable Door' 62 CLJ 548 (*Mirvahedy*).

North, P. M. (1972), *The Modern Law of Animals*, Butterworths.

20

Trespass to the person

Objectives

After reading this chapter you will:

1. Appreciate the concepts underlying the action of trespass to the person.
2. Appreciate the distinction between assault and battery and understand the legal rule applying to actions for these two torts.
3. Understand the legal rules applying to an action for false imprisonment.
4. Have a critical knowledge of the history and present significance of the rule in *Wilkinson* v *Downton*.

Example

Bob and David are arguing about football when Bob says, 'I'll kill you for that.' He then throws a punch at David but misses and hits Eric who is standing nearby. David then pushes Bob into a room and locks the door. Bob suffers from claustrophobia and suffers mental distress as a result.

Introduction

Objective 1

The gist of trespass to the person is that it involves an infringement of an individual's personal integrity. It is concerned with protecting a person from unjustifiable interference rather than with physical damage.

Trespass to the person has now ceased to be a tort in the mainstream of personal injuries litigation. This function is now performed almost exclusively by negligence.

There is some overlap between criminal cases and trespass to the person. Where the defendant's act amounts to a criminal offence, the claimant may prefer a criminal prosecution to be brought, rather than face the hazards of litigation. If the defendant is convicted, the claimant may be able to obtain compensation through the Criminal Injuries Compensation Scheme. This scheme awards compensation to a person who has suffered personal injury as a result of crimes of violence. The amount of compensation is unlikely to be as high as that obtainable in a tort action. The courts now have means of awarding compensation to the victims of crime.

Compensation may not be the primary motive in bringing a trespass to the person action. The state prosecutor may have refused to bring a criminal action or an action may have failed. (See, for example, *Ashley v Chief Constable of Sussex Police* [2008] UKHL 25.) However, if a criminal assault and battery charge has been dismissed (or upheld) in the magistrates' court, civil proceedings in the same cause will be barred. (Offences Against the Person Act 1861 s 45.) The standard of proof in a criminal action (beyond reasonable doubt) is higher than that in a civil action (on the balance of probabilities).

The remaining importance of trespass to the person is in the area of civil liberties. It offers some protection against the over-officious police officer (and the possibility of exemplary damages), the practical joker and the office wolf.

Trespass to the person encompasses the three torts of battery, assault and false imprisonment. Although not a trespass, the rule in *Wilkinson v Downton* [1897] 2 QB 57 will also be dealt with here. This tort is concerned with those who suffer psychiatric damage or other emotional harm as a result of another person's intentional conduct.

Trespass has certain features which will be examined first.

Actionable *per se*

For torts actionable *per se*, see Chapter 1.

All trespasses are actionable *per se*. This means that the claimant does not have to prove actual damage as part of their case. The tort protects personal integrity, which is regarded as being so important that it is protected even in the absence of damage. An unwanted contact may amount to trespass to the person even though there is no physical injury to the claimant.

Direct and physical

The trespass action is derived from the ancient writ of trespass. One of the requirements of the writ was that the defendant's act had to be direct and physical. Where the infringement is caused by an indirect act, there may be a remedy in a tort derived from case, such as nuisance or negligence, but not in trespass. If the defendant throws a log and it hits the claimant, this is trespass. If the log lands in the road and the claimant later trips over it, this is case (negligence).

Scott v Shepherd (1773) 2 W Bl 892

> The defendant threw a lighted squib into a crowded market place. It landed on a market stall and was thrown on. It landed on another stall and exploded, injuring the claimant. The defendant was held liable for the injuries to the claimant as they were a direct result of the defendant's act. The act of throwing the squib on did not break the link between the defendant's act and the claimant's injury, as it was instinctive.

Defendant's state of mind

For strict liability, see Chapter 1.

At one time it was thought that trespass to the person was a tort of strict liability, in the sense that it did not require any fault on the part of the defendant. This view was rejected in *Stanley v Powell* [1891] 1 QB 86, where it was held that trespass to the person was not actionable in the absence of intention or negligence. The decision confirmed that trespass is a fault-based tort, but left open the question of burden of proof.

Fowler v *Lanning* [1959] 1 QB 426

A shot from the defendant's gun hit the claimant. The claimant's statement of claim alleged simply that the defendant shot the clamant. The defendant applied to have the action struck out as disclosing no cause of action. Diplock J ruled that the burden of proof in a trespass action was on the claimant, who had to show that the defendant acted either intentionally or negligently. The decision was controversial as there was authority in both directions, but it removed one of the supposed major advantages of the trespass action, that the defendant had to prove he was not at fault.

For intent and negligence, see Chapter 1.

The argument over the state of mind required continued. At first it was a question of whether there was actually such a thing as a negligent trespass, or whether trespass was solely an intentional tort.

Letang v *Cooper* [1965] 1 QB 232

The claimant was sunbathing on a hotel car park. The defendant negligently drove his car over her legs and caused injury. The action was brought more than three years after the incident. The defendant said that the action was statute barred by limitation. The claimant said that her cause of action was in battery and that the limitation period there was six years. The Court of Appeal held that as the action was for a failure to take reasonable care, it was, for the purposes of the Limitation Act, an action in negligence.

Lord Denning was of the opinion that where the act causing the damage was intentional, the correct cause of action was trespass. Where the act was negligent, the cause of action was in negligence. There was no overlap between trespass and negligence (Danckwerts LJ agreed). This view seems to have been accepted in **Wilson v Pringle** [1986] 2 All ER 440 (see below).

Diplock LJ was not prepared to hold that a trespass could not be committed negligently, but proceeded to eliminate any advantages that the claimant might have in suing in trespass. He said the burden of proof in terms of fault was on the claimant in trespass and actual damage is a necessary ingredient in unintentional trespasses.

The view of Lord Denning was upheld by the Court of Appeal in *Iqbal* v *Prison Officers Association* [2009] EWCA Civ 1312: 'All forms of trespass require an intentional act. An act of negligence will not suffice.' (Smith LJ.)

This still leaves the question of what is meant by *intention*. Intention can mean:

1 Intentional conduct can mean willed voluntary conduct. If a person has an epileptic fit and strikes someone then they cannot have acted intentionally in this sense.

2 Intending the consequences of one's willed actions. This version can be illustrated by the example of a security guard who locks a door when a person is inside. Has this person been falsely imprisoned?

  (a) If the security guard knows the person is in the room then he intends the consequences of his action.

  (b) If he has been told by a colleague that there might be a person in the room and that he should check but does not, then he is reckless.

  (c) If he thinks that there is a possibility that there may be someone in the room and does not check then at most he is negligent. In (b) and (c) the security guard is aware that his conduct may bring about a particular result without intending that result.

In *Iqbal* the Court of Appeal held that intention in trespass to the person also includes subjective recklessness. This is where the defendant foresees the relevant consequences of their actions but goes ahead regardless.

Battery

Objective 2

For battery and medical practitioners, see Chapter 15.

A battery is the direct and intentional application of force to another person without that person's consent. The application of the force must be voluntary and intentional. The original force may be unintentional but a failure to rectify the situation may render it a battery. Thus, when the defendant unintentionally stopped his car on a policeman's foot, there was no battery but when he refused to remove it there was. (**Fagan** v **Metropolitan Police Commissioner** [1969] 1 QB 439.)

The requirement of intent creates some problem. If I fire an arrow from a bow then I intend to do this. If a person walks into a fenced off area where the target is situated while the arrow is in in flight then I intend to fire the arrow but do not intend to hit anyone. Unless I have been reckless it is unlikely that a battery action will succeed.

Mental state required for battery

The courts have always been faced with the problem of distinguishing those contacts which are part of everyday life and those which are unacceptable and illegal.

This presents difficulties for the courts. Contact between persons ranges from violent assaults through to accidental bumps in crowded streets. In between are people who play practical jokes, people who indulge in sexual harassment and doctors who need to treat unconscious patients. How is a court to draw a line?

Collins v Wilcock [1984] 3 All ER 374

Goff LJ stated that the court started with the fundamental principle that every person's body is inviolate. Interference with a person's body will generally be lawful where they consented to it. There is also a broad exception to allow for the exigencies of everyday life such as jostling in the street and social contact at parties. This is a question of physical contact which is generally acceptable in the ordinary conduct of everyday life.

In 1986 the Court of Appeal attempted a test to make the distinction.

Wilson v Pringle [1986] 2 All ER 440

The defendant, as a practical joke, pulled the claimant's schoolbag from his shoulder, causing injury. The Court of Appeal held that the act of touching the claimant had to be intentional and the touching had to be a hostile touching. The relevant intention was the intention to do the act. There need be no intention to cause damage. A blow struck by a person undergoing an epileptic fit would therefore not be trespass, as there would not be the relevant intent.

Hostility was not to be construed as malice or ill-will and would be a question of fact in each case. The act of touching in itself might display hostility. If not, then the claimant must plead the facts which they claim demonstrate that the touching was hostile.

The intention of the Court of Appeal was to remove the necessity for the courts to find implied consent in some cases where they did not wish to hold that a touching was a battery. The requirement of hostility was supposed to remove the need for implied consent because a touching which is hostile can scarcely be said to be consented to.

The attempt to frame a test of this nature has not been particularly successful. The first problem is what is meant by hostile. The Court of Appeal gave a number of examples of what it is not, but only one example of what it is. A police officer who touches a person with the intention of restraining them, with no legal power to do so, is acting with a hostile intent. (See also *Collins* v *Wilcock* above.)

Battery has always operated against the person who pushed unwanted attention on a person as well as against the violent person. The unwanted kiss is as actionable as the unwanted punch. If hostile is taken in its literal sense, then the practical joker and the molester could be immune in this tort. The dividing line in *Wilson* v *Pringle* was drawn at what was generally acceptable in the ordinary conduct of daily life. However, what is perfectly acceptable to one person may be totally repugnant to another.

See also Chapter 15 for *F* v *West Berks*.

The hostility test has not been particularly well received by the House of Lords. One of the areas in which it was thought it could operate was medical cases. Where a doctor had to touch a person in an emergency, instead of saying there was an implied consent, the court would say that there was no hostility on the part of the doctor and therefore no battery. This view has now been rejected by the House of Lords. (*F* v *West Berkshire Health Authority* [1989] 2 All ER 545.) Lord Goff stated:

> and it has recently been said that the touching must be hostile . . . I respectfully doubt whether that is correct. A prank that gets out of hand, an over-friendly slap on the back, surgical treatment by a surgeon who mistakenly thinks that the patient has consented to it, all these things may transcend the bounds of lawfulness, without being characterised as hostile . . . In *Wilson* v *Pringle* the Court of Appeal considered that treatment or care of such persons [the mentally disordered] may be regarded as falling within the exception relating to physical contact which is generally acceptable in the ordinary conduct of everyday life. Again, I am, with respect, unable to agree. That exception is concerned with the ordinary events of everyday life, jostling in public places and such like, and treatment, even treatment for minor ailments, does not fall within that category of events. The general rule is that consent is necessary to render such treatment lawful.

See also Chapter 22 for *Wainwright*.

See Chapter 15 for battery in medical practice.

The approach of Lord Goff was confirmed in *Wainwright* v *Home Office* [2003] 4 All ER 969 by Lord Hoffmann.

The present position is not clear. In medical cases the hostility requirement has been rejected. In order to avoid an action for battery, a doctor must show either that consent was given for the touching, or that the touching was necessary in the best interests of the patient. In other cases it appears that Lord Goff's general exception for everyday contact may take precedence over hostility.

Contact

As battery is derived from the writ of trespass it must be direct and physical. This means that there must be some contact with the claimant before a battery is committed. Merely obstructing a person's progress without any contact is not a battery.

Assault

An assault is an act which causes another person to apprehend the infliction of immediate, unlawful force on his person. (*Collins* v *Wilcock*.)

The torts of assault and battery normally go together. If a person waves their fist, this is an assault. If the blow is struck, that is a battery. If the claimant is unaware of the impending blow – for example, if they are struck from behind or are unconscious – then only battery is committed.

For assault to be committed, the claimant must be in reasonable apprehension of an immediate battery. The test for reasonable apprehension is an objective one. If the defendant does not have the means to carry out the threat, then no assault is committed. Violent gestures by pickets at colleagues who are still working and pass by in buses protected by a police cordon is not an assault. (***Thomas* v *National Union of Mineworkers*** [1985] 2 All ER 1.) However, where the defendant attempts to land a blow on the claimant but is restrained by a third party, the tort of assault is committed. (***Stephens* v *Myers*** (1830) 4 C&P 349.) Passive obstruction, such as where a police officer blocks a person from entering a room, is not assault. (***Innes* v *Wylie*** (1844) 1 C&K 257.)

Where a loaded gun is pointed at the claimant, an assault is committed. Is there an assault if the gun is unloaded? In principle the answer should be yes, provided the claimant is unaware of the fact the gun is not loaded. There is dictum to the effect that this is not an assault (***Blake* v *Barnard*** (1840) 9 C&P 626), but in a criminal case it was stated that it was an assault (***R* v *St George*** (1840) 9 C&P 483). Most commentators take the view that the latter case is correct.

There is some difficulty with whether words alone can amount to an assault. The problem dates back to an old case where it was said that no words or singing are equivalent to an assault. (***R* v *Meade*** (1823) 1 Lew CC 184.) Many commentators feel that this is wrong and where words spoken by the defendant induce fear in the claimant, this should be actionable. (See ***Khorasandjian* v *Bush*** [1993] 3 WLR 476.) Support for this can be found in a criminal case where it was considered that the words, 'get out knives', would constitute an assault. (***R* v *Wilson*** [1955] 1 WLR 493.)

What would be the position with a series of silent phone calls which induce fear in the victim? If words cannot amount to an assault, how could silence? The issue was raised in a criminal case (***R* v *Ireland*** [1998] AC 147) and Lord Steyn doubted the statement in *Meade* as being 'unrealistic and indefensible'. If this is the case, then a person who intends by their silence to cause fear and that fear leads to an apprehension of immediate personal violence, then the caller may be guilty of an assault.

What is clear is that words may negative what would otherwise have been an assault.

Turberville v *Savage* (1669) 1 Mod Rep 3

> The claimant and defendant were involved in an argument. The defendant placed his hand on his sword and said, 'if it were not assize time I would not take such language from you'. It was held that the words negatived what would otherwise have been an assault.

Defences to assault and battery

Consent

For consent (volenti) generally, see Chapter 10.

Following ***Wilson* v *Pringle*** there is some dispute as to the extent to which consent is a defence to trespass to the person, or whether it is a part of the tort itself. The argument centres around the requirement of hostility. If the contact must be made with hostile intent, then any consent to the contact would negate an inference of hostility. (See 'Battery' above.) The substantive importance lies in the burden of proof. Does the claimant have to prove a lack of consent or does the defendant have to establish there was consent? There is no clear answer to this, but the preferable view in the light of developments in the medical cases is that consent is a defence and the burden of proof is on the defendant.

See Chapter 15 for battery action in medical practice.

Express consent does not present problems where the claimant is legally capable of giving it. A surgeon will be protected from an action in battery by the signing of a consent form by the patient.

Implied consent presents more difficulties. It has been rejected in favour of necessity in medical cases. (See above.) A participant in a sporting event is said impliedly to consent to contacts in accordance with the rules of the game. A punch thrown at an opponent will not be within the rules and there will be a battery committed. (*R v Billinghurst* [1978] Crim LR 553.) In boxing no action will lie for a punch within the rules, as a participant consents to this by getting into the ring. But a foul punch is not consented to and may give rise to a battery action.

For consent in medical cases, see Chapter 15.

Any consent given will be limited to the act for which permission is given. A customer going to the hairdresser consents to having their hair cut and any other treatment they specifically agree to. But a customer who gives consent for a permanent wave does not agree to a tone rinse. The hairdresser will be liable in battery. (*Nash v Sheen* [1953] CLY 3726.)

The consent must be real and not induced by duress, fraud or misrepresentation.

Self-defence

Self-defence is a defence where reasonable force is used in defence of the claimant's person, property or another person. The burden of proof in self-defence in civil proceedings is on the defendant. What amounts to self-defence will be a question of fact in each case but the basic principle is that the force used must be reasonable in proportion to the attack.

Lane v Holloway [1968] 1 QB 379

The claimant and defendant were neighbours. The claimant had been drinking and was talking to a friend outside his house. The defendant's wife shouted, 'you bloody lot'. The claimant replied, 'shut up you monkey faced tart'. The defendant heard this and said he wanted to see the claimant on his own. The claimant came out and, thinking he was about to be hit, hit the defendant on the shoulder. The defendant hit the claimant in the eye, which needed 19 stitches. The defendant's blow was held to be out of proportion to the circumstances and the action succeeded.

The defence of *volenti non fit injuria* also failed, as, although a participant in a fight takes the risk of injury, they do not accept the risk of a savage blow out of proportion. Where the violence used is in proportion, then the claimant may be defeated by either *volenti non fit injuria* or *ex turpi causa*.

See Chapter 10.

The next case is interesting, as it deals not only with self-defence in tort but also contrasts the role of the defence in civil and criminal law.

Ashley and others v Chief Constable of Sussex Police [2008] UKHL 25

Armed police shot and killed the deceased during a raid on a house. It was admitted that the deceased had not been armed at the time. The responsible officer was charged with murder and manslaughter but acquitted following a submission of no case to answer. The deceased's father and son brought a civil action under the Fatal Accidents Act 1976. The causes of action alleged included assault and battery, or alternatively negligence, by the officer who had done the shooting. The defence to the battery claim was that the officer had been acting in self-defence when he shot the deceased.

Held: For civil law purposes, an excuse of self-defence based on non-existent facts that were honestly but unreasonably believed to exist had to fail. The belief had to have been reasonably held, and it might be that even that would not suffice to establish the defence. The plea for consistency between the criminal law and the civil law (the defendant had argued that the defence should be the same in civil and criminal law) lacked cogency, for the ends to be served by the two systems were very different.

The case demonstrates a key difference between tort law and the criminal law. The core function of the criminal law is to punish bad people. The policeman may have made a serious mistake but he was not bad in the criminal sense. He thought he was doing the right thing when he shot Ashley. Tort law exists to vindicate people's rights. Had the policeman violated Ashley's rights in shooting him? The fact that he honestly thought he was doing the right thing in shooting Ashley did not mean that he did do the right thing in shooting Ashley.

If Ashley had positively done something to make the policeman reasonably (but incorrectly) think that he was a threat, then the policeman would have done no wrong in shooting Ashley. But if Ashley had done nothing himself to give that impression, and the policeman only reasonably thought that Ashley was a threat because of briefings he had received before the drugs raid started, then Ashley would still have had a right not to be shot.

Contributory negligence

For contributory negligence, see Chapter 10.

Whether the Act applied to trespass to the person was formerly a matter of dispute although it is difficult to see why fault is a defence to an intentional tort concerned with a person's integrity rather than a compensatory tort concerned with apportionment of loss. The issue was considered by the Court of Appeal in *Co-operative Group (CWS) Ltd* v *Pritchard* [2011] EWCA Civ 669. It was held that the 1945 Act would not allow damages to be reduced by virtue of a party's alleged contributory negligence in cases where claims were based on the tort of assault and battery.

False imprisonment

Objective 3

False imprisonment is the unlawful imposition of constraint on another's freedom of movement from a particular place.

The tort does not require incarceration as such and can be committed by any unlawful detention. Forcing a person to remain in a field by threatening them with a gun would be false imprisonment. It could also be an assault.

The commonest modern examples of the tort are wrongful arrest by police officers or shop detectives. In such cases it is necessary to consider the powers of arrest of the defendant and whether they have been complied with.

The restraint must be total

Bird v *Jones* (1845) 7 QB 742

The defendants wrongfully roped off part of the footpath on a bridge. The claimant was prevented from crossing the bridge by this route. This was held not to be false imprisonment as the restraint was not total. Lord Denman dissented and was of the opinion that if a person had a right to go somewhere and was prevented from doing so, then that should be false imprisonment. (See also *Austin* v *Commissioner of Police of the Metropolis* (2009).)

The decision means that if a person has a reasonable means of escape, the tort will not be committed. But if the means of escape involves any danger, it is not reasonable to expect a person to take it. If the door to a room is locked but there is an open French window at ground level, this would not be false imprisonment. But it would not be reasonable to expect a person to climb from a second-floor window.

The House of Lords has considered the position of a person serving a term of imprisonment and whether such a person has an action for false imprisonment if the conditions of his detention are altered.

Hague v *Deputy Governor of Parkhurst Prison; Weldon* v *Home Office* [1991] 3 All ER 733

In one case the governor of the prison had ordered the transfer of a prisoner to another prison and his segregation from other prisoners. In the other case a prisoner alleged that he had been placed in a strip cell without lawful authority. The House of Lords held that a person lawfully committed to prison had no residual liberty which could be protected by private law remedies, since while in prison he had no liberty to be in any place other than where the prison regime required him to be. He therefore had no liberty capable of deprivation by the prison regime which could constitute the tort of false imprisonment.

A prisoner who is subjected to intolerable conditions of detention which are seriously prejudicial to their health has a public law remedy by way of judicial review. They may also sue in negligence if they suffer actual injury to their health.

The question of restraint comes up in connection with mental health patients. In *R v Bournewood Community and Mental Health NHS Trust ex p L* [1998] 3 All ER 289 the House of Lords held (by a bare majority) that there was no false imprisonment when an informal mental health patient was kept on an unlocked ward and showed no desire to leave. An order for his detention under the Mental Health Act 1983 would have been applied for had he tried to leave. This was a potential rather than an actual restraint. The majority held that he had not been detained against his will although he had been sedated. An application was then made under Article 5 of the European Convention on Human Rights. The article provides that 'everyone has the right to liberty and security of the person but is subject to a number of derogations of which the relevant one is 'the lawful detention of persons of unsound mind'. The European Court of Human Rights held that the applicant had been detained contrary to Article 5. The court refused to accept the House of Lords' distinction between actual restraint and restraint which was conditional on a person seeking to leave. As a result of the gap between the common law and the Convention, applications under the latter are likely to become more common than actions for false imprisonment.

The circumstances in which a mentally ill patient can be detained have been clarified by the Mental Capacity Act 2005. In the light of the legislation and the decision of the ECHR it is unlikely that *Bournewood* will be followed.

Knowledge of the detention

Does the claimant have to be aware that they have been falsely imprisoned? If they were asleep, unconscious, drunk or insane at the time of the detention, they might not have been aware they were detained. This raises the question of which interest is protected by the tort: freedom of movement as such, or the mental stress caused by knowledge of detention?

415

In a nineteenth-century case it was held that a child kept behind at school as his parents had not paid the fees had no action, as he was unaware of the detention. (*Herring* v *Boyle* (1834) 1 Cr M&R 377.) However, modern authority indicates that knowledge is not a necessary ingredient of the tort.

Meering v *Grahame-White Aviation Co Ltd* (1920) 122 LT 44

The claimant was suspected of theft and was taken to his employer's offices. Two policemen remained close to him while he was questioned. The defendants, in an action for false imprisonment, argued that the claimant was unaware of any detention. Atkin LJ stated that knowledge of the detention was irrelevant to whether the tort had been committed. Knowledge might, however, be relevant to the assessment of damages.

This view has now been approved by the House of Lords in *Murray* v *Ministry of Defence* [1988] 2 All ER 521. Where a person was unaware of their detention and had suffered no actual harm, they would receive only nominal damages. The US view that knowledge was necessary was rejected because of the importance of liberty of the individual.

The restraint must be unlawful

A person may be able to impose a lawful restraint on a person. An occupier of premises may be able to stipulate certain restrictions on a visitor, including the method by which they are to leave.

Robinson v *Balmain Ferry Co Ltd* [1910] AC 295

The claimant paid one penny to enter the defendants' wharf, intending to leave by ferry. He missed a ferry and wished to leave the wharf via the turnstile. The defendants refused to let him out unless he paid a penny. This was held not to be false imprisonment. The condition that a penny should be paid was a reasonable one and the claimant had contracted to leave the wharf by another way.

This decision does not give a general right to imprison to enforce contractual rights. An innkeeper who locked up the claimant when he refused to pay his bill was held liable in false imprisonment. (*Sunbolf* v *Alford* (1838) 3 M&W 248.)

Herd v *Weardale Steel, Coal and Coke Co Ltd* [1915] AC 67

A coalminer, in breach of contract, refused to continue with his work and demanded to be taken to the surface. His employers refused for some time. This was held not to be false imprisonment. The miner had consented to remain underground until the end of his shift and was not entitled to be taken to the surface until then.

Although the case was decided on the basis of consent, an alternative explanation is that the defendant had omitted to act, rather than acting positively, and that this is not trespass. Would this mean that a failure to let a person out of a locked room was not false imprisonment?

What these cases establish is that a passenger on a bus cannot insist on getting off except at a scheduled stop.

The issue arose again in *Iqbal* v *Prison Officers Association* [2009] EWCA Civ 1312. Prison officers went on an unlawful strike and the claimant was locked in his cell for longer than normal. The Court of Appeal held that the prison officers' actions amounted to an omission and did not constitute false imprisonment. In the absence of a specific duty to act, a failure to act would not constitute the tort. Sullivan LJ dissented on the basis that the Prison Officers Association's action in calling a strike could not be called a mere omission as opposed to a positive act. The court said that the appropriate action would be misfeasance in public office.

The question of lawfulness of restraint has arisen in the context of demonstrations. These have raised the problem of ensuring a balance between the requirements of the police in protecting property and lives and those of individual liberty. The European Convention on Human Rights is also in play.

Austin and another v *Commissioner of Police of the Metropolis* [2007] EWCA Civ 989 (CA); [2009] 2 WLR 372 (HL)

A came to take part in a demonstration on May Day 2001. *S* came to London on his employer's business and was caught up in the events of the day. Neither of them acted other than lawfully throughout.

Both were detained within a police cordon at Oxford Circus for many hours. After their requests to leave had been refused by individual police officers, neither made any attempt to break through the police cordon.

The claimants claimed under common law for false imprisonment and s 7 of the Human Rights Act 1998 for unlawful detention contrary to Article 5 of the European Convention on Human Rights. The judge rejected their claims under both heads.

The Court of Appeal considered both the common law and Convention actions.

1 On the common law action: there was an interference with the claimants' liberty which amounted to the tort of false imprisonment unless it was lawful. A threshold test of imminence had to be passed before action could be taken to prevent a breach of the peace and once the test of imminence was passed, action which was both reasonably necessary and proportionate to prevent a breach of the peace could be taken.

    The court concluded that in this very exceptional case, on the basis of the judge's finding that what the police did in containing the crowd was necessary in order to avoid an imminent breach of the peace, the actions of the police were lawful at common law, even though the police did not reasonably suspect that the individual claimants were about to commit a breach of the peace.

2 On the Convention action, the Strasbourg cases on Article 5 of the Human Rights Convention had drawn a distinction between a restriction of liberty of movement as opposed to a deprivation of liberty: see *Guzzardi* v *Italy (Application No 7367/76)* (1980) 3 EHRR 333.

    Mere restrictions on liberty were governed by Article 2 of Protocol 4, not by Article 5 of the Convention. The difference between the two was merely one of degree or intensity, not one of nature or substance. The United Kingdom had not ratified Article 2 of Protocol 4. Its provisions were not part of the law of England and Wales.

There was an appeal to the House of Lords on the Convention action but not on the common law action.

Held: No reference was made in Article 5 to the interests of public safety or the protection of public order as one of the cases in which a person might be deprived of his liberty. But the importance that would have to be attached in the context of Article 5 to measures taken in the interests of public safety was indicated by Article 2 of the Convention, as the lives of persons affected by mob violence might be at risk if measures of crowd control could not be adopted by the police. That was a situation where a search for a fair balance was necessary if those competing fundamental rights were to be reconciled with each other. The ambit that was given to Article 5 as to measures of crowd control would have to take account of the rights of the individual as well as the interests of the community. So any steps that were taken would be resorted to in good faith and would have to be proportionate to the situation which had made the measures necessary. That was essential to preserve the fundamental principle that anything that was done which affected a person's right to liberty should not be arbitrary. If those requirements were met, however, it will be proper to conclude that measures of crowd control that were undertaken in the interests of the community would not infringe the Article 5 rights of individual members of the crowd whose freedom of movement was restricted by them.

In the instant case, Article 5(1) of the Convention was not applicable. The restriction on the claimants' liberty which had resulted from them being confined within the cordon by the police had met the criteria, and was not the kind of arbitrary deprivation of liberty that was proscribed by the Convention.

The question of lawfulness of detention arose in different circumstances in the following case.

R (on the application of Lumba) v *Secretary of State for the Home Department; R (on the application of Mighty)* v *Secretary of State for the Home Department* [2011] UKSC 12

The claimants were foreign nationals who entered the United Kingdom and were subsequently convicted of serious offences. After they had served their prison sentences the Home Secretary notified them of the intention to deport them and they were detained pending deportation. The secretary of state's published policy on the detention of foreign national prisoners was that there was a presumption in favour of release although detention could be justified in some circumstances. In fact, during that period, the secretary of state adopted a quite different unpublished policy which imposed a near blanket ban on release and admitted of exceptions only on compassionate grounds. The claimants sued for false imprisonment.

Held: The unpublished policies which were applied to the claimants were unlawful because they had not been published and also because they included a presumption of detention. The claimants' detention would have been inevitable since they both posed a risk of absconding and reoffending. In response to the defence argument that if they had applied the published policy the defendants would still have been detained (i.e. a causation test), the important question was whether it was right to apply a causation test and for that reason to hold that the detentions were lawful. The introduction of a causation test in the tort of false imprisonment was held to be contrary to principle both as a matter of the law of trespass and of administrative law. Neither recognised any defence of causation so as to render lawful what was in fact an unlawful authority to detain, by reference to how the executive could and would have acted if it had acted lawfully, as opposed to how it did in fact act. Trespassory torts such as false imprisonment were actionable *per se* regardless of whether the victim suffered harm and even if the victim did not know that they were imprisoned. All that a claimant had to prove was that they were directly and intentionally imprisoned by the defendant, whereupon the burden shifted to the defendant to show that there was lawful justification for doing so. There was no lawful justification in this case so the defendants were liable in false imprisonment.

If the power could and would have been lawfully exercised, that was a powerful reason for concluding that the detainee had suffered no loss and was entitled to no more than nominal damages. But that was not a reason for holding that the tort had not been committed. The claim for exemplary damages was rejected.

Lawful arrest

Where the defendant is carrying out a lawful arrest no tort is committed. The correct procedure must be carried out in order to make an arrest. The arrested person must be told the true grounds on which they are being arrested and, unless they are physically seized, must be told that they are being arrested. Exceptions are provided where a person makes it impossible to inform by resisting and, in the case of citizens' arrests, no reason need be given where it is obvious. If a private citizen makes an arrest, they must hand the arrested person over to the police within a reasonable time. (***Lewis v Tims*** [1952] AC 676.)

The question of power of arrest is a complex one and will only be dealt with in outline here.

A police officer arresting with a warrant will be protected from an action for false imprisonment. Any defects in the warrant are not their concern.

The main powers of arrest without a warrant are found in the Police and Criminal Evidence Act 1984.

Anyone may arrest a person who is in the act of committing an indictable offence or anyone whom they have reasonable grounds for suspecting to be committing such an offence.

A police officer may arrest anyone who is committing or about to commit an offence, or anyone whom he believes on reasonable grounds to be doing either of these things. Where an offence has been committed, anyone may arrest a person whom they have reasonable grounds for suspecting to be guilty of it. This applies even where the wrong person was arrested, provided there were reasonable grounds for suspecting them.

A police officer is protected where no offence has been committed but where they have reasonable grounds for suspecting that it had. A private citizen who arrests where no offence had been committed is guilty of false imprisonment.

There is also a common law power for any person in whose presence a breach of the peace is being committed, or is about to be committed, to make an arrest.

Intentional infliction of emotional or physical harm

The rule in *Wilkinson* v *Downton*

Objective 4

Closely associated to trespass is the rule in ***Wilkinson* v *Downton*** [1897] 2 QB 57. The defendant, as a practical joke, told the claimant that her husband had broken both legs in an accident. As a result the claimant suffered nervous shock. The court held the defendant liable for the damage. Wright J laid down a principle:

> The defendant has . . . wilfully done an act calculated to cause physical harm to the plaintiff, – that is to say, to infringe her legal right to personal safety, and has in fact thereby caused physical harm to her. That proposition without more appears to me to state a good cause of action, there being no justification alleged for the act.

The action could not have been brought in trespass as there was no contact made or physical force used. At the time there was no liability in negligence for nervous shock, which has since been introduced. This perhaps explained the paucity of reported decisions on the principle. The case has only been fully followed twice. In ***Janvier* v *Sweeney*** [1919] 2 KB 316 the claimant recovered damages after the defendant told her that her husband was a German spy and she suffered nervous shock. In ***Khorasandjian* v *Bush*** [1993] 3 WLR 476 the defendant made unwanted telephone calls to the claimant inflicting stress but no physical injury. An injunction was granted to restrain the defendant under the rule.

The so-called 'rule' in ***Wilkinson* v *Downton*** has had a chequered history. There are a number of reasons for this. First and foremost is that it is a tort based on *intention* and where claimants have been blocked from bringing an action by the rules of another tort they have attempted to base an action on intention.

See Chapter 4 for psychiatric damage.

The development of the rules on nervous shock in negligence meant that there was no scope for the 'rule' to develop in that direction. However, the rule that a claimant in an action for psychiatric damage caused by negligence must prove an identifiable psychiatric injury has given rise to attempts to bring actions for mental distress falling short of this under the 'rule'. The potential of the action for introducing a tort based on intention has not been taken up despite suggestions that it should be tortious to intentionally inflict mental distress which falls short of nervous shock.

See Chapter 17 for *Hunter*.

In *Hunter* v *Canary Wharf Ltd* [1997] 2 All ER 426 Lord Hoffmann (at 452, *obiter*) saw no reason why the rule had to be restricted by rules in negligence that required the claimant to suffer a recognisable psychiatric injury. However, in *Wong* v *Parkside Health NHS Trust* [2003] 3 All ER 932 the Court of Appeal stated that the damage which must occur is physical damage or a recognisable psychiatric injury. Rudeness and unfriendliness in the workplace did not infringe the claimant's right to personal safety unless the conduct was such that physical damage or recognisable psychiatric damage was so likely to result that the defendant could not be heard to say that he did not mean it to do so. Despite Lord Hoffmann's statement, English law did not recognise a tort of intentional harassment going beyond the intentional infliction of harm.

Partial success came in the following case.

C v *D* [2006] EWHC 166 (QB)

The claimant alleged that his headmaster had touched his penis whilst drying him on occasions when the class had gone swimming; filmed his class in the shower; and stared at his genitals after taking him to the infirmary. The claimant sued for damages for distress and psychiatric injury contending that the defendant had intended to cause harm such that he could recover damages for mental distress *in addition to* psychiatric injury.

Held: There was no authority to support the proposition that a genuine intention to cause 'mere distress' gave rise to tortious liability. Even if harm was caused it was only actionable if the harm suffered was a recognised psychiatric injury. The video incident was not actionable as its impact did not go beyond distress. However, the claimant did suffer from a state of mental abnormality and a more than trivial cause was the infirmary incident, which was a gross invasion of his personal integrity at a time when he was especially vulnerable. Furthermore, behaving as he did during that incident, the defendant had been reckless as to whether he caused the claimant psychiatric injury. Accordingly, the defendant was liable for that conduct.

In *A* v *Hoare* [2006] the Court of Appeal (in a largely unrelated case) added a footnote which stated: 'it seems preferable for the law to develop along conventional modern lines rather than through recourse to this obscure tort, whose jurisprudential basis remains unclear.'

The major modern statement on the 'rule' came in *Wainwright*.

Wainwright v *Home Office* [2003] 4 All ER 969

See also Chapter 22 for *Wainwright*.

The first claimant together with her son, the second claimant, went to visit another son in prison. There was a drug smuggling problem in the prison and a prison officer told the claimants that they would have to be strip-searched. They reluctantly agreed and prison officers took them to separate rooms where they were asked to undress. They did as they were asked but both found the experience upsetting. They were examined by a psychiatrist who concluded that the second claimant, who had physical and learning difficulties, had been so severely affected by his experience as to suffer post-traumatic stress disorder. The first claimant had suffered emotional distress but no recognised psychiatric illness. The strip searching was held to be an invasion of their privacy which exceeded what was necessary and proportionate to deal with the drug smuggling problem and that the prison authorities had not adhered to their own rules. The claimants contended that the House of Lords should declare that there was a tort of invasion of privacy under which the searches of both of the claimants were actionable and damages for emotional distress recoverable. Alternatively, they submitted that damages for distress falling short of psychiatric injury could be recovered if there was an intention to cause it, that the prison officers did acts calculated to cause distress to the claimants and therefore should be liable on the basis of imputed intention. The appeal was dismissed.

The infliction of humiliation and distress by conduct calculated to humiliate and distress, without more, was not tortious at common law. There was no remedy for distress which did not amount to recognised psychiatric injury and, so far as there might be a tort of intention under which such damage was recoverable, the necessary intention in the instant case was not established. If a principled distinction were to be drawn which justified abandoning the rule that damages for mere distress were not recoverable, imputed intention would not do. The defendant must actually have acted in a way which he knew to be unjustifiable and intended to cause harm or at least acted without caring whether he caused harm or not.

For the privacy claim, see Chapter 22.

Lord Hoffmann:

> I do not resile from the proposition that the policy considerations which limit the heads of recoverable damage in negligence do not apply equally to torts of intention. If someone actually intends to cause harm by a wrongful act and does so, there is ordinarily no reason why he should not have to pay compensation. But I think that if you adopt such a principle, you have to be very careful about what you mean by intend. In *Wilkinson v Downton* RS Wright J wanted to water down the concept of intention as much as possible. He clearly thought, as the Court of Appeal did afterwards in *Janvier v Sweeney* [1919] 2 KB 316, that the plaintiff (claimant) should succeed whether the conduct of the defendant was intentional or negligent. But the *Victorian Railway Comrs* case 13 App Cas 222 prevented him from saying so. So he devised a concept of imputed intention which sailed as close to negligence as he felt he could go.
>
> If, on the other hand, one is going to draw a principled distinction which justifies abandoning the rule that damages for mere distress are not recoverable, imputed intention will not do. The defendant must actually have acted in a way which he knew to be unjustifiable and intended to cause harm or at least acted without caring whether he caused harm or not . . . The judge made no finding that the prison officers intended to cause distress or realised that they were acting without justification in asking the Wainwrights to strip. He said . . . that they had acted in good faith and . . . '. . . the strip-searches were, in my judgment, not intended to increase the humiliation necessarily involved but merely sloppiness.'
>
> Even on the basis of a genuine intention to cause distress, I would wish, as in *Hunter*'s case [1997] AC 655, to reserve my opinion on whether compensation should be recoverable. In institutions and workplaces all over the country, people constantly do and say things with the intention of causing distress and humiliation to others. This shows lack of consideration and appalling manners but I am not sure that the right way to deal with it is always by litigation. The Protection from Harassment Act 1997 defines harassment in section 1(1) as a 'course of conduct' amounting to harassment . . . The requirement of a course of conduct shows that Parliament was conscious that it might not be in the public interest to allow the law to be set in motion for one boorish incident. It may be that any development of the common law should show similar caution.
>
> In my opinion, therefore, the claimants can build nothing on *Wilkinson v Downton* [1897] 2 QB 57. It does not provide a remedy for distress which does not amount to recognized psychiatric injury and so far as there may be a tort of intention under which such damage is recoverable, the necessary intention was not established. I am also in complete agreement with Buxton LJ, . . . that *Wilkinson v Downton* has nothing to do with trespass to the person.

> Counsel for the Wainwrights submit that unless the law is extended to create a tort which covers the facts of the present case, it is inevitable that the European Court of Human Rights will find that the United Kingdom was in breach of its Convention obligation to provide a remedy for infringements of Convention rights. In addition to a breach of Article 8, they say that the prison officers infringed their Convention right under Article 3 not to be subjected to degrading treatment.
>
> I have no doubt that there was no infringement of Article 3. The conduct of the searches came nowhere near the degree of humiliation which has been held by the European Court of Human Rights to be degrading treatment in the cases on prison searches to which we were referred: see *Valasinas* v *Lithuania* Application No 44558/98 (unreported) 24 July 2001 (applicant made to strip naked and have his sexual organs touched in front of a woman); *Iwanczuk* v *Poland* Application No 25196/94 (unreported) 15 November 2001 (applicant ordered to strip naked and subjected to humiliating abuse by guards when he tried to exercise his right to vote in facilities provided in prison); *Lorsé* v *The Netherlands* Application No 52750/99 (unreported) 4 February 2003 (applicant strip searched weekly over six years in high security wing without sufficient security justification).
>
> Article 8 is more difficult. Buxton LJ thought . . . that the Wainwrights would have had a strong case for relief under section 7 if the 1998 Act had been in force. Speaking for myself, I am not so sure. Although Article 8 guarantees a right of privacy, I do not think that it treats that right as having been invaded and requiring a remedy in damages, irrespective of whether the defendant acted intentionally, negligently or accidentally. It is one thing to wander carelessly into the wrong hotel bedroom and another to hide in the wardrobe to take photographs. Article 8 may justify a monetary remedy for an intentional invasion of privacy by a public authority, even if no damage is suffered other than distress for which damages are not ordinarily recoverable. It does not follow that a merely negligent act should, contrary to general principle, give rise to a claim for damages for distress because it affects privacy rather than some other interest like bodily safety.
>
> Be that as it may, a finding that there was a breach of Article 8 will only demonstrate that there was a gap in the English remedies for invasion of privacy which has since been filled by sections 6 and 7 of the 1997 Act. It does not require that the courts should provide an alternative remedy which distorts the principles of the common law.

The House of Lords here were unwilling to extend the tort beyond claims for indirectly inflicted physical and recognised psychiatric injury. The concern was that to do so would be to open the floodgates to litigation from people who were the victims of things said with the intention of causing distress and humiliation.

The difficulties here are created by the different requirements of different torts. These actions cannot be brought in trespass because of the requirements of direct and physical conduct. If they are brought under the *Wilkinson* v *Downton* principle then they run into the difficulty of proving the necessary physical damage. This treatment effectively subsumes the rule within the law on the negligent infliction of nervous shock, although Lord Hoffmann left the way open for the creation of a tort of intention but not one based on imputed intention.

The facts of *Wainwright* arose before the Human Rights Act 1998 came into force and it may be that the prison authorities could have had a duty as a public authority to respect the claimant's privacy under Article 8. If this was the case it would raise a problem as this would affect the general principle that there is no liability for negligent conduct causing distress falling short of a recognised psychiatric illness.

Harassment

One possible development of *Wilkinson* v *Downton* could generally be described as *harassment*. This is the area to which Lord Hoffmann was referring when he stated in *Wainwright*:

In institutions and workplaces all over the country, people constantly do and say things with the intention of causing distress and humiliation to others. This shows lack of consideration and appalling manners but I am not sure that the right way to deal with it is always by litigation.

A remedy has been granted in respect of claimants being harassed by unwanted telephone calls. The introduction of the Protection from Harassment Act 1997 creates criminal offences and civil remedies in respect of harassment. Harassment is not defined by the Act, but it will catch cases such as *Khorasandjian v Bush* [1993] 3 WLR 476, where the harassment does not cause the claimant to fear that violence will be used. There must be more than one act of harassment, as the Act refers to 'a course of conduct' (s 1(1)). A series of articles in a newspaper can amount to a course of conduct (*Thomas v News Group Newspapers Ltd* [2002] EMLR 4) and mental illness on the part of the defendant is not a defence. (*R v Colohan* [2001] 2 FLR 757.) It will be a defence that the conduct was pursued for the purpose of detecting a crime, under a legal requirement or was reasonable in the circumstances (s 1(3)).

If harassment is shown, the remedies available are damages and/or an injunction and the damages can cover anxiety and financial loss (s 3). Foreseeability of the injury or loss sustained by a claimant in a case of harassment is not an essential element in the cause of action. (*Jones v Ruth* [2012] 1 WLR 1495).)

An interesting use of the statutory action came in the following case:

Ferguson v British Gas Trading Ltd [2009] EWCA Civ 46

The claimant used to be customer of the defendant company and for a long time after she ceased to be a customer the defendant sent the claimant bill after bill and threatening letter after threatening letter. Nothing the claimant did could stop the letters or the bills. The threats were threefold in nature: namely, to cut off her gas supply, to start legal proceedings and to report her to credit rating agencies. The claimant wrote letter after letter pointing out that she had no account with the defendant and made telephone calls, with difficulties of getting through, but to no avail. Mainly, her letters received no response. Occasionally, she received apologies and assurances that the matter would be dealt with, but the bills and threats continued. The claimant made a complaint to 'Energy Watch', and she wrote to the chairman of the defendant twice, with no response. She claimed that she had wasted many hours and had been brought to a state of considerable anxiety, not knowing whether the 'gas man' would come at any time to cut her off, whether she would have legal proceedings served upon her or whether she would be, or had already been, reported to credit rating agencies. Even when her solicitor wrote on her behalf about an unjustified bill, no response was received. She brought civil proceedings claiming that the defendant's conduct amounted to unlawful harassment, contrary to the Protection from Harassment Act 1997. She intended to 'bring British Gas to book' and stated that it should 'not simply blame information technology'. The defendant contended that it had done nothing wrong and that the particulars of claim disclosed no reasonable ground for bringing the claim. It applied to strike out the claim. The judge refused the application. The defendant appealed.

It accepted that what it had done to the claimant amounted to a 'course of conduct' for the purposes of the Act. However, it contended that it was not enough even arguably to amount to harassment. It submitted that harassment was both a civil wrong and a crime, and so the impugned conduct had to be rather serious, so that otherwise merely annoying or aggravating matters of everyday life would be criminalised, which could not have been the intention of Parliament. It contended that the claimant had known that the claims and threats were unjustified. Moreover, it submitted that the correspondence had been computer generated and so the claimant should not have taken it as seriously as if it had come from an individual.

Held: The appeal would be dismissed.

A course of conduct had to be grave before the offence or tort of harassment was proved, and the only real difference between the crime and the tort was the standard of proof to be applied, namely, the balance of probabilities in the case of the tort, and the usual criminal standard in respect of the crime.

In the circumstances of the instant case, it could not be said that the impugned conduct was incapable of satisfying that test of gravity. On the contrary, it was strongly arguable that it did and one could reasonably conclude that the persistent and continued conduct pleaded was on the wrong side of the line, as amounting to 'oppressive and unacceptable conduct'. It would be entirely proper for a prosecutor such as trading standards to bring criminal proceedings in respect of a case where there had been such a period of persistent conduct and such threats as pleaded in the instant case.

What the defendant had been threatening was undoubtedly serious. It was absurd to say that the claimant had known the claims and threats were unjustified. A victim of harassment would almost always know that it was unjustified.

As to the suggestion that the correspondence was computer generated, real people were responsible for programming and entering material into the computer. It was the defendant's system which, at the very least, had allowed the impugned conduct to happen. Moreover, the threats and demands were to be read by a real person, not by a computer. A real person was likely to suffer real anxiety and distress if threatened in the way in which the claimant had been; and a real person was unlikely to take comfort from knowing that the claims and threats were unjustified or that they were sent by a computer system.

The Court of Appeal has stated that the Act has rendered it unnecessary to develop a common law tort of harassment. (***Wong v Parkside NHS Trust*** [2003] 3 All ER 932.)

? Question

Alan was invited to a party by Bob. Christine, one of the guests, dressed up as a ghost and jumped out at Alan, who was of a nervous disposition. Alan passed out, and was carried into a spare bedroom by David, another guest. Some time later Bob saw that the bedroom door was open and, without looking inside, locked the door, as the room contained his priceless collection of country and western records. David and Christine later went to see if Alan was all right but found the door locked. They asked Bob for the key, but he refused as he was busy tuning his banjo. One hour later he opened the door. Alan was still unconscious, but as Bob poured cold water over him, he swung his fist in a reflex action and knocked some of Bob's teeth out.

What torts, if any, have been committed and which defences do you consider to be relevant?

Suggested approach

With a question of this nature it is best to take each incident separately. Start by defining the three relevant torts.

With the ghost incident, two torts may have been committed. Could there be an action under the principle in ***Wilkinson v Downton***? There has been an intentional act without lawful justification but has Alan suffered damage? If he suffered nervous shock, then yes. Likewise, if he received physical injuries. Otherwise the decision in ***Wainwright*** would block such an action. There may be an action in assault. The advantage of this tort is that it does not require damage (actionable *per se*). Was Alan placed in immediate fear of a battery?

When David carries Alan is there a battery? If there is a requirement of hostile intent, then no, as the act is performed for Alan's benefit. If hostility is not required for the tort then David will need to find a defence. This could be implied consent or necessity.

Placing Alan in the room does not constitute false imprisonment as there is a means of escape through an unlocked door. When Bob locks the door, does he commit false imprisonment? He is unaware of anyone's presence in the room and cannot have intended to commit the tort. Was he negligent in not checking and can the tort be committed negligently? Recent case law on state of mind in trespass has concentrated on battery, but it appears that the tort can only be committed intentionally. If this is the case in false imprisonment, the tort would appear not to have been committed.

Does Bob commit the tort when he refuses to open the door? This raises the question of whether false imprisonment can be committed by an omission. See *Herd* v *Weardale*.

Does Bob commit a battery when he pours water on Alan? Again consider the question of hostility. If this element is not required then Bob would appear to have committed a battery. He could defend on the grounds of either implied consent or necessity.

Alan's punch would appear not to be a battery as he does not intend to do the act. His action is similar to an epileptic striking a person during a fit.

Summary

This chapter deals with the tort of trespass to the person and the rule in *Wilkinson* v *Downton*.

- Trespass to the person covers the actions for battery, assault and false imprisonment.

- Trespasses have certain features. They are actionable without proof of damage; the act must be direct and physical; the action requires either intention or (possibly) negligence on the part of the defendant.

- Battery is the direct and intentional application of force to another person without consent. The Court of Appeal in *Wilson* v *Pringle* attempted to introduce a requirement of 'hostile intent' into the tort but this has not proved popular and certainly does not apply in medical cases. (*F* v *West Berkshire Health Authority*.) There must be some contact.

- Assault is an act which causes another person to apprehend the infliction of immediate force. The claimant must have been in reasonable apprehension of an immediate battery. Words alone cannot amount to an assault but they may negative what would otherwise have been one.

- Defences to assault and battery include consent and self-defence.

- False imprisonment is the unlawful imposition of constraint on another's freedom of movement. The restraint must be total and it is not necessary that the claimant was aware that he was being detained. The restraint must be unlawful and the tort is not committed where a lawful arrest takes place.

- The rule in *Wilkinson* v *Downton* is where a person intentionally performs an act with the intention of causing physical damage to another and does cause such damage. The rule has had little success in England. The development of rules of negligence on psychiatric damage and the legislation on harassment have left it little scope for operation.

Further reading

Cane, P. (2000), 'Mens Rea in Tort Law' 20 OJLS 533.

Cooke, R. (1994), 'A Development in the Tort of Private Nuisance' 57 MLR 289.

Lunney, M. (2002), 'Practical Joking and its Penalty: *Wilkinson* v *Downton* in context' 10(3) *Tort Law Review* 168.

Tan, K. F. (1981), 'A Misconceived Issue in the Law of Tort' 44 MLR 166. (Trespass and civil liberties – *Herd* and *Robinson*.)

Trinidade, F. A. (1982), 'International Torts: Some Thoughts on Assault and Battery' 2 OJLS 211. (Characteristics of a trespass action.)

21

Defamation

Objectives

After reading this chapter you will:

1. Have a critical knowledge of the role of the jury in a defamation action.
2. Appreciate the distinction between libel and slander.
3. Understand the legal rules governing an action in defamation.
4. Have a critical knowledge of the public interest defence.
5. Appreciate the role played by human rights, particularly freedom of speech.

Introduction

The torts of libel and slander are collectively known as defamation and protect a person's interest in their reputation. Defamation presents particular problems, as any law which protects reputation will also impinge on freedom of speech. A good law should draw a balance between these competing interests. The English law on defamation has historically been criticised for favouring protection of reputation at the expense of freedom of speech, and adverse comparisons have been drawn with the law in the United States, where freedom of speech is protected by the constitution. Any protection which is given to freedom of speech in England is provided by the defences to defamation (see 'Freedom of speech' below) and Article 10 of the European Convention on Human Rights. A preliminary point for students to note is that these are as important as the requirements for the claimant's case. A frequent error in defamation answers is to ignore the defences.

Example

A newspaper publishes a story which states that it would be impossible for a cyclist to win the Tour de France without taking performance-enhancing drugs. They are sued for libel by the winner of the previous Tour de France.

In the libel action the court must establish whether the statement was defamatory. (And in what sense.) Did the defamatory statement refer to the claimant and was it published by the defendant?

> If this is proved then to avoid liability the defendant must prove that the statement was true (if factual) or an honest comment (if opinion) or covered by privilege.
>
> The issues at stake here are the cyclist's reputation balanced against freedom of speech. The freedom of speech issue is the public interest in the fair conduct of sport.

Reform

Defamation is a controversial subject and there have been frequent attempts to reform it. Two factors have driven reform recently. The first is the influence of human rights through the Human Rights Act 1998, which places a greater emphasis on freedom of speech based on Article 10 of the European Convention on Human Rights. The second is the change in methods of communicating. Most of the current law on defamation was created in the era when the printed word was the chief method of communication. The advent of the internet and social media has changed the landscape and the law now faces of the challenge of adapting.

The most recent reform is the Defamation Act 2013 which came into force on 1 January 2014. Commentators generally think that the legislation does not make major changes to the law so the old law is still relevant.

Features of defamation

Jury trial

Objective 1

Historically, defamation was usually tried by jury. The use of a jury has gradually been eroded. The Defamation Act 1996 introduced a new summary procedure for defamation actions whereby a judge alone would decide whether the case should be heard summarily or go to a full jury trial. The advantages of the summary procedure are an opportunity for an early clarification of the issues and to test the strength of both claim and defence. However, the maximum amount of damages recoverable through the summary procedure is £10,000. There is currently a recommendation to increase this to £20,000.

The Defamation Act 2013 s 11 abolishes the presumption in favour of jury trials on the basis of decreasing costs. A judge is still able to order a jury trial. It is envisaged that this will be limited to cases involving senior figures in public life where their public credibility is at stake.

Many of the cases discussed in this chapter were tried by jury and some of the law involved which questions were for the judge and which for the jury. In the light of the virtual demise of the jury it should be remembered that these questions are now usually for the judge alone.

Death of claimant

A person's reputation does not survive their death and a defamation action will terminate on the death of the claimant.

Libel tourism

Concerns have been expressed about 'libel tourism' where cases with a tenuous link to England and Wales are brought in this jurisdiction. There appears to be a perception that

English courts have become the forum of choice for those who wish to sue for libel and that this has a chilling effect on freedom of expression. For example, a Russian newspaper publishes an article which is possibly defamatory. The paper sells a million copies in Russia and 50 in England. The claimant commences libel proceedings in London. The allegedly claimant-friendly libel laws in England have led to some jurisdictions refusing to enforce judgments in their own jurisdictions. However, evidence suggests that not a great number of libel claims are actually brought by such people but that threats of litigation have the effect of stifling investigative journalism.

In the United States the SPEECH (Securing the Protection of our Enduring and Established Constitutional Heritage) Act was passed in 2010 to prevent foreign libel judgments being enforced in the United States.

In cases where the defendant is not domiciled in a member state, English courts have at common law a discretion to decline to assume jurisdiction.

Any change to the law has to take into account European legislation on jurisdictional matters. The victim of a libel in a newspaper article distributed in several contracting states in the European Union can bring an action in the place where the publisher of the defamatory statement is established (which has the jurisdiction to award damages for all the harm caused) or in any state in which the publication was distributed. (*Shevill* v *Presse Alliance* [1998] 2 AC 18.)

The Defamation Act 2013 s 9 changes the law so that a court does not have jurisdiction to hear a claim to which the section applies unless it is satisfied that, of all the places in which the statement complained of has been published, England and Wales is clearly the most appropriate jurisdiction in which to bring an action in respect of the statement. Whilst this appears sensible, it is easy to see that in an age of global business and media conglomerates its application to the facts may not always be straightforward. One test could be to assess the harm caused in this country against that caused in other jurisdictions.

Actionable *per se*

Libel was historically actionable *per se* (without proof of damage). If a statement could be shown to be defamatory then it was presumed that the claimant had suffered damage. From case law it appears that the courts have power to strike a case out if it does not pass a 'threshold of seriousness' and there needs to be a 'real and substantial wrong'. (*Thornton* v *Telegraph Media Group Ltd* [2010] EWHC 1414; *Jameel* v *Dow Jones & Co* [2005] EWCA Civ 75.)

The Defamation Act 2013 s 1 provides that a statement is not defamatory unless its publication has caused or is likely to cause 'serious or substantial harm'. Any case which failed to make this threshold should be struck out at an early stage.

The new test may be significant in relation to claims for defamation published on the internet. The courts appear to take the view that publication, for example in chat rooms, does not have the gravity of a libel in written form. The likelihood is that defendants will increasingly argue that in certain instances not too much weight should be attached to what appears on the internet and that the threshold of serious harm is not triggered.

In the case of a body which trades for profit 'serious harm' means serious financial loss (s 1(2)). In practice, proving such financial loss is likely to be very difficult for companies. The mere fact that the company's share price may have fallen is insufficient.

Is libel still actionable *per se*?

Cost of bringing an action

A frequent criticism of defamation is that it is only available as a remedy to the wealthy as legal aid is not available. This was challenged in **Steel & Morris** v **United Kingdom** (2005) 18 BHRC 545, and the European Court of Human Rights held that in complex cases assistance should be provided.

It has been calculated that the cost of libel actions is 140 times higher than the European average. (*A Comparative Study in Defamation Proceedings Across Europe*, Centre for Socio-Legal Studies, University of Oxford (2009).)

However, it is possible to litigate in defamation by using a conditional fee arrangement, or 'no win no fee', whereby a 'success fee' is added to the lawyer's costs. Such an arrangement is not a breach of Article 10. (**Campbell** v **Mirror Group Newspapers Ltd (No 2)** [2005] 4 All ER 793.)

The issue of cost is a complex one and applies right across the civil justice system. In the particular context of defamation one of the objectives of the 2013 Act is to bring down costs by simplifying procedures.

It may be possible to get round the lack of legal aid for defamation by bringing some other action.

Joyce v Sengupta [1993] 1 WLR 337

A false allegation was made that the claimant had stolen letters belonging to the Princess Royal and given them to a national newspaper. The claimant sued for malicious falsehood, for which legal aid is available. The Court of Appeal refused to strike out the claim as an abuse of the process of the court.

Damages

In cases where a jury is used in a defamation action it is the jury that determines the award of damages to the claimant. English defamation law fell into disrepute in the 1980s, when excessive amounts of damages were awarded in some cases. The problem was compounded by the fact that the Court of Appeal had no power to amend a jury decision on quantum and had to order a new trial which (if only on the grounds of costs) would be disadvantageous to the parties. This situation was changed by statute in 1990 and the Court of Appeal now has the power to substitute an award of damages instead of ordering a new trial in cases where the damages awarded by a jury are excessive or inadequate. (Courts and Legal Services Act 1990 s 8.) However, awards still tended to be high in comparison with awards for personal injuries and it was held by the European Court of Human Rights that one award of £1.5 million contravened Article 10 (freedom of speech) of the European Convention on Human Rights. (**Tolstoy Miloslavsky** v **United Kingdom** [1996] EMLR 152.)

To counter this criticism there is now a ceiling on general damages of £200,000 with a generous margin to be left at the upper end of the scale to accommodate more serious libels. (**Campbell** v **Newsgroup Newspapers** [2002] All ER (D) 513 (Jul).) There will inevitably be some libels which are so serious that the upper limit will have to be breached but the perceived advantage of the limit is to give greater clarity and consistency so that the consequences of conduct can be said to be 'prescribed by law' and will encourage settlement. To encourage jury compliance with realistic figures the modern practice is for the judge to give guidance to the jury. The guidance will usually consist of: awards approved or substituted by the Court of Appeal; awards made in personal injuries cases for pain and suffering; a suggested 'bracket' considered appropriate by the judge.

John v MGM Ltd [1996] EMLR 229

Elton John was awarded £75,000 in general damages and £275,000 in exemplary damages. These sums were reduced by the Court of Appeal to £25,000 and £50,000 respectively. The Court of Appeal directed that guidance on damages should be given in the future to juries. This guidance should make juries aware of awards approved or substituted by the Court of Appeal, damages usually awarded in personal injury cases for pain, suffering and loss and a figure or a range of damages considered appropriate by the judge of a case.

The unpredictability of a damages award by a jury in defamation cases was one factor which dissuaded settlement of the action and encouraged 'gold digging' claimants to bring and continue proceedings. The virtual abolition of the jury by the 2013 Act means that damages will almost always be awarded by a judge.

Jury verdict

In cases where a jury is used in a libel action, an appeal court is extremely reluctant to overturn a jury verdict on the grounds that it is perverse.

Grobbelaar v News Group Newspapers Ltd [2002] 1 WLR 3024

The claimant was a professional footballer who was accused of accepting bribes from a person in pursuance of a corrupt agreement and letting in goals. The jury found for the claimant and awarded £85,000 in damages. The Court of Appeal found that the jury verdict was perverse and quashed it. The House of Lords held that they had been wrong to quash the verdict as the verdict of the jury was on the basis that he had not let any goals in, which was the sting of the libel, but the claimant was a person shown to have no reputation worthy of legal protection and the award of damages was reduced to £1. The difference between finding a jury verdict perverse and reducing a jury award of damages was stressed.

Lord Bingham:

> The oracular utterance of the jury contains no reasoning, no elaboration. But it is not immune from review. The jury is a judicial decision-maker of a very special kind, but it is a judicial decision-maker nonetheless. While speculation about the jury's reasoning and train of thought is impermissible, the drawing of inevitable or proper inferences from the jury's decision is not, and is indeed inherent in the process of review.

Lord Hobhouse:

> Many juries would in these circumstances make a substantial award of damages. An award of £85,000 is within the range of awards which a jury might erroneously think appropriate. It is wrong to treat it as evidence of perversity. The conclusion that a jury has acted perversely, that is to say in breach of their oath, is a serious matter and not lightly to be inferred. If there is another more plausible explanation of their verdict, it should certainly be preferred. To assume perversity unworthily discredits an integral and honourable part of the justice system.

Lord Millett:

> In my view an appellate court ought not to find the verdict of a jury on liability to be perverse unless there is no rational explanation for it. There is not the same constraint against finding an award of damages to be excessive.

Lord Phillips in **Spiller v Joseph** [2010] UKSC 53 has stated (prophetically):

> Finally, and fundamentally, has not the time come to recognize that defamation is no longer a field in which trial by jury is desirable? The issues are often complex and jury trial simply invites expensive interlocutory battles, such as the one before this court, which attempt to preempt issues going before the jury.

Libel and slander

Objective 2

A defamatory meaning can be conveyed by any medium, but it is the choice of medium which determines whether an action lies in slander or libel. If the defamatory meaning is conveyed in a permanent form, then the action is in libel. If it is in a temporary form, then slander. Modern technology has created difficulties in drawing the distinction, but there are some established examples of each tort.

Libel is committed where writing or printing is used. The placing of a wax effigy in the chamber of horrors by mistake has also been stated as libel. (**Monson v Tussauds Ltd** [1894] 1 QB 671.)

Youssoupoff v Metro-Goldwyn-Mayer Pictures Ltd (1934) 50 TLR 581

The defendants made a film which falsely imputed that the claimant had been raped or seduced by Rasputin. The defamatory matter was in the pictorial (as opposed to the soundtrack) part of the picture and was held to be libel. It must therefore be regarded as unsettled whether a defamatory soundtrack is libellous or slanderous.

Slander is generally committed by speech or gestures.

Certain areas are settled by statute. The Defamation Act 1952 s 1 provides that words or visual images broadcast for general reception are libel. This will cover BBC, ITV and other commercial broadcasts, but not police radio or CB broadcasts. The Theatres Act 1968 provides that the publication of words in the course of performance of a play shall be treated as libel. Some areas are still uncertain, such as reading aloud letters, sky writing, gramophone records and sign language.

The importance of the distinction

See Chapter 1 for torts actionable per se.

There are two important distinctions between libel and slander.

A libel which tends to provoke a breach of the peace is a crime. Slander is only tortious.

Libel has historically been actionable *per se* (without proof of actual damage) There is now a requirement of 'serious damage' under the Defamation Act 2013 and in the case of bodies trading for a profit damage must be shown. (Defamation Act 2013 s 1). Slander is actionable only on proof of actual damage, except in the following circumstances.

1 *Imputation of a criminal offence.* The offence must be punishable with imprisonment, but a specific offence need not be mentioned. 'I know enough to put you in gaol', is therefore a slander actionable *per se*.

2 *Imputation of unfitness or incompetence.* This exception relates to allegations of unfitness, incompetence or dishonesty in any profession, trade, calling or business held or carried on by the claimant.

There were previously two further exceptions – *imputation of a disease* and under the Slander of Women Act 1891 *imputation of unchastity or adultery to any woman or girl*. The Defamation Act 2013 s 14 repeals the Slander of Women Act 1891 and the exception on the grounds of contagious or infectious disease on the grounds that they are outdated and potentially discriminatory.

The Defamation Act 1952 s 2 states:

> In an action for slander in respect of words calculated to disparage the plaintiff in any office, profession, calling, trade or business held or carried on by him at the time of the publication, it shall not be necessary to allege or prove special damage, whether or not the words are spoken of the plaintiff in the way of his office, profession, calling, trade or business.

The effect of this section is that it is no longer necessary for the words to slander the claimant in the context of their office provided that the words are likely to injure them within it.

The claimant's case

Objective 3

In order to establish an action in defamation the claimant must prove three things:

1 that the words were defamatory and caused serious harm to the claimant;

2 that they referred to themselves;

3 that they were published by the defendant.

Defamatory meaning

As it is impossible to produce a list of words which are defamatory, there needs to be a general test which can be applied to the alleged defamatory statement. It is important to remember that the words must be taken in the context in which they were used and that words change their meaning over time. In the past it has been held to be defamatory to call a person a German or a Catholic. Neither of these words would now carry a defamatory meaning. Until recently, the word 'gay' had a universally complimentary meaning. To describe a person as gay today might be to invite proceedings for defamation.

The most generally accepted definition of a defamatory statement is that of Winfield: 'Defamation is the publication of a statement which tends to lower a person in the estimation of right thinking members of society generally; or which tends to make them shun or avoid that person.'

Three things should be noted at this stage.

1 Defamation is essentially an attack on reputation. If a person says that a businessman runs his business dishonestly or incompetently, this is defamatory. But, if it is stated that the business has closed down, this is not defamatory, although financial loss may be caused. (An action may lie in malicious falsehood.) Likewise, it is not defamatory to say that a pop star has joined a closed order of monks, as this will not affect his reputation, although it may affect his bookings.

2 Defamation need not impute moral turpitude. This is shown by the *Youssoupoff* case and cases where it has been held to be defamatory to allege insanity.

3 Words have to be interpreted in their context and the claimant is not allowed to select passages which are prima facie libellous if the passage taken as a whole is not defamatory. This is apparent in the relationship between newspaper headlines and articles.

Charleston v News Group Newspapers [1995] 2 All ER 313

The defendant newspaper published two photographs in which the heads of the claimants, an actor and actress who played the parts of a husband and wife in a TV serial, were superimposed on the bodies of two people engaged in intercourse or sodomy. On the same page there was a photograph in which the first claimant's head was superimposed on a woman dressed in a tight leather outfit with a headline: 'Strewth! What's Harold up to with our Madge?' A smaller headline read: 'Porn Shocker for Neighbours Stars'. The captions under the photographs and the text made it clear that the photographs had been produced as part of a pornographic computer game in which the claimant's faces had been used without their knowledge or consent and described them as victims.

The claimants alleged that the photographs and headlines were libellous in their ordinary and natural meaning that they had posed for pornographic photographs. This meaning was dismissed for two reasons.

A prominent headline or photograph could not found a claim in libel in isolation from the related text of an accompanying article which was not defamatory when considered as a whole, because it was contrary to: (a) the law of libel for the claimant to sever, and rely on, an isolated defamatory passage in an article if other parts of the article negated the effect of the libel; and (b) the principle that if no legal innuendo was alleged then the single natural and ordinary meaning to be ascribed to the words of an allegedly defamatory publication was the meaning which the words taken as a whole conveyed to the mind of the ordinary, reasonable, fair-minded reader. Accordingly, a claimant could not rely on a defamatory meaning conveyed only to a limited category of readers who only read headlines.

Function of judge and jury

Where a defamation case is tried by judge and jury, the judge's functions are:

1 to direct the jury on the legal meaning of defamation;

2 if the judge thought that no reasonable person could regard the words as defamatory, the case had to be withdrawn from the jury; and

3 if the words were obviously defamatory, then the judge could indicate to the jury that the evidence could not bear any other interpretation.

Every defamation action must come before a judge at an early stage so that they can decide whether it is suitable for disposal under summary procedure or if it must go for a full trial. The summary procedure enables a judge to dismiss weak claims if they think that no reasonable person would regard the words as defamatory. In the case of strong claims, they may make an award of up to £10,000 in the claimant's favour if they feel this would provide adequate compensation. This limit is likely to be raised to £20,000 in the near future.

The judge may decide that a claim must go for a full trial if there is an arguable defence or that the claimant will not be adequately compensated through the summary procedure. The judge may also refer cases which involve complex issues or where the allegations are considered too grave to be dealt with by the summary procedure.

It is possible to apply on a preliminary application for a judge to fix before trial the *permissible* meanings of the allegedly defamatory words, so as to ascertain the degree of injury to the claimant's reputation and to evaluate any defences raised.

Mapp v *News Group Newspapers Ltd* [1998] 2 WLR 260

The headline 'Drug Quiz Cop Kills Himself' and an article on a police sergeant who had committed suicide after being ordered to give information on eight police officers alleged to have been involved in drug dealing was held to be incapable of bearing the meaning of imputing guilt to the officers. There were various meanings a reasonable reader could ascribe to the words.

The case illustrates the importance of the distinction between imputations of guilt and statements of reasonable suspicion of guilt. The words complained of were merely statements of suspicion, and the reference to the suicide did not transform these into imputations of guilt. (See *Lewis* v *Daily Telegraph*, below.)

If a case goes for a full trial, then whether the words are in fact defamatory is a question for the jury if there is one.

Capital and Counties Bank Ltd v *Henty* (1882) 7 App Cas 741

The defendants had a disagreement with the managers of the claimant bank and sent out a circular telling their customers they would not take cheques drawn on the claimant bank. The claimants contended that the circular implied insolvency on their part. It was held that the circular taken in conjunction with the circumstances in which it was published did not constitute evidence from which reasonable persons would infer the imputation. There was therefore no case to go before a jury. If more than one defamatory meaning is alleged then the judge must rule whether the words are capable of bearing each, and, if so, which, of those meanings.

Lewis v *Daily Telegraph* [1964] AC 234

The defendant newspaper stated that the fraud squad were investigating the affairs of a company and named the chairman, one of the claimants. The claimants alleged that the statement meant not only that the company was being investigated for fraud but also that they were guilty of fraud. The House of Lords held that the statement was not capable of bearing that alternative meaning. To have ruled otherwise would have meant that crime investigations could not be reported. (See also *Stern* v *Piper* [1996] 3 All ER 385; *Mapp* v *News Group Newspapers Ltd*.)

Clearly, a case can be shaped and defined by the permissible meaning or meanings that a judge determines that the words can have. An example is where a person is accused of having committed some illegal act. There are three levels of defamatory meaning that can be attached ('chase' meanings). In descending levels of seriousness these are: that the claimant is guilty of the accusation; that there are reasonable grounds to suspect him; that there are grounds for investigating whether the claimant has been responsible for such an act. The way in which a story will be written will depend on the nature of the evidence available to prove justification. If the media have conclusive evidence of guilt then an accusation of guilt can be made. Where they do not, a formula is frequently used of referring to 'questions which need answering'. If the formula is successful the defendant can draw the 'sting' of the libel by justifying this meaning. If the judge excludes this meaning, the defendant's task in justification is much more difficult.

The principles on defamatory meaning were helpfully summarised in *Jeynes* v *News Magazines Ltd* [2008] EWCA Civ 130:

The governing principles relevant to meaning . . . may be summarised in this way:

(1) The governing principle is reasonableness.
(2) The hypothetical reasonable reader is not naïve but he is not unduly suspicious. He can read between the lines. He can read in an implication more readily than a lawyer and may indulge in a certain amount of loose thinking but he must be treated as being a man who is not avid for scandal and someone who does not, and should not, select one bad meaning where other non-defamatory meanings are available.
(3) Over-elaborate analysis is best avoided.
(4) The intention of the publisher is irrelevant.
(5) The article must be read as a whole, and any 'bane and antidote' taken together.
(6) The hypothetical reader is taken to be representative of those who would read the publication in question.
(7) In delimiting the range of permissible defamatory meanings, the court should rule out any meaning which, 'can only emerge as the produce of some strained, or forced, or utterly unreasonable interpretation . . .'.
(8) It follows that 'it is not enough to say that by some person or another the words might be understood in a defamatory sense'.

Innuendo

Words may be self-evidently defamatory or defamatory in the light of additional facts or circumstances known only to the persons to whom the words are published. Where the words are alleged to have this hidden meaning, this is known as an innuendo. The claimant must specifically plead the meaning they attribute to the words used and must prove the existence of facts to support that meaning.

A distinction is drawn between the false innuendo and the true innuendo. The former is where the claimant pleads that the words in their natural and ordinary meaning have a particular meaning which can be discovered without the need for additional evidence. An example of the false innuendo is ***Lewis v Daily Telegraph*** (see above).

Allsop v Church of England Newspaper Ltd [1972] 2 QB 161

> The claimant was a well-known broadcaster. The defendant newspaper referred to his 'pre-occupation with the bent'. The claimant sued on the ordinary meaning of the word 'bent'. It was held that as the word was used as slang in the context of pornography, its meaning was not precise and the claimant had to plead all the meaning he claimed to be inherent in the words.

The 'true' innuendo is where extrinsic evidence (outside of the publication) needs to be introduced in order to establish defamatory meaning.

Identifying possible innuendoes is one of the most difficult tasks facing a defamation lawyer. The following cases are illustrations.

Tolley v Fry & Sons Ltd [1931] AC 333

> The claimant was a well-known amateur golfer. The defendants, without the claimant's knowledge, produced an advertisement using the claimant to show that their chocolate was as good as his golfing ability. The claimant sued for libel. The innuendo was that he had accepted money for the advertisement and thereby lost his amateur status.
>
> The extrinsic factors here were that people would know that the claimant was an amateur golfer and would lose his amateur status if he accepted money for playing golf.

Cassidy v *Daily Mirror Newspapers Ltd* [1929] 2 KB 331

The defendants published a picture of a couple, with a caption, stating that it was Mr *C* and Miss *X*, whose engagement had just been announced. Mrs *C* sued for libel, claiming that people who knew them would interpret the article as meaning she was not married to Mr *C*. The claimant's action succeeded.

The extrinsic factors here were that people who knew Mrs *C* would think that she had been living in sin as married people do not normally get engaged.

Byrne v *Deane* [1937] 1 KB 818

Police raided a golf club and took away an illegal fruit machine. A verse appeared on the club notice-board: 'but he who gave the game away may he byrne in hell and rue the day.' The claimant sued the golf club, alleging that the verse imputed that he had informed the police. The action failed, as the statement would not lower the claimant in the eyes of right-thinking members of society, who would have informed the police of the commission of a criminal offence.

The case is useful for a number of reasons. Firstly on defamatory meaning. Secondly, on publication (the golf club). Thirdly, on innuendo.

Baturina v *Times Newspapers* [2011] EWCA Civ 308

The defendant newspaper published an article which stated that the claimant (the wife of the mayor of Moscow) had purchased an expensive house in London through a front company. The claimant submitted that Russian citizens would realise that, as the wife of the mayor of Moscow, she would be obliged to comply with a declaration issued by the Russian president in May 2009, requiring all officials and civil servants of the Russian Federation to make information available as to their assets and income. She submitted that Russian readers of the article who were aware of the declaration would conclude that she had used the front company to hide her interest in the property.

The Court of Appeal held: it was not necessary for the evidence which made the apparently innocent statement defamatory to be known to the person who wrote the allegedly defamatory statement; the claimant would be required to specify the persons who had the particular knowledge required from which they could draw the defamatory meaning.

This was an early stage of the case and the court noted that there were 400,000 Russians in England and Wales. The claimant would be required at trial to identify readers of the article in England and Wales who understood the innuendo being made. A critical question would be whether a sensible reader of the article would have considered that the claimant had declined to list the property dishonestly rather than merely selectively. The meaning and effect of the published words would have to be decided by the court rather than the claimant producing a series of witnesses to say what they had made of the publication.

Linked publications

Can the claimant put together a defamation action from two or more publications?

Hayward v Thompson [1981] 3 WLR 471

In the first article, the defendants stated that the police had the names of two more people associated with the 'Scott' affair and that one was a wealthy benefactor of the Liberal party. The affair referred to was an alleged murder plot. The second article, a week later, named the claimant and stated that the police wanted to interview him. The claimant was a wealthy man who had given large sums of money to the Liberal party. The Court of Appeal upheld the trial judge's ruling that the jury could look at the second article to see to whom the first article referred.

Reference to the claimant

It is essential that the defendant's statement is shown to refer to the claimant. The defendant need not have intended the statement to refer to the claimant, provided that people who know the claimant understand that they were pointed at by the words used. It is not necessary that everybody should know that the claimant was referred to, provided that reasonable people knowing the claimant would believe that they were referred to. The reference may be latent rather than express.

There are a number of recurring situations which raise problems in this area.

The fictional name

What is the position where the defendant uses a name for a character who is supposed to be fictional and a real person with the same name claims to have been defamed?

Hulton & Co v Jones [1910] AC 20

The defendants published an article containing defamatory statements of 'Artemus Jones', a church-warden from Peckham. The article was alleged to be fictitious. A barrister named Artemus Jones from North Wales sued for libel as some of his friends thought that the article referred to him. The defendants were held liable although they had not intended to defame the claimant.

Two people with the same name or picture

What is the position where the statement is intended to refer to one person but another person with the same name claims that it refers to them?

Newstead v London Express Newspapers Ltd [1940] 1 KB 377

Harold Newstead, a 30-year-old unmarried hairdresser of Camberwell, sued for libel in respect of a statement published by the defendants that Harold Newstead, a 30-year-old Camberwell man, had been convicted of bigamy. The statement was true of one Harold Newstead, but clearly not of the claimant. The defendants were held liable.

This is the reason why court reports always contain the address, age and occupation of the accused.

It should be noted that liability is strict. It does not matter that the defendant did not intend to refer to the claimant. However, this principle could amount to a breach of Article 10 of the European Convention on Human Rights, which defends freedom of expression.

O'Shea v *MGN Ltd* [2001] EMLR 40

An advert for an adults-only internet site contained a picture of a well-known glamour model. It was alleged that the picture was a look-alike of the claimant and was defamatory of her as it suggested she was promoting a pornographic website. The judge held that Article 10 applied as a form of expression. The strict liability principle at common law represented a restriction on freedom of expression and the question was whether this restriction could be justified under Article 10(2). To do this it needed to be necessary in a democratic society for the protection of the reputation of others. 'Necessary' meant that there had to be a pressing social need and the restriction had to be proportionate to the legitimate aim pursued. The judge concluded that there was no pressing social need as this was the first case on look-alike pictures. Strict liability did not apply to a look-alike picture as it would impose an impossible burden on a publisher if they were required to check whether a picture resembled someone else. It would be an unjustifiable interference with the defendant's right to freedom of expression and disproportionate to the legitimate aim of protecting freedom of expression. In the ***Newstead*** case it was possible to check and avoid liability by including sufficient information.

No person named

Where no person is named in the article but the claimant alleges that persons who know them think the article refers to themselves, can they succeed?

Morgan v *Odhams Press Ltd* [1971] 1 WLR 1239

A newspaper article alleged that a girl had been kidnapped by a dog-doping gang and kept at a house in Finchley. No one was mentioned by name in the article except the girl. At the relevant time the girl had been staying with the claimant in Willesden. The claimant sued for libel and called six witnesses who thought the article referred to the claimant. The House of Lords held there need be no key or pointer in the words themselves and that the claimant could introduce extrinsic evidence to show that he was referred to. On these facts there was sufficient material to leave to the jury. In determining the impression on the mind of the reader, regard should be had to the character of the article and the class of reader likely to read it.

For the situation where the defamatory material appears in one article and the claimant is identified in another, see *Hayward* v *Thompson* (above).

The Defamation Act 1996 (ss 2–4) now provides a procedure to enable cases of unintentional defamation to be resolved through an 'offer to make amends'. The person who has published a statement alleged to be defamatory of another may offer to make amends by publishing a suitable correction or an apology to the defamed person and to pay compensation and/or costs. Any offer of amends must be made before the serving of any defence and, if accepted, will end the defamation proceedings.

Non-acceptance of an offer of amends by an aggrieved party may be relied on in subsequent proceedings as a defence by the defendants. (See 'Defences' below.)

Class defamation

A statement may be defamatory of a class of people: for example, 'All doctors are quacks'. The question then arises as to whether any individual doctor may sue.

Knupffer v London Express Newspaper Ltd [1944] AC 116

The defendants published an article which referred to an émigré Russian movement and linked it with Fascism. The movement had a membership of about 2,000 and the United Kingdom branch had 24. The claimant, a Russian resident in London, sued for libel, alleging that the article referred to him. The House of Lords laid down that the crucial points were as follows:

1 Were the words published of the claimant, in the sense that he can be said to be personally pointed at?
2 Normally, where the statement is directed to a class of persons no individual belonging to that class is entitled to sue.
3 The words may be actionable if there is something which points to a particular claimant or claimants.
4 If the reference is to a small group, then each member of the group will be able to sue: for example, the trustees of a trust. This is if the words may be said to refer to each member.

The claimant's action failed as the words were defamatory of a class and there was nothing to point to him as an individual.

The law on class defamation is confusing and involves questions as to how small a group must be before each member may sue. The Court of Appeal has marked its disapproval of class defamation (*Orme* v *Associated Newspapers Ltd* (1981) Times, 4 February), and it may be preferable simply to apply the general rules on reference to the claimant.

Publication

Publication is the communication of words, pictures, visual images, gestures or any other method of signifying meaning to at least one person other than the person defamed. The defendant must be responsible for publication, either by publishing themselves or asking others to do so. Under the Defamation Act 1996 s 1, those having primary responsibility for publication have been defined as authors, editors and commercial publishers.

A person cannot be defamed in their own eyes, so the defendant will be liable only when they are responsible for the communication of defamatory material to a third party. It is the publication, not the composition, of the defamatory material that is the actionable wrong.

The publication need not consist of a positive act. If a person refrains from removing defamatory material from their premises they may be responsible for publication. An example of this can be seen in *Byrne* v *Deane* (see above), where the golf club were the appropriate defendants as they failed to remove the offending material.

A communication between husband and wife is not a publication as it is covered by privilege. If *H* says to *W* that *X* is a thief, *X* has no action against *H*. But if *X* says to *H* that *W* is a thief, then *W* will have an action against *X*.

The rules on publication can be illustrated by defamatory statements sent through the post. If *X* sends a letter to *Y* which is defamatory of *Y*, then *Y* will have no action. The only person who is entitled to open the letter is *Y*. If *Y* communicates the contents of the letter to a third party then it is *Y* who is responsible for the publication, not *X*. But if a statement is sent on a postcard then *Y* would have an action as there is a presumption that a postcard has been read during the course of its journey. A similar principle would apply if the defamatory material was on the envelope rather than in the letter.

Negligent publication

Where the defendant intends to publish the words about and concerning the claimant, there is no great difficulty with the publication requirement. But can the defendant be liable where the publication has occurred as a result of his negligence?

Theaker v *Richardson* [1962] 1 WLR 151

> The defendant and the claimant were members of a local council. The defendant wrote a letter which stated that the claimant was 'a lying, low down brothel keeping whore and thief'. The letter was sealed in an envelope and put through the claimant's letter box. The claimant's husband opened and read the letter, thinking that it was an election address. The jury found that the defendant anticipated that someone other than the claimant might open and read the letter and it was probable that the claimant's husband might do so. There had therefore been a publication and the defendant was liable.

Huth v *Huth* [1915] 3 KB 32

> The defendant posted a letter in an unsealed envelope to the claimant. The claimant's butler opened the envelope and read the letter. This was held not to amount to publication as the butler's behaviour was not a direct consequence of sending the letter.

If a defamatory letter sent to a businessperson is opened by their secretary, this would amount to publication. The way to avoid this would be to mark the letter 'Personal' or 'Private'.

Repetition

Every repetition of defamatory words is a fresh publication and creates a fresh cause of action against each successive publisher. Thus a libel which is printed will bring liability to the author, printer and publisher. In theory, this liability could extend to secondary publishers such as newsagents and booksellers. To mitigate the hardship that this would bring, the courts introduced the defence of innocent dissemination.

Vizetelly v *Mudie's Select Library Ltd* [1900] 2 QB 170

> The publishers of a book had asked for its return as it contained defamatory material. The defendants, who operated a circulating library, were held liable for allowing people to use the book after they had received the warning. The court stated that secondary publishers (distributors), relying on a defence of innocent dissemination, would not be liable if they could show that:
>
> 1 they were innocent of any knowledge of the libel contained in the work in question;
> 2 there was no reason for them to be aware that the work contained libellous material; and
> 3 they were not negligent in failing to know that the work was libellous.

The introduction of the statutory defence known as the 'distributor's defence' in the Defamation Act 1996 s 1 superseded but did not replace the common law defence of innocent dissemination. (*Metropolitan International Schools Ltd* v *Designtechnica Corporation* [2009] EWHC 1765.)

The 'distributor's defence' is available to printers, publishers, sellers and those involved in the production of film, audio and electronic publications. The new defence also takes account of defamatory material which might be outside the control of the broadcaster, for example, live television programmes.

The defence is not available to a defendant who knew that their act involved or contributed to a publication defamatory of the claimant and will only be available if the defendant had taken all reasonable care and had no reason to think that their act would have had a defamatory effect.

Godfrey v Demon Internet [1999] 4 All ER 342

An Internet Service Provider (ISP) was not the 'publisher' within the meaning of the Defamation Act 1996 s 1 of defamatory messages posted on a Usenet. The ISP was therefore entitled to use s 1. However, the defendant had been notified of the defamatory content of the messages and had not removed them. (within ten days) This was held to amount to a failure to exercise reasonable care when they knew (or had reason to believe) that what they had done had contributed to the publication of a defamatory statement. At common law their position was said to be similar to a library which allowed books to go out knowing they contained defamatory material.

Where the ISP is unaware of defamatory material they will not be a publisher. An internet service provider which performed no more than a passive role in facilitating postings on the internet could not be deemed to be a publisher at common law. (*Metropolitan International Schools Ltd* v *Designtechnica Corporation*.) It was essential to demonstrate a degree of awareness or at least an assumption of general responsibility, such as had long been recognised in the context of editorial responsibility, in order to impose legal responsibility under the common law for the publication of words. Although it was not always necessary to be aware of defamatory content to be liable for defamatory publication, there had to be knowing involvement in the process of publication of the relevant words. It was not enough that a person had played merely a passive instrumental role in the process. (*Bunt* v *Tilley* [2006] 3 All ER 336. See also *Tamiz* v *Google Inc* [2013] EWCA Civ 68.)

A notice attached to the material warning against treating it as the truth would normally suffice to remove any defamatory sting. (*Loutchansky* v *Times Newspapers (No 2)* [2002] 1 All ER 653.)

The single publication rule

Historically the principle in English law was that each publication gave rise to a separate cause of action. *Godfrey* raised a problem for newspapers and other media that maintain archives of their material. Such material would normally be available on the organisation's internet site. The Court of Appeal held that a claimant may sue for libel for material published on an internet site even if the action is brought more than one year after the initial publication This principle was held not to be in breach of Article 10 as it was not a disproportionate restriction on freedom of expression. Archive maintenance did have a social utility but this was a comparatively insignificant aspect of freedom of expression. This decision was supported by the European Court of Human Rights (*Times Newspapers Ltd (Nos 1 and 2)* v *United Kingdom* (2009) Times, 11 March), which held unanimously that a court's finding that Times Newspapers Ltd had libelled G.L. by the continued publication on its internet site of two articles was not a disproportionate restriction on the newspaper's freedom of expression, as guaranteed by Article 10 of the European Convention on Human Rights.

The Defamation Act 2013 s 8 states that the single publication rule should protect anyone who republishes the same material in a similar manner after it has been in the public domain for more than one year. This is unless the subsequent publication is substantially different in terms of prominence or extent of publication.

Libel and internet publication

The question of libel and the internet is an extremely complex one. From the point of view of the claimant there is a need to be able to identify the person responsible for the allegedly libellous statement and from the point of view of the defendant to reduce the pressure on hosts and service providers to take down material whenever it is challenged as being defamatory (in order to protect freedom of speech). There is also a need to encourage site owners to moderate content written by users.

Proposals for reform include:

1 Where complaint is received about allegedly defamatory material written by an identifiable author the service provider should publish a notice of complaint alongside that material. The notice reduces the sting of the alleged libel but protects free speech by not requiring the provider to take down what has been said.

2 The complainant to be able to apply to court for a take-down order. If this order is granted the material must be taken down or the service provider faces an action for libel.

3 Where the material is written by an unknown person then it should be taken down on receipt of a complaint unless the author responds positively to a request to identify themselves. In this case a notice of complaint should be attached. If the ISP believes there are significant public interest reasons for publishing – e.g. whistleblowers – it should have the right to apply to a judge for an exemption from the take-down order and secure a leave-up order. An ISP should not be liable for anonymous material if it has complied with these requirements.

The following reforms have been implemented:

Defamation Act 2013 s 5

s 5(2)
It is a defence for the operator of the website to show that they were not the person who posted the statement.

s 5(3)
(a) The defence is defeated if it is not possible for the claimant to identify the person who posted the statement. (sufficient to bring proceedings)
(b) The claimant gave the operator a notice of complaint about the statement and;
(c) The operator failed to respond to the notice of complaint.

Malice will defeat this defence.

Details of notices of complaint are to be laid down in a statutory instrument.

Defamation Act s 13

Where a claimant obtains a judgment for defamation the court can make an order to the operator of the website to remove the statement.

Example

Mary operates a political internet site. A posting on the site states that the Member of Parliament for the Utopia constituency has been involved in child pornography. The MP denies this and wishes to take action for libel. The first step would be to obtain the identity of the person who posted on the site and sue them as they are the publisher. Mary then has a defence under s 5. If the person cannot be identified, the MP must then give Mary a notice of complaint. If Mary fails to respond then the MP has an action for libel against Mary.

Repetition

A person who makes a defamatory statement may be liable for any damage caused by a reasonably foreseeable repetition of the libel by a third party.

Slipper v British Broadcasting Corp [1991] 1 QB 283

The claimant sued for libel in respect of a film which was broadcast by the defendants. The Court of Appeal refused to strike out his claim for damages arising from reviews of the film in the press which repeated the libel. The law on republication was said to be an aspect of *novus actus interveniens*. If the republication is unauthorised then prima facie the chain of causation is broken. On the facts the defendants could arguably foresee that the libel would be repeated in the reviews.

Defences

Defamation should be a balance between protection of reputation and freedom of speech. Such a balance as exists in England is given by the defences to defamation. There are four major defences, which are dealt with below. A few preliminary matters will be dealt with first.

Offer of amends

The 'offer of amends' procedure was introduced by the Defamation Act 1996 ss 2–4. Under this procedure a defendant may make an offer, in writing, to a claimant to publish an apology or correction and pay damages, even before a writ is served on them. The offer may be in relation to a statement generally or to a specific defamatory meaning within a statement, in which case it is called a 'qualified offer'. The offer must be made before a defence is served, however, because an offer cannot be made in conjunction with any other defence and will not succeed if the defendant seeks to rely on any other defence. If the offer is made before the claimant starts proceedings, then any future proceedings will be treated as a follow-up to the offer.

If the claimant accepts the offer, then the matter is settled by agreement between the parties and the court will intervene only if necessary, to adjudicate as to the amount of compensation due or on the nature of the apology or correction to be published by the defendant. Acceptance of an offer will terminate any defamation proceedings against a particular defendant in relation to a particular publication.

If the offer is not accepted by the claimant, then the defendant may withdraw the offer and issue a new offer, or they may let the offer stand and rely on the fact that an offer was made as a defence. A defendant may withdraw their offer altogether and choose instead to rely on another defence, for example, justification.

Consent

For consent (*volenti*) generally, see Chapter 10.

If the claimant has agreed to the publication then no action will lie.

Chapman v Lord Ellesmere [1932] 2 KB 431

A horse trainer's licence was granted subject to a condition that the licence might be withdrawn and that this would be published in the Racing Calendar. Such a publication was held not to be actionable as the claimant had consented to its publication.

Journalists are frequently advised to show a copy of what is to be published to the subject of the article and to incorporate a statement from the subject explaining his side of the story.

Truth (justification)

English law does not permit a claimant to recover damages in respect of an injury to a character which he does not possess. For this reason a successful plea of justification was an absolute defence to a claim in libel because it showed, as a matter of objective fact, that a claimant is not entitled to the unblemished reputation which he claims to have been damaged by the publication of which complaint is made.

Section 2 of the Defamation Act 2013 states that the defence of justification is replaced with a statutory defence of 'truth'. This applies if the defendant could show that the imputation conveyed by the statement is 'substantially true'. The section also repeals and replaces s 5 of the Defamation Act 1952.

In effect s 2 codifies the existing law of justification. The repetition rule survives, as does the requirement that the burden of proof remains upon the defendant.

For a plea of truth to succeed, there must be a final finding on the merits by a court on admissible evidence that the defamatory 'sting' of the allegation complained of is objectively true as a matter of fact. The defendant does not have to prove that every word he published was true. He has to establish the essential or substantial truth of the 'sting' of the libel. To prove the truth of some lesser defamatory meaning does not provide a complete defence.

The burden of proving justification rests on the defendant. Although the standard of proof is the balance of probabilities, the more improbable an allegation the stronger must be the evidence that it did occur before, on the balance of probabilities, its occurrence will be established.

A defendant must set out in his statement of case the defamatory meaning he seeks to prove to be essentially or substantially true. The claimant (and the court) will therefore know unequivocally what meaning the defendant is seeking to justify. The defendant must then give proper particulars of the facts on which he relies to justify that meaning.

At the trial the jury must undertake a two-stage process. They must first decide whether, on the admissible evidence called by the parties, the defendant has proved to their satisfaction, according to the appropriate standard of proof, all or at least some of the factual propositions asserted by the particulars of justification. They must then decide whether the whole of the facts which they have found to be proved are such as to establish the essential or substantial truth of the 'sting of the libel'.

The 'sting' of a libel may be capable of meaning that a claimant has in fact committed some serious act. Alternatively, it may be suggested that the words mean that there are reasonable grounds to suspect that he has committed such an act. A third possibility is that they may mean that there are grounds for investigating whether he has been responsible for such an act ('chase' meanings).

A defence of truth based upon reasonable grounds for suspicion has three principles. First, it must focus upon some conduct of the individual claimant that in itself gives rise to the suspicion. Secondly, it is not permitted to rely upon hearsay. If a defendant repeats a libel he has heard from others, a plea of truth will only succeed if he can prove by admissible evidence that what they said was substantially true. Finally, a defendant cannot plead as supposed grounds matters post-dating publication. This poses a particular problem for the media, who for a number of reasons, including commercial pressure to break a story, the threat of an injunction, or the anonymity of sources, may wish to publish before they have conclusive evidence of justification.

Notice that the burden of proof here is on the defendant to prove that the words are true rather than on the claimant to show that they were untrue.

Example

A newspaper publishes a story on performance-enhancing drugs in professional cycling. The article states that it would be almost impossible for a cyclist to win the Tour de France without performance-enhancing drugs and is sued for libel by the previous year's winner.

The first question is whether the statement is defamatory and in what sense. Does it accuse the cyclist of guilt (level one); raise reasonable grounds for suspicion (level two); or mean that there are questions to be answered (level three)? Once the court has fixed the meaning this establishes what the defendant has to prove is true. If the court says it is a level one meaning then the defendant must prove that the cyclist took performance-enhancing drugs. If they cannot do this then the only defence available would be public interest privilege. (See below.)

The words must be true in substance and fact and, if an innuendo has been pleaded, the truth of that must also be proved. The success or failure of the defence will turn on the interpretation of the facts.

Wakley v *Cooke and Healey* (1849) 4 Exch 511

The defendant called the claimant a 'libellous journalist'. In evidence the defendant proved that the claimant had once been successfully sued for libel. The defence of justification (truth) failed as the court took the view that in context the words meant that the claimant habitually libelled people. The defendant had failed to justify this meaning.

When a defendant pleads truth they must particularise the meaning of the words which they allege to be justified. (**Lucas-Box v News Group Newspapers Ltd** [1986] 1 WLR 147.)

Difficulty arises where the defendant wishes to argue that their words imported a general rather than particular charge.

Williams v *Reason* [1988] 1 All ER 262

> The claimant was an amateur rugby player. The defendants published a book alleging that he had breached the amateur code by writing a book for money while he was still playing. The defendants were granted leave to introduce new evidence to prove that the claimant had accepted 'boot-money' as the sting of the libel was that the claimant was guilty of 'shamateurism'.

Bookbinder v *Tebbitt* [1989] 1 All ER 1169

> It was alleged that during an election meeting the defendant had defamed the claimant by calling a policy of a council (of which the claimant was leader) a 'damn fool idea'. The policy was to overprint stationery with the words 'Support Nuclear Free Zones'.
>
> The claimant alleged a natural meaning that irresponsible conduct had resulted in large-scale squandering of public money. The Court of Appeal refused to allow evidence in relation to a wide range of council activities alleged to constitute overspending of public money. The words, in the context in which they were used, were not capable of raising this general charge.

The issues in a defence of truth are likely to be what the words mean and whether that meaning can be proved to be substantially true. If the defendant can prove that part but not all of what he said was substantially true the issue would then arise whether that part of the defamatory statement has or would be likely to cause serious harm (s 2(3)). Section 5 of the Defamation Act 1952 which had previously dealt with the situation where only part of the defamatory statement could be shown to be true is now otiose.

For example, the claimant is described as a murderer, rapist, arsonist, thief and liar. The defendant proves the truth of the first four charges but is unable to justify the last.

Honest opinion

 Introduction

Whereas truth provides a defence on questions of fact, the common law defence of honest (fair) comment defended opinions which by their nature cannot be true or false. Sometimes called the critics' defence, it was previously called fair comment and defended honest and fair criticism. The Supreme Court stated that it be renamed 'honest comment'. (*Joseph* v *Spiller* [2010] UKSC 53.)

Section 3 of the Defamation Act 2013 provides for a new statutory defence of honest opinion. Four conditions need to be met:

1 The statement made would need to be one of opinion and not an assertion of fact.

2 The statement indicated, whether in general or specific terms, forms the basis of the opinion.

3 The opinion must be one that an honest person could have held on the basis of a fact which was in existence at the time the statement was published or a privileged statement published before the statement complained of. Privileged statement includes defences under s 4 and s 16.

4 The defence is defeated if the claimant shows that the defendant did not hold the opinion. If the defendant publishes a statement made by another person (the author) the defence is defeated if the defendant knew or ought to have known that the defendant did not hold that opinion.

Section 3 largely incorporates the changes to the defence made in *Joseph* v *Spiller* [2010] UKSC 53 by the Supreme Court.

The word 'critic' comes from ancient Greek and means one who offers reasoned judgement or analysis, interpretation or observation. Not all criticism is reasoned and some can be positively vitriolic. The defence has to draw the line between what used to be called 'fair' and unfair comment but was described as 'honest' comment by the Supreme Court. (*Joseph* v *Spiller*.) The reason for the change was that a comment may be unfair but can still be protected by the defence provided it is honest.

Example

To say that '*X* is a thief and is therefore unsuited to be a bank manager' requires the defendant to justify '*X* is a thief' and to prove honest opinion for the remainder of the statement.

The statutory defence

1 The statement made would need to be one of opinion and not an assertion of fact

What is fact and what is opinion is not always easy to determine. In *Kemsley* v *Foot* (see below for the facts) the issue was whether the words 'lower than Kemsley' were fact or opinion. The House of Lords found that there was a generic reference to the Kemsley Press and this was sufficient to attract the defence.

Telnikoff v *Matusevitch* [1992] 2 AC 343

The claimant wrote an article in the *Daily Telegraph* criticising the BBC Russian Service for over-recruiting from Soviet ethnic minorities. The defendant published a reply in the same paper accusing the claimant of racism.

The majority of the House of Lords held that in considering whether a statement in the defendant's letter was fact or comment, the letter must be considered without reference to the original article for context. It was likely that large numbers of persons who read the letter would not have read the article.

The majority argued that a letter writer had to make clear that he was writing comment and not misrepresenting the content of the article. Lord Ackner (dissenting) felt that the freedom to comment on matters of public interest was vital to the functioning of a democratic society and that it should be sufficient for the defendant to give an honest opinion and identify the publication on which he was commenting.

2 The statement indicated, whether in general or specific terms the basis of the opinion

The defence originated in respect of comments about artistic works such as books, plays, theatrical performances, musical compositions and concerts. Comments in relation to such matters necessarily identified the work to which they related, or they would have been meaningless. The matters commented on were matters of public interest. They had been placed by their authors or performers in the public domain. Where what was criticised was the artistic merit of the work, the only issue that could arise was as to the question of malice. There was no question but that the statement made was comment. There was no doubt about the matter to which the comment related. No issue arose as to the truth of the facts, for there were none. No issue was likely to arise as to whether the comment was 'fair', for beauty is in the eye of the beholder. The critic was doing no more than purporting to express his subjective reaction to what he had seen or heard. The only issue was malice. Was the critic fairly expressing his honest opinion, or was the opinion that he expressed dishonest, or motivated by spite or ill-will?

Where the criticism did not relate to the artistic merit of the work product, but the comments made amounted to an attack on the character of the author, then the element of fairness might have been in issue in as much as some cases identified a requirement that the inferences drawn by the comments made should be reasonable.

A number of developments complicated the defence of fair comment. It was extended to cover the conduct of individuals, where this was of public interest. It thus became possible to make a derogatory comment about a person which was inferentially based on his conduct, without expressly identifying the facts upon which the comment was based. Sometimes the conduct was notorious and thus in the public domain. Then the comment might inferentially identify the conduct on which it was based and no difficulty would arise in relation to evaluating the various elements of the defence. But it might not be possible to identify by inference the conduct in relation to which the comment was made. Indeed that conduct might not even be in the public domain. It might be known only to the person making the comment.

The following case raised some of these issues:

Kemsley v Foot [1952] AC 345

The defendant published an article which referred to one of the Beaverbrook newspapers under the heading, 'Lower than Kemsley'. Kemsley was the owner of another group of newspapers. Was this fact or opinion? The House of Lords decided that as the conduct of the Kemsley Press was the fact on which the comment was made the defence of fair comment was available. It was not necessary that the facts on which the comment is based should be stated in the alleged libel.

The issue was whether the plea of fair comment should be allowed to stand in circumstances where the article itself set out no facts at all that related to the claimant or his newspapers. The House of Lords held that it could.

The Supreme Court later had to interpret the difficult judgments in **Kemsley** in the context of whether a *bare comment* which infers the existence of discreditable conduct but does not identify it could attract the defence of fair comment (honest opinion). They found that the defence of fair comment (honest opinion) could be raised where the comment identified the subject matter of the comment generically as a class of material that was in the public domain. There was no need for the commentator to spell out the specific parts of that material that had given rise to the comment. (*Joseph* v *Spiller* [2010] UKSC 53.) The Kemsley press had been identified generically and this was sufficient for the defence to be raised.

3 The opinion must be one that an honest person could have held on the basis of a fact which was in existence at the time the statement was published or a privileged statement published before the statement complained of

The facts on which the opinion is alleged to be based must be facts which were in existence at the time the comment was made. The defendant cannot rely on facts which occurred after the comment.

If the facts are untrue but were stated on a privileged occasion, then honest opinion can succeed as a defence. This could occur if the facts were stated in court and subject to absolute privilege.

The issue of the facts on which the defendant wished to rely was in issue in the following case. The narrower issue for the Supreme Court was whether the defendants could rely on a fact to which no reference was made in the article complained of.

Joseph v *Spiller* [2010] UKSC 53

The claimants were members of a musical group and appointed the defendants to promote their performances. The parties entered into a contract under which any further bookings at the same venue in the following 12 months had to be made through the defendants. The defendants arranged a booking and the claimants agreed to perform again at the same venue three weeks later without reference to the defendants. The defendants e-mailed the claimants, complaining about the breach of contract. The first claimant responded that the contract was 'mearly [sic] a formality and holds no water in legal terms', and that they were not bound by the contract. The defendants then posted a notice on their website announcing that they were no longer representing the claimants, stating that the claimants were 'not professional enough to feature in our portfolio and have not been able to abide by the terms of their contract', and advising others not to deal with them. The claimants brought proceedings in libel in respect of that notice.

The defendants pleaded a number of defences including fair comment. (honest opinion) The defence of fair comment (honest opinion) was based upon an alleged earlier breach of contract by the claimants with a hirer in December 2005.

The Supreme Court held that where, expressly or by implication, general criticism was made of a play, a book, an organ of the press or a notorious course of conduct in the public domain, the defendant was likely to wish in his defence to identify particular aspects of the matter in question by way of explanation of precisely what it was that led him to make his comment. Those particular aspects would be relevant to establishing the pertinence of his comment and to rebutting any question of malice, should that be in issue. The comment did not have to refer to those particular aspects specifically and it was not necessary that all that were pleaded should be accurate, provided that the comment was supported by at least one that was. Strasbourg authority was to the effect that even where a statement amounted to a value judgement, there had to exist a sufficient factual basis to support it. The defence of honest comment required the commentator to identify, at least in general terms, the nature of that factual basis.

In the instant case, the posting by the defendants referred to the breach of contract, and to the claimants' e-mail, and those facts could be relied upon. The email arguably evidenced a contemptuous approach to the claimants' contractual obligations to the claimants and to contracts in general. It would be a matter for the jury to decide. The defence should therefore be reinstated.

The issue in this case is the extent to which the subject matter of the comment must be identified by the comment, at least in general terms. The underlying justification for the creation of the fair comment (honest opinion) exception was the desirability that a person should be entitled to express his view freely about a matter of public interest. That remains a justification for the defence, albeit that the concept of public interest has been greatly widened. If the subject matter of the comment is not apparent from the comment this justification for the defence will be lacking. The defamatory comment will be wholly unfocused.

In the words of Lord Phillips:

> it may be thought desirable that the commentator should be required to identify at least the general nature of the facts that have led him to make the criticism. If he states that a barrister is 'a disgrace to his profession' he should make it clear whether this is because he does not deal honestly with the court, or does not read his papers thoroughly, or refuses to accept legally aided work, or is constantly late for court, or wears dirty collars and bands.

4 The defence is defeated if the claimant shows that the defendant did not hold the opinion

This must be read in conjunction with the previous point. The opinion must be one that an honest person could have held and can be defeated if the defendant did not actually hold that opinion.

This means that the comment must be an honest expression of the defendant's opinion: 'would any fair man, however prejudiced he may be, however exaggerated or obstinate his views, have said that which this criticism has said.' (*Merivale* v *Carson* (1888) 20 QBD 275 at 281.)

The test of honesty (fairness) is an objective one, in the sense that any person, however prejudiced and obstinate, could honestly have held the views expressed. (*Telnikoff* v *Matusevitch*.) If the comment is shown to be objectively fair, the court will presume the statement of opinion is honest unless malice can be proved.

Malice

For malice generally, see Chapter 1. Since 1906, the defence was able to be defeated by malice. Originally malice meant spite or evil motive but it now has a wider and more objective meaning. (See *Joseph* v *Spiller* below.) The key factor is now whether the defendant acted 'honestly' no matter how obstinate and prejudiced they may have been.

Thomas v *Bradbury, Agnew & Co Ltd* [1906] 2 KB 627

A book reviewer for *Punch* wrote a very critical view of the claimant's book. The defendant's malice was ascertained from the review itself and his conduct in the witness box. The defence of fair comment (honest opinion) failed because of the defendant's malice.

It was not clear whether one defendant's malice could infect a co-defendant's plea of fair comment: for example, if a newspaper printed a letter and both the letter writer and the newspaper are sued. Both pleaded honest opinion, but the writer's defence failed because of malice. Could the newspaper have succeeded in its defence?

The modern position of malice in a fair comment (honest opinion) defence was described by Lord Phillips in *Joseph* v *Spiller* [2010] UKSC 53:

> In recent cases the area of inquiry in relation to the defence of fair comment has been expanded. The scope of public interest has been greatly widened. If *Cheng* is accepted as correctly setting out the test of malice, the scope of malice has been significantly narrowed. The fact that the Defendant may have been motivated by spite or ill-will is no longer material. The only issue is whether he believed that his comment was justified. In practice this issue is seldom likely to be explored, for the burden is on the Claimant and how can he set about proving that the Defendant did not believe what he said? The subjective nature of the defence of fair comment has diminished. The issue is no longer the subjective one – did the Defendant honestly believe that the facts on which he commented justified his comment? Instead the focus has been on the objective question: could an obstinate and prejudiced person have honestly based the comment made by the Defendant on the facts on which the Defendant commented?

It is difficult to see that malice will play any significant part in future defences on comment. The burden of proof for the defence is on the defendant to prove that the comment was 'honest' in the objective sense that any person, however prejudiced, could have held the views expressed. The burden of proof then passes to the claimant to establish malice. As the defendant has already established 'honesty' it would be an exceptional case where this could be proved.

The key issue is now the objective one of 'honesty' rather than the subjective one of spite or ill-will. It is also established that malice has a different meaning in qualified privilege from that in fair comment.

Honest (fair) opinion has historically been a notoriously complex defence to run in a libel action. The following cases give an example of some of the issues which can arise.

Burstein v *Associated Newspapers Ltd* [2007] 4 All ER 319

> The claimant was the composer and co-librettist of an opera called 'Manifest Destiny', performed at the Edinburgh Festival. The opera was about suicide bombers and was plainly anti-American. A review of the opera was published by the defendant in its *Evening Standard* newspaper. In the final sentence of the review, the reviewer wrote: 'But I found the tone depressingly anti-American, and the idea that there is anything heroic about suicide bombers is, frankly, a grievous insult.'
>
> The claimant alleged that the article conveyed the defamatory meaning that he was a sympathiser with terrorist causes and actively promoted them in his work or that he applauded the action of suicide bombers and raised them to a level of heroism.
>
> The defendant denied that the words were capable of bearing the defamatory meanings alleged and also pleaded that words were fair comment (honest opinion) on a matter of public interest.

The Court of Appeal held:

> WHAT WAS THE MEANING?
>
> The test to be applied was what the words would convey to the ordinary reasonable reader. The judge's role was confined to deciding whether the words used were capable of bearing the meaning or meanings contended for and, if so, whether any of the those meanings was legally capable of being defamatory.
>
> The theme of an opera or play might be described as insulting, without implying any motive or viewpoint held by the author. The judge had therefore been wrong to conclude that the word 'insult' arguably attributed a motive to the author and the first of the alleged meanings could not be attached to the words used in the review by any reasonable jury. As to the second pleaded meaning, the words were just capable, if given a restricted interpretation, of meaning that in this opera the claimant applauded the action of suicide bombers and raised them to a level of heroism. That could still have been seen as defamatory of the claimant.

COMMENT OR FACT?

The sense of comment was something that was or could reasonably be inferred to be a deduction, inference, conclusion, criticism, remark or observation.

The words were contained in a press article, which was obviously a review by a critic expressing the subjective views of the writer. The final sentence in the review was patently intended as a summary of and a commentary on the factual description of the opera set out in the preceding part of the review and no reasonable person could read it as a statement about the claimant in respect of any matter not contained in that review. There was no suggestion that the reviewer was otherwise acquainted with the claimant.

Moreover, the reader would expect a review to contain a subjective commentary by the critic. The words also embodied powerful elements of value judgments and the final sentence followed other sentences full of evaluative words. That too would influence how a reasonable reader would see the final sentence. Such value judgments were not something which a writer should be required to prove were objectively valid.

A jury might regard the words as attributing a 'motive' to the author, but that could not suffice to take the case out of the category of comment, when any such 'motive' could only be an inference drawn from the factual material set out earlier in the article. In the present case the words complained of carried the unmistakable badge of comment and no reasonable jury could treat them as a statement of fact.

WAS THE COMMENT FAIR?

The requirement that the comment be objectively 'fair' meant simply that the opinions expressed in the review could be honestly held by someone who had seen the opera. The court was not required to ask whether it was a reasonable opinion. The law protected the frank expression of views on matters of public interest, so long as they were not actuated by 'malice' in the sense used in the jurisprudence of defamation. The opera dealt with matters upon which strong opinions could legitimately be held and upon which any jury would expect strong opinions to be held without any scintilla of dishonesty on the part of those who held them. Since the claimant did not point to any factual inaccuracies in the earlier part of the review which summarised the events portrayed in the opera and since the events were clearly a matter of public interest, all the requirements of the fair comment defence were satisfied.

Accordingly, the appeal was allowed and summary judgment was granted in favour of the defendant.

This case illustrates the link between defamatory meaning and the defences. (In this case honest comment.) What the defendant has to establish will be determined by the meaning ascribed to the alleged defamatory words.

Would the decision be any different in the light of *Joseph* v *Spiller*? Undoubtedly not, as the emphasis in that case was on the objective 'honesty' of the comment.

British Chiropractic Association v *Singh* [2010] EWCA Civ 350

The claimant was the British Chiropractic Association, a company whose objects included promoting and maintaining high standards of conduct and practice among the United Kingdom's chiropractors. It contended that it had been defamed by the defendant, a scientist and science writer, who published an article in a newspaper's 'Comment and Debate' page which included the following passage: 'The British Chiropractic Association claims that their members can help treat children with colic, sleeping and feeding problems, frequent ear infections, asthma and prolonged crying, even though there is not a jot of evidence. This organisation is the respectable face of the chiropractic profession and yet it happily promotes bogus treatments.' By agreement between the parties, the judge was asked to determine two preliminary issues. The first was what defamatory meaning the words bore. The second was whether they constituted assertions of fact or comment. The judge held that the words would mean to a reasonable reader: (i) that the claimant had claimed that chiropractic was effective help to treat children with colic, sleeping and feeding problems, frequent ear infections, asthma and prolonged crying, although it knew that there was absolutely no evidence to support its claims; and (ii) that by making those claims the claimant had knowingly promoted bogus treatments. He went on to hold that the defendant's remarks were factual assertions and were verifiable and were not expressions of opinion. If so, the defendant at trial had to prove that the meanings were factually true or lose. The defendant appealed.

He submitted that the judge had elided the issues of meaning and comment when, though related, they were distinct and used an unwarranted 'verifiable fact' test to eliminate comment as a defence.

The appeal would be allowed.

The subject-matter of the defendant's article had been an area of epidemiology in which the relationship of primary fact to secondary fact, and of both to permissible, was heavily and legitimately contested. The issue posed by the judge was in reality two distinct issues: first, had there been any evidence to support the material claims?; and second, if there had not, had the claimant's personnel known that? If the first issue was one of opinion and not of fact, the second issue ceased to matter. The judge had erred both in conflating those two elements of the claim and, more particularly, in treating the first of them as an issue of verifiable fact. The material words, however one represented or paraphrased their meaning, were an expression of opinion. The opinion might have been mistaken, but to allow the party which had been denounced on the basis of it to compel its author to prove in court what they had asserted by way of argument was to invite the court to become an Orwellian Ministry of Truth.

The natural meaning of the passage was not that the claimant was promoting what it knew to be bogus treatments but that it was promoting what the defendant contended were bogus treatments without regard to the want of reliable evidence of their efficacy.

This case goes some way to resolving a problem whereby libel actions were brought to attempt to stifle debate in scientific matters. The correct approach to these matters was given by an American judge: 'scientific controversies must be settled by the methods of science rather than by the methods of litigation . . . more papers, more discussion, better data, and more satisfactory models.' (Easterbrook J in *Underwager* v *Salter* 22 Fed 3d 730 (1994).) This is the 'marketplace of ideas' approach and the Court of Appeal clearly had this in mind when they contemplated members of the public having access to information that would enable them to make informed choices concerning healthcare.

Further moves towards the protection of academic debate can be seen in the extension of qualified privilege to peer reviewed statements in academic journals by the Defamation Act 2013 s 7 (see 'Qualified privilege' below).

Absolute privilege

There are certain occasions where freedom of speech outweighs protection of reputation. On these occasions privilege is granted to the statement. Privilege may be absolute or qualified. The distinction is that absolute privilege is not affected by malice, whereas a defence of qualified privilege is destroyed by malice.

Parliamentary privilege

The privilege of free speech is extended to all members of both Houses of Parliament under Article 9 of the Bill of Rights 1688, which states:

That the freedom of speech and debates or proceedings in Parliament ought not to be impeached or questioned in any court or place out of Parliament.

This privilege is limited to the confines of Parliament and will not protect an MP outside the House. No action will lie against an MP for defamation in respect of anything said in parliamentary proceedings, either in debate or committee or in petitions to Parliament.

Church of Scientology of California v Johnson-Smith [1972] 1 QB 522

The claimants sued the defendant MP for a libel alleged to have been made in a television interview. The defence was fair comment. The claimants pleaded malice. To establish malice they wanted to use extracts from *Hansard*. It was held that this evidence could not be used because of parliamentary privilege.

Allason v Haines [1996] EMLR 143

The claimant MP sued over an article which was alleged to have inferred that he had abused his parliamentary privilege by making unproven allegations in Parliament. The defendants pleaded justification and argued that without the protection of parliamentary privilege the claimant might have been more careful about his facts. The claimant argued in reply that he had taken care and that his allegations were not unproven. The action was stayed on the grounds that, since the defendants were unable to raise the defence of justification because of parliamentary privilege, it would be unjust to allow the claimant to proceed with the action.

The Defamation Act 1996 s 13 has since amended the rules of evidence and parliamentary proceedings in that there is a provision which now enables an MP to waive the privilege so that they can pursue an action over defamatory allegations about their conduct within Parliament.

This has been criticised as allowing MPs to waive parliamentary privilege when it is to their advantage to do so, but also to hide behind it when it suits them.

Hamilton v Al Fayed [2000] 2 All ER 224

The House of Lords held that the privilege was that of Parliament, not of an individual MP. Once an MP had waived the privilege then any evidence given to a Parliamentary Committee could be challenged in a defamation action without it being regarded as infringing the autonomous jurisdiction of Parliament.

Judicial privilege

Statements which are made in the course of judicial proceedings by judge, juror, counsel, solicitor, parties or witnesses are absolutely privileged. The privilege also applies to documents used. The statement must be connected with the case and does not extend, for example, to interruptions from the public gallery.

Judicial proceedings covers ordinary courts of law and tribunals acting judicially. Military inquiries, courts martial and disciplinary hearings of the Law Society are covered. The privilege does not extend to the activities of administrative bodies and so would not cover proceedings of the licensing justices.

A fair, accurate and contemporaneous newspaper or broadcast report of public judicial proceedings in the United Kingdom, the European Court of Justice, the European Court of Human Rights and any international criminal tribunal established by the Security Council of the United Nations or by international agreement to which the United Kingdom is a party, is absolutely privileged. (Defamation Act 1996 s 14.)

Section 7 of the Defamation Act 2013 extends the privilege attached to reports of court proceedings to such proceedings anywhere in the world.

To be *fair*, the report must present a summary of both sides of the case. If only the prosecution case has been heard then the report should say 'continuing' at the end.

To be *accurate*, the report should contain no material inaccuracies: for example, it should not identify someone who is a witness as the defendant. The proceedings do not have to be reported verbatim.

To be *contemporaneous*, the report should be in the first issue of the newspaper after the hearing. Non-contemporaneous reports carry qualified privilege.

Communications between solicitor and client attract privilege although it is not certain whether this is absolute or qualified.

A reporter must be careful not to 'jump the gun'. In **Stern v Piper** [1996] 3 All ER 385 a newspaper published an article quoting allegations against *S* made in an affirmation in a pending action in the High Court. *S* sued for libel for the newspaper's repetition of the remarks. The Court of Appeal held that privilege only protected reports of legal proceedings in open court and was no defence when the publisher anticipated those proceedings. A plea of justification was rejected as this defence did not apply to the publication of extracts from documents prepared for pending legal proceedings.

The extent of the defence was considered in **Waple** (below).

Waple v *Surrey County Council* [1998] 1 All ER 624

A child had been placed with foster parents by the local authority and a notice to contribute to the child's maintenance was issued to the child's adoptive parents. The adoptive parents asked the local authority why they had initiated the removal of their child and the solicitor for the authority replied that the mother had said that, unless the boy was removed, she would lock him in his room.

It was held that absolute privilege applies to statements made in judicial and quasi-judicial proceedings. It extends to other statements made by witnesses, even prior to the issue of a writ, provided the statement was made for the purposes of a possible action and at a time when a possible action was being considered. No privilege would apply to a local authority after a contribution notice had been sent, as this did not inevitably mean that judicial proceedings would ever start, and the letter did not have an immediate link with possible proceedings.

However, a document created during the course of an investigation by a financial regulator attracts absolute privilege as otherwise the flow of information to financial regulators might be seriously impeded if informants thought they might be harassed by libel proceedings. (*Mahon v Rahn (No 2)* [2000] 4 All ER 41.)

Executive privilege

Statements made by one officer of the state to another in the course of duty are absolutely privileged. There is some doubt as to how high ranking the official has to be in order to attract this privilege.

Qualified privilege

Qualified privilege is a complex area of law. It differs from absolute privilege in that it can be defeated by malice. Owing to its increasing complexity it is sensible to divide it into three separate groups.

Privileged reports

Parliamentary proceedings

Fair and accurate reports of parliamentary proceedings are covered by qualified privilege (Defamation Act 1996 s 15). The whole debate does not need to be reported and the reporter may select only those bits which are of public interest.

Cook v Alexander [1974] QB 279

> The claimant had been a teacher at an approved school and his criticism of the school had led to it being closed by the Home Secretary. The closure order was debated in the House of Lords. The *Daily Telegraph* reported the debate and published a parliamentary sketch of those parts of the debate which the reporter thought were of public interest. The Court of Appeal held that the sketch was privileged as it was made fairly and honestly.

Reports of judicial proceedings

Fair and accurate reports of public judicial proceedings which are not covered by absolute privilege attract qualified privilege. This covers reports which are not contemporaneous and are not made in a newspaper.

Reports privileged under the Schedule to the Defamation Act 1996 (as amended)

The Schedule to the Defamation Act 1996 (as amended by the Defamation Act 2013) provides that a number of reports are covered by qualified privilege. These are divided into Part I and Part II reports.

Part I reports are privileged without explanation or contradiction provided they are fair and accurate and are made without malice. These reports are:

1 A fair and accurate copy of, extract from or summary of a notice or other matter issued for the information of the public by or on behalf of–

    (a) a legislature or government anywhere in the world;
    (b) an authority anywhere in the world performing governmental functions;
    (c) an international organisation or international conference.

2 '*Governmental functions*' includes police functions.

Part II provides that certain reports are privileged subject to explanation or contradiction, provided they are fair and accurate and without malice and issued for the benefit of the public such as:

1 A copy or extract from a notice issued by:

    (a) any Parliament of a member state of the European Union or the European Parliament;
    (b) the government of any member state or any government department (including police), or the European Commission;
    (c) international organisations or conferences.

2 A copy or extract from a document made available by a court anywhere in the world or a judge or officer of those courts.

3 Reports of the following carry qualified privilege:

   (a) local authorities (including committees and sub-committees) and the equivalent bodies in European Union member states;

   (b) licensing justices;

   (c) tribunals open to the public;

   (d) local inquiries;

   (e) inquiries set up under any statutory provision;

   (f) a fair and accurate report of proceedings at a press conference held anywhere in the world for the discussion of a matter of public interest.

4 A fair and accurate report of proceedings at any public meeting held anywhere in the world. A *'public meeting'* means a meeting bona fide and lawfully held for a lawful purpose and for the furtherance or discussion of a matter of public interest, whether admission to the meeting is general or restricted.

   In this case the privilege applies to the proceedings. A meeting is public for this purpose if the organisers issued a general invitation to the press. Press conferences and press releases (even if not read out at the meeting) are therefore covered by the privilege. (*McCartan Turkington Breen (a firm)* v *Times Newspapers Ltd* [2000] 4 All ER 913.) (See also (f) above.)

5 A fair and accurate report of proceedings at a general meeting of a listed company. *'Listed company'* has the same meaning as in Part 12 of the Corporation Tax Act 2009.

6 A fair and accurate copy of, extract from or summary of any document circulated to members of a listed company.

7 A report of the findings and decisions of the following bodies is privileged. A report of the proceedings is not. Bodies concerned with:

   (a) art, science, religion or learning;

   (b) trade, business, industry or the professions;

   (c) games, sports or pastimes;

   (d) charities.

8 A fair and accurate report of proceedings of a scientific or academic conference held anywhere in the world, or copy of, extract from or summary of matter published by such a conference.

It should be noted that Part II reports are privileged subject to explanation or contradiction.

Example

A reporter attends a meeting of the licensing justices. *X* has applied for a licence to sell alcoholic drinks. The police object to the granting of the licence because of *X*'s known criminal associates. The reporter's paper carries a report of the proceedings. This is privileged under Part II. *X* writes to the newspaper and asks the paper to publish his letter, which sets out his side of the story. If the paper does not publish the letter, then it risks losing privilege. (For the relationship between privilege attached on this basis to notices issued by the police and public interest privilege see *Flood* v *Times Newspapers* [2012] UKSC 11.)

What is the situation where privileged and non-privileged material are mixed? In *Curistan* v *Times Newspapers* [2007] 4 All ER 486 the Court of Appeal stated that when considering the question of when the qualified privilege which in principle attaches to a fair and accurate report of parliamentary proceedings under s 15 of and para 1 of Sch 1 to the Defamation Act 1996 is lost because of the addition of extraneous non-privileged material in the same article or report three considerations are important in deciding whether a particular report qualifies as 'fair and accurate', namely: (i) the amount of the extraneous non-privileged material which has been added to and mixed with the privileged material; (ii) whether the typical reader of the particular publication would be able to distinguish the passages which constitute reportage from the unprivileged material added by the publisher; and (iii) the extent to which it can be said that the extraneous additional material is connected with the privileged reportage.

See also 'Reportage' below.

Common law privilege

This area will still be treated separately from public interest privilege (see below) although it is arguable the two are moving together. This is 'old style' common law privilege.

A statement which is made in the performance of a duty will attract qualified privilege provided that the person making the statement has a legal, moral or social duty to make the statement and the person receiving it has an interest in doing so. The court will also look at the nature, status and source of the material and the circumstances of the publication. (***Reynolds v Times Newspapers Ltd*** [1999] 4 All ER 609.) A simple example of this is a reference given by a present employer to a potential future employer. However, if a reference contains defamatory statements, the subject of the reference may have an action for negligence against the author.

Watt v Longsdon [1930] 1 KB 130

The defendant, a director of a company, received a letter from the foreign manager of the company. The letter made allegations of drunkenness, dishonesty and immorality about the claimant, also an employee of the company. The defendant showed the letter to the other directors and to the claimant's wife. It was held that the publication to the directors was covered by qualified privilege but the publication to the claimant's wife was not, as the defendant had no duty to make the communication.

Bryanston Finance Co Ltd v de Vries [1975] 2 All ER 609

The defendants issued a writ against the claimants, with whom they had had business dealings. To force a settlement the defendants had documents prepared alleging that the claimants had committed serious misdemeanours against Bryanston Co. They threatened to send these documents to the shareholders. A letter was drafted to go out with the documents. The documents were dictated to a typist and then handed to an office boy for copying, but never sent out. The claimants sued for libel.

The defendants claimed that the publication to the typist was privileged. The Court of Appeal held that such a publication was privileged, but was divided as to whether the privilege was an original one or an ancillary one. If the former view is correct, then it does not matter whether the intended publication (in this case to the shareholders) was privileged or not.

What is the position where a defamatory statement is made by mistake and an apology tendered which is in itself defamatory?

Watts v Times Newspapers Ltd [1996] 1 All ER 152

The defendants published in their newspaper an item suggesting that the claimant author had plagiarised another author. By mistake, a photograph, intended to be of the author, but in fact of a property developer of that name, was printed. The property developer demanded an apology and the defendants agreed, suggesting a neutral form of wording. However, at the insistence of the property developer's solicitors, a different wording was published, including a statement that the article and photograph suggested that the property developer had been a plagiarist.

The claimant alleged that not only the original article but also the apology were defamatory to him. The defendants claimed that the apology was protected by qualified privilege.

The Court of Appeal held that as the general principle on which common law privilege was based was the public interest, each party's claim to privilege should be looked at separately. Where an apology tendered in mitigation of a libel was itself defamatory of a person other than the victim of the original libel, the question of whether the apology was protected by qualified privilege had to be considered separately in relation to the person publishing the apology and the person at whose instance it was published. The defendants were not rebutting an attack on themselves and could have published a simple retraction and could have made a statement in open court which would have been protected by absolute privilege. In these circumstances the defendants could not claim any derivative privilege through the property developer, and the publication of the apology with the defamatory words was not warranted, so the defendants had no privilege.

The property developer (and his solicitors) were entitled to qualified privilege as the property developer as the victim of the attack was entitled to a right of reply, so long as he did not overstep the bounds and include entirely irrelevant and extraneous material. The words used did not overstep these bounds and both the property developer and the solicitors were protected by qualified privilege.

Clift v *Slough BC* [2010] EWCA 1484

The claimant was placed on a potentially violent persons register by the defendant local authority and this information was circulated to a number of people including local authority employees and 'partner organisations'. The defendants pleaded qualified privilege as a defence but the Court of Appeal held that the circulation to some employees and 'partner organisations' was too wide and breached the claimant's rights under Article 8. (The local authority being a public authority.) This was held to deprive the defendants of the defence in respect of those publications.

Public interest privilege

Objective 4

The defence of qualified privilege is one aspect of the question as to whether public figures should be able to sue in defamation or whether there should be some public interest defence in English law so that debate on matters of public importance is not censored by the prospect of a libel action. This can be done by a number of methods but in England the debate has centred on whether there should be a 'public interest' version of qualified privilege. Historically, qualified privilege was confined to specific occasions such as reports of meetings and to duty–interest situations such as references (see above). The restricted ambit of the defence can be partly ascribed to its drastic effect. Once the privilege has been established, the only way that the claimant can succeed is by proving malice on the part of the defendant. Attempts to introduce a duty–interest privilege attaching to the media were largely rejected on the basis that if the media uncovered wrongdoing, their duty was to report it to the relevant authorities rather than publishing it to the public. (For an exception, see *Webb* v *Times Publishing Co Ltd* [1960] 2 QB 535.)

English law resisted the introduction of any form of 'public interest' privilege which would apply to the media until recently, partly as a result of the Human Rights Act 1998 and the freedom of speech requirements in Article 10 of the European Convention on Human Rights. The present law is now on a statutory basis.

Section 4 of the Defamation Act 2013 states that it is a defence to an action for defamation for the defendant to show:

(i) that the statement complained of is, or forms part of, a statement on a matter of public interest; and

(ii) the defendant acted responsibly in publishing the statement complained of.

See Chapter 1 for
tort law and human
rights generally.

In determining this latter test, matters are listed to which the court may have regard.

The common law defence is abolished and the Act makes certain changes to the previous common law defence which will be discussed first.

The origins of the defence lie in the House of Lords' decision in the following case:

Reynolds v Times Newspapers Ltd [1999] 4 All ER 609

The claimant became Prime Minister of Ireland in February 1992, heading a coalition of his own party and Labour, under S. During the course of the coalition the claimant and S did much to promote the Northern Ireland peace process, and the future of the coalition was thus a matter of public interest in Great Britain as well as in Ireland. In November 1994 S decided to end the coalition as a result of a political crisis caused by the appointment to the office of President of the High Court of the former Attorney General and his handling, whilst still Attorney General, of a request to extradite a Roman Catholic priest from Eire to Northern Ireland to answer charges of sexual abuse of children. On 17 November the claimant resigned as Prime Minister, and as leader of his party soon afterwards. On 20 November the defendants published an article in the British mainland edition of their Sunday newspaper about the political crisis and the claimant's resignation. The claimant took strong exception to the article, and issued proceedings claiming damages for libel. In the statement of claim it was pleaded that the words complained of in the article meant and were understood to mean that the claimant had deliberately and dishonestly misled Parliament and his Cabinet colleagues, particularly S, by withholding from them information about the handling of the extradition request, and that he had lied to them about when the information had come into his possession. In their defence the defendants claimed, inter alia, qualified privilege at common law. At the end of the trial the claimant was awarded 1p damages. In relation to qualified privilege, the Court of Appeal held that a newspaper would have to satisfy a three-stage test. There had to be a legal, social or moral duty to the general public to publish the material in question (the 'duty test'). The general public had to have a corresponding interest in receiving the information (the 'interest test'). The defendant had to establish that the nature, source and status of the material and the circumstances of its publication were such as to warrant the protection of privilege (the 'circumstantial test').

On appeal to the House of Lords, the Lords refused to find a generic qualified privilege for political information. This was despite argument for the defendants on Article 10 of the European Convention on Human Rights. They held that the standard test of duty in disseminating the information and duty to receive it should continue to apply. In determining this, ten matters were identified as having to be taken into account:

1 the seriousness of the allegation;
2 the nature of the information and the extent to which the subject matter is of public concern;
3 the source of the information;
4 the steps taken to verify the information;
5 the status of the information;
6 the urgency of the matter;
7 whether comment was sought from the claimant;
8 whether the article contained the gist of the claimant's story;
9 the tone of the article; and
10 the circumstances of the publication including the timing.

As this was a hard-hitting article and the defendants had omitted to give Reynolds' explanation to the Dail, the article was not privileged.

This case was concerned with political information and, although the House of Lords refused to find a generic qualified privilege for political information, they did extend the protection given to dissemination of public interest information by the media on individual stories, provided certain criteria were satisfied. This protection has been arguably widened by subsequent decisions. It is, for example, clear that the privilege extends beyond political information in the narrow sense, to other material which is of serious public concern and is, for example, capable of applying to sporting issues. (*Grobbelaar* v *News Group Newspapers Ltd* [2002] 1 WLR 3024.)

The case law developed a three part test:

1 Was the material on a question of public interest?

2 Was it necessary to include the alleged defamatory statement?

3 Was it responsible journalism?

The basis of the test was one of responsible journalism with a balance drawn between setting the standard of journalistic responsibility too low and encouraging the publication of defamatory material and setting the standard too high and deterring the media from their proper function of keeping the public informed.

In determining whether the standard of journalism was responsible, the courts drew a distinction between an expressly defamatory statement and one where the words are ambiguous. In the latter they may be prepared to overlook a failure to inquire into the truth of the statement or refer to the claimant's side of the story. (*Bonnick* v *Morris* [2003] 1 AC 300; *Jameel* v *Wall Street Journal Europe SPRL* [2005] 4 All ER 356.) A contrast can be drawn with non-media defendants who do not have to show that they acted responsibly.

Other jurisdictions have adopted a different approach, usually from the different starting point that the integrity and competence of elected politicians is a matter of constitutional law and the dominant concern is that of the electorate in receiving true information on politicians. Subsidiary to this is the reputation of politicians and freedom of the press. In the United States the test is 'actual malice', under which the claimant must prove that the defendant knew the story was false or was reckless as to its truth. (*Sullivan* v *New York Times* (1964) 376 US 254.) In Australia, the defendant has to prove that there was no negligence in failing to establish falsity. (*Lange* v *Australian Broadcasting Co* (1997) 2 BHRC 513.) In New Zealand, *Reynolds* was rejected as too uncertain and restrictive. (*Lange* v *Atkinson (No 2)* (2000) 8 BHRC 500.) The New Zealand Court of Appeal favoured the generic head of privilege rejected by the House of Lords, where all that had to be proved was the absence of malice and that a genuine political discussion was involved. They regarded the *Reynolds* approach as having a chilling effect on the media and reducing the vital role of the jury in freedom of speech cases. The English press may have been the victims of their own practices here, as the court observed that New Zealand newspapers were more responsible than English ones.

The advent of this form of privilege opened up a Pandora's box in libel litigation. The limits and exact principles of the defence were still being tested before the Act but some principles had emerged. The advantage for the media was that in appropriate cases they did not have to run the difficult defence of justification. Whether or not the article was true is not relevant to the question of responsible journalism. What had to be considered is whether it was responsible to publish the article having regard to the risk that the defamatory imputation in the article might prove to be untrue. Relevant to that question was the information given to the publishers by the sources of the article, the nature of the sources, and the extent to which they backed that information.

One recurrent problem for the media is time. When a story breaks quickly, a decision now has to be made as to whether there is sufficient public interest in running the story at this time and whether it would amount to 'responsible journalism' if they do. Not surprisingly, the question has arisen as to whether after-acquired information can be used in the sense of whether the defence can incorporate facts which supported their case of which they had been unaware at the time of publication but subsequently became aware. However, the Court of Appeal has held that all the factors for consideration have to be determined on the basis of the defendant's state of knowledge at the time of publication. Some of the factors, including steps taken to verify the information, the urgency of the matter and the circumstances of publication would lose their potent effect if a publisher was allowed to rely on after-acquired information.

Loutchansky v *Times Newspapers Ltd (No 2)* [2002] 1 All ER 653

An allegation was made that the claimant was the boss of a major Russian crime organisation involved in money laundering and the smuggling of nuclear weapons. This was posted on a newspaper website. The case raised a number of issues including the extent of qualified privilege.

1 The traditional approach to qualified privilege was whether the occasion was privileged, not the publication. (See, for example, *Watts*.) The privilege in *Reynolds* appears to apply to the publication itself.
2 Once *Reynolds* privilege has been established, it is difficult to see what scope there is for malice to operate. The defendant's conduct must be taken into account when determining whether the privilege applies and if he has been reckless as to the truth (the basic test for malice) then there will be no privilege. As malice is usually a question for the jury, this involves a shift of power in the courtroom.
3 What would amount to responsible journalism? An objective test will be applied in the light of what was known to the defendant at the time of the publication. Whether the publication was true or not is irrelevant and it is not appropriate to speculate what further information might have been uncovered if the publisher had made further inquiries. The question is whether the public was entitled to know the information without the publisher making further inquiries. (*GKR Karate (UK) Ltd* v *Yorkshire Post Ltd* [2000] 1 WLR 2571.) The more ambiguity there is, the greater benefit of doubt to be given to the journalist. The more obvious the defamatory meaning and the more serious the libel, the less benefit of doubt that should be given.
4 The tone of the article can be crucial. In *Grobbelaar* v *News Group Newspapers Ltd* [2001] 2 All ER 437 the defendants were unable to use this version of privilege because of the tone of their coverage which went far beyond responsible journalism.

The Privy Council stated that the *Reynolds* privilege was available to non-media defendants. (*Seaga* v *Harper* [2008] 1 All ER 965.) The Act makes it clear that the statutory defence is available to all defendants.

Another recurrent problem for the media with the 'responsible journalism' test was that they frequently had to defend the anonymity of their sources. This made it difficult to establish justification and raised the question of whether relying on anonymous sources amounted to 'responsible journalism' and made it difficult to establish malice.

Jameel v *Wall Street Journal Europe SPRL* [2005] 4 All ER 356 (CA); [2006] 3 WLR 642 (HL)

The alleged defamatory statement was that the Jameel group of companies was on a list supplied by the US government to the Saudi Arabian government and were being monitored for terrorist ties. The defendants stated that they had five anonymous sources. The jury held that the article had a defamatory meaning and that there were no reasonable grounds to suspect the defendants. In order to determine whether the article carried qualified privilege the jury were asked to determine factual matters relating to the defendants' dealings with their anonymous sources. The jury did not accept that four of the sources had confirmed the first source's story or that the defendants had taken reasonable steps to contact the claimants. The trial judge asked the question of whether the publisher would have been open to legitimate criticism if it had failed to publish the article. This test had, however, been disapproved by the Court of Appeal in *Loutchansky* as it supplanted the *Reynolds* duty. On this and other grounds the judge found that qualified privilege did not apply. On the question of qualified privilege, the Court of Appeal held that the phrase 'responsible journalism' was insufficiently precise to constitute the sole test for *Reynolds* privilege. It was also necessary to demonstrate that the subject matter of the publication was of such a nature that it was in the public interest that it should be published. The defendants in this case had not satisfied the test of responsible journalism. A key factor was the gravity of the allegation which demanded a high degree of care.

The ruling appeared to conflict with the greater latitude given to the media in *Loutchansky* when the courts were urged to give journalists the benefit of the doubt and be slow to conclude that publication was not in the public's interest to know.

The House of Lords, in a media-friendly judgment, overturned the Court of Appeal decision.

In deciding whether the newspaper could rely on the *Reynolds* defence, the first question was whether the subject matter of the article was a matter of public interest, and that was a question for the judge. In answering that question, it was not helpful to apply the classic test for the existence of a privileged occasion and ask whether there was a duty to communicate the information and an interest in receiving it. The *Reynolds* defence was developed from the traditional form of privilege by a generalisation that, in matters of public interest, there could be said to be a professional duty on the part of journalists to impart the information and an interest in the public in receiving it. That generalisation having been made, it should be regarded as a proposition of law and not decided each time as a question of fact. If the publication was in the public interest, the duty and interest were taken to exist. If the article as a whole concerned a matter of public interest, the next question was whether the inclusion of the defamatory statement was justifiable. On that question, allowance had to be made for editorial judgment. The inquiry then shifted to whether the steps taken to gather and publish the information were responsible and fair. In *Reynolds*, Lord Nicholls gave his well-known non-exhaustive list of ten matters which should in suitable cases be taken into account in deciding the issue of responsible journalism. They were not tests which the publication had to pass. The standard of conduct required of the newspaper had to be applied in a practical and flexible manner. In this case, there was no basis for rejecting the newspaper's *Reynolds* defence.

Was *Reynolds* (common law public interest) privilege a different creature to traditional privilege? On this their Lordships were divided. Lord Bingham and Lord Hope felt that it emanated from traditional qualified privilege at common law. Baroness Hale and Lord Hoffmann (with whom Lord Scott agreed) felt that the new defence was different and advocated the dropping of the reference to 'privilege'.

Baroness Hale:

> It should by now be entirely clear that the *Reynolds* defence is a 'different jurisprudential creature' from the law of privilege, although it is a natural development of that law. It springs from the general obligation of the press, media and other publishers to communicate important information upon matters of general public interest and the general right of the public to receive such information. It is not helpful to analyse the particular case in terms of a specific duty and a specific right to know. That can, as experience since *Reynolds* has shown, very easily lead to a narrow and rigid approach which defeats its object. In truth, it is a defence of publication in the public interest.

The end result of *Jameel* was that a three-stage test would be applied where the defendant raised a defence of public interest: determining what was in the public interest; inclusion of the defamatory statement; and asking what is responsible journalism.

1 What is in the public interest?

The article should be considered as a whole rather than isolating the defamatory statement. The question of whether the material concerned a matter of public interest is decided by the judge. As has often been said, the public tends to be interested in many things which are not of the slightest public interest and the newspapers are not often the best judges of where the line should be drawn. The publication in *Jameel* easily passed that test. The thrust of the article as a whole was to inform the public that the Saudis were cooperating with the US Treasury in monitoring accounts. It was a serious contribution in measured tone to a subject of very considerable importance. It is not helpful to apply the classic test for the existence of a privileged occasion and ask whether there was a duty to communicate the information and an interest in receiving it. The *Reynolds* defence was developed from the traditional form of privilege by a generalisation that, in matters of public interest, there can be said to be a professional duty on the part of journalists to impart the information and an interest in the public in receiving it. This is a proposition of law and not decided each time as a question of fact. If the publication is in the public interest, the duty and interest are taken to exist. (See also *Flood v Times Newspapers* [2012] UKSC 11, below.)

2 Inclusion of the defamatory statement

If the article as a whole concerned a matter of public interest, the next question was whether the inclusion of the defamatory statement was justifiable. The fact that the material was of public interest did not allow the newspaper to drag in damaging allegations which served no public purpose. They had to be part of the story. The more serious the allegation, the more important it was that it should make a real contribution to the public interest element in the article. But whereas the question of whether the story as a whole was a matter of public interest had to be decided by the judge without regard to what the editor's view may have been, the question of whether the defamatory statement should have been included was often a matter of how the story should have been presented. And on that question, allowance had to be made for editorial judgement. If the article as a whole was in the public interest, opinions may reasonably differ over which details were needed to convey the general message. The fact that the judge, with the advantage of leisure and hindsight, might have made a different editorial decision should not have destroyed the defence. That would make the publication of articles which are, *ex hypothesi*, in the public interest, too risky and would discourage investigative reporting.

In *Jameel*, the inclusion of the names of large and respectable Saudi businesses was an important part of the story. It showed that cooperation with the US Treasury's requests was not confined to a few companies on the fringe of Saudi society but extended to companies which were by any test within the heartland of the Saudi business world. To convey this message, inclusion of the names was necessary. Generalisations such as 'prominent Saudi companies', which can mean anything or nothing, would not have served the same purpose.

3 What is 'responsible journalism'?

If the publication, including the defamatory statement, passed the public interest test, the inquiry then shifted to whether the steps taken to gather and publish the information were responsible and fair. The question in each case was whether the defendant behaved fairly and responsibly in gathering and publishing the information. In this case, Eady J said that the concept of responsible journalism was too vague. He said it was 'subjective'. The standard of responsible journalism is as objective and no more vague than standards such as 'reasonable care' which are regularly used in other branches of law. Greater certainty in its application is attained in two ways. First, a body of illustrative case law builds up. Secondly, just as the standard of reasonable care in particular areas, such as driving a vehicle, is made more concrete by extra-statutory codes of behaviour like the Highway Code, so the standard of responsible journalism is made more specific by the Code of Practice which has been adopted by the newspapers and ratified by the Press Complaints Commission (the Press Complaints Commission closed on 8 September 2014 and has been replaced by the Independent Press Standards Organisation (IPSO)). This, too, while not binding upon the courts, can provide valuable guidance.

Eady J at first instance was said to have rigidly applied the old law, insisting that *Reynolds* had changed nothing. It was not in his opinion sufficient that the article concerned a matter of public interest and was the product of responsible journalism. It was still necessary to show that the newspaper was under a social or moral duty to communicate to the public at large not merely the general message of the article (the Saudis were cooperating with the US Treasury) but the particular defamatory statement that accounts associated with the claimants were being monitored. Some of their Lordships felt that it was unnecessary and positively misleading to go back to the old law on classic privilege. Had the newspaper satisfied the conditions of responsible journalism? This was divided into three topics: the steps taken to verify the story, the opportunity given to the Jameel group to comment and the propriety of publication in the light of US diplomatic policy at the time. (See also *Flood* v *Times Newspapers Ltd* [2012] UKSC 11 (see below); *Prince Radu of Hohenzollern* v *Houston* [2008] EWCA Civ 921.)

The statutory defence

To what extent does the statutory defence in the Defamation Act 2013 s 4 change the common law defence? It is arguable that this defence does not belong under qualified privilege any more as the section simply states 'it is a defence'.

In the original Bill the *Reynolds* defence was effectively codified and, had it been enacted, the *Reynolds* criteria would have been part of the ten factors reduced to eight.

The public interest defence as now adopted is wider than the *Reynolds* defence and more flexible. It also has the potential advantage of reducing the likelihood of preliminary issues as to how the material came to be published.

The ingredients of this defence are:

1 That the statement complained of was or formed part of a statement on a matter of public interest. This is not defined in the Act.

2 The defendant must have reasonably believed that publishing the statement was in the public interest. In determining whether the defence is made out, the court is directed to have regard to all the circumstances of the case. The court in having regard to all circumstances is likely to be looking to see if the journalism was conducted in a responsible manner and is likely to apply an approach which is not dissimilar to that adopted in the *Reynolds*, *Jameel* and *Flood* cases.

How will the courts determine 'public interest' in the absence of a statutory definition? The choice would appear to be taking a wide view and deferring in significant measure to editorial judgement or taking the more restrictive view of the European Court of Human

Rights that the article must be said to add to public debate. It seems reasonably certain that the court would be inclined to the view that matters of celebrity gossip would not amount to public interest and would clearly differentiate from matters that simply happened to interest the public. However, there are grounds to think that a reasonably wide view would be taken of what constitutes public interest. There is both a subjective element in that the defendant must believe that the statement was in the public interest and an objective element, namely that the court must be satisfied that the statement was on a matter of public interest and that the defendant's belief was reasonable.

In deciding whether the defendant's belief was reasonable the court is likely to look at a number of the *Reynolds* factors.

A starting point could be the statement of Lord Brown in *Flood*:

> could whoever published the defamation given what they knew (and did not know) and whatever they had done (and had not done) to guard so far as possible against the publication of untrue defamatory material, properly have considered the publication in question to be in the public interest?

Under s 4(4) the court in determining whether it was reasonable for the defendant to believe that the statement complained of was in the public interest should make such allowance for editorial judgement as it considers appropriate. One of the original criticisms of the *Reynolds* defence was that it was applied in too strict a fashion and almost involved putting a judge in the editor's office.

Reportage

One of the issues which arose in qualified privilege as a result of the introduction of the public interest defence in *Reynolds* was the defence of reportage. This defence is the disinterested reporting of the fact that the statements had been made, without adopting the truth of them. In *Charman v Orion Publishing Group Ltd* [2008] 1 All ER 750 a police informant had made allegations of police corruption at his trial. The defendants published a book on police corruption which mixed reporting of the trial (statutory qualified privilege) with other material. The claimant, a former police officer, sued for libel and the defendant claimed reportage and public interest privilege. The Court of Appeal held that the reportage defence would be established where, judging the thrust of the report as a whole, the effect of the report was not to adopt the truth of what was being said, but to record the fact that the statements which were defamatory had been made. The protection was lost if the journalist adopted what had been said and made it his own or if he failed to report the story in a fair, disinterested, neutral way. To justify the attack on the claimant's reputation, the publication should always meet the standards of responsible journalism, the burden being on the defendants. As the book went much further than simply reporting and mixed other material based on the defendant's researches, the defence failed. However, a public interest defence was successful based on the *Jameel* principles.

In *Roberts v Gable* [2008] QB 502 an article published in a magazine reported a feud between two factions of the British National Party. There was held to be a defence of reportage. The article concerned political life, and judged as a whole was clearly a matter of public interest. The judge had been correct to decide that the effect of the article was to report that the allegations had been made, not that they were true, and that the allegations had not been adopted. Therefore, responsible journalism had not required verification of the truth. In all the circumstances, and considering the factors identified in *Reynolds*, the article had met the standards of responsible journalism.

Reportage is a special, and relatively rare, form of privilege. It arises where it is not the content of a reported allegation that is of public interest, but the fact that the allegation has been made. It protects the publisher if he has taken proper steps to verify the making of the allegation and provided that he does not adopt it. *Jameel*'s case was analogous to reportage because it was the fact that there were names of substantial Saudi Arabian companies on the blacklist that was of public interest, rather than the possibility that there might be good reason for the particular names to be listed. Just as in the case of reportage, the publishers did not need to verify the aspect of the publication that was defamatory.

The position is quite different where the public interest in the allegation that is reported lies in its content. In such a case the public interest in learning of the allegation lies in the fact that it is, or may be, true. It is in this situation that the responsible journalist must give consideration to the likelihood that the allegation is true. Public interest privilege absolves the publisher from the need to justify his defamatory publication, but the privilege will normally only be earned where the publisher has taken reasonable steps to satisfy himself that the allegation is true before he publishes it.

> In most cases the Reynolds (public interest privilege) defence will not get off the ground unless the journalist honestly and reasonably believed that the statement was true but there are cases ('reportage') in which the public interest lies simply in the fact that the statement was made, when it may be clear that the publisher does not subscribe to any belief in its truth. (Lord Hoffmann in *Jameel* v *Wall Street Journal* [2007] 1 AC 359.)

Section 4(3) of the Defamation Act 2013 recognises the common law doctrine of reportage.

Flood v *Times Newspapers Ltd* [2012] UKSC 11

The claimant, a serving police officer, brought an action in defamation against the defendants after the publication of an article in the newspaper and on its website concerning allegations of corruption against the claimant. The article included information in a press statement issued by the police, and in addition named the claimant who had not been identified in the police statement and included the details of the allegations made to the police against him. A police investigation was initiated but no evidence was found to support the allegations against the claimant. After the conclusions of the investigation were communicated to the defendant, the original article remained on its website unamended.

The website
The defendant relied on a defence of qualified privilege in relation to the website version of the article. The trial judge held that the website publication attracted qualified privilege at the time of publication, but that the website publication had ceased to be privileged after the defendant learned of the conclusions of the police investigation. This was upheld by the Court of Appeal.

The newspaper article
The publication of the police statement came within the statutory privilege in section 15(1) of the Defamation Act 1996.

The Supreme Court held that it was impossible to publish the details of the article without disclosing to those close to the claimant that he was the officer to whom it related. He would be identified as such by the other members of the Extradition Unit and anyone else who knew that he had been removed from that unit. If he were not named, other members of the Extradition Unit might come under suspicion.

The publication of the allegations (which were not within the police statement) was defended on the basis of public interest privilege. The Court of Appeal held that the journalists had failed to take sufficient steps to verify the details of the allegations so that their publication did not constitute 'responsible journalism' and did not attract qualified privilege.

The Supreme Court held, that qualified privilege existed where the public interest justified publication notwithstanding that it carried the risk of defaming an individual who would have no remedy.

A balance had to be struck between the desirability that the public should receive the information and the potential harm which might be caused if the individual were defamed; that the overriding test was that of responsible journalism; that, since the story in the present case, if true, was of high public interest which lay not only in the fact of police corruption but also in its nature and concern that the allegations might not be properly investigated, and since the allegations themselves were the whole story and it would have been impossible to publish the article without identifying the claimant as the officer against whom the allegations had been made or publishing the facts supporting the allegation, it had been in the public interest that both the accusation against the claimant and the facts supporting it, including the claimant's identity, should be published.

The public interest lay in the content of the allegations and the fact that they might be true, the publisher would be absolved from the need to justify the defamatory publication only if reasonable steps had been taken before publishing to verify that the allegations were true and if he reasonably believed that there were grounds for believing that they were; that, on the facts, the defendant's journalists had been justified in concluding on the basis of the information available that there was a strong circumstantial case against the claimant and that there was a serious possibility that he was guilty of corruption; and that, accordingly, the requirements of responsible journalism were satisfied in respect of the newspaper article and the defendant was entitled to qualified privilege.

At the heart of the case was the question of verification. Public interest privilege tends to arise where the facts cannot be proved to be true or false and the question is whether it is responsible journalism to publish the facts. The steps taken by the journalist to check the facts are one of the factors going towards responsible journalism. Each case will turn on its own facts but in this case the journalists had been reasonably satisfied, on the basis both of the 'supporting facts' and of the action of the police that there was a serious possibility that Sergeant Flood had been guilty of corruption. They were therefore found to have acted responsibly.

This was not a case of 'reportage' as the defamatory allegation lay not in the fact that a defamatory allegation had been made but in the content of the allegation. (See above.)

Malice

For malice generally, see Chapter 1.

A defence of qualified privilege will be defeated by malice. A statement will be made maliciously where the publisher does not have a positive belief in its truth, where the maker is reckless as to truth or falsity. Alternatively, the defendant may have had an honest belief in his statement but misused the publication for a purpose other than that for which the privilege is granted in order to vent ill feeling towards the person who is the subject of the statement.

Horrocks v Lowe [1974] 2 WLR 282

The claimant and defendant were elected members of a local authority. The defendant made defamatory remarks about the claimant at a council meeting. The defendant pleaded privilege. The claimant claimed that the privilege was destroyed by malice. The House of Lords held that, as the defendant honestly believed that his statement was true, there was no malice. Malice would exist only if it could be shown that he had been actuated by spite or ill will.

Angel v H Bushel Ltd [1968] 1 QB 813

> The claimant dealt in scrap and was introduced to the defendants by a mutual friend. The parties did business together but things went wrong. The defendants wrote to the mutual friend alleging that the claimant was 'not conversant with normal business ethics'. The defendants pleaded qualified privilege, but it was held that the privilege was destroyed by malice. The letter was unnecessary and written out of anger.

Malice and public interest privilege

Whether the publication carries qualified privilege is a question of law for the judge. Whether publication is activated by malice is a mixed question of law and fact and therefore one for the judge and jury, where one is used. One effect of the introduction of public interest privilege was to move certain factors which previously went to malice, to the question of whether the publication was privileged and therefore for the judge. This marked a shift in power in the courtroom. Several of Lord Nicholls' factors raised matters which are normally associated with malice, previously an issue for the jury in a libel case. *Reynold* has the effect of transferring these factual issues to the judge to decide and also moved the burden of proof on certain issues from the claimant to the defendant. This was one of the reasons why *Reynolds* was rejected in New Zealand. Qualified privilege applied to press coverage of the political activities of politicians, leaving the question of how the story was produced for the jury to determine at the malice stage.

The effect of the Court of Appeal's decision in *Loutchansky* would appear to remove any jury involvement in the issue of qualified privilege and transfer the burden of proof on recklessness from the claimant to the defendant. It would appear that the burden will vary according to the nature of the story. This can be done on the basis of a spectrum running from political information at one end to entertainment, including sporting issues, at the other. At one end of the spectrum, if the story is concerned with political information, the defendant would only appear to have to meet the test of not having been reckless. At the other end of the spectrum, it appears that the defendant will have to discharge the heavier burden of proving that they were not negligent.

Remedies

The normal remedy in a defamation action is a suitable correction or apology and/or damages. Damages are awarded by a judge through the summary procedure, or by a judge or jury if the case goes to a full trial.

The amount of damages awarded by juries in defamation actions became a problem which has now been rectified by statute and case law. (See 'Introduction' above.) There is now a ceiling on general damages of £200,000, with a generous margin to be left at the upper end of the scale to accommodate more serious libels. (*Campbell* v *Newsgroup Newspapers* [2002] All ER (D) 513 (Jul).) There will inevitably be some libels which are so serious that the upper limit will have to be breached but the perceived advantage of the limit is to give greater clarity and consistency so that the consequences of conduct can be said to be 'prescribed by law' and will encourage settlement.

See Chapter 28 for exemplary damages. Punitive or exemplary damages may be awarded in a libel action where the defendant decided to publish a libel, calculating that the possible damages would not be exceeded by the profit they would make on the book. (*Cassell & Co Ltd* v *Broome* [1972] AC 1027.)

If the alleged libel comes to the claimant's attention before publication, they may seek an injunction to prevent publication. An interlocutory injunction will generally not be granted where the defence is that the words are incapable of any defamatory meaning, the claimant is not referred to, or justification. If the Human Rights Act 1998 s 12(3) applies to a defamation action, on an application to restrain publication, the court is required to take into account whether the applicant is 'likely' to succeed in its application at trial before any such restraint can be granted. This appears to dilute the requirement at common law which is that the applicant has 'no realistic chance of success'. (*Bonnard* v *Perryman* [1891] 2 Ch 269.) However, in *Greene* v *Associated Newspapers* [2005] QB 972 the Court of Appeal held that s 12(3) had no application to defamation as the section is concerned with freedom of expression and could not therefore be taken to reduce the common law test.

See Chapter 28 for injunctions.

Parties

A corporation can sue for defamation where the statement affects its corporate reputation. It is not possible for local authorities or departments of central government to sue.

Derbyshire County Council v Times Newspapers Ltd [1993] AC 534

The defendant newspaper published articles questioning the propriety of investments by the claimant council in superannuation funds. The House of Lords held that no action lay, although proceedings could be brought for malicious falsehood by a council, or in defamation by an individual councillor.

The reason behind the decision was that it would be unduly inhibiting on freedom of speech in a democracy to allow such bodies to sue to protect their governing reputation.

The principle has been used to deny a political party an action in defamation. (*Goldsmith* v *Bhoyrul* [1997] 4 All ER 286.)

A trade union cannot sue for defamation, as it is an unincorporated association. (*EEPTU* v *Times Newspapers Ltd* [1980] 1 All ER 1097.)

Rehabilitation of Offenders Act 1974

The Act provides that after a period of time a criminal conviction is spent and should not be referred to. Whether a conviction is spent depends on the sentence passed: for example, sentences of more than two-and-a-half years in prison are never spent; prison sentences of six months to two-and-a-half years are spent after ten years; prison sentences of less than six months are spent after seven years.

The Act affects defamation in two ways. Where a claimant's spent conviction is referred to, then the defendant can still plead justification as it is a fact that the conviction existed at one stage. But in these circumstances malice will destroy the defence of justification: i.e. that the defendant's major motive in revealing the spent conviction was to injure the claimant's reputation.

Second, where a spent conviction is referred to in court and is held inadmissible, the defendant cannot plead privilege.

Defamation and the Human Rights Act 1998

Objective
5

See Chapter 1 for
tort law and human
rights.

Two of the Articles in the European Convention on Human Rights are relevant to defamation.

Article 10 of the European Convention on Human Rights provides:

1 Everyone has the right to freedom of expression: This right shall include freedom to hold opinions and to receive and input information and ideas without interference by public authority regardless of formalities . . .

2 The exercise of these freedoms, since it carries with it duties and responsibilities, may be subject to such formalities, conditions, restrictions and penalties as are prescribed by law and are necessary in a democratic society . . . for the protection of the reputation or rights of others . . .

Article 10 can be invoked directly in a defamation action in England. (Human Rights Act 1998.) Article 10(1) gives a right to freedom of expression which is subject to a number of derogations in Article 10(2), of which the relevant one is the protection of reputation. Any such restriction must be 'prescribed by law', in the sense that it is sufficiently certain for a citizen to obey it, and must be 'necessary in a democratic society' for the relevant purpose. The latter means that the restriction must be proportionate to the aim that it pursues and there must be a pressing social need. This means that any restriction on free speech must be justified and English law has to draw a balance between the two protected rights.

The Article therefore requires national law to draw a balance between freedom of speech and protection of reputation. The question is whether English law does this. The battleground is in the areas of qualified privilege and burden of proof. On the former, look at *Reynolds* and ask whether the House of Lords was justified in rejecting a generic defence of dissemination of political information. On the latter, the question is whether it should be up to the defendant to prove that the statement was true or whether the claimant should have to prove that it was untrue.

English defamation law has already been found wanting and changed in accordance with Article 10. (See *Tolstoy Miloslavsky* v *United Kingdom* (1995) 20 EHRR 442.) It has also made efforts to adapt to the balancing of interests required by Article 10 (see *Derbyshire County Council* v *Times Newspapers Ltd* [1993] AC 534) by preventing governmental bodies from suing in libel, and the House of Lords has said that it is satisfied that English law in this area is consistent with the requirements of Article 10. (*Reynolds* v *Times Newspapers Ltd* [1999] 3 WLR 1010.)

The second article is Article 8, which protects a person's privacy. Any protection given to the media in relation to freedom of speech may impinge on a person's right to privacy. This may raise the difficult question of the amount of protection that should be given to a public figure, such as a politician, when balanced against the right of the media to report. At what point does public life end and private begin?

In areas where, as the Lord Chancellor said, the common law is still developing, the courts will inevitably be influenced by Article 8 in the choice which they have to make as to direction. The days when the courts eschewed making new law are past. The pace of the modern world and the application of the law in ever new contexts have led to a franker acknowledgement that courts do make and develop new law. The development has not always been coherent or consistent. The step-by-step approach of the common law has sometimes seemed to approximate to one step forward, the next back, or to an enormous circle, as in the field of liability in negligence for economic loss unaccompanied by any bodily injury or physical damage. Privacy is an area where the common law has been slow to act. The Convention scheduled to the 1998 Act has the merit of setting out the different balancing considerations which are relevant when courts make decisions in this area. As under Article 8, so at common law, one may expect to find courts considering and evaluating both the manner and circumstances in which potentially private material was obtained and also the purpose for which it is deployed, both when assessing whether common law protection should be available and when assessing whether the public interest or some countervailing private interest outweighs any prima facie claim to privacy.

However, the Act does not authorise or oblige the courts simply to abandon previously established legal principles and to start afresh with directly enforceable rights prescribed by the Convention. Parties must bring their cases according to law, and English courts have to work within English common law, which in the last analysis may, of course, be changed by Parliament if necessary to reflect the Convention. The Act does not introduce directly enforceable rights between private individuals, and, where the parties have clearly established legal rights and duties, the courts must give effect to those rights and duties.

Has the advent of the Human Rights Act 1998 made any difference to this area of law? An English court must now give explicit consideration to the right of freedom of expression (Human Rights Act 1998 s 12(4)) and to the relevant jurisprudence of the European Court of Human Rights (s 2(1)).

Reform

It appears doubtful, given the decisions in *Reynolds*, *Jameel*, *Derbyshire* and *John*, that English courts will go much further towards freedom of expression in this area. Arguments put to courts are likely to centre around the development of a *Sullivan* defence as used in the United States (*New York Times* v *Sullivan* 376 US 254 (1964)) where, if the claimant is a 'public figure', it is necessary for them to prove 'actual malice' against the defendant. This means that, even if the defamatory statement is untrue, the claimant will fail unless the defendant made it maliciously. English law has so far refused to accept this principle and it is at least arguable that the more limited protection offered by qualified privilege is sufficient.

However, English libel law is under severe pressure as a result of modern methods of communication. A system which was designed for nineteenth-century methods of communication is proving unsuitable in the twenty-first century. The international nature of modern media means that statements can be made in one country and accessed anywhere in the world. England and Wales have faced accusations that libel law here gives rise to 'libel tourism' where a claimant with no obvious link to this country brings proceedings here. This has led to courts in the United States refusing to enforce English libel judgments and US media outlets threatening to bar access to their internet sites to users in this country. New York State passed the Libel Terrorism Protection Act (2008) ('Rachel's Law') which states that foreign libel judgments are unenforceable unless the foreign law grants the defendant the same First Amendment protections which are available in New York State.

Do the reforms implemented in the Defamation Act 2013 go far enough? Much of the Act appears to be codification of existing case law. However, two sections attempt to address perceived problems in the law of defamation.

1 The 'single publication rule' – the current law provides that each time a reader views an internet publication online the one-year limitation period is reset. Prior to the internet, publishers could derive comfort from the expiration of the limitation period, but such

comfort no longer exists when articles are available online and some publishers will have a significant archive on the internet. The Act now (s 8) provides that, for limitation purposes, the date of first publication would be the date when the limitation period commences.

2 'Libel tourism' – where parties with little connection to this jurisdiction become involved in libel proceedings in England and Wales. The extent to which libel tourism exists is rather unclear, but this section (s 9) provides that the court must be satisfied that, of 'all' the places in which the statement complained of has been published, England and Wales is 'clearly' the most appropriate place in which to bring an action in respect of the statement. Whilst this seems entirely sensible, it is easy to see that in an age of global business and media conglomerates its application to the facts may not always be straightforward.

However, the Act fails to address the most important issue in publication cases, namely costs. Until such time as the government takes action and amends the law on recoverable costs, it is ignoring the most fundamental issue at play.

? Question

Peter, a political agent, had an argument with Helen, the constituency MP. Peter dictated a speech on to a dictaphone, intending to make the speech at a constituency meeting. In the speech he said that 'ignorance, vanity and corruption are all too common in politics today; the virtues of honesty and adherence to the law are rarely adhered to'.

Peter gave the tape to his secretary, James, to type up, but by an error James sent the tape to Helen. The parcel was opened by Helen's husband, Alfred, who played the tape. Helen is also a barrister. Advise Helen.

Suggested approach

There are three major issues in a defamation answer. Is the statement slander or libel? The three elements in the claimant's case. Are there any relevant defences?

Libel is where a defamatory meaning is conveyed in a permanent form. Slander is where a temporary form such as speech is used. The old maxim was 'slander to the ear and libel to the eye'. However, modern means of communication have made this uncertain. There is no direct authority on tape recordings or dictaphones, so the case could be either slander or libel. The major distinction is that libel is actionable *per se*, without proof of damage. Slander requires proof of damage except in two cases. It would appear that the words used here would come within the exception in the Defamation Act 1952 s 2.

Helen must prove that the words used were defamatory, that they referred to her and that they were published by the defendant.

The test for whether words are defamatory should be stated and applied to the facts of the question. The words 'ignorance, vanity and corruption' would appear to be defamatory on the face of them, as would the words 'honesty and adherence to the law are rarely adhered to'. The latter two may also be defamatory by virtue of innuendo. Helen is a barrister and this fact is known to Alfred.

The words must refer to the claimant. Helen is not mentioned by name, but this is not necessary. Neither is it necessary for everyone who might hear the words to be able to identify her. The test is that laid down in *Morgan v Odhams Press* (1971). Alfred's special knowledge would be relevant here.

If a class of persons is defamed, then normally no member of the class may sue unless the class is small enough or there is something which particularly identifies the claimant. Politics and law are probably too large as groups.

Publication identifies the defendants to the action. Peter has published to James and to Alfred. James has also published to Alfred. With regard to James he would appear to have a defence under the Defamation Act 1996 s 1 concerning responsibility for publication. (State the requirements and apply.) The publication by Peter to James may attract qualified privilege. The publication to Alfred will come under negligent publication. Had Helen opened the parcel there would have been no publication. Apply *Huth* v *Huth* and *Theaker* v *Richardson*.

Peter may offer to make amends and if this is acceptable publish an apology to Helen and pay her an agreed sum in damages. If his offer is not accepted then he may rely on that offer as a defence. He may decide to withdraw his offer and plead truth or honest opinion as defences. If the statement is factual then truth is appropriate. If opinion, then honest opinion. (Apply the relevant points.) As the parties have previously had bad relations then malice may be relevant, in which case any defence of qualified privilege will be defeated. Could malice be avoided by running a 'public interest' defence? In *Kearns* v *General Council of the Bar* [2003] 2 All ER 534 the Court of Appeal stated that the defence only applied to media defendants but this has been disapproved by the Privy Council in *Seaga* v *Harper* (2008). If the defence did apply then Peter would have to establish that the speech was on a subject of public interest, and that the defendant must have reasonably believed that publishing the statement was in the public interest.

Helen could apply for an injunction to restrain delivery of the speech but, as reference to the claimant is likely to be raised, it is unlikely to be granted. If the case is dealt with by a judge under the summary procedure then they may award Helen damages up to a statutory ceiling, order Peter to publish a statement to the effect that Helen's claim against him has been upheld and grant an injunction restraining Peter from delivering the speech. If the judge is satisfied that Helen's claim has little chance of success or that there is no reason for a trial, they will dismiss the case. If they consider that there is no arguable defence or that Helen would not be adequately compensated under the terms of the summary procedure, then they will refer the case for a full trial with jury.

Summary

This chapter is concerned with the tort of defamation.

- Defamation consists of the torts of libel and slander. Slander is where a defamatory meaning is conveyed in a transitory form such as speech. Libel is where it is in a permanent form. Libel is actionable without proof of damage (*per se*), whereas damage must be proved in a slander action except in two circumstances.

- Defamation protects a person's interest in their reputation and does not require a particular state of mind on the part of the defendant.

- Defamation has a number of oddities: there is still a provision for trial by jury; an action will terminate on the claimant's death; proceedings can be brought wherever the defamatory statement is published; there is no legal aid; and where a jury is used the jury determines the damages. Libel damages grew to be excessive and statute and case law now control the amount of damages. Jury trial will now only be used in very limited circumstances.

- A claimant must prove that the words used were defamatory; that they referred to the claimant; and that they were published by the defendant.

- The test for defamatory meaning is 'the publication of a statement which tends to lower a person in the estimation of right thinking members of society generally; or which tends to make them shun or avoid that person'. The words must be taken in context. It is the function of the jury to determine whether the words are defamatory. The judge directs the jury on the meaning of defamation and in certain cases can withdraw the case from the jury. There is now a summary procedure available in defamation cases for minor claims. The limit for damages is £10,000. Where the words have more than one literal meaning the claimant must plead and prove the meaning he alleges. This is known as the false innuendo. Where the words have a hidden meaning this is known as an innuendo.

- The claimant must prove that he is the person referred to in the defamatory statement. In the case of fictional names, where a real person claims to have been identified the defence of offer of amends can be used. If two people have the same name the publisher must be careful to identify the one he is referring to. Extrinsic evidence can be admitted to prove reference. (*Morgan* v *Odhams Press*.) Where a group of people are referred to (class defamation) either an individual must be identifiable or the group must be small enough for each person to sue.

- The defamatory statement must be published by the defendant to a third party. Every repetition of a defamatory statement is fresh publication. There is a statutory distributor's defence in s 1 of the Defamation Act 1996 available to secondary publishers. The secondary publisher must have taken all reasonable care. There are now specific provisions on internet publication. (Defamation Act 2013 s 5.)

- A defence of offer of amends was brought in by the Defamation Act 1996.

- There is a defence of truth on statements of fact if the defendant could show that the imputation conveyed by the statement is 'substantially true.' The defendant must remove the 'sting' of the libel. The words must be true in substance and fact.

- Where the statement is one of opinion, there is a defence of 'honest opinion'. The statement made would need to be one of opinion and not an assertion of fact; it must indicate the basis of the opinion; and the opinion must be one that an honest person could have held on the basis of a fact which was in existence at the time the statement was published.

- Absolute privilege is a complete defence to defamation. It applies to statements made in Parliament by MPs and peers; to statements made in court by participants; to fair, accurate and contemporaneous reports of court proceedings; statements made by one officer of state to another; and possibly to solicitor–client communications.

- Qualified privilege can be destroyed by malice in its traditional form. There are privileged reports, such as reports of proceedings in Parliament and reports privileged under the Defamation Act 1996. There is a common law qualified privilege based on reciprocal duties such as the giving of a reference.

- A new defence called 'public interest privilege' has recently been created, although it is arguable whether it is a form of privilege. It is a defence to an action for defamation for the defendant to show that the statement complained of is, or forms part of, a statement on a matter of public interest; and the defendant acted responsibly in publishing the statement complained of. (Defamation Act 2013 s 4.) The remedies for defamation are damages or an injunction.

Further reading

Descheemaeker, E. (2011), '"Veritas non est defamatio"? Truth as a Defence in the Law of Defamation' *Legal Studies* 1.

Gibbons, T. (1996), 'Defamation Reconsidered' 16(4) *Oxford Journal of Legal Studies* 587.

Index on Censorship Report on Libel Reform – www.libelreform.org/the-report.

Ministry of Justice, 'Draft Defamation Bill (Consultation Paper CP3/11).

Ministry of Justice, 'The Government's Response to the report of the Joint Committee on the Draft Defamation Bill' (Cm 8295).

Kaye, J. M. (1975), 'Libel or Slander: Two Torts or One?' 91 LQR 524.

Loveland, I. (1994), 'Defamation of Government: Taking Lessons from America' *Legal Studies* 206 (*Sullivan*).

Mullis, A. and Scott, A. (2009), 'Something Rotten in the State of English Libel Law? A Rejoinder to the Clamour for Reform of Defamation' *Communications Law* 173.

Trinidade, F. (2000), 'Defamatory Statements and Political Discussions' 116 LQR 185 (*Reynolds*).

Williams, J. (1997), 'Reforming Defamation Law in the United Kingdom' *Tort Law Review* 206.

Yang L.K. (2014), 'Reynolds Privilege Transformed' 130 LQR 24 (s 4 Defamation Act 2013).

22

Privacy

Objectives

After reading this chapter you will:

1. Appreciate the concept of privacy.
2. Understand the various methods by which privacy is protected in English law.
3. Have a critical knowledge of the development of privacy law through the law on breach of confidence.
4. Appreciate the methods by which privacy is balanced against freedom of speech.
5. Have a critical knowledge of the role played by human rights in framing privacy laws.

Introduction

Objective 1

Privacy is notoriously difficult to define. For present purposes it will be treated as facts about a person which most individuals do not want widely known about themselves. A privacy claim is usually founded on true facts but if the facts are untrue a person has an action for defamation.

Example

An article in a newspaper states that a famous actress has an addiction to cocaine and is being treated for drug dependency. If the story is untrue then the actress will have an action for libel. If the story is true then she may have an action for invasion of her privacy through the action for breach of confidence.

Privacy is an area where the common law has been slow to act and the courts have inevitably been influenced by Article 8 of the European Convention on Human Rights in the choice which they have to make as to direction. The days when the courts eschewed making new law are past. The pace of the modern world and the application of the law in ever new contexts have led to a franker acknowledgement that courts do make and develop new law. The development has not always been coherent or consistent. The Convention scheduled to the Human Rights Act 1998 sets out the different balancing considerations which are relevant when courts make decisions in this area. Under Article 8 and at common law, the courts are considering and evaluating both the manner and circumstances in which potentially private material was obtained and also the purpose for which it is deployed, both when assessing whether common law protection should be available and when assessing whether the public interest or some countervailing private interest outweighs any prima facie claim to privacy.

However, the Act does not authorise or oblige the courts simply to abandon previously established legal principles and to start afresh with directly enforceable rights prescribed by the Convention. Parties must bring their cases according to law, and English courts have to work within English common law, which in the last analysis may, of course, be changed by Parliament if necessary to reflect the Convention. The Act does not introduce directly enforceable rights between private individuals, and, where the parties have clearly established legal rights and duties, the courts must give effect to those rights and duties.

The relationship between national law and Strasbourg jurisprudence raises two major questions. Article 8 is primarily directed against state interference with the right to a private life but does this impose a positive obligation on the state to provide a remedy when one party invades the privacy of another? Secondly, how is the apparent clash between freedom of speech and privacy to be dealt with?

Other jurisdictions in the world have taken radically different stances in relation to privacy. France has very strong privacy laws and gives high levels of protection to people, including major public figures. The United States, influenced by the First Amendment, gives protection for truthful privacy-invading disclosures if there is a public interest justification.

What is privacy?

The most comprehensive enquiry into privacy in the United Kingdom was the Calcutt Report in 1990. The report was primarily concerned with self-regulation of the press but a key issue concerning the press was invasion of privacy.

Calcutt Report (1990)

1 A working definition

3.5   A working definition of privacy, however imprecise, is, nevertheless needed as a yardstick against which to measure complaints and solutions. Privacy could be regarded as the antithesis of what is public: hence everything concerning an individual's home, family, religion, health, sexuality, personal legal and personal financial affairs. French privacy law generally adopts this approach. On the other hand, an individual is a member of society and, as such, cannot expect to enjoy total privacy. The formulation 'the right to be let alone' is too simplistic. There is a mismatch between what an individual might regard as private and what might be regarded as such by his neighbours, including the press.

3.6   Most stories in the press about individuals are liable to be regarded by them as an intrusion into their privacy unless they themselves have sought publicity or have consented to publication. The most obvious examples are favourable stories put out by publicity agents or press officers to promote authors or others who wish to be in the public eye. The fact that someone has consented to give an interview or to be photographed does not, however, mean that he surrenders all claims to privacy. The real issue is not whether there has been intrusion, but whether the intrusion is unwarranted.

3.7 For working purposes we have adopted a formulation of privacy similar to that in paragraph 3.2. Our formulation is: the right of the individual to be protected against intrusion into his personal life or affairs, or those of his family, by direct physical means or by publication of information. We discuss in paragraph 3.12 the extent to which this right needs to be offset against other rights.

3.8 A right to privacy could include protection from:

(a) physical intrusion;
(b) publication of hurtful or embarrassing personal material (whether true or false);
(c) publication of inaccurate or misleading personal material; and
(d) publication of photographs or recordings of the individual taken without consent.

2 Accuracy

3.9 We received a number of complaints about inaccuracies (including alleged libels). In some cases witnesses considered that they had been misquoted, treated unfairly or even deceived. However, inaccuracy alone does not determine that there has been an intrusion into privacy. We would not necessarily regard a distorted account of an interview as such an intrusion (even though, in some American states, presenting someone in false light is covered by the tort of invasion of privacy).

3 Taste

3.10 We are also sent cuttings of stories which we considered to be in exceptionally bad taste. A story which gives offence on grounds of taste does not, however, necessarily constitute an intrusion into privacy. Conversely such an intrusion is not necessarily in bad taste. Public taste may, nevertheless, influence attitudes about the amount of privacy particularly individuals should enjoy.

3.11 It is not our task to comment on matters of taste as such. In this context we note that argument put by, among others, the editor of the *Sun* (Mr Kelvin MacKenzie):

> Tabloid journalism cannot be condemned simply because it is brash or noisy or declamatory. It must only be called to order if it is false, irresponsible or reports untruths.

4 Freedom of speech

3.12 Individual privacy cannot be considered in isolation. It must be weighed along-side freedom of speech and expression. This is recognised in countries with privacy laws, sometimes expressly. In the United States of America the tort of invasion of privacy is always seen in the context of the constitutional right to free speech. Similar rights are to be found in those European countries which have privacy laws. The European Convention on Human Rights provides in Article 10 that 'everyone has the right to freedom of expression'; Article 8 provides that 'everyone has the right to respect for his private and family life, his home and his correspondence'.

The interest which underlies privacy laws is autonomy. This has been recognised by the House of Lords.

What human rights law has done is to identify private information as something worth protecting as an aspect of human autonomy and dignity . . . the right to control the dissemination of information about one's private life. (***Campbell* v *Mirror Group Newspapers (No 2)*** (2005) 4 All ER 793.)

Once the ability to exercise informational control about one's own life is given, this has the effect of protecting personal dignity and avoiding feelings of shame and embarrassment.

The values that are in issue have been summed up as:

[Privacy] provides space for individuals to think for themselves and to engage in creative activity, free from observation and supervision. Further, personal relationships could not develop if participants felt that every move was watched and reported . . . privacy is an aspect of human dignity and autonomy. It enables individuals to exercise some degree of independence or control over their lives. (Barendt)

The general principle

Article 8 of the European Convention on Human Rights provides:

1 Everyone has the right to respect for his private and family life, his home and his correspondence.

2 There shall be no interference by a *public authority* with the exercise of this right except such as is in accordance with the law and is necessary in a democratic society in the interests of national security or the economic well-being of the country, for the prevention of disorder or crime, for the protection of health or morals, or for the protection of the rights and freedoms of others.

The position in English law

Objective 2

It is well known in English law there is no right to privacy and the facts of the present case are a graphic illustration of the desirability of Parliament considering whether and in what circumstances statutory provision can be made to protect the privacy of individuals.

This case nonetheless highlights, yet again, the failure of both the common law of England and statute to protect in an effective way the personal privacy of individual citizens.

[A right to privacy] has so long been disregarded here that it can be recognised now only by the legislature . . . it is to be hoped that the making good of this signal shortcoming in our law will not be long delayed. (***Kaye* v *Robertson*** [1991] FSR 62.)

I would reject the invitation to declare that since at the latest 1950 there has been a previously unknown tort of invasion of privacy. (***Wainwright* v *Home Office*** [2003] 4 All ER 969.)

English law, historically, did not recognise a right to privacy in the sense of a tort of invasion of privacy. Any protection was given incidentally by other causes of action. This is not the case in many other jurisdictions. However, the difficulty of defining a general right to privacy as opposed to specific instances such as the right not to have your medical records disclosed, has made the English courts reluctant to use the forum of litigation to create such a right. The debate on privacy is ongoing and was brought sharply into the mainstream media by the phone hacking scandal at the News of the World and the subsequent Leveson inquiry.

Progress towards a statutory right to privacy

The debate on the adequacy of existing legal principles to protect the privacy of individuals began in the United States as long ago as 1890, with an article published by Samual D. Warren and Louis D. Brandeis in the *Harvard Law Review* (1890) 4 Harv LR 193. They suggested that it was possible to generalise certain cases on defamation, breach of copyright and breach of confidence as being based on the protection of a common value called privacy and that the courts should declare the existence of a general principle which protected a person's appearance, sayings, acts and personal relations from being exposed in public. US courts began to develop a jurisprudence of privacy but it became apparent that it could not be confined within a single principle. What emerged was a complex of four different torts:

1 intrusion upon the claimant's physical solitude or seclusion – this would include unlawful searches, telephone tapping, telephoto lens photography and telephone harassment;

2 public disclosure of private facts;

3 publicly putting the claimant in a false light;

4 appropriating the claimant's name or likeness.

You may wish to contrast these with the possible areas to be covered by privacy identified in the Calcutt Report at para 3.8.

In the twentieth century in England, the debate gave rise to a report produced by JUSTICE in 1970, which recommended the introduction of a right to privacy, the interference with which would be a new tort.

There followed an unsuccessful attempt to introduce the necessary legislation by private member's Bill, in the absence of government support.

Subsequent reports, however, have rejected the need for a general right of privacy which is protected by a new tort.

Parliament has proved reluctant to create a tort of privacy and this has proved to be a major problem in English law when developing protection for privacy.

Limited recognition of the existence of a right to privacy

Existence of a right to privacy has received limited statutory recognition in England by entrusting Ofcom with the task of considering and adjudicating on complaints of unwarranted infringement of privacy in or in connection with the obtaining of material included in sound or television programmes.

The lack of legal development in this area did not mean that it was not hotly and repeatedly discussed, and certain extra-legal protections exist, expressly directed to the protection of legitimate interests of privacy, which may be regarded either as part of the price of or a reason for the absence of legal protection. The most prominent involve Ofcom (for broadcast material) and the Press Complaints Commission.

The Press Complaints Commission, for example, applies a code, which is of value for the principles that it identifies but suffers from the absence of direct sanctions, whether by way of injunction or damages, which private law can supply.

Clause 3 deals with privacy.

3 *Privacy
(i) Everyone is entitled to respect for his or her private and family life, home, health and correspondence, including digital communications.

(ii) Editors will be expected to justify intrusions into any individual's private life without consent. Account will be taken of the complainant's own public disclosures of information.

(iii) It is unacceptable to photograph individuals in private places without their consent.

Note – Private places are public or private property where there is a reasonable expectation of privacy.

Some clauses of the code (including Clause 3) can be derogated from if it is in the public interest to do so.

The public interest

There may be exceptions to the clauses marked * where they can be demonstrated to be in the public interest.

1 The public interest includes, but is not confined to:
   (i)   Detecting or exposing crime or serious impropriety.
   (ii) Protecting public health and safety.
   (iii) Preventing the public from being misled by an action or statement of an individual or organisation.
2 There is a public interest in freedom of expression itself.
3 Whenever the public interest is invoked, the PCC will require editors to demonstrate fully that they reasonably believed that publication, or journalistic activity undertaken with a view to publication, would be in the public interest.
4 The PCC will consider the extent to which material is already in the public domain, or will become so.
5 In cases involving children under 16, editors must demonstrate an exceptional public interest to over-ride the normally paramount interest of the child.

This form of self-regulation has been supported by governments until recently. It has the advantage of being quick and cheap. The drawbacks are that there are no sanctions on the press other than a published retraction and apology and retraction, and it appears as if the press are policing themselves.

A number of scandals involving the press, particularly the *News of the World*, led to an inquiry being set up by the Prime Minister into press regulation. The inquiry (the Leveson Inquiry) reported in 2012 (*Report into the Culture, Practices and Ethics of the Press* (2012)) and made a number of recommendations. These included:

(i)   A new independent regulatory body with no serving editors
(ii) A Standards Code which recognized the importance of freedom of speech and publication in the public interest
(iii) The new body to have the right to award financial penalties and order apologies and corrections
(iv) The system to be underpinned by legislation.

Predictably this produced strong opposition from the press, who objected to legislation being introduced on the grounds of freedom of speech.

Protection of privacy through other means

There are four routes by which the absence of a remedy for an invasion of privacy could be remedied:

1 To leave matters in the hands of the Press Complaints Commission and Ofcom and their codes. However, they have no compensatory or restraining powers.

2 For Parliament to introduce a general statutory right of privacy.

3 For the courts to introduce such a right through development of a new free-standing common law tort.

4 For the courts to continue to develop existing remedies under the influence of the Human Rights Act. This is the route that English law has taken. Prior to human rights law having an effect, claimants resorted to a variety of other causes of action in an attempt to obtain redress for what is in essence an invasion of their privacy:

(a) *infringement of copyright* where the defendant has copied a literary or other work of the claimant in which copyright subsists;

See Chapter 21 for defamation.

(b) *defamation* for oral or written false statements about the claimant which lower them in the esteem of right-thinking people;

See Chapter 23 for malicious falsehood.

(c) *malicious falsehood* for oral or written statements maliciously made about the claimant and which cause them financial loss;

See Chapter 20 for trespass to the person.

(d) *trespass to the person, trespass to property and nuisance* where the invasion amounts to an assault or battery, to unlawful entry on private property or unlawful interference with the enjoyment of property;

See Chapter 23 for passing off.

(e) *passing off* where the defendant misrepresents something of their own as associated or connected in some way with the claimant;

(f) *breach of confidence* where equity will restrain the use or disclosure of confidential information imparted to or acquired by the defendant in circumstances importing an obligation of confidence; and

(g) *Protection from Harassment Act 1997*.

Often, in such cases, it was apparent to the court that what the claimant was really complaining about was an invasion of their privacy. This was expressly recognised by Bingham LJ in **Kaye v Robertson** (below).

Kaye v Robertson [1991] FSR 62

P was a well-known actor who had undergone extensive surgery after suffering a head injury driving during a storm. *D1* was editor of *The Sunday Sport*. *D2* was publisher of *The Sunday Sport*.

Journalists from *D2*'s newspaper got into *P*'s hospital room ignoring notices prohibiting entry and interviewed and took photographs of *P*. *P* apparently agreed to be interviewed and did not object to the photographs. *D1* and *D2* announced their intention to publish the interview and photographs and *P* sued seeking an interlocutory injunction to prevent publication. *P* relied on:

(i) malicious falsehood;
(ii) libel;
(iii) passing off; and
(iv) trespass to the person.

The basis of (i) and (ii) was that the statement that he had consented to the interview was false as, to the journalists' knowledge, he had not been in a fit state to consent.

In the first case it was alleged that this was libellous in that it would lower *P* in the esteem of
See Chapter 21 for *Tolley v Fry*.
right-thinking people, by analogy with ***Tolley v Fry & Sons Ltd*** [1931] AC 333. In the second case it had caused damage by the loss of ability to be paid for his interview.

The basis of (iii) was also the false statement of consent, i.e. that the proposed article would falsely be represented to the public as having been consented to by *P*.

The basis of (iv) was that the use of flash photography in such circumstances was a battery.

P was granted an interlocutory injunction by Potter J which restrained use or publication of the photographs or interview, based on (i), (ii) and (iii).

On appeal, the Court of Appeal (Glidewell, Bingham and Leggatt LJJ) held that no injunction could be granted based on (ii), because of the rule in libel that an interlocutory injunction could only be granted in the clearest cases, which this was not.

Further, no injunction could be based on (iv), since the injunction sought aimed at the fruits of the trespass not at preventing a repetition of the trespass.

The court held that (iii) was not seriously arguable, as *P* was not in the position of a trader with regard to his interest in the story.

However, an injunction restraining further publication could and should be based on (i).

It is to be noted that this would not and did not prevent the newspaper printing the photographs and so-called interview as such, provided it made it clear that the actor had not consented.

Trespass and nuisance turn primarily upon the claimant being the legal occupier and the defendant infringing his occupation of the land. They may thus protect a landowner from invasion of or interference with the enjoyment of their property, for example, by the press or other persons physically intruding on the property or doing acts off the property which affect its enjoyment (including harassment by a former lover involving loitering, watching and besetting the house), but they will not assist their spouse (unless they are co-occupier in law), children, au pair or visitor who are residing with them, but do not have any legal interest in the property.

Harassment not involving any property interest gives rise, since the Protection from Harassment Act 1997, to both criminal liability and civil remedies (in the form of both a restraining order and damages for mental anxiety or financial loss). The Act applies where someone pursues a course of conduct which amounts, and which they know or ought to know amounts, to harassment. It was introduced to deal with stalkers, but is capable of wider application, for example, to the press.

Breach of confidence

Objective 3

The most promising of all existing English torts in the context of privacy must now be regarded as that protecting against breach of confidence. This tort commonly arises in circumstances where there is or has been some relationship or transaction between the parties: for example, one of employment, marriage, or even sale and purchase. An example from marriage is *Duchess of Argyll* v *Duke of Argyll* [1967] Ch 302, where, after the parties' divorce, the Duke was restrained from publishing articles disclosing marital secrets. Another is *Pollard* v *Photographic Co* (1888) 40 ChD 345, where a woman commissioned a photographer to take and supply her with some photographs, later to find, to her surprise, that the photographer was incorporating her image in Christmas cards for general sale.

Coco v AN Clarke (Engineers) Ltd [1968] FSR 415

Confidence will be breached where:

(a) the information has the necessary quality of confidence;
(b) the information has been imparted in circumstances importing an obligation of confidence;
(c) there is an unauthorised use of the information to the detriment of the original communicator of the information.

Traditionally, breach of confidence was confined to cases of prior relationship or transaction. This would clearly be an obstacle to using the tort to protect privacy as in many cases where it is alleged that there has been an unwarranted invasion of privacy there will have been no prior relationship between the parties. However, it is now clear that a duty of confidence may arise in equity independently of such cases. (See per Lord Goff in *Attorney General v Guardian Newspapers (No 2)* [1990] 1 AC 109 (the second *Spycatcher* case) at 281.) The conditions for its application identified by Lord Goff were that there should be confidential information, which:

> . . . comes to the knowledge of a person (the confidant) in circumstances where he has notice, or is held to have agreed, that the information is confidential, with the effect that it would be just in all circumstances that he would be precluded from disclosing the information to others.

Lord Goff said that he had:

> . . . expressed the circumstances in which the duty arises in broad terms, not merely to embrace those cases where a third party receives information from a person who is under a duty of confidence in respect of it, knowing that it has been disclosed by that person to him in breach of his duty of confidence, but also to include certain situations, beloved of law teachers – where an obviously confidential document is wafted by an electric fan out of a window into a crowded street, or where an obviously confidential document, such as a private diary, is dropped in a public place, and is then picked up by a passer-by.

Lord Goff also left open whether and if so what sort of detriment was always required to be shown. He went on, however, to identify the qualification, which applies to any claim to protect confidence, whereby the court must consider whether there is any countervailing public interest which on a balance of all relevant factors outweighs the claimant's interest in protecting their confidence.

The essence of the tort is that the information should be and be known to be confidential. Where information relates to matters of an obviously private nature, the conditions for its application may well exist. English law has not yet developed the full implications of this. But there are signs that it is pointing in a direction which may bring it closer to some continental systems. A well-known dictum in this sense is that of Laws J in *Hellewell v Chief Constable of Derbyshire* [1995] 1 WLR 804 at 807:

> If someone with a telephoto lens were to take from a distance and with no authority a picture of another engaged in some private act, his subsequent disclosure of the photograph would, in my judgment, as surely amount to a breach of confidence as if he had found or stolen a letter or diary in which the act was recounted and proceed to publish it. In such a case, the law would protect what might reasonably be called a right of privacy, although the name accorded to the cause of action would be breach of confidence. It is, of course, elementary that, in all such cases, a defence based on the public interest would be available.

The question of what constitutes a private act is, of course, left open by this formulation. Breach of confidence was not raised by the claimant in *Kaye v Robertson*. The Lord Chief Justice, who had been a member of the Court of Appeal in that case, has expressed doubt whether it could have been, together with some unease about appropriating causes of action to purposes quite alien to their original object. His preference was for legislation but he also made clear the belief that, in default of legislation, the courts would develop the law to give relief in obvious and pressing cases of invasion of privacy.

Case law and principles on privacy since the Human Rights Act 1998

Case law on privacy since the Human Rights Act 1998 has established the following principles:

1 There is no English domestic law tort of invasion of privacy.

2 In developing a right to protect private information, including the implementation in the English courts of Articles 8 and 10 of the European Convention on Human Rights, the English courts have to proceed through the tort of breach of confidence, into which the jurisprudence of Articles 8 and 10 has to be 'shoehorned'.

3 One difficulty is that the action for breach of confidence is employed where there was no pre-existing relationship of confidence between the parties, but the 'confidence' arose from the defendant having acquired by unlawful or surreptitious means information that he should have known he was not free to use. The verbal difficulty referred to has been avoided by the rechristening of the tort as *misuse of private information*.

4 Where the complaint is of the wrongful publication of private information, the court has to decide two things. First, is the information private in the sense that it is in principle protected by Article 8? If no, that is the end of the case. If yes, the second question arises: in all the circumstances, must the interest of the owner of the private information yield to the right of freedom of expression conferred on the publisher by Article 10?

The facts of the following case arose before the coming into force of the Human Rights Act but it contains an important statement of principle and rewards careful reading.

Wainwright v *Home Office* [2003] 4 All ER 969

See also Chapter 20 for *Wainwright* and trespass to the person.

The claimants were a mother and son who had been subjected to a strip search on a visit to prison. The claim was for battery and invasion of privacy. In relation to the latter claim the judge concluded that requiring the claimants to take off their clothes was a form of trespass to the person and that the law of tort should give a remedy for any kind of distress caused by an infringement of the right of privacy protected by Article 8. This part of the judgment was set aside by the Court of Appeal and the claimants appealed to the House of Lords.

The House of Lords held that there was no common law tort of invasion of privacy. There was a great difference between identifying privacy as a value which underlay the existence of the rule of law and privacy as a principle of law itself. Nor was there anything in the jurisprudence of the European Court of Human Rights which suggested that the adoption of some high level principle of privacy was necessary to comply with Article 8. Where the 1998 Act applies, Article 8 may justify a monetary remedy for an intentional invasion of privacy by a public authority even if no damage is suffered other than distress for which damages are not ordinarily recoverable. A merely negligent act should not give rise to a claim for damages because it affects privacy rather than some other interest like bodily safety.

Lord Hoffmann:

The claimants placed particular reliance upon the judgment of Sedley LJ in *Douglas v Hello! Ltd* [2001] QB 967. Sedley LJ drew attention to the way in which the development of the law of confidence had attenuated the need for a relationship of confidence between the recipient of the confidential information and the person from whom it was obtained – a development which enabled the UK government to persuade the European Human Rights Commission in *Earl Spencer v United Kingdom* (1998) 25 EHRR

CD 105 that English law of confidence provided an adequate remedy to restrain the publication of private information about the applicants' marriage and medical condition and photographs taken with a telephoto lens. These developments showed that the basic value protected by the law in such cases was privacy. Sedley LJ said, at p 1001, para 126:

> ... What a concept of privacy does, however, is accord recognition to the fact that the law has to protect not only those people whose trust has been abused but those who simply find themselves subjected to an unwanted intrusion into their personal lives. The law no longer needs to construct an artificial relationship of confidentiality between intruder and victim: it can recognise privacy itself as a legal principle drawn from the fundamental value of personal autonomy.

I read these remarks as suggesting that, in relation to the publication of personal information obtained by intrusion, the common law of breach of confidence has reached the point at which a confidential relationship has become unnecessary. As the underlying value protected is privacy, the action might as well be renamed invasion of privacy. 'To say this' said Sedley LJ, at p 1001, para 125, 'is in my belief to say little, save by way of a label, that our courts have not said already over the years.'

I do not understand Sedley LJ to have been advocating the creation of a high-level principle of invasion of privacy. His observations are in my opinion no more (although certainly no less) than a plea for the extension and possibly renaming of the old action for breach of confidence. . . .

See Chapter 21 for *Derbyshire CC v Times Newspapers*.

There seems to me a great difference between identifying privacy as a value which underlies the existence of a rule of law (and may point the direction in which the law should develop) and privacy as a principle of law in itself. The English common law is familiar with the notion of underlying values – principles only in the broadest sense – which direct its development. A famous example is **Derbyshire County Council v Times Newspapers Ltd** [1993] AC 534, in which freedom of speech was the underlying value which supported the decision to lay down the specific rule that a local authority could not sue for libel. But no one has suggested that freedom of speech is in itself a legal principle which is capable of sufficient definition to enable one to deduce specific rules to be applied in concrete cases. That is not the way the common law works.

Nor is there anything in the jurisprudence of the European Court of Human Rights which suggests that the adoption of some high level principle of privacy is necessary to comply with article 8 of the Convention. The European Court is concerned only with whether English law provides an adequate remedy in a specific case in which it considers that there has been an invasion of privacy contrary to article 8(1) and not justifiable under article 8(2) . . .

Counsel for the Wainwrights relied upon **Peck**'s case as demonstrating the need for a general tort of invasion of privacy. But in my opinion it shows no more than the need, in English law, for a system of control of the use of film from CCTV cameras which shows greater sensitivity to the feelings of people who happen to have been caught by the lens. For the reasons so cogently explained by Sir Robert Megarry in **Malone v Metropolitan Police Comr** [1979] Ch 344, this is an area which requires a detailed approach which can be achieved only by legislation rather than the broad brush of common law principle.

Furthermore, the coming into force of the Human Rights Act 1998 weakens the argument for saying that a general tort of invasion of privacy is needed to fill gaps in the existing remedies. Sections 6 and 7 of the Act are in themselves substantial gap fillers; if it is indeed the case that a person's rights under article 8 have been infringed by a public authority, he will have a statutory remedy. The creation of a general tort will, as Buxton LJ pointed out in the Court of Appeal, at [2002] QB 1334, 1360, para 92, pre-empt the controversial question of the extent, if any, to which the Convention requires the state to provide remedies for invasions of privacy by persons who are not public authorities. For these reasons I would reject the invitation to declare that since at the latest 1950 there has been a previously unknown tort of invasion of privacy.

Following this high level refusal to create a free-standing right of privacy any judicial developments in this area in the foreseeable future had to come through the action for breach of confidence. The decision sends a clear message to the legislature that the courts will not create a tort as this would pre-empt the question as to what remedies, if any, should be provided for invasions of privacy by persons who are not public authorities.

The facts of the case arose before the coming into force of the Human Rights Act 1998. No argument could therefore have been made on the basis of the prison authorities' breach of Article 8 as a public authority. Neither was there any need to address the argument based on the duties of the courts (as a public body) when interpreting and developing the law. This point was addressed by Lord Hoffmann, however. He appeared to say that privacy only became a legal principle (as opposed to a value underlying a legal principle) where it is made directly actionable under the Human Rights Act against public authorities. Otherwise, it is for the courts to develop the common law as they feel appropriate and for Parliament to respond to any deficiencies. This approach would appear to raise two questions. First, does this adequately address the obligations placed upon courts as public bodies under the Human Rights Act? (See *Von Hannover* below.) Secondly, will other judges take their cue from the House of Lords or will they show more enthusiasm for involving Convention considerations in developing the common law?

The next case is the major authority in England on the position where the defendant is not a public authority but the Human Rights Act is in play.

Campbell v *Mirror Group Newspapers* [2002] All ER (D) 448 (Mar) (QB); [2003] 1 All ER 224 (CA); [2004] 2 All ER 995 (HL)

Naomi Campbell, the model, sought damages for breach of confidence and compensation under s 13 of the Data Protection Act 1998 in respect of articles and photographs published in the *Mirror*. The gist of the stories was that, contrary to her previous assertions, she was a drug addict and attending Narcotics Anonymous. Photographs of her leaving a meeting of Narcotics Anonymous were published. Distress, embarrassment and anxiety aggravated by later stories and the defendant's conduct at the trial were also cited. The original claim for infringement of privacy was not pursued.

The articles complained about revealed the following matters:

(i) the claimant was a drug addict;
(ii) she was receiving treatment for her addiction;
(iii) she was attending Narcotics Anonymous;
(iv) details of that treatment;
(v) a visual portrayal by means of photographs.

In order to establish a claim for breach of confidence she had to show:

1 that the details given by the publications complained of about her attendance at Narcotics Anonymous had the necessary quality of confidence about them;
2 that those details were imparted in circumstances importing an obligation of confidence; and
3 that the publication of the details was to her detriment.

At first instance the claim was successful. However, on appeal, it was held that the fact that the claimant was attending meetings of Narcotics Anonymous was not, in its context, sufficiently significant to amount to a breach of the duty of confidence owed to the claimant. The information published by the defendant was justified in order to provide a factual account of the claimant's drug addiction that had the detail necessary to carry credibility. Provided that publication of particular confidential information was justified in the public interest, a journalist had to be given reasonable latitude as to the manner in which that information was conveyed to the public, or his right to freedom of expression under Article 10 would necessarily be inhibited.

Although the claim was framed in confidence, it was stated by counsel that it had more to do with privacy. A distinction was made between infringement of privacy as a free-standing tort and infringement of privacy as a species of breach of confidence. The former occurred where there was an intrusion into privacy which did involve the disclosure of private facts. No claim was made to attempt to establish that this species of tort was recognised by English law. The latter involved the misuse or disclosure of private or personal information. The photographs of Ms Campbell themselves may have been invasive but did not convey any information that was confidential. If they had been captioned 'Miss Campbell out in the street', then a free-standing tort of privacy would have had to have been resorted to. It was the captions on the photographs and the articles that conveyed the information that was alleged to be confidential.

The degree of difficulty in assessing what information is confidential can be seen in the differing conclusions of the first instance judge and the Court of Appeal.

The Court of Appeal stated that whether the claim is framed in privacy or breach of confidence there would be a public interest defence for the media. As Ms Campbell was a celebrity and was on public record as saying that she was not a drug addict, the *Mirror* was entitled to set the record straight and publish that her denials of drug addiction were deliberately misleading. However, consistent with Article 8, details which have the badge of confidentiality should be protected from publication unless, despite the breach and the private nature of the information, the publication is justifiable. Article 10 is not an unqualified right as Article 10(2) requires respect for the right to privacy. Striking a balance between Article 8 and Article 10 and bearing in mind s 12(4), Ms Campbell was not entitled to damages for breach of confidence. What happened here is that the *Mirror* had not overstepped the mark. They were entitled to show that Naomi Campbell had lied about her drug addiction and their intrusion into her private life in publishing photographs and details about her sessions at Narcotics Anonymous was necessary to give credibility to the story.

Ms Campbell appealed to the House of Lords and the principal issue was the way in which the balance was to be struck between the right to respect for private and family life and the right to freedom of expression. It was held (Lords Nicholls and Hoffmann dissenting) that the appeal would be allowed.

(i) The underlying issue in cases where there was alleged to be a breach of confidence was whether the information disclosed was public or private. In this case the information was private. The assurance of privacy at meetings such as Narcotics Anonymous was essential. Despite the fact that no objection could be taken to the first two elements in the article, this did not mean that they could be left out of consideration as to whether disclosure of the other elements was reasonable. The article had to be read as a whole along with the photographs. The context was that of a drug addict who was receiving treatment and it was her sensibilities that needed to be taken into account.

(ii) The right to privacy that lay at the heart of an action for breach of confidence had to be balanced against the right of the media to impart information to the public. Each right was of equal value in a democratic society. The tests were whether publication of the material pursued a legitimate aim and whether the benefits that would be achieved by its publication were proportionate to the harm that might be done by the interference with privacy. There were no political or democratic values at stake, nor was any pressing social need identified. The potential for the disclosure to cause harm was an important factor. There had been an infringement of the claimant's right to privacy and she was entitled to damages.

The difficulties of performing this balancing act are shown by the disagreements among the senior judiciary as to where the balance should be drawn on the facts of this case. The majority of the House of Lords leaned towards protection of Ms Campbell's privacy but the minority were in favour of a degree of journalistic latitude in respect of this information.

Issues arising from *Campbell*

Terminology

One difficulty raised by the use of breach of confidence is that of terminology. Some of the judges in *Campbell* used the expression breach of confidence, an action used to protect privacy interests. However, these judges appear to use the words 'private' and 'confidential' interchangeably. Other judges acknowledged that the concepts of privacy and confidence have merged in cases which involve the disclosure of personal information. Lord Nicholls took the seemingly logical step and argued that the tort should be renamed misuse of private information.

There would now appear to be two versions of breach of confidence: the traditional one; and one which applies where the disclosure of private information is the issue. Breach of confidence has simply become an action that protects against unauthorised publicity given to private facts.

> Now the law imposes a 'duty of confidence' whenever a person receives information he knows or ought to know is fairly and reasonably to be regarded as confidential. (Lord Nicholls)

> If the information is obviously private, the situation will be one where the person to whom it relates can reasonably expect his privacy to be respected. (Lord Hope)

What is private information?

Campbell is concerned with when private information will be protected by the action for breach of confidence but this raises the question: what is private information?

Three tests were suggested in the case. The first is the reasonable expectation of privacy test. (Lord Nicholls and Baroness Hale.) This is whether in relation to the disclosed facts the person in question had a reasonable expectation of privacy (Lord Nicholls) or whether the defendant knew or ought to have known that the claimant had a reasonable expectation that the information would remain private. As any restriction on publishing facts may bring Article 10 and freedom of speech into play, Baroness Hale said:

> the exercise of balancing Article 8 and Article 10 may begin when the person publishing the information knows or ought to know that there is a reasonable expectation that the information in question will be kept confidential.

These tests echo the ones used in two significant Court of Appeal cases.

A v B (a company) [2002] 2 All ER 545

The claimant was a Premier League footballer who was married with children. He had adulterous relationships with C (second defendant) and another woman, D. C and D sold their stories to the first defendant, a national newspaper and the claimant sought an interim injunction to prevent publication. The injunction was granted and, when considered on the merits, upheld. On appeal, the Court of Appeal held that the judge at first instance had failed to recognise that any interference by way of injunction had to be justified. It was not sufficient to find that the claimant had a right to privacy and that publication should be restrained unless there was a public interest. There was a very real difference between marriage and the relationship that the claimant had had with the two women. The fact that the women had chosen to disclose their relationships affected his right to protection of the information and a conclusion to the contrary would not recognise their right to freedom of expression. There was also a public interest in the proposed publications and the injunction was therefore discharged.

> Lord Woolf CJ laid down the guidelines for interim privacy applications. The claimant had to establish an interest capable of being the subject of an action for privacy or some interest of a private nature and then establish a duty of confidence. This would happen whenever a party was in a position where he knew or ought to have known that the other person can reasonably expect his privacy to be protected.

Douglas v *Hello! Ltd* [2001] 2 WLR 992

MD and *C Z-J* sold exclusive rights to publish their wedding photographs to *OK* magazine. *Hello!* obtained unofficial photographs, publication of which the claimants sought to restrain. An injunction was granted at first instance but discharged by the Court of Appeal as damages would be an adequate remedy at trial.

One question for the court was whether the Human Rights Act 1998 could found claims against private parties as well as public authorities, i.e. did the Act have 'horizontal effect'?

The claimants had a strong prima facie case on breach of confidence, but if the photographer was an intruder with whom no relationship of trust and confidence could be established then a claim based on breach of confidence would probably fail. If that was the case, could the claimants' privacy be protected independently of breach of confidence?

Sedley LJ:

> Domestic law has now evolved to the extent that it now recognises and will appropriately protect a right of personal privacy even where no relationship of trust and confidence exists.

He cast privacy as a legal value in its own right which permitted judicial protection of personal autonomy openly rather than by artificial recourse to confidence. It protects not only those persons whose trust has been abused but also those subject to an unwarranted intrusion into their lives. The right could be inferred from domestic jurisprudence but the Human Rights Act 1998 gives the final impetus. (But see Lord Hoffmann's interpretation of this speech in *Wainwright*.)

Brooke LJ:

> Article 1 of the ECHR provides that positive steps must be taken to enable individuals to enjoy Convention rights in horizontal as well as vertical situations.

(*NB:* Article 1 is not in the Human Rights Act 1998 – see s 1(1).) It would have been arguable that Article 1 required United Kingdom courts to develop a concept of privacy and allow its enforcement against private as well as public authorities. As Article 1 was not in the Act (and therefore incapable of triggering horizontality in domestic law), s 6 requires all public authorities (including courts) to act compatibly with Convention rights and may act as a trigger. (Also favoured by Sedley and Keene LJJ.)

Keene LJ doubted whether s 6 permitted new causes of action but required the development of common law in accordance with the Convention. He therefore favoured breach of confidence.

It should be noted that s 12 applied, therefore Article 10 was in play. Section 12 cannot in itself found a privacy-based claim, as it only applies when the court is considering the grant of relief.

This litigation has been extremely lengthy and in a later hearing concerned with the defendants' appeal against the damages award made to the third claimants (*OK* magazine), (*Douglas* v *Hello! Ltd (Nos 5 and 6)* [2006] QB 125), Lord Phillips stated that whether information is private depends on whether the defendant knew or ought to have known that the claimants had a reasonable expectation that the information would remain private.

The second test is the highly offensive to a reasonable person of ordinary sensibilities test. (Lord Hope.) This is a mixed objective/subjective test:

the question is what a reasonable person of ordinary sensibilities would feel if she was placed in the same position as the claimant and faced with the same publicity.

The third test is the second part of Lord Hope's test and is whether the information was *obviously private*. This would be where the information can be easily identified as private. From the *Campbell* case it would appear that all medical information is 'obviously private'. Facts concerning sexual relations or a person's address, and photographs of the interior of a home are also confidential.

What is the 'harm' caused by privacy infringements?

As this action develops it is important to identify what the harm is that is caused by privacy infringements. Again, the House of Lords was divided on this issue.

Lords Nicholls and Hoffmann felt that protection of privacy was important as it helped to preserve an individual's dignity, personality and well-being and should therefore be protected for its own sake.

The majority felt that the emotional and psychological effect that the publications had on the claimant was more important. The problem with this approach is that the absence of such harm does not mean that a claimant's privacy interest should not be protected or that it should carry less weight in the balance between privacy and freedom of speech.

How is privacy to be balanced with freedom of speech?

Objective
4

The principles to be taken into account when a conflict arises between Article 8 and Article 10 were set out in *McKennitt v Ash* (see below).

1 Neither article has, as such, precedence over the other.

2 Where conflict arises between the values under Articles 8 and 10, an 'intense focus' is necessary upon the comparative importance of the specific rights being claimed in the individual case.

3 The court must take into account the justifications for interfering with or restricting each right.

4 So, too, the proportionality test must be applied to each.

The Strasbourg approach

Objective
5

The narrow majority in *Campbell* appear to be supported by an important decision of the European Court of Human Rights. The case is of particular interest as it looks at the crucial issue of the balance between the right to privacy and the media's freedom to publish photographs. The case also tackles the question of the role of the state in protecting privacy in cases where a public authority is not directly involved.

Von Hannover v Germany (2005) 40 EHRR 1

The applicant, Princess Caroline of Monaco, had on several occasions unsuccessfully applied to the German courts for injunctions to prevent any further publication of photographs which had appeared in certain German magazines. She claimed that the photographs infringed her right to protection of her private life and her right to control the use of her image. In December 1999 the Federal Constitutional Court allowed her appeal regarding the photographs in which she appeared with her children. However, it considered that, as a 'figure of contemporary society', she had to tolerate the publication of photographs of herself in a public place, even if they showed her in scenes from her daily life rather than engaged in official duties. The court referred to the freedom of the press and to the public's legitimate interest in knowing how such a person behaved in public. The applicant complained that the decisions of the German courts infringed her right to respect for her private and family life, as guaranteed by Article 8 of the Convention.

The court held unanimously that there had been a violation of Article 8.

1 The concept of 'private life' extends to aspects relating to personal identity, such as a person's name or picture. Furthermore, it includes a person's physical and psychological integrity. There is a zone of interaction with others, even in a public context, which may fall within the scope of 'private life'. In certain circumstances, a person has a legitimate expectation of protection and respect for his or her private life. And the publication of photos of the applicant in her daily life fell within the scope of her private life. (See also *Niemietz* v *Germany* (1993) 16 EHRR 355.)

2 Although the object of Article 8 is essentially that of protecting the individual against arbitrary interference by public authorities, it does not merely compel the state to abstain from such interference. There may be positive obligations inherent in an effective respect for private or family life. That also applies to the protection of a person's picture against abuse by others. Although the boundary between the state's positive and negative obligations cannot be defined precisely, the applicable principles are similar. Regard must be had to the fair balance to be struck between the competing interests of the individual and of the community as a whole, and the state enjoys a margin of appreciation.

3 The protection of private life must be balanced against the freedom of expression guaranteed by Article 10. Although the press must not overstep certain bounds, particularly in respect of the reputation and rights of others, its duty is to impart in a manner consistent with its obligations and responsibilities information and ideas on all matters of public interest.

4 Although freedom of expression extends to the publication of photos, this is an area in which the protection of the rights and reputation of others assumes particular importance. The present case concerns images containing very personal, even intimate 'information' about an individual. Furthermore, photos appearing in the tabloid press are often taken in a climate of harassment which induces in the person concerned a very strong sense of intrusion or even of persecution. In cases where the court has had to balance the protection of private life against the freedom of expression, it has always stressed the contribution made by photos or articles in the press to a debate of general interest.

5 The photos show the applicant in scenes from her daily life, engaged in activities of a purely private nature. As a member of the Prince of Monaco's family, she represents the family at certain cultural or charitable events but does not exercise any function within or on behalf of the State of Monaco.

6 A fundamental distinction must be drawn between reporting facts capable of contributing to a debate relating to politicians in the exercise of their functions, and reporting details of the private life of an individual who does not exercise official functions. In the former case the press exercises its vital role of 'watchdog' in a democracy, whereas in the latter case it does not do so. Although the public has a right to be informed, which in certain circumstances can extend to aspects of the private life of public figures, particularly where politicians are concerned, this is not the case here. The situation does not come within the sphere of any political or public debate. The publication of the photos and articles, the sole purpose of which was to satisfy the curiosity of a particular readership regarding the applicant's private life, does not contribute to any debate of general interest even though she is known to the public. In these circumstances freedom of expression calls for a narrower interpretation.

In the judgment of the ECHR, the 'functional' and 'spatial' tests were employed.

The ECtHR first considered the classification by the domestic courts of the Princess as a public figure 'par excellence', pursuant to s 23(1) of the German Copyright (Arts Domain) Act, what the court terms the 'functional' test. The court appears to have accepted the account of her role offered by the Princess as someone who does not exercise any official functions on behalf of the state, concluding that, as a result, the Princess was not properly considered a 'public' figure. As the court explained:

> ... although the public has a right to be informed, which is an essential right in a democratic society that, in certain special circumstances, can even extend to aspects of the private life of public figures ... this is not the case here.

Although the court found that the classification of a public figure 'par excellence' may be appropriate for a politician exercising an official function, given that such a classification removes nearly all protection from one's private life, it could not be justified in the case of the Princess, the public interest in whom stems solely from her membership of the royal family.

The court then considered the one test which the German courts were willing to apply in protection of the private life of the Princess, what the ECtHR terms the 'spatial' test. Accepting the submissions of the Princess on this point, the court concluded that, although the test was superficially attractive, it was, '... in reality too vague and difficult for the person concerned to determine in advance'. This points to one of the most immediate effects of **Von Hannover** for the United Kingdom, the need to consider reform of the Code of Practice of the Press Complaints Commission, as it relies on very similar criteria to determine when the photography of individuals without their consent is inappropriate.

In its opinion the court repeatedly emphasised the need to balance the protection of individual privacy against the right to free expression found in Article 10 ECtHR, which it refers to as 'one of the essential foundations of a democratic society'. Indeed, the court offers an extremely strong defence of the role of the press in democratic society, stating that 'its duty is nevertheless to impart in a manner consistent with its obligations and responsibilities information and ideas on all matters of public interest'. However, the court concluded that:

> ... the publication of the photos and articles in question, of which the sole purpose was to satisfy the curiosity of a particular readership regarding the details of the applicant's private life, cannot be deemed to contribute to any debate of general interest to society despite the applicant being known to the public.

Taking into account the continuing climate of harassment in which the photographs of the Princess were taken, the court found that:

> ... the public does not have a legitimate interest in knowing where the applicant is and how she behaves generally in her private life even if she appears in places that cannot always be described as secluded and despite the fact that she is well known to the public.

The ECtHR concluded that the German courts did not strike a fair balance between the competing rights at issue, concluding that 'the criteria on which the domestic courts based their decisions were not sufficient to protect the applicant's private life effectively'.

This was not the end of the affair. The paparazzi continued to take photographs of the Princess and she returned to Strasbourg to complain that Germany had failed to execute the first judgment. The Strasbourg Court did not make any major statement of policy as it was simply concerned with whether the German Courts had applied the relevant criteria. The application failed. (**Von Hannover v Germany (No 2)** [2012] EMLR 16.)

The question of photographs in public places was considered by the Court of Appeal in **Murray v Express Newspapers plc** [2008] Fam Law 732. A photograph had been taken with a telephoto lens of the one-year-old child of a well-known author in a pushchair on the street. The defendant applied for summary judgment and at first instance the judge held that there was no reasonable expectation of privacy and that Article 8 was not engaged. The Court of Appeal overruled this and stated (applying *Von Hannover*) that there was a reasonable expectation of privacy and that Article 8 was engaged. The case was therefore sent back for trial (unless the parties settled) on the balance between Articles 8 and 10. The key factor here was that the photograph was of a child. Children of celebrities do not court publicity for themselves; therefore they have a legitimate expectation of privacy.

If the victim was not a child then various factors come into play in determining a reasonable expectation of privacy. If the information was already in the public domain then relief may be denied. (*Theakston* v *MGN Ltd* [2002] EWHC 137 (QB).) However the publication of photographs on a friend's Facebook page may not constitute the public domain. (*RocknRoll* v *News Group Newspapers* [2013] EWHC 24 (Ch).)

The issue of public interest in publication may also determine this issue. The publication of pictures and CCTV footage of the daughter of Mick Jagger and the son of George Best having sex outside a night club was injuncted. Although the couple were in a public space they had no knowledge that they were being filmed and publication would not be in the public interest. (*Jagger* v *Darling* [2005] EWHC 683 (Ch).)

The approach used in *Von Hannover* was adopted in the English decision in the following case.

McKennitt v Ash [2006] All ER (D) 02 (Feb) (QB); [2007] 3 WLR 194 (CA)

The claimant (*M*), a folk musician who had sold millions of records, sought a declaration that the defendant (*N*), an author and former friend, had breached her privacy and confidence by publishing a book about her containing private information. *M* also sought damages and an injunction to prevent the book being published in its current form. The specific passages to which *M* objected contained information concerning her personal and sexual relationships; her feelings, particularly those relating to her deceased fiancé and the circumstances of his death; her health and diet; her emotional vulnerability; and earlier litigation between her and *N* which concerned the purchase of a property and had been settled privately. *N* contended that *M*'s right to respect for her private life under the Human Rights Act 1998, Article 8 was not engaged because the information was either not confidential, too trivial to attract a duty of confidence, in the public domain, or a matter of public interest. She also maintained that *M*'s attempt to interfere with her right to freedom of expression under Article 10 was an attempt at censorship.

The applications were granted at first instance. The court considered the relationship between privacy and freedom of speech.

Where a person's Article 8 rights conflicted with another's right to freedom of expression, neither right had an inherent precedence over the other and it was essential to focus intensely on their comparative importance in the individual case and apply the proportionality test when considering restricting either. The court should adopt a two-stage approach. It was necessary to establish, first, whether there was a reasonable expectation of privacy so as to engage Article 8. If that initial test was satisfied, it was then necessary to consider any 'limiting factors', namely whether the information was in the public domain, whether it was trivial, and whether there was a public interest in disclosure. Regarding the first stage, a person could have a reasonable expectation that his privacy would be protected because of the nature of the information itself or the circumstances in which the information had been voluntarily imparted to others. He could have a reasonable expectation of privacy concerning even quite trivial matters. However, the trivial nature of the information would be taken into account at the second stage when considering the proportionality of imposing an injunction. The protection of privacy extended to relations with other people and could embrace a social dimension. (*Von Hannover* v *Germany*.) When weighing the conflicting rights at the second stage of the test, the court would also consider whether intrusive references to an individual's private life were justified by considerations of public concern or bore on a matter of general importance. However, in order for the public interest defence to be triggered a very high degree of misbehaviour had to be demonstrated. Where a genuine public interest existed alongside a commercial interest in the media in publishing articles or photographs, sometimes such interests would have to yield to the individual citizen's right to the effective protection of his private life. In the instant case, a number of the passages to which *M* had objected did not give rise to a reasonable expectation of privacy, such as those referring to friendships with various men; but many others did, such as those giving details of *M*'s emotional reaction to her fiancé's death. Some information was too anodyne, general or unintrusive to require protection, and some was in the public domain. However, the publication of a number of the disputed passages did need to be restrained by an injunction. *M* would also be awarded £5,000 in damages.

The defendant appealed and the first instance judgment was upheld.

A very useful summary of the current law of privacy was given by Buxton LJ:

(i)   There is no English domestic law tort of invasion of privacy.

(ii) In developing a right to protect private information, including the implementation in the English courts of Articles 8 and 10 of the European Convention on Human Rights, the English courts have to proceed through the tort of breach of confidence, into which the jurisprudence of Articles 8 and 10 has to be 'shoehorned': *Douglas v Hello! (No 3)* [2005] 4 All ER 128.

(iii) One difficulty is that the action for breach of confidence is employed where there was no pre-existing relationship of confidence between the parties, but the 'confidence' arose from the defendant having acquired by unlawful or surreptitious means information that he should have known he was not free to use: as was the case in *Douglas* and also in *Campbell*.

(iv) The verbal difficulty referred to in (iii) above has been avoided by the rechristening of the tort as misuse of private information: per Lord Nicholls of Birkenhead in *Campbell*.

(v)   In *McKennitt* the complaint was old-fashioned breach of confidence by way of conduct inconsistent with a pre-existing relationship, rather than simply of the purloining of private information.

In a case such as *McKennitt* where the complaint is of the wrongful publication of private information, the court has to decide two things. First, is the information private in the sense that it is in principle protected by Article 8? If no, that is the end of the case. If yes, the second question arises: in all the circumstances, must the interest of the owner of the private information yield to the right of freedom of expression conferred on the publisher by Article 10? The latter enquiry is commonly referred to as the 'balancing exercise'.

In relation to the first question, the judge had restrained information on the following matters: Ms McKennitt's personal and sexual relationships; her personal feelings and, in particular, in relation to her deceased fiancé and the circumstances of his death; matters relating to her health and diet; matters relating to her emotional vulnerability.

The judge had stressed that a crucial factor in this case was the pre-existing relationship of confidence between the parties and that the defendant was only too aware, at the time of and prior to publication, that much of the content of the book would cause concern and distress to Ms McKennitt because of its intrusive nature. Accordingly, not only a reasonable person standing in her shoes, but the defendant herself would be conscious that she was thereby infringing the 'trust' and 'loyalty' to which she referred in the book. This information was therefore private.

In relation to the second question:

1   Neither article has, as such, precedence over the other.

2   Where conflict arises between the values under Articles 8 and 10, an 'intense focus' is necessary upon the comparative importance of the specific rights being claimed in the individual case.

3   The court must take into account the justifications for interfering with or restricting each right.

4   So, too, the proportionality test must be applied to each.

The judge at first instance thought that there was little legitimate public interest in the matters addressed by the book, and certainly no public interest sufficient to outweigh Ms McKennitt's Article 8 right to private life. That conclusion was contested under this head, on appeal, in two respects, which it was necessary to keep separate.

The first argument was that there was a legitimate public interest in the affairs of Ms McKennitt because she was a public figure, and for that reason alone. The second argument was that if a public figure had misbehaved, the allegation in the present case being of hypocrisy, the public had a right to have the record put straight. The parallel for that argument was the case of Ms Campbell, who could not retain privacy for the fact that she was a drug addict because she had lied publicly about her condition.

The first of the arguments involved consideration of two recent authorities, **Von Hannover** and **A v B**. (The latter case now had to be read in the light of the decision in the former.) First, as to the position of Ms McKennitt, she clearly did not fall within the first category mentioned by Lord Woolf (in **A v B**) and 'hold a position where higher standards of conduct can be rightly expected by the public': that is the preserve of headmasters and clergymen, who according to taste may be joined by politicians, senior civil servants, surgeons and journalists. Second, although on one view Ms McKennitt comes within Lord Woolf's second class, of involuntary role models, the Court of Appeal doubted the validity of that concept; and it would in any event seem difficult to include in the class a person such as Ms McKennitt, who had made such efforts not to hold herself out as someone whose life is an open book. Third, it is clear that Lord Woolf thought that role models were at risk, or most at risk, of having to put up with the reporting of disreputable conduct: such as was the conduct of the claimant in **A v B** Ms McKennitt did not fall into that category.

Was exposure legitimate to demonstrate improper conduct or dishonesty? Weight has to be given to the commercial interest of newspapers in reporting matter that interests the public. A view on this was given in the defamation case of *Jameel v Wall Street Journal* [2006] 3 WLR 642 by Baroness Hale:

> there must be a real public interest in communicating and receiving the information. This is, as we all know, very different from saying that it is information that interests the public – the most vapid tittle-tattle about the activities of footballers' wives and girlfriends interests large sections of the public but no-one could claim any real public interest in our being told all about it.

There was therefore no public interest in the disclosure of the private material in the book.

The issue of sexual conduct and public interest was raised in the case of *Mosley* v *News Group Newspapers* [2008] All ER (D) 322. The claimant, the son of the fascist politician Oswald Mosley and President of the Formula 1 racing organisation was photographed during a sado-masochistic session with five prostitutes. The pictures and an article were published by the *News of the World*, which alleged that the session had Nazi overtones. Mosley sued for invasion of privacy. There was no doubt that the information was private. The issue was whether the publication was in the public interest. The newspaper argued that because of the Nazi overtones and possible Holocaust denial it was. However, their key witness failed to appear and the issue became simply whether the fact that Mosley had been involved in a sado-masochistic session was in the public interest. The judge held it was not as it was a private act between consenting adults and awarded £60,000 in damages. He refused to award exemplary damages.

A further case which received wide publicity was concerned with an application for an injunction to restrain the publication of information about a well-known businessman. This case was similar to *McKennitt* in that it involved a previous relationship between the parties but differed in that some of the information which it was sought to protect was personal and some business.

The court in this case was not conducting a trial but considering an application for an interlocutory injunction. Under s 12(3) of the Human Rights Act, the question for decision in relation to each such piece of information is whether the court is satisfied that the applicant is likely to establish, presumably at a trial, that publication should not be allowed. For the purposes of this case, the relevance of s 12(4) is simply that the court must have regard to the importance which the Convention attaches to freedom of expression.

Lord Browne of Madingley v Associated Newspapers Ltd [2007] EWHC 202 (QB)

The claimant was chief executive of BP. During 2002, he became involved in a relationship with C, a Canadian individual. The claimant provided C with a luxurious lifestyle for the duration of the relationship. C's visa was due to run out early in the relationship and the claimant took various steps to enable him to remain in the country, including paying for a university course from 2003 so that he would acquire student status. He also helped C to set up a company. When the relationship ended, in 2006, C found himself in financial difficulties. He sent various requests for financial assistance, and eventually decided to go to the press and supply them with various pieces of information about the claimant and their relationship. He contacted the defendant. The claimant applied to restrain publication by the defendant of C's allegations, most of which he said were false or misleading, on the ground that they were matters in respect of which he had a 'reasonable expectation of privacy' and/ or because they had been communicated to journalists in breach of a duty of confidence arising from an intimate personal relationship. The issue also arose as to whether the claimant should be denied injunctive relief because he had admitted lying to the court over the circumstances under which he had met C. The particular allegations that the defendants wished to publish, and which the claimant sought to suppress, were: (a) an allegation about BP strategy being discussed with a third party; (b) the alleged misuse of BP's resources and manpower to support or assist C, which included (i) the use of BP computers, (ii) BP staff assisting in setting up a company for C and (iii) the use of a senior BP employee to run a personal errand for the claimant by delivering cash to C; (c) the bare fact of the claimant's relationship with C; (d) the alleged breach of confidentiality by the claimant in discussing with C confidential BP matters and documents; and (e) the claimant's relationships with colleagues in BP. The judge ruled that publication of categories (a) and (e) would be enjoined, but categories (b), (c) and (d) would not. The claimant appealed.

Held: The appeal would be dismissed.

The judge's approach had been correct. It was necessary for the court first to consider whether Article 8 was engaged. It should then consider whether the right to freedom of expression under Article 10 was engaged and, critically, whether the applicant seeking relief had shown that he was likely to establish at a trial that publication should not be allowed within the meaning of s 12(3) of the Human Rights Act 1998. On the facts of the instant case, it was for the claimant to persuade the judge, in respect of each category, that his prospects of success at trial were sufficiently favourable to justify such an order being made in the particular circumstances of the case, the general approach being that the courts should be exceedingly slow to make interim restraint orders where the applicant had not satisfied the court that he would probably (more likely than not) succeed at the trial. On the facts, the judge had not been in error regarding the disputed categories.

There was some discussion in the course of the argument as to whether it was sufficient for the claimant to show that there was a relationship of confidence and whether, once such a relationship is shown, all information obtained in the course of the relationship is confidential without regard to the nature of the information. The answer was no. On Lord Nicholls' formulation of the test, namely whether in respect of the disclosed facts the claimant has a reasonable expectation of privacy, the test must be applied to each item of information communicated to or learned by the person concerned in the course of the relationship.

The nature of the relationship is of considerable importance. For example, the mere fact that the piece of information can be regarded as trivial is not to be decisive against answering Lord Nicholls' question in the affirmative. It may or may not be. The question whether any particular piece of information qualifies as private, and the claimant has a reasonable expectation of privacy in respect of it, requires a detailed examination of all the circumstances on a case-by-case basis. The circumstances include the nature of the information itself and the circumstances in which it has been imparted or obtained. (See also *Re Guardian News and Media Ltd* [2010] UKSC 1 where it was held that freedom of expression outweighed a terrorist suspect's right to anonymity.)

Limits to protection

The development of breach of confidence as the major litigation route for dealing with invasion of privacy inevitably means that the action is restricted to confidential information. One of these limitations was demonstrated in *Wainwright v Home Office* [2003]. The badly performed strip search of the claimant did not involve private information and did not therefore fall under the heading of breach of confidence and the House of Lords confirmed that there was no tort of invasion of privacy to protect the claimant. The facts of *Wainwright* arose before the Human Rights Act 1998 came into force and it has subsequently been confirmed by the European Court of Human Rights that an action would now lie against the Home Office for breach of Articles 8 and 13. (*Wainwright v UK* (2006) 44 EHRR 809.)

The gaps in protection were also demonstrated by the following case.

Peck v United Kingdom (2003) 36 EHRR 41

A local council released CCTV footage to media organisations of an individual on a main road carrying a knife. It later became known that the individual had just attempted suicide. Peck alleged a breach of Article 8. The UK government argued that as the individual's actions were already in the public domain, having taken place on a main road, there could be no breach. The Strasbourg court held that there is 'a zone of interaction of a person with others, even in a public context, which may fall within the scope of "private life"'. Whilst the CCTV recording was lawful, as it was to prevent crime, the further disclosure of the CCTV footage to the media was held to be an invasion of Mr Peck's privacy.

The court also found that the United Kingdom had breached Article 13, the right to an effective remedy. The Broadcasting Standards Commission and ITC, the then regulatory bodies, could not offer an effective remedy because they had no power to award damages.

Peck established that for a public authority to release footage portraying private acts without consent to the media is a prima facie breach of Article 8 subject to a freedom of expression defence. The later case of *Von Hannover v Germany* (2005) 40 EHRR 1 established that Article 8 is engaged by the failure of the state to afford victims a proper remedy for invasion of privacy where the defendant is not a public authority.

Remedies

Damages

The normal remedy for an invasion of privacy through the action for breach of confidence is damages. There is some dispute about the interest protected by illegal invasions of privacy. In *Campbell* the House of Lords were divided on the issue. Lords Nicholls and Hoffmann felt that protection of privacy was important as it helped to preserve an individual's dignity, personality and well-being and should therefore be protected for its own sake. The majority, however, felt that the emotional and psychological effect that the publications had on the claimant was more important. The problem with this approach is that the absence of such harm does not mean that a claimant's privacy interest should not be protected or that it should carry less weight in the balance between privacy and freedom of speech.

Quantum of damages in these cases is somewhat erratic. The highest award given in England appears to be the £60,000 awarded to Max Mosley (see above).

Injunctions

The major issue in remedies is whether an interim injunction should be awarded to prevent publication. In a defamation case an interim injunction will not be granted where the defendant intends to plead justification. This is on the basis that the damage done by publication can be repaired by a finding that the allegation was false, which has the effect of restoring a damaged reputation. However, where private or confidential information is published, the invasion of privacy cannot be repaired by an award of damages. An interim injunction (awarded before publication) is therefore the only effective remedy.

Parliament provided a 'sweetener' to the media when the Human Rights Act 1998 was passed who were concerned that stories would be injuncted on the basis of Article 8. Section 12 provides that if a court is considering to grant any relief which might affect the exercise of freedom of expression that no such relief should be granted unless the applicant is likely to establish that such publication should not be allowed and that the court should have particular regard to the right to freedom of expression.

The major problem with this remedy is that it requires the publisher to notify the claimant before publication. In the Mosley case the *News of the World* had published a video of the events on its website, which was viewed by 1.4 million viewers before they notified him.

See Chapter 21 for defamation. In defamation cases where a defendant seeks to invoke public interest privilege it was in the defendant's interest to notify the claimant in order to satisfy the 'responsible journalism' test.

If a notification requirement was brought in the fear is that this would stifle investigative journalism. However, the court hearing an application for an interim injunction would have to take account of s 12 of the Human Rights Act 1998 (see above).

An attempt was made by Max Mosley to convince the European Court of Human Rights that there should be a notification requirement on the media. (*Mosley* v *United Kingdom* [2011] ECHR 48009/08; [2011] All ER (D) 66 (May).) The application was rejected. The court emphasised the importance of a prudent approach to the state's positive obligations to protect private life in general and of the need to recognise the diversity of possible methods to secure its respect. Where measures under Article 8 would have an impact on freedom of expression, regard had to be had to Article 10, which merited, in principle, equal respect.

The court emphasised the pre-eminent role of the press in informing the public and imparting information and ideas on matters of public interest in a state governed by the rule of law.

Methods of objective and balanced reporting might vary considerably and it was therefore not for the court to substitute its own views for those of the press as to what technique of reporting should be adopted. However, editorial discretion was not unbounded. There was a distinction to be drawn between reporting facts – even if controversial – capable of contributing to a debate of general public interest in a democratic society, and making tawdry allegations about an individual's private life. It was commonly acknowledged that the audiovisual media often had a much more immediate and powerful effect than the print media. The nature and severity of any sanction imposed on the press in respect of a publication were relevant to any assessment of the proportionality of an interference with the right to freedom of expression.

Finally, while Article 10 did not prohibit the imposition of prior restraints on publication, the dangers inherent in prior restraints were such that they called for the most careful scrutiny on the part of the court.

The court noted that the conduct of the newspaper was open to severe question. Having regard to the chilling effect to which a pre-notification requirement risked giving rise, however, to the significant doubts as to the effectiveness of any pre-notification requirement and to the wide margin of appreciation in that area, Article 8 did not require a legally binding pre-notification requirement.

Super injunctions

The question of injunctions granted for prospective invasions of privacy has been complicated by the rise of so-called 'super injunctions' (although this expression is used in different ways). If a person applies for an interim injunction to prevent the publication of material which they claim would constitute an invasion of their privacy then the case may be reported in such a way as to hide the identity of the applicant. A similar method is used in cases involving children. However, applicants have now taken to applying for an order where the terms include the fact that the existence of the order itself cannot be reported. This contravenes the principle of open justice and may also contravene Article 6.

The number of such orders is said to run into hundreds but little is known about the law governing the grant of such orders. There is no known authoritative court ruling justifying, explaining or describing the legal principles at work. The reason for this lack of information seems to be connected to the risk of adverse costs orders in this type of litigation. Applications for super injunctions are made by applicants with deep pockets against media organisations, such as newspapers. Although such orders are interim only, pending the outcome of the claim for a permanent injunction, in practice they amount to a knock-out blow to the respondent who will be undertaking a prohibitive costs risk if it took the case all the way to trial. Respondents are deterred by the risk of losing on the merits and having to pay the claimant's costs, especially where the applicants are represented on a conditional fee basis, in which case a losing defendant may end up having to pay twice the claimant's costs as well as their own lawyers' fees. Since an adverse costs order could well run into many hundreds of thousands of pounds and more, media organisations have concluded that it makes no economic sense to defend their right to publish. It would therefore appear that such orders have succeeded not only in suppressing curiosity but in stifling the respondents' cases altogether.

For an example see *LNS* **v** *Persons Unknown* [2010] EWHC 119 (QB). The applicant (the footballer John Terry) applied for an *ex parte* order which sought not only a secret injunction but also without giving anyone the right to be heard. The judge held in this case that an injunction was not necessary or proportionate having regard to the level of gravity of interference with the applicant's private life.

Conclusions on privacy

As can be seen from this brief discussion, the development of privacy laws in England and Wales are at an early stage.

What can be said with confidence at this stage is that the courts are not willing to develop a general tort of invasion of privacy. The view is that if this is to be done it is a job for Parliament and not the courts. Development has therefore taken place within the action for breach of confidence, although a more accurate description of the action when used to protect privacy would be *misuse of private information.*

In order to establish that there is an action, the claimant has to show that the relevant information was private. A number of tests have been suggested for this but the preferable one is that of a *reasonable expectation of privacy.* There must be some detriment to the claimant as a result of the disclosure and this may be either damage to honour and dignity or emotional stress. If the claimant meets these requirements then the court must balance the privacy needs of the claimant against the free speech needs of the defendant. Article 8 and Article 10 should have equal weight. Some guidance can be drawn from the *Von Hannover* case where the classification of someone as a 'public figure' would give greater freedom to publish information about them.

The argument over 'horizontality' appears to have been resolved and it is now clear that the state has a duty to implement laws which protect 'private life' between ordinary citizens. The defendant state (Germany) in *Von Hannover* already had such laws in place but these were declared inadequate by the Strasbourg court.

English law probably does not go as far as *Von Hannover*, as the pictures were taken in a public place (although, on photographs of children, see *Murray* **v** *Express Newspapers plc* [2008] Fam Law 732) and did not relate to a key item of personal information such as medical history (as in *Campbell*). *Von Hannover* therefore appears to hold that a person can have a reasonable expectation in a public place in relation to everyday events such as shopping or having a cup of coffee. The key factor here appears to be the purpose for which the photograph was taken. If it is simply a photograph for private use which happens to include a particular person then there is no protection. If it is taken for the purpose of circulation in the media then protection is given by *Von Hannover* but not by *Campbell* unless the photograph is taken where there is a reasonable expectation of privacy. A famous model coming out of a dependency clinic is protected. A famous model walking to Tesco is not. English law does not extend this far.

Summary

This chapter deals with the law on privacy.

- Privacy is notoriously difficult to define. The Calcutt Report in 1990 defined it as the right of the individual to be protected against intrusion into his personal life or affairs, or those of his family, by direct physical means or by publication of information.

- A right to privacy could include protection from:
  (a) physical intrusion;
  (b) publication of hurtful or embarrassing personal material (whether true or false);
  (c) publication of inaccurate or misleading personal material; and
  (d) publication of photographs or recordings of the individual taken without consent.

- Any privacy law must be balanced against the right to freedom of speech.

- Historically, English law did not have any specific protection for privacy rights. Such protection as there was was given incidentally by other actions such as trespass, nuisance, defamation and passing off. The lack of protection was illustrated in the case of ***Kaye* v *Robertson*** (1991).

- Development of privacy law has taken place in the context of the action for breach of confidence. Confidence will be breached where: (i) the information has the necessary quality of confidence; (ii) the information has been imparted in circumstances importing an obligation of confidence; (iii) there is an unauthorised use of the information to the detriment of the original communicator of the information. Traditional breach of confidence actions require a pre-existing relationship between the parties but this is no longer necessary.

  The impetus for the development of a privacy law has come through the Human Rights Act 1998 and specifically through the need for the legal system to comply with Article 8.

  English law has developed the following principles:

  (i) there is no English domestic law tort of invasion of privacy;
  (ii) in developing a right to protect private information, including the implementation in the English courts of Articles 8 and 10 of the European Convention on Human Rights, the English courts have to proceed through the tort of breach of confidence;
  (iii) there is no need for a pre-existing relationship between the parties;
  (iv) the tort is now called misuse of private information;
  (v) where the complaint is of the wrongful publication of private information, the court has to decide two things: first, is the information private in the sense that it is in principle protected by Article 8? If no, that is the end of the case. If yes, the court must carry out a 'balancing exercise' between Article 8 and Article 10;
  (vi) in relation to the second question:
      (a) neither article has, as such, precedence over the other;
      (b) where conflict arises between the values under Articles 8 and 10, an 'intense focus' is necessary upon the comparative importance of the specific rights being claimed in the individual case;
      (c) the court must take into account the justifications for interfering with or restricting each right;
      (d) so, too, must the proportionality test be applied to each.

Further reading

Bennett, T. (2010), 'Re-Examining Horizontal Effect: Privacy, Defamation and the Human Rights Act'; Part 1, 21(3) *Entertainment Law Review* 96; Part 2, 21(4) *Entertainment Law Review* 145.

Brazell, L. (2005), 'Confidence, Privacy and Human Rights: English Law in the Twenty-First Century' 27(11) EIPR 405.

Eady, Mr Justice (2009), 'Speech at University of Hertfordshire' 10 November (Judiciary of England and Wales website).

Fenwick, H. and Philipson, G. (2006), *Media Freedom under the Human Rights Act* (Oxford University Press), chs 13–15.

Moreham, N. A. (2005), 'Privacy in the Common Law: A Doctrinal and Theoretical Analysis' 121 LQR 628.

Phillipson, G. (2003), 'Transforming Breach of Confidence? Towards a Common Law Right of Privacy under the Human Rights Act' 66(5) *Modern Law Review* 726.

Phillipson, G. (2009), 'Max Mosley goes to Strasbourg: Article 8, Claimant Notification and Interim Injunctions' 1 *Journal of Media Law* 73.

Pillans, B. (2007), 'McKennitt v Ash: The Book of Secrets' 12(3) *Communications Law* 78.

Wragg, P. (2014), 'Leveson's Vision for Press Reform: One Year On' 19(3) *Communications Law* 6 (Leveson Report)

23

Deceit, malicious falsehood and passing off

Objectives

After reading this chapter you will:

1. Understand the legal rules relating to the tort of deceit.
2. Have a knowledge of the legal rules relating to the tort of malicious falsehood.
3. Understand the legal rules relating to the tort of passing off.

Deceit

Introduction

Objective
1

See Chapter 5 for negligent misstatement.

The tort of deceit is committed when the defendant makes a false statement to the claimant, knowing it is false, or reckless as to its truth, with the intention that the claimant acts on it, the claimant does act and suffers damage as a result. (*Pasley* v *Freeman* (1789) 3 TR 51.)

The tort is related to the action for negligent misstatement. The distinction is that the latter action is based on negligence and covers statements of fact and opinion, whereas deceit is based on fraudulent misrepresentation and covers only statements of fact.

False statement of fact

For deceit to be committed there must be a false representation of fact. The representation must generally be a positive act made by words or conduct. The words may be oral or written. This rule is in support of the point that there is usually no duty of disclosure in English law.

Students of contract law will be familiar with this principle if they have studied misrepresentation. They will also be familiar with the point that if a statement of fact was made which was true at the time but later became false, a failure to correct the misrepresentation is actionable. (*With* v *O'Flanagan* [1936] Ch 575.) In the case of contracts *uberrimae fidei*, such as an insurance contract, there may also be a duty to disclose any material fact.

The statement must be one of existing fact and not opinion. This distinction may not be easy to make.

Bisset v *Wilkinson* [1927] AC 177

> The vendor of land in New Zealand said that the land would support 2,000 sheep. This turned out to be incorrect, but the statement was held to be one of opinion and not fact and therefore not a misrepresentation. Two factors appear to have been important in the decision. The land had never been used for sheep before and neither of the parties had any special knowledge of sheep.
>
> It would appear that if the maker of the statement has special knowledge, the statement is more likely to be held to be one of fact. An example of this can be seen in **Esso Petroleum Co Ltd v Mardon** [1976] QB 801.

Knowledge of the falsity of the statement

To be liable in deceit, the defendant must have knowledge that the statement is false or be reckless as to whether it is true or false.

Derry v *Peek* (1889) 14 App Cas 337

> Directors of a company issued a prospectus stating that they had the right to run trams on steam power. Board of Trade approval was necessary to do this and such approval had not been obtained. The directors believed that such approval would be given as a matter of course, but the Board of Trade refused to give its approval. The company was wound up and the claimant, who had bought shares in the company relying on the prospectus, brought an action in deceit. The House of Lords held that such an action did not lie. In order to succeed in deceit, the claimant had to prove fraud. Fraud would arise where a false representation of fact had been made:
>
> 1 knowingly;
> 2 without belief in its truth;
> 3 recklessly, careless as to whether it was true or false.

See Chapter 5 for *Hedley Byrne* v *Heller*. This case had a long-lasting effect on English law in the area of statements. Until ***Hedley Byrne* v *Heller*** (1964), it was authority for the point that no action lay on a careless but honest statement. It is now possible for a claimant to sue for damages on a statement in the tort of negligence or under the Misrepresentation Act 1967 s 2(1). Both of these actions are easier to prove than establishing fraud for the purpose of deceit.

Intention that the statement be acted on

The defendant must intend that the statement be acted on. Only those persons or class of persons whom the defendant intended to act on the statement can sue. The easiest way of establishing this is to prove that the defendant made the statement to the claimant, but this is not necessary to establish liability. It is sufficient that the claimant was a member of a class to whom the statement was addressed.

Langridge v *Levy* (1837) 2 M&W 337

> The claimant's father purchased a gun from the defendant, whom he told he was going to pass the gun on to his son. The defendant knowingly and falsely said that the gun was sound. The father gave the gun to his son, the claimant, who was injured when the gun burst. The defendant was held liable in deceit.

The claimant must act on the statement

The claimant must prove that they acted on the statement to their detriment. It must be reliance on the statement that caused the claimant's loss. The statement need not be the only or indeed the decisive factor in causing the claimant to act in the way that they did, provided that it was a material factor.

Damage to the claimant

For remoteness, see Chapter 9.

The remoteness test for deceit is directness and not reasonable foreseeability, and the aim of the damages award is to put the claimant into the position they would have been in if no false representation had been made.

Doyle v *Olby (Ironmongers) Ltd* [1969] 2 QB 158

The claimant had been induced by the defendant's fraudulent misrepresentation to buy a business for £4,500 plus stock at a value of £5,000. After the claimant discovered the fraud, he had to remain in business as best he could and after three years sold the business for £3,500.

The Court of Appeal treated the claimant as having lost £9,500 less £3,500 (for the sale) and £3,500 other benefits acquired plus consequential losses of £3,000 in respect of liabilities incurred in running the business. Total damages of £5,500.

Smith New Court Securities Ltd v *Scrimgeour Vickers Ltd* [1996] 4 All ER 769

The House of Lords laid down that a victim of fraud was entitled to all the actual loss, including consequential loss directly flowing from the transaction induced by the deceit of the wrongdoer.

The remoteness test for deceit is directness and not reasonable foreseeability.

Claims for deceit will frequently arise in the context of the purchase of a company. The claim in deceit may typically be combined with a claim in misrepresentation and/or breach of contract. One of the most difficult questions in these cases is the calculation of damages. The following case illustrates the principles and difficulties involved and illustrates that damages are available for loss of chance in deceit.

4 Eng Ltd v *Harper* [2008] EWHC 915 (Ch)

The claim arose out of the purchase of a company, Excel Engineering Ltd, by the claimant. The defendants owned Ironfirm Ltd, which owned Excel. On the sale of Excel the defendants had given the typical vendors' warranties, such as that the accounts were a true reflection of Excel's finances, and that they knew of nothing that would cause Excel's principal customer (Mars UK Ltd) from continuing to do business with it. In fact both defendants had participated in a corrupt scheme in which Mars employees had been bribed to invent or inflate invoices for work done by Excel, which Excel then submitted to Mars for payment. As a result, Excel's accounts did not show the true state of its finances, since it owed Mars £1.8 million under a constructive trust; Mars also had a very good reason to cease doing business with Excel.

The damages were claimed under five heads:

1 the purchase price paid for Excel;
2 the costs of acquisition;
3 salaries paid to two senior personnel appointed to manage Excel after the takeover;

4   the costs of investigating the corrupt scheme;

5   the lost opportunity to acquire another company.

Heads **2** and **4** were recoverable as straightforward consequential losses directly flowing from the fraud. Recovery of the purchase price was slightly more problematic, as the defendants argued that credit should be given for the value of Excel at the date of acquisition (i.e. before the corrupt scheme was brought to light). The judge held that the date of acquisition was not the correct date to value Excel. The date of acquisition was inappropriate because, as a result of the corrupt scheme, Excel was not a readily marketable asset.

The most difficult claim concerned the fifth head of damage – the lost opportunity to enter an alternative transaction (to purchase a company called Tarvale). This head overlapped with the third head, in that, if the alternative transaction had been accomplished, the claimant would have appointed the same two senior personnel (who were effectively its controlling minds) to run the newly acquired business. Hence, the claimant conceded that an award under the fifth head would exclude an award under the third head, because any profit made in the alternative business would take account of expenses such as salaries.

The judge held that, as a matter of principle, damages for loss of the alternative purchase were recoverable, and that they represented damages for loss of a chance.

The claimant needed to show two things: first, that it would have purchased the alter-native business; secondly, that the shareholders would have agreed to sell. The first requirement had to be shown on the balance of probabilities; the second, involving an assessment of how a third party would have acted, was to be estimated as a chance. On the facts it was held that, on the balance of probabilities, the claimant would have been able to arrange finance for the purchase. The first requirement was, therefore, satisfied. As for the shareholders' likelihood of selling, that was assessed at 80 per cent. The claimant was, therefore, entitled to recover 80 per cent of the profit that it would have made from Tarvale; it was also entitled to recover 20 per cent of the salary costs set out in the third head of damage.

Malicious falsehood

Introduction

Objective
2

This tort was originally called slander of title, as it involved a statement which questioned a person's title to land, with the result that the land was unsaleable. In the nineteenth century the tort was extended to slander of goods and passing off. (See below for 'Passing off'.)

For malice, see Chapter 1.

At the end of the nineteenth century, the Court of Appeal fused an action of general application.

Ratcliffe v Evans [1892] 2 QB 524

The defendant newspaper proprietor published an article that implied the claimant's firm had gone out of business. The article was false and was published with malice. The claimant sued to recover his resulting business losses. The action would lie for a false statement which was maliciously published with the intention of causing damage. The tort was not actionable *per se*, so the statement must have actually caused damage.

For defamation, see Chapter 21.

How does this tort differ from defamation and deceit?

Defamation is concerned with protecting a person's reputation. It is not defamatory to say that a firm has stopped trading or that a pop star has entered a closed order of monks.

Neither of these statements would lower the claimant in the eyes of right-thinking members of society. Malicious falsehood (sometimes called injurious falsehood) is generally concerned with the claimant's economic interests, and the tort can be committed without impugning reputation. However, the scope of the tort has been expanded by two Court of Appeal cases.

Kaye v Robertson [1991] FSR 62

The claimant was an actor famous for his part in 'Allo 'Allo. He suffered serious head injuries during a storm and was photographed in a hospital bed without his consent. The defendant newspaper published the story as having been obtained with his consent. This was held to be capable of being malicious falsehood as it prevented the claimant from marketing the story himself.

Joyce v Sengupta [1993] 1 WLR 337

The defendant newspaper accused the claimant of stealing personal letters from the Princess Royal while in her employment. The Court of Appeal held that her claim in malicious falsehood was not an abuse of process as her future employment prospects might be prejudiced.

The effect of these cases is that individual economic interests as well as commercial interests are protected by the tort.

It should be noted that the 'single meaning rule' in defamation does not apply in malicious falsehood cases. (*Ajinomoto Sweeteners Europe SAS* v *Asda Stores* [2010] 2 All ER 311.)

Deceit is concerned with false statements made to the claimant with the intention that they should act on them. Malicious falsehood is concerned with false statements made to third parties about the claimant with the intention that loss will be caused to the claimant.

There are three requirements for the tort:

1 a false statement of fact;

2 malice; and

3 damage.

False statement

The defendant must make a false statement of fact to some person other than the claimant. As with deceit, it must be a statement of fact rather than a statement of opinion. This causes problems with distinguishing a trade puff and an actionable misrepresentation. A considerable amount of advertising is based on the merits of a product while impliedly denigrating the quality of rival products. Provided that a person sticks to the qualities of their own goods, even if this includes saying that they are superior to other products, the tort is not committed. But if false reasons are given for the lack of quality in another person's goods, then the statement may be actionable.

De Beers Abrasive Products Ltd v International General Electric Co of New York [1975] 1 WLR 972

Both parties made diamond abrasives which were used for cutting concrete. The defendants, to boost sales, published a pamphlet with what purported to be a laboratory report comparing the parties' products. This report contained adverse comment on the claimant's product. The test to be applied was whether a reasonable person would take the claim being made as a serious claim or not.

> An indication that the claim was meant to be taken seriously was a claim that a rival's goods had been subjected to a proper scientific test. To say that your goods are better than those of a rival is acceptable. But to denigrate the goods of a rival without grounds was a falsehood.

 ## Malice

See Chapter 1 for malice.

The statement must be made with malice. Malice means without just cause or excuse and with some indirect, dishonest or improper motive. The burden of proof is on the claimant to establish malice.

If the defendant makes the statement knowing it is false or if they are reckless as to the truth of the statement, then the statement is made with malice. Where the defendant honestly believes that the statement is true but it is false, there is no malice.

Damage

The claimant must prove that they suffered damage as a result of the defendant's statement. This is usually done by proving a general loss of business.

The Defamation Act 1952 s 3 provides:

> . . . it shall not be necessary to allege or prove special damage:
>
> (a) if the words upon which the action is founded are calculated to cause pecuniary damage to the plaintiff and are published in writing or some other permanent form; or
> (b) if the said words are calculated to cause pecuniary damage to the plaintiff in respect of any office, profession, calling, trade or business held or carried on by him at the time of publication.

Passing off

Introduction

Objective 3

Passing off is normally considered as a separate tort from malicious falsehood, but some writers treat it as part of malicious falsehood.

The tort is committed by the defendant passing off their goods as the claimant's. The claimant's interest which is protected is his financial interest in his property.

The basis of the action is:

1 a reputation (or goodwill) acquired by the claimant in the goods, name, mark etc.;

2 a misrepresentation by the defendant leading to confusion (or deception) causing;

3 damage to the claimant (***Consorzio del Prosciuttodi Parma* v *Marks & Spencer plc*** [1991] RPC 351).

The modern version of the tort was set out in the following case.

Even Warnink BV v Townend & Sons (Hull) Ltd [1979] AC 731

> The claimants made a drink called advocaat. The defendants began to make a drink called Old English Advocaat. The claimants applied for an injunction to restrain the defendants from using the name advocaat. Lord Diplock identified five essential elements of the tort:

1 a misrepresentation;
2 made by a trader in the course of his trade;
3 to prospective customers of his or ultimate consumers of goods or services supplied by him;
4 which is calculated to injure the business or goodwill of the trader by whom the action is brought or will probably do so;
5 which causes actual damage to a business or goodwill of the trader by whom the action is brought or will probably do so.

As the name which was used by the claimants distinguished the claimants' product from any others, the claimants were entitled to the injunction.

The claimant has to establish a goodwill or reputation attached to the goods or services which he supplies in the mind of the purchasing public. It is not possible to provide a complete list of the circumstances in which an action will succeed and the cause of action is still evolving.

Methods of committing the tort

Using the claimant's name

This may be done by using the claimant's actual name where that name has a particular connection with the claimant's business. It is not possible to open a French restaurant with the name Maxim's, as the public would think it had a connection with the famous restaurant of that name in Paris. (*Maxim's Ltd* v *Dye* [1977] 1 WLR 1155.) What if the defendant had been called Maxim? Would they be entitled to use their own name? A person is generally entitled to use their own name unless that name is so closely associated with the name of the claimant's goods that the public would be misled.

Alternatively, the defendant may use a name similar to the name of the claimant's goods as in the advocaat example above. Similarly, an injunction was granted to prevent wine being called Spanish Champagne. The name champagne referred to a particular area of France and only producers in that area were entitled to use the name on their product. (*J Bollinger* v *Costa Brava Wine Co Ltd* [1960] Ch 262.)

If the name applies to a type of goods, such as vacuum cleaners, the name is not protected.

If the parties are not in the same trade, it is difficult to obtain an injunction. A well-known children's broadcaster called Uncle Mac failed to prevent a cereal company calling a breakfast cereal Uncle Mac's Puffed Wheat. (*McCullough* v *May* [1947] 2 All ER 845.)

Imitating the appearance of the claimant's goods

Not only the name of the goods is protected, but also the physical appearance and the way the goods are advertised. If the claimant has used an advertising campaign linking their goods to a virile sporting image and can establish that the public exclusively link that image with their product, the defendant can be prevented from using a similar image. (*Cadbury-Schweppes Pty Ltd* v *Pub Squash Co Pty Ltd* [1981] 1 WLR 193.)

Claiming that the claimant's goods belong to the defendant

This is one of the original forms of the tort and is committed when the defendant claims ownership of goods which in fact belong to the claimant.

Remedies

See Chapter 28 for injunctions.

The normal remedy in passing off is an injunction to prevent the defendant from using a name, etc. The claimant may also claim damages or an account of profits.

Summary

This chapter deals with the torts of deceit, malicious falsehood and passing off.

- Deceit is where the defendant makes a false statement to the claimant, knowing it is false or being reckless as to its truth, with the intention that the claimant acts on it, the claimant does act and suffers damage as a result.
- There must be a false statement of fact not opinion.
- The defendant must have knowledge that the statement is false or be reckless as to whether it is true or false.
- The defendant must intend that the statement be acted on.
- The claimant must act on the statement.
- There must be damage to the claimant. The remoteness test is directness. The aim of damages is to put the claimant in the position they would have been in if no false representation had been made. (For the calculation of damages see *4 Eng Ltd* v *Harper* (2008).)
- Malicious falsehood involves a statement which questions a person's title to land, slanders their goods or involves passing off. There must be malice and damage as a result. The tort is concerned with economic interests but can extend to reputation.
- There must be a false statement of fact, malice and damage. Damage can be proved by showing general loss of business; it is not necessary to show special damage.
- Passing off is generally considered to be a separate tort from malicious falsehood. It is committed by the defendant passing off their goods as the claimant's.
- The claimant must prove: reputation or goodwill acquired by the claimant in the goods; a misrepresentation by the defendant leading to confusion or deception; damage to the claimant.
- The modern version of the tort was set out in *Even Warnink BV* v *Townend* (1979):
  1. a misrepresentation;
  2. made by a trader in the course of his trade;
  3. to prospective customers of his or ultimate consumers of goods or services supplied by him;
  4. which is calculated to injure the business or goodwill of the trader by whom the action is brought or will probably do so;
  5. which causes actual damage to a business or goodwill of the trader by whom the action is brought or will probably do so.

Further reading

Weir, T. (2004), *Casebook on Tort* (10th edn), Sweet & Maxwell, ch 15.

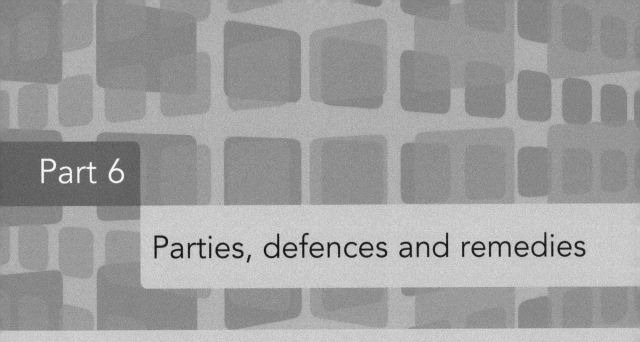

Part 6

Parties, defences and remedies

24

Vicarious liability

Objectives

After reading this chapter you will:

1. Appreciate the concept of vicarious liability.

2. Understand the justifications for imposing vicarious liability.

3. Understand the legal rules on vicarious liability.

Introduction

Objective 1

See Chapter 15 for medical negligence.

Vicarious liability is where one person is made liable for the tort of another person. It is important to draw a distinction between primary liability and vicarious liability. This can be illustrated by the medical negligence cases. A health authority may be vicariously liable for the torts of its employees and it may also be primarily liable where it fails to provide adequate levels of staffing in one of its hospitals and an accident results.

The commonest example of vicarious liability in tort is that of an employer for the torts of their employee. Two things are necessary for such liability to arise. There must be a particular relationship between the employer and the employee. A distinction is drawn here between employees and independent contractors. The employer is liable for the torts of the former but not those of the latter. Secondly, the tort committed must be referable to the employment relationship. This is expressed by saying that the tort must be committed in the course of employment.

Example

Andrew was run over and injured by a lorry driven by Brian. The vehicle was being driven negligently at the time. Brian was employed as a lorry driver by Charles and if Brian was in the course of his employment, then Charles will be vicariously liable for Brian's negligence. If Brian was on what is sometimes called a frolic of his own, then Brian will be outside the course of his employment and Charles will not be vicariously liable.

If the vehicle was a taxi which had been stopped by Charles, then Brian, the driver, will be an independent contractor in relation to Charles, and Charles will prima facie not be liable for Brian's negligence.

Vicarious liability is not a static doctrine. Types of employment change over time and it is clear that the doctrine extends beyond contracts of employment. In can exist in partnership cases, principal and agent relationships, and relationships 'akin to employment' such as bishops and priests.

In *E v English Province of Our Lady of Charity* [2011] EWHC 2871; [2012] EWCA Civ 938, the question was whether a diocesan bishop could be vicariously liable for the torts of a priest. Vicarious liability, in a relationship akin to employment, could arise where the relationship between the defendant and the tortfeasor was so close in character to the relationship of employer and employee that it was just and fair to hold the employer liable. In this case, although not an employment relationship, or a contractual relationship, the relationship between the bishop and B had been nevertheless sufficiently akin to that of employment given the degree of control and connection, and given the objectives of the bishop in B's appointment to promote the spiritual well-being of parishioners within the diocese, which it had been intended B should further and promote. Vicarious liability in respect of B's activities in the parish was thus capable of arising. The test was the nature and closeness of the relationship.

The issue was considered by the Supreme Court;

Various Claimants v *Institute of the Brothers of the Christian Schools* [2012] UKSC 56

The claimants alleged abuse by staff at their former school. For the relevant period the school was run by a board of managers. Some, but not all, of the school's teachers were supplied by the Institute of the Brothers of the Christian Schools, an unincorporated association. The question was whether the Institute, in addition to the school management, was liable for the acts of abuse committed by the brothers who were employed by the managers. The defendants were held to be vicariously liable on the basis of a relationship 'akin to employment'.

This is an important case as it is rare that a vicarious liability case reaches the Supreme Court.

Vicarious liability is an example of strict liability, in the sense that there need be no fault on the part of the employer before they can be made liable. What, therefore, is the justification for imposing vicarious liability?

Justification for imposing vicarious liability

Objective 2

Although the doctrine of vicarious liability is accepted in English law, there is no clear and convincing rationale for its imposition. A number of theories have been put forward to explain the deviation from the prevalent fault-based theory of liability.

The employer is best placed to reduce workplace accidents and intentional wrongdoing by employees. It has been suggested that the employer is in control of the behaviour of their employee. This is no longer convincing as many employees perform skilled tasks which the employer is incapable of understanding. To say that a health authority chief executive controls the work of a consultant is stretching the meaning of the word.

Alternative suggestions have included the fact that the employer may have been careless in selecting the employee. However, liability is not based on this premise and a perfectly competent employee is capable of behaving negligently at some stage in their employment.

The modern approach is entirely pragmatic and is based on social convenience and rough justice. The imposition of liability is based on the employer's greater ability to pay any damages and the fact that this involves loss spreading. The employer is the best insurer against liability, and any extra cost to the employer can be passed on to the public in the form of higher prices. This may encourage accident prevention, as a firm which raises its prices too high will go out of business.

> . . . Vicarious liability is a loss distribution device based on grounds of social and economic policy. Its rationale limits the employer's liability to conduct occurring in the course of the employee's employment. 'The master ought to be liable for all those torts which can fairly be regarded as reasonably incidental risks to the type of business he carries on' . . . 'the ultimate question is whether or not it is just that the loss resulting from the servant's acts should be considered as one of the normal risks to be borne by the business in which the servant is employed.' (Lord Millett in *Dubai Aluminium Co Ltd* v *Salaam* [2003] 2 AC 366.)

> . . . the policy objective underlying vicarious liability is to ensure, in so far as it is fair, just and reasonable, that liability for tortious wrong is borne by a defendant with the means to compensate the victim. (Lord Phillips in *Various Claimants* [2012].)

Lord Phillips invoked insurance, loss spreading, a deep pockets argument, acting on behalf of employer, enterprise and risk creation, and control justifications.

The doctrine can be justified on a moral basis if the employee inflicts loss on the claimant while pursuing the employer's business interests. As the employer obtains a benefit from the employee's work, they should also bear the costs of accidents arising out of it.

The difficulty with all of these arguments is that they run counter to the main thrust of tort law and do not sit well with the actual case law on vicarious liability. If a form of strict liability is being imposed then why does the employee have to commit a tort before the employer is liable? Why not just impose strict liability on employers for all damage committed by their employees? Tort law is not in general designed to spread losses, so why pursue this objective in one part of the law of tort and not others?

The strength of the doctrine is reflected in the House of Lords decision in *Majrowski* v *Guys and St Thomas NHS Trust* [2006] 4 All ER 395. The claimant had brought a claim against his former employers under the Protection from Harassment Act 1997 on the grounds of their vicarious liability for his former line manager's homophobic bullying. The House of Lords dismissed the employer's claim that the legislation was of a public order nature and was not intended to impose a burden on employers. Where the harassment was carried out in the course of employment the employer could be vicariously liable.

See Chapters 17 and 22 for Protection from Harassment Act 1997.

Who is an employee?

Objective 3

Although vicarious liability extends beyond the employer–employee situation most cases have arisen in this context. Perhaps the question should now be 'for whose torts is another person liable'?

An employer is vicariously liable for the torts of an employee committed in the course of their employment, but not for those of an independent contractor. This has caused severe difficulties for the courts and continues to do so. Where employment does not fall into a traditional pattern, even the parties may be unaware of their employment relationship. This may happen with casual workers, for example. Employers may also attempt to avoid their legal liabilities by attempting to classify employees as independent contractors. It is clear that the label attached to the relationship by the employer is not conclusive.

A number of tests have been used to attempt to draw a distinction. Traditionally, a distinction was made between a contract of service (employee) and a contract for services (independent contractor). This distinction is no help in telling which is which.

For a time the control test was popular. If the employer retained control over the work and told a person how to do it, that person was an employee. The test reflected a society where ownership of the means of production coincided with the possession of technical knowledge and skill. The typical employer would be the Victorian engineer who knew all aspects of the work done in his firm. As so many employees are now skilled, the employer may be able to tell them what to do but not how to do it. The computer specialist, lawyer or accountant employed by a firm does not fit the control test.

> ... many employees apply a skill or expertise that is not susceptible to direction by anyone else in the company that employs them. (Lord Phillips in *Various Claimants* [2012].)

The problems with the control test led the courts to search for alternatives. One suggestion was the business integration test put forward by Lord Denning. (*Stevenson, Jordan and Harrison Ltd v McDonald and Evans* (1952) 1 TLR 101.) A person would be an employee if their work was an integral part of the business. An independent contractor would work for the business, but as an accessory rather than an integral part of it. On this basis it would be possible to distinguish between a chauffeur and a taxi driver and a staff reporter and a newspaper contributor. In practice, the test proved too vague to apply, as did a variation of whether the person was in business on their own account. (*Market Investigations Ltd v Minister of Social Security* [1969] 2 QB 173.)

The courts have now abandoned the search for any single factor to act as a test and will look at all the circumstances of the particular case.

Ready Mixed Concrete (South East) Ltd v Minister of Pensions [1968] 2 QB 497

The following criteria for a contract of service were put forward:

1 the employee agrees, in return for a wage or other remuneration, that they will provide their work and skill for the employer;
2 the employee agrees expressly or impliedly to be subject to their employer's control; and
3 the other terms of the contract are consistent with there being a contract of employment.

These three factors are not all the courts will look at. If the parties have specified that a person will be self-employed and the terms of the contract reflect self-employed status, then the contract will be regarded as a contract for services.

O'Kelly v Trusthouse Forte plc [1983] ICR 728

Wine butlers who worked at the Grosvenor House Hotel were described as regular casual workers and only worked when required. They could refuse work if they wanted. They were held not to be employees for the purpose of employment protection legislation, but what would the position have been if one of them had negligently injured a guest or his property? The economic reality of the situation surely dictates that they would be employees for the purpose of vicarious liability. As the objective of vicarious liability is to enable the claimant to satisfy a judgment, the risk-bearing capacity of the parties and the solvency of the employees would point towards this solution.

It could be argued that too narrow a view has been taken of control and that a combination of (an extended) control plus integration is more satisfactory. This looks at the question of whether or not a tortfeasor is part of the defendant's team (integrated). This is not just an issue of control over the task, but instead what day-to-day control is (or can be) exercised, by A over B.

Lending an employee

What is the position where an employer A lends their employee B to another employer C and B commits a tort within the course of this employment? Who will be vicariously liable, A or C?

Mersey Docks and Harbour Board v *Coggins & Griffith (Liverpool) Ltd* [1947] AC 1

A employed B as a mobile crane driver and hired B and the crane to C. The contract between A and C provided that B should be the employee of C. However, B continued to be paid by A who also had the power to dismiss. A person was injured as a result of B's negligent handling of the crane. The House of Lords laid down principles to determine whether A or C was vicariously liable for B's negligence:

1. a term in the contract between A and C is not decisive;
2. the burden of proof is on the permanent employer A to show that C was B's employer for the purposes of vicarious liability; and
3. where labour only is lent, then it is easier to infer that the hirer is the employer. Where labour and plant is hired, it is more difficult to rebut the presumption, as the hirer may not have control over the way the plant is used.

On the facts, A had failed to rebut the presumption and remained B's employer for the purposes of vicarious liability.

Where a nightclub bouncer was hired to a nightclub by his employers and committed an assault on a customer, it was held that the nightclub were vicariously liable as they had sufficient control over the employee. (*Hawley* v *Luminar Leisure Ltd* [2006] EWCA Civ 18.) The Court of Appeal asked the question: 'who was entitled and therefore obliged to control (the bouncer's) act so as to prevent it.' The answer was the nightclub.

The Court of Appeal has now ruled that in very limited circumstances there may be dual vicarious liability and both the permanent and temporary employer may be vicariously liable.

Viasystems (Tyneside) Ltd v *Thermal Transfers (Northern) Ltd* [2006] QB 510

The claimants engaged the first defendants to install air conditioning in their factory. The first defendants sub-contracted ducting work to the second defendants. The ducting work was being carried out by a fitter and his mate, supplied to the second defendants by the third defendants on a labour-only basis, under the supervision of a fitter working for the second defendants, when the fitter's mate negligently caused the fracture of the fire protection sprinkler system, resulting in severe flood damage to the factory. The judge gave judgment for the claimants against the first defendants, pursuant to a contractual indemnity, dismissed the claim against the second defendants and found the third defendants vicariously liable for the fitter's mate's negligence.

On appeal by the third defendants it was held, allowing the appeal, that vicarious liability was liability imposed by a policy of the law on a party who was not personally at fault, and, in the case of a negligent employee, derived from the employer's responsibility to control the careful execution of his employees' duties; that the concept of transference of employment, in cases such as the present, was misleading and it was more appropriate to concentrate on the relevant negligent act and whose responsibility it was to prevent it; that, while there had been a long-standing assumption that dual

> vicarious liability was not possible, it provided a coherent solution to the problem of the borrowed employee, and was permissible, where, on the facts, there were two employers each in theory obliged to control the employee's negligent act; that, on the facts, both the second and third defendants were entitled, and in theory obliged, so to control the fitter's mate as to stop his negligent act and, accordingly, should be jointly vicariously liable; and that, in the absence of any personal fault on the part of either employer, the just and equitable division of contribution under s 1 of the Civil Liability (Contribution Act) 1978 should be equal.
>
> May LJ focused the court's attention on the question of control. He did not envisage a finding of dual vicarious liability in many factual situations. Rix LJ, however, doubted that the doctrine of vicarious liability should depend solely on the question of control and suggests a broader test of 'whether or not the employee in question is so much part of the work business or organisation of both employers that it is just to make both employers answer for his negligence'.

This decision was considered by the Supreme Court in **Various Claimants** [2012]. Lord Phillips considered May LJ's approach too stringent and preferred Rix LJ's approach. Little explanation was given for this conclusion, although it may stem from Lord Phillips' brief criticism of control. Consequently he stated that the facts of the case of **Viasystems** would support dual vicarious liability.

It is possible that, where an employee is lent out, the permanent employer will remain personally, rather than vicariously, liable when the employee is injured. (**McDermid v Nash** [1987] AC 906.)

See Chapter 14 for McDermid v Nash.

In the course of employment

The employer will only be liable for torts which the employee commits *in the course of their employment*. These are probably the most litigated words in the English language and it is arguable that each case will be a question of fact.

NB. Cases prior to 2002 should now be read in the light of the House of Lords decision in **Lister v Hesley Hall Ltd** [2001] 2 All ER 769.

The policy factors include the desire to secure compensation for the victim of the tort by having a solvent defendant (the employer) to sue. There are also economic issues involved, including the employer's ability to spread the risk through insurance and providing incentives for the employer to reduce risks (enterprise risk).

> The underlying legal policy is based on the recognition that carrying on a business enterprise necessarily involves risks to others. It involves the risk that others will be harmed by wrongful acts committed by the agents through whom the business is carried on. When those risks ripen into loss, it is just that the business should be responsible for compensating the person who has been wronged. (**Dubai Aluminium Co Ltd v Salaam** [2003] 2 AC 366, per Lord Nicholls.)

The courts have often used a test suggested by Salmond, that an act is in the course of employment if it is either:

1 a wrongful act authorised by the employer; or

2 a wrongful and unauthorised mode of doing some act authorised by the employer.

This test should be treated with some caution. The first limb of the test has more to do with employer's primary, rather than vicarious, liability. If the employer authorised the tort then he would be primarily liable.

The second leg of the test has caused problems. An employer can clearly be liable for an act which he has forbidden, otherwise the employer could avoid liability simply by issuing instructions. The courts have looked at this question broadly, taking into account all the surrounding circumstances. The fact that the employee was doing his job negligently does not necessarily take him outside the scope of his employment.

Century Insurance Co v *Northern Ireland Road Transport Board* [1942] AC 509

The employee was employed by the defendants as a petrol tanker driver. While he was unloading his tanker he threw away a lighted match, which caused a fire and explosion. The defendants were held vicariously liable for his negligence as he was doing his job at the time of the accident, even if he was doing it in a negligent way. '. . . negligence in starting smoking and throwing away a lighted match in that moment is plainly negligence in the discharge of the duties on which he was employed . . .'

The second limb of the test has been rejected by the House of Lords in *Lister* v *Hesley Hall Ltd* [2002] (see below). However, it is still a useful starting point for discussion.

Express prohibition

It is possible for the employer to be vicariously liable for an act if the prohibition applies to the way in which the job is done, rather than the scope of the job itself. A bus driver is therefore within the scope of his employment when he races other buses when expressly prohibited from doing so. (*Limpus* v *London General Omnibus Co* (1862) 1 H&C 526.) The driver was still doing what he was paid to do, driving a bus.

A number of cases have involved giving lifts to people.

Rose v *Plenty* [1976] 1 WLR 141

The defendants had prohibited their employees from carrying boys on their milk floats. The 13-year-old claimant was injured while being carried on a milk float, due to the negligence of an employee. It was held that the defendants were vicariously liable as the prohibition had not affected the course of the employee's employment, simply the method by which he could do his job.

There is clearly a problem with distinguishing the earlier cases of *Conway* v *George Wimpey & Co Ltd* [1951] 2 KB 266 and *Twine* v *Bean's Express Ltd* (1946) 62 TLR 458. The majority in the Court of Appeal (Denning MR and Scarman LJ) said that in *Twine* the claimant was a trespasser and owed no duty of care. This point was no longer valid in the light of case law that held that a limited duty of care was owed to a trespasser. Secondly, in *Twine* the lift was not given for a purpose beneficial to the employer, but in *Rose* the boy was assisting with the delivery of milk.

Despite the efforts of the Court of Appeal, it may be that the cases are irreconcilable and *Rose* represents a pragmatic approach to the question of course of employment. Previous case law had demonstrated the latitude given to the court when it asked the questions 'what was the employee paid to do?' and 'what was he doing at the time of the accident?' The modern approach may be to define the scope of employment in wide terms, so as to enable the claimant to satisfy judgment.

Detours

A number of cases have involved drivers who make a detour from their authorised route and are involved in an accident. Are they still within the course of their employment? One test is whether they are on a frolic of their own or still on the employer's business.

An employer was held not liable when the driver completed his work and then went to visit a relative. This was a new and independent journey which had nothing to do with his employment. (*Storey* v *Ashton* (1869) LR 4 QB 476.)

Whether a lunch break is within the course of employment will depend on whether the employee is authorised to take one. The question of fact in each case will be whether the driver was going about the employer's business or not. Therefore, a bus driver who detoured while carrying children, in order to please the children, was still within the course of his employment. (*Williams* v *Hemphill Ltd* 1966 SLT 259.)

Accidents on the way to work have been considered.

Smith v Stages [1989] 2 WLR 529

Stages and another employee were travelling to their homes in the Midlands after working in South Wales. The car crashed and both men were injured. The employers were paying travelling expenses, but did not stipulate the means of travel, and the men were paid for the day they travelled. The House of Lords held that the men were in the employer's time and were therefore within the course of their employment. However, most journeys to and from work by employees will be outside the scope of employment, unless a person is on the employer's business.

Close connection test

The House of Lords attempted to solve some of the problems with this issue and particularly with the problem caused by claimants attempting to make employers vicariously liable for intentional torts caused by employees. In some instances the intentional conduct would be criminal.

Lister v Hesley Hall Ltd [2002] 1 AC 215

The warden of a boarding-house school for children with emotional and behavioural problems systematically sexually abused the claimants who were children in the boarding house. The question was whether the employers could be held vicariously liable for the warden's sexual abuse. What the warden did could not be described as an unauthorised method of doing some act authorised by the employers. It was the opposite of what he was employed to do. The school were, nevertheless, held vicariously liable. This was done by applying Salmond's extension on the second limb of his test that: 'a master ... is liable even for acts which he has not authorised, provided they are so connected with acts which he has authorised that they may rightly be regarded as modes – although improper modes – of doing them.' The question was therefore whether:

> ... the warden's torts were so *closely connected* with his employment that it would be fair and just to hold the employers vicariously liable. On the facts of the case the answer is yes. ... the sexual abuse was inextricably interwoven with carrying out by the warden of his duties ... (Lord Steyn.)

Lord Hobhouse stated that the employer's liability was grounded in the assumed relationship between the employers and the claimants which imposes specific duties upon the employer in relation to the person they entrust with the performance of those duties.

> There has to be a nexus or closeness of connection between the tortious conduct of the employee and their employer. The fact that the warden had access to the premises as a groundsman would not have been sufficient. It was the warden's position of responsibility to the boys in his care that created the nexus between the work and the sexual abuse.

The 'close connection' test is easier to state than to apply. In order to establish the necessary connection the court will examine the nature and purpose of the job and the circumstances and context in which the acts took place. The House of Lords stated that private acts of passion or resentment or spite were outside the principle.

The principle in *Lister* was tested and applied in *Mattis* v *Pollock* [2003] 1 WLR 2158. A serious assault was committed by a doorman on a customer at a night club. The doorman had been motivated by a desire for revenge and had injured the claimant a long time after an incident at the club the same night. The Court of Appeal held that as the employee had been encouraged by his employer to keep order by violent behaviour the employer would be vicariously liable. The court were clearly swayed by the employer's knowledge and encouragement of the bouncer's violent behaviour and found a close connection between the attack and what the bouncer was employed to do.

This test was applied where a semi-professional rugby player playing under contract for his club punched another player, causing damage (*Gravil* v *Carroll* [2008] EWCA Civ 689) and where a Roman Catholic priest sexually assaulted a juvenile parishioner (*Maga* v *Roman Catholic Archdiocese of Birmingham* [2010] EWCA Civ 256).

The difficulties are illustrated by two cases involving policemen. In *Weir* v *Chief Constable of Merseyside Police* [2003] EWCA Civ 111, a policeman was helping his girlfriend move house when he found the claimant going through her possessions. He identified himself as a police officer and threw the claimant down a flight of stairs before locking him in a police van he had borrowed. There was held to be a 'close connection' as he had identified himself as a police officer. In *N* v *Chief Constable of Merseyside Police* [2006] EWHC 3041, a police officer who raped a woman who was drunk and made a video film of the assault was held to be outside the course of his employment despite the fact that he was in police uniform and had showed a warrant card.

The close connection test has been criticised because it offers no guidance on the type or degree of connection that is required. (Lord Nicholls in *Dubai Aluminium Co Ltd* v *Salaam* [2003] 2 AC 366.) Justice may have been achieved in *Lister* but at the expense of certainty (both practical and theoretical). It has blurred the distinction between the employer's primary duties and vicarious liability. It has been suggested that a two stage test should be used when considering whether to impose vicarious liability for intentional torts. Stage one is that the employee must have been entrusted with a protective or fiduciary duty to be exercised at the employee's discretion. Stage two is that the act must take place as part of their purported exercise of this discretion (Gilliker, 2010).

The Supreme Court, in considering the second stage of vicarious liability met in *Various Claimants* [2012], upheld the 'close connection' test from *Lister* and clarified the role that risk plays in this test, which was previously unclear. Close connection entails a 'strong causative link'; risk creation is not just a policy consideration, it is also a factor in establishing close connection, although it is not by itself enough.

In cases of dishonesty, the fact that the offence was committed for the employee's benefit will not take them outside the course of their employment. (*Port Swettenham Authority* v *TW Wu* [1979] AC 580.) The question will still be, what was the employee paid to do and what were they doing at the time of the offence?

Lloyd v Grace Smith & Co [1912] AC 716

> A solicitor's clerk was held to have acted within the scope of his employment when he fraudulently induced a client to convey properties to him. As the clerk was paid to do conveyancing, he was within the course of employment.

Credit Lyonnais Bank Nederland NV v Export Credits Guarantee Dept [1999] 1 All ER 929

> An employer cannot be liable for the fraudulent conduct of their employee unless all the features of the tort occurred in the course of the employee's employment.

The House of Lords has now confirmed that there might be vicarious liability between partners in respect of the torts of partners where the partner was acting in the ordinary course of the firm's business. The test for this would be the principle in *Lister*. (*Dubai Aluminium Co Ltd v Salaam* [2003] 2 AC 366.)

The employer's indemnity

For joint tortfeasors, see Chapter 25.

The employer and employee are joint tortfeasors. This means that each will be fully liable to the claimant, who may choose whom to sue. It is normally the employer who is sued. As the employee is jointly liable, the employer is entitled to sue them and recover an indemnity.

Lister v Romford Ice & Cold Storage Ltd [1957] AC 555

> A lorry driver knocked over his father who was acting as his mate on the lorry. The father recovered damages on the basis of the employer's vicarious liability for the driver's negligence. The damages were paid by the employer's insurers, who then exercised their right of subrogation to bring proceedings against the driver for an indemnity. The House of Lords held that there was an implied term in the employee's contract of employment that he would perform his contractual duties with reasonable care. He had broken this and the insurers were entitled to recover the money which they had paid to the father.

Since this case, the result of which received considerable criticism, the employers' insurance companies have reached a gentlemen's agreement, that they will not pursue their rights under the *Lister* principle unless there is evidence of collusion or misconduct. The decision in *Lister* did seem to undermine the principle of vicarious liability, that the employer is the best person to insure against such losses. Allowing the insurance company to get its money back from the employee looks like having your cake and eating it. The employers pay a premium for the insurer to take a non-existent risk.

It should be noted that the gentlemen's agreement was made before the statutory right to an indemnity under the Civil Liability (Contribution) Act 1978 s 1.

Employers and independent contractors

The basic rule is that an employer is not liable for the torts of their independent contractors. There are, however, occasions where the employer will be primarily responsible where damage was caused by their independent contractor.

The employer may be under a non-delegable duty which cannot be discharged by entrusting work to an independent contractor. Examples of this are the employer's personal duty of care to their employees; liability under the rule in **Rylands v Fletcher**; work done by an independent contractor on or over the highway.

Non-delegable duties have historically been little used in English tort law but the complexities of modern business relationships have led the Supreme Court to examine them and lay down guidelines. This is not *vicarious* liability but rather *primary* liability on the defendant.

The essential feature of a duty of reasonable care which a defendant cannot delegate to a third party is that the defendant has control over a vulnerable claimant for the purpose of performing a function for which the defendant had assumed responsibility.

Woodland v Swimming Teachers Association [2013] UKSC 66

A schoolgirl had sustained serious brain damage when involved in a near drowning incident while taking part in a swimming lesson organised by her school but taking place at a municipal pool and supervised by an independent swimming instructor. The Supreme Court held that the education authority owed her a duty of care.

Her injuries had been due to the negligence of the swimming teacher and the lifeguard, neither of whom had been employed by the education authority but had been provided by an independent contractor who carried on an unincorporated business and had contracted with the education authority to provide swimming lessons to its pupils.

The issue arose out of an allegation in the claimants' pleadings that the education authority owed her a 'non-delegable duty of care', with the result that it was liable in law for any negligence on the part of the swimming instructor and the lifeguard.

The factors involved were characterised by the following defining features:

(1) The claimant was a patient or a child, or for some other reason was especially vulnerable or dependent on the protection of the defendant against the risk of injury. Other examples were likely to be prisoners and residents in care homes.

(2) There was an antecedent relationship between the claimant and the defendant, independent of the negligent act or omission itself (i) which placed the claimant in the actual custody, charge or care of the defendant, and (ii) from which it was possible to impute to the defendant the assumption of a positive duty to protect the claimant from harm, and not just a duty to refrain from conduct which would foreseeably damage the claimant.

It was characteristic of such relationships that they involved an element of control over the claimant, which would vary in intensity from one situation to another, but was clearly very substantial in the case of school children.

(3) The claimant had no control over how the defendant chose to perform those obligations, i.e. whether personally or through employees or through third parties.

(4) The defendant had delegated to a third party some function which was an integral part of the positive duty which he had assumed towards the claimant; and the third party was exercising, for the purpose of the function thus delegated to him, the defendant's custody or care of the claimant and the element of control that went with it.

(5) The third party had been negligent not in some collateral respect but in the performance of the very function assumed by the defendant and delegated by the defendant to him.

The essential element was not control of the environment in which the claimant had been injured, but control over the claimant for the purpose of performing a function for which the defendant had assumed responsibility.

Principal and agent

It is possible for a principal to be vicariously liable for the tort of their agent where the agent commits a tort in the course of their employment.

Ormrod v Crossville Motor Services [1953] 1 WLR 1120

The owner of a car asked a friend to drive the car to Monte Carlo from Birkenhead. The owner planned to compete in a car rally in Monte Carlo and the two were to go on holiday together afterwards. The friend caused damage to the claimant's bus in an accident caused by his negligence. It was held that the owner was liable for his friend's negligence, even though the friend was going on the journey partly for his own purposes.

Morgans v Launchbury [1973] AC 127

A husband sometimes used his wife's car. The wife was concerned about the husband's drinking habits and said he had to get a friend to drive him home if he had too much to drink. The husband did this and the friend negligently caused an accident. An action was brought against the wife, claiming she was vicariously liable. The House of Lords held that the husband was using the car for his own purposes and not hers. The driver was therefore not an agent of the wife.

Conclusion

Vicarious liability is not 'infinitely extendable' but the Supreme Court has not given guidance as to what the limits on the doctrine are; they will have to be determined through further appellate decisions.

The 'akin to employment' category recognises the changing nature of employment and the range of occupational activities between the statuses of employee and independent contractor. *Various Claimants* [2012] will lead to a broadening of vicarious liability, for example within the voluntary sector, with franchisers and franchisees, and between foster carers and local authorities, amongst others. Voluntary sector organisations will need to carefully consider their volunteer recruitment, training, retention and insurance policies. The broadening of who one can be vicariously liable for should be met with a reassessment of what one is vicariously liable for. Whilst the close connection test may be entirely appropriate in relationships of employment, it may not be appropriate where the relationship between *A* and *B* is far less proximate.

Summary

This chapter deals with the rules on vicarious liability.

- A person can be either primarily liable for a tort or vicariously liable.
- The commonest example is that an employer may be vicariously liable for a tort committed, in the course of his employment, by an employee. The doctrine is being expanded to relationships such as bishop and priest.

- A distinction is drawn between employees and independent contractors. An employer is not generally liable for the torts of the latter. The courts have now abandoned the search for a single factor to determine into which category a person falls and will look at the circumstances of the particular case but will also look at factors such as: whether the employee agreed, in return for a wage or other remuneration, that they would provide their work and skill for the employer; whether the employee agreed expressly or impliedly to be subject to their employer's control; and whether the other terms of the contract are consistent with there being a contract of employment.

- Where an employee is lent by one employer to another there is a problem as to who is liable if the employee commits a tort. The courts will consider the following factors: a term in the contract between *A* and *C* is not decisive; the burden of proof is on the permanent employer *A* to show that *C* was *B*'s employer for the purposes of vicarious liability; and where labour only is lent, then it is easier to infer that the hirer is the employer.

- Where labour and plant is hired, it is more difficult to rebut the presumption, as the hirer may not have control over the way the plant is used. It is now possible for both the permanent and temporary employer to be vicariously liable. (***Viasystems*** v ***Thermal Transfers*** [2006].)

- The employee must commit the tort in the course of his employment. The classic test is that of Salmond. An act is in the course of employment if it is either: a wrongful act authorised by the employer; or a wrongful and unauthorised mode of doing some act authorised by the employer. Modern case law suggests that the second part of the test may need to be modified to a 'closeness of connection' test. (***Lister*** v ***Hesley Hall*** [2002] and ***Various Claimants*** [2012].)

Further reading

Cane, P. (2002), 'Liability for Sexual Abuse' 116 LQR 21.

Gilliker, P. (2009), 'Making the Right Connection: Vicarious Liability and Individual Responsibility' 17 *Torts Law Journal* 35.

Gilliker, P. (2010), 'Lister Revisited: Vicarious Liability, Distributive Justice and Course of Employment' LQR 521.

McBride, N. (2003), 'Vicarious Liability in England and Australia' CLJ 255.

McIvor, C. (2006), 'The Use and Abuse of the Doctrine of Vicarious Liability' (2006) 35 *Common Law World Review* 268.

Morgan P. (2013), 'Vicarious Liability on the Move' LQR 139 (*Various Claimants*.)

Tan D. (2013), 'A Sufficiently Close Relationship Akin to Employment' LQR 30.

Weekes, R. (2004), 'Vicarious Liability for Violent Employees' 63 CLJ 53.

25

Joint and several liability

Objectives

After reading this chapter you will:

1. Understand the concepts of joint and several liability.
2. Have a knowledge of the legal rules relating to successive actions.
3. Understand the rules on contributions between tortfeasors.

Introduction

Objective 1

If there is more than one breach of duty which causes the claimant damage, the liability of the defendants may be independent, several or joint.

Independent liability arises where the claimant suffered damage as a result of two completely separate torts. Each tortfeasor is liable for the damage they inflict. If *A*'s car is damaged on the right-hand side by *B*'s negligence and a week later *C* drives negligently into the left-hand side of the car, *B* and *C* are independently liable for the damage they inflicted.

If more than one tortfeasor acts independently to cause the same damage to the claimant, then they are severally liable. An example would be where two careless motorists collide and injure a pedestrian. In cases of several liability, each tortfeasor is separately liable in respect of the damage, but the claimant may recover damages only once.

Joint liability may arise in a number of ways. If two or more tortfeasors commit a joint breach of duty or act in furtherance of a common design, then they are joint tortfeasors.

Brooke v Bool [1928] 2 KB 578

The claimant leased a shop from the defendant who remained entitled to enter the premises. A lodger in the shop told the defendant he could smell gas and both men investigated. The lodger was told to light a match by the defendant and there was an explosion. The defendant was held jointly liable for the damage caused by the lodger's negligence.

See Chapter 24 for vicarious liability.

Joint liability also arises where an employer is held to be vicariously liable for the negligence of their employee. The employer and the employee are joint tortfeasors. Similarly, where the employer is under a non-delegable duty and damage is caused by the tort of their independent contractor and in principal–agent cases.

In cases of joint liability each tortfeasor is liable for the full amount, but the claimant can recover only once.

Two problems are raised by joint and several liability: successive actions by the claimant and contribution between defendants. The position has now been changed by statute, but it is still relevant to look at common law.

Successive actions

Objective
2

If two or more persons were found to be joint tortfeasors at common law then two consequences followed.

A judgment against one tortfeasor barred a subsequent action against the others. This was so even if the judgment was unsatisfied. Judgment also meant that the claimant could not continue the action against other tortfeasors. This rule was reversed by the Law Reform (Married Women and Tortfeasors) Act 1935 s 6 (now the Civil Liability (Contribution) Act 1978 s 3).

Judgment recovered against any person liable in respect of any debt or damage shall not be a bar to an action, or to the continuance of an action, against any other person who is (apart from any such bar) jointly liable with them in respect of the same debt or damage.

If the claimant does bring a second action against a joint or several tortfeasor, then s 4 provides that they shall be refused costs in the later action unless the court is satisfied that there was reasonable ground for bringing it.

The statutory provision removed an important distinction between joint and several liability, as the common law rule against successive actions did not apply to several (concurrent) tortfeasors.

Where the claimant sues joint or several tortfeasors together, one judgment is given for a single sum.

The second consequence of joint liability at common law was that the release of one joint tortfeasor had the effect of releasing the other tortfeasors. This was based on the reason that in cases of joint liability only one tort was committed. Where liability was several, the release of one tortfeasor did not affect the liability of the others. The severity of the rule in cases of joint liability has been mitigated by courts drawing a distinction between an agreement not to sue, which preserves the cause of action against the rest, and a release, which extinguishes the liability of the rest. In practice, the courts are very reluctant to find that there has been a release; and, even where there has been a release, this does not extinguish the action if there is an express or implied reservation of the action against the others.

In the case of concurrent liability the House of Lords has now held that where the claimant has entered into a 'full and final' settlement with *D1* then they cannot maintain a claim against *D2* for the same liability. (***Jameson v Central Electricity Generating Board*** [1999] 2 WLR 141.) In this case *D1* was not a joint tortfeasor and the claimant can, as part of the settlement with *D1*, reserve the right to claim against other concurrent tortfeasors. It should be noted that in ***Jameson*** the 1978 Act is irrelevant, as after *D1*'s settlement *D2* has no liability to the claimant and therefore no need to seek a contribution. The agreement between the claimant and *D1* is not intended to confer any benefit on *D2*; the claimant no longer has any loss which requires compensation. (***Heaton v Axa Equity & Law Assurance Society Ltd*** [2002] 2 All ER 961.)

Contribution between tortfeasors

At common law the rule was that a joint or several tortfeasor could not recover a contribution or indemnity from other tortfeasors in the absence of an agreement between them to the contrary.

This rule was reversed by statute and is now contained in the Civil Liability (Contribution) Act 1978 ss 1 and 2.

Section 1 provides:

> Subject to the following provisions of this section, any person liable in respect of any damage suffered by another person may recover contribution from any other person liable in respect of the same damage (whether jointly liable with him or otherwise).

The person seeking a contribution must be actually or hypothetically liable.

Section 1(6) provides:

> References in this section to a person's liability in respect of any damage are references to any such liability which has been or could be established in an action brought against him in England or Wales by or on behalf of the person who suffered the damage.

Therefore, if the claimant could not establish liability, for example, because the action was statute barred, no contribution is recoverable. However, if the person has paid the claimant, then s 1(2) provides that they will be entitled to a contribution even though they have ceased to be liable to the claimant, provided they were liable immediately before they made the payment. There is a two-year limitation period from the date of judgment or settlement in which a contribution can be sought.

The person from whom the contribution is sought will be liable to make the contribution even though they are no longer liable to the original claimant. This is unless the claim for contribution itself is defeated by the two-year limitation period.

If the claimant's action against the person from whom contribution is sought is blocked by a limitation period, this does not stop another tortfeasor claiming a contribution unless their action is blocked by the two-year limitation period (s 1(3)).

A complication arises in respect of s 1(5). This states:

> A judgment given in any action . . . by or on behalf of the person who suffered the damage in question against any person from whom contribution is sought . . . shall be conclusive in the proceedings for contribution as to any issue determined by that judgment in favour of the person from whom the contribution is sought.

This section would appear to contradict s 1(3), as literally interpreted it would mean that a court's judgment on limitation, in an action between the claimant and the person from whom contribution is sought in the latter's favour, would be conclusive that no contribution could be claimed.

Section 1(4) provides:

> A person who has made or agreed to make any payment in bona fide settlement or compromise of any claim . . . shall be entitled to recover contribution in accordance with this section without regard to whether or not he himself is or ever was liable in respect of the damage, provided, however, that he would have been liable assuming that the factual basis of the claim against him could be established.

This section recognises the fact that most civil actions are settled and do not go to trial. Provided the settlement is bona fide and not collusive, then the person settling is entitled to a contribution.

Section 2 deals with the amount of contribution a person may be entitled to. This is the amount that the court finds to be just and equitable having regard to that person's responsibility for the damage in question. The court has to take into account all the relevant circumstances, such as the degree of blameworthiness and the parties' role in bringing about the damage.

Fitzgerald v Lane [1989] AC 328

> The claimant stepped out into traffic on a busy road. He was struck by a vehicle driven by *D1*. This pushed him into the path of a vehicle being driven by *D2*. *D1* and *D2* were held to have been negligent. The House of Lords held that the claimant's conduct had to be looked at in the light of the totality of *D1* and *D2*'s conduct. The claimant was held to be 50 per cent to blame. Then the court had to decide the amount of contribution payable. It was held that *D1* and *D2* were equally to blame and they had to contribute equally to the remaining 50 per cent of the claimant's damages.

The court may also exempt a party from having to pay a contribution, or may order a party to pay a complete indemnity.

The amount which can be recovered by contribution is limited to the amount that the claimant could have recovered from that particular defendant.

See Chapter 9 for asbestos cases. The principle has caused problems in the asbestos cases and in **Barker v Corus UK Ltd** [2006] 3 All ER 785 the issue that arose in all three appeals was whether under the **Fairchild** exception a defendant is liable, jointly and severally with any other defendants, for all the damage consequent upon the contraction of mesothelioma by the claimant or whether he is liable only for a share, apportioned according to the share of the risk created by his breach of duty, and determined that the latter was the case. This meant that a defendant was only severally liable for the portion of the damage for which he was responsible.

See also Chapter 9. This part of the judgment was swiftly reversed by legislation in s 3 of the Compensation Act 2006, which makes each defendant jointly and severally liable.

Example

A collision occurs between three cars driven by *D1*, *D2* and *D3*. As a result, a pedestrian, *P*, is injured.

P has a choice as to whether to sue *D1*, *D2* or *D3*, or he could issue a single writ against all three.

If *P* chose to sue *D1* and was successful, recovering £30,000 in damages, *D1* could then bring contribution proceedings against *D2* and *D3* within two years. The court would then have to determine the relative contributions of the three parties. If *D1* was held to be 25 per cent to blame then he could recover £22,500 from *D2* and *D3*. If *D2* was found to be 50 per cent to blame, then *D1* would recover £15,000 from him and the remainder from *D3*.

Suppose *P* sued all three defendants and was awarded £30,000. He would then have a choice as to which defendant(s) to enforce the judgment against. That person would then have to seek a contribution from the others. This leaves the claimant with the option of enforcing against a solvent defendant.

Summary

- If there is more than one breach of duty which causes the claimant damage, the liability of the defendants may be independent, several or joint.

- Independent liability arises where the claimant suffered damage as a result of two completely separate torts.

- If more than one tortfeasor acts independently to cause the same damage to the claimant, then they are severally liable.
- Joint liability may arise in a number of ways. If two or more tortfeasors commit a joint breach of duty or act in furtherance of a common design, then they are joint tortfeasors.
- In cases of joint liability each tortfeasor is liable for the full amount, but the claimant can recover only once.
- Joint liability also arises where an employer is held to be vicariously liable for the negligence of their employee.
- Civil Liability (Contribution) Act 1978 s 3: judgment recovered against any person liable in respect of any debt or damage shall not be a bar to an action, or to the continuance of an action, against any other person who is (apart from any such bar) jointly liable with them in respect of the same debt or damage.
- At common law the rule was that a joint or several tortfeasor could not recover a contribution or indemnity from other tortfeasors in the absence of an agreement between them to the contrary. This rule was reversed by statute and this is now the Civil Liability (Contribution) Act 1978 ss 1 and 2. Section 2 deals with the amount of contribution a person may be entitled to. This is the amount that the court finds to be just and equitable having regard to that person's responsibility for the damage in question. The court has to take into account all the relevant circumstances, such as the degree of blameworthiness and the parties' role in bringing about the damage.

Further reading

Markesinis, B. and Deakin, S., *Tort Law*, Oxford University Press, ch 26.

Limitation

After reading this chapter you will:

1. Appreciate the concept of limitation barring the remedy.

2. Understand the rules on accrual of causes of action.

3. Have a critical knowledge of the limitation periods in actions for personal injuries, death and trespass to the person.

4. Understand the limitation rules on latent damage.

Introduction

Objective 1

A defendant ought not to have the threat of litigation hanging over them indefinitely and there are therefore statutory limitation periods within which the claimant must either serve their writ or lose their remedy. The present complex law is contained in the Limitation Act 1980 (as amended).

The legal effect of the expiration of a limitation period is to bar the remedy, but not the right: for example, where a debt is owed but the limitation period has expired, the creditor cannot sue for the money but the debt is still owed.

The major difficulty in fixing limitation periods is to draw a fair line between the defendant's interest in having a clearly defined and short limitation period and not barring the claimant before he is aware that he has an action. This problem arises particularly in two areas.

Where the claim is for personal injuries, but the nature of the claimant's illness means he is not aware of it for many years: for example, X worked in Y's factory from 2000–2008. In 2014 X discovers that he is suffering from asbestosis contracted during his employment by Y. Should X be allowed to claim?

See Chapter 9 for asbestos cases.

See Chapter 11 for defective buildings.

If the claim is for a defective building, the damage may take many years to manifest itself: for example, X builds a house in 1999. The house is purchased by Y in 2003. In 2014 large cracks appear in the walls of the house and Y discovers that these are due to faulty foundations. Should Y be able to sue X?

Accrual of causes of action

Objective 2

See Chapter 1 for torts actionable *per se*.

The limitation period starts to run when the cause of action accrues. Where the tort is actionable *per se* (without proof of damage), time starts to run from the date of the defendant's act. Where the tort is actionable only on proof of damage, the cause of action accrues when the damage is sustained. If the tort is of a continuing nature, such as nuisance, then a fresh cause of action arises each time that damage is inflicted.

In the asbestosis and defective building examples given above there may be problems in ascertaining when damage occurred. This problem is widespread and it is a question of fact in each case whether damage has been established: for example, it has been held that damage occurs when burglars enter premises rather than when a defective safety gate was installed. (**Dove** v **Banhams Patent Locks** [1983] 1 WLR 1436.) A further problem is that if the damage was unobservable (latent) when it occurred then the claim could be statute barred before the claimant is aware of it. This problem is dealt with by the legislation.

See Chapter 2 for concurrent liability.

In some cases the claimant may have a choice of action in either contract or tort. One of the factors which may affect their decision is the relevant limitation period. Limitation periods in contract accrue when a breach of contract occurs.

Midland Bank Trust Co Ltd v *Hett, Stubbs and Kemp (a firm)* [1979] Ch 384

The claimant was given an option to purchase a farm. The defendant solicitor negligently failed to register the option. More than six years later the farm was sold to a third party. The damage for the purposes of a negligence action was held to occur when the farm was sold. The negligence action was therefore not statute barred. The contract action was also held not to be barred as the breach of contract was an omission which continued until the sale of the farm. Had the breach of contract been an act then the limitation period would have run from then.

Limitation periods

 ### Normal periods

Objective 3

The basic rule is that a tort action must be brought within six years of the accrual of the cause of action. (Limitation Act 1980 s 2.)

What would happen if the cause of action was contingent on something happening in the future?

Law Society v *Sephton* [2006] 3 All ER 401

A member of the defendant firm of accountants had prepared reports and certified that a solicitor had complied with the Solicitors' Account Rules. In fact the solicitor had been misappropriating moneys held in his client account. A client complained to the Law Society over a delay in payment and the Society's investigating accountant discovered the deficiency. The Society maintained the Solicitors' Compensation Fund for the purpose of making grants for the relief of loss caused by dishonesty on the part of a solicitor. The first claim on the compensation fund made by a former client of the solicitor was made on 8 July 1996. Others followed. The Society wrote to the defendant saying that it proposed to hold the firm liable for payments which had to be made out of the compensation fund, which it said were attributable to the negligent reports. The claim form was issued on 16 May 2002. The defence pleaded that the claims were statute barred under the Limitation Act 1980 as the cause of action had accrued more than six years earlier. A preliminary issue was tried as to the date that the cause of action accrued. The judge ruled against the Society holding that the cause of action had accrued before 16 May 1996. The Court of Appeal reversed that decision. The defendant appealed contending that the Society suffered damage in consequence of the accountant's negligence whenever the solicitor had misappropriated client's money after a negligent accountant's report had been delivered as that misappropriation gave the client a right to make a claim on the compensation fund and liability to such a claim was damage.

Held: A contingent liability was not as such actionable damage until the contingency occurred. No actual damage would be sustained until the contingency was fulfilled and the loss became actual, and until that happened the loss was prospective and might never be incurred. In the instant case, by virtue of the terms of the compensation fund rules, the solicitor's misappropriations gave rise to the possibility of a liability to pay a grant out of the fund, contingent upon the misappropriation not being otherwise made good and a claim in the proper form being made. Such a liability would be enforceable only in public law, by judicial review, but would still count as damage. But until a claim was actually made, no loss or damage was sustained by the compensation fund. It followed that the cause of action did not accrue in the Society's favour against the defendant until it first received a claim on its fund from one of the solicitor's clients. Accordingly, the appeal would be dismissed.

Damages for personal injuries and death

Where the damages claimed by the claimant consist of or include a claim for damages for personal injuries, the limitation period is three years from either the occurrence of the damage or the date of knowledge of the injured party. (Limitation Act 1980 s 11(4).) The latter provision was inserted to avoid the injustice shown in cases such as the one that follows.

Cartledge v *E Jobling & Sons Ltd* [1963] AC 758

The claimant contracted pneumoconiosis as a result of the defendant's breach of duty. He did not know he had the disease until well after the three-year time period had expired. It was held that his action was statute barred. The damage occurred when the lung tissue was scarred, although a medical examination might not have revealed the damage at that stage.

The obvious injustice of this decision was almost immediately reversed by statute (now the Limitation Act 1980 s 11(4)). This allowed the claimant to claim within three years of the date of knowledge.

Knowledge is defined by s 14 as knowledge of certain facts:

1 that the injury in question was significant;

2 that the injury was attributable in whole or in part to the act or omission which is alleged to constitute negligence, nuisance or breach of duty;

3 the identity of the defendant;

4 if it is alleged that the act or omission was that of a person other than the defendant, the identity of that person and the additional facts supporting the bringing of an action against the defendant. (This would cover cases of vicarious liability.)

An injury is significant:

> if the person whose date of knowledge is in question would reasonably have considered it sufficiently serious to justify his instituting proceedings for damages against a defendant who did not dispute liability and was able to satisfy a judgment (s 14(2)).

The relevant knowledge required is of facts not of law (s 14(1)). Therefore, it is irrelevant whether or not the claimant was aware that the defendant's act or omission amounted to a tort. It also means that incorrect legal advice will not stop time running against the claimant. If the claimant is aware of the facts but is advised that they have no cause of action, time will run against them. (But the court may apply the discretion.)

Knowledge may be either actual or constructive (s 14(3)). It therefore includes facts observable or ascertainable by them, and facts ascertainable by them with the help of medical or other appropriate expert advice which is reasonable for them to seek. If the claimant has symptoms of, for example, asbestosis, and fails to seek medical advice, then they will have constructive knowledge. However, if they have sought medical advice but the doctor has failed to ascertain the appropriate facts and diagnose the condition, then time will not run against them.

The court is given a power to disapply the provisions relating to personal injuries or death (s 33). In deciding whether to apply this discretion, the court must have regard to certain factors:

1 the length of, and the reasons for, the delay on the part of the claimant;
2 the effect of the delay on the cogency of the evidence in the case;
3 the conduct of the defendant after the cause of action arose, including their response to the claimant's request for information;
4 the duration of any disability of the claimant arising after the cause of action;
5 the extent to which the claimant acted promptly and reasonably once they knew of the facts which afforded them a cause of action;
6 the steps taken by the claimant to obtain medical, legal, or other expert advice and the nature of any such advice received.

This equitable discretion was originally supposed to be limited to exceptional cases. However, it has been given a broad interpretation by the courts. (*Thompson* v *Brown* [1981] 1 WLR 744.) But the discretion can only be applied where the claimant is prejudiced by the operation of the provisions of the Act. It will not apply where prejudice is caused by failure to serve the writ or where the action is discontinued.

A v Hoare and other appeals [2008] 2 All ER 1

(For facts see under 'Trespass to the person' below.)

As well as the issue of whether **Stubbings v Webb** ought not to be followed, one of the appeals concerned the meaning of 'significant' injury in s 14(2). The dispute concerned how much account, if any, ought to be taken of personal characteristics of the claimant, either pre-existing or consequent on the injury he had suffered.

The test for 'significant injury' in s 14 was as provided in s 14(2). The material to which that test applied was generally 'subjective' in that it was applied to what the claimant knew of his injury rather than the injury as it actually was. Even then, his knowledge might have to be supplemented with imputed 'objective' knowledge under s 14(3). But the test itself was an entirely impersonal standard: not whether the claimant himself would have considered the injury sufficiently serious to justify proceedings but whether he would 'reasonably' have done so. The questions to be asked were: (i) what the claimant knew about the injury he had suffered; (ii) what knowledge about the injury might be imputed to him under s 14(3); and (iii) whether a reasonable person with that knowledge would have considered the injury sufficiently serious to justify his instituting proceedings for damages against a defendant who did not dispute liability and was able to satisfy a judgment. That did not mean that the law regarded as irrelevant the question of whether the actual claimant, taking into account his psychological state in consequence of the injury, could reasonably have been expected to institute proceedings. Rather, it dealt with that question under s 33, which provided specifically in s 33(3)(a) that one of the matters to be taken into account in the exercise of the discretion was 'the reasons for the delay on the part of the plaintiff'. Thus, consideration of the inhibiting effect of sexual abuse upon certain victims' preparedness to bring proceedings in respect of it should be considered under s 33, not s 14(2).

Judges should not have to grapple with the notion of the reasonable unintelligent person. Once it had been ascertained what the claimant knew and what he should be treated as having known, the actual claimant dropped out of the picture. Section 14(2) was simply a standard of the seriousness of the injury and nothing more. Standards were in their nature impersonal and did not vary with the person to whom they were applied. Section 14(2) assumed a practical and relatively unsophisticated approach to the question of knowledge. Section 33 was the right place to consider the actual claimant; it enabled the judge to look at the matter broadly and not have to decide the highly artificial question of whether knowledge which the claimant had in some sense suppressed counted as knowledge.

The application of the rules was seen in the following case.

AB v Ministry of Defence [2012] UKSC 9

The actions concerned military veterans who had been in the vicinity of nuclear tests in the 1950s and had developed serious health problems which they claimed were related to negligent exposure to nuclear radiation. They took two issues to the Supreme Court. The first was the appropriate date for knowledge within s 14. The second was the application of the discretion. The cases were held to be statute barred. The claimants had the relevant knowledge under s 14 and the time period had now expired. The court also refused to apply the discretion. The court was heavily influenced by the fact that the claimants would have virtually no chance of success if the actions went ahead as they faced serious problems with proving causation. They could not keep their claims on ice for an indefinite period in the hope that one day the right evidence might turn up. On the discretion it would have been absurd for the Court of Appeal to have exercised the discretion to disapply s 11 of the Act so as to allow the appellants to proceed in circumstances in which the next stage of the litigation would have been likely to have been their failure to resist entry against them of summary judgment.

Trespass to the person

See Chapter 20 for *A v Hoare* and trespass to the person.

Difficulties were caused by the fact that personal injuries actions can also be brought in the tort of trespass to the person where there was a fixed limitation period of six years. This caused problems in the case of sexual assaults where the victim was outside the six-year period. Were the provisions in s 14 and s 33 applicable to actions brought in trespass to the person? The House of Lords had held in *Stubbings v Webb* [1993] AC 498 that they did not.

In the following case the Court of Appeal had found that it was bound by the previous decision of the House of Lords.

A v Hoare and other appeals [2008] 2 All ER 1

Six appeals before the House concerned the question of whether claims for sexual assaults and abuse which took place many years before the commencement of proceedings were barred by the Limitation Act 1980. All of the actions were therefore outside the six-year limitation period prescribed by s 2 of the Act. They sought to bring themselves within s 11 of the Act and argued that either their know-ledge had not arisen within the relevant three-year period, or that the discretion under s 33 should be exercised in their favour. In the lower courts, all of the claims failed because the courts considered themselves bound by the decision of the House of Lords in *Stubbings v Webb* [1993] 1 All ER 322, in which it was held that s 11 did not apply to a case of deliberate assault, including acts of indecent assault. An action for an intentional trespass to the person was not an action for 'negligence, nuisance or breach of duty' within the meaning of s 11. Therefore, a claim based on an intentional sexual assault was subject to a non-extendable six-year limitation period under s 2. The claimants all con-tended that *Stubbings v Webb* had been wrongly decided and that the House should depart from it. They relied on the Law Commission's report (Law Com No 270) which recommended a uniform regime for personal injuries, whether the claim was made in negligence or trespass to the person.

The appeals were allowed.

Actions for personal injury deriving from intentional trespass to the person fell within s 11 of the 1980 Act and therefore the court had a discretion under s 33 of the Act to extend the time in the claimants' favour.

Parliament could not have intended to exclude the benefit of s 33 from those who had been intentionally injured. Otherwise, anomalies would arise such as *S v W (child abuse: damages)* [1995] 1 FLR 862, in which it was held that a claimant suing out of time was able to pursue a claim against her mother for failing to protect her against sexual abuse by her father, but not a claim against the father himself.

Stubbings v Webb [1993] 1 All ER 322 overruled; *Letang v Cooper* [1965] 1 QB 232 approved.

Defective buildings and latent damage

Objective
4

Just as disease in a person may not manifest itself for a lengthy period of time, so a building may outwardly seem healthy but have serious latent defects. The legal problem raised is not to prejudice the claimant by fixing a cut-off point before they realise they have a cause of action and avoiding making the defendant liable decades after the alleged breach of duty.

The law is now contained in the Latent Damage Act 1986. A three-stage analysis is made:

1 Initially, the limitation period runs for six years from the date of the damage. (Limitation Act 1980 s 14A(4)(a).) This confirms the House of Lords decision in *Pirelli General Cable Works Ltd v Oscar Faber & Partners* [1983] 2 AC 1. The difficulty here is that where the original defect about which the complaint is made is, for example, in the foundations, no damage may be observable until the six-year period has expired.

2 The second period runs for three years from the earliest date on which the claimant or their predecessor first knew, or could have known, of the facts required to commence proceedings. (Limitation Act 1980 s 14A(4)(b).) This discoverability test comes from *Sparham-Souter v Town and Country Developments* [1976] 1 QB 958. The claimant must be aware of all relevant facts before the period begins to run: i.e. they must be aware of the defect or should reasonably be aware of it. The claimant is not endowed with the knowledge of an expert and the damage must be sufficiently serious to justify the implementation of proceedings.

3 The third provision is a long-stop which prevents the discoverability test operating indefinitely. No action may be commenced in cases of latent damage beyond 15 years of the breach of duty which causes the damage. (Limitation Act s 14B.) The relevant breach of duty will usually be when the building is completed.

> ### Example
>
> *A* Ltd build a house and construction is completed in July 2003. The house is purchased by *B. A* Ltd have failed to dig the foundations to the appropriate depth. Damage to the building commenced immediately, so the initial six-year period runs from July 2003. *B* is unaware of the damage as there are no external signs to put him on his guard. In July 2011 a large crack appears in the gable end wall. The three-year discoverability period will run from this date. *B* will have until July 2014 in which to serve his writ. The 15-year period runs until July 2026, so *B* is unaffected by this.

See Chapter 11 for defective buildings.

NB. The above example assumes that *B* does have an action in tort against *A* Ltd. Defective premises actions may also be brought in contract, when the limitation period is six years from the date of the breach of contract, or under the Defective Premises Act 1972 where the limitation period is six years from when the building was completed. (Defective Premises Act 1972 s 1(5).)

Miscellaneous limitation periods

See Chapter 12 for Consumer Protection Act.

Actions under the Consumer Protection Act 1987 must be brought within three years of suffering the relevant damage or within three years of acquiring the necessary knowledge, if this is later (Consumer Protection Act 1987 s 5(5) and Sch 1). The Act also provides a long-stop provision of ten years from when the defendant supplied the product to another.

See Chapter 28 for effect of death.

In cases of personal injury followed by death, if the claimant dies after the expiration of the limitation period the claim does not survive for the benefit of their estate. The personal representatives may ask the court to exercise the discretion. Where the claimant dies before the expiration of the limitation period, a new limitation period begins to run for three years from the date of death or the date of the personal representatives' knowledge, whichever is later. (Limitation Act 1980 s 11(5).)

Fraud or concealment

Where the claimant's action is based on the defendant's fraud or where any fact relevant to their right of action is concealed by the defendant, the limitation period does not begin to run until the claimant has, or ought with reasonable diligence to have, discovered the fraud or concealment. (Limitation Act 1980 s 32(1).)

Summary

This chapter deals with the rules on limitation of actions.

● There are statutory limitation periods within which the claimant must either serve their writ or lose their remedy. The present law is contained in the Limitation Act 1980 (as amended).

- The legal effect of the expiration of a limitation period is to bar the remedy, but not the right.

- The limitation period starts to run when the cause of action accrues. Where the tort is actionable *per se* (without proof of damage), time starts to run from the date of the defendant's act. Where the tort is actionable only on proof of damage, the cause of action accrues when the damage is sustained.

- The basic rule is that a tort action must be brought within six years of the accrual of the cause of action. (Limitation Act 1980 s 2.)

- Where the damages claimed by the claimant consist of or include a claim for damages for personal injuries, the limitation period is three years from either the occurrence of the damage or the date of knowledge of the injured party. (Limitation Act 1980 s 11(4).)

- The court is given a power to disapply the provisions relating to personal injuries or death (s 33).

- The rules on date of knowledge and s 33 also apply to actions for personal injuries brought in trespass to the person. (*A v Hoare* (2008).)

- The law on limitation in relation to defective buildings is now contained in the Latent Damage Act 1986. A three-stage analysis is made.

- Initially the limitation period runs for six years from the date of the damage. (Limitation Act 1980 s 14A(4)(a).)

- The second period runs for three years from the earliest date on which the claimant or their predecessor first knew, or could have known, of the facts required to commence proceedings. (Limitation Act 1980 s 14A(4)(b).)

- The third provision is a long-stop which prevents the discoverability test operating indefinitely. No action may be commenced in cases of latent damage beyond 15 years of the breach of duty which causes the damage. (Limitation Act 1980 s 14B.) The relevant breach of duty will usually be when the building is completed.

- Actions under the Consumer Protection Act 1987 must be brought within three years of suffering the relevant damage or within three years of acquiring the necessary knowledge, if this is later. (Consumer Protection Act 1987 s 5(5) and Sch 1.) The Act also provides a long-stop provision of ten years from when the defendant supplied the product to another.

- In cases of personal injury followed by death, if the claimant dies after the expiration of the limitation period, the claim does not survive for the benefit of their estate. The personal representatives may ask the court to exercise the discretion. Where the claimant dies before the expiration of the limitation period, a new limitation period begins to run for three years from the date of death or the date of the personal representatives' knowledge, whichever is later. (Limitation Act 1980 s 11(5).)

Further reading

Capper, D. (2008), 'The Limitation Defence in Sexual Abuse Claims – The Working Out of A v Hoare', 27 *Civil Justice Quarterly* 445.

Limitation of Actions, Law Commission Report No 270 (July 2001).

27

General defences

See Chapter 21 for fair comment.

See Chapter 16 for distress damage feasant.

See Chapter 10 for *volenti*/contributory negligence/*ex turpi causa*.

See Chapter 15 for medical negligence.

Objectives

After reading this chapter you will:

1. Understand the law on the general defence of mistake.

2. Understand the law on the general defence of inevitable accident.

3. Understand the law on the general defence of necessity.

Introduction

Defences in tort actions can be divided into two categories. First, those which are only applicable to particular torts. Examples would include fair comment in a defamation action and distress damage feasant in a trespass to land action. These defences can be found in the chapter on the relevant tort.

The second group of defences are those which have general application in tort cases. The defences of *volenti non fit injuria*, contributory negligence and illegality may arise in a number of torts, but have a particular importance in negligence actions. For this reason, they were dealt with in a separate chapter in the negligence section. The remainder of the general defences will be dealt with here.

Mistake

Objective 1

Mistake is not generally a defence to a tort action, as a mistake as to law or fact will not usually exclude the defendant from liability. For example, it is not a defence to trespass to land for the defendant to argue that they mistakenly thought that the land was theirs. Neither is it a defence in a medical negligence action for the defendant doctor to claim that they made a mistake in diagnosing the patient's condition, if that mistake amounted to negligence.

Mistake may be relevant where reasonableness is required. A reasonable mistake of fact may be relevant to a defence. Where a police officer arrests a person and has reasonable grounds for suspecting that an arrestable offence has been committed, the tort of false imprisonment is not committed, even if no such offence has been committed.

The next case is interesting as it deals not only with self defence in tort but also contrasts the role of the defence in civil and criminal law.

Ashley v Chief Constable of Sussex Police [2008] 3 All ER 573

See also Chapter 20 for *Ashley*.

In 1998, armed police shot and killed the deceased during a raid on a house. It was admitted that the deceased had not been armed at the time. The responsible officer was charged with murder and manslaughter but acquitted following a submission of no case to answer. No other criminal proceedings were instigated. The deceased's father and son brought a civil action under the Fatal Accidents Act 1976 as dependants of the deceased. The causes of action alleged: (i) assault and battery, or alternatively negligence, by the officer who had done the shooting; (ii) negligence and misfeasance in public office regarding preparation for the raid; and (iii) negligence and misfeasance in public office regarding the post-shooting conduct of the police. The Chief Constable denied battery. His defence to the battery claim was that the officer had been acting in self-defence when he shot the deceased. The judge gave summary judgment for the Chief Constable in respect of the claim for battery. The claimants appealed. The Court of Appeal ruled that, in civil proceedings, the burden of proving self-defence lay upon the defendant; and a defendant who had mistakenly but honestly thought it was necessary to defend himself against an imminent risk of attack could not rely on self-defence if his mistaken belief although honestly held had not been a reasonable one. The Chief Constable appealed.

The issues on appeal were, first, whether self-defence to a civil law claim for tortious assault and battery, in a case where the assailant acted in the mistaken belief that he was in imminent danger of being attacked, required that the assailant's belief was not only honestly but also reasonably held. The second issue was whether in all the circumstances the assault and battery claims in the instant case should be allowed to proceed to a trial. The Chief Constable contended that the criteria for self-defence in civil law should be the same as in criminal law. He also contended that the assault and battery claims constituted an abuse as no damages could be recovered in addition to those already recoverable due to the admitted negligence.

The appeal would be dismissed (Lord Carswell and Lord Neuberger dissenting in part).

For civil law purposes, an excuse of self-defence based on non-existent facts that were honestly but unreasonably believed to exist had to fail. The belief had to have been reasonably held, and it might be that even that would not suffice to establish the defence.

The plea for consistency between the criminal law and the civil law lacked cogency, for the ends to be served by the two systems were very different. One of the main functions of the criminal law was to identify, and provide punitive sanctions for, behaviour that was categorised as criminal because it was damaging to the good order of society. It was fundamental to criminal law and procedure that everyone charged with criminal behaviour should be presumed innocent until proven guilty and that, as a general rule, no one should be punished for a crime that he or she did not intend to commit or be punished for the consequences of an honest mistake. There were of course exceptions but that explained why a person who honestly believed that he was in danger of an imminent deadly attack and responded violently in order to protect himself from that attack should be able to plead self-defence as an answer to a criminal charge, whether or not he had been mistaken in his belief and whether or not his mistake had been, objectively speaking, a reasonable one for him to have made. The greater the unreasonableness of the belief, however, the more unlikely it might be that the belief was honestly held. The function of the civil law of tort was different. Its main function was to identify and protect the rights that every person was entitled to assert against, and require to be respected by, others. It was one thing to say that if a person's mistaken belief was honestly held he should not be punished by the criminal law. It would be quite another to say that his unreasonably held mistaken belief would be sufficient to justify the law in setting aside the victim's right not to be subjected to physical violence by that person.

1 The case demonstrates a key difference between tort law and the criminal law. The core function of the criminal law is to punish bad people. The policeman may have made a serious mistake but he was not bad in the criminal sense. He thought he was doing the right thing when he shot Ashley. Tort law exists to vindicate people's rights. Had the policeman violated Ashley's rights in shooting him? The fact that he honestly thought he was doing the right thing in shooting Ashley did not mean that he did do the right thing in shooting Ashley.

2 If Ashley had positively done something to make the policeman reasonably (but incorrectly) think that he was a threat, then the policeman would have done no wrong in shooting Ashley. But if Ashley had done nothing himself to give that impression, and the policeman only reasonably thought that Ashley was a threat because of briefings he had received before the drugs raid started, then Ashley would still have had a right not to be shot.

See Chapter 28 for deceit.

In the tort of deceit, if the defendant honestly believed the truth of his statement, there is no liability.

Inevitable accident

Objective 2

See Chapter 20 for trespass to the person.

An accident will be inevitable where it was not intended by the defendant and could not be avoided by the use of reasonable care. In a fault-based tort this only means that the defendant was not at fault. As the burden of proof is on the claimant to establish fault, inevitable accident is not a defence. At the time when the burden of proof in actions for trespass to the person was on the defendant, they could avoid liability by proving that the event complained of was an inevitable accident. This is no longer the case.

Necessity

Objective 3

The defence of necessity is usually raised in connection with actions for intentional interference with persons or property. The defence is essentially that the defendant's action was necessary to prevent greater damage to the defendant or a third party.

Where self-defence is used, the defendant has responded to the claimant's threatened or actual tortious behaviour. With necessity, the claimant may well be an innocent third party.

The courts seem to take the view that where personal injury is threatened, then any necessary damage to property will be justified. If a ship is threatened with sinking in a storm, the decision to throw goods overboard to try and save the ship's crew could be defended by necessity.

In battery cases involving lack of consent on the part of a patient, where the patient is incapable of giving a valid consent, the test is whether the treatment was in the best interests of the patient. (*F* v *West Berkshire Health Authority* [1989] 2 All ER 545.) If the patient

See Chapters 15 and 20 for consent and battery.

is capable of giving a valid consent and refuses, then the doctor must abide by that refusal or face a battery action.

Where property damage is threatened, the question is whether the defendant acted in the way that a reasonable person would have done. If they see a fire on the claimant's land which they reasonably think is liable to spread to their own land and cause damage, they may enter the claimant's land and attempt to extinguish the fire.

Would it make any difference if the fire was started by the defendant's own negligence? In *Rigby* v *Chief Constable of Northamptonshire* [1985] 2 All ER 985, it was stated that where the need to act was brought about by the defendant's negligence, then necessity would not be a good defence. Necessity can therefore never be a defence to negligence.

It should be noted that the courts are very hesitant about allowing a defence of necessity, as it means inflicting loss on the claimant. The Court of Appeal, for example, has refused to accept necessity as a defence to squatting. (*Southwark London Borough Council* v *Williams* [1971] Ch 734.)

Under the Access to Neighbouring Land Act 1992 a court order may be obtained to allow access to land to carry out work necessary to preserve the applicant's land.

Summary

This chapter deals with the general defences to tort actions.

- Mistake is not generally a defence to a tort action, as a mistake as to law or fact will not usually exclude the defendant from liability. Mistake may be relevant where reasonableness is required. A reasonable mistake of fact may be relevant to a defence.

- As the burden of proof is on the claimant to establish fault, inevitable accident is not a defence.

- The defence of necessity is usually raised in connection with actions for intentional interference with persons or property. The defence is essentially that the defendant's action was necessary to prevent greater damage to the defendant or a third party. In battery cases involving lack of consent on the part of a patient, where the patient is incapable of giving a valid consent, the test is whether the treatment was in the best interests of the patient.

- The courts are very hesitant about allowing a defence of necessity, as it means inflicting loss on the claimant.

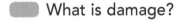

28

Remedies

Objectives

After reading this chapter you will:

1. Appreciate the concept of damage in a personal injuries action and understand the distinction between compensatory and non-compensatory damages.

2. Have a critical knowledge of the circumstances in which non-compensatory damages can be awarded.

3. Have a critical knowledge of the principles applying to the award of damages for personal injuries.

4. Understand the legal rules governing actions by the estate and dependants of a deceased person.

5. Understand the legal rules on the award of injunctions.

Introduction

See Chapter 16 for distress damage feasant.

See Chapter 17 for abatement of a nuisance.

Remedies in tort are classified as either judicial or extra-judicial. Judicial remedies are the sort that a judge may make, such as an award of damages or an injunction. Extra-judicial remedies comprise some form of self-help, such as distress damage feasant or abatement of a nuisance.

Damages

What is damage?

Objective 1

Where a tort requires damage to be actionable it is normally easy to say whether damage has occurred or not. However, there are cases where it may be difficult for the court to determine whether there has been any damage which can be compensated. This may be the case in a negligence action where the defendant has been in breach of duty and exposed the claimant to a risk that he will be ill in the future. This was the problem in the next case,

547

which dealt with the issue of whether a claimant could aggregate two or more consequences, neither of which on their own would constitute damage in order to make a claim.

Rothwell v Chemical and Insulating Co Ltd [2007] 4 All ER 1047

See also Chapter 4 on *Rothwell*.

Each of the claimants had been negligently exposed by his defendant employer to asbestos dust. That exposure had had three foreseeable consequences. The claimant had developed pleural plaques; the claimant was at risk of developing one or more long-term asbestos-related diseases; and the claimant had suffered anxiety at the prospect that he might suffer such disease. It was common ground that none of those consequences, if experienced on its own, would constitute damage capable of founding a cause of action in negligence.

The common issue was whether, by aggregating with pleural plaques one or both of the other consequences, sufficient damage could be demonstrated to found a cause of action.

One of the claimants, G, had suffered not merely anxiety but a recognised psychiatric illness, clinical depression, in consequence of his being told that the pleural plaques indicated a significant exposure to asbestos and the risk of future damage.

Held (House of Lords): A person who had been negligently exposed to asbestos in the course of his employment could not sue his employer for damages on the ground that he had developed pleural plaques. The symptomless plaques were not compensatable damage and proof of damage was an essential element in a negligence claim. The risk of future illness, which was not consequent on the plaques, or anxiety about the possibility of that risk materialising, did not amount to damage for the purpose of creating a cause of action. The plaques did not become damage when aggregated with the risk which they evidenced or the anxiety which that risk caused. It followed that the development of pleural plaques, whether or not associated with the risk of future disease and anxiety about the future was not an actionable injury, nor was a psychiatric illness caused by contemplation of that risk. Psychiatric illness constituted damage for the purpose of founding an action in negligence, so that the question in the case of G was not whether he suffered damage but whether the defendants owed him a duty of care in respect of psychiatric illness caused by his anxiety at the risk of a future illness. On the facts of G's case there was no basis for a finding that it was reasonably foreseeable that the event which actually happened – the creation of a risk of an asbestos-related disease, not itself actionable – would cause psychiatric illness to a person of reasonable fortitude. Accordingly, the appeals would be dismissed. (See also ***Yearworth* v *North Bristol NHS Trust*** [2009] EWCA 37.)

Damages in tort may be either compensatory or non-compensatory.

Non-compensatory damages

Objective 2

Non-compensatory damages may be nominal, contemptuous or exemplary.

Nominal damages

See Chapter 1 for torts actionable *per se*.

Nominal damages are awarded for a tort actionable *per se*, i.e. where a legal right has been violated but the claimant has suffered no actual loss. The damages are awarded for the wrong itself rather than any loss suffered. (See ***R (on the application of Lumba)* v *Secretary of State for the Home Department*** [2011] UKSC 12.) The amount awarded will be small, normally £2, and the fact that nominal damages have been awarded does not mean that the claimant should be regarded as a successful claimant for the purposes of costs.

Contemptuous damages

Contemptuous damages are usually awarded only in defamation actions. They consist of an award of the least valuable coin of the realm. Contemptuous damages acknowledge that

See Chapter 21 for
Grobbelaar.

the claimant's legal rights have suffered a technical infringement but express derision of their conduct in the matter. A claimant who is awarded contemptuous damages is unlikely to recover costs. (See *Grobbelaar* v *News Group Newspapers Ltd* [2002] 1 WLR 3024.)

Exemplary (or punitive) damages

Exemplary or punitive damages are awarded to punish the defendant for their conduct and are in addition to compensatory damages. Where the claimant has suffered no damage then exemplary damages cannot be awarded. (*Watkins* v *Secretary of State for Home Department* [2006] 2 All ER 353.) The award of exemplary damages in tort is controversial as many people feel that the punitive function of the law should be performed by the criminal rather than the civil law.

The award of exemplary damages in tort actions has been considered by the House of Lords and the principles are laid down in *Rookes* v *Barnard* [1964] AC 1129. The House was generally unhappy with the award of exemplary damages as this tended to confuse the respective roles of civil and criminal law. Exemplary damages were therefore confined to three categories. Statute and precedent prevented their abolition. The three categories were confirmed by the House of Lords in *Cassell & Ltd* v *Broome* [1972] AC 1027.

1 *Conduct calculated to make a profit.* Such damages are usually awarded in defamation cases and are primarily to reverse unjust enrichment but may also take into account the claimant's difficulties in litigating.

Cassell & Co Ltd v Broome [1972] AC 1027

The claimant was a retired naval officer. The defendant published a book about a wartime convoy with which the claimant was involved. The claimant sued for libel and was successful. The jury awarded £25,000 exemplary damages which was upheld by the House of Lords because of the profit which the defendant would have made. It was not necessary that the defendant calculated that the profit would exceed the damages. The major factor was that the defendant was prepared to hurt somebody in order to make a profit.

For libel, see
Chapter 21.

No precise mathematical calculation need take place. The defendant must be aware that what he was proposing to do was against the law (or be reckless as to that fact) but had proceeded in the belief that the prospect of material advantages outweighed the possibility of material loss. Most of the successful actions have taken place in libel claims where the defendant has published a statement which he knows is defamatory but calculates that he will, for example, increase his sales beyond the amount he will have to pay in damages.

2 *Oppressive conduct by government servants.* This category covers not only government servants in the strict sense, but also persons exercising governmental functions, such as police officers.

In *AB* v *South West Water Services Ltd* [1993] 1 All ER 609, a nationalised corporation which contaminated drinking water and failed to warn the public was held to be not exercising governmental power. The Court of Appeal held that exemplary damages could not be awarded for public nuisance or any tort for which exemplary damages had not been awarded before *Rookes* v *Barnard*. (The 'cause of action' test.)

The 'cause of action' test was criticised by the Law Commission (Law Commission Reports Nos 132 (1993) and 247 (1997)) and the cause of action test has now been overruled. (*Kuddus* v *Chief Constable of Leicestershire Constabulary* [2001] 3 All ER 193.)

The test is now the nature of the conduct, not the basis of the cause of action. The conduct must still fit into one of the two categories. It was also suggested (by Lord Nicholls) that the two categories ought to be reconsidered.

A court may award exemplary damages where there has been oppressive, arbitrary or unconstitutional action by government servants. It does not extend to private individuals or corporations, although Lord Nicholls in *Kuddus* doubted whether the exclusion of non-governmental oppression remains appropriate in the modern world.

This category covers wrongful arrest. The circumstances in which exemplary damages could be awarded against the police in cases of wrongful arrest were considered by the Court of Appeal in *Thompson* (below).

Thompson v Commissioner of Police for the Metropolis [1998] QB 498

The jury should be told that in exceptional cases it was possible to award damages to punish the defendant where there was conduct (including oppressive or arbitrary behaviour) which deserved exceptional remedy. Such damages were unlikely to be less than £5,000 and might be as much as £25,000, with an absolute maximum of £50,000 in cases where an officer of at least the rank of superintendent had been directly involved in the misconduct.

3 *Express authorisation by statute.* The only clear example of this is the Reserve and Auxiliary Forces (Protection of Civilian Interests) Act 1951 s 13(2). There has been some discussion as whether the Copyright, Designs and Patents Act 1988 s 97(2) authorises the award of exemplary damages but there is no clear answer. Following the abolition of the 'cause of action' rule in *Kuddus*, it is no longer a bar to awarding exemplary damages in an action for statutory breach of copyright.

The relationship of exemplary damages to compensatory damages was considered by Lord Nicholls in *Kuddus* v *Chief Constable of Leicestershire Constabulary* [2001] 3 All ER 193:

Exemplary damages are a controversial topic, and have been so for many years. . . . Awards of damages are primarily intended to compensate for loss, whether pecuniary or non-pecuniary. Non-pecuniary loss includes mental distress arising from the circumstances in which the tort was committed, such as justified feelings of outrage at the defendant's conduct. Damages awarded for this type of loss are sometimes called *aggravated damages*, as the defendant's conduct aggravates the injury done. Sometimes damages may also be measured by reference, not to the plaintiff's (claimant's) loss, but to the profit obtained by the defendant from his wrongdoing. Exemplary damages or punitive damages, the terms are synonymous, stand apart from awards of compensatory damages. They are additional to an award which is intended to compensate a plaintiff (claimant) fully for the loss he has suffered, both pecuniary and non-pecuniary. They are intended to punish and deter.

The question of exemplary damages was referred to the Law Commission who recommended that they should be retained but renamed punitive damages and put on a more rational basis. They concluded that both the categories test in *Rookes* v *Barnard* and the cause of action test in *AB* v *South West Water Services* should be abolished. (Which it was in *Kuddus*.) Punitive damages should be available for any tort where the defendant deliberately and outrageously disregarded the claimant's rights. They should not be awarded if the defendant had been convicted of a criminal offence involving the conduct in question. In assessing quantum the court should take into account the defendant's means and damages should be proportionate to the gravity of the wrong. (Law Commission Report No 247 (1997).)

Support for these views (although not precedent) can be found in the House of Lords decision in *Kuddus* v *Chief Constable of Leicestershire Constabulary* [2001] 3 All ER 193.

There was a suggestion in the Leveson Report (ch 16.3) that exemplary damages could become more common for invasions of privacy by the media but this is likely to be strongly opposed.

Aggravated damages

It is convenient at this point to discuss the expression 'aggravated damages'. This is an expression used by judges and some confusion surrounds the question as to whether they are compensatory or non-compensatory. They are awarded where there is outrage to person or property and are best regarded as compensatory. They are to compensate for injury to the claimant's pride or feelings. They may be awarded in deceit (*Archer* v *Brown* [1984] 2 All ER 267) or cases involving rape or sexual assault. (*W and D* v *Meah* [1986] 1 All ER 935.)

Some confusion is caused by the fact that they are reflected in the claimant's general damages. (*AB* v *South West Water Services* [1993] 1 All ER 609.)

The award of aggravated damages must not violate the overall principle of compensation and the Law Commission (*Aggravated, Exemplary and Restitutionary Damages* (1997), para 2.42) recommended that they should be seen as a species of mental distress damages or damages for injured feelings. This has not yet been implemented.

Compensatory damages for personal injuries

Introduction

Objective 3

The basis of an award of compensatory damages in a tort action is that the claimant should be awarded such a sum of money as will, as nearly as possible, put them in the position they would have been in if they had not sustained the injuries. Historically, the damages have been awarded on a once and forever basis in the form of a lump sum. However, there are signs that this is now changing.

The expression 'personal injuries' covers physical harm to the person, disease and illness (including psychiatric illness).

Damages for personal injuries are normally treated separately as they raise problems not encountered with other types of loss. Where damage to property is caused then financial compensation is adequate. Where a person is deprived of a leg by tortious conduct, money is the only compensation available, but this requires the court to fix the market value of a leg and to engage in the difficult task of assessing damages for intangibles such as pain, shock and suffering. Other serious difficulties are posed by the problems of calculating future pecuniary losses and estimating future medical condition.

Example

Emma was a talented law student aged 22. She was expected to have a good career as a solicitor when she was seriously injured in a road accident caused by the negligent driving of Andrew. Andrew has admitted negligence but contests the amount of damages claimed. This is a typical claim in practice where the issue at stake is normally quantum of damages rather than liability. Emma has brought an action for damages and has claimed *compensatory damages*.

(i) *Pecuniary losses.* Emma's injuries are so severe that she will never work so she will be awarded compensatory damages for *loss of earnings* for the rest of her life. This is calculated by working

---

> out how much she would have earned and then calculating her life expectancy. If her average earnings over a lifetime would have been £50,000 per annum and she would have worked for a period of 40 years, the court will calculate her damages from these figures. They do not just multiply the yearly loss by 40 but apply a figure called the multiplier to take account of a large capital sum. In Emma's case the multiplier would be in the region of 15. Her damages for loss of earnings would therefore be **£50,000 × 15**.
>
> (ii) *Non-pecuniary losses.* Emma will be compensated for any *loss of amenity*. This covers damages for the injury itself and any inability to enjoy life. Damages will also be awarded for any pain and suffering she has suffered.

Classification of damages

Damages in personal injuries cases are divided into pecuniary and non-pecuniary losses. Pecuniary damages are those that can be estimated in monetary terms, such as loss of earnings, medical and other expenses. Non-pecuniary damages cover intangibles such as loss of physical amenity, pain, shock and suffering.

Form and basis of the award

The judge is required to itemise the award, showing how much has been awarded for each head of loss. The reason for this is that different rates of interest are applied to pecuniary and non-pecuniary damages. The advantage of the system in practical terms is that practitioners are aware of the going rate for each type of loss and this encourages out-of-court settlements.

The basis of the award is full compensation. The claimant must be compensated for all pecuniary losses which they have suffered as a result of the tort. The system of full compensation is subject to a number of criticisms.

The first is that a high cost is involved for small claims. This could be avoided by excluding compensation for the first few days.

Secondly, there is no incentive for the victim to recover and return to work. This only applies if the compensation is paid in a lump sum. If it is paid by periodical payments then these can be varied or terminated to take account of changing conditions. (See below.)

See the discussion of the proposals of the Pearson Report in Chapter 1.

Thirdly, is the idea that full compensation can lead to over-compensation. Awards of damages can overlap with social security and private insurance payments. This is not really a problem with the principle of full compensation but with the failure to have effective rules which deal with the interrelationship between the three systems.

It should also be noted that certain factors tend to prevent full compensation being achieved. The most important of these is inflation. An award made in the 1990s, which might have seemed generous at the time, will now have been considerably diminished by subsequent inflation.

The lump sum

The lump sum is said to have the advantages of enabling the claimant to concentrate on recovery without reducing their entitlement to compensation, enabling the insurer to pay up and incur no further inconvenience, and enabling the claimant to plan their life, taking into account any disability suffered.

The disadvantages are that the claimant may use the capital unwisely; no account can be taken of any improvement or deterioration in the claimant's medical condition and it is difficult to take account of inflation, which may erode what at the time was adequate compensation. (See *Wells* v *Wells* [1998] 3 All ER 481.)

The lump sum has, historically, been the method for awarding tort damages. However, it has come under increasing criticism and is now being eroded as the principal method of awarding compensation. The first step was the possibility of a structured settlement agreed between the parties. (See below.) There is now a coherent scheme for the award of damages in the form of periodical payments but it is still too early to calculate how effective this will be.

Structured settlements

The haphazard effect of the lump sum award of damages in personal injuries cases has brought about many calls for reform. The claimant is generally at a disadvantage because of the difficulty of estimating the amount that will be awarded at trial. This, combined with delay and the stress of the litigation process, leads to claimants accepting low figures in negotiated settlements.

The structured settlement works by the insurer buying an annuity which covers the liability involved and is held for the injured person. This pension can be varied and the payments structured over a period of time. The system offers direct benefits to the claimant. The income which is generated can be guaranteed against erosion by inflation, and the income is paid free of tax to the claimant. The latter factor increases by a quarter the value of the lump sum paid by the insurer. Payments are exempt from the social security recoupment scheme.

The first part of a structured settlement is a lump sum to cover financial losses incurred up to the date of settlement. The second part is a pension which will usually last for the remainder of the claimant's life. This pension covers future loss of income, non-pecuniary losses, medical expenses and the cost of future care.

Prior to the coming into force of the Courts Act 2003 ss 100–101 the court had no power to order a structured settlement, so these were available only where the parties agreed. Under the legislation the court may make orders for future pecuniary loss to be made in the form of periodical payments. Where there is consent by the parties, the court may make an order under which damages are wholly, or partly, to take the form of periodical payments. (Damages Act 1996 s 2.) A second limitation is that they are only appropriate in connection with future losses; they are not appropriate to past losses. The damages must be large enough to justify using a structured settlement. At present, cases must be worth at least £50,000 to make it worthwhile.

Periodical payments

The discussion on lump sum or periodical payments for damages for personal injuries has been a long one. The Courts Act 2003 ss 100–101 (see also the Damages (Variation of Periodical Payments) Order 2005) now give the courts the power to award a periodic payment order in relation to future income loss (but not past pecuniary loss or damages for pain and suffering) without the consent of the parties. (Damages Act 1996 s 2(1) (substituted by Courts Act 2003 s 100).)

A court awarding damages in an action for personal injury may, with the consent of the parties, make an order under which the damages are wholly or partly to take the form of periodical payments.

In order to do this the court has to be satisfied that the continuity of payment under the order is reasonably secure. This would be satisfied if, for example, the defendant was a government body or health service authority.

Any settlements reached out of court will escape the duty to consider compensation in the form of periodical payments. Any scheme of periodical payments is more expensive for the insurers who meet virtually all damages claims. It is therefore likely that there will be more out-of-court settlements in the future as this will be cheaper for the insurers.

Where such an award is made the courts will determine the amount payable and the frequency and duration of the payments. The starting point is to work out the current and future needs of the claimant without attempting to work out his longevity. This is known as the 'bottom-up' approach. The insurer must then decide how to satisfy the order in future. One potential problem is the ability of the payer to meet the order in future. This is one of the factors which the court has to take into account when deciding whether to make such an order. If the payer is, for example, the National Health Service, the risk is assumed to be so small as to be non-existent. The periodical payment can be made variable in the future. (For the conditions for variation see the Damages (Variation of Periodical Payments) Order 2005 and *Thompstone* v *Tameside and Glossop Acute Services NHS Trust* [2008] EWCA Civ 5.)

These provisions have the potential to revolutionise the award of damages in tort actions. They avoid some of the problems of structured settlements such as the need to calculate a lump sum. The major question would appear to be whether the insurance industry is able to cope with it.

The advantages of periodical payments are:

1 They are less wasteful as they do not require a calculation of the claimant's life expectancy which may turn out to be wrong.

2 They do not require the claimant to seek investment advice and cannot be spent at once.

3 They can be increased or decreased as a result of a change in circumstances.

Periodical payments do not provide answers to all of the problems, however:

1 They are more expensive to administer.

2 The claimant does not obtain a capital sum to invest.

Provisional damages

There is now a statutory power to award provisional damages. (Senior Courts Act 1981 s 32A.) If there is a chance that, at some future time, the injured person may develop some disease or suffer deterioration in their physical or mental condition, they may be awarded damages on the basis that this will not occur, with a proviso that further damages will be awarded at a later date if it does occur. The section must be specifically pleaded by the claimant, who may be awarded a higher amount at trial if they do not plead the provision. The right to have the award adjusted may only be exercised once.

The example envisaged was that of a child whose skull was fractured in an accident and appeared to have made a full recovery. However, with cranial injuries there is always a chance of subsequent epilepsy. If nothing is claimed at trial for the feared epilepsy the claimant can reserve the right to come back to court later and claim for the feared event if it subsequently develops.

The provision has not proved popular with claimants and has been conservatively interpreted by the courts.

Willson v *Ministry of Defence* [1991] 1 All ER 638

Provisional damages were refused on the ground that serious deterioration refers to a clear and severable event rather than an ordinary continuing deterioration, such as a typical osteoarthritic condition.

Three requirements must be satisfied before the court will sanction provisional damages:

1 there must be a chance of the feared event materialising at some future date;
2 there must be a serious deterioration of the claimant's physical condition – not just an ordinary deterioration or progression of the disease or illness;
3 the judge must be satisfied that the case justifies him in giving the claimant the right to return at a later date for more; or that is best resolved by once-and-for-all damages.

Interim damages

Interim damages may be awarded at the interlocutory stage where the defendant admits liability but contests quantum. The defendant must be insured, or be a public body, or have the resources to make an interim payment. (Senior Courts Act 1981 s 32.)

Pecuniary losses

1 Loss of earnings

Damages for loss of earnings come in two categories. Loss of earnings suffered by the claimant before the trial have to be pleaded as special damages. The claimant must show what their net loss has been as a result of their injury. At this stage inflation can be taken care of, for example, if the accident occurred in 2011 and the trial in 2015, if the claimant was earning £20,000 per annum in 2011 and, but for the accident, would have been earning £25,000 in 2015, then an average figure of £22,500 will be taken and multiplied by five.

Future loss of earnings (i.e. from the trial onwards) are claimed as general damages. This causes severe problems for the courts as it involves guessing what would have happened to the claimant had the accident not occurred.

The multiplicand

The first stage in calculating future loss of earnings is to take the claimant's net annual loss, i.e. the difference between what they would have earned and what they are earning. This is known as the multiplicand. The court will then adjust this figure to take into account factors such as promotion prospects. This inevitably involves some guesswork.

Dixon v *Were* EWHC 2273 (QB)

The claimant was born in 1976. He attended Radley college, where he gained ten GCSEs and three A-levels: two Cs and one D. In 1994, he commenced a course at Newcastle University for a combined honours degree in accountancy and mathematics. He subsequently transferred to a degree in economics. He was described as being of average ability and predicted a lower second. In 1997, he was involved in a road traffic accident in a car driven by the defendant, and suffered severe physical injuries and brain damage. Liability was admitted, subject to a deduction of 27.5 per cent in respect of contributory negligence.

Only quantum was at issue. During the course of the trial, an award for pain, suffering and loss of amenity was agreed in the sum of £147,500. Issues remained as to loss of earnings.

Evidence was adduced that pre-accident, the claimant was charismatic, confident and full of energy; he aspired to work in the City and to make a lot of money; he had the benefit of some contacts in City circles. It was submitted that the claimant would have been likely to have had a career which would have been successful and well remunerated. The defendant invited a cautious approach, in particular highlighting the need to contrast the 'hard evidence' with the 'dreams'.

The court ruled:

On the evidence, the claimant's likely career path would have led to employment in the financial services sector. He had an attractive personality which, together with his background, the fact of his degree and to some extent his contacts, would have secured entry into a good job at above national average figures. Regard, however, had to be had to the defendant's submissions, and the likely fact that the work ethic was not his foremost characteristic. The argument that the claimant had lost a chance of achieving very high earnings was speculative, and nothing extra would be awarded under such a head.

On that basis, the appropriate future multiplicands were: (i) £45,000 gross at the date of trial; (ii) £50,000 gross from October 2005, (iii) £55,000 gross from October 2011; (iv) £65,000 gross from October 2021.

The multiplier

The second stage is to apply the multiplier to this figure. The multiplier is calculated by working out the number of years that the disability is likely to continue. This figure is then reduced to take into account the contingencies of life, i.e. the claimant might not have lived or worked until retirement age and they have received a capital sum which can be invested and make money which would otherwise not be available to them.

The use of the multiplier is controversial. If a person has been living on income then the income would have increased to take account of inflation. A capital sum, however, is fixed and the courts do not make an allowance for future inflation. The claimant will, however, be able to invest the capital and earn interest on it. One of the factors in calculating the appropriate multiplier is therefore the amount of interest that the claimant could earn on their capital. The House of Lords ruled that this is to be on the basis that the claimant had invested in index-linked government securities (ILGS). The average rate of interest on ILGS is 3 per cent and this should be the discount rate. (*Wells* v *Wells* [1998] 3 All ER 481.) This was later amended by statutory instrument to 2.5 per cent. (Damages (Personal Injury) Order 2001.)

The effect of the decision in *Wells* means that there has been an increase in the multiplier. In the case itself, the application of a 3 per cent rate led to an increase in awards of £300,000 in the case of a six-year-old and £186,000 to a 28-year-old. The subsequent fixing of the rate at 2.5 per cent confirms the trend towards an increase in the size of damages awards. The courts would also appear to be extremely reluctant to hear that a different rate would be appropriate. (*Warriner* v *Warriner* [2003] 3 All ER 447; *Cooke* v *United Bristol Healthcare NHS Trust* [2004] 1 All ER 797.)

At this stage a simple example would be useful.

Example

The subject is a 27-year-old man who has been rendered totally unfit for work by a negligently caused accident. Before the accident he worked as a roofer and earned £20,000 per annum. The accident took place in 2014 and the trial in 2015. Had the accident not occurred he would have been earning £22,000 in 2014.

1. Pre-trial loss of earnings, £21,000 less tax and National Insurance which would have been paid:
   £14,000 × 3 = £42,000
2. Future loss of earnings (assuming no promotion prospects): net annual loss of £14,000. Multiplier of **15 = £210,000.**

The objective of this exercise is that the claimant should receive a sum, which when invested will produce a figure equal to the lost sum.

Where the claimant is a child below working age, the court will take into account national average earnings during early working years and apply a low multiplier. The reason for the low multiplier is that the child might never have become a wage earner. (*Croke* v *Wiseman* [1981] 3 All ER 852.)

The lost years. One problem which may evolve in calculating damages for future loss of earnings are the so-called lost years. This occurs where the claimant's life expectancy is reduced by the accident. Damages for loss of earnings are based on the claimant's life expectancy before the accident (*Pickett* v *British Rail Engineering Ltd* [1980] AC 136) but a deduction is made for the amount that the claimant would have spent on their own support during the lost years.

If our subject in the above example had his life expectancy reduced in that he would now die at 40, damages are recoverable by him for the period 40–65 years of age, but subject to a deduction for his living expenses.

No damages are recoverable for loss of expectation of life itself but non-pecuniary damages may be awarded for mental suffering caused by the knowledge that life has been cut short.

Loss of earning capacity. Damages are available for the situation where the claimant can carry on working but his earning capacity has been reduced as a result of the accident. The damages are awarded for being handicapped in the job market. (*Smith* v *Manchester Corpn* (1974) 17 KIR 1.)

Loss of pension rights. This raises the question of whether the claimant would have remained in employment long enough to obtain a pension and what test should be employed to answer this question: balance of probabilities or degree of likelihood.

Brown v *Ministry of Defence* [2006] All ER (D) 133 (May)

The claimant enlisted in the army in February 1998, aged 24. Eight weeks into her service she suffered a serious fracture of her left ankle in the course of basic training. Although she did her best to regain her fitness, it became clear that she would be unable to complete her training and she was eventually discharged in October 1999. The claimant began proceedings against the defendant for negligence. She claimed, among other things, compensation for loss of pension rights calculated on the assumption that she would have remained in the army for the full service term of 22 years, which would have qualified her for an immediate pension instead of having to wait until the age of 60. The defendant argued that since at the time of her enlistment the average length of service of female recruits was a little over six years, a claim for loss of pension rights based on 22 years' service could not be sustained.

The Court of Appeal held that the first instance judge had erred in making findings about the way the claimant's military career would have developed by reference to the balance of probabilities, rather than by assessing the chances of its developing in one way rather than another. The court had, therefore to consider the matter afresh. Having regard to the evidence of her enthusiasm and commitment, the chances that the claimant would have left the army of her own volition after only six years' service were negligible. After that the position became more difficult to assess because over the next few years other factors might well have begun to play a more important part in her thinking. The period between the ages of 30 and 36 was one that could well see significant changes in her personal and family situation of a kind that could have a profound effect on her approach to continuing a full-time military career. The chances of her completing 12 years' service could not be put at higher than 50 per cent. The next ten years were even more difficult to assess, partly because they lay farther in the future, but as she began to approach the end of her 22 years' service the incentive to complete them would obviously increase. Taking everything into consideration, the chances of her completing that further period of ten years should be assessed at 60 per cent. On that basis, the chances of her obtaining the additional benefit represented by the right to an immediate pension on completing 22 years' service was 30 per cent. The conclusion that the claimant would have reached the rank of staff sergeant was not challenged, and the fairest course was to assume that she would have achieved promotion to that rank after the average period of service at which that was achieved, namely 14 years and 6 months. The highest at which the chance of her reaching the rank of warrant officer first class could be put was 15 per cent.

2 Other pecuniary losses

The claimant can recover any expenses reasonably incurred as a result of treatment of their injuries. Any medical expenses reasonably incurred may therefore be recovered. The claimant has a choice as to whether they are treated privately or not. (Law Reform (Personal Injuries) Act 1948 s 2(4).) But if the claimant is treated by the National Health Service, then the living expenses which they save are set off against their loss of earnings. (Administration of Justice Act 1982 s 5.)

If a friend or relative has incurred financial loss in caring for the claimant, then the claimant can recover this amount as damages. This is the claimant's loss because of his need for care. (***Housecroft* v *Burnett*** [1986] 1 All ER 332.) The award reflects the claimant's obligation to hold this part of the damages on trust for the person providing the services. (***Hunt* v *Severs*** [1994] 2 All ER 385.) A person who has previously looked after a disabled relative but is no longer able to do so as a result of the defendant's negligence is entitled to damages for the cost of the care he previously gave. (***Lowe* v *Guise*** [2002] QB 1369.)

Where the services are gratuitously rendered by the tortfeasor, the claimant cannot recover the cost of those services by way of damages. (***Hunt* v *Severs*.**)

Non-pecuniary losses

1 Loss of amenity

The claimant may recover damages for the injury itself and any consequent inability to enjoy life. These damages are calculated on an objective basis and do not take into account the claimant's inability to appreciate the disability. Unconscious claimants may therefore recover for loss of amenity. (***West* v *Shephard*** [1964] AC 326.)

> The fact of unconsciousness is therefore relevant in respect of and will eliminate those heads or elements of damage which can only exist by being felt or thought or experienced. The fact of unconsciousness does not, however, eliminate the actuality of the deprivations of the ordinary experiences and amenities of life which may be the inevitable result of some physical injury. (Lord Morris in ***West* v *Shephard*.**)

Loss of amenity may include loss of capacity to enjoy sport or other pastimes which the claimant engaged in before the injury. Impairment of one of the five senses, inability to play with one's children, diminution of marriage prospects, impairment of sexual life and destroyed holidays may also be compensated under this heading.

The courts work from a tariff which is laid down by the Court of Appeal. The tariff figure can be adjusted in the light of the particular circumstances of the claimant.

The most serious injuries fall within a bracket of £150,000–£200,000, with, for example, £175,000 as the appropriate figure for an average case of tetraplegia. (***Heil* v *Rankin*** [2000] 2 WLR 1173.)

The Law Commission had argued that damages were too low for non-pecuniary loss in personal injuries cases (Law Commission Report No 257 (1999)) and this was accepted by the Court of Appeal in *Heil v Rankin* with respect to the most serious cases but not for those awards assessed at under £10,000. In future, the figures will increase in line with the retail price index.

2 Pain and suffering

The court will award damages for any pain and suffering which can be attributed to the injury itself and to any consequential surgical operations. The award will cover past and any future pain. Compensation neurosis may also be compensated. This is a medically recognised condition caused by awaiting the outcome of litigation.

An unconscious claimant cannot recover damages for pain and suffering. A conscious claimant may recover for any mental suffering caused by the knowledge that life has been cut short (Administration of Justice Act 1982 s 1(1)(b)) or that their ability to enjoy life has been diminished by physical handicap.

Damages for nervous shock are awarded as damages for pecuniary loss and as damages for pain and suffering and loss of amenity.

Damages for bereavement are only awarded in actions under the Fatal Accidents Act 1976 to certain classes of dependants. (See below.) No damages can be awarded for grief or sorrow. (*Hinz v Berry* [1970] 2 QB 40.) However, there may be a claim under the Human Rights Act 1998. (*Rabone v Pennine Care NHS Trust* [2012] UKSC 2.)

Deductions

A victim of an accident may be in receipt of money from sources other than tort damages. As the objective of the damages award is to compensate the claimant for losses incurred as a result of their injury, it is necessary for the courts to work out to what extent these other sources must be set off against damages. The claimant may be entitled to state benefits as a result of their injuries and may also have private insurance or become entitled to payments by their employer.

The philosophy employed by the courts is not to punish a thrifty claimant. On this basis, personal accident insurance money is generally non-deductible, as are pensions. (*Parry v Cleaver* [1970] AC 1.) If an employee has received sick pay or wages from an employer, then this will be deducted unless the sick pay has to be repaid out of any damages received.

There has been considerable controversy over whether social security benefits should be deductible from tort damages for personal injuries. It should be remembered that social security payments are the main source of compensation for accident victims. Parliament has now accepted the case against double compensation. The law is now contained in the Social Security (Recovery of Benefits) Act 1997. Certain social security payments can be recouped by the Department of Social Security. The compensator (who will normally be an insurance company) must pay benefits received by the claimant before a compensation payment is made. The system applies to settlements out of court.

Prior to the 1997 Act, the amount of benefits received was simply deducted from the claimant's damages. The new approach is to correlate the type of benefit received to the particular head of damages. For example, any benefits to provide for the cost of care can only be deducted from the claimant's damages for cost of care. Any damages for pain and suffering are effectively protected from recoupment as there is no social security benefit which corresponds to this head.

> **Examples**
>
> 1 *X* is awarded £50,000 damages and has received £12,000 in benefits. *X* will receive £38,000 in damages.
> 2 *X* is awarded £20,000 in damages reduced by 50 per cent for contributory negligence and has received £10,000 in benefits. *X* will receive nothing in damages.

Damages under the Human Rights Act 1998

Damages may be awarded by a court when a public authority has acted in a way which is incompatible with a Convention right. Section 8(1) states that a court 'may grant such relief or remedy, or make such order, within its powers as it considers just and appropriate'.

By virtue of s 8(3) no damages award is to be made unless the court is satisfied that the award is 'necessary to afford just satisfaction' to the claimant.

Under s 8(4) the court must take into account, in deciding whether to award damages and the amount of those damages, the principles applied by the European Court of Human Rights.

Damages are therefore not available as of right for a wrong under the 1998 Act and can be refused if other appropriate remedies render an award of damages unnecessary. In ***Dennis*** v ***Ministry of Defence*** [2003] EWHC 793 (QB) no damages were awarded for infringement of a Convention right because compensatory damages had been awarded in the tort of nuisance.

See Chapter 16 for *Dobson*.

In ***Dobson*** v ***Thames Water Utilities Ltd*** [2009] EWCA Civ 28 the Court of Appeal held that it would not normally be necessary for those with a proprietary interest in land who had made a successful claim in nuisance to have their damages 'topped up' under the Human Rights Act. However, a person who had no proprietary interest in the land affected and therefore no claim in private nuisance might have an action but damages would probably be nominal because of the basis on which private nuisance damages for interference with amenity were assessed.

See Chapter 17 for nuisance.

See below for bereavement claims. (***Rabone*** v ***Pennine Care NHS Trust*** [2012] UKSC 2.)

The principles on which damages are awarded were stated in the following case:

R (on the application of Greenfield) v *Secretary of State for Home Department* [2005] UKHL 14

Domestic courts, when exercising their power to award damages under s 8 of the 1998 Act, should not apply domestic scales of damages.

1 The 1998 Act was not a tort statute; its objects were different and broader . . . a finding of violation . . . would be an important part of his remedy and an important vindication of the right he had asserted. Damages did not need ordinarily to be awarded to encourage high standards of compliance by member states since they were already bound in international law to perform their duties under the Convention in good faith.
2 The purpose of incorporating the Convention in domestic law through the 1998 Act had been to give (claimants) the same remedies that they could recover in the ECHR without the concomitant delay and expense.
3 The awards made by the ECHR were not precisely calculated but judged by it to be fair in the individual case. Judges in England and Wales had also to make similar judgments in the cases before them. (See also ***R (KB)*** v ***Mental Health Review Tribunal*** [2003] 3 WLR 185.)

Lord Bingham:

> It is evident that under art 41 there are three preconditions to an award of just satisfaction: (1) that the court should have found a violation; (2) that the domestic law of the member state should allow only partial reparation to be made; and (3) that it should be necessary to afford just satisfaction to the injured party.

It can be anticipated that there may be problems involved in awards for mental distress and pure economic loss as Strasbourg principles on these are different to those in English domestic law.

(See *Damages under the Human Rights Act 1998*, Law Commission Report No 266 (2000).)

Effect of death on an award of damages for personal injuries

Introduction

Objective 4

If the defendant in a tort action dies then the cause of action will usually survive against their estate. Where the claimant dies, their cause of action will generally survive for the benefit of their estate and a new cause of action will be created for their dependants. An important exception to this principle is in actions for defamation, where the death of a party terminates the action.

The estate's action (Law Reform (Miscellaneous Provisions) Act 1934)

At common law the action did not survive the death of the claimant. The introduction of compulsory third-party insurance for motor cars made it unjust that if the defendant killed their victim instead of maiming them, they could escape civil liability. The 1934 Act removed the rule that the action did not survive death.

The Act does not create liability. It preserves the deceased's subsisting action for the benefit of their estate (s 1(1)). The action is the one that the deceased would have brought had they lived.

This principle does not create difficulties for damages accruing during the deceased's lifetime: for example, the deceased was injured in a car accident caused by the defendant's negligence and died three months later. The estate will recover damages for pecuniary and non-pecuniary losses based on the normal principles.

Problems do arise with losses accruing after the death. There is a difficulty with overlap with the dependant's action. To avoid this, the Act provides (s 1(2)) that no damages may be recovered by the estate for loss of earnings for the lost years. It is also provided that no damages may be recovered by the estate for bereavement (s 1A).

The action is not for death caused by the defendant and so the defendant need not be responsible for the death. But where the defendant's wrong has caused the death, then any losses or gains to the estate consequent on the death are ignored in the calculation of damages (s 1(4)). An example of a loss would be the termination of an annuity. An example of a gain would be an insurance payment. One exception to this rule is that the court may award the estate any funeral expenses incurred.

The dependant's action (Fatal Accidents Act 1976)

Who can claim?

A definition of dependants is given in s 1(3) of the Act. The normal action will be brought by the surviving spouse and children, but parents and other ascendants, siblings, uncles and aunts and their issue are included. One category which deserves special mention is cohabitees. If the claimant had lived with the deceased as husband or wife for a period of at least two years, then that person is classed as a dependant.

The action is brought by the personal representatives of the deceased or after six months of the appointment of the personal representatives, by any dependant on behalf of themselves or others.

The nature of the action

This is a new right of action given to the dependants and is not a survival of the deceased's right of action. The death must have been caused by the tortious act of the defendant (s 1(1)) and the dependants have to show that the deceased had a right of action in order to be able to claim. This means that if the deceased had settled the claim or obtained judgment, the dependants have no claim. But the dependants will not be bound by any limitation on the amount the deceased could have claimed. Where the deceased had been awarded provisional damages and then died, this does not operate as a bar to a claim under the Fatal Accidents Act 1976. However, these damages are taken into consideration when assessing compensation for the dependants. (Damages Act 1996 s 3.)

The action is often said to be for the loss of a breadwinner. Where a spouse is deprived of the other spouse's earnings or a child is deprived of a parent's earnings, there will be a claim. The loss of a spouse's 'housekeeping services', rendered gratuitously, is also recoverable. (*Berry* v *Humm & Co* [1915] 1 KB 627.) Children are able to recover for the loss of a mother's services in order to meet the cost of a housekeeper (*Hay* v *Hughes* [1975] QB 790) but lower damages will be awarded if the mother was unreliable. (*Stanley* v *Saddique* [1992] QB 1.)

The amount recoverable

The main head of damages is the pecuniary loss suffered by the dependants from the date of death. The method of assessing damages was stated by Lord Wright in *Davies* v *Powell Duffryn Collieries Ltd* [1942] AC 601.

The starting point is the amount of wages which the deceased was earning, the ascertainment of which to some extent may depend upon the regularity of their employment. Then there is an estimate of how much was required or expected for their own personal and living expenses. The balance will give a datum or base figure which will generally be turned into a lump sum by taking a certain number of years' purchase. That sum, however, has to be taxed down by having due regard to uncertainties.

An award may be made from the date of death up to the date of trial. The earnings the deceased would have made are calculated and the sum they would have spent on their own support is deducted. The second stage is to assess losses into the future. The annual value of dependency is estimated (the multiplicand) and the appropriate multiplier used. The aim is to give a lump sum which, when invested, will produce an income equivalent to the dependant's loss of income over the period of dependence. This will give a global figure which is available for distribution between the dependants.

Dependence

The dependence must not arise from a business relationship. In *Malyon v Plummer* [1964] 1 QB 330, the claimant had been paid £600 per annum for services rendered to her husband's company. The value of these services was calculated at £200 per annum. The balance was attributable to her relationship with the deceased. Her loss of dependence was therefore £400 per annum.

Where the court is calculating the damages to be awarded to a cohabitee, it must take into account the fact that the dependant had no enforceable right to financial support by the deceased (s 3(4)).

When assessing a wife's claim in respect of her husband's death, the court must take no account of her remarriage or prospects of remarriage (s 3(3)).

Bereavement

Damages for bereavement may be awarded to certain classes of dependants. The spouse of the deceased or the parents of an unmarried child may claim. The damages are for mental distress at the death and are fixed by statute at £11,800 for deaths occurring after 1 January 2008. There is no attempt to reflect the subjective level of grief.

The Ministry of Justice consultation document (*The Law on Damages* (2009)) proposes an extension of the persons eligible to claim to include children of the deceased under 18 years at the time of the death or a person who had lived with the deceased as husband or wife (or same sex couple) for two years before the accident. It also proposes a fixed sum of £5,000 for each eligible child.

In *Rabone v Pennine Care NHS Trust* [2012] UKSC 2 the Supreme Court held that the parents of an adult daughter who killed herself while on leave from a mental hospital were held to have an action as their daughter's right to life under Article 2 had been infringed. The fact that the parents had already received £7,500 from a common law claim against the defendants (under the Law Reform (Miscellaneous Provisions) Act 1934) was held not to be sufficient. They had received nothing for bereavement. This decision would appear to circumvent the rule in the Fatal Accidents Act that the parents of grown up children could not sue for bereavement damages.

> We are here because the ordinary law of tort does not recognize or compensate the anguish suffered by parents who are deprived of the life of their adult child. (Lady Hale)

Deductions

In assessing the damages in respect of a person's death, any benefits which have accrued or may accrue to any person from his estate or otherwise as a result of death are disregarded (s 4). Therefore, any insurance money, pensions or damages for pain and suffering inherited as part of the deceased's estate are disregarded. Social security benefits are not deducted.

For all its seeming simplicity, s 4 raises complications. This is illustrated by two Court of Appeal cases.

In *Stanley v Saddique* [1992] QB 1 it was held that in assessing a child's damages for the death of his mother, the advantages to the child from the father's subsequent marriage to a woman who provided much better mothering than the natural mother was a benefit accruing as a result of the death under s 4 and was to be disregarded. This gave the word 'benefit' a wide meaning not confined to money or money's worth. However, in *Hayden v Hayden* [1992] 4 All ER 681, a majority of the Court of Appeal held that where the tortfeasor was the father of the infant claimant and had given up work to look after the claimant, the value of his services was not a benefit that accrued as a result of the death under s 4 and was to be deducted from the claimant's damages.

The courts have generally shown a preference for **Stanley**. (See **R v Criminal Injuries Compensation Board ex p K (minors)** [1999] QB 1131.) In **MS v ATH** [2003] QB 965 the children had been cared for by their father after the death of their mother. The parents had been divorced and the father lived separately with a new wife and had offered no financial support for the children prior to the death. **Hayden** was distinguished by the Court of Appeal as it could not be argued that the father was discharging a pre-existing parental obligation. His care was a 'benefit' which resulted from the death and could therefore be disregarded by the court. The situation would have been different had the parents been living together before the death or the father had provided support.

At present the situation is unsatisfactory as it appears to penalise people who took their parenting duties responsibly. The Law Commission proposed (*Claims for Wrongful Death*, Law Commission Report No 263 (1999)) that s 4 should be repealed and the position be rationalised with that in personal injury claims and making clearer which benefits are or are not to be deducted.

Defences

If the deceased could have had a defence raised successfully against them by the defendant, then the dependants may have the same defence raised against them. *Volenti* or *ex turpi causa* will therefore bar the claim. Any contributory negligence on the part of the deceased will be reflected in a deduction of damages.

Example

Fred was injured in an accident at work due to negligence and breach of statutory duty on the part of Gareth, his employer. The accident rendered Fred unfit for work and he died, as a result of his injuries, two years after the accident.

Fred is survived by his wife Sally and two children, Alan (aged nine years) and Becky (aged seven years). At the time of the accident Fred earned £15,000 per annum (net). His employment prospects were good, but he was unlikely to earn a higher salary later in his working life.

Six months after Fred's death, Sally started proceedings in tort against Gareth, and two years after the claim form was issued a judge approved a settlement of the action on the following basis.

The estate

Fred had died intestate and his property therefore devolved to his wife and children.

Pecuniary losses: two years' loss of earnings	=	*£30,000*
Other losses	=	*£6,000*
Non-pecuniary losses: pain, shock and suffering	=	*£9,000*
Loss of amenity	=	*£8,000*
Damages to the estate	=	*£53,000*

The dependants

Fred's only dependants were his wife and two children.

Pecuniary losses: from date of death to date of trial (2½ years) from the trial (settlement)	=	*£37,500*
Multiplicand of 15,000; multiplier of 20	=	*£300,000*
Damages for bereavement to Sally	=	*£7,500*
Damages to the dependants	=	*£345,000*

Injunctions

Objective 5

An injunction is a court order requiring that the defendant do some act or refrain from doing some act.

The injunction may be mandatory, ordering the defendant to do something, or prohibitory, ordering them not to do something.

A mandatory injunction requires the defendant to undo something which they have done in breach of a tortious obligation. There must be a strong probability of grave damage to the claimant and damages must be inadequate. Mandatory injunctions are not granted as a matter of course, and the court will take into account any hardship which would be caused to the defendant and the defendant's behaviour.

Prohibitory injunctions are granted to prevent continuing tortious misconduct. They are normally used in trespass to land and nuisance actions to protect the claimant's proprietary interest. They are also granted in other torts which can be repeated, such as trespass to the person and defamation. The principle behind the prohibitory injunction is that the defendant should not be allowed to buy the right to inflict damage. They are granted more readily than mandatory injunctions and hardship to the defendant is not a ground for the court refusing the injunction.

See also Chapters 16 and 17 for injunctions.

The injunction may be final or interlocutory. A final injunction is awarded at the end of the trial to the successful party. An interlocutory injunction is awarded pending trial of the action. This is done to prevent harm to the claimant where damages would not be an adequate remedy if they succeeded in their action.

Specific restitution

The remedy of specific restitution is available in actions for conversion. If the defendant is found liable, the court has a discretion to order the return of the claimant's goods. This remedy is unlikely to be exercised where the goods are of no special value.

Self-help

See also Chapter 27 for self-help.

There are areas of tort where the claimant may avail themselves of self-help, although it is fair to say that the law does not generally favour this. Details of self-help can be found in the individual torts.

In actions for trespass to land, the claimant may exercise a right of re-entry on to the land. Where chattels have come on to his land, he may exercise a right of distress damage feasant.

In actions for nuisance, it may be possible for the claimant to take steps to abate the nuisance.

? Question

Alan and Bob went on a pub crawl together. Alan offered Bob a lift home in his car, which Bob accepted although he knew Alan was drunk. On the way home, they stopped at an off-licence and threw a brick through a window. Disturbed by a policeman, Alan drove off at high speed and, due to Alan's negligent driving, collided with a car driven by Charles.

> Bob, who was not wearing a seat belt, was badly injured and Charles suffered serious injuries to his legs. Charles refused a blood transfusion at the hospital as it was contrary to his religious beliefs. As a result, he had to have one leg amputated. Depressed by this, Charles committed suicide three months later.
>
> Advise Bob, and Charles' wife, Diana, as to their prospects of succeeding in a tort action against Alan.

Suggested approach

Bob's action

In normal circumstances Bob would have a relatively straightforward action against Alan in negligence. On the facts of this case Bob may have a problem in establishing that he was owed a duty of care by Alan because of the maxim *ex turpi causa*. A duty of care may not be owed to a person who suffers damage while participating in a criminal activity (*Pitts v Hunt*). The facts are similar to the case of *Ashton v Turner* where it was held at first instance that one of the grounds for denying the claimant an action was *ex turpi causa*.

If a duty of care was owed to Bob in respect of Alan's driving, there is an established breach of duty and reasonably foreseeable damage caused as a result. Are there any defences which Alan could raise?

Volenti non fit injuria is a possible defence to negligence. Bob was aware that Alan had been drinking and might not be capable of driving safely. Was he *volenti* by getting into the car with Alan? There is no express agreement between the parties that Bob will assume the risk of harm. Would the court imply such an agreement? From the cases it would appear not. (See *Nettleship v Weston*; *Owens v Brimmell*.) The claimant may be aware of the risk, but does not consent to the act of negligence which causes their injury. In *Pitts v Hunt* it was held by the Court of Appeal that the Road Traffic Act 1988 s 149 meant that *volenti* was not available where a passenger in a car sues the driver in circumstances where insurance is compulsory.

Has Bob been contributorily negligent? In order to establish this as a defence, the defendant must prove that the claimant failed to take reasonable care for their own safety and that this failure was a cause of their injuries. It appears that Bob may have been contributorily negligent in getting into the car with a driver whom he knew was incapable and by failing to wear a seat belt. In either case the court will have a power to reduce Bob's damages by the proportion for which he was responsible under the Law Reform (Contributory Negligence) Act 1945.

Diana's action

Diana may be able to bring an action as Charles' estate and/or as his dependant. Charles was owed a duty of care by Alan as one road user to another and Alan was in breach of that duty by driving negligently. The problem in the action by the dependant is establishing the chain of causation between the original action and the death.

Alan would have been liable for the original damage to Charles' legs as this was caused by his breach of duty and was not too remote. Would he have been liable for the amputation? Assume that the amputation would not have been necessary, but for the refusal of the blood transfusion. Was the amputation too remote? The test for remoteness in a negligence action is whether the kind of damage suffered by the claimant was reasonably foreseeable (*Wagon Mound (No 1)*). If the extent of the damage was due to a physical characteristic of the claimant then the defendant is liable even if they could not have foreseen the extent of the damage. This is known as the egg-shell skull rule (*Smith v Leech Brain & Co*). It is not known whether this principle extends to non-physical characteristics in civil law. If it does, then Alan would be liable for the amputation.

Would Alan be liable for Charles' suicide? The courts seem to have abandoned public policy as a method of denying relief to the estate of a suicide (*Reeves v Commissioner of Police for the Metropolis*). The question would be whether the suicide was caused by the breach of duty using the 'but for' test. This would appear to be satisfied on the facts. Would the suicide be too remote? It has been held that a suicide is not too remote (*Corr v IBC Vehicles*). If it is a reasonably foreseeable consequence.

Diana's action as the estate is essentially the action which Charles would have had, had he lived. Alan will be liable for all pecuniary and non-pecuniary losses between the breach of duty and the death. (Law Reform (Miscellaneous Provisions) Act 1934.) This would depend on the court's finding as to causation and remoteness, as discussed above. Any loss of earnings, expenses and damages for pain, shock and suffering may be recovered. No damages are recoverable for the period after the death.

Diana's action as a dependant is under the Fatal Accidents Act 1976 and is essentially for loss of a breadwinner. She would have to establish that the death was caused by the breach of duty. Diana as a spouse is a dependant and has two heads of damage to claim for. She would be entitled to £11,800 for bereavement. She could also claim for loss of dependency. This would be the amount in monetary terms which she could have expected to receive from Charles had he lived. This is done by taking Charles' net income and deducting the amount he would have spent on his own support had he lived. The appropriate multiplier is then applied and the resulting figure is the amount available for distribution to the dependants.

Summary

This chapter deals with remedies in tort.

- Remedies in tort are classified as either judicial or extra-judicial. Extra-judicial remedies comprise some form of self-help.

- The usual remedy in a tort action is damages. If the tort is actionable *per se* no damage need be proved. The claimant cannot aggregate two or more consequences, neither of which on their own would constitute damage in order to make a claim. (**Rothwell v Chemical and Insulating Co.**)

- Damages in tort may be compensatory or non-compensatory.

- Non-compensatory damages may be nominal, contemptuous or exemplary.

- Nominal damages are awarded for a tort actionable *per se*, i.e. where a legal right has been violated but the claimant has suffered no actual loss. The amount awarded will be small, normally £2.

- Contemptuous damages acknowledge that the claimant's legal rights have suffered a technical infringement but express derision of their conduct in the matter. Lowest coin of the realm awarded.

- Exemplary or punitive damages are awarded to punish the defendant for their conduct and are in addition to compensatory damages. They are awarded in three categories. (**Rookes v Barnard**.) Conduct calculated to make a profit; oppressive conduct by government servants; or where their award is expressly authorised by statute.

- Aggravated damages are awarded where there is outrage to person or property and are best regarded as compensatory. They are to compensate for injury to the claimant's pride or feelings. They may be awarded in deceit (**Archer v Brown**) or cases involving rape or sexual assault. (**W and D v Meah**.)

- Compensatory damages for personal injuries. The basis of an award of compensatory damages in a tort action is that the claimant should be awarded such a sum of money as will, as nearly as possible, put them in the position they would have been in if they had not sustained the injuries. The expression personal injuries covers physical harm to the person, disease and illness (including psychiatric illness).

- Damages in personal injuries cases are divided into pecuniary and non-pecuniary losses. Pecuniary damages are those that can be estimated in monetary terms, such as loss of earnings, medical and other expenses. Non-pecuniary damages cover intangibles such as loss of physical amenity, pain, shock and suffering.

- The basis of the award is full compensation. Once the claimant has succeeded in an action, then damages have historically been awarded in the form of a lump sum.

- The lump sum has historically been the method for awarding tort damages. However, it has come under increasing criticism and is now being eroded as the principal method of awarding compensation. The first step was the possibility of a structured settlement agreed between the parties. The court may now award damages in the form of periodical payments for future income loss and can award provisional damages.

- Pecuniary losses: loss of earnings. Damages for loss of earnings come in two categories. Loss of earnings suffered by the claimant before the trial have to be pleaded as special damages. Future loss of earnings (i.e. from the trial onwards) are claimed as general damages. The first stage in calculating future loss of earnings is to take the claimant's net annual loss, i.e. the difference between what they would have earned and what they are earning. This is known as the multiplicand. The second stage is to apply the multiplier to this figure. The multiplier is calculated by working out the number of years that the disability is likely to continue. This figure is then reduced to take into account the contingencies of life. One of the factors in calculating the appropriate multiplier is therefore the amount of interest that the claimant could earn on their capital. The House of Lords has now ruled that this is to be on the basis that the claimant had invested in index-linked government securities (ILGS). The average rate of interest on ILGS is 3 per cent and this should be the discount rate. (*Wells* v *Wells* [1998] 3 All ER 481.) This was later amended by statutory instrument to 2.5 per cent. (Damages (Personal Injury) Order 2001 (SI 2001/2301).)

- The effect of the decision in *Wells* means that there has been an increase in the multiplier.

- Other pecuniary losses: the claimant can recover any expenses reasonably incurred as a result of treatment of their injuries. Any medical expenses reasonably incurred may therefore be recovered. The claimant has a choice as to whether they are treated privately or not. (Law Reform (Personal Injuries) Act 1948.)

- If a friend or relative has incurred financial loss in caring for the claimant, then the claimant can recover this amount as damages. This is the claimant's loss because of his need for care. Where the services are gratuitously rendered by the tortfeasor, the claimant cannot recover the cost of those services by way of damages. (*Hunt* v *Severs*.)

- Non-pecuniary losses: loss of amenity. The claimant may recover damages for the injury itself and any consequent inability to enjoy life. These damages are calculated on an objective basis and do not take into account the claimant's inability to appreciate the disability. The courts work from a tariff which is laid down by the Court of Appeal. The tariff figure can be adjusted in the light of the particular circumstances of the claimant.

- Pain and suffering: the court will award damages for any pain and suffering which can be attributed to the injury itself and to any consequential surgical operations. An unconscious claimant cannot recover damages for pain and suffering. A conscious claimant may recover for any mental suffering caused by the knowledge that life has been cut short (Administration of Justice Act 1982 s 1(1)(b)) or that their ability to enjoy life has been diminished by physical handicap.

- Deductions. Personal accident insurance money is generally non-deductible, as are pensions. (*Parry* v *Cleaver*.) Certain social security payments can be recouped by the Department of Social Security. Any damages for pain and suffering are effectively protected from recoupment as there is no social security benefit which corresponds to this head.

- Damages may be awarded by a court when a public authority has acted in a way which is incompatible with a Convention right. Section 8(1) states that a court 'may grant such relief or remedy, or make such order, within its powers as it considers just and appropriate'. Damages are available as of right for a wrong under the 1998 Act and can be refused if other appropriate remedies render an award of damages unnecessary. Where damages are appropriate it would appear that the principles on which they are awarded are essentially the same as compensatory damages in tort.

- Effect of death. If the defendant in a tort action dies then the cause of action will usually survive against their estate. Where the claimant dies, their cause of action will generally survive for the benefit of their estate and a new cause of action will be created for their dependants.

- The Law Reform (Miscellaneous Provisions) Act 1934 preserves the deceased's subsisting action for the benefit of their estate (s 1(1)). The action is the one that the deceased would have brought had they lived.

- The Fatal Accidents Act 1976 provides a cause of action for the dependants of the deceased. This is a new right of action given to the dependants and is not a survival of the deceased's right of action. The death must have been caused by the tortious act of the defendant (s 1(1)) and the dependants have to show that the deceased had a right of action in order to be able to claim.

- The action is often said to be for the loss of a breadwinner.

- The main head of damages is the pecuniary loss suffered by the dependants from the date of death.

- Damages for bereavement may be awarded to certain classes of dependants. The spouse of the deceased or the parents of an unmarried child may claim. The damages are for mental distress at the death and are fixed by statute at £11,800.

- Injunctions. An injunction is a court order requiring that the defendant do some act or refrain from doing some act.

- The injunction may be mandatory, ordering the defendant to do something, or prohibitory, ordering them not to do something.

Further reading

Aggravated, Exemplary and Restitutionary Damages, Law Commission Report No 247 (1997).

Claims for Wrongful Death, Law Commission Report No 263 (1999).

Damages for Personal Injury: Non-pecuniary Loss, Law Commission Report No 257 (1999).

Damages under the Human Rights Act 1998, Law Commission Report 266 (2000).

Harris, D. *et al.* (1984), *Compensation and Support for Illness and Personal Injury*, Clarendon.

Kemp, D. (1998), 'Damages for Personal Injuries: A Sea Change' 114 LQR 570 (*Wells* v *Wells*).

Law of Damages, Ministry of Justice Consultation Report (2009) www.justice.gov.uk.

The Law on Damages (2007), Department for Constitutional Affairs Consultation Paper.

Lewis, R. (2001), 'Increasing the Price of Pain' 64 MLR 100 (*Heil* v *Rankin*).

Lewis, R. (2006), 'The Politics and Economics of Tort Law: Judicially Imposed Periodical Payments of Damages' 69 MLR 418.

Glossary of terms

Act of God Defence to an action in *Rylands* v *Fletcher*.

Assault Form of trespass to the person. An unlawful act which causes another person to apprehend the infliction of a battery.

Battery Form of trespass to the person. The infliction of unlawful force on another person without consent.

Breach of duty Term used in tort of negligence to determine whether a person has been negligent.

Causation The necessary link between the defendant's conduct and the claimant's damage.

Claimant The person who brings an action in tort.

Compensation One objective of tort law. To compensate the victims of torts.

Concurrent liability Where liability may arise on the same facts in either contract or tort.

Consent Agreement.

Contributory negligence Claimant fault which contributes to the damage.

Damage Where a person suffers loss. This may take a number of forms including damage to the person, property or pocket.

Damages Money awarded by a court to a successful claimant.

Damnum sine injuria Where harm is caused without a legal wrong.

Defendant The person against whom an action in tort is brought.

Dependant Person who can bring action on death of another.

Deterrence One of the objectives of tort law is to deter tortious conduct. This is known as individual deterrence. May also take the form of market deterrence which is designed to reduce the costs of accidents.

Distress damage feasant Right to retain items which have unlawfully come on hand.

Duty of care Device used by courts in tort of negligence to determine who owes whom a duty to take reasonable care.

Economic loss Financial loss which may be consequential on damage to the person or property (consequential economic loss) or pure economic loss.

Egg-shell skull rule Rule for damages for 'sensitive' claimants.

Exemplary damages Damages awarded to punish the defendant for his conduct.

Ex turpi causa non oritur actio From a bad cause no action arises – for example, where the claimant is injured whilst engaged in a criminal act.

Fair comment Defence to defamation.

False imprisonment Form of trespass to the person. The unlawful imposition of restraint on another's freedom of movement.

Foreseeability Where the defendant foresees a result at the time of the alleged negligent conduct.

Informed consent Term used in medical negligence to denote the information that must be given to a patient.

Injunction Court order to a person to do or refrain from doing something.

Intention Where a person desires to produce a result forbidden by law.

Justification Defence to defamation.

Libel A defamatory meaning conveyed in permanent form.

Limitation Time period when a tort action may be brought.

Malice Either: (a) the intentional doing of some wrongful act without proper excuse; or (b) to act with some collateral or improper motive. The term usually refers to (b).

Minor Person under the age of eighteen years.

Misfeasance A positive act.

Negligence Either the tort of negligence or a form of fault where the defendant is careless.

Neighbour test Test used in negligence to determine whether a duty of care exists.

Nervous shock Where the claimant suffers recognised psychiatric injury as a result of the defendant's negligence.

No-fault scheme Where compensation is paid by the state or an insurance company regardless of fault.

Nonfeasance An omission or failure to act.

Non-natural user Requirement in tort of *Rylands v Fletcher*.

Novus actus interveniens An act which breaks the chain of causation.

Nuisance Tort committed against a person's use or enjoyment of land.

Objective Where conduct is judged by a standard extrinsic to the defendant.

Per se Liability without the need to prove damage.

Personal injuries Damage to the person which may include psychiatric injury.

Post-traumatic stress disorder A psychiatric illness.

Primary victim Person placed in danger who suffers psychiatric illness.

Privilege Defence to defamation – may be absolute or qualified.

Proximity Literally closeness. In order for a court to find a duty of care there must be a proximate or sufficiently close relationship between claimant and defendant.

Psychiatric damage This is where there is damage to the mind rather than the body. Lawyers have traditionally used the expression 'nervous shock' to describe this condition. However, the Court of Appeal has indicated that the expression 'psychiatric damage' is preferable.

Quantum (of damages) Amount awarded.

Reasonable man test Objective test used to determine whether defendant was negligent.

Reliance May mean specific reliance by one person on another or general reliance where the defendant had some power which could have been exercised in the claimant's favour.

Remoteness (of damage) Damage in tort can only be recovered if it is not too remote or distant from the claimant's conduct.

Res ipsa loquitur Literally, the thing speaks for itself. Term used in proof of negligence.

Rylands v *Fletcher* Tort protecting land.

Scienter *rule* Historic form of strict liability for damage caused by animals.

Secondary victim Person who suffers psychiatric injury as a result of fear for the safety of another.

Slander A defamatory meaning conveyed in a temporary form.

Statutory duty Duty imposed by legislation.

Strict liability Where liability is imposed without proof of fault.

Tort A civil wrong other than a breach of contract.

Trespass Generic term for unlawful interference with the person, property or land.

Trespasser Unlawful entrant on premises.

Vicarious liability Where one person is made liable for the tort of another person.

Visitor Lawful entrant on premises.

Volenti non fit injuria Where a person voluntarily agrees to undertake the legal risk of harm at his own expense.

Voluntary assumption of responsibility Where one person assumes responsibility for another's welfare.

Index

Page numbers in **bold** relate to entries in the Glossary.